EDWARDIAN BLOOMSBURY

EDWARDIAN BLOOMSBURY

The Early Literary History of the Bloomsbury Group

Volume 2

S. P. Rosenbaum

Emeritus Professor of English Literature
University of Toronto

St. Martin's Press   New York

First published in the United States of America in 1994

Printed in Hong Kong

ISBN 0–312–23909–2

Library of Congress Cataloging-in-Publication Data
Rosenbaum, S. P. (Stanford Patrick), 1929–
Edwardian Bloomsbury / S. P. Rosenbaum.
p. cm.
Continuation of: The early literary history of the Bloomsbury
group, vol. 1, Victorian Bloomsbury.
Includes bibliographical references and index.
ISBN 0–312–23909–2
1. Bloomsbury group. 2. English literature—20th century—History
and criticism. 3. Bloomsbury (London, England)—Intellectual
life—20th century. I. Rosenbaum, S. P. (Stanford Patrick), 1929–
Victorian Bloomsbury. II. Title.
PR478.B46R673 1994
820.9'00912—dc20   93–14044
                                                              CIP

This history is dedicated to

Naomi Black

Contents

List of Plates   viii
Explanation of References and Abbreviations   ix
Preface   xiv

PART ONE   EARLIER EDWARDIAN

   Introduction   3
1 Independent Reviewers   9
2 E. M. Forster's Earlier Short Writings   30
3 The First Book of Bloomsbury   61
4 E. M. Forster's First Novel   76
5 Desmond MacCarthy at the Court Theatre   97
6 Lytton Strachey and the Prose of Empire   117
7 Virginia Woolf: Beginnings   140
8 Roger Fry and the Early Aesthetics of Bloomsbury   194

PART TWO   LATER EDWARDIAN

    Introduction   217
 9 E. M. Forster's Refutation of Idealism   226
10 Desmond MacCarthy and the *New Quarterly*,
    Clive Bell and the *Athenaeum*   259
11 Lytton Strachey and the *Spectator*   285
12 E. M. Forster: Rooms and Views   311
13 Virginia Woolf and the Proper Writing of Lives   339
14 Leonard Woolf's Ceylon Writings   391
15 E. M. Forster: Ends and Means   438

    Notes   489
    Bibliography   514
    Index   534

List of Plates

I   Roger Fry: End-papers, E. M. Forster, *The Celestial Omnibus* (1912)   46

II   Carrington: Wrappers, Leonard Woolf, *Stories of the East* (1921)   402

Explanation of References and Abbreviations

Note numbers in the text refer to substantive notes at the end of the book. References to books or papers given in parentheses in the text refer to the Bibliography listed after the notes. These parenthetical references are of two types.

(1) The most frequently cited writers and books are given by initials only, with a slash separating author and title; volume and page numbers follow. Periodical works by these frequently cited authors are given short titles after the slash. References to collections of papers are indicated by a lower case 'p' and initials indicating their location. Unpublished letter citations include their dates when known. (Citations of Virginia Woolf's Reading Notebooks refer to Brenda Silver's index of them.)

(2) Other references give the author's last name, a short title when there is more than one work by an author of that name, then volume and page numbers.

References omit indications of authors or works when they are supplied by the context. All citations are given in the Bibliography.

Examples of references

LS/*EV*, p. 309	Lytton Strachey, *Eminent Victorians*, p. 309.
VW/*D*, II 123	*The Diary of Virginia Woolf*, vol. II, p. 123.
10.viii.05, LW/pT	Unpublished letter of Leonard Woolf, 10 August 1905, Leonard Woolf papers, University of Texas.
DM/'Irish Plays', p. 252	Desmond MacCarthy, 'The Irish Plays', p. 252.
Laing, *RF*, p. 237	Donald A. Laing, *Roger Fry: An Annotated Bibliography of the Published Writings*, p. 237.

ABBREVIATIONS

1 *Bloomsbury authors and works*

CB   Clive Bell

	C	*Civilization*
	OF	*Old Friends*
	PB	*Pot-Boilers*
	pH	Papers, Huntington Library
	pKC	Papers, King's College, Cambridge
	pTC	Papers, Trinity College, Cambridge

VB   Vanessa Bell

	pKC	Papers, King's College, Cambridge
	pNY	Papers, New York Public Library
	pT	Papers, University of Texas

EMF   E. M. Forster

	AE	*Albergo Empedocle and Other Writings*
	AH	*Abinger Harvest*
	AN	*Aspects of the Novel*
	AS	*Arctic Summer and Other Fiction*
	CB	*Commonplace Book*
	CO	*The Celestial Omnibus and Other Stories*
	CSS	*Collected Short Stories*
	EM	*The Eternal Moment and Other Stories*
	GLD	*Goldsworthy Lowes Dickinson*
	HD	*The Hill of Devi and Other Writings*
	HE	*Howards End*
	HEMSS	*The Manuscripts of Howards End*
	L	*Selected Letters of E. M. Forster*
	LJ	*The Longest Journey*
	LN	*The Lucy Novels*
	LTC	*The Life to Come and Other Stories*
	M	*Maurice*
	pB	Papers, University of Bristol
	pKC	Papers, King's College, Cambridge
	pNY	Papers, New York Public Library
	pT	Papers, University of Texas
	RV	*A Room with a View*
	2CD	*Two Cheers for Democracy*

WAFT   *Where Angels Fear to Tread*

RF   Roger Fry
    FFBA   *French, Flemish, and British Art*
    L   *Letters of Roger Fry*
    pKC   Papers, King's College, Cambridge
    VD   *Vision and Design*

DG   Duncan Grant
    pBL   Papers, British Library
    pHG   Papers in possession of Henrietta Garnett

JMK   John Maynard Keynes
    CW   *Collected Writings*
    pKC   Papers, King's College, Cambridge

DM   Desmond MacCarthy
    CT   *The Court Theatre, 1904–1907: A Commentary and Criticism*
    E   *Experience*
    H   *Humanities*
    M   *Memories*
    P   *Portraits*
    pCU   Papers, Cambridge University Library
    pM   Papers, Lilly Library
    S   *Shaw*
    T   *Theatre*

LS   Lytton Strachey
    BC   *Books and Characters, French and English*
    CC   *Characters and Commentaries*
    EV   *Eminent Victorians*
    LSH   *Lytton Strachey by Himself*
    LVWLS   *Virginia Woolf and Lytton Strachey: Letters*
    pBL   Papers, British Library
    pKC   Papers, King's College, Cambridge
    pNY   Papers, New York Public Library
    pP   Papers, Princeton University
    pST   Papers, Strachey Trust
    pT   Papers, University of Texas
    RIQ   *The Really Interesting Question*

	SE	*Spectatorial Essays*
	SS	*The Shorter Strachey*
LW	Leonard Woolf	
	BA	*Beginning Again*
	DAW	*Downhill All the Way*
	DC	*Diaries in Ceylon*
	E	*Essays on Literature, History, Politics, Etc.*
	G	*Growing*
	IC	*Imperialism and Civilization*
	JNAM	*The Journey Not the Arrival Matters*
	L	*Letters of Leonard Woolf*
	pH	Papers, Huntington Library
	pS	Papers, University of Sussex
	pT	Papers, University of Texas
	S	*Sowing*
	SE	*Stories of the East*
	VJ	*The Village in the Jungle*
VW	Virginia Woolf	
	CE	*Collected Essays*
	CR1	*The Common Reader*, first series
	CR2	*The Common Reader*, second series
	CSF	*The Complete Shorter Fiction of Virginia Woolf*, second edition
	CW	*Contemporary Writers*
	D	*The Diary of Virginia Woolf*
	E	*The Essays of Virginia Woolf*
	EJ	*The Early Journals of Virginia Woolf*
	L	*The Letters of Virginia Woolf*
	LVWLS	*Virginia Woolf and Lytton Strachey: Letters*
	MB	*Moments of Being*, second edition
	P	*The Pargiters*
	pNY	Papers, New York Public Library
	pS	Papers, University of Sussex
	RF	*Roger Fry*
	RN	*Reading Notebooks*
	RO	*A Room of One's Own*
	W&F	*Women & Fiction*

2 *Other authors, works, periodicals*

DNB	*Dictionary of National Biography*
EMFCH	*E. M. Forster: The Critical Heritage*, ed. Philip Gardner
MH/*LS*	Michael Holroyd, *Lytton Strachey*
MH/*LSBG*	Michael Holroyd, *Lytton Strachey and the Bloomsbury Group*
OED	*Oxford English Dictionary*
PNF/*EMF*	P. N. Furbank, *E. M. Forster*
QB/*VW*	Quentin Bell, *Virginia Woolf*
TLS	*The Times Literary Supplement*
VWCH	*Virginia Woolf: The Critical Heritage*, ed. Robin Majumdar and Allen McLaurin

Preface

Edwardian Bloomsbury is a continuation of the early literary history of the Bloomsbury Group that I began with *Victorian Bloomsbury* in 1987. That volume described the Group's nineteenth-century origins and Cambridge education as reflected in their writings. The present volume can nevertheless be read independently as an account of Bloomsbury's literary history during the first decade of the twentieth century. At the end of *Victorian Bloomsbury* I indicated hopefully that *Edwardian Bloomsbury* would continue through the writing of Virginia Woolf's first novel, which she finally finished in 1913. The extent and diversity of Bloomsbury's Edwardian writings and the repercussions of the first post-impressionist exhibition make the end of 1910 a better stopping point. A third volume, entitled *Georgian Bloomsbury*, will trace the consequences of post-impressionism and then the First World War for the Group's writings.

The emphasis of *Edwardian Bloomsbury* remains on the literary writings rather than the lives of E. M. Forster, Virginia Woolf (or Virginia Stephen as she still was), Lytton Strachey, Desmond MacCarthy, Leonard Woolf, Roger Fry, Clive Bell, and, to a lesser extent, Thoby and Adrian Stephen, John Maynard Keynes, and Saxon Sydney-Turner. The particular nature of the Bloomsbury Group as a collectivity of friends and relations whose ideas and attitudes display a family resemblance is set forth in the introduction to *Victorian Bloomsbury* along with the range of intertextual connections between their works. It is worth repeating again that the general intention of this group literary history is to describe a historical sequence of Bloomsbury's early interrelated literary texts for the purpose of interpreting them analytically and comparatively. The inclusive conception here of a literary text that encompasses not just fiction, poetry, or drama but also varieties of non-fiction is also explained at the beginning of *Victorian Bloomsbury*.

Scepticism about even the possibility of literary history continues to exercise theorists – though the notion of literary history arranged in smaller clusters than periods or nations is seldom considered. Bloomsbury, too, had its doubts about literary history. In a recently discovered review of 1909, Virginia Woolf wrote,

> From books it seems that artists in any great movement were a little body, made one by a single aim. The history of literature as we look back seems to fall asunder into chapters. But at the present moment we can detect no school turning the talent of the age upon one subject; either our fathers did not state the truth with sufficient emphasis for us to demolish it, or we have no clear view of our own desire. Happily the more one reads of books the more one distrusts the history of them; the more likely it appears that they were written in separate garrets, from different points of view, and that our classifications are only to be made from a height and with very nervous fingers. . . . Whatever shape it will wear in the end, we must know that there is a movement going on among us, and that we live as hotly as our ancestors.
>
> ('Masques and Phases')

The classifications in *Victorian Bloomsbury* and *Edwardian Bloomsbury* are eclectic and contextual, but they have not been made from a remote theoretical or narrative distance. The particular nature of a work takes precedence over *a priori* patterns into which it may be fitted. The similarities and differences that can be displayed from the comparison of texts are the bases for Bloomsbury's literary history. But these have been handled nervously so as not to obscure either the separateness of Bloomsbury's works and viewpoints, or the heat with which the Group lived their literary movement.

Versions or parts of some chapters of *Edwardian Bloomsbury* have been published in *Twentieth Century Literature, The Times Literary Supplement, Virginia Woolf Miscellany*, and the *Charleston Magazine* as well as in the following collections: *E. M. Forster: A Human Exploration*, edited by G. K. Das and John Beer; *Leon Edel and Literary Art*, edited by Lyall H. Powers; and *Essays for Richard Ellmann: Omnium Gatherum*, edited by Susan Dick *et al.*

My debts to the people and institutions that have made the writing of both *Victorian Bloomsbury* and *Edwardian Bloomsbury* possible are set forth in the acknowledgements of the first volume. Additional help that I have received is referred to in the notes to this volume, but mention should be made here of the essential support I have received from the University of Toronto and the

Killam Program of the Canada Council. And I am particularly grateful to Richard Garnett for his careful reading of the typescript, and to Andrew McNeillie for helpful criticism.

For permission to quote from Virginia Woolf's unpublished writings in the Monks House Papers at the University of Sussex, copyright 1992, I am grateful once more to Quentin Bell. For permission to quote from the unpublished letters of Leonard Woolf in the Monks House Papers at the University of Sussex, the British Library, the Berg Collection of the New York Public Library, and the Humanities Research Center at the University of Texas, I am indebted again to Trekkie Parsons. Quotations from E. M. Forster's *The Longest Journey* and *Howards End* are by permission of King's College, Cambridge and the Society of Authors as the literary representative of the E. M. Forster estate, and also by permission of Alfred A. Knopf, Inc., in the United States. Roger Fry's illustration for E. M. Forster's *The Celestial Omnibus* has been reproduced by permission of Sidgwick & Jackson. The wrapper illustration for Leonard Woolf's *Stories of the East* has been used by permission of the author's estate and the Hogarth Press. Unpublished material from the E. M. Forster papers, copyright 1992, has been granted by the Society of Authors on behalf of the Provost and Scholars of King's College, Cambridge. Unpublished material from Lytton Strachey's Papers in the possession of the Strachey Trust, the Berg Collection of the New York Public Library, the Humanities Research Center at the University of Texas, the Monks House papers at the University of Sussex, and the Robert E. Taylor Collection at Princeton University, copyright 1992, has also been quoted with permission of the Society of Authors on behalf of the Strachey Trust.

Toronto   S. P. R.

Part One
Earlier Edwardian

Introduction

Once again it was Virginia Woolf, who, looking back from a 1920 Memoir Club paper entitled 'Old Bloomsbury', divided the early history of the Group into two 'chapters' (*MB*, p. 195). The first ended with the death of Thoby Stephen in November 1906; the second began with the marriage of Vanessa and Clive Bell a few months later and concluded with the first post-impressionist exhibition in December 1910. The Earlier and Later Parts of *Edwardian Bloomsbury* correspond to these two chapters. A further chapter of Old Bloomsbury, referred to by Woolf, closed with the First World War. It belongs to the literary period she called Georgian.

The first chapter of Bloomsbury's literary history had several beginnings. One was in 1899, when Lytton Strachey, Leonard Woolf, Saxon Sydney-Turner, Clive Bell, and Thoby Stephen all entered Trinity College, Cambridge. Another beginning was the election in 1902 of Strachey, Woolf, and Sydney-Turner as Cambridge Apostles, whose older members included Roger Fry, Desmond MacCarthy, and E. M. Forster; Keynes would be elected the next year. October 1903 saw the publication of G. E. Moore's *Principia Ethica*, that so influenced Bloomsbury's ethical beliefs, and also of the first issue of the *Independent Review*, which printed the early reviews and stories of Strachey, Forster, MacCarthy, Woolf, and Fry. The death of Leslie Stephen in February 1904, and the move of his daughters and sons to the district that gave the Group its name was still another beginning. Sometimes the start of the Group is put as late as 1905 when Thoby began to hold his Gordon Square Thursday evenings at which his sisters encountered Strachey, Bell, Sydney-Turner, and MacCarthy (Leonard Woolf had departed for Ceylon the previous October) for a continuation of the kinds of discussion the men had been having in Cambridge (see *Victorian Bloomsbury*, pp. 248–9). It was also in 1905 that Vanessa organised the Friday Club for the discussion of literary and aesthetic topics and the exhibition of art. This first of Bloomsbury's clubs suggests how the Group would

3

take visual art as seriously as they took literature. During its Edwardian years the Friday Club heard papers from Thoby Stephen, MacCarthy, Fry, and Forster, among others. Again in 1905 Clive Bell and Sydney-Turner arranged for the publication of *Euphrosyne: A Collection of Verse,* Forster published his first novel, MacCarthy started as a theatre critic, Roger Fry brought out his edition of Sir Joshua Reynolds's *Discourses* , and Virginia Woolf began writing reviews and essays regularly for publication.

If the beginnings of Bloomsbury's first chapter are various, the end was quite definite. Thoby Stephen's death brought together his family and friends in a series of loving friendships that lasted all their lives. Thoby was twenty-six when he died, and it is worth remembering for Bloomsbury's early literary history how young the members of the Group were. At the midpoint of *Edwardian Bloomsbury,* Virginia Woolf was twenty-four, Leonard twenty-five, Strachey twenty-six, Forster twenty-seven, and MacCarthy twenty-nine. Only Fry, the oldest, was approaching middle age at thirty-nine. (The jacket photographs to this volume are a reminder of Bloomsbury's Edwardian youth.)

In chapter one of Old Bloomsbury, E. M. Forster was the earliest to establish himself as a writer. His essays, stories, and novels dominate the Group's Edwardian literary history, though his relations with Bloomsbury did not extend much beyond Apostolic friendships with Strachey and Woolf until the end of the decade. Forster's development contrasts with that of Desmond MacCarthy, who also did not figure very much in Bloomsbury until he became an editor in 1907. MacCarthy was trying futilely to write a great novel while his gregarious charm and discriminating catholicity of taste were making him into a successful literary critic instead. Roger Fry's Edwardian writings on art were crucial in the formation of Bloomsbury aesthetics; his arrival in Bloomsbury also did not occur until the end of the decade, but he knew Forster and MacCarthy from Cambridge, had met Vanessa, and spoken at the Friday Club before going to New York's Metropolitan Museum in 1906. Clive Bell came to know the Stephen sisters early through his close friendship with Thoby, and he started proposing to Vanessa in 1905. Bell's poetry, wide reading, interest in art, and familiarity with past and present French culture, along with his undoubted charm and ability to cause even Sydney-Turner to shine, made Bell important for Bloomsbury's development in several respects. But person-ally the most influential member in the growth of Edwardian

Bloomsbury was Lytton Strachey. Strachey's relationships with Thoby and his sisters, with Woolf in Ceylon, with Keynes in Cambridge, with Grant, Bell, Forster, MacCarthy, and Sydney-Turner in London did more than anything else to establish the network of friendships out of which Bloomsbury grew. Some of his influence was a consequence, in Leonard Woolf's later words, of 'the semi-real, semi-unreal personal drama' that Strachey imposed on personal relations (*L*, p. 559). This combined with the iconoclastic honesty and irreverent humour of his homosexuality to give him moral authority in Cambridge and Bloomsbury. Though Strachey did not become famous as a writer until the end of the First World War, his knowledge of English and French literature, and the early maturity of his elaborate prose style impressed his Bloomsbury friends, most of whom were also hoping to become writers. Nobody in Bloomsbury was better read in English literature, however, than the youngest daughter of Leslie Stephen. Her earlier Edwardian role in Bloomsbury was largely a family affair. The influence of Cambridge on her development, which began with her father, was renewed through Thoby's Thursday evenings, just as she was starting to make her mark as a reviewer and essayist.

Bloomsbury's developing personal interrelations are part of what makes the comparative analysis of the Group's writings so illuminating. Their private and public responses to each other's works began in the early years of their literary history. Strachey and Leonard Woolf's correspondence about Forster's novels as well as the reviews of them by Virginia Woolf and later Clive Bell, provide a valuable historical context for Forster's literary progress and of Bloomsbury as a whole. Virginia and Thoby's differing opinions of the verse published anonymously by Bell, Sydney-Turner, Strachey, and Leonard Woolf reveal his interested, and her detached views of the literary attitudes of Cambridge men. The enthusiastic or ironic early reviews by Lytton Strachey led Bloomsbury and Strachey himself to hope he would soon be writing poetic or dramatic masterpieces even without the fellowship Trinity College had failed to award him for his dissertation on imperial history. MacCarthy's friends were also confident, with even less reason, of his capacity to write a great novel. Virginia Woolf, though she had written little, was regarded with more justification as a potential genius by some of her friends and relatives.

Bloomsbury's earlier Edwardian literary history consists of more than aspirations, personal relations, and apprentice work. The

Group's writings during this period include reviews, essays of different types, short stories, drama criticism, diaries, letters, a collection of verse, a novel, a dissertation. In these varieties of writing, Bloomsbury sought forms through which they could express their emerging un-Victorian experience. The search for suitable modern literary forms makes their early literary history more coherent than the diversity of their texts might suggest. Yet only Forster was really able to establish himself in his early work. For the others, there were many dead ends and much incomplete work. But now and then in the reviews of Strachey, the essays and stories of Virginia Woolf, the criticism of MacCarthy and Fry, and the fiction of Leonard Woolf, one begins to hear their distinctive voices.

The originality of the Bloomsbury writers developed, as it usually does, through the modification of their predecessors' genres. The Group's literary background has been described in Part Two of *Victorian Bloomsbury*. *Edwardian Bloomsbury* will record again the literary presence in the Group's early criticism and fiction, of Leslie Stephen, Henry James, George Meredith, and Samuel Butler. In poetry, Swinburne and Meredith remained the most impressive Victorians for them, along with Whitman and more recently Housman, while their critical responses to aestheticism were involved in different ways with the work of Pater, Wilde, Symonds, Beerbohm, and Berenson.

Bloomsbury's search for new kinds of writing led them to early experiments in the mixing of the factual and the fictive in their essays and stories. Such generic combinations remained characteristic of much of their prose. Bloomsbury wanted to extend the boundaries of literature by making all their writing literary, which meant making it worthwhile in itself as writing. The Group never accepted in their literary theory the modernist separation of the aesthetic from the cognitive. In their earlier Edwardian writing they were already beginning to challenge readers who were accustomed to texts that provided entertainment or information, truth or beauty, but not all together.

How and what the Group wanted to write was affected, of course, by the editors and publishers who paid for and printed them. It is important in the early literary history of Bloomsbury to distinguish between their private, unfinished or unpublished texts and those written directly for publication. The published Edwardian reviews, essays, and stories that Forster, Strachey, MacCarthy,

Virginia Woolf, and Fry wrote were significantly conditioned by the periodicals for which they were intended. What the establishment *Athenaeum*, or the fledgling *Times Literary Supplement* expected from their reviewers was quite different from the work that the New Liberal *Independent Review* and *Speaker*, or the women's pages of the Church *Guardian* wanted to publish. Interesting early work of both Forster and Virginia Woolf was rejected by editors who sometimes cut and rewrote what they did accept. All this is relevant to the interpretation of texts, as are such simple journalistic facts as how much space the reviewers were allowed, how much they were paid, and whether their reviews were signed or anonymous. Equally pertinent are the circumstances under which Bloomsbury's Edwardian books were published. The title for Forster's first novel was rejected by his publishers; their royalties were also small but at least Forster did not have to pay for publication, as Clive Bell did for the verse he and his friends wrote.

The conditions of publication are an essential aspect of literary history, and they show that Bloomsbury's search for new directions in writing cannot be isolated from what the members of the Group were attempting to express in that writing. I. A. Richards, who understood the Cambridge origins of Bloomsbury very well, thought that Forster's distinctive quality as a novelist was 'his fiercely critical sense of values' (p. 162). That sense is also fundamental to the work of both of the Woolfs, to Strachey, Fry, Bell, and even MacCarthy. Defining that sense of values is essential for the description of Bloomsbury's literary texts. Crucial to those values is what Strachey described in a 1905 Cambridge paper on the Gospels as 'the most important and far-reaching of all ethical distinctions – that between good as an end and good as a means' (p/ST). The discrimination of intrinsic and instrumental values – the most basic of principles in *Principia Ethica* – recurs in the Group's earlier Edwardian texts, from the first essays and stories of Forster and Strachey in the *Independent Review* to MacCarthy's influential criticism of Shaw's plays. Throughout their literary history Bloomsbury's writing seeks what ends are ideally valuable for their own sakes, and what are the best ways of realising them. Fundamental to this search is the Group's critique of goals that are valuable only as means to ends of unexamined or trivial worth.

The sense of values that makes the work of Bloomsbury illuminating to analyse and compare is not confined to ethical ideals or philosophical distinctions. They reappear in the Group's concerns with imperialism, economic inequality, the situation of women, and what today is known as sexual orientation. Bloomsbury's involvement with these issues was expressed not only through writing and talk. Leonard Woolf spent seven years and J. M. Keynes two years as practising, if increasingly disillusioned, imperial civil servants. Various members of the Group taught for different periods at adult education institutions for working men and women, sometimes using the knowledge they had acquired as upper-middle-class English travellers in Europe. Forster began teaching Latin at the Working Men's College in 1902; he also gave Cambridge University extension lectures on Italian history and culture for eight years. Virginia Woolf spent three years teaching history, literature and writing at Morley College evening classes, where Vanessa, Thoby and Adrian Stephen, and also Clive Bell also taught briefly.

At the end of the introduction to *Victorian Bloomsbury*, I suggested, along the lines of Bloomsbury's own principles, that there were, in the history of modern English literature, both extrinsic and intrinsic justifications for such a detailed study of the Group's early literary history (pp. 16–18). In the descriptions that follow of how Forster, MacCarthy, Strachey, and Virginia Woolf began their earlier Edwardian careers, the extrinsic justification for modern English literary history appears primarily in the various conditions of publication to which they had to conform, in the politics of the time that influenced them, and in their literary attitudes toward the writers who were their precursors and contemporaries. But also in these early Bloomsbury texts, the intrinsic worth of the Group's writing begins to emerge and calls for responses from readers to both rational and visionary kinds of literary value without sacrificing one for the other. The early Edwardian literary history of Bloomsbury is among other things the story of that emergence.

1 Independent Reviewers

I

Both Lytton Strachey and E. M. Forster thought October 1903 marked the start of a new age. For Strachey, the publication of *Principia Ethica* heralded 'the beginning of the Age of Reason' (MH/LS, p. 207), and for Forster it was the appearance of first number of the *Independent Review*. Like G. E. Moore's book, the review was a product of the Cambridge that shaped Bloomsbury. The *Independent Review* was controlled by Cambridge Apostles. G. M. Trevelyan, Goldsworthy Lowes Dickinson, and Nathaniel Wedd made up a majority of its editorial committee, which also included C. F. G. Masterman. Trevelyan and his brother Robert helped finance the review, Roger Fry designed a cover of Greek columns and a frieze, and Strachey bought shares in the journal and published his first essay in the first issue. In the second issue, Forster made his first appearance as an essayist outside of student magazines, and his essay was accompanied by the earliest of Desmond MacCarthy's important reviews of George Bernard Shaw's plays. The fourth issue of January 1904 carried a review by 'L. S. Woolf', the first he had published. By the time it ceased publication five years later under the title the *Albany Review*, the journal had printed eleven stories, essays, and reviews by Forster, another eleven reviews and essays by Strachey, nineteen reviews by MacCarthy, an essay by Fry, and the review by Woolf.

The *Independent Review* was the first of many periodicals with which Bloomsbury writers would be associated together, and it was an auspicious beginning. Accompanying them in the review were a number of well-known Edwardian authors. In addition to the editorial committee's contributions there were works by Hilaire Belloc (a novel), Edward Carpenter, W. B. Yeats ('Red Hanrahan'), Bertrand Russell ('A Free Man's Worship'), J. G. Frazer, G. K. Chesterton, Thomas Hardy (a poem), H. G. Wells, A. C. Bradley, and many others including the jurist and Apostle, Sir Frederick Pollock who wrote an obituary on Leslie Stephen comparing him to G. E. Moore.[1]

Yet the primary purpose of the *Independent Review* was political, not literary. It was a journal of the New Liberalism, opposed to the imperialism and protectionism of Joseph Chamberlain. It advocated, according to Forster's account in his biography of Dickinson, a sane foreign policy and a constructive domestic one.[2] The review, Forster thought, was 'an appeal to Liberalism from the Left to be its better self.' And if it did not have much impact on the government, it at least influenced a number of Liberals who felt,

> that the heavy, stocky body of their party was about to grow wings and leave the ground. . . . Can you imagine decency touched with poetry? It was thus that the *Independent* appeared to us – a light rather than a fire, but a light that penetrated the emotions. (*GLD*, p. 95–6)

None of Bloomsbury's contributions to the *Independent Review* was very political, but they were associated with and often quite compatible with the values and attitudes of a liberalism that was close to socialism. Desmond MacCarthy, too, whose early work was published in various periodicals associated with liberalism, would have been responsive to a New Liberal journal in which decency was touched with poetry. Strachey was more sceptical of the *Independent Review*'s political aims. He felt it important to be included in the first issue yet thought Trevelyan was trying to turn the Apostles into a political party. The *Independent Review* should have been called the *Phenomenal Review*, he suggested in Apostolic language that equated phenomena with unreality (Putt, p. 80). Strachey continued to publish his most substantial early work in the review but considered his final contribution to be an attack on the ineffectiveness of the journal's policies.

Whatever the feelings of the Bloomsbury Apostles about the policies of the *Independent Review* or the worth of some of its contents, it was in the liberal context of the *Independent Review* that they were first published and read together beyond Cambridge. In this early writing the mixed genres so characteristic of later Bloomsbury writing can first be seen. The literary history of these beginnings will be described in Strachey's reviews and essays first, more briefly in MacCarthy's reviews, and continued in the next chapter on the early factual and fictional narratives Forster published in the *Independent Review* and elsewhere.

II

The first issue of the *Independent Review* that contained Strachey's remarkable prose début began with a series of Liberal calls for greater individual freedom, more distribution of wealth, increased accessibility to higher education, more equitable treatment of the colonies, greater co-operation with Germany, and less institutionalised religion, the last being urged by Lowes Dickinson in the first of a series of articles. Also in this issue was the beginning instalment of Hilaire Belloc's *Mr Burden*, an ironic novel about imperialism that may have influenced Forster. Among reviews of Gilbert Murray's translation of Euripides and James Bryce's biographical sketches was a carefully wrought account by 'G. L. Strachey' of an anthology of Vauvenargues and La Bruyère.

From its opening epigram – 'The greatest misfortune that can happen to a witty man is to be born out of France' – to the final Jamesian question of how La Bruyère conveys 'the whole dismal fatality of things', Strachey's 'Two Frenchmen' reflects both his own life and the prose he is discussing (CC, pp. 71, 78). Part of Strachey's review is inevitably about a third Frenchman, La Rochefoucauld, 'the cleverest duke who ever lived'. La Bruyère too is described as 'one of the great writers of the world'. (La Bruyère and Vauvenargues were both also character writers, a genre familiar in Cambridge through Jebb's edition of Theophrastus, and one which would influence Bloomsbury's biographical writings.) Strachey's knowledge of French literature, his ability to translate sensitively and generalise widely, are impressive for a young man of twenty-three, even if some of the generalisations are facile – his observation, for example, that the aphorism dominates French as imagination does English literature. The remark illustrates the truth of another by Strachey himself, who was practising aphorisms around this time: 'there are few things more difficult to write than a good aphorism; and one of them is to write a true one' (Merle, p. 912). Another aphorism in 'Two Frenchman' asserts that it is as difficult perhaps for an Englishman 'to translate a French epigram as to compose an English one'. Strachey surmounts this difficulty but not the unfortunate anthologist whom he chose to review.

James Strachey has suggested that his brother never reprinted this first review because it was an unkind attack on an insignificant anthology (*CC*, p. v). But the review was not forgotten. On the basis of it H. A. L. Fisher persuaded his colleagues several years later to invite not the ubiquitous Edmund Gosse but the unknown G. L. Strachey to write *Landmarks of French Literature* for the Home University Library (Sanders, *Strachey*, pp. 32–3).

Strachey's *Independent Review* texts were the first substantial published critical writings by a member of Bloomsbury, and an early formative influence on some of the Group. He had more space, more scope, in these reviews than in those he was doing a little later for the *Speaker* or the *Spectator*. Some of the *Independent Review* pieces were ephemeral, but Strachey thought well enough of them to reprint five of the texts later in *Books and Characters, French and English*, a title that well summarises his central preoccupations as a writer from the *Independent Review* onwards.

An example of Strachey's influence on Bloomsbury appears in the fourth number of the *Independent Review*, which was published in January 1904. Leonard Woolf's first review of a not very good biography of Voltaire is similar to Strachey's review in subject, treatment, and style. (Woolf's letters to Strachey mention that he began a review of something by Chesterton, then the editors changed their mind about it; he then hoped to do Shaw's *Man and Superman* but that was given to MacCarthy.) Characteristic of Woolf's own later development is his complaint that the biographer has followed Carlyle too much, and not brought out the relation of Voltaire's life to his times. But the language of the review is more aphoristic than Woolf's later astringent prose, and his interpretation of Voltaire's life depends upon a Stracheyan paradox. Voltaire was both a revolutionary before the revolution – 'the French Revolution began when Voltaire first put pen to paper' – and also a typical eighteenth-century thinker as incapable as his fellow *philosophes* of understanding Rousseau when he 'whirled out of the next century into their midst' ('Voltaire', pp. 681–2). Voltaire's belief in the power of reason reconciled this contradiction; but for Leonard Woolf and Lytton Strachey living in the century after Rousseau, subjective emotion is as necessary and valuable as rational analysis. Nothing more was published by Leonard Woolf for eight years, except for an article on preserving game in Ceylon, where he went in October 1904, with a dog and ninety beautiful, large eighteenth-century volumes of Voltaire (*G*, p. 12).[3]

The literary history of Bloomsbury is prefigured at several places in Strachey's second contribution to the *Independent Review* of February 1904. 'The Wrong Turning' is a review of *English Men of Letters: Fanny Burney (Madame D'Arblay)* by the poet and critic Austin Dobson. Playing with the antinomies of the title, Strachey dismisses, as we now would not, the contradiction of a woman as a man of letters and then develops his review around her double literary identity as Fanny Burney the novelist and Madame D'Arblay the diarist. Strachey continues the periodic, epigrammatic style of his first review, praising Dobson as a delightful guide to eighteenth-century London but an unsatisfactory critic of Burney's novels because he follows Macaulay's 'metallic way' of devoting more attention to her life than her literature. Strachey's own rhetorical way is to treat Burney's novels as an enigma: proclaimed by Johnson and others as a novelist comparable to Richardson and Fielding, Strachey finds she is unread today. The mystery is explained with a theory of the novel. During Burney's time the English novel was in eclipse because the novelists between Oliver Goldsmith and Jane Austen were not 'character mongers' in Johnson's phrase. Strachey asserts that what makes Sterne immortal 'is not his sentiment, nor his indecency, nor his asterisks, but his Mr Shandy and his Uncle Toby' (*CC*, p. 82). So Macaulay was right after all; Burney's characters are only caricatures. Some imaginative, psychological analysis began to appear in *Evelina* before the influence of the novelist's brilliant circle of friends turned her away from it, but fortunately Fanny Burney changed into Madame D'Arblay, author of one of 'the great diaries of literature'. Who would not substitute all of *Cecilia* for the diary description of Warren Hastings' trial? Strachey asks (*CC*, p. 86). Certainly not the reviewer, absorbed in his fellowship dissertation on Hastings. Strachey's review was read by the two incipient Bloomsbury novelists, Woolf and Forster, who in their different ways would later affirm theories of the novel that emphasised character and psychological representation. And one of them was a woman led astray by a circle of brilliant admirers, it is sometimes claimed, who would also write another of the great diaries of literature.

An earlier eighteenth-century writer, to whom Strachey would return a number of times throughout his career, was the subject of his third review for the *Independent Review*. Strachey thought that the world of Horace Walpole's correspondence was particularly attractive when seen across 'an age of barbarous prudery' whose

Victorian relics survived in the unprintable omissions blotting the edition of letters Strachey was reviewing (*CC*, p. 88). Again the metallic Macaulay (he seems to obsess Strachey at this time) is used to define the contrasts between the eighteenth and nineteenth centuries – and implicitly between the nineteenth and the early twentieth. Strachey does not disagree with Macaulay's characterisation of Walpole's letters but he finds 'the great reviewer's' epigrammatic sentences and Catherine-wheel paragraphs completely fail to convey the affectionate nature beneath Walpole's malice and quarrels. Macaulay is incapable of appreciating a world of cards, verses, confidences, conversation and letters. Nothing less than the true value of reality, so central to Bloomsbury's writings, is at question here for Strachey. 'Are these things really less real', he inquires Apostolically with Walpole, '. . . than shouting at elections and writing articles for the magazines?' (*CC*, p. 95).

Strachey did not reprint his Walpole review either, but he used bits of it for the long essay on English letter writers which he submitted unsuccessfully for a Cambridge essay prize (*Victorian Bloomsbury*, pp. 136–7). Cambridge was also the testing ground for his next contribution to the *Independent Review*; it was read to the Cambridge Sunday Essay Society before being published in August 1904.[4] 'Shakespeare's Final Period' is the first of Strachey's iconoclastic texts to be published, the earliest text he chose to reprint, and one of the first to attract attention over time. Like 'Voltaire's Tragedies' that followed, it is an essay rather than a review, freer and more discursive in its range. The icon to be smashed is the theory that Shakespeare's inner life during his final play-writing years was one of quiet serenity as mirrored in the late romances, just as the great tragedies had reflected his gloomy middle age. Strachey does not find the late plays serene. Indeed, some of the poetry he quotes from *The Winter's Tale* and *Cymbeline* in the reprinting of his essay was apparently so gross that it could only be summarised in the *Independent Review*. As for characters, Strachey holds up Prospero: 'to an irreverent eye, the ex-Duke of Milan would perhaps appear as an unpleasant crusty personage, in whom a twelve years' monopoly on the conversation had developed an inordinate propensity for talking' (*BC*, p. 63). The irreverent eye of Strachey makes 'Shakespeare's Final Period' among his most amusing early writings and clearly anticipates the irreverent gaze of his biographies. In place of serenity Strachey offers boredom as an explanation of Shakespeare's state of mind in his final period. The literary assumptions behind this rather silly alternative are nevertheless important for Strachey's and Bloomsbury's future ideas about literature, but first the satirical intention of the explanation should be noted. In suggesting boredom as a motive for the late plays, Strachey is mocking the bardolaters with a too human image of Shakespeare. (A passage cut when the essay was reprinted derides Sidney Lee's depiction of Shakespeare as too stupid to realise how clever he was – Sanders 'Revisions', p. 228.) The literary evidence that Strachey educes for Shakespeare's boredom is that his plays from *Coriolanus* onwards ceased to be 'essentially realistic' (*BC*, p. 57). Realism is the basis for Shakespeare's aesthetic, moral, and psychological greatness, and Strachey finds a gulf in his development between the characters of Bottom in *A Midsummer Night's Dream* and Caliban in *The Tempest*. But because Strachey's notion of realism remains undefined, we are left only with another mark of the value with which Bloomsbury invested the word *real* and its cognates. The other basic literary assumption of 'Shakespeare's Final Period' repudiates the notion 'that the character of any given drama is, in fact, a true index to the state of mind of the dramatist composing it' (p. 48). But then Strachey accepts this very idea for the purposes of his critique. S. Schoenbaum has noted that Strachey trembled on the brink of critical modernity here, but turned away to follow his idea of the bored Bard because he was not interested in critical theory. Strachey's Apostle papers around this time actually show him very interested in the way a work's organic unity could transform the aesthetic significance of its parts, including its characters (see *Victorian Bloomsbury*, pp. 230, 256–7). Moore's particular concept of an organic whole may indeed have helped Strachey to question the general view that the mind and character of the artist can be inferred from his or her art. Schoenbaum is right that Strachey merely stands the simplistic serenity theory of Dowden and others on its head, but then Schoenbaum proceeds to infer the critic's character from his writing. He posits a bored Strachey recognising a bored Shakespeare. Boredom, Schoenbaum says neatly, 'may be a cynic's version of serenity' (Schoenbaum, p. 665). But Strachey was an ironist, not a cynic. Boredom for him was *funeste* – the opposite of the passion he idealised.

The Strachey family had been associated with Shakespeare ever since an ancestor wrote one of the sources for *The Tempest* . (As an example to himself, Malvolio in *Twelfth Night* recalls that 'the Lady

of the Strachey married the yeoman of the wardrobe' – II. v.
ll. 37–8.) In the course of his career Lytton wrote more reviews and
essays about Shakespeare than anyone else. His last writing project
was a study of the plays beginning with *Othello*. The humorous
intention of 'Shakespeare's Final Period' can be brought out, perhaps, by a comparison with the introduction to George Rylands's
Words and Poetry that Strachey wrote in 1928. There he argues
Shakespeare gave up realism with *Coriolanus* and became 'a
glorious gramophone' (in the early essay the phase, borrowed from
Uncle Walter Raleigh, was 'a melodious megaphone') not from
boredom but because he now cared only for style (*CC*, p. 307). As
an account of the late work, this may not be much of an improvement, but it may suggest the comic purpose of the bored-
Shakespeare theory.

After Shakespeare Voltaire was the author whom Strachey most
frequently wrote on. His first Voltaire essay was a discussion of his
tragedies in April 1905. The *Independent Review* setting of the essay
again reveals the associations that make that journal significant in
the early literary history of Bloomsbury. 'Shakespeare's Final
Period' had been published in the same issue as Forster's 'The
Story of a Panic'; 'Voltaire's Tragedies' appeared with Forster's
essay on Cardan and also a review by Lowes Dickinson of Oscar
Wilde's *De Profundis*. Strachey again anticipates his own later
biographical techniques, not by belittling Voltaire's tragedies –
their stature was already quite small – but by viewing them
paradoxically. The frame of the essay is a theory of literary history,
epigrammatically set forth in the first sentence:

> The historian of Literature is little more than a historian of
> exploded reputations. What has he to do with Shakespeare, with
> Dante, with Sophocles? Has he entered into the springs of the
> sea? Or has he walked in the search of the depth? . . . His
> business is with the succeeding ages of men, not with all time.
>
> (*BC*, p. 139).

The God-like critic's questioning of the Job-like literary historian is
a good Bloomsbury theme: those parts of the literary past that do
not represent great states of mind and their consequences ought to
be of concern only to 'the geologist of literature'. What makes the
theory incongruous after the exaggeration and the imagery is that
Strachey then proceeds to spend the whole essay on Voltaire's

exploded reputation as a tragedian. Through an extended summary that deftly weaves together French quotations and English translations, he exhibits Voltaire's *Alzire, ou Les Américains* for the readers of the *Independent Review*. Comparisons with Shakespeare, Sophocles and Racine show how preposterous were the praises of contemporaries and Voltaire's own conviction that he was Racine's successor. He lacked the poetry, the psychology, had only the passion of the great French dramatist, and even this failed him because he had no dramatic sense.[5] Reading Strachey's criticism in the light of the plays he himself was trying to write at the time (*Victorian Bloomsbury*, pp. 270–4), it is difficult not to see here some self-criticism. Racine triumphed in the constricting classical tradition but for Voltaire it was fatal. The conclusion of Strachey's literary historical excursus is a shapely periodic irony:

> The Classical tradition has to answer for many sins; perhaps its most infamous achievement was that it prevented Molière from being a great tragedian. But there can be no doubt that its most astonishing one was to have taken – if only for some scattered moments – the sense of the ridiculous from Voltaire. (p. 155)

III

Signed reviews in the *Independent Review* of Sir Thomas Browne, William Blake, and Samuel Johnson, all written in 1906, and reprinted in *Books and Characters* in the 1920s, show Lytton Strachey's increasing maturity as a prose stylist, critic, and ironist. While writing the first of these reviews he said of his style in a letter to his sister Dorothy Bussy,

> My ideal in writing is the non-flamboyant – unless one's Sir Thomas Browne; but I'm annoyed to find that every time I write I become more flamboyant than before. It's so difficult to be amusing unless one does plunge into metaphors, 'paradoxes', 'brilliant epigrams', etc. etc. etc. – unless one's Swift.
> (MH/*LSBG*, p. 55)

The humorous function of Strachey's metaphors, paradoxes, epigrams – one could add clichés – is indicated here. Strachey's amusing flamboyance in his review of Browne himself is at the expense of Edmund Gosse. Thus began Bloomsbury's mutually uncongenial association with a leading member of the English literary establishment. Gosse's study of Browne was another *English Men of Letters* volume, and Strachey found it so entertaining and discriminating he thought that readers would be unable to separate the biographer and his subject. After this and other less ambiguous compliments about Gosse's understanding of Browne's life, Strachey makes his main criticism: Gosse is incapable of appreciating the most important thing about Sir Thomas Browne, which is his style. As a critic of Browne's work he is devastatingly compared by Strachey to the Frenchman who, ignoring the double-column format of the *L'Encyclopédie*, read straight across the page for a whole volume and observed that the work was excellent 'mais un peu abstrait' (Sanders, 'Revisions', p. 229).

A private correspondence with Gosse ensued over the respective merits of biography and criticism, and the value of Browne's Latinisms, which Strachey had rightly argued in his review could not be judged apart from his style as a whole. The aggrieved Gosse complained that Strachey had not read his book, but was assured he had and carefully (Spurr, pp. 244–5). When Strachey reprinted the review, however, he deleted his French comparison and toned the review down to a discussion of Browne's style (Sanders, 'Revisions', p. 229). (Another unsigned, much shorter, and more dismissive review of Gosse's book was written by Strachey for the *Speaker* but never reprinted.) In the revised text, Strachey's chief complaint is still of Gosse's insensitivity to Browne's style and influence. He maintains that Browne's 'uncommon sentiments', in Johnson's words, could not have been expressed in the spondaic rhythms of Saxon prose, which are more suitable for describing the atmosphere of everyday life. Browne did not, as Gosse claimed, eschew barbarous Saxon terms but used them at times to set off his Latin ones. Strachey agrees that not until Coleridge and Lamb, was Browne's inner spirit recognised, yet his prose influenced the great neo-classical stylists. Then with Gosse's aid, Strachey outlines the history of a century of English prose that is interesting in Bloomsbury's literary history for the range of writers and styles that Strachey appreciates. According to Strachey, the prose of Shaftesbury (this was later revised to Locke) and Bishop Butler became loose and flat before Samuel Johnson went back to Browne, and ended by transforming the clarity and force of Swift's Doric into Gibbon's clear and forceful Corinthian – a transformation that also produced Johnson's great style as well as those of Hume, Reynolds, Walpole, and Burke.[6] Such are the sources of what Cyril Connolly has identified as Bloomsbury's own 'new Mandarin' style (*Enemies*, pp. 57–61). Connolly is mistaken, however, in describing the pages where Strachey's description first appeared as those of 'a dull review'. For Bloomsbury writers and readers the *Independent Review* was anything but dull in 1906.

Strachey's defence of Browne's style is relevant to his own in two further ways. He draws an analogy between Browne's vocabulary and the brushwork of Rubens, Velasquez or the impressionists that has to be seen as part of the whole picture, not judged by itself in isolation. The same could be said of Strachey's diction, particularly his use of clichés. In Browne, and Strachey too sometimes, the relation of the part to the whole is intentionally grotesque. As if to emphasise this, Strachey closes his review with an autobiographical Brownean pastiche. He is speculating fancifully on the best English setting for Browne and decides it must be some ancient university, perhaps the cloisters of Trinity where 'the present writer' (Strachey almost never uses the first-person singular) recalls few happier moments that those rolling out the periods of *Hydrotaphia* in the darkness to nightingales. On further reflection, however, the present writer concludes it is really Oxford where Sir Thomas Browne belongs, with its old gardens, hidden streets, quiet waters, and 'that strange company of faces which guard, with such a large passivity, the circumference of the Sheldonian' (*BC*, p. 44). Some may find self-indulgent prose like this inappropriate in a review but that was not the only genre of Strachey's flamboyant text. Leonard Woolf, for one, appreciated the autobiographical aspects of the review in a letter to Strachey but thought the satire rather elusive (28.ii.06, LS/pBL).

Editions of Blake's poetry were the subject of Strachey's next review to appear in the *Independent Review* in 1906. He moves from them through a discussion of Blake's ideas, about which he has reservations, to a consideration of his poetry, about which he has none. Strachey praises highly the first accurate edition of Blake's poems; Shakespeare might be repunctuated with impunity, 'but add a comma to the text of Blake, and you put all Heaven in a rage' (*BC*, p. 212). For Strachey Blake's most persistent quality was his 'triumphant freedom from conventional restraints' such as rational consistency. Strachey disagrees with Professor Walter Raleigh's claim, in the introduction to one of the editions under review, that

Blake's work was a complete exposition of anarchy. Blake was far too unreasonable for that, and Strachey gently mocks his relative and former teacher for regarding Blake as a dangerous thinker. How dangerous can a poet be who argues that wickedness does not exist, and that it is wicked of people to think it does? Particularly interesting for Bloomsbury are the comments on Blake's mysticism. Strachey objects not to its unreasonableness but its 'lack of humanity. . . . What shall it profit a man, one is tempted to exclaim, if he gain his own soul, and lose the whole world?' (p. 219). Forster, in the midst of writing *The Longest Journey*, would incorporate these words as the conclusion to the essay that is Chapter 28 of the novel and also pose the question in his unpublished story 'The Rock', while Virginia Woolf would echo them later in a review (see pp. 59, 239, 353). The response of Forster, Virginia Woolf, and Bloomsbury to such a mysticism is epitomised in words that Strachey quotes (and alters)[7] from Charles Lamb:

> Sun, and sky, and breeze, and solitary walks, and summer holidays, and the greenness of fields, and the delicious juices of meats and fishes, and society, and the cheerful glass, and candle-light, and fireside conversations, and innocent vanities, and jests, and *irony itself* – do these things form no part of your Eternity? (p. 220)

They were certainly part of Bloomsbury's, particularly the italicised *irony*, which may be the most persistent quality of Strachey's work. Strachey on Blake was also read by Leonard Woolf, who had written an undergraduate essay on mysticism and compiled a list of mystics for a collaborative book with Strachey and other Cambridge friends (see *Victorian Bloomsbury*, pp. 131–3). He wrote to Strachey from Ceylon, 'do you know that I believe middle age is beginning to touch you?' (13.v.06, LS/pBL).

Blake's poetry, rather than his prophecy, his nature rather than his eternity, are what Strachey responds to. After finishing the review, he told Duncan Grant that Blake was the equal of the greatest poets but felt he had not managed to bring this out in his review (MH/LS, p. 308). Strachey does say in his review that Blake's poems have a natural loveliness and power, sometimes exquisitely simple, sometimes disturbingly elemental. And at the end he dwells on the sense of ruin that Blake's poetry can express, comparing it to the annihilation foretold 'when the drum and the violin mysteriously come together, in one of Beethoven's Symphonies' – another remark that Forster would remember, this time in *Howards End* (*BC*, p. 222).

Strachey's briefer review of an erudite, ponderous and ugly edition of Johnson's *Lives of the Poets* is among the earliest of Bloomsbury's published writings on critical theory. One sentence from it is frequently quoted: 'Johnson's aesthetic judgments are almost invariably subtle, or solid, or bold; they have always some good quality to recommend them – except one: they are never right' (*BC*, p. 68). Strachey's hyperbole has deflected attention from his praise of Johnson's power and independent thought, his sense of the actual, and his combination of sanity and paradox. What Strachey objects to most in Johnson, and later in Matthew Arnold, and even in Leslie Stephen, is the lack of sympathy with what the writers they criticised were trying to do. The first obligation of a critic for Strachey and the school of Sainte-Beuve in which he enrols himself is 'not to criticise, but to understand the object of his criticism' (pp. 69–70). Arnold and Stephen considered themselves followers of Sainte-Beuve too, but Strachey thought them preoccupied with evaluating rather than understanding literature. Sympathy, not judgement, is what we now need from critics, though in this development Strachey is also aware that something essential to criticism has been lost. Sympathetic critics sometimes forget to ask whether the works they understand in terms of its age, environment, and author have any value. 'It is then one cannot help regretting the Johnsonian black cap' (p. 70).

Toward its conclusion Strachey's review attempts to explain why the unimaginative Johnson undertook to judge poetry at all. The explanation reveals once more that Bloomsbury's fondness for the eighteenth century was importantly qualified by Romanticism. According to Strachey, Romanticism had nothing to do with the return to nature – all eighteenth-century authorities wanted that – rather, it was concerned with 'the discovery of the Unknown' (p. 72). Romanticism clarifies Strachey's dislike of Johnson's criticism as well as Arnold's and Stephen's. When Strachey referred to the wrongness of Johnson's 'aesthetic judgments', he used a word not to be found in Johnson's dictionary. *Aesthetic* is a Romantic, Kantian term involving the attention to feeling and the interrelation of the arts. For Strachey and most of the other members of Bloomsbury, literary responses were analogous to pictorial and musical experiences and to be judged accordingly.

IV

Before describing the last reviews Lytton Strachey wrote for the
Independent Review, mention should be made of two others which
appeared in 1906 for the *Speaker,* that other New Liberal paper
which published Bloomsbury writers early. In addition to books on
Lyly and Browne, Strachey reviewed a guidebook on Versailles, in
which he again displayed his ambivalence towards the classical
tradition. The book did not sufficiently appreciate the magnificently
arrogant, almost divine, spiritual failure that Louis XIV's palace and
age were. And in reviewing two books on Sir Walter Scott, Strachey
attacked another member of the Edwardian literary establishment,
Andrew Lang, for whom Bloomsbury had little respect. And not
only Bloomsbury, for Strachey's mother wrote urging him to
trounce Lang's book (Merle, p. 41). He did, finding Lang's study of
Scott not only slovenly written like the Versailles guide, but also
affected, obscure, slipshod in expression – not, in short, an honest
piece of work like the other book on Scott under review, which was
a straightforward condensation of Lockhart's early Victorian
biography which Strachey thought immortal.

The final three reviews Strachey wrote for the *Independent Review*
and its short-lived successor, the *Albany Review,* which ceased
publication in 1908, belong with Bloomsbury's later Edwardian
writings, but are better described in the context of the earlier writings he did for the first journal to publish Bloomsbury's writings.
All three texts were biographical rather than literary, and Strachey
reprinted none of them. The review of a good biography of Mademoiselle de Lespinasse in September 1906, recounts somewhat
melodramatically a life of epistolary passion. Strachey's account is
almost too sympathetic; it lacks the subtlety of the essay-review on
Madame du Deffand he wrote in 1913 for the *Edinburgh Review.* He
celebrates Mademoiselle de Lespinasse's salon in terms that
describe Bloomsbury's ideal of social friendship. One could find
there 'a sense of freedom and intimacy which was the outcome of a
real equality, a real understanding, a real friendship such as have
existed, before or since, in few societies indeed' (CC, p. 106). The
reiteration of *real* suggests how close we still are to the Cambridge
Apostles in the *Independent Review.* The word recurs as an adverb in
the description of the Comte de Guibert, to whom Mademoiselle de
Lespinasse wrote her immortal love letters: 'He was really a clever
man; he was really well-meaning and warm-hearted; but that was

all' (p. 109). (This might have been a description of Maynard Keynes as Strachey jealously viewed him around this time.) Mademoiselle de Lespinasse's letters are, for Strachey, 'the most complete analysis the world possesses of a passion which actually existed in a human mind' (p. 100). The review ends with an epitaph on her from the second circle of Dante's *Inferno*. In Wallace Stevens's description of Strachey entering heaven Mademoiselle de Lespinasse is one of the figures he hopes to meet there (Stevens, *Opus Posthumous*, p. 39).

Reviewing a biography of Mary Wortley Montagu in 1907, Strachey shows how he was preparing for his literary life's work through the reading and writing he was doing for the *Independent Review* and other journals. His comments in this review touch on a central preoccupation of his later writing: the badness of English biography. The wording and even the syntax of one passage read like a early draft of the preface to *Eminent Victorians*:

> The book, with its slipshod writing, its uninstructed outlook, its utter lack of taste and purpose, is a fair specimen of the kind of biographical work which seems to give so much satisfaction to large numbers of our reading public. Decidedly, 'they order the matter better in France', where such a production could never have appeared. (*CC*, p. 125)

The biographer has no understanding of Lady Mary, so Strachey undertakes to defend her as a moralist and wit, though admitting that she lacked the sympathetic feelings we now think the essence of goodness; love and revenge were her two great pleasures. Much of the review consists of a lively retelling of her life, and it concludes with Strachey admiring her honest and brave acceptance of 'the worthlessness of things' (p. 133). Leonard Woolf, reading the *Independent Review* in Ceylon (he also read the *TLS*), was unconvinced that she was really all that supreme (29.ix.07, LS/pBL), and Strachey himself was dissatisfied with the way the piece turned out.

In March 1907, the last issue of the *Independent Review* under that name carried a remarkable essay-review by Strachey on the letters of the Indian Viceroy Lord Lytton, who wrote verse under the name Owen Meredith and also happened to be the reviewer's godfather and namesake. (Both Virginia Woolf's and Lytton Strachey's godfathers were poets.) But that is not all that makes the review so unusual. 'The First Earl of Lytton' is unique among Strachey's writings as a panegyric on an eminent Victorian. The editors of the *Independent Review* may have asked Strachey to review the letters because of his dissertation on the first Governor General of India, Warren Hastings. What they got was a defence of Indian imperialism. Strachey argues that the popular idea of Lytton 'as a minor poet masquerading as a Viceroy, who scribbled verses when he should have been composing dispatches, is a glaring travesty of the facts. The antithesis, however, is delightful, like all antitheses' even when supported by the English prejudice that a witty man cannot be a wise one (*CC*, p. 119). Strachey does not deny that Owen Meredith had a fatal facility for minor verse; he chooses rather to defend him from the obloquy he has received as Viceroy. Lytton's domestic administration at least was highly beneficent and forward-looking in its achievement, for instance, of giving free trade to India. Strachey wrote to his sister Dorothy that he considered his review such a violent attack on the editors of the *Independent Review* and was surprised they printed it (10?.v.07, LS/pP). It is hard to find much violence in the review now but presumably Strachey felt his praise for a Disraeli-appointed and much-denigrated Indian imperialist might have been an embarrassment for the editorial board of New Liberals.

In the nineteenth century, Stracheys and Stephens were importantly involved in colonial administration. Bloomsbury's complex responses to imperialism appear and reappear throughout the Group's literary history, as we shall see in their monographs, novels, biographies and autobiographies. Strachey's account of Lytton's letters, for example, is an implicit autobiographical text as well as a review. Lord Lytton was not only a much admired friend of his mother's, he was also close friends with the Stephens' uncle, Sir James Fitzjames Stephen. Here is Strachey's account of the relationship:

> The friendship is remarkable for something more than its swift beginning: it was a mingling of opposites such as it is a rare delight to think upon. Sir James Stephen was eminently unromantic. His qualities were those of solidity and force; he preponderated with a character of formidable grandeur, with a massive and rugged intellectual sanity, a colossal commonsense. The contrast is complete between this monolithic nature and the mercurial temperament of Lord Lytton, with his ardent

imagination, his easy brilliance, his passionate sympathy, his taste for the elaborate and the coloured and the rococo. (pp. 116–17)

This is also the description of a friendship between another Stephen and another Lytton – Thoby, who died the previous year, and the reviewer who loved him.

V

The liberalism of the *Independent Review* apparently presented no difficulties for Desmond MacCarthy, who maintained friendly relations with liberals like the Asquiths through the First World War. MacCarthy published in the second issue of the *Independent Review*, a notable review of Shaw's printed play *Man and Superman* which may have led to his becoming drama critic for the *Speaker* in 1904. He continued to do occasional reviews both elsewhere and in the *Independent Review*, becoming a more regular reviewer after 1907, when the *Speaker* turned into the *Nation*. But he was not well paid by the *Independent Review*, (nor presumably were Strachey or Forster), receiving only twenty-five shillings for 3000 words (Cecil, p. 68).

Although MacCarthy is one of the best Edwardian drama critics, largely because of his discerning criticism of George Bernard Shaw, his reviews do not generally justify the attention of literary history as much as Lytton Strachey's critical essays do. MacCarthy's urbane, sensible prose has the restricted but valuable aim of being perceptive about the work he is criticising. Yet his reviews do not illuminate his more substantial literary texts because he wrote none. MacCarthy's genre is primarily the review, and his reviews, like Leonard Woolf's, are mainly interesting not for their own sake as writing but for the attitudes and ideas they display. The critical opinions of MacCarthy have a considerable importance for the literary history of Bloomsbury, which can be presented more selectively in summary than can Strachey's, Forster's, or Virginia Woolf's. Though MacCarthy's range as a critic could be as wide as anyone's in Bloomsbury, as a weekly reviewer and then columnist he was often confined to the writings of his contemporaries. Strachey by contrast almost never reviewed twentieth-century writers. Among the authors MacCarthy reviewed for the *Independent Review* were Shaw, James, Butler, Conrad, Gissing, Belloc,

Wells, Chesterton, A. C. Benson, Hudson, Symons, Gosse, and W. H. Davies. MacCarthy's criticism of these and other writers embodies Bloomsbury values and attitudes while representing a more traditional literary point of view than is to be found in the criticism of other Bloomsbury members. His reviews, especially of Bloomsbury works are therefore important in the Group's literary history because they often indicate how the Group's writing struck their contemporaries. The basic criticisms that have been made, for example, of the truth of Strachey's biographies or the forms of Virginia Woolf's fiction were often first and best expressed by MacCarthy. He was more of a common reader than anyone else in Bloomsbury, and more of a common reviewer too. But MacCarthy was also a Cambridge Apostle devoted to Moore, and a member of Bloomsbury whose friendship and judgement were highly valued by Forster, Fry, and the Woolfs.

All but one collection of MacCarthy's reviews are now out of print; indeed only two or three volumes of them were ever reprinted. Of the critics he influenced outside of Bloomsbury, only Cyril Connolly and perhaps David Cecil are still read today. Yet for the literary historian, MacCarthy's wide sympathies and clear critical discrimination provide much insight into Bloomsbury's writing.

MacCarthy's review of *Man and Superman* in the November 1903 issue of the *Independent Review* was the beginning of an extensive, ambivalent commentary on Shaw's ideas that illuminates those held by Bloomsbury. Wittily entitled 'The New St Bernard', the review implicitly indicates what Moore and his followers would have thought of the play's ideas. Within a month of the publication of *Principia Ethica*, MacCarthy was writing of the fatal defect in Shaw's wit: 'He cannot see that men and women are lovable, and therefore he cannot value for their own sakes the emotions which they arouse in each other, or rather, he simply does not believe in them.' Don Juan's Hell is to be found in the Apostolic and Bloomsbury Ideal of 'personal affections and beauty' ('New St.', pp. 350, 352). MacCarthy appreciates *Man and Superman* as an interesting play (in a later review he will call it a brilliant one), but he is more concerned in the *Independent Review* to discuss the play's ideas as these are what Shaw cared about, 'for Art's sake he could never have penned a line . . . ' (p. 349). What MacCarthy has to say about Shaw's self-criticism in the play's dedicatory epistle applies to his own literary criticism: 'All criticism which is not purely technical cannot help being an exposition of the writer's philosophy . . . ' (p. 346). MacCarthy's Moorean assumptions reject the asceticism of this new St Bernard's loveless world. Instead of martyrdom, however, he thinks Shaw deserves another kind of suffering – the discovery that his ideas are not 'worth a dump as a philosophy of life' (p. 352).

The most striking Bloomsbury characteristic of the twenty reviews by MacCarthy that followed in the *Independent Review* was his adaptation of the fundamental distinction between good means and ends in *Principia Ethica* as a method of critical evaluation. Reviewing Henry James's *The Golden Bowl*, and later *The American Scene*, for instance, MacCarthy says that James's moral philosophy could be summarised in the sentence, 'There are no short cuts to a good end' ('American Scene', p. 114). Novels like *The Awkward Age* show the consequences of trying to storm the ideals of refinement and intimacy. The admiration with which James's late works were read in Cambridge by MacCarthy and other Apostles is qualified a little by 1905, because James is found to have overvalued subtle personal relations, caring more for them than for his characters. Yet MacCarthy still finds James a realist whose influence extends to a novel like Conrad's *The Secret Agent*, which MacCarthy praised for its Balzacian energy and masterful representation of the psychology of violent emotion.

One of MacCarthy's most valuable functions as a Bloomsbury critic is to be found simply in the works he was assigned or chose to bring to the attention of his readers. His recognition of the quality of Edmund Gosse's anonymous autobiography *Father and Son* illustrates MacCarthy's critical talent for appreciation. He is kinder to Gosse than Strachey, but then he was not reviewing one of Gosse's literary studies. MacCarthy's description of Gosse the son as 'a fluid, attaching character' is a nicely mixed metaphor for the man he would eventually succeed as the influential critic of *The Sunday Times* ('Anonymous', p. 337). Gosse's book brings out an amusing, rueful confession from his reviewer:

> Long after we have given up as impracticable the intentions of becoming philosophers, charmers of hearts, warriors, poets, philanthropists, society wits, and romantic recluses at the same time we hanker after the notion that somehow or other, if we could only behave better, we might combine in our moral natures, say, the generous diffused humanity of Shakespeare and

the austere discriminative insight of Tolstoi, or the friendliness of
Lamb with the concentrated devotion of Saint Augustin.

(pp. 337–8)

Such an autobiographical passage is worthy of the model for
Bernard in Woolf's *The Waves*.

In two *Independent Review* notices of books on nineteenth-century
Russian literature, MacCarthy anticipated what would be a literary
revelation for Bloomsbury. (The second review appeared in the
same issue as Strachey's piece on Lord Lytton.) MacCarthy was the
first of the Group to express in print his enthusiasm for Turgenev,
Tolstoy, Dostoevsky, and Chekhov; he was soon followed by
Strachey and later by the Woolfs and Forster. MacCarthy's view of
Russian culture may not have been very informed but his
recognition of its fiction's ethical significance is unmistakably
characteristic of Bloomsbury:

> No authors remind the world so often or so vividly as the
> Russians of difference between the actions which are merely
> important as means, and those actions and feelings which are
> ends in themselves. Standing half outside civilisation, they often
> see clearer what is necessary and what is superfluous.
>
> ('Russian Literature', pp. 355–6)

Russian realism, psychological and physical, was far more
stimulating for MacCarthy and Bloomsbury than various expressions of aestheticism which were appearing in the early twentieth
century. Two reviews of Arthur Symons's books by MacCarthy
commended his sensitivity but objected in good Cambridge fashion
to his mysticism and praise for the decadents. MacCarthy appears
unaware of the importance of Symons's book on the symbolist
movement for modern poetry, although elsewhere in the *Independent Review* MacCarthy appreciated Verlaine's poetry. In another
review that helps relate Bloomsbury to modernism, MacCarthy
thought Nietzsche also regarded the world from the aesthetic rather
than the moral point of view, and this explained some of his current
influence. MacCarthy was reviewing A. R. Orage's introduction to
Nietzsche. Realising of course that Nietzsche is a moralist urging us
to live dangerously, MacCarthy cannot take him or Schopenhauer
seriously as philosophers. They may blunder on truth more than
carefully reasoning philosophers, but that does not matter because

we read philosophy he says, echoing F. H. Bradley, 'not to swallow truths on trust, but to discover good reasons for holding what we already suspect to be true' ('Nietzsche', p. 91).

MacCarthy was not the only early Edwardian writer in Bloomsbury to criticise aestheticism; Forster too was satirising it in early fiction, some of which was published in the *Independent Review*. Forster's and MacCarthy's literary values were close in the Group. They shared, for example, an enthusiasm for the work of Samuel Butler, whom MacCarthy had known. MacCarthy's essay-review on *Erewhon* (it appeared in the *Independent Review* in 1904 along with an essay by Fry on technique and a translation from Nietzsche by Forster's Apostle friend H. O. Meredith) singles out ideas of Butler that are also to be found in Forster's fiction. These include the convictions that man's whole duty consists in serving God and Mammon, and that self-deception, priggishness, and lack of candour are among the chief causes of evil in life. MacCarthy preferred the irony of *Erewhon* to the pure satire of *The Way of All Flesh* – a preference Forster may have shared – and he developed this distinction several years later in another discussion of Butler's irony in the *Independent Review*. *Erewhon* was the best of several utopias reviewed by MacCarthy in the *Independent Review*, better, he thought, than H. G. Wells's *In the Days of the Comet* or W. H. Hudson's *Crystal Age*, neither of which show how human relations actually proceed in their imagined worlds. This is a criticism Forster could have made. Also Forsterian was MacCarthy's dissatisfaction with A. C. Benson's popular essays *From a College Window*, (also dismissed later by Virginia Woolf). The book's popularity is a bad sign, MacCarthy thinks, for it is a tired book of 'wistful blandness' that displays 'the smoothness of the transition from the snug to the sublime' ('Recent Books', pp. 231–2). Sometimes MacCarthy's criticism suffers also from blandness, but not here, where a caustic phrase marks the limit of his critical tolerance.

The format of the monthly *Independent Review* may have allowed MacCarthy too much space for his reviews, which he often filled up with summaries. Strachey's early texts, on the other hand, become more interesting when they can expand into little narratives instead of being confined to reviews in the weekly columns of the *Spectator*. E. M. Forster also did some of his best early work for the *Independent Review*, where like Strachey he was allowed a generic freedom to mix reviewing and narrating, describing and imagining, fact and fiction.

2 E. M. Forster's Earlier Short Writings

I

So grateful was E. M. Forster for the *Independent Review* that he dedicated his first collection of stories, *The Celestial Omnibus*, to its memory in 1912. Four of the six stories in it had been published in the *Independent Review*, whose editorial board included his Cambridge mentors Dickinson and Wedd, and he would use another as the title story for his second collection, *The Eternal Moment*, in 1928. But it was not as a short-story writer that Forster began to be read by his contemporaries in the New Liberal journal which touched decency with poetry. The first two contributions of Forster's to appear in the *Independent Review* were informal essays. Over the next five years he contributed five short stories, two brief historical biographies, a travel sketch, and a review. The diversity of these texts brought inquiries as to whether 'E. M. Forster' was a pseudonym, perhaps, of Hilaire Belloc's. An editorial note in the October 1905 issue asserted firmly that 'all Mr. Forster's contributions to this Review are signed by his own name' (PNF/*EMF*, I 109). As with Strachey's early work, the mixture of genres in these texts and the circumstances of their publication are part of Bloomsbury's literary history. Fiction or non-fiction is not an adequate classification for the stories, fantasies, allegories, myths, satires, essays, biographies, histories, travelogues, and reviews that he was writing. Short narratives may be the most comprehensive classification of this cross-genre writing that Forster practised all his life, though it does not include all of his essays, or his lectures and reviews (Herz, *Narratives*[1]).

Forster's début in the second number of the *Independent Review* shows the difficulties inherent in separating his fiction and non-fiction. 'Macolnia Shops' is a humorous prose ode on a Grecian toilet case. The Keatsean similarities add a suppressed self-mockery to the text. Forster fished the toilet case out of the stream of history when he saw it in a Roman museum (*AH*, p. v). On the basis of an inscription he re-creates its purchase by a Roman matron and then describes the sylvan scene from the Argonauts that is engraved on the case. The heroes are sharing water denied them by a boxer who has been vanquished and tied naked to a tree. Praise of water is the outward motive of the toilet case, in Forster's interpretation; the inner meaning is praise of friendship in a scene from which both classical self-consciousness and Christian self-denial are absent. Forster's narrator links the motives in the moral he draws from the case: 'when the body is feeble, the soul is feeble: cherish the body and you will cherish the soul' (*AH*, p. 169). The most beautiful figures of the engraving (the least attractive is Athena, the only female present) lean on their spears together after having shared another labour together – but from this reverie the poet-essayist is summoned back by Macolnia whose shopping has teased him out of thought. She scoffs at his descriptions, had bought the case because she thought it pretty; that praise may please its maker, the narrator admits, more than his own high thoughts and feelings about the beautiful Mediterranean past, nature, the body, and male love.

'Macolnia Shops' was one of what Forster called his 'sentimental articles' (PNF/*EMF*, I 90). Several of these early texts, which he left unpublished, display more explicitly the persona of his early travel writings. A piece on Syracuse grants that sentiment can be enervating, pernicious, even ludicrous; but those lacking the knowledge of archaeologists or the genius of poets must invoke it to dream even inaccurately of the past's greatness. In another, called 'The Amateur among the Mountains', the narrator searches for a name and occupation. Avoiding the conventionally bohemian 'vagabond' of Stevenson, he adopts 'the disused profession of pilgrim', though what he seeks beyond man's relation to nature is admittedly vague (pKC). Among the ancestors of Forster's sentimental pilgrims are Laurence Sterne's sentimental journeyers and Henry James's passionate pilgrims. Emotional and inhibited, intelligent yet ineffective, they appear as comically self-conscious moral commentators in both his articles and his stories.

Forster's second publication in the *Independent Review* was another sentimental article. 'Cnidus' is an autobiographical travel narrative about not seeing the seaport in Asia Minor, famous for

Praxiteles's lost statue of Aphrodite. Rain and darkness keep the conscientious tourists from images that could connect Cnidus to reality, and therefore the place lies defenceless to 'the sentimental imagination' that ceaselessly re-creates the city at cloudless midday. In a sentence cut when Forster reprinted 'Cnidus' in *Abinger Harvest*, the authorial narrator adds that because he saw nothing when he was there, self-respect will not allow him to write what he sees now. Perhaps the remark was dropped because twice the narrator does let his sentimental imagination go at Cnidus. The first occasion is over the Cnidian Demeter, who appeals to Forster more than the famous Aphrodite. Warm, dry, and regularly dusted in the British Museum, she will become the symbol of natural, maternal beauty and love three years later in *The Longest Journey*. In 'Cnidus' she is the occasion for rapture touched with irony:

> Demeter alone among gods has true immortality. . . . To her, all over the world, rise prayers of idolatry from suffering men as well as suffering women, for she has transcended sex. And Poets too, generation after generation, have sung in passionate incompetence of the hundred-flowered Narcissus and the rape of Persephone, and the wanderings of the Goddess, and her gift to us of corn and tears; so that generations of critics, obeying also their need, have censured the poets for reviving the effete mythology of Greece, and urged them to themes of living interest which shall touch the heart of to-day. (p. 172)

The *Independent Review* was full of living-interest themes; in the same March 1904 issue as 'Cnidus', for example, Bertrand Russell's laudatory review of *Principia Ethica* appeared. But Forster would continue to sing, with passionate incompetence at times, in the pages of the *Independent Review* and elsewhere during the Edwardian period of effete Greek myths, as he tried to relate them to the undeveloped hearts of his contemporaries.

The second time the sentimental imagination comes into play at Cnidus is when the tourists are embarking for their ship. An extra person appears among them, peering into their faces, offering to help them into the boats.

> It is well known (is it not?) who that extra person always is. . . . He made no answer to our tremulous greetings, but raised his

hand to his head and then laid it across his breast, meaning I understand, that his brain and his heart were ours.

Over this extra person the narrator's brain cannot keep steady (pp. 173–4). The fantasy introduced here at the end of what seemed at first to be a realistic travel essay invokes an even more important and complex mythological symbol in Forster's subsequent short writings, whose representation in another British Museum sculpture also had aesthetic and personal significance for Forster. God of travellers and of dreams, father of Pan, 'messenger, thief, and conductor of souls to a not too terrible hereafter', Hermes symbolises fantasy itself in Forster's *Aspects of the Novel* (p. 77), and later in *The Collected Short Stories*, which Forster rededicates to him. As Hermes Psychopompos, the conductor of the dead, he is also the dedicatee of *Pharos and Pharillon*, Forster's Egyptian writings, where history and imagination are fused again (Herz, 'Hermes').

II

At the end of 1904, Forster gloomed in his diary, 'Independent going smash, no one else takes my things' (PNF/*EMF*, I 121). He had tried to publish pieces in such places as the prestigious *Blackwood's* but succeeded in placing only two other pieces in magazines which would both cease publication shortly. The *Independent Review* did not smash for another four years, but even by the end of its first year, it had published two of Forster's most remarkable stories: 'The Road from Colonus' in June 1904 and 'The Story of a Panic' in August. In printing them, however, the editor, a jurist named Edward Jenks, enraged his young author by criticising his punctuation and changing his commas to semicolons (PNF/*EMF*, I 107, 113). Forster had to wait until their republication in *The Celestial Omnibus* to change them back again.

In the light of recent interpretations that emphasise Forster as a homosexual author, it is a little comical that his first story in the *Independent Review* was connected with Oedipus but had little to do with sex. Yet 'The Road from Colonus' is the most modern of Forster's early Edwardian stories. The ironic juxtaposition of classical myth and contemporary life relates it to work of Joyce and Eliot that was still to come. Mr Lucas is an anti-Oedipus at Colonus; his Antigone conspires to force him from the scene of an impending, transcendent death to a trivial and querulous old age in London. Life-in-Death wins Mr Lucas from Death, as she won the Ancient Mariner. His daughter's conclusion that 'such a marvellous deliverance does make one believe in Providence' is worthy of Strachey (*CO*, p. 164). 'The Road from Colonus' is not only a satire however. What has become perhaps Forster's most distinctive subject – the philistine hypocrisy and brutality of the English abroad – is certainly satirised in a manner quite compatible with the anti-imperialism of the *Independent Review*, but there is more to the story. Other important aspects of it to which Forster will return in his novels and later stories are Mr Lucas's growing desire to contradict the logic of his ageing and die somehow triumphantly, and his revelation in a tree-shrine at Colonus. That mystical experience is especially noteworthy in the literary history of Bloomsbury, for it is the first published account in the Group's writings of a visionary moment of being.

> So he lay motionless, conscious only of the stream below his feet, and that all things were a stream, in which he was moving.
> He was aroused at last by a shock – the shock of an arrival perhaps, for when he opened his eyes, something unimagined, indefinable, had passed over all things, and made them intelligible and good. (pp. 148–9)

In Forster's and Virginia Woolf's works such mystical shocks, which are often Romantically associated with the spirit of a natural place, continue to be good both in themselves and for their transforming consequences. But Mr Lucas's 'arrival' is short-lived. His daughter turns up and compares him not to Sophocles's tragically sacred Oedipus but to Tennyson's Merlin. Mr Lucas is able to describe the scene of his experience only in pompous, tepid clichés. 'Such is the form in which a revelation is announced to the world', comments the narrator unnecessarily in a sentence deleted when the story was republished in *The Celestial Omnibus*.

'The Road from Colonus' may be the best of Forster's early short fictions. The satiric and the visionary are interrelated more thoroughly, maybe even too thoroughly at the end, in a modern, realistic yet fantastic, amusing yet moving narrative. It is free from the naïve and sentimental sexual encounters that occur in other early texts of his such as the one that appeared two months later in the *Independent Review*.

'The Story of a Panic', the first story that Forster ever wrote, is an attempt to connect what Forster in 'Cnidus' called 'the effete mythology of Greece' with Edwardian life. The limited point of view of the story emphasises the satiric rather than the fantastic. In much of Forster's best writing the authorial narrative voice that critics have sought recently to define is not restricted to a dramatised narrator but given more scope for omniscient description and reflection. Still, in a story of sexual awakening it is useful to have as an insensitive narrator, 'a plain, simple man, with no pretensions to literary style' (*CO*, p. 1), but quite a few to moral judgement. Priggish complacency confronting the supernatural is a stock situation in Forster's early Edwardian fiction; the familiar cast of characters usually includes fatherless sons, matriarchs, uncles, curates, aesthetes, and lower-class native males. What makes 'The Story of a Panic' exceptional is the story of the panic itself – a panic that will have its artistic culmination in the Marabar Caves of *A Passage to India*. Forster's inspired transformation of a picnic into a panic begins with didactic bullying and chatter about nature, art, and the death of Pan; it ends with the terrifying sound of Eustace's whistle and a catspaw of wind (ominously described in mixed metaphors) coming down one of the green fingers of the valley. The remaining two-thirds of the story Forster said he added later, but his original inspiration must have included the discovery of the changed fourteen-year-old Eustace (*CSS*, p. v). Mr Tytler, the Dickensianly-named narrator, tells how he, the curate, and the aesthete who destroyed Eustace's whistle try to cope with the goatish boy and his new friend Gennaro, a young waiter who understands what has happened. The waiter insists Eustace will die if he is not allowed, as Gennaro says, to 'run through the woods, and climb the rocks, and plunge into the water until I had accomplished my desire' (p. 39). Gennaro is nevertheless bribed to betray Eustace, which he does unsuccessfully before becoming the first of Forster's characters to drop dead of moral rather than natural causes. Beyond the need to be affectionate to Gennaro, to run, climb, and swim, the exact nature of the escaping Eustace's Pan-induced desire is left undefined by the narrative form of the story.

The prevalence of Pans in late nineteenth, and early twentieth-century literature has often been noticed. Lytton Strachey's essay on Shakespeare's last period, which appeared in the same issue of the *Independent Review* as 'The Story of a Panic', concludes with a comparison of Caliban to Victor Hugo's vast Pan. At the end of 1904 a much smaller one named Peter appeared famously on the London stage. Forster complained in his unpublished sentimental article 'The Amateur among the Mountains' that it had taken centuries to domesticate Pans and satyrs so that ladies and curates could listen to their pipes (pKC). Yet how far did Forster understand the implications of his Pan in 'The Story of a Panic'? When D. H. Lawrence read the story later in *The Celestial Omnibus* he objected to Forster's splitting love and sex and confusing Pan with universal or Christian love instead of connecting him with sexual feeling, as Lawrence would later in some of his own fiction (*Letters*, II 275). And Forster himself in a 1920s Memoir Club paper told how one Cambridge reader of the *Independent Review* maliciously interpreted to Keynes the displaced sexuality of the story as an account of buggery with a waiter followed by bestiality with a goat!

> Of course Maynard flew chirruping with the news. It seemed to him great fun, to me disgusting. . . . In after years I realized that in a stupid and unprofitable way he was right and that this was the cause of my indignation. (*LJ*, p. 302)

The *Church Times* also took note of the story (which mocks Christianity in several ways) and thought it very foolish (PNF/ EMF, II 113–4). Clearly Forster was being read in the *Independent Review* not just in Cambridge and Bloomsbury, and not just as a satirist of imperial attitudes like Belloc. Satire is present in 'The Road from Colonus' and 'The Story of a Panic', but it is the emotional poverty of the English as much as their arrogant exploitation of the natives that Forster exposes.

A third story that Forster published in the *Independent Review* in 1904 leaves the realistic settings of Greece and Italy for an allegorical world in which the travellers are not tourists, but pilgrims measuring their progress along the road of life. In 'The Other Side of the Hedge' dropouts like the narrator pass through the thorny hedge bordering the road and the cold water of a moat to find themselves in the heaven of G. E. Moore's Ideal. Only with difficulty do they understand it is a realm of ends where competitive progress is pointless. 'What does it all mean?' asks the narrator after seeing a runner but no race, and is told by his guide 'It means nothing but itself . . . ' (*CO*, p. 48). *Independent Review* topics such as the Boer War, the Fiscal Question, Radium and Christian Science are of no interest to the inhabitants in this afterlife of pastoral peace, beauty, and regained brotherly love, whose setting again owes something to Keats's odes and also the underworld of Virgil's *Aeneid*, which Forster was annotating for the Temple Classics (Stape, 'Myth' pp. 375–8). 'The Other Side of the Hedge' is the simplest of Forster's utopian fantasies that relate nature, art, and brotherhood with death. But how bored Bloomsbury would have been there. The two sides of the hedge are connected only through the gates of true and false dreams. Yet the Group would have agreed with the ethical principle of Forster's allegory – as they did with MacCarthy's criticisms of Shaw's hell and heaven in *Man and Superman* – that doing in life needs to be justified by being that is greatly good in itself.

III

In 1905 the *Independent Review* published another form of Forster's writing. Two essays in historical biography appeared under his name; it was at the end of the second that the editor found it necessary to state Forster was signing all his contributions with his own name. Several months before, the *Independent Review* had serialised, in three instalments, Forster's longest short story, 'The Eternal Moment'. Critics have paid little attention to these biographical essays yet they belong to the genre of Bloomsbury brief lives that descends from Leslie Stephen and includes Strachey's major writing and some of Virginia Woolf's best essays. The possible varieties of short biography are almost as diverse as those of the short story. Neither of Forster's biographical essays on Cardan and Gemistus Pletho are in the ironical mode that Strachey created later. Still, there are distinct similarities in tone, for example, with Strachey's 'Voltaire's Tragedies' that appeared in the same issue of the *Independent Review* as 'Cardan'. In their personal point of view and colloquial style, however, Forster's brief biographies are unlike the formality of Strachey's mandarin prose treatments, in which the narrator maintains his distance. In this respect Virginia Woolf's biographical texts are closer in form to Strachey's than Forster's, though quite different in style. In this Bloomsbury genre, however, the three display a family resemblance in their critical sense of values.[2]

Italian humanist values of the fifteenth and sixteenth centuries are the focus of Forster's interest in Jerome Cardan and Gemistus Pletho. (Forster had begun giving Cambridge University extension lectures on Italian history in 1903.) Both subjects are historically rather remote but Forster's humorous, serious moral inquiries show their relation to Bloomsbury's later work. 'Cardan' is about the sixteenth-century Italian mathematician, physician, and philosopher, mainly as he revealed himself in his remarkable autobiography. Forster finds that Cardan's ability to express sincere, unsentimental egotism rescues him from oblivion; he can make us 'blush sometimes for him, and more frequently for ourselves' (*AH*, p. 188). His learned superstitiousness becomes a source of comedy in the essay as he casts one wrong horoscope after another. But Forster also sees Cardan's astrology as an attempt to connect the spiritual with everyday life in the wake of Catholicism's disintegration. The consequences are described acidulously in contemporary metaphors: 'A little later, and the Jesuits put an end to private enterprise in superstition, and reorganized it in the interests of the Church' (p. 192). In the inquisition's atheist tripos Cardan got only a second class and was therefore not elected to a martyrdom.[3] Cardan's was not an easy life, personally or professionally. The great Scaliger attacked him and then, misinformed that his polemic had been fatal, wrote an unneeded funeral oration. This was, says Forster, who shares Bloomsbury's delight in the absurdities of scholarly controversy, 'the greatest joke of the sixteenth century' (p. 195).

'To raise up a skeleton, and make it dance, brings indeed little credit either to the skeleton or to us', Forster writes at the end of his sketch of Cardan. 'But those ghosts who are still clothed with passion or thought are profitable companions' (*AH*, p. 198). This is the moral intention of 'Cardan', as it is of Strachey's biographies later. Forster does not exaggerate his importance; Michelangelo and Cellini are more interesting, and Sir Thomas Browne was sounder on immortality. Cardan did not care how he was remembered just as long as he was. It is just this honest autobiographical self-knowledge that makes him a profitable ghost for biography for Forster – and for Bloomsbury. Thirty years later, Keynes was still recommending Cardan's candid autobiography to BBC readers (*CW*, XXVIII 332).

'Gemistus Pletho' begins as a travel essay on ancient Sparta, then turns into the biography of a philosopher who mediated Plato and

Greek religion to the Italian Renaissance. It ends with the bio-grapher/traveller/narrator contemplating, before Gemistus' tomb in Rimini, the significance of a thinker who believed, as Forster did, that truth 'might be in the past rather than the present' (*AH*, p. 176). Gemistus' career as a government official involved him in the politics of religious controversy, which was a subject Forster relished even more than scholarly polemics. He could no more pass up a church council than Strachey could. The Patriarch Joseph, whom Gemistus advises, is reduced to a modern tourist worrying about his luggage at the disastrous Council that was to unite the Greek and Roman churches. The Patriarch 'lost his labours quite as much as he had lost his temper', died in Florence, and was buried with an epitaph falsely proclaiming his happiness (p. 181). The abiding significance of the Council lay not in the machinations of pope and patriarch, however, but in the philosopher Gemistus's explanations to the Florentine intelligentsia of the differences between Plato and Aristotle. 'Hitherto it had not been known that there was any difference . . . ' (p. 179). Forster's tone remains irreverent as he writes about matters that were important in Cambridge. Eclectic Florence got Plato all wrong, but the Forsterian biographer, glancing maybe at Dickinson and his philosophical friends, adds that 'a nation of artists is perhaps seldom sound in its philosophy, and is apt to produce masterpieces which have no metaphysical justification'. (Roger Fry felt the same way about the thought of Dickinson and McTaggart.) But in one respect Florence got Plato right. Forster's description of it relates Florence to the Cambridge Conversazione Society with deliberate anachronism:

> Through him they recaptured for the world one of the secrets of ancient Greece – the secret of civilized conversation. The Middle Ages had separated serious discussion from daily life, confining it to the study and the lecture room and the hall of disputation. Florence, like Athens, summoned it into the open air, and bade it take its chance against birds and trees, evolve, if it could, from a dinner or a game of fives, yield, if it must, to a dance or to a song.
>
> (p. 180)

In Clive Bell's *Civilization*, ancient Greece and Renaissance Italy remained exemplars of civilisation, and in Gemistus' work Forster tries to relate both to modern life. Gemistus' later attempt to fashion a new religion by adapting Greek mythology to philosophy is treated more critically by Forster. It ultimately did not matter, however, for the gods 'who have, in the idle additions of the poets, an immortality which Gemistus did not suspect, could endure the philosophy of that day, just as they will endure the archaeology of this' (pp. 184–5).

Gemistus Pletho died and was buried in Greece. Sismondo Malatesta of Rimini brought his honoured remains back to Italy, driving the Turks out of Arcady in the process. The symbolic background of this posthumous return is explored by Forster in a short story of some 10,000 words that pre-dates his essay. While he was writing 'The Tomb of Pletone' (which uses the Italian spelling of Gemistus' last name), Forster aptly described it to a friend as 'the impossible – a short historical story' (*AS*, p. xi). Its rejection by several editors seems to have confirmed his opinion. The story, which has survived in a manuscript now lacking an ending, was one of only two historical fictions that Forster wrote. In his fantasies and realistic stories Forster can effectively combine satire and imagination; in biographical and topographical essays he derives satire from the retelling of history and the evoking of places. But in 'The Tomb of Pletone' these different purposes appear to interfere with each other. The historical identities of the soldier Sismondo, the young banker Astorre, and his friend the scholar Jacobo remain rather vague. Pletone, the betrayal of the honest, affectionate Astorre (he is an ancestor of Maurice) by the soldier and the scholar, the finding of Pletone's sarcophagus which crushes Astorre – all are left undeveloped. Forster seems to be suggesting that Astorre is somehow closer to the fused mysticism and rationalism of Pletone, whose tomb he discovers, than the active Sismondo or the learned Jacobo. The story's irony is too unfocused, perhaps. Writing at one point of Astorre's admiration for Pletone's new religion, in which he did not believe, the narrator warns that 'such were the thoughts of a commonplace man of the fifteenth century. Let the man of the twentieth pause ere he unsheathe his ready wit' (p. 98). This sounds a little like self-criticism. The most engaging aspect of 'The Tomb of Pletone' is Forster's representation of fifteenth-century ideas and behaviour in such a way as to make them into criticisms of modern attitudes. What, for example, was called 'the shameless inconsistency' of the times in the biography of Gemistus (*AH*, p. 184) is described in a physical image in the fictional 'The Tomb of Pletone': 'The men of the past stepped naked from one emotion to the other, caring nothing for the old garment when the reason for wearing it was over. Because of this abruptness we fancy them more inconsistent than ourselves' (*AS*, p. 112). The essay on Pletho is a more engaging historical re-creation of the past than the story of Pletone. For some time Forster had wanted to write a historical novel; his reading of Anatole France's *Thaïs* in 1905 provided an impetus, but nothing came of it (*L* 1 79). A sustained ironic treatment of the past such as France's would have involved Forster in a very different kind of literary work. In Bloomsbury's writings, the sense of the past is created largely through ironic biography. Only in Virginia Woolf's *Orlando* and *Flush* was biography combined with satire and fantasy in full-length works of historical fiction.

IV

Two of the four remaining pieces published by Forster in the *Independent* or *Albany Review* before it finally went smash in 1908 became the title stories of Forster's two short-story collections. The third was an unreprinted *Baedeker* visit (complete with grading of inns) to the northern German towns of Rostock and Wismar, which can be summed up with the judgement of Rostock: 'If the tourist is happy here . . . he will be happy elsewhere' (*AE*, p. 97). German merchant culture has little appeal for Forster. They 'never builded better than they knew. They never stray into immortality, like the Italians' (p. 99). The fourth text, also uncollected by Forster, was his only review to appear in the *Independent Review*. In it an un-promising book on literary eccentrics is turned into a discussion of kinds of literature. Through the topographical metaphor of bypaths diverging from the highway of standard literature, he describes one route that wanders into the chaos of daily life where there is no ordering art, and another that leads into the country of eccentricity, where we are soon up the creek with sirens and the like. The geography and theory are sketchy but the reviewer's preference is clear; if he cannot have standard literature (whatever that may comprise) he prefers eccentric fantasy to inartistic realism. Later this would be Virginia Woolf's preference as well.

Between 'The Celestial Omnibus' – an allegorical fantasy of child-hood and literature – and 'The Eternal Moment' – a long, artistic and realistic story of middle-aged tourists in the Italian Alps – lies the wide range of Forster's *Independent Review* fiction. And the contrast between these two stories' genres brings out their shared criticism of English life.

'The Eternal Moment' was serialised over three months in the summer of 1905, just before the publication of *Where Angels Fear to Tread*, with which it had clear affinities. *Blackwood's Magazine* had rejected the story but it was phenomenally successful in the *Independent Review*, Forster wrote to Leonard Woolf in the jargon of the Apostles (28.viii.05, EMF/pNY). Forster's later description of 'The Eternal Moment' as a Tyrolean village meditation that was almost a yarn (*CSS*, p. vii) suggests that its satirical travel-essay setting dominates the story of love and time. Connecting the two is the consciousness of the novelist-heroine who reflects most of the narrative. Like *Where Angels Fear to Tread*, 'The Eternal Moment' is Jamesian in outline. A genteel, middle-aged writer, travelling with the slightly unconventional companions of a maid and a loving, confidant colonel, returns to the scene of her first literary triumph. There Miss Raby discovers that she has misunderstood the personal significance of the literary success whose public consequences have turned the village into a deplorable tourist attraction. The realisation of her failure entails the loss of Colonel Leyland's love (he must be a relative of the aesthete Leyland in 'The Story of a Panic') and a new kind of sacrificial triumph for her. But the action of 'The Eternal Moment' is so unlike James's fiction as to be almost a parody. Miss Raby amusingly disconcerts, even insults, the English, Germans, and Italians in her dismay at the venal bad taste of the natives and the arrogant vulgarity of the foreigners. Her discovery that she has been 'an unskilful demiurge, who makes a world and beholds that it is bad' (*EM*, p. 172) is essentially comic.

The world that Miss Raby believes she has created began with 'the eternal moment' she experienced twenty years ago and used as the central event as well as the title of her popular novel. Given the importance of the timeless moment in the literature of Bloomsbury and their contemporaries, it is worth taking a close look at its changing meanings in Forster's story. Miss Raby's youthful moment is more ambiguous than old Mr Lucas's one in 'The Road from Colonus'. She remembers a young Italian guide's falling in love with her as a farce of second-hand proposals, screams, tears and sprained ankles. Yet it resulted in a book

written round the idea that man does not live by time alone, that an evening gone may become like a thousand ages in the courts of heaven – the idea that was afterwards expounded more philosophically by Maeterlinck. She herself now declared that it was a tiresome, affected book, and that the title suggested the dentist's chair. (p. 149)

The remembered moment (which interpretations of Bloomsbury's writings would later locate in Bergson rather than Maeterlinck) is again altered by the heroine's understanding of it near the end of the story:

The incident upon the mountain had been one of the great moments of her life – perhaps the greatest, certainly the most enduring: she had drawn unacknowledged power and inspiration from it, just as trees draw vigour from a subterranean spring. Never again could she think of it as a half-humorous episode in her development. There was more reality in it than in all the years of success and varied achievement which had followed, and which it had rendered possible. (pp. 178–9)

Yet for all this moment's inspirational significance, Miss Raby does not realise until she sees the guide Feo again – now a ridiculously middle-aged concierge with 'his greasy stoutness, his big black kiss-curl, his waxed moustache, his chin which was dividing and propagating itself like some primitive form of life' (pp. 171–2) – that she had also once been in love with him. It was one of Miss Raby's convictions that the only thing worth giving away was oneself, for such self-exposure helped one transcend the spiritual barriers of class. A book of hers had been on this subject. In her guilt as an unskilled creator she gives herself away again, offering to adopt a child of Feo's. The disgusted colonel and the alarmed concierge sink to the same spiritual level in their belief that the unbalanced woman still loves Feo. In her recognition that she had been in love, Miss Raby experiences a final eternal moment that is very different from both the comically remembered eternal moment of her book and her later inspirational understanding of it. Miss Raby's last eternal moment is one of failure in which she nevertheless attains a vision of having lived worthily: 'she was conscious of a triumph over experience and earthly facts, a triumph magnificent, cold, hardly human, whose existence no one but herself would ever surmise' (pp. 186–7). The perishing beauty of the Tyrolean village with its campanile sliding slowly and silently (the morning bells have been stopped by tourist complaints) into the valley becomes finally remote for Miss Raby. She now looks forward to a more satisfactory old age than Mr Lucas's. The eternal moment of 'The Eternal Moment' has turned out to be quite transient after all.

The characteristically serious and satirical treatment of the moment, together with love, class, and the English abroad makes Forster's longest short story much closer to his novels than his fantasies, though it lacks a novelistic development of the various meanings of the moment that might have made the story's yarn and meditation aspects more fully interrelated.

'The Celestial Omnibus', Forster's final contribution to the *Independent* or *Albany Review* is also a story about the consequences of literature. It is the only one of his texts for that journal that has an earthly setting entirely in England. The title's comic yoking of heaven and public transport presents a different kind of paradox than that of an eternal moment. Unlike Forster's other fantasies, the humour of the story is not primarily satirical because 'The Celestial Omnibus' is a fairy tale. Forster's narration focuses on the child's point of view; the allusions and parodies of different omnibus drivers such as Sir Thomas Browne or Jane Austen are presented through his understanding. The imagery of the journey is Shelleyan and Wagnerian, the boy's ignorance Keatsean, his heavenly friends Homeric and Dickensian. What keeps the celestial idealism of the tale from cloying is the literary comedy. The puns and allusive settings of 'The Celestial Omnibus' turn it into an early modern allegory of reading. Literature is misused in the philistinism of Agathox Lodge, (where poetry is punishment) and in the aesthetic pretentiousness of Mr Bons (the cultural goods his name proclaims spell snob backwards). 'I am the means and not the end. I am the food and not the life', Bons is told by Dante, who seems to have been reading *Principia Ethica* (p. 82). Writing is a celestial omnibus whose end is the reader – the boy crowned with 'TELOS'. Those whose good excludes beauty and the imagination are left earthbound in Suburbiton; those who use good snobbishly are destroyed, leaving the boy to heaven.[4] He has been conducted there under the guidance once again of Hermes. (The caduceus appears on the Celestial Omnibus Company's announcement of the reduction of services to sunrise and sunset – literature does not pay.)

When 'The Celestial Omnibus' was reprinted in 1912 together with 'The Road from Colonus', 'The Story of a Panic', 'The Other

Side of the Hedge', and two fantasies published in other journals, Roger Fry did an illustration for the end-papers of the volume. The drawing depicts a rainbow rising out of a suburbia of houses and billboards that proclaim 'Practical Culture' and 'Imperial Culture' below a heaven of mountains, mist, and sun (Plate I). The illustration reflects the critical New Liberal values Forster thought the *Independent Review* and its editors, friends of Fry and himself, stood for. It is a fitting visual Bloomsbury comment in a volume dedicated to the memory of the review that gave Forster his start as a writer.

V

'The Celestial Omnibus' is a work of Bloomsbury's later Edwardian years. We need to return to the earlier fantasies that Forster was publishing, or trying to publish, in periodicals quite different from the *Independent Review*. The first short story that Forster ever published appeared a month after 'Macolnia Shops' in the December 1903 issue of the *Temple Bar*, a magazine 'for town and country readers' that consisted mainly of fiction and was not identified with any particular political view. (It ceased publication in 1906.) Forster's début there as an author of fiction was in a characteristically satirical and supernatural story of a young English tourist's psychic self-discovery in Italy. Forster considered including 'Albergo Empedocle' in The Celestial Omnibus (*LTC*, p. viii) but it remained his only uncollected early story, perhaps because its elements are more discordant than in similar stories like 'The Story of a Panic'.[5] The first-person narrator who frames the tale, but merges with an omniscient, even authorial voice in the middle, tells of Harold's discovery that he has a transmigrated soul at the Sicilian birthplace of Empedocles (identified as the philosopher who believed in the psychic transmigration). The absence of Harold's loving friend, who is the narrator, and the presence of his unloving, hypocritical fiancée Mildred Peaslake and her philistine family turn the comic fantasy into a tale of pitiful insanity. At first Harold's emerging Greekness is farcical; he cries 'the sea! the sea!' without knowing why. His is a simple, if reincarnated soul – Maurice is another of his reincarnations – and his lack of imagination strengthens the Forsterian virtues that the narrator says are Harold's power to love and his desire for truth. These virtues

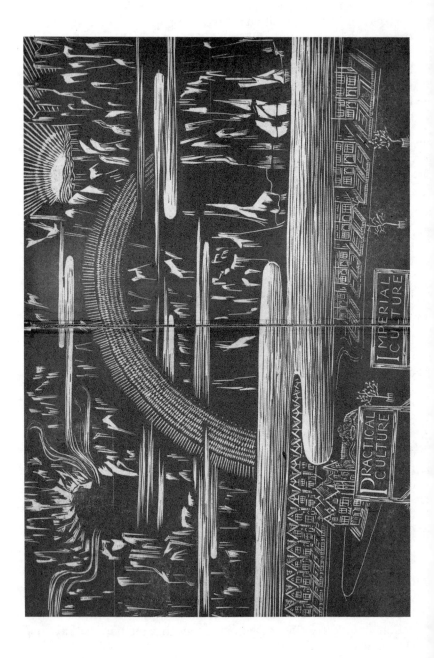

support an uncanny sympathy with the past that transcends Mildred's self-conscious historical imagination. The psychological tricks that Harold somewhat unconvincingly plays on himself combine with the dishonest Mildred's incomprehension of his loving truthfulness to make her fiancé metempsychotically mad. The homosexual implications of his madness are rather sinisterly hinted at by the narrator, who can never forgive Mildred for what he thinks she has done to his friend. He continues to visit the institutionalised Harold. 'Last time, when I entered the room, he got up and kissed me on the cheek. I think he knows that I understand him and love him: at all events it comforts me to think so' (*LTC*, p. 35).

'Albergo Empedocle' is, if anything, less ambiguously about sexuality than 'The Story of a Panic'. (It would be amusing to know what Keynes thought of it, but he probably did not read the *Temple Bar*.) The fantasy of transmigration symbolises not just the presentness of the past, but homosexual self-realisation, and the results are sadder for Harold than Eustace. 'If you think I'm mad', Harold says to the Peaslakes and their ilk before losing his modern identity completely, 'I am mad. That's all it means' (p. 32). In this pathos the satire and the fantasy of the story disintegrate.

Even closer to 'The Story of a Panic', and a better story than either it or 'Albergo Empedocle', is 'The Story of the Siren', which the *Temple Bar* nevertheless rejected early in 1904 (*LTC*, p. ix). The story remained unpublished until 1920, when Virginia and Leonard Woolf printed it in tropical turquoise marble covers as the ninth publication of the Hogarth Press and the first by a member of the Bloomsbury Group other than themselves. Virginia did not think 'The Story of the Siren' would sell very well, and Roger Fry, unaware of when it was written, complained to her, that 'It's always the same theme; I wish he could get something new and more solidly constructed. He exploits too much his fancy' (RF/L, II 486). Katherine Mansfield reviewed the pamphlet very favourably but recognised the familiar cast of characters in Forster's fiction, which she delightfully described as 'alive with aunts and black with chaplains' (*EMFCH*, p. 185). One need not go as far as a later critic and claim that 'The Story of the Siren' is 'the archetype of all his fictions' (Thomson, p. 88) to see that it displays some recurrent features of Forster's Edwardian writings, including Apostolic ruminations on the nature of reality. As in 'The Story of a Panic', the opening narrator is a priggish Englishman abroad, though a

student this time. Instead of Pan, the Siren is the sexual deity
who induces an awakening that is more disastrous than sexual
liberation. The Siren's story also brings tourism to the locale, as the
novel did in 'The Eternal Moment'. Conventional actuality and
fantastic reality interact again when an English student, an aunt, a
clergyman, and a colonel approach the marvellous. From satirising
a tourist excursion to a Mediterranean grotto, the story opens with
the narrator's dissertation notebook on the Deist Controversy after
it has fallen into in the water. The narrator stays behind with a
young Italian boatman 'in a magic world, apart from the all
commonplaces that are called reality. . . . Here only the fantastic
would be tolerable' (*EM*, p. 118). As he dries the notebook that the
beautiful diving boatman has retrieved, he listens to the story of
how the Siren appeared to the boatman's brother Giuseppe – a
story that 'for all its absurdity and superstition, came nearer to
reality than anything I had known before' (p. 125). The effect of the
Siren on Giuseppe was to make him supernaturally sensitive to the
mortality of living creatures; the effect of the story on the narrator is
a fleeting desire to help others. 'The Story of the Siren' ends
symbolically with the returning boat of the tourists darkening
the grotto.

In the 1947 introduction to his *Collected Short Stories* Forster
observed how 'Fantasy to-day tends to retreat or to dig herself in or
become apocalyptic out of deference to the atom bomb'; his own
Edwardian fantasies flitted with Hermes through holidays or into
the future (p. v). 'The Story of the Siren' is more apocalyptic than
these. After Giuseppe has married a girl named Maria who has also
seen the Siren, it is prophesied that their child will become the
Antichrist and bring the Siren's song out of the sea to 'destroy
silence and save the world!' (*EM* p. 129). Before this can happen,
Maria is killed by a priest, Giuseppe dies in Liverpool searching for
someone else who has seen the Siren, and the Siren remains in the
sea. But the boatman is still hopeful that 'silence and loneliness
cannot last for ever' (p. 129). This is the beneficent if vague
apocalyptic significance of the Siren. Many years later, when
writing of a siren of Lampedusa's, Forster added that his own early
siren would destroy primness and cruelty along with silence and
loneliness when she finally saved the world (Lampedusa, p. 15).

One can imagine what the *Church Times* might have said about
'The Story of the Siren', had it been published in the *Temple Bar* in
1904. Criticism of the story's anti-clericalism came from a very

different source when it was finally printed. In a review for the *New Statesman*, Rebecca West objected to the boatman's remark that 'Love is everywhere since the death of Jesus Christ'. The remark is made as the Italian explains to the English youth that love is not happiness, for anyone can get love (p. 125). West thought it a Protestant not a Catholic kind of comment from someone diving for Karl Marx rather than a Siren (*EMFCH*, pp. 188–9). Forster seems to have agreed, and when the story was reprinted in *The Eternal Moment* the sentence was dropped.

The other early Edwardian stories that Forster wrote around 1904 or 1905 are unapocalyptic English fantasies whose publication in various magazines after his early novels testified to Forster's developing reputation. In 1907, 'The Curate's Friend' appeared, complete with illustrations, in the glossy *Pall Mall Magazine*, which also ran poetry, and articles on public affairs, socialites, fashion, and travel. By contrast 'Other Kingdom' was accepted by Ford Madox Ford for the distinguished *English Review* in 1909 (after Ford had apparently refused 'The Machine Stops'). Forster's story appeared there along with works by Belloc again, Bennett, Conrad, Galsworthy, Hardy, Hudson, Meredith, and Pound. (The only authors still read who were published in the *Pall Mall Magazine* around the time of Forster's story are Jack London and John Masefield.)

'The Curate's Friend' must also have seemed very foolish to the *Church Times* but the only public response appears to have been its republication in the New York *Putnam's Monthly* – the first of Forster's writings to appear in America. The story differs from Forster's other Pan and Siren works in being entirely an English comedy with the narrator as protagonist, though again there is a mythological figure who brings about a conversion in the feelings of a truthful man susceptible to animistic nature. A faun is not to be confused with Pan, according to Pan's modern literary historian (Merivale, p. 184), but the curate's faun friend is nonetheless a sexual deity who changes from a naked youth (mistaken by the curate for one of his parishioners until he sees his tail) into 'the great pagan figure of the Faun' (*CO*, p. 138) towering like Hugo's Pan above the curate's intended and her 'little friend'; he manipulates them like puppets, before turning back into an endearing youth who helps the curate become a successful, unmarried priest (the faun did offer to provide him with wives) in touch with nature as he has never been before, though unable to tell of his revelation without risking prison. What Forster's Cambridge readers made of this relationship is not recorded either, but an interpretation of the fantasy's sexual import should include the role of the reflexive narrator. The comedy of 'The Curate's Friend' is the curate's, and the satire is retrospectively directed at himself. Before the advent of his friend he says 'I was facetious without humour and serious without conviction' (p. 130). Afterwards he can mock his ineffective parish labours and his ludicrous attempt to exorcise the faun. He no longer deceives himself but the nature of his experience requires that he deceive his readers. Instead of the congenial lyrical rhetoric of the sermon he is forced 'to use the unworthy medium of narrative, and to delude you by declaring that this is a short story, suitable for reading in the train' (p. 142). The allusion to Gwendolyn Fairfax's description of her diary in Wilde's *The Importance of Being Earnest* – 'One should always have something sensational for reading on the train' – has been pointed out (Summers, *Forster*, p. 251).

Complaints about the repetitive domestication of Greek myths in Forster's fantasies have been made even by sympathetic readers such as Leonard Woolf or Lionel Trilling. Forster himself realised by the time of *Howards End* that Pan was, if not dead, at least Victorian (*HE*, p. 106). Earlier he parodied himself mildly with the stories of Rickie Elliot in *The Longest Journey*. One of Rickie Elliot's *Pan Pipes* about a modern dryad is a much simplified version of Forster's 'Other Kingdom', which also connects with other texts of Forster's. The heroine and her lover resemble Lucy Honeychurch and George Emerson in *A Room with a View*. The businessman Mr Worters is clearly related to Mr Wilcox; his house and wood are in the same county as *Howards End*. The way Worters tries to possess a wood is the subject of Forster's later self-parody of possession, 'My Wood'. In *The Longest Journey* Agnes's résumé of the story for Stephen is 'Allegory. Man = modern civilization (in bad sense). Girl = getting in touch with Nature' (p. 119). Earlier Rickie had to explain to her that the girl who escapes her intended and disappears into the wood is a dryad. Agnes's equations partly describe the metamorphosis of 'Other Kingdom' but Rickie's story apparently lacks the subplot of the young man (named Ford by a odd coincidence) whose guardian is Worters and whose love is Worters's fiancée. There is also no mention of the sardonic, servile tutor who acts as narrator and chorus in the story.[6] It is Ford who says the classics are full of tips on how to dodge things, and that is just what Evelyn Beaumont learns to do. After Worters buys her the wood and then dismisses Ford, she dodges Worters, and, calling for her lover, turns into a dryadic tree. 'Other Kingdom' is again, like 'The Other Side of the Hedge' and 'The Celestial Omnibus', a story of transformation to an ideal world from which there is no returning, no connecting of passion with prose (Wilde, *Art and Order*, p. 69). Yet 'Other Kingdom' is the only one of Forster's fantasies concerned with the transformation of a woman. Her free spirit rebelling against the sham of rights and status, the egoistically possessive Worters, the ironic narrator, and the young man who keeps a notebook of sayings, poems, and drawings, the English setting – all manifest the influence of George Meredith on Forster's work at this time. Rupert Brooke thought it 'the best story ever written' (*Letters*, p. 173). Later at Grantchester, he was more sceptical:

> And clever modern men have seen
> A Faun a-peeping through the green,
> And felt the Classics were not dead,
> To glimpse a Naiad's reedy head,
> Or hear the Goat-foot piping low. . . .
> But of these are things I do not know.
> (*Collected Poems*, p. 150)

The basically comic narratives of 'The Curate's Friend' and 'Other Kingdom' keep Forster's Edwardian Anglicising of Greek myths in these fantasies from being too sentimental. Recent interpretations of their latent homosexual plots have may have added to their significance (Summers, *Forster*; Herz, *Narratives*). But they still lack the interest and even something of the power of stories like 'The Story of a Panic' and 'The Story of the Siren'. Exported to England, Pans and Sirens decline into fauns and dryads. The imperial theme of Forster's satire is also missing from them. His best later stories like 'The Machine Stops' or 'The Point of It' are still ironic fantasies but not mythological ones.

VI

In his literary development E. M. Forster differs from Lytton Strachey and Virginia Woolf as well as Desmond MacCarthy in not beginning as a literary critic. Forster the influential critic came after, rather than before or along with Forster the novelist. His fiction helped to shape Bloomsbury's fiction; their criticism contributed to his criticism. Before turning to Forster's unpublished early short narratives, however, there are three early published critical texts of Forster's that should be noted.

In addition to his *Independent Review* piece on literary eccentrics, Forster wrote an introduction and notes for an edition of the *Aeneid* (1906), and two papers for the Working Men's College on pessimism in modern literature, and on Dante that he gave in 1906 and 1907.[7] The *Aeneid* was a bilingual edition for the Temple Classics series that Lowes Dickinson and H. O. Meredith were editing. Forster's introduction held up well enough for it to be revised with the help of another Kingsman and reprinted with a different translation in 1957. The approach of Forster to the *Aeneid* is not particularly sympathetic; he prefers the gentler, more philosophical and joyful Georgics to a poem that is patriotic rather than human, and which continues to interest the English because European civilisation descends from Rome. For Forster, Virgil is a 'spasmodic' spiritual guide. His hell is illogically arranged, his heaven uncertain: 'Are we our own masters or do [the gods] flick us into right and wrong?' (pp. xvi–xvii). *Flick* is a perfect word here – colloquial and disdainful. As for the poem's structure, Forster advises the reader to take the good things as they appear and not seek too closely for connections between them. Aeneas is hardly a Bloomsbury hero. His piety makes him almost colourless; his function 'is not so much to do and to feel as to originate' (p. xi). Once, for a moment with Dido, he speaks and acts like a man instead of an ancestor 'and a most contemptible man he proves' (p. xv). In the final paragraph of the introduction Forster comes to the unVictorian conclusion that Virgil is being threatened by admiring readers who, among other things, make him too Tennysonianly tearful and mellow. Fifty years later the threat was gone, and Forster omitted the last paragraph.

Forster's two papers for the Working Men's College journal that the Apostle F. D. Maurice and fellow Christian socialists established a half century before are of a genre between the lecture and the essay. They are interesting for the simple, uncondescending way they exhibit Forster's assumptions about literature and life. The exposition of Dante, Forster rather surprisingly remembered later, came to him 'as of a living thing developing', and the flaws in its argument did not diminish the satisfaction he felt in doing it (*CB*,

p. 52). In his old age Forster wrote that *The Divine Comedy* together with *The Decline and Fall of the Roman Empire* and *War and Peace* were the three great books that extended him, even though they did not exert an influence like that of *Erewhon* (*2CD*, pp. 212). The nature of Dante's extension may be reflected in the three fundamental moral questions that Forster sees Dante's work as answering, questions to do with our behaviour towards people we know, towards people we do not, and towards 'the Unknowable' (*AE*, p. 146). Dante's *The New Life* answers the first question, but unsatisfactorily because it uses people as a means, even though the end is God. The utopian *Empire* (or *Monarchia*) answers the second question admirably, Forster thinks, because a balance is struck 'between monotony and war – between the bloodiness of Mr. Rudyard Kipling and the greyness of Mr. Sidney Webb' (p. 160). By the time Forster reaches *The Divine Comedy* and the response to the unknowable, he almost gives up trying to summarise Dante. But the importance of his comparing conduct toward the unknowable with conduct towards strangers or friends remains, for his own work if not Dante's. It is interesting that Forster's comparison here of the punishment of Brutus and Cassius with that of Judas (they betrayed Caesar and he, Christ) is not the one he gave later. In 1938, he saw their punishment as Dante's response to the betrayal of a friend, which led to Forster's famous choice between betraying one's country or one's friend (*2CD*, p. 66).

The paper 'Pessimism in Literature' encompasses a considerable range of modern literature; Zola, Ibsen, Tolstoy, Stevenson, Gissing, Hardy, James, Shaw, Barrie, Pinero, and Wagner are all mentioned. But more significant is Forster's sharp distinction between literature and life, and his use of the end as a basis for separating them. And by *end* here Forster means ending not telos, though something of the second meaning remains. In life, endings are unimportant ('the journey not the arrival matters', as Leonard Woolf, quoting Montaigne, called the last volume of his autobiography) but in books they are crucial. Optimistic modern life is possible but not, Forster argues, in works of permanent literary art. Separation is the note on which modern plays and novels end pessimistically. One of the illustrations Forster offered his audience of former students at the Working Men's College in 1906 is revealing for Bloomsbury's literary history:

The early Victorian woman was regarded as a bundle of goods.

She passed from the possession of her father to that of her husband. Marriage was a final event for her: beyond it, she was expected to find no new development, no new emotion. And so the early Victorian novelist might reasonably end his book with a marriage. The social feeling of the period approved him. But the woman of today is quite another person. She is by no means a bundle of goods. She may throw herself flat on the floor of the House of Commons and resemble a bundle, but she does it to give more trouble to the police. She may marry, but her marriage is most certainly not an *end*, either for herself or for her husband. Their courtship was but a prelude: their wedding is but the raising of the curtain for the play. The drama of their problems, their developments, their mutual interaction, is all to come. And how can the novelist of today, knowing this, end his novel with a marriage? (*AE*, pp. 135–6)

The incipient feminist formalism of 'Pessimism in Literature' would be developed later by Virginia Woolf but it was not an enduring conviction of Forster's. By 1927, Forster was denying in *Aspects of the Novel* that there was any organic connection between the women's movement and the development of the novel (p. 13). His denial provided part of the impetus two years later for *A Room of One's Own* (Rosenbaum, 'Aspects', pp. 79–81).

VII

Finally, a group of Forster's unpublished early stories are interesting for their relevance to the autobiography of the author or to the short-story genres he was experimenting with.[8] 'Ansell' and 'Ralph and Tony' are very early quasi-autobiographical texts, whereas 'The Helping Hand' and 'The Purple Envelope' are somewhat later attempts at familiar late Victorian and Edwardian forms of short fiction; 'The Rock' is a Jamesian story that Forster described as his last inspired piece of writing.

In the very early 'Ansell', Forster used his memory and the name of a garden boy and childhood friend he would commemorate again variously in *The Longest Journey*, *Howards End*, *Maurice*, and *Marianne Thornton*. The narrator bears Forster's own first name, which may endorse the narrative's personal source. Ansell, who is perhaps the earliest gamekeeper in modern English fiction, provides the weak, scholarly Edward with a vacation of physical experiences in place of the lost fellowship dissertation on which he was supposed to be working. These are recurrent antitheses in Forster's fiction, and they are presented awkwardly by the first-person narrator, who ends his narrative saying ' . . . I have not yet realized what has happened' (*LTC*, p. 9). What saves the story, however, is the narrator's humour. Here is his description of the loss of his box of books and notes whose weight almost pulled himself, Ansell, and their horse and cart into the ravine:

> About halfway down [the box] hit a projecting rock, opened like a water-lily, and rained its sweetness upon the deep. Most of the books were heavy and plunged like meteors through the trees into the river. One of two of the smaller ones roosted coyly for a minute on the branches before they too slipped through and disappeared.

His Greek lexicon remained on the rock:

> In dry weather an invisible person rapidly turns over the leaves, hurrying from one word to another. But in the damp his ardour flags. There is something rather poetical in the idea of this un-embodied searcher after knowledge, and I would write a Greek epigram on him, but I am forgetting the words.
>
> (pp. 6, 8–9)

The metamorphosis of books into beauty, mind into nature, reappears, complete with disembodied reader, in the opening image of 'The Story of the Siren'. And in both stories the witty commentary keeps the transformation from being Romantically hackneyed. Ansell too becomes a diver for the lost research materials. Edward's dissertation was to be on the Greek optative – a mood for the expression of wishes, choice, and sometimes hypothetical statements; his education with Ansell proceeds in the present indicative. Ansell's relation to the topic is confined, the narrator notes, to a primitive form of the accusative case: 'Them books' (p. 4).

The equally early but much longer, untitled story published posthumously as 'Ralph and Tony' was originally classified as a fragment of a novel, even though it has a certain completeness.

Again the story is about two young Englishmen, one 'effeminate and unorthodox' in appearance (*AS*, p. 77), the other apparently healthy and heroic. The weak Ralph is accompanied by an ineffective mother, the mountain-climbing Tony by a sister with whom Ralph falls in love as a surrogate for her brother. The setting of the story is the Tyrol, as in 'The Eternal Moment', but there is little satire. The narrative traces Ralph's triumphant quest for love and justice and the failure of Tony's violent contempt, yet the conflict between them remains sentimentally vague. Ralph's 'sore place' and the nature of the justice he seeks are both indistinct, while Tony's sudden heart disease seems but a moral malady. The love Ralph has for Tony and his sister anticipates a central concern of *The Longest Journey* when Ralph proclaims that he does not know whether he loves the brother or sister best:

> I don't believe in liking people best. . . . People say that three can't live together – that there will be jealousy. They don't know what love is. It doesn't deal in quantities. It's nothing to do with sex or relationship. (p. 80)

However, Tony's peculiar beatings of Ralph together with the violence and the collapses manifested in their mutual mountain rescuing are sadomasochistic. Ralph's dream, developed later in 'The Other Side of the Hedge', that success comes from loving and understanding others, not outstripping them in the climb to the top, is left unreconciled with this relationship in the humourless omniscient narration. 'Ralph and Tony' may be a fragmentary novel after all.

What Bloomsbury would have made of 'Ansell' and 'Ralph and Tony' might be imagined from the sceptical comments Lytton Strachey made later about the future of Maurice's relationship with Alec in the novel *Maurice* (*M*, p. 238). Less self-revealing were the stories about writers or ghosts that were in demand by magazine readers and editors around the turn of the century. 'The Helping Hand' is a brief, derivative Jamesian story about the consequences of plagiarism in art history. Women are the undoing of the modest, ironic historian of the tale, first the noble lady who steals his ideas for her monograph on a fifteenth-century Italian painter, and then the historian's wife who gets the credit back for him after his theory turns out to be wrong. The world of 'The Helping Hand' is not unlike Roger Fry's around this time; indeed Fry may have suggested the idea, directly or indirectly, for he complained to R. C. Trevelyan in 1901 that his Italian lectures had been plagiarised by a woman for her book on Florentine painting. The story is not about Fry in any particular respect, but he would have also found little to disagree with in its criticisms of the art-history world.[9]

In *The Longest Journey* the editor who gently rejects Rickie's Pan fantasies tells him 'Write a really good ghost story and we'd take it at once' (p. 144), and in 'The Purple Envelope' Forster tried to write one. He wrote to Leonard Woolf in 1905 while writing the story that 'it does require a mind of extraordinary frivolity to frighten people, and I'm rather pleased to find that I can't do it' (*L*, I 64). When he finally finished the story no editor would take it. 'The Purple Envelope' is of significance in Forster's development for the subject of its plot, the character of its hero, and the topic of its satire. As a ghost story about the inheritance of an estate whose rightful heir – named Howard – is defrauded by the concealment of an old woman's will, the work obviously looks forward to *Howards End*, but the narrator, who emerges only at the end of the story to admit his incompetence, practically destroys any interest in who will own the estate. Whatever suspense 'The Purple Envelope' has, involves ghostly mirror-writing done by the guilty, sleep-walking cousin who has appropriated Howard's house and land; there is no explanation of the mysterious woman who gives Howard the oval shotgun that kills the villain. In another letter to R. C. Trevelyan, Forster acknowledged the influence of Ibsen's *The Wild Duck*, adding again 'I somehow think I am too refined to write a ghost story' (*L*, I 62). Yet another source may well have James's ghost stories – not the refined Henry's, but those of M. R. James, Dean at King's during Forster's time and later Provost, whose well-known *Ghost Stories of an Antiquary* were published in 1904. The work of Maeterlinck also appears again in the story. Howard's cousin presents him on his twenty-first birthday with a set of Maeterlinck's works and proceeds to expound and then exemplify Maeterlinck's notion of the inexorable justice that our real selves exact in response to our misdeeds. The cousin's hypocrisy is part of the satire that the story directs toward the humanitarians, vegetarians, aesthetes, and psychical researchers who surround the good-hearted, boorish Howard (*LTC*, pp. 36–54).

In certain ways the last of the early stories Forster never published is the most remarkable. It was described by him as a complete flop that no editor would look at and an object lesson in the limits of inspiration. The inspiration for 'The Rock' had been as genuine in Cornwall as it had been in Italy with 'The Story of a Panic' and in Greece with 'The Road from Colonus' – except for the results. To read 'The Rock' after Forster's dismissive summary is a surprising experience, for his account leaves out its moral centre. Forster stated that the theme of his story was a question: how much was the life of a man worth who had been pulled from a rock in the sea by the lifeboat crew of a Cornish village? The man cannot decide, according to Forster's account, and after encouraging the greedy hopes of the village, he sells off everything, gives them nothing, and then lives on their cruel charity. But in the actual story none of this is presented directly. 'The Rock' consists of an intimate conversation between the man's wife and the sympathetic narrator. Its form together with the ambiguous ironies that surround the tale is manifestly derived from Henry James this time. In describing his inspiration Forster said the only thing he had to improvise was the rescued man's wife, 'a very understanding woman' (*CSS*, p. vi). She is so understanding that the 'mysterious tragedy', which she bears 'not only with patience but actually with joy' (*LTC*, p. 62), is partly of her own creating. The narrator makes a point of her Roman Catholicism, and the story is suffused with religious language. Questions such as the value of the saved man's life spring 'straight out of the infinite'; after the rescue everything is 'transfigured because he has been saved'. The wife and 'all that she said was a rock in the tideway' for the narrator, which lets the title of the story refer to the wife and her church as well as the place of the man's rescue (p. 63). The narrator remains stubbornly practical, however, asking if there was not a tariff for rescues. There is, but for the wife such questions lead only to the conclusion, shared by her husband, that because no value can be placed on his life, it is worth nothing. She is nevertheless aware that this conviction contributes to her husband's suffering and their separation. The narrator sums up in the final paragraph:

> This conversation taught me that some of us can meet reality on this side of the grave. I do not envy them. Such adventures may profit the disembodied soul, but as long as I have flesh and blood, I pray that my grossness preserve me.

And he dreams of the couple meeting at rare intervals and shattering 'their spiritual communion by one caress' (p. 64).

The narrator's conclusion about what profits a disembodied soul echoes again the inverted question asked by Strachey in his Blake review about the profitability of losing the world to gain one's soul (see p. 20). In 'The Rock', Forster imagines this happening and suggests its various Jamesian ironies before presenting the narrator's unambiguous judgement. But none of these complications are mentioned in Forster's account of the story, nor does he indicate that unlike 'The Story of a Panic' and 'The Road from Colonus', his third and last inspired story is an unJamesianly brief anecdote of about 1500 words. Still, the form of the story, its absence of satirical humour or fantasy, and the spiritual question that is posed and answered all make 'The Rock' a surprising early narrative for Forster to have written and then so misleadingly remembered.

VIII

After eating a mango for the first time in India, E. M. Forster wrote to his mother, 'as they said of my short stories "it didn't compel" but had a subtle and delicate flavour which pleased me' (*HD*, p. 201). The stories pleased their author so much, however, that he told Edward Garnett and others he thought better of them than of his long books (Heilbrun, pp. 139–40). As early as 1905, Forster was trying to publish a collection that included 'The Road from Colonus', 'The Story of a Panic', 'The Other Side of the Hedge', 'The Eternal Moment', 'Albergo Empedocle', 'The Purple Envelope', and 'The Helping Hand'. He sent them to the firm of Virginia Woolf's half-brother Gerald Duckworth, but despite a favourable report by Garnett, they were rejected (Jefferson, p. 102). Only after the success of *Howards End* was he finally able to publish half a dozen stories in a book.

No critic I know of has agreed with Forster's preference for his stories over his novels. Their mixture of fantasy with travel writing, myth with satire, fiction with biography and autobiography, display that regrettable yet unavoidable eclectic double vision that Forster spoke of later in *Aspects of the Novel* (and which Virginia Woolf criticised in his novels). 'When real things are so wonderful', the autobiographical Rickie Elliot asks himself about one of his unfinished Pan pipings in *The Longest Journey*, 'what is the point of pretending?' (*LJ*, p. 60). It was a paradox easily appreciated by the Apostles in Cambridge and on the *Independent Review*, however, that the real could be represented in fantastic as well as realistic genres. The novels that Forster was also writing along with these short texts, though less eclectic and fantastic, cannot very usefully be categorised as realistic either. The one that he finally completed in 1905 after several fragmentary beginnings was the first novel to be written by a member of the Bloomsbury Group, though not the first book. Judging from the critical response to the novel over nearly three generations now, *Where Angels Fear to Tread* appears to have compelled. Before turning to it, however, we should look first at a book that came out of Bloomsbury shortly before it.

3 The First Book of Bloomsbury

Early in August 1905 there appeared in Cambridge and London an anonymous book of poems entitled *Euphrosyne*. Its title page described the volume as 'A Collection of Verse' published and sold by the Cambridge bookseller Elijah Johnson. Unsigned notices of *Euphrosyne* were printed in the London *Graphic* and then in the *Cambridge Review*, where two pseudonymous correspondents carried on a discussion of the review and the poems for several weeks. After that the volume disappeared from literary history. Some sixty years later, *Euphrosyne* began to reappear in the footnotes and appendices of Bloomsbury biographies and in the lists of some of the Group's bibliographies, which noted that *Euphrosyne* included poems by Clive Bell, Saxon Sydney-Turner, Lytton Strachey, and Leonard Woolf.

Euphrosyne could be called the first book of Bloomsbury. But its unique character along with the responses it evoked within the Group also made it in another sense the last book of Bloomsbury. Never again did members of the Group publish any joint literary works. Fittingly, the idea for a collection of some of the Group's undergraduate verse appears to have originated with the most obscure member of the Group, Saxon Sydney-Turner. In the spring of 1905, Lytton Strachey wrote to Leonard Woolf in Ceylon that Sydney-Turner hoped to persuade Clive Bell to finance an anthology of poetry by themselves and their friends; Strachey did not mind contributing 'under the strictest veils of anonymity' and asked Woolf if he would: 'Mightn't it be rather fun? But quite, quite mad' (3.iv.05, LS/pT). The potential contributors to *Euphrosyne* were not, it seems, very prolific poets, and as Sydney-Turner wrote to Bell, others besides their Trinity College friends would have to be

61

found to fill up the pages of the projected book (CB/pKC). This explains why two of the poets in *Euphrosyne*, both from Brighton where Sydney-Turner's family lived, were unknown to other members of the Group. *Euphrosyne* was published at Bell's expense, Strachey wrote to Woolf in August, adding that he hoped Woolf did not mind that three of his undergraduate poems from the *Cambridge Review* had been included in the collection (10.viii.05, LS/pT). Later in the month, Bell, having proposed and been rejected by Vanessa Stephen, wrote gloomily to Sydney-Turner asking him to take over all the arrangements for distributing *Euphrosyne*, which he did (CB/pH).

For the price of a shilling, the reader was offered a ninety-page paper-covered anthology of some fifty poems divided into eight sections. Most of the poems are lyrics, the main exception being the long dramatic monologue 'At the Other Bar' that occupies Section II. Section VI consists of translations; the poems of Section VII are all identified by their verse or rhyme forms. Other sections consist of love poems and other dreamily reflective, descriptive, or denunciatory lyrics. After love, time is the favourite subject. The prevailing mood is melancholy reverie, which possibly makes the title a little ironic. Euphrosyne was one of the three graces and usually represents joy. Spenser calls her 'mylde' in the *Faerie Queene* (VI.X.xxii), and Goethe gave her name to the title of an elegy for a young actress, but her English poetic fame mostly derives from Milton's *L'Allegro* where she is 'heart-easing mirth', the 'buxom, blithe, and debonair' daughter of Venus and Bacchus or maybe Aurora and Zephyr. On the whole, however, the poets of *Euphrosyne*, with the possible exception of Clive Bell are *e penserosi*. But *Euphrosyne* is not really a whole. Individual poems and poets are greater than the whole collection. *Euphrosyne* is significant for literary history rather than literature, now that the survival of several marked copies makes it possible to remove the veils of anonymity almost completely, as Table 1 shows.[1]

II

The authorship of *Euphrosyne* reveals the anthology to be largely the work of Sydney-Turner, who wrote nearly half of its poems, and Clive Bell, who wrote about a quarter of them. The poems they solicited from the Brighton outsiders consisted of a Miltonic sonnet

Table 1 The authorship of *Euphrosyne*

Title	Page	Author
	Section I	
Last Night	6	Arthur Francis Bell
The Song of the Beasts	8	Leonard Woolf
Lines Written at Dusk in the Great Court	9	Clive Bell
Ningamus Serta Rosarum	11	Lytton Strachey
Life	12	Saxon Sydney-Turner
Three Lyrics from 'Melusine'	13	Saxon Sydney-Turner
Sonnet	18	Walter Lamb
Sonnet	19	Clive Bell
Dead Leaves	20	Leonard Woolf
	Section II	
At the Bar	23	Arthur Francis Bell
	Section III	
Dreamland	38	Saxon Sydney-Turner
A Prisoner's Complaint	39	Saxon Sydney-Turner
Pereunt et Imputantur	40	Clive Bell
Dreams	42	Saxon Sydney-Turner
Narcissus	45	Saxon Sydney-Turner
Sonnet: To —	47	Walter Lamb
A Dream	48	Walter Lamb
Casanova	49	Clive Bell
Sonnet (To Miss R—.)	50	Saxon Sydney-Turner
	Section IV	
The Two Comings	52	Saxon Sydney-Turner
In the Days of Utter Night	54	Clive Bell
Hang Me Jewels in the Sun At Dawn	55	Saxon Sydney-Turner
	56	Clive Bell
Aurea Sidera	57	Saxon Sydney-Turner
Rain at Night after a Day of Heat	58	Clive Bell
The Trinity Ball	59	Clive Bell
PYRRHA	60	Saxon Sydney-Turner

Title	Page	Author
Section V		
Andromeda	62	Saxon Sydney-Turner
When We Are Dead a Thousand Years	64	Lytton Strachey
A Lady Smoking a Cigarette	65	Clive Bell
Song of the Water- Spirits	66	Saxon Sydney-Turner
The Cat	68	Lytton Strachey
Section VI [Translations]		
Meleager	71	Saxon Sydney-Turner
L'Andalouse	74	Clive Bell
Section VII		
Sestina	77	Saxon Sydney-Turner
Curtailed Sonnet. George Meredith	79	Clive Bell
Assonance	81	Clive Bell
Roundel	81	Saxon Sydney-Turner
Triolet	82	Saxon Sydney-Turner
Roundel	83	Clive Bell
Section VIII		
Sonnet	85	J. S. R.
Song (The Duchess, at her wedding . . .)	86	Walter Lamb
After a Dance (Madame de Montmartre)	87	Clive Bell
Dedication	89	Saxon Sydney-Turner

invoking Cromwell by someone whose initials were J. S. R. and two contributions by one Arthur Francis Bell, who was unrelated to Clive. The first of this Bell's poems was a lyric of evening regrets for lost youthful promise and morning hopes of a new day. The second, punningly entitled 'At the Other Bar', was a Browning-esque monologue of nearly four-hundred lines in which an alcoholic hack explains to a barmaid how he went wrong with debts at

Oxford, abandoned the girl he loved for a overseas job in which he failed, and returned to find his former love a prostitute. The blank verse is fluent but the banality of the Oxford man's story suggests the difficulty that the editors of *Euphrosyne* found in filling the pages of their Cambridge anthology. The song and three love sonnets by Walter Lamb, a Trinity College contemporary, and later suitor of Virginia Woolf's, are closer in form and subject to the poems of Bell and Sydney-Turner, though the love imagery is almost comic in places. Two of the sonnets are addressed to rose-like lovers who are unaware of the passions that wrack the poet dreaming in one poem of a bride's 'devastating fires' that leave him 'The desert of my infinite desires' (p. 18). In another dream sonnet the passion for a dead friend is detailed in images of warm limbs, kisses, laughter, flinging, and fondling.

Leonard Woolf originally offered Sydney-Turner a poem on dreams and his dramatic monologue of Lucian or 'some other twaddle' (7.v.05, pH) but later wrote that he had no energy to copy out anything for the book. Sydney-Turner, Strachey, and Bell did not include 'Lucian' (see *Victorian Bloomsbury*, p. 266), though it was a far better monologue than 'At the Other Bar'; they selected instead three of the five poems Woolf had published in the *Cambridge Review*. The poems are characteristic of Woolf's undergraduate verse. 'The Song of the Beasts' is a Swinburnian chant about the vanished 'old red days' of bestial domination with a satirical thrust at the end (p. 8). The anapestic 'Dead Leaves' personifies its subject as shrivelled tongues of the forest who mock the poet as he treads on them and tells them to be quiet in their grave. The dreams of Woolf's 'Dreams' are of un-Forsterian Pan music beckoning the dreamer 'To golden Death and silver sleep', of a maiden whose soul flees his hot embraces, and of a dead poet. The derivative diction and *fin-de-siècle* mood of this verse is illustrated in the last stanza:

> Fill me then full the fiery red
> Sweet cup of Death empotionèd
> For I would join the peopled dead
> Away out on your silver shore,
> And there upon the marge of Time
> With rhythmic feet and ghostly rhyme
> Dance in a whirl of dreams sublime
> Upon the mystic ocean floor. (p. 44)

'I was never a poet', Woolf had truthfully written to Sydney-Turner when *Euphrosyne* was being planned, '& now I'm a Ceylon Civil Servant' (16.vii.05, pH).

Leonard Woolf's and Lytton Strachey's poems are closer in their subjects than anyone else's in *Euphrosyne*. Two of Strachey's three contributions also first appeared in the *Cambridge Review*. His animal poem 'The Cat' is the only poem in the anthology ever to be reprinted. Again in a dream, the poet is led by a cat into some vague splendour of the South where he turns into a cat following the cat who has now turned into a woman. The light tone of the double metamorphosis keeps the verse from cloying with its imagery of mysteries that glare and gleam, gleam and glare (pp. 68–9). Strachey's *carpe diem* 'Ningamus Serta Rosarum' has the same over-familiar imagery ('The endless stars that gloam and gleam'), the same expressed desires to dream, escape, and die amidst love and flowers. The one new poem of Strachey's, 'When We Are Dead a Thousand Years', is among the best in the collection. E. M. Forster was so impressed that he copied the poem into his diary, and it may eventually have influenced his story, 'The Point of It'. In the poem late seventeenth rather than late nineteenth-century English literature is echoed – the prose of Browne and the poetry of Marvell:

> When we are dead a thousand years,
>   And 'mid tumultuary things
> Are vanished all our hopes, our fears,
>   Our loves, and our imaginings;
>
> When scattered through essential dust
>   Falls the thin powder of our bones,
> And through the enormous air our lust
>   Is rolled with sempiternal stones

And so on, through three stanzas of subordinate clauses before the main one states simply that then 'some dilatory hand' will sift our sand (p. 64). The poem is accomplished but when the sea's surge is called 'incorrigible', it is apparent that sound takes precedence over sense here and elsewhere in the melancholy tetrameters of Euphrosyne's time-mesmerised poets.

III

The verses of Clive Bell and Saxon Sydney-Turner that make up
three quarters of *Euphrosyne* differ most from each other in their
tones. Sydney-Turner's tend to be melancholy. Bell too writes sadly
of love and time; his roundel and Sydney-Turner's were not easily
distinguishable even in the marked copies that have survived. But
Bell's love poems are more amorous and violent than Sydney-
Turner's. An autumn poem, 'Pereunt et Imputantur', moves from
the clearing of crops to 'sad brain-ghosts' or memories 'of the
passions that were strangled when the heart was young and brave'
(p. 41). The imagery here undermines the sadness of the thoughts.
'Lines Written at Dusk in the Great Court' contrasts the passion-
laded night air 'when lovely Nature sinks/ Into her lover's arms'
(p. 9) with the cold cloister where the monkish past had given way
to a classical faith in love and youth. There is a Shakespearean
sonnet to a woman the poet dares to love only in dreams, and a
dawn poem of a bereft lover in Venice, which ends with the sun
raping the virgin sky. Another poem uses heat and rain as
metaphors for a made-up quarrel with a friend. *Euphrosyne* also
contains some poems of denunciation and despair by Bell that are
closer to the work of Woolf than Sydney-Turner. One called 'In the
Days of Utter Night' urges us to let go of the afterglowing past and
accept the dark present and endless death as the hope of future
ages. Another poem, deceptively entitled 'The Trinity Ball', uses this
occasion for five stanzas of midnight curses on 'God and His
crapulous spawn' (p. 59). 'Curtailed Sonnet' is a thirteen-line poem
on George Meredith that compares his work with the littleness of
men around the poet. Sydney-Turner found this poem obscure and
asked if it were a curtailed sonnet, which seems to have led to the
poem's title. (Hopkins's curtal sonnets had not yet been published.)
     Clive Bell's best verse is lightly erotic. He was the only one of the
Euphrosyne poets to publish poetry later, and all of it was light.
Milton's Euphrosyne presides more fittingly over Bell's poems than
anyone else's. A sonnet to Casanova expresses the hedonistic pose
Bell liked to assume: the poet laments these evil days of prudery
and continence and wishes he

>   Might live a living life of ecstasy,
>   Careless of Fate or Future, when or why;

> To spend one moment in eternity,
> And leave a dry-sucked orange when I die.
>
> (p. 49)

Four of Bell's poems are devoted to women. The most interesting of
them is an impressionistic description of a lady smoking a cigarette
in a boat – a sketch that reminded one of the few public commentators on *Euphrosyne* of Renoir and Monet (Oxon, '*Euphrosyne*',
p. 66). The influence of Whistler may have been closer to home at
this time. While Sydney-Turner characteristically translated from
the Greek Anthology in *Euphrosyne*, Bell was rendering de Musset's
celebration of his Andalusian mistress's 'wine-deep eyes', 'yielding
zone', 'milky thighs', glowing breasts, kisses, bites, and stretched
clothes (pp. 74–5). 'After a Dance', the last of Bell's poems in
Euphrosyne, is addressed with self-mockery to Madame de Mont-
martre, an experienced woman who, like the poet, does not blush at
kisses or leave 'Swinburne in the lurch/ To dream their virgin loves
in church'. Swinburne leads to other poets, and the last two stanzas
acknowledge a poetic influence that is not as strong in *Euphrosyne* as
might have been expected:

> Along with J. K. S. and Mat
> We two sophisticated sinners
> Suffer from wisdom, knowing that
> Our souls are far beneath our dinners –
> That 'life's a jest, and love's a trinket;
> We knew that once but now we think it.'
>
> I know myself, without within,
> Too clever far from earliest days,
> I never could be taken in
> By pretty, stupid, artless ways;
> I rather think I know you, too,
> The daintiest thing this earth possesses,
> A charming, witty woman, who
> Has learnt a world of men and dresses.
>
> (pp. 87–8)

These lines are much more characteristic of Bell's later verse than
any of the poems of dreaming, cursing, pleasuring, or dying that he
included in *Euphrosyne*. The Mat referred to is not Arnold but Prior,

the source of the quotation being J. K. Stephen's 'Senex to Matt. Prior', which in turn is an adaptation of John Gay's epitaph (Stephen, *Quo Musa Tendis?* p. 60). The nineteenth-century Cambridge tradition of light verse that began with Praed and Calverley and mostly ended with Leslie Stephen's nephew is largely missing from *Euphrosyne*, except for poems like 'The Cat' and 'After a Dance'. In Clive Bell's later verse he would adopt Stephen's metres and tones to the subject of love, which Stephen usually avoided.

Saxon Sydney-Turner was generally acknowledged in Bloomsbury to be the most accomplished of the *Euphrosyne* poets. Leonard Woolf called his verse 'pale' when he first read *Euphrosyne* (*L*, p. 100) then described it as 'elegant' in an obituary letter to *The Times* ('Sydney-Turner'). The pale elegance of Sydney-Turner's poems is the prevailing mood of the volume. Beauty, dreams, love, friendship, death are the recurring desires in his poetry, and summer gardens or woods, legends, fairytales, and the classical past are their recurring contexts. The garden of 'Life', his first poem in the collection, has pleasant hours of flowers, weeds of misdeeds, and escape grapes for those preferring death. In 'Dreamland' there are 'laughing lovers flushed and fleet' (p. 38) but they are an exception to the peace enjoyed by the other lotus-eaters in the garden. 'Hang Me Jewels in the Sun' is a sensuous exercise in synaesthesia which transposes colours into music. 'Aurea Sidera' is another sun poem of serenity. A sonnet to a lady begins with a vision of a rose in flames and ends in a hidden bower of gentle peace. In a sestina the fairies come out when summer afternoon turns to evening in the woodlands. The first two 'Melusine' lyrics, presumably translated from Grillparzer, are songs about confinement and liberty sung by the fool in the garden; the third lyric, sung by Melusine herself, is an inconclusive Arthurian dream of a hero, an ivory boat, a lake islet, a wounded youth, and a band of virgins. The 'Song of the Water-Spirits' celebrates the capturing of a human child for fairyland, like Yeats's 'The Stolen Child'. Indeed the reveries of early Yeats are what the reader of modern poetry is likely to be reminded of in Sydney-Turner's poems rather than, for example, the passionate intensity and simplicity of Joyce's *Chamber Music*, which was published two years after *Euphrosyne*.

In addition to Sydney-Turner's translations of Meleager from the Greek Anthology, which are all laments of love's pains or for dead lovers, four of his other poems have classical settings. The monologue of Narcissus contemplating the face among the lilies expresses a languorous self-love that appears in some of the other summer garden poems. The diction here (and elsewhere, as in the courtly love lyric 'A Prisoner's Complaint') is affectedly archaic at times, yet the subject of Narcissus suits the temperament of Sydney-Turner's muse. The reveries of 'Andromeda', ending melodramatically with the monster rising from the sea and Perseus dropping from the sky, have more erotic vitality than those of his other love poems, which usually associate love with frustration or death. Despite its paternalistic touch, the best of Sydney-Turner's classical poems may be the brief meditation on a Roman dancer's epitaph:

PYRRHA

Faint fragrance from the buried years
Clings round your name and tomb, my child,
Who danced and played till grave Rome smiled,
Grave Rome that you could move to tears
Or long loud laughter at your will.

Those before whom you danced are gone
Long ages since beneath the earth:
The high-born women, men of worth,
All are forgotten, every one:
The dancer is remembered still.
No Roman name can stir me so
Save yours, of whom I only know
That on your tomb these words were writ:
PYRRHA • SALTAVIT • PLACVIT.

(p. 60)

The most interesting of Sydney-Turner's classical poems, however, is probably his 'Two Comings' because of its revealing contrast to some of Yeats's later poems, particularly 'Two Songs from a Play'. Dionysus and Christ are the two divine comings in both poems. The poet in Sydney-Turner's is a follower of Dionysus, who laments the languorous ecstasies of summer afternoons and riotous nights that are now but memories because Dionysus has been replaced by a pale god, 'Bringing to men a newer happiness,/ In quiet life and death's long quietness' (p. 53). No cycles of history determine the comings in 'Two Comings'; its lengthier description lacks the apocalyptic force of Yeats's compressed lines that describe the deaths of gods instead of their differing dispensations. Yeats's poet is a spectator of history; his conclusion – 'Whatever flames upon the night/ Man's own resinous heart has fed' (*Poems*, p. 240) – gives his poem an expanding significance far beyond the Swinburnian moral implicit in Sydney-Turner's poem. The last poem in *Euphrosyne* is Sydney-Turner's 'Dedication'. Borrowing from Gilbert Murray's translation of Oedipus's speech to Theseus at Colonus about how time disquiets all things but the gods, the ballade dedicates the anonymous verses of *Euphrosyne*'s to the poet's friends and to the one thing that shall endure for him, 'the mem'ry of these later years'. That refrain identifies the value of *Euphrosyne* for its authors, which lay not in the negligible quality of its poetry so much as in the poetic expression of feelings, thoughts, and fantasies that Bell, Sydney-Turner, Strachey, and Woolf shared during their 'later years' at Cambridge.[2]

IV

A few years after the publication of *Euphrosyne*, Lytton Strachey reviewed for the *Spectator* a collection of modern poetry which he criticised for its lack of inspiration and for the romantic bondage that kept all its verse but Kipling's out of touch with real life ('Modern Poetry'). When Leonard Woolf reviewed another anthology of recent poetry in the Twenties, he observed, as Ezra Pound had before him, that the standard of published poetry was lower than that of prose. Among the prose writers he cited were Strachey and Forster (who left their poetry unpublished). Woolf thought the trouble was formulaic: the poetic frame of mind, which everyone falls into sooner or later, leads to hackneyed expression (*E*, pp. 94–6). All of this applies to *Euphrosyne*, as does Pound's vigorous description of the state of English poetry before his and Eliot's poetic revolution:

> The common verse of Britain from 1890 to 1910 was horrible agglomerate compost, not minted, most of it not even baked, all legato, a doughy mess of third-hand Keats, Wordsworth, heaven knows what, fourth-hand Elizabethan sonority blunted, half-melted, lumpy. (*Essays*, p. 205)

Also stirred into *Euphrosyne* were Victorians (Tennyson, Browning, Fitzgerald), later Victorians (Swinburne above all, but also Meredith, Dobson, Henley, and Thomson), as well as some French *Symbolistes* (Verlaine, Mallarmé). That there was no influence of Whitman indicates the consistency of the compost. Housman seems to have affected only Forster's verse.

Derivative as the forms and contents of *Euphrosyne* are, the collection is a significant text in the literary history of Bloomsbury. First of all, it is Bloomsbury's most decadent work. The influences of *fin-de-siècle* English and French poets are unmistakable. Bloomsbury's writings have been connected with the decadents, often by unsympathetic critics who exaggerate the Group's aestheticism and ignore their puritan, utilitarian, and liberal aspects. That *Euphrosyne* is the best example of such a connection emphasises how undecadent the Group's prose work really is. *Euphrosyne* also discloses what Woolf later noted, that the quality of Bloomsbury's Cambridge poetry was inferior to that of their prose. Nothing of the humorous and radical ethical criticism of their Apostle papers is to be found in the poems' conventional despair and dreams. The literary discrimination shown in some of their Cambridge essays finds no application in the verse either. Forster's and Strachey's undergraduate prose attracted attention at Cambridge but aside from Strachey's 'Cat', the only aspect of *Euphrosyne* that appears to have provoked comment outside the Group was the volume's atheism, or so Keynes wrote to Strachey (9.ix.05 JMK/pKC). Later anthologies of Cambridge poetry, which included the work of such Apostolic friends as R. C. Trevelyan and H. O. Meredith, took nothing from *Euphrosyne*. The anthology did not even provide fodder for the protocols of I. A. Richards's *Practical Criticism* (as a poem by the Apostle and Hogarth Press poet G. H. Luce did). As a privately financed, anonymous group endeavour that also included outsiders, *Euphrosyne* might also be seen to anticipate certain Bloomsbury developments, but perhaps the most interesting indication of the Group's future nature was the kind of criticism that the collection elicited from one of the members.

Euphrosyne appears to have received only two brief unsigned reviews. One was in the London paper, the *Graphic*.[3] The other, in the *Cambridge Review*, is the first example in its literary history of a Bloomsbury work being reviewed by a member of the Group. The reviewer was Thoby Stephen, and the editor of the magazine, the *Euphrosyne* contributor Walter Lamb.

Stephen's brief review praised poems by Woolf, Sydney-Turner, Strachey, Bell, and Lamb as, 'marked for the most part by originality of imagination, felicity of diction, skilful technique, and a finely audacious vocabulary'. This was generous but it stops short of the claims for immortality that Virginia Woolf recalled her brother making for his poet friends (*MB*, pp. 192–3). (Less generous was the paradoxical description of A. F. Bell's long monologue as immature and derivative – but also forceful and original in dramatic vigour.) Stephen asserts Johnsonianly, 'If the excellences of this book are many, its faults will be readily discovered, . . . ' but instead of specifying either, he passes to the consanguinity of the poems in *Euphrosyne*, which he says were plainly written by half a dozen poets. That consanguinity shows a distinct Cambridge decadence which manifests itself in 'a quick perception of curious and unauthorised beauties, a defiance of vulgar condemnations, a resolute recognition of the unpleasant, and a due appreciation of the value of technique' ('Cambridge Muse'). The manifestation of these moral and aesthetic attributes – decadent or not – will reappear in a good deal of Bloomsbury's future writing.

About his review, Stephen wrote to Bell, 'I say little about the poems themselves but enlarge a good deal on decadence & say it is an unmistakable product of modern Cambridge – hope it will rouse some discussion' (J. T. Stephen, Cambridge papers). Unspontaneous discussion was aroused in replies that were hardly more disinterested than the reviewer's. The first reply by 'A Cambridge Graduate' came from the editor himself, according to Stephen, and the second by 'Oxon', who was invited to comment by the editor. When Stephen was challenged in the correspondence columns by 'A Cambridge Graduate' over whether *Euphrosyne* was really a manifestation of Cambridge decadence, he expanded his definition:

. . . 'the decadents' are simply those who in a society that is ruled by convention possess independence of thought, and still care for art at a time when for most men it has ceased to exist. That the reflections of such minds should be somewhat melancholy is inevitable, and that they should desire to express what they feel I take to be evidence rather of candour than of perversity.

('*Euphrosyne*')

While not a very comprehensive definition of decadence, Stephen's letter together with his review is noteworthy as an early attempt by a proto-member of Bloomsbury to explain and defend in print the independent qualities of his friends' minds and their high valuation of art. The differences between these friends and someone like Lamb, who was only associated with them, point forward again to Bloomsbury's development as a Group.

All of Thoby Stephen's praise except that for Sydney-Turner's work was dismissed by 'Oxon' in a long, condescending letter to the *Cambridge Review*. The writer even questioned the volume's decadence, suggesting that esurience or hypochondria might more accurately lie behind some of the poems. A few other verses were moderately admired, and Strachey's 'The Cat' yielded a parody by Oxon in the next issue. 'The Cambridge Graduate' replied again, this time defending Cambridge's devotion to poetry and questioning Oxford's, which produced another long letter from Oxon citing an Oxford parallel to *Euphrosyne* entitled *Semiramis*. Lamb then reappeared in his editorial guise and declined to publish any more letters on the two universities' muses.

Euphrosyne caused no more public commentary but private criticism continued for a time in Bloomsbury. After receiving a copy of *Euphrosyne* in Ceylon, Woolf described it to Sydney-Turner as 'rather an astounding production' (he wondered if Clive was also the author of A. F. Bell's 'At the Other Bar' – 3.IX.05, pH). Woolf wrote more frankly to Strachey that the only poems he wanted to reread in the book were Strachey's, though Sydney-Turner's were not bad; Bell's on the other hand made him almost as sick as his own (*L*, pp. 100–1). Two years later Woolf still thought Strachey's poems had youth in them (*L*, p. 132). But when he came to write his autobiography, Leonard Woolf made no mention of *Euphrosyne*. Nor did Bell in his memoirs. The reticence that descends on this youthful literary indiscretion in the private and published writings of Bloomsbury would have been complete, were it not for Thoby's sister Virginia. Her first mention of the collection is in a letter accompanying a copy she sent to Lady Robert Cecil. 'The ever youthful poets . . . are rather a melancholy company', she says, and contrasts their verse to 'a real poem' that she had just seen in a newspaper, where it was described as a suicide note by a madwoman. Such poetic mania is not to be found among seven poets in *Euphrosyne*, she observes. The real poem is actually the well-known housewife's epitaph that begins 'Here lies a poor woman who always was tired', and ends 'Dont mourn for me now, dont mourn for me never; I'm going to do nothing for ever and ever' (*L*, I 202–3).

The response of Virginia Woolf to *Euphrosyne* is developed in her unfinished commentary, begun in May 1906, that uses the book to criticise the universities. This fragment has already been mentioned in *Victorian Bloomsbury* (p. 278) and will be referred to again, for it is an early text on that central topic of Woolf's, the education of women. Her approach, of course is ironic:

> Among the advantages of that sex which is soon, we read, to have no [dis]advantages, there is much to be said surely for that respectable custom which allows the daughter to educate herself at home, while the son is educated by others abroad.

The drawbacks of university education from which custom shields the daughters of educated men are then considered as they are found in certain pale graduates whose initials – which appear in certain marked copies of *Euphrosyne* – are S. T., G. L. S., C. B., and W. L. (but no L. W.). The last illusion of these disillusioned young men is their own ability, and what they most admire are certain unprinted and unprintable works of their friends. But when some of their songs and sonnets recently appeared, she continues, the reader of the opposite sex found the poets singing 'of Love & Death, & Cats, & Duchesses, as other poets have sung before, & may, unless the race is extinct, sing yet again.' As for the melancholy of these productions, it was (as Thoby had said hopefully) a illustration of decadence; but for Virginia, *Euphrosyne's* decadence 'was beyond the decadence of Swinburne himself . . . the last & lowest tide of decadence' (QB/VW, I 205–6).

Euphrosyne is not mentioned by name in the mockingly discreet commentary of Virginia Woolf. In her published writings, however, the memory of Bloomsbury's Cambridge muse was not permitted to disappear quite as completely as the poets might have wished. In her first novel, *Euphrosyne* becomes the name of the ship in which the heroine voyages out to encounter, among others, two characters important for her education who resemble the *Euphrosyne* poets Bell and Strachey. And later in *Orlando*, it is the Lady Euphrosyne, duly mentioned in the book's index, to whom Orlando writes his sonnets.[4]

4 E. M. Forster's First Novel

Two months after the appearance of *Euphrosyne* William Blackwood and Sons of Edinburgh and London published E. M. Forster's first novel, *Where Angels Fear to Tread*. The beginnings of Forster's early novels are all intertwined. The first one that was published in 1905 was actually Forster's third attempt at a novel. Earlier he had written fragmentary drafts of the Italian and English halves of his *The Lucy Novels* which eventually became *A Room with a View* in 1908, the year after Forster's second novel, *The Longest Journey*, appeared. And while still at Cambridge in 1899, Forster had started a novel that was abandoned two years later in Italy for the first of the Lucy drafts, and this in turn was dropped for *Where Angels Fear to Tread*, or *Monteriano* as it was originally called.

Forster's literary history as a novelist actually begins then with the 25,000-word fragment of a novel that has been posthumously published as *Nottingham Lace*, a title taken from the novel's opening sentence. Set in the school town of Sawston, the novel reads a little like a prologue to *The Longest Journey*. The various problems that prevented Forster from finishing *Nottingham Lace* can serve in a different way as an introduction to *Where Angels Fear to Tread*, which also begins at Sawston.

The main character of *Nottingham Lace* views his own story as a drama not of action but of 'the Soul's Awakening, so dear to the modern mind' (*AS*, p. 26). Edgar Carruthers's aunt and uncle, with whom he lives, have a reproduction of that famous Victorian painting of a young girl with a prayer-book. Edgar does not anticipate so comfortable an awakening; he has not been able to stick at Sawston's school even as a day-boy and carries on his own education by reading Pater, Swinburne, and Fitzgerald until Mr

Manchett, his bullying uncle, suggests that the new schoolmaster who has just moved in across the street might take his education in hand. Sidney Trent's frankness and common sense please the uncle at first, but Edgar is disturbed by the schoolmaster's lack of reticence: 'he criticized things and people they met freely, and it was difficult to say whether good judgement or ill-breeding predominated' (pp. 21–2). Trent clearly resembles Ansell in *The Longest Journey*, but not yet present in *Nottingham Lace* is the distinction drawn in that novel between the coarseness of revealing something and the vulgarity of concealing it (*LJ*, p. 207). Edgar concludes that Trent lacks ideals. Trent's 'only true occupation was to "go on observing people till he died"', and the narrator adds that this was also true of Edgar, though he did not know it (p. 35). It remains the chief occupation and limitation of Philip Herriton in *Where Angels Fear to Tread*. Edgar's awakening in *Nottingham Lace*, his discarding of snobbish, hypocritical ideals, remains undeveloped, however. Not until *The Longest Journey* would Forster base an education novel on the criticism of idealism.

Sidney Trent's lack of reserve – always a sign of salvation in Forster's fiction – is accompanied by an aesthetic sensibility that also contributes to Edgar's education. Refinement, rather than being a condition for aesthetic enjoyment and discrimination, can inhibit and corrupt them, as Forster's Italian novels will suggest. Like his creator, Trent is a connoisseur of landscape (he also plays Wagner by heart on the piano) and the ridge of hills beyond Sawston provides the primary source of aesthetic value in *Nottingham Lace*. Trent's appreciation of them shows he has been profitably reading Oscar Wilde, whereas the snobbery of the Pater that Edgar reads is likened by the narrator to the attitudes of Edgar's aunt. Edgar tries to contend with Trent's aesthetic and unrefined moral insight by separating his own family life from his artistic impulses. 'There had been little connection between them in the past and there should be none in the future' (p. 26). The plan for this double life fails when the separated parts come into conflict. After the discovery that Sidney Trent is the son of a Jewish draper, the Manchetts in their middle-class insecurity try to detach their nephew from him. (Trent's character, like Ansell's in *The Longest Journey*, seems to owe something to Forster's Apostolic brother and close friend H. O. Meredith, but his Jewishness and first name suggests associations with Leonard Sidney Woolf whom Forster had possibly not yet met in 1899.) But Edgar, unable and finally unwilling to divide up his life, takes his family troubles to Trent, who counsels self-reliance. *Nottingham Lace* is Forster's first sustained attempt at the great theme of his English fiction that reaches its culmination in *Howards End*: 'the continuity of England and the desirability of her continuance' is the way he described this theme in a late lecture (*HD*, p. 294). In *Nottingham Lace* Forster tries to connect Edgar's worlds with those of the Manchetts and Trent. There is not much hope for Edgar's uncle and aunt but Trent also needs to connect more. Despite his frank vulgarity, he wants to conceal his social origins, and is dismayed for his less educated, less free sisters and mother when the family background becomes known. Not enough of *Nottingham Lace* was written to show how Forster planned the connections in his novel. After Edgar's double life falls apart, Forster unconvincingly introduces love; a woman flirtatiously attracts Edgar, and his cousin Jack becomes entangled along with a sister of Trent's in the proprieties of Sawston. Edgar hears from his father in India that he cannot have the financial independence he longs for, and the novel breaks off as a friendship starts between him and Jack.

The possibility of Edgar's falling in love with a woman excites his aunt's dull life at one point in the novel; their relationship

> made her think she was living in that realm of modern fiction, where the love of woman for man and of man for woman can alone produce startling situations and heroic deeds, and alone bring happiness and misery to the characters concerned.
>
> (*AS*, p. 54)

This was not to be the realm of Bloomsbury's modern fiction. The dissatisfaction of Forster and Virginia Woolf with the novel's traditional subject of heterosexual love in society is reflected in their theories of fiction and their careers as novelists. Forster's tutor at Cambridge, Nathaniel Wedd, thought he possessed the novelist's 'special and unusual apparatus', but Forster was not so sure and recalled later in a Memoir Club paper on his books that *Nottingham Lace* proceeded 'but feebly, and dreamily' (*LJ*, p. 301). At the time he wrote to his other mentor Lowes Dickinson

> I'm very discontented with the novel. I've tried to invent realism, if you see what I mean: instead of copying incidents & characters that I have come across, I have tried to imagine others equally

commonplace, being under the impression that this was art, and by mixing two methods have produced nothing. I think I shall have a try at imagination pure & simple: though the result will be unsuccessful it will perhaps be more profitable. I think I have the photo-graphic gift of which you spoke: but till I'm sure I can do no better, I don't mean to use it unreservedly. (*L*, I 51)

In the short writings that he began publishing a few years later in the *Independent Review* and elsewhere, Forster mixed his methods more successfully and without abandoning the comedy of manners and morals that makes *Nottingham Lace* distinctively and enjoyably Forsterian. Examples of his comedy are Edgar's bully of an uncle struggling to write a letter home because 'his personality, like himself, did not travel well' (p. 35), or that judge of gentility, Miss Lucy Carr Davis, known as the 'L. C. D.' because she never errs in detecting the lowest of common denominators, which is vulgarity' (p. 10). But they are not enough. The narrator's facetious allusions to Greek tragedy, which Forster would extend in his parodies of Verrall (*Victorian Bloomsbury*, pp. 275–6), suggest how little dramatic conflict was to be found in the awakening of Edgar's soul.[1]

After Cambridge, while travelling in Italy with his mother, Forster began to envisage a different kind of conflict than the one he had been trying to represent between aesthetic and bourgeois English life in *Nottingham Lace*. He started to think of an international conflict, a comedy in which England and Italy, reason and feeling, realism and imagination might be connected. Separate early versions of the Italian and English halves, which eventually became Forster's third novel, were written between 1901 and 1903. Then a 'sorry bit of twaddle' overheard in an Italian pension early in 1904 (*HD*, p. 291) appears to have coalesced with a masterpiece on the international theme that Henry James had published the previous fall. Within the year Forster had finally completed the draft of a novel.

II

One of the troubles Forster said he had while writing his first novel was what to call it (PNF/*EMF*, I 123). He referred to it revealingly as

his 'Gino novel' and considered 'Rescue' as a title before deciding
on *Monteriano,* which his publisher Blackwood rejected. Two more
titles, *From a Sense of Duty* and *Where Angels Fear to Tread,* were
suggested by Forster's friend the musicologist E. J. Dent, another
fellow of King's College at this time who had helped introduce
Forster to Italy. Later Forster said in his Memoir Club paper that
about two-thirds of Dent became the central character Philip
Herriton (*LJ,* p. 304). Yet in a passage cancelled in the proofs of the
novel, Philip is described as 'my true and tried acquaintance, who
on this occasion, as on so many others, feels and behaves as I do'
(*WAFT,* p. 158). It is possible, of course, that Forster is comparing
Philip with the narrator rather than the author himself. Yet the
description of Philip's face as 'all confusion' below his good
forehead, eyes, and nose, so that 'those people who believe that
destiny resides in the mouth and chin shook their heads when they
looked at him' (p. 54) fits Forster himself, not Dent.[2]

From a Sense of Duty was also rejected as a title by Forster's
publisher, and thus the novel became *Where Angels Fear to Tread.* 'I
quite agree it isn't "me"', Forster wrote to his mother about the
title, adding, 'with all its faults – and it has many – it has the merit
of describing the contents' (*WAFT,* p. xii). Still, when he sent a copy
to Leonard Woolf in Ceylon, he crossed out the printed title and
wrote in *Monteriano.*[3] The hackneyed partial quotation that Forster
settled for does indeed describe the moral inaction of the novel's
hero that contributes to the tragic consequences of his fool sister's
rushing in, and there are other inactive angels and busy fools in the
novel as well. Santa Deodata, the patron saint of Monteriano, so
holy that she would not help after the devil had thrown her mother
downstairs, is another angel in a novel that is as much about the
relations of parents and children as about England and Italy. Forster
described *Where Angels Fear to Tread* as 'a novel of contrasts' (*HD,*
p. 291) but the static place name he wanted for his title emphasises
only the Tuscany hill town (based on San Gimignano) without suggesting how the beauty, love, cruelty, and vulgarity of Monteriano
are partly defined by the civility, security, complacency, and
pretence of Sawston.

A title Forster might have used to bring out the contrasts
expressed in the novel's language of diplomacy was no longer
available to him after the publication in September 1903, of Henry
James's *The Ambassadors.* For all the differences in age and achievement between the authors and heroes of *Where Angels Fear to Tread*

and *The Ambassadors*, between the length, prose style, point of view, plot structure, character types, settings, comedy, manners, and morals of these two texts, there are still some remarkable similarities which, together with the differences, show how Forster assimilated the influence of the greatest novelist then writing in English. Both novels tell stories of 'poor sensitive gentlemen', as James once described his heroes (*Criticism*, p. 1250), who are sent abroad by matriarchs to rescue relatives in love with foreigners. Under the aesthetic and moral influence of life abroad, the gentlemen fail honourably as ambassadors through their unwillingness to act, and are succeeded by the more simple-minded and effective daughters of the matriarchs. The gentlemen meanwhile have changed sides and end up futilely in love themselves. In each novel the quest of the hero includes similar scenes. Philip dramatically encounters Gino, as Strether does Chad, in the theatre. Revelatory interviews with Caroline Abbott and Madame de Vionnet take place in church; both women finally weep openly before the loving, appalled gentlemen. There are stylistic echoes of James in *Where Angels Fear to Tread*. 'All the wonderful things are over', Caroline Abbott says in the last chapter. 'That is just where it is' (p. 144). Earlier in the church she says to Philip 'You do understand wonderfully', which is pure James, and then adds 'you are the only one of us who has a general view of the muddle', which is pure Forster (p. 119). Despite their melodramatic plots, the drama of each novel is one of consciousness, perception, understanding. Yet what is perceived and understood in *Where Angels Fear to Tread* is very different from *The Ambassadors*. James showed Forster how the growth of moral awareness could be represented through a sustained narrative of personal relations in conflicting cultures. But neither the relations nor the cultures in Forster's and James's novels are alike.

In his strictures on *The Ambassadors*, written a quarter of a century later in *Aspects of the Novel*, Forster complained that James had castrated his characters: 'their clothes will not take off, the diseases that ravage them are anonymous, like the sources of their income' Forster concluded that unique as James's achievement was, 'I do not want more of his novels, especially when they are written by someone else' (pp. 110, 112). No one takes off any clothes in Forster's first novel (though they do in his third); Lilia has a baby, it almost seems, without being pregnant, and the cause of her first husband's death is as anonymous as the source of the Herritons' money. Nevertheless, it could not be said that *Where Angels Fear to Tread* is a James novel written by Forster. No critic before Lionel Trilling appears to have noticed the resemblance, perhaps because the manner of narration and the tone of Forster's novel are so unJamesian. Though Philip's consciousness is reflected in a great deal of *Where Angels Fear to Tread,* there are scenes, even whole chapters, where he is absent; and when present, he is always accompanied by that deceptively whimsical, penetratingly judgemental narrator whose voice unmistakeably links Forster's fiction and essays.

By not being concentrated on one angle of vision, Forster's novel can develop a story of contrasts between Sawston and Monteriano more easily. Mrs Herriton's ruthlessly proud management of appearances – including the public manifestations of her family's behaviour – and the pathetic story of Lilia's fate in *Monteriano* have no counterparts in *The Ambassadors,* where Mrs Newsome never appears and Chad's French life remains a mystery almost to the end. Flat characters such as Harriet appear flatter in omniscient narration than do Waymarsh or Mrs Pocock from Strether's perspective. The ironies of *Where Angels Fear to Tread* are more satirical than the ambiguous ones of a restricted Jamesian point of view. Forster's scenes of farce, such as the night at the opera, derive from a delighted, uninvolved narrator, whereas the scenic intensity of James comes from the actors in his dramas. The views of provincial town life that the narrator, Philip, Harriet, Lilia, and Gino all provide are also more diverse than Strether's vision of Paris and the countryside. Their views are also less complex. Monteriano's beauty contrasts with Sawston, as Paris's does with New England's, but the ways that art helps to create this beauty are quite different in the two novels. Scenes in and around Paris appear to Strether as beautiful paintings. In *Where Angels Fear to Tread* the frescoes of Santa Deodata and the opera *Lucia di Lammermoor* are represented comically; they are part of the unJamesian, even unBloomsburian satire of aestheticism in Forster's Edwardian fiction. Love in different forms, not just in the appreciation of beauty, is what Philip must learn. This is finally his most important difference from Strether. *The Ambassadors* is a middle-aged book, which makes Strether's appreciation of Paris and the love of Chad and Madame de Vionnet all the more moving. *Where Angels Fear to Tread* is a novel of young men and women whose discoveries of love are more urgent and uncertain.

III

Philip's discovery of love begins with beauty. 'All the energies and enthusiasms of a rather friendless life had passed into the championship of beauty', we are informed by the narrator after Philip's first visit to Italy. But he achieves nothing at Sawston and falls back on his second gift, a sense of humour. He did not know, adds the narrator, 'that human love and love of truth sometimes conquer where love of beauty fails' (pp. 54–5). Philip's progress in *Where Angels Fear to Tread* is the discovery of these loves. 'The object of the book is the improvement of Philip' Forster replied to his friend the Apostle R. C. Trevelyan's criticisms of the novel; his intention was that Philip 'grows large enough to appreciate Miss Abbott, and in the final scene he exceeds her' (*WAFT*, p. 149). This somewhat surprising final judgement of his characters reveals an ambivalence towards physical love in the novel. Philip, whose very name incorporates the word love, is described in the final chapter as having 'reached love by the spiritual path', while the object of his love confesses herself to be 'crudely' in love with Gino. Caroline can tell Philip this because she still believes he is 'without passion' – a sexual angel in effect. Shocked by his mistaking her love, Philip imagines it mythically, first as Pasiphaë's infatuation with a bull and then – after she speaks of how Gino's regarding her as a goddess had saved her from the follies of Lilia's love – as the Moon's love for Endymion. Caroline insists Philip must get over thinking of her as refined, but even as she speaks she is transfigured beyond refinement for him: 'Out of this wreck there was revealed to him something indestructible – something which she, who had given it, could never take away' (pp. 141, 145–7).

Despite Forster's expressed intention, Philip's Platonic understanding of love remains ambiguous at the end of *Where Angels Fear to Tread*. The 'almost alarming intimacy' of his relationship with Gino (p. 140) emerges as a clear homoerotic complement to his love for Caroline and her passion for Gino. As the focus of all these characters' love, including Lilia's, Gino is the most powerful character in the novel, and it is not surprising Forster began by calling *Where Angels Fear to Tread* his Gino novel. Philip, like Caroline, has been saved, but by love rather than from it – and not just by the love of beauty, but by 'human love and love of truth' as well. The culminating scene of his salvation begins in a sado-masochistic encounter with Gino; after being rescued by Caroline, he watches her maternal consolation of Gino and is converted. The description of the conversion is often quoted:

> Philip looked away, as he sometimes looked away from the great pictures where visible forms suddenly became inadequate for the things they have shown to us. He was happy; he was assured that there was greatness in the world. There came to him an earnest desire to be good through the example of this good woman. He would try henceforward to be worthy of the things she had revealed. Quietly, without hysterical prayers or the banging of drums, he underwent conversion. He was saved. (p. 139)

The sacrament of milk shared with Gino completes the conversion.

Forster's concern for moral salvation runs throughout in his writing. 'Two people pulling each other into salvation is the only theme I find worthwhile', he wrote in his *Commonplace Book* in 1930 (p. 55). There are several aspects of this scene worth noting with regard to Bloomsbury's literary history. First, there is use of religious language and imagery to describe a fundamental shift in attitude. In the early years of Bloomsbury at Cambridge, important changes in intellectual, moral, or aesthetic states of mind were frequently described in terms of conversion and salvation. Three months after the publication of *Where Angels Fear to Tread*, for example, J. M. Keynes wrote to Lytton Strachey about an important epistemological paper of G. E. Moore's as follows:

> Oh! I have undergone conversion. I am with Moore absolutely and on all things – Even secondary qualities. . . . But as the whole thing depends on intuiting the Universe in a particular way – I see that now – there is no hope of converting the world except by Conversion, and that is pretty hopeless. It is not a question of argument; all depends upon a particular twist in the mind.[4]
> (Harrod, p. 113)

The evangelical heritage of Bloomsbury is an obvious source for such descriptions; often they are ironical, but not always. Philip is saved by love but not the love of Christ. *Where Angels Fear to Tread* satirises the Christianity of both Harriet's violent Protestantism and

Monteriano's effete Catholicism. Philip's is a Platonic conversion. Human love and love of truth lead him up from his love of beauty to love of the good. Before being saved by the love of good, Philip had been 'trivial' in his moral passivity. Even Harriet had not been that. In Sawston he had led a more sophisticatedly divided life of pretence and reality than Edgar managed in *Nottingham Lace*. Philip had urged it on Caroline as a way of living in an invincible society of dullness and spite, while retaining one's ideals of splendour and beauty. Her reply, 'Surely I and my life must be where I live', illustrates for Philip 'the usual feminine incapacity for grasping philosophy' (p. 62). In Italy, Philip's kind of idealism collapses. Forster's next completed novel, *The Longest Journey* traces the failure of this idealism in England.

Philip's conversion to a Platonic type of idealism is also given a significant iconic form in *Where Angels Fear to Tread*. Caroline holding Gino appears to Philip as a goddess of infinite pity and majesty like those he had seen in great pictures. When Philip found Caroline, Gino, and the baby together earlier in the novel, he saw 'to all intents and purposes, the Virgin, and Child, with Donor', and babies by Bellini, Signorelli, and Lorenzo di Credi are all invoked by the knowledgeable narrator for comparison (p. 112). No particular painter is associated with the Mater Misericordiae image of Caroline that leads to Philip's conversion; she is simply likened to great pictures whose 'visible forms' are inadequate for the greatness represented. In the formalist aesthetics of Bloomsbury which would develop out of post-impressionism later in the decade, it was the form of a good picture that made its content irrelevant. The qualified formalism that Forster eventually espoused is only implicit in his first novel's use of pictorial analogies to express feeling, the feeling being predominantly comic. Santa Deodata's frescoes, admired by Philip with his sense of beauty and sense of humour, mock his own inaction. Like the saint he does not accomplish much (p. 119).[5] Painting analogies in *Where Angels Fear to Tread* illustrate Philip's growth from aesthetic to moral awareness. This is done through the representation of family relationships that comment seriously and humorously on the nature of love in a novel whose international conflicts are mostly familial. Maternal feeling, or the lack of it, along with paternal affection are the dominant and limited forms of love that the novel presents critically. *Where Angels Fear to Tread* is even more of a Bloomsbury novel in its criticism of the family than in its aesthetic attitudes.

IV

The strongest love, according to the narrator of *Where Angels Fear to Tread*, is that of parents for children, or at least fathers for sons. Gino's love for his son is called

> the strongest desire that can come to a man – if it comes to him at all – stronger even than love or the desire for personal immortality. All men vaunt it, and declare that it is theirs; but the hearts of most are set elsewhere. It is the exception who comprehends that physical and spiritual love may stream out of him for ever. Miss Abbott, for all her goodness, could not comprehend it, though such a thing is more within the comprehension of women. (p. 109)

Mothers in the novel are rather unloving, however. Lilia easily abandons her daughter for a new husband. Mrs Herriton's soulless devotion to the pretence of family pride wastes her son, Caroline tells him (p. 120). Philip is allowed to say what he wants as long as he does what his mother wants (p. 9). He can rebel only by doing nothing like Santa Deodata. Yet the love of fathers and sons is contingent upon the unfortunate asymmetry that the narrator sees in family relations. He observes that

> a wonderful physical tie binds the parents to the children; and – by some sad, strange irony – it does not bind us children to our parents. For if it did, if we could answer their love not with gratitude but with equal love, life would lose much of its pathos and much of its squalor, and we might be wonderfully happy.
>
> (p. 111)

'Equal love' in *Where Angels Fear to Tread* only appears in Philip's vaguely fraternal relationship with his sister-in-law's new husband Gino. (The novel never refers to the relationship between Philip and his elder dead brother.) Philip's love for Caroline is Platonically filial. Her worship of Gino would not lead to a much more equal alliance than Lilia's or the 'English' marriage that Gino had arranged with a countrywoman to take care of his son.

Beneath all the domestic comedy of international manners in the first sustained piece of writing that is associated with the Bloomsbury Group, marriage and the family appear to offer little love or happiness. Instead there is manipulation, deceit, isolation, apathy, kidnapping, and death. Some of this results from misunderstanding between the northern woman and the Latin man, but much is inherent in the structures of English matriarchy and Italian patriarchy. Neither adequately answers what the narrator calls, in a remarkable essayistic passage on the difficulties of Lilia's marriage, 'the great question of our life'. The answer is to be found not in the hierarchy of the family but in the democracy of the café or the street, where the brotherhood of man is real. 'There one may enjoy that exquisite luxury of socialism – that true socialism which is based not on equality of income or character, but on the equality of manners' (pp. 35–6). In the early Edwardian years of this century Forster believed the ideals of social justice and love could be connected by means of equality in personal relations. There was nevertheless a price for Monteriano's 'true socialism' that makes its equality of manners far from ideal. The brotherhood of man

> is accomplished at the expense of the sisterhood of women. Why should you not make friends with your neighbour at the theatre or in the train, when you know and he knows that feminine criticism and feminine insight and feminine prejudice will never come between you! Though you become as David and Jonathan, you need never enter his home, nor he yours. . . .
> Meanwhile the women – they have, of course, their house and their church. . . . Occasionally you will take them to the *caffè* or theatre, and immediately all your wonted acquaintance there desert you, except those few who are expecting and expected to marry into your family. It is all very sad. But one consolation emerges – life is very pleasant in Italy if you are a man. (p. 36)

The homoerotic implications of this passage have been noted (Wilde, *Horizons*, p. 57) but more remarkable is the surprisingly modern feminist criticism from a man who, after Virginia Woolf's death, would call her feminism old-fashioned (*2CD*, p. 249). Forster's shifting opinions about feminism are as unsystematic as his attitudes towards aesthetics.

Forster's representation of the pleasant life in Italy for men – and for 'that privileged maniac, the lady tourist' (p. 36) – in his early Italian fiction and essays gives them a good deal of their charm. It is understandable why he wanted to call his first novel *Monteriano*, for the town is depicted as an urban idyll of masculine life with its numerous phallic towers (Summers, *Forster*, p. 32). To reach it Philip has to leave the English realm of common sense, not for a fantasy world where there are no dentists, but for a classless society of brothers (pp. 15, 19). 'There is no knowing who is who in Italy', observes the narrator when Philip is pulled into a party of Gino's friends at the opera (p. 97). The remark is an English one, however, for the Italians know who they are. The real subjects of Forster's Italian novels and shorter Edwardian writings are the English in Italy. With Gino's character, his domestic arrangements and his Italian friendships, Forster tried to imagine Italians apart from the English, yet even here the Englishness of the narrator conditions his point of view. Monteriano's true socialism is an English perception of the contrast between Italian equality of manners and English snobbery. The contrast is frequently comic, sometimes as a result of the incongruity between the perceiver's role and what is being perceived. *Baedeker*'s description of Monteriano's fortifications, as quoted by Forster, is good illustration of the touristic perspective: 'The view from the Rocca (small gratuity) is finest at sunset' (p. 12). In Monteriano Philip's senses of beauty and humour expand. They do not require him to live a divided life, as in Sawston, and he wonders if the tower that he contemplates reaching from advertisements in the dark street up to the radiant sunshine is symbolic of the town (p. 90). In his relationship with Gino the brotherhood of man becomes more personal. From him Philip learns human love and from Caroline love of the good. He had considered himself an ambassador of civilisation; they help him realise that the behaviour of the Herritons in Monteriano is ultimately barbaric.

The realism that Forster told Dickinson he had failed to invent in his first attempt at a novel is created successfully in *Where Angels Fear to Tread* through the mixture of experienced English and imagined Italian worlds. In the novels Forster would go on to write, the structures of those dealing with the conflict of cultures are aesthetically more complete than those set entirely in England. *Where Angels Fear to Tread* does not have a shape like the hour-glass form Forster admired and regretted in *The Ambassadors* (*AN*, p. 109) but the pattern of contrasts in his first novel is original and well made. The English/Italian shifts allow Forster both a realism so specific that Virginia Woolf thought that social historians would find the book informative (*CE*, I 342), and also a fantasy that comprises the farcical and the surreal. There are Italian scenes where trainmen play touch-you-last and divas in the midst of tragic opera throw bouquets back to the audience. There are others of madness and violence with idiot messengers and night journeys; twice Gino turns into a kind of monster. Through the use of allusions and other parallels Forster extends his realism again both humorously and seriously. On two occasions Philip ironically heralds changes at Sawston by alluding to Dante's *La Vita Nuova* (pp. 3, 57), and the dark wood of the novel's catastrophe is related to the opening of *The Divine Comedy* (p. 24).[6] A subtler analogue in some ways is Donizetti's transformation of Sir Walter Scott's *The Bride of Lammermoor* – a novel of tragic conflict in marriage and the family. (The opera's adaptation of the novel, it is worth remembering, drops Lucia's dominant and destructive mother from the story and substitutes Lucia's brother as the villain.) In *Where Angels Fear to Tread* this Italian Scottish opera is a brilliant example of the interaction of northern and southern cultures, with a literary tradition of comic reception that goes back, the narrator reminds us, to *Madame Bovary* (p. 95). Forster concluded in *Aspects of the Novel* that fiction was likely to find its nearest parallel in music (p. 116), and no less an authority than Benjamin Britten has observed that the structure especially of *Where Angels Fear to Tread* owes something to the musical form of opera:

> The construction of Forster's novels often resembles that of 'classical' opera (Mozart–Weber–Verdi) where recitatives (the deliberately un-lyrical passages by which the action is advanced) separate arias or ensembles (big, self-contained set pieces of high comedy or great emotional tension). . . . The purpose of the big musical episode in *Where Angels Fear to Tread* is to dent deeper Philip's defences by confronting him with Gino at his gayest and most ingenuous. The scene, *Lucia di Lammermoor* at the Monteriano opera house, is long and gloriously funny. . . . But, as always with Forster (as with Mozart, too), under the comedy lies seriousness, passion, and warmth: the warmth of the Italians loving their tunes, being relaxed and gay together, and not being afraid of showing their feelings – not 'pretending', like Sawston.
>
> (pp. 82–3)

The recitatives of the narrator's voice (which at times are also lyrical), the arias of Philip and Caroline, their touching duets, the trios with Gino – all composed into a melodramatic story expressive

of comedy and passionate seriousness – do make the Italian life in
Where Angels Fear to Tread operatic, in contrast to the careful Sawston
life of pride and prejudice which derives from the English novel's
tradition of ironic domestic realism.

The originality of Forster's first novel appears largely in his
combination of these different national life-styles. It is not surprising that his first readers were bewildered by the mixture – by
the way these cultures tend to subvert each other in the text. Critical
disagreement still persists as to whether *Where Angels Fear to Tread* is
a comic masterpiece or a sad, even cold book.

V

The reception of the novel Forster wanted to call *Monteriano* begins
with the conditions of its publication. As with his shorter writings,
Forster's first novel was affected by a magazine. In the hope that it
would be serialised, Forster sent the manuscript to the famous
nineteenth-century periodical, *Blackwood's Edinburgh Magazine*. Of
the fiction that 'Maga', as it was familiarly called, published in the
early years of the century, only Conrad's 'The End of the Tether'
(1902) could be said to continue Blackwood's great Victorian
reputation. Why Forster chose a Tory Scottish magazine instead of a
liberal London one is not certain. It probably had to do with the
difficulties he had been having in placing his essays and stories.
The very hospitable *Independent Review* was already scheduled to
serialise, in the summer of 1905, the three parts of Forster's *The
Eternal Moment*, which *Blackwood's* had turned down. (The story
reads at times like a middle-aged sequel to Caroline Abbott's role in
Where Angels Fear to Tread.) *Blackwood's* had also refused another
story and an article of Forster's, so that their declining to serialise
the unconventional novel of new young writer could not have been
unexpected. But then surprisingly William Blackwood and Sons,
the firm that published the magazine, accepted *Monteriano* for
publication as a book. Forster had intended to send the book to
Methuen (publishers of *The Ambassadors*) or Heinemann (*L*, I 67).
The terms that Blackwood offered were poor,[7] the title changed, and
the novel unhelpfully advertised after the first reviews as 'a story
which puzzles the critics' (*WAFT*, p. xiv). Still, Forster considered
himself wonderfully lucky to get a first ten-chapter novel published
by Blackwood (*L*, I 78).

Years later, Forster recalled in a review of the plays of Edward Garnett that he and C. F. G. Masterman were the only critics to take any notice of his first novel ('Man Behind', p. 4). There was in fact a third, the anonymous reviewer in the *Speaker*. (The reviewer was almost certainly not Desmond MacCarthy, who had become the *Speaker*'s drama critic earlier in the year.) The *Speaker* critic described as 'brilliantly original' Forster's exposure of 'Sawston's ideals and ways of life in the glare of the vertical Italian sun'; he thought that the novel was perhaps the first of a series of 'quiet, refined, satirical studies' and hoped for a sequel that would restore Philip to Sawston's bosom (*EMFCH*, pp. 50–1). Masterman, a founding editor of the *Independent Review*, knew Forster's early shorter work. His reviews of Forster's first three novels praised them highly, and Forster in turn used Masterman's political writings in *Howards End*. Masterman's review of *Where Angels Fear to Tread* for the *Daily News*, of which he had become the literary editor, stressed, like the *Speaker*'s review, the contrasts of Sawston and Monteriano. He saw the novel as a delightfully humorous liberal critique of both English and Italian life, but made little of Philip's particular moral development (*EMFCH*, pp. 52–5). The reviewer for the conservative *Spectator* – edited by Lytton's cousin St. Loe Strachey, who was beginning to print some of his young relative's reviews – foreshadowed the general critical disagreement over the impact of *Where Angels Fear to Tread* by finding the novel's story exceedingly clever but also 'decidedly painful'. Forster was nevertheless a writer to be reckoned with. This was the best encouragement a young writer could have, for the anonymous reviewer was Edward Garnett (Jefferson, p. 101). More than anyone else of his time, Garnett had the ability to recognise new literary genius. Before Forster he had helped to discover Conrad and afterwards D. H. Lawrence. Garnett was also to be the publisher's reader who recommended to Gerald Duckworth that he publish his half-sister's first novel. Thus he was present and influential at the novelistic débuts of both Forster and Virginia Woolf, and all this before his son David became the most prominent member of Bloomsbury's younger literary generation. Garnett's review found several orthodox lessons in *Where Angels Fear to Tread*, such as 'the futility of ill-considered rebellion against convention'. The dominant impression left on him by the book was 'that under the stress of opportunity primitive instincts reassert themselves in the most carefully educated and studiously repressed natures'. (Garnett describes Gino as half faun and half satyr.) This appreciation of Forster's first novel suggests links with Lawrence but Garnett does not bring out the comic implications of the instincts and their repression in *Where Angels Fear to Tread*. At the end of his review he called not for another refined satire but 'a story in which the fallibility of goodness and the callousness of respectability are less uncompromisingly insisted upon' (*EMFCH*, pp. 56–8).

The divergence of these early serious, favourable reviews concerning the tone and the form of *Where Angels Fear to Tread* as well as the moral development of its hero was continued in the responses of Forster's friends and acquaintances. A Darwin aunt of Gwen Raverat may have been referring to *Where Angels Fear to Tread* when she complained 'his novel is really *not* good; and it's too unpleasant for the girls to read. I very much hope he will turn to something else, though I am sure I don't know what' (Raverat, p. 273). Forster recalled in another memoir that the Countess von Arnim, author of the popular *Elizabeth and her German Garden*, who engaged him for several months in 1905 as a tutor for her children in Germany, was alternatively disgusted and charmed by the realism and sentiment of the book (*WAFT*, pp. xi–xii). Julia Wedgwood, the family friend whose book on the ideal of love Forster helped to revise, remained uncertain whether the novel was trying to be a tragedy or a comedy (*WAFT*, p. xiii). Similar responses came from various Apostolic brothers of Forster, and their reactions are more important for the literary history of *Where Angels Fear to Tread* because they shared Forster's intellectual milieu. But private opinions in letters or diaries have not the same status as public judgements in reviews; they are less considered, more spontaneous but still conditioned by the contexts in which they are made.

The most detailed criticism of Forster's novel by a brother Apostle came from the poet R. C. Trevelyan. In his friendly, energetic, and obtuse way Trevelyan criticised the mixture of atmospheres in the book as well as Forster's facetiousness and style. With the style it was not only the Jamesian conceits that Trevelyan objected to but the 'jarring modern notes and journalistic idiom' that he had also found in the writings of their friends Roger Fry and Desmond MacCarthy. 'You ought always to try deliberately to write beautifully, . . . ' he argued with little awareness of what Forster's and Bloomsbury's evolving prose styles were trying to do and what they were rebelling against (*WAFT*, p. 151). Forster's reply characteristically deprecates his own abilities as an artist or thinker while making an early and important statement of his artistic intentions as a writer. After asserting that the object of the novel was Philip's improvement, Forster admits to difficulties with the 'surprise' method of plotting that springs Philip's love for Caroline on the reader, but he disliked sticking finger-posts of implication around the book. As a novelist he had not yet developed very fully the 'rhythm' of repeated images and motifs that give coherence to his later works. But he felt the suggestion that a book should have but one atmosphere 'pedantic':

> Life hasn't any, and the hot and cold of its changes are fascinating to me. I determined to imitate in this and let the result be artistic if it liked. Naturally it did not like. (*WAFT*, p. 149)

Forster's conviction that art should imitate life in the mixing of atmospheres remains a characteristic of all his writing, not just his novels and stories. It is a defining characteristic of Bloomsbury's modernism and reflected in the eclectic pluralism of their art, thought, and lives.

Trevelyan also reported to Forster that Lowes Dickinson and Maynard Keynes had liked *Where Angels Fear to Tread* a great deal, and so had Desmond MacCarthy. Trevelyan was particularly glad MacCarthy had liked it because 'he never likes anything without very good reasons, and is the best critic of modern novels I know' (*WAFT*, p. 152). Another Apostle who had written to Forster about *Where Angels Fear to Tread* was his close friend H. O. Meredith, who would become a partial model for characters in Forster's next two novels, as he was in *Nottingham Lace*. Meredith read the work in manuscript and compared it with that of his namesake, George Meredith – a comparison that has been made by others. Meredith thought Forster might have managed subordinate scenes and unpleasant characters better but felt Forster really understood tragedy and comedy (*WAFT*, p. xii). An older Apostle, Bertrand Russell, found the novel clever and the novelist certainly talented, but he complained that the work was too farcical at times and too sentimental at the end (*Autobiography*, I 180).

The least sympathetic criticism of *Where Angels Fear to Tread* among the Apostles came from two members of Bloomsbury. Leonard Woolf and Lytton Strachey were unprepared at this point in their careers for Forster's success as a novelist. Their views of Forster's novels as expressed in their correspondence constitutes an important Edwardian commentary on the development of Bloomsbury's thought and character. Strachey had nicknamed Forster the 'Taupe', Leonard Woolf explained in a passage from his autobiography that illuminates his early criticism of Forster,

> partly because of his faint physical resemblance to a mole, but principally because he seemed intellectually and emotionally to travel unseen underground and every now and again pop up unexpectedly with some subtle observation or delicate quip which somehow or other he had found in the depths of the earth or of his own soul. (*S*, p. 172)

On 29 October 1905, Leonard Woolf wrote to Strachey:

> The Taupe sent his book last week. It is really extraordinary that it is as amusing as it is. It is a queer kind of twilight humour don't you think. I can imagine the taupes in their half lit burrows making jokes to one another in it or old ladies in musty close smelling suburban rooms revelling in it if they ever had any humour at all. He is, I suppose, certain to 'make a name' for everyone will call it clever. What enraged me in the book was the tragedy. If it is supposed to *be* a tragedy it's absolutely hopeless; if it's supposed to be amusing, it simply fails. (*L*, p. 105)

To Sydney-Turner, Leonard Woolf wrote more succinctly that the novel had amused and annoyed him a good deal (30.x.05, LW/pH).

Strachey was very much in agreement with Leonard Woolf's criticism and reported a meeting with Forster in January 1906 which Strachey came away from feeling that Forster's acknowledged success was an unmistakable sign of their lapse; if they ever did succeed, how ashamed they would be (LS/pNY). The Apostles' and Bloomsbury's contempt for success seems infused with jealousy here. Leonard Woolf's career as a civil servant had begun in Ceylon because of his relatively poor examination marks, and Strachey had again just failed to win a Trinity College fellowship with his dissertation. Leonard Woolf's attempt to define Forster's humour is nevertheless significant. He begins by admitting the novel is funny, but after trying to define the distinctiveness of the humour he concludes that *Where Angels Fear to Tread* fails to be amusing. The claim of tragedy, which Forster does not make in the novel, deflects Woolf's appreciation of the novel's humour. Exalted conceptions of the tragic and the real run through the criticisms of Forster's Edwardian novels that Woolf sent Strachey. Jaffna and Hambantota were a long way from Monteriano.

VI

The critical reception of *Where Angels Fear to Tread* was, like any writer's work, affected by Forster's subsequent books. The wider scope of *The Longest Journey, Howards End,* and *A Passage to India* increased the appreciation and influence of the Italian novels' more elegant limits. (L. P. Hartley's *Simonetta Perkins* in 1925 is an example of a writer combining aspects of Forster's two Italian novels and transferring them to Venice.[8]) The minor success of a play made from the novel by Elizabeth Hart in the 1960s was followed in the nineties by a film version. The play opens only after Lilia's death, and all the scenes take place in rooms of Mrs Herriton, the Italian hotel's, or Gino's house. As with *A Room with a View* from which it derives, the film by Charles Sturridge follows the book much more closely than the play and is able to use railway stations, opera houses, churches, and the wonderful outdoors of San Gimignano. Forster thought the character of Gino in the play was acted with all 'the charm, coarseness, tenderness, and explosive power' of the original, and wrote to *The Times* to say so ('Where Angels', p. 11). In the film of a later generation the sexuality of the novel is somewhat more explicit, though not its homoeroticism. The mood of the film is more melodramatic, less comic than the novel, and the ending with Caroline and Philip embracing implies more of a *rapprochement* than in the novel.

It was in the late 1920s that Virginia Woolf made the most comprehensive assessment of Forster's career in Bloomsbury. What she admired in Forster's first novel was 'its fantasy, its penetration, its remarkable sense of design', and she saw it in literary history as a descendant of Jane Austen and Thomas Love Peacock (*CE*, I 344). (Meredith and James are missing from the genealogy.) In her reading notes for the article, Woolf admired Forster's ability to create real characters, like Gino or Aziz in *A Passage to India* (*RN*, p. 90). The fantasy, penetration and design of Forster's writing have been widely discussed and much praised since Woolf's essay but sometimes without her qualification that Forster's was a divided talent. Many common readers of Forster will probably continue to agree with the late view of Desmond MacCarthy, however. He wrote to G. E. Moore (who had been rereading Forster's novels in old age and finding fault with them) that next to the last, he rather felt the most enjoyable of Forster's novels was the first (17.vii.48, Moore, Cambridge Papers).

5 Desmond MacCarthy at the Court Theatre

I

The year of *Where Angels Fear to Tread* and *Euphrosyne* was also significant for the career of Desmond MacCarthy. In September of 1905 MacCarthy reviewed a play at the Court Theatre for the *Speaker*, a New Liberal weekly that belongs with the *Independent Review*, the *Athenaeum*, and *The Times Literary Supplement* as a notable periodical for the publication of Bloomsbury's early writing. The conjunction of reviewer, theatre, and journal led, two years later, to the publication of MacCarthy's *The Court Theatre, 1904–1907: A Commentary and Criticism*. The only one of MacCarthy's books to be reprinted after his death, *The Court Theatre* has been described as 'one of the best bodies of analytical writing on the Edwardian drama' (Weintraub, p. xx). The unmistakeable Cambridge, liberal assumptions of MacCarthy's dramatic criticism make it part of Bloomsbury's early literary history, even though it was written prior to MacCarthy's close association with the Group.

T. S. Eliot, looking over his own career as a critic, distinguished four kinds of critics: the professional, the advocate, the academic, and the creator. He included himself in the last group, Richards and Leavis as philosophical and moralist types of academic critics, and Saintsbury and Quiller-Couch as examples of critics who advocated, often with gusto, second-rate writing. The professional critic Eliot defined a writer as someone

whose literary criticism is his chief, perhaps his only title to fame. This critic might also be called the Super-Reviewer, for he has often been the official critic for some magazine or newspaper, and the occasion for each of his contributions the publication of some new book.

Examples were Sainte-Beuve and his old friend Paul Elmer More. He continued,

> another old friend of mine who was a Professional Critic, of both
> books and theatre, Desmond MacCarthy, confined his literary
> activity to his weekly article or review and employed his leisure
> in delightful conversation instead of devoting it to the books he
> never wrote. (Eliot, *Critic*, pp. 11–12)

If Eliot's distinctions were more widely accepted, the different functions of criticism might be less invidiously distinguished and MacCarthy's achievements as a critic made clearer. MacCarthy was certainly a professional critic and super-reviewer; he could also be an advocate critic, and, though no academic, he could on occasion be a philosophical and a moralising one too. But MacCarthy was never, to his great regret, a creator critic. Throughout the Edwardian and Georgian years, and even into the Twenties, MacCarthy continued to hope he would write something more than criticism. As he said in a letter to himself aged twenty-two, written from his fifties,

> some day, when you came upon a hushed space in life, away
> from journalism, away from the hubbub of personal emotions, I
> know you fully intended to listen to yourself; and discovering
> what you thought about the world to project it into a work of
> art – a play, a novel, a biography. But confess, you were too
> careless to prepare that preliminary silence, and too indolent to
> concentrate. (*P*, p. ix)

After his pass degree at Cambridge (awarded when he was too ill to take the examinations), MacCarthy made a further attempt to study philosophy there with Moore as his tutor. He then spent a term at Leipzig University improving his German and visiting his maternal grandfather, a half-mad Prussian aristocrat. MacCarthy was supposed to be preparing for a clerkship in the House of Lords, which his mother wanted him to take. While in Leipzig, he recalled in a brief memoir, he attended the philosophical psychologist Wilhelm Wundt's lectures and associated with social pariahs rather than the student corps. What he mainly learned, however, was the art of sponging from having had it practised on him. (MacCarthy with an income of £150 a year from his father's estate felt wealthy in Leipzig.) It was, he thought, the most useful accomplishment he brought back to England. At Leipzig MacCarthy happened to see a performance of Frank Wedekind's *Erdgeist* and was fascinated by its 'curious combination of crude, energetic realism and of poetic disregard of literal truth'. Later Van Gogh's paintings gave him the same feeling. MacCarthy met Wedekind but was not yet interested enough in drama, alas, to do anything more:

> If I had only had my wits about me then, or dreamt I should ever be interested in drama, I might, as long ago as the beginning of the century, have been the harbinger of 'Expressionism' to these shores. (*E*, p. 182)

Nevertheless, a few years later MacCarthy did become at least one of the harbingers of Shaw's drama.

On returning to England MacCarthy began to read extensively, studying such writers as Coleridge, Arnold, and Ruskin, to prepare himself as a novelist. He often saw Samuel Butler, cultivated Henry James, became acquainted with Leslie Stephen and later attended Thoby's Thursday evenings in Gordon Square. MacCarthy's novels would never be written, but the reading served him very well as a critic. By 1903, when MacCarthy had begun to review for the *Independent Review*, he was also trying to write for *The Times*; R. C. Trevelyan wrote to Leonard Woolf in 1904 that the paper kept sending MacCarthy proofs of his work without ever publishing any of it (8.iv.04, LW/pNY).[1]

MacCarthy's career as a literary journalist really began not with the monthly *Independent Review*, but with the weekly *Speaker* that had been started in 1890 and then re-founded in 1899 under J. L. Hammond to oppose the imperialism of St. Loe Strachey's *Spectator*. J. A. Hobson's influential book on *Imperialism* first appeared as articles in the *Speaker*, and there were other contributions by G. M. Trevelyan, Edward Garnett, W. B. Yeats, Ford Madox Hueffer, H. O. Meredith, and Bertrand Russell. Reviews by two young Bloomsbury writers were also published in the *Speaker* thanks to MacCarthy: Strachey's four reviews have been mentioned; another four by Virginia Woolf will be discussed in chapter 7. MacCarthy admired Hammond's gentle eloquence and was made to feel by his editor 'that whatever happened it was always worth while to have lived to be on the side of right' (*H*, p. 16), which in this case was the side of the New Liberalism. Hammond eventually gave up full-time

journalism to write with his wife their distinguished social histories
of the English labourer.

MacCarthy is inconsistent in his various brief memoirs about
the year he started reviewing for Hammond, but his signed
contributions began appearing in the spring of 1905. That summer
the *Speaker* lost its drama critic and Hammond replaced him with
MacCarthy, who had been paid thirty shillings a review and
now received a fixed salary of one hundred pounds a year to
supplement his own dwindling capital (*E*, p. ix; *H*, p. 15). The
circulation of the *Speaker* was small – MacCarthy thought about
3000. By 1907, MacCarthy had become the assistant literary editor
of the *Speaker* but in March the paper underwent another metamorphosis and turned into the *Nation*. H. W. Massingham, the new
editor, whose political columns had followed the theatre reviews in
the *Speaker*, made the mistake of dropping MacCarthy (*H*, p. 16),
whose subsequent adventures in Edwardian journalism involved
various papers, including his own *New Quarterly*. Finally in 1913
MacCarthy became a drama critic again, not for a liberal paper this
time but for the newly founded Fabian *New Statesman*. Periodical
publication thus continued to shape Bloomsbury's early literary
history. Perhaps nowhere is this clearer than in MacCarthy's
reviews of the Edwardian theatre, especially where Bloomsbury's
values encountered those of Shaw and the Fabians for the first but
not the last time.

II

Although most of the more than forty signed reviews MacCarthy
wrote for the *Speaker* had to do with drama, only about a third of
them were about Court Theatre productions. The others often
reflect the poor quality of the London theatre, which caused
MacCarthy to describe himself after a year of play-reviewing as a
'disenchanted frequenter of the theatre' ('Verse', p. 574). His
disillusionment came from the unreality of the plays, productions,
and acting that he watched. In Bloomsbury 'reality' was a
indefinable standard – as indefinable as 'the good' – a standard by
which imaginative art as well as moral life were to be judged. The
tyranny of the well-made play's contrived plots combined with the
still dominant actor-manager system, and the results were plays

striving for impact rather than truth. As MacCarthy wrote at the beginning of his book on the Court Theatre, the managers

> have no artistic faith; they are interested, not in human nature, but in dramatic effects; they prefer plays which 'show power'; and in consequence they are obliged to train their actors and themselves so as to disguise the weaknesses of such plays, and to avoid natural acting for fear of challenging in the spectator a standard of reality. (p. 5)

Several of MacCarthy's reviews were devoted to productions of the most able actor-manager of the day, Herbert Beerbohm Tree, whose biographer called MacCarthy 'his most perceptive critic' (Pearson, p. 194). (Beerbohm Tree's half-brother Max and daughters Viola and Iris all figure in Bloomsbury's history.) None of Tree's productions was actually a well-made play; MacCarthy reviewed few of these for the *Speaker*. But Tree's theatre was disillusioningly unreal in other familiar ways. His sentimental adaptation of Thackeray's *The Newcomes*, for example, was a mixture of 'cheap effects and gleams of insight', which made MacCarthy regret that this imaginative actor picked such bad plays to do ('Tears', p. 269). MacCarthy had high praise for a matinee of Tree's production of Ibsen's *The Enemy of the People* and begged to have it put on again as a regular performance instead of the other plays like Stephen Phillips's verse drama *Nero*. Fleet Street reviewers enthused over Tree's revival of poetic drama, while MacCarthy quietly analysed the thin, repetitious, easily declaimed verse that had made Phillips popular with actor-managers and the press. In another review, this time of a Court Theatre verse play, MacCarthy called Maurice Hewlett's *Pan and the Young Shepherd* 'an artistic fake' with its heated and swollen rhetoric so incongruous in a pastoral myth ('The Theatre', p. 523).

MacCarthy was not dismissive of all modern poetic drama. One of his most interesting, unsatisfactorily brief reviews was of the seven plays put on during two days in London by the Irish Theatre Society, the only other English-speaking theatrical company of the day comparable in importance to the Court Theatre. Two Synge plays, two Yeats plays, and one each by Lady Gregory and William Boyle are mentioned, but MacCarthy despairs of suggesting the spirit of the plays. He quotes Yeats's prose instead, makes a few remarks as an Irishman on their Irishness (distinguishing, for example, between Irish blarney and English humbug), finds a lack of concentrated passion in Synge's and Yeats's peasants, and then draws a dramatic moral about the production of these plays that will be repeated in various ways in his Court Theatre notices:

> Art so sincere, frugal, and imaginative is a criticism, more deadly than critics can forge, of the congested, over-staged, commercially cooked-up drama that is played nightly in most of our theatres.
>
> ('Irish Plays', p. 252)

Five of the poetic dramas MacCarthy saw while he was drama critic for the *Speaker* were by Shakespeare. His reviews of them reveal his recurring critical concerns with the sound of the spoken poetry, with the staging and acting, and with the moral significance of the plays. The first performance MacCarthy reviewed for the *Speaker* was *The Taming of the Shrew*. 'Years afterwards', he wrote with characteristic self-deprecation of his notice, 'I was dismayed to find that it was quite up to the standard of my later work'; he thought he had become a better judge of acting but not of a play's possibilities (*S*, p. 212). MacCarthy had liked this production because the audience did not have to depend for its enjoyment on the costumes or console themselves that Shakespeare's plays are improving when not entertaining. But MacCarthy was critical of the acting that made the happy ending depend upon the breaking of Kate's spirit instead of the developing love between her and Petruchio. Desmond MacCarthy was one of the less responsive members of Bloomsbury to the feminism of his time, as his controversies with Virginia Woolf show. Here, MacCarthy's *Speaker* reviews were up to the standard of his later work. A performance of *Othello* in which the last act was utterly ruined by the acting and cutting was also criticised by MacCarthy. The review is amusing because MacCarthy wants to damn the production further but feels restrained by libel laws, so he contents himself with repeating that the last act is utterly ruined and hopes the readers will take this as an understatement. Here once more MacCarthy writes on the moral interest of the play, observing that if *Hamlet* can be simplified as a play about the consequences of thinking too much, *Othello* ought to be viewed as just the opposite. Beerbohm Tree's production of Antony and Cleopatra was also ruined for MacCarthy by the badly spoken poetry, made more inaudible by an accompanying orchestra; Cleopatra was not very various, and Tree's Antony was limp.

One of MacCarthy's Shakespeare pieces concentrated almost entirely on the meanings of the play. Entitled 'Poetic Injustice', MacCarthy's review of *Measure for Measure* assumes the *Speaker*'s readers are well read in English literature. This is the kind of dramatic criticism he would have liked to write more often if the quality of the performances being reviewed had permitted him to – the kind of criticism he approached more closely in his reviews of Shaw at the Court Theatre. Swinburne, Coleridge, and Pater are all quoted on the question of Angelo's just deserts, and MacCarthy agrees most with Pater, arguing that Shakespeare was not much concerned with questions of justice, but did feel 'beauty of character as an end in itself' ('Poetic', p. 56). Philosophers have suggested the same thing about G. E. Moore's ethics.

Two notices of plays by Oscar Wilde need to be mentioned before coming to the more important reviews of the Court Theatre plays, for they reveal some of the differences between MacCarthy's and Bloomsbury's aestheticism, and Wilde's. After seeing *An Ideal Husband*, MacCarthy praised the dramatic construction and dialogue but found Wilde's marvellous wit basically undramatic and confined to inessential places, as in *The Importance of Being Earnest* (which, however, he thought the best farce in English). The essential places where Wilde's characters discuss their emotions or act are 'sentimental, conventional, and stilted' because Wilde lacked interest in human or social nature. This did not matter in comic society plays but it was fatal to what MacCarthy calls philosophical drama ('Ideal', p. 11). It is not surprising, then, that MacCarthy considered *Salome*, admirably staged by Charles Ricketts and Sturge Moore, a mediocre play. Its mixture of Flaubert, Maeterlinck, and the *Song of Songs*, showed that Wilde lacked creative imagination; he was not an artist, only a prophet of art for its own sake. MacCarthy gives no credit here to the creative imagination required for the writing of good social comedy and excellent farce.

The review of *Salome* was the only one of MacCarthy's in the *Speaker* to elicit a published complaint. Wilde's friend and editor Robert Ross attacked MacCarthy for his unoriginal praise and failure to expose the incompetence of the actors, calling his remarks on Wilde's artistry parrot-like; MacCarthy was little more than an insolent Hibernian who mutilated the dead and flattered the living ('*Salome*', p. 337). MacCarthy's mild reply sensibly defends his review, and concludes wistfully, 'as for being a literary moonlighter, an utterer of "insolent Hibernianisms" – I must try to live that reputation down, for I cannot very well argue it away' ('Court Theatre', p. 362).

III

TOUCHSTONE. Wast ever at the Court, shepherd?
CORIN. No, truly.
TOUCHSTONE. Then thou art damned.

Were it not for the Court Theatre, Desmond MacCarthy's *Speaker* notices of Beerbohm Tree, verse drama, Shakespeare, or Oscar Wilde would scarcely fill a chapter of Bloomsbury's early literary history. The above quotation from *As You Like It*, used by MacCarthy as the epigraph for *The Court Theatre, 1904–1907: A Commentary and Criticism*, conveys how blest he felt himself to be as a London drama critic during two of that theatre's three famous Vedrenne–Barker seasons. *The Court Theatre* is dedicated to J. L. Hammond, who, as the *Speaker*'s editor, gave MacCarthy the opportunity to be on the side of right in the theatre, as well as politics. The *Speaker* is not directly mentioned in the book, however, and the only other indication of how much of its contents first appeared as newspaper reviews is in the introduction's complaint about the haste with which drama notices have to be turned out. Haste affected the book too, for according to MacCarthy's correspondence he had less than a month in which to prepare it while he was getting the first issue ready of his own journal, the *New Quarterly*. Since MacCarthy had not reviewed the first season of the Court, he had somehow to make thirteen reviews into a discussion of some thirty plays. The result is not the familiar crafted work of Bloomsbury criticism but a very uneven book, some of whose parts are more notable than the whole. MacCarthy's subtitle, *A Commentary and Criticism*, succinctly describes his usual critical procedure of combining analysis and evaluation with discussions of subjects that are sometimes only tangentially related to the work being criticised. The charm and intelligence of MacCarthy's discursiveness keeps his criticism interesting in short texts of around a thousand words. But a book's chapters of commentary and criticism customarily require a more sustained organisation, and this MacCarthy had difficulty providing. Transitions are lacking, play summaries intrude into general discussions, one play is noticed by someone else because MacCarthy never saw it, and he acknowledges missing the performances of several others. Aside from the tables and reprinted programmes in the appendix (which occupies 50 of the book's 170 pages), there is little indication of the sequence of performances. *The Court Theatre* remained Desmond MacCarthy's only book-length critical work. All the rest were collections. Yet despite its flaws the book is a valuable critical record of the first artistic revolution that members of Bloomsbury were to be involved in during their Edwardian years. It was not simply a coincidence that MacCarthy also participated just a few years later in the second one, helping Fry to organise the first post-impressionist exhibition and writing the important introduction for the catalogue. MacCarthy's involvement in both the Court Theatre and the first post-impressionist exhibition is an early instance of the connections between writing and painting in Bloomsbury.

The short introductory essay to *The Court Theatre* on the influence of dramatic criticism describes how the Court's success came after a decade of criticism by men like Shaw, Beerbohm, Archer, and Walkley, who kept complaining about the hackneyed, vapidly sentimental English theatre. MacCarthy did not believe, however, that drama criticism could or should affect the success of a play. For this he was grateful because it meant his criticism might fulfil its main function, which was not to make or break the public's theatrical taste, but simply to stimulate 'impartial scrutiny and interest in the minds of those who concern themselves with works of art' (p. xiv). If this sounds a little naïve about the potential consequences of theatre reviews, at least it shows *The Court Theatre* to be a work of good Bloomsbury critical theory, though not practice. Vedrenne and Barker were very fortunate to have along with MacCarthy in their stalls such critics as Max Beerbohm, who had succeeded Shaw at the *Saturday Review*; William Archer, the translator of Ibsen, who wrote for yet another liberal paper, the *Tribune*; and A. B. Walkley of *The Times*. But it was on Shaw the playwright as well as director and critic of his own plays, that the fame of the Court largely depended.

Shaw's protégé, the actor and director Harley Granville Barker, had persuaded the management of the Court to stage some matinées of *Candida* in the spring of 1904. Their favourable reception led to the Court's first repertory season in the autumn.

The topical success early in the season of *John Bull's Other Island* (written by Shaw originally for Yeats and the Abbey Theatre) effectively began the Court's transformation of modern English drama. Prime ministers and kings came and enjoyed a play that, MacCarthy noted, had neither plot nor star, presenting instead recognisable characters involved in a natural series of events which left the audience with much to laugh and think about (*CT*, pp. xiii–xiv). How Shaw dominated the Court is shown in the statistical tables in the appendix: eleven of his plays were given over seven hundred performances during the Court seasons; next were three plays of Euripides, translated by Gilbert Murray, with nearly fifty performances. Shaw dominates *The Court Theatre* too; the two longest of the book's four chapters are given over to his plays.

IV

The first two chapters of *The Court Theatre* mix general commentary on the theatre's acting, productions, and dramaturgy with criticism of the particular plays performed there by dramatists other than Shaw. Chapter 1 begins with a brief account of how Barker started at the Court, using Ibsen's theory of the stage to present plays in which the acting and settings were simple, natural, truthful. Discussing the Court's unostentatious scenery, MacCarthy mentions the influence of Japanese theatre, and this brings him to the Court's revivals of Euripides as translated by Gilbert Murray. Murray's and the Court's way of reviving ancient drama was to present the plays as if they had been written for the modern stage. MacCarthy thought this worked well with a dramatist like Euripides who seems much in sympathy with modern feeling; only in the chorus of lugubrious chanting ladies did he find the Court not following their guiding principle of truth rather than effect. T. S. Eliot later dismissed Murray as an insignificant pre-Raphaelite poet whose translations were 'a vulgar debasement of the eminently personal idiom of Swinburne' (*Essays*, p. 48). MacCarthy disliked the dramatic verse of Binyon, Phillips and Hewlett, but in his wish for a drama that challenged our standards of reality, he was uncritical of Murray's versions, which he thought 'rare and beautiful' (*CT*, p. 10). His praise of them reveals, as *Euphrosyne* had, how unmodern was Bloomsbury's earlier Edwardian taste in poetry.

MacCarthy starts his second chapter with a perceptive discussion of the young English dramatists whose work was performed at the Court, including the work of Hankin, Hewlett, Galsworthy (whose *The Silver Box* he liked), Fenn, the Harcourts, and Granville Barker himself. He stresses the breadth of the Court's sympathies; Shaw's dominance had not limited its productions to one movement of dramatic thought. When he turned to the particular plays of the Court, however, MacCarthy often fell back on the summaries that fill a good part of his reviews. Foreign plays are mentioned after the English ones, *The Wild Duck* and then *Hedda Gabler* being given the fullest treatment. MacCarthy criticises Barker's acting in the former, which Shavianised the play by stressing the ironies of the different view points too much. *The Wild Duck* MacCarthy saw as Ibsen's satire on his own philosophy and idealistic followers. (At the end of *The Court Theatre* he expresses the wish that Shaw write a Wild Duck about the Shavians.) If he had to summarise in a sentence the aesthetic influence of the Court Theatre through these plays, MacCarthy thinks he would have to say

> that it has expanded enormously the conception of what kind of story is suitable for the stage; in short, that it has enlarged the meaning of the word 'dramatic', for that adjective signifies nothing but a quality in actions and persons which would make them impressive on the stage. (p. 17)

Well-made plots became less important than the moral and emotional situation of characters in the Court plays because the theatre's playwrights realised again 'that action may be internal as well as external'. The development in psychology or morals must be dramatised, however; otherwise it remained more suitable to the novelist's art than the dramatist's (pp. 19–20).

These and other observations by MacCarthy about the aesthetic significance of the Court Theatre plays of English playwrights as well as those of Ibsen, Maeterlinck, Schnitzler, and Hauptmann, as well as Murray's Euripides offer some grounds on which to compare the two Edwardian artistic revolutions MacCarthy witnessed and wrote about. Court Theatre plays cannot really be described as post-impressionist dramas. Shaw did not make MacCarthy think of Van Gogh the way Wedekind did. Nevertheless there are some noteworthy similarities between the two arts. The conspicuous production of highly finished, technically ornate Royal

Academy paintings and actor-manager extravaganzas were abandoned by the modern artists. Historical subjects gave way to the
aesthetic, psychological, or moral realities of present-day life.
Middle-class materialism ceased to be rendered and celebrated as
much, and social injustice became a major subject in the drama.
Avant-garde painters and playwrights enlarged the accepted
boundaries of their arts, stressing less the primacy of story and
sentiment in pictures and plays. Post-impressionism turned away
from mimetic realism to the emotional significance of form as the
essential aspect of art, while modern drama became more concerned with the thoughts and feelings, the states of mind, of its
characters – as did Bloomsbury's later fiction and non-fiction,
which MacCarthy would also comment upon and criticise.

V

Desmond MacCarthy wrote more criticism on George Bernard
Shaw than on any other author, living or dead (*S*, p. vii). He once
even told Shaw he was going to write his life, which Shaw knew
was just talk (VW/*D*, IV 106). A year after Shaw's death and a year
before his own, MacCarthy did publish a collection of writings on
Shaw that he had written over a period of forty years. The
twentieth-century volume of the *Oxford History of English Literature*
asserted in 1963 that MacCarthy's collected theatre notes 'still
constitute the only consistently intelligent artistic discussion of
Shaw' (J. Stewart, p. 170). *The Court Theatre* discussions of Shaw
express the essential admiration and dissatisfaction that MacCarthy
continued to feel for his genius over the years. And the methods of
MacCarthy's early criticism of Shaw are characteristic of the kind of
Bloomsbury criticism MacCarthy would continue to practice. By
dividing the Shaw half of *The Court Theatre* into a chapter on his
characters and their emotions and then a chapter on the plays,
MacCarthy indicates that, like Forster and Virginia Woolf (at times),
he considered character as significant an aspect of drama and
fiction as artistic form. In *The Court Theatre*, MacCarthy's version of
this commonplace critical assumption leads him to attend to the
characters' emotions. His analysis of Shaw's use of emotion is more
acute and original than his comments on either the reality of Shaw's
women, the Dickensian vividness of the minor characters, or the
social origins of Shaw's psychological caricatures. MacCarthy sees

that the emotional instability of Shaw's excitable yet detached characters makes his plays rather fantastic. In his analysis of the sexual emotion so important yet oddly isolated in plays like *Man and Superman*, MacCarthy displays Apostolic skill in describing and evaluating states of mind:

> This emotion must be distinguished from lust on the one hand, and from love on the other; for in the first place, it is imaginative as well as sensual, an excitement of the mind as well as of the body – of the whole living being in fact – and, in the second, it does not include a desire for the other person's welfare, nor the conscious contemplation of what is good. (*CT*, p. 60)

One of the values of Shaw's plays for MacCarthy is that they help us to distinguish our emotions, even though these opportunities are limited by Shaw's exaggeration of human stupidity. The philosopher in Shaw overrides the artist who would represent more the emotional complexities of life. For all their sexuality, the general impression left by his plays is that of a loveless world.

In the last chapter of *The Court Theatre* on Shaw's plays, MacCarthy returns to the critical format of the *Speaker*. Plots are summarised, acting and production commented upon, ideas briefly analysed, scenes or dialogue praised, and the play as a whole evaluated. The organisation is not quite chronological by play performance because MacCarthy wants to end with a discussion of Shaw's philosophy as expressed in *Major Barbara* and *Man and Superman*. He begins with *Candida*, the first of Shaw's plays to be put on at the Court and for MacCarthy one of his best, with its clear embodiment of Shaw's ruthlessly idealistic socialism. *John Bull's Other Island* illustrates the new drama where the emphasis is on contrasting temperaments rather than plot. MacCarthy's account of *You Never Can Tell* was largely repeated from the *Speaker*. Added, however, was a paragraph on the audience's comic reception of Shaw's Schopenhauerian vitalism here and in *Man and Superman*. This last play MacCarthy considered Shaw's most brilliant but he says little about its philosophy of sex. When MacCarthy reviewed *Captain Brassbound's Conversion* in the *Speaker* he talked about the obligation of critics to respect the art but question the philosophy of such a play; in the book, however, MacCarthy is more favourably disposed to the work and thinks Shaw's emotional asceticism completely justified in a drama that exposes the vulgarity and silliness of revenge. Two *Speaker* reviews and ten pages of *The Court Theatre* are devoted to *The Doctor's Dilemma*, a play MacCarthy does not really like, though the performance was excellent. The first review is rather self-conscious, about what other critics are writing, and the second, mostly reprinted in *The Court Theatre*, attacks the play's trivialising epilogue and the formulaic characterisation of the painter Dubedat. Dubedat allows MacCarthy an aside on English aestheticism: he is '"the artistic temperament", that dismal relic of the art for art's sake movement, so wretchedly barren itself in England' (a criticism Shaw took exception to in a later letter to MacCarthy on his Court Theatre book – CT, p. 101; DM/pM). Forster was saying something similar in *Where Angels Fear to Tread* the year before. *The Philanderer*, MacCarthy thinks a queer play but for the odd reason that as a satire on the 'new woman' it is out of date in 1907 – like Ibsen's *The Doll's House*! *The Philanderer* may not be much of a feminist play, but MacCarthy's awareness of the Edwardian women's movement is very limited here.

When MacCarthy reviewed *Major Barbara* at the Court in December 1905, he wished he had the space of four articles to do justice to it. After recounting the play in *The Court Theatre* and praising the wonderful second act in the Salvation Army shelter, he concentrates on Shaw's philosophy there, and also in the *Don Juan in Hell* dream from *Man and Superman* that was performed separately at the end of the Court Theatre seasons in 1907. MacCarthy makes his criticism of Shaw as a philosophic dramatist the culmination of his Court Theatre book, not because he valued Shaw's philosophy higher than his art, but because he thought Shaw did. In his critique of Shaw MacCarthy develops the ethical point he made in the *Independent Review* when he reviewed *Man and Superman* back in 1903:

His great defect as an artist-philosopher is that he does not distinguish between those things which are bad as means and those which are bad in themselves, or between what is good as an end and what is only good as a means to that end. . . . But it is certain that qualities and things which are valuable as means are not necessarily worth having for their own sakes, and that things very good in themselves may not at the same time be important as means to something else worth having. And since this is indubitably true, it follows that any one who judges the values of things from the point of view of their results, and hardly ever asks himself whether they have any value in themselves, must often get his scale of values wrong. This is the most general criticism which can be brought against the morality of the Shavian drama. A great part of that originality of view which underlies the plays is due to the fact that he judges goodness and badness by their results alone. The transvaluation which follows is often startling. (pp. 113–14)

Thus Shaw extols the useful virtues – vitality, honesty, courage, benevolence – and devalues the ultimate ends of personal affection and the appreciation of beauty. That is how Shaw so paradoxically reverses heaven and hell in *Man and Superman*: his community of saints, 'the masters of reality', are really just a community of reformers trying to improve everyone, while his damned are left to contemplate unreal goodness and beauty in hell.

VI

Desmond MacCarthy's analysis of a transvaluation that exalts instrumental goods and ignores or belittles intrinsic ones is derived directly, of course, from *Principia Ethica* and it demonstrates the continuing influence of Moore's ethics on MacCarthy's criticism. The dramatic criticism of MacCarthy also reveals fundamental differences in the scales of value not just between himself and Shaw but between Bloomsbury and the Fabians. Disagreements about the significance of ultimate ethical ends are usually implicit and sometimes explicit in the encounters that took place over the years between members of Bloomsbury and those associated at one time or another with the Fabian Society. They underlie the disagreements between MacCarthy and Shaw about the character of Caesar in *Caesar and Cleopatra* (1913), between Roger Fry and Shaw over the worth of virtuosity in painting (1913), between Bell, Shaw, and MacCarthy about ultimate values in *Back to Methuselah* (1922), between Keynes, Shaw, and Wells over Stalin's communism (1934). They can be found in *Heartbreak House* which Shaw said he always connected with Virginia Woolf (LW/BA, p. 126) and also in his *A Village Wooing* which dramatises a Strachey-like character's trans-formation into a village storekeeper (Holroyd, 'Fabians', pp. 45–6). In the 1930s Beatrice Webb put the difference between Bloomsbury and Fabian values with exaggerated clarity in a letter to E. M. Forster about his biography of Lowes Dickinson:

> Why don't you write another great novel (analogous to the *Passage to India*) giving the essence of the current conflict all over the world between those who aim at exquisite relationships within the closed circle of the 'elect' and those who aim at hygienic and scientific improvement of the whole of the race?
>
> (EMF/*GLD*, p. 224)

The controversies between members of Bloomsbury and the Fabian Society are more rewarding than those with Wyndham Lewis, for instance, because basically both Groups agreed about ethical means worth pursuing. Both attacked Victorian idealism and the ethics of duty, agreeing that good actions were to be measured by their results and disagreeing about the standards of measurement. Bloomsbury would certainly have concurred with MacCarthy when he concluded a summary of the virtues of Shaw's plays at the Court Theatre with this praise: 'almost every play he has written stimulates that social consciousness of communal responsibility upon which the hopes of reformers depend' (*CT*, p. 118). As for Shaw, he thought highly of MacCarthy's dramatic criticism. When the Webbs established the Fabian *New Statesman* in 1913, it is not surprising that they asked a liberal like MacCarthy to be its dramatic critic. MacCarthy thought he owed the job to Shaw (*H*, p. 15).

That the Fabians and some of Bloomsbury's political opinions overlapped for quite a while is shown in the political writings of Leonard Woolf. As he would write in his autobiography, 'we found ourselves always on the same side of the barricades with Shaw, Wells, and Bennett'[2] (*BA*, p. 124). This remained true until the Thirties, when the admiration of the Webbs, Shaw, and Wells for what Stalin had accomplished brought out a political difference, sometimes anticipated in MacCarthy's *Speaker* reviews, between Bloomsbury liberalism and Fabian socialism. Very broadly, the difference is between the virtues of individualism versus collectivism. Dissention occurred within the Bloomsbury Group itself not so much about ultimate ends as about the best means to attain them. In the early 1920s Virginia Woolf wrote ironically to her former teacher Janet Case about an argument in the park with Leonard over Shaw and the Edwardians' moral heritage. She was in the midst of working out the differences between the Edwardians and the Georgians for her own literary purposes:

> Leonard says we owe a great deal to Shaw. I say that he only influenced the outer fringe of morality. Leonard says that the shop girls wouldn't be listening to the Band with their young men if it weren't for Shaw. I say the human heart is touched only by the poets. Leonard says rot, I say damn. Then we go home. Leonard says I'm narrow. I say he's stunted. But don't you agree with me that the Edwardians, from 1895 to 1914, made a pretty poor show. By the Edwardians, I mean Shaw, Wells, Galsworthy, the Webbs, Arnold Bennett. We Georgians have our work cut out for us, you see. There's not a single living writer (English) I respect. . . . How does one come by one's morality? Surely by reading the poets. And we've got no poets. Does that throw light upon anything? Consider the Webbs – That woman has the impertinence to say that I'm a-moral: the truth being that if Mrs Webb had been a good woman, Mrs Woolf would have been a better. Orphans is what I say we are – we Georgians.   (*L*, II 529)

Yet Virginia herself derived an important part of what she calls her morality from the same work of Edwardian ethics as her husband and Desmond MacCarthy, a work whose *summum bonum* of love and beauty, Shaw placed in hell.

VII

Aside from his cogent criticism of Shaw's ethical principles, how good a drama critic was MacCarthy at the Court Theatre? How well did his criticism fulfil its main function, which he said was to stimulate 'impartial scrutiny and interest in the minds of those who concern themselves with works of art'? (*CT*, p. xiv) In the brief conclusion to his book MacCarthy worried that he had been too carping of Vedrenne and Barker's achievement, but he felt the customary 'strain of almost obituary benevolence' found at the end of critical works was inappropriate for dramatic enterprise about to move to another theatre and try (vainly as it turned out) for commercial success (p. 119). MacCarthy was, if anything, less critical and more enthusiastic than the other discriminating reviewers of the Court productions. One way of evaluating the early critical performance of Bloomsbury's 'super-reviewer' may be to compare it briefly with those of Archer, Beerbohm, and Walkley, all of whom, like MacCarthy, used their Court Theatre reviews in books of dramatic criticism.

After the Court's first season William Archer brought out *The Vedrenne–Barker Season, 1904–5: A Record and a Commentary*. This brief pamphlet of comments, photographs, and programmes may well have given MacCarthy the idea for his book. Archer has the highest praise for the Court's efforts. He particularly likes Murray's translations; only the theatre's emphasis on Shaw disquiets him. Archer is aware that the actor-managers' timidity has stimulated the demand for Shaw's plays, but he wants more different kinds of plays at the Court. MacCarthy liked Shaw's plays rather more than Archer, perhaps, but he agreed with him that some of the foreign plays should have had a better reception.

MacCarthy complained at the beginning of *The Court Theatre* that he was given little time – usually varying from forty to a hundred minutes – in which to write his copy for the *Speaker* (p. xi). Haste, often caused by procrastination, would always deprive Mac-Carthy's writing of finish. What he said later of his broadcasts applies to all of MacCarthy's writing: 'I put work of any kind off till the last moment, otherwise I spend a preposterous amount of time titivating' (Cecil, p. 286). Max Beerbohm had much more time for his weekly column, and more space too. His Court reviews are more graceful, coherent, and polished, more elegant and entertaining and self-conscious than MacCarthy's. 'I have the satiric temperament', he wrote at the beginning of *Around Theatres* to explain why he should not have become a critic: 'when I am laughing at any one I am generally rather amusing, but when I am praising any one, I am always deadly dull' (I 5). Like Walkley and MacCarthy, Beerbohm thought the task of a critic was to report on his impressions. But in his criticism the reviewer's impressions tend to replace the play that gave rise to them. As a critic Beerbohm has little to say about ideas, even when reviewing Shaw's plays; he wants to be sympathetic to Shaw but this intellectual limitation makes his reviews of Shaw less stimulating than those of the other Court critics. He also wavered as to whether plays like *Man and Superman* were really plays at all, a topic that futilely exercised Walkley as well. But Beerbohm recognised the value of Mac-Carthy's criticism. He read his weekly *Speaker* reviews because MacCarthy's 'austere sobriety of judgment was surprisingly expressed in terms of youthful ardour'. The appreciation of Shaw in *The Court Theatre* Beerbohm considered 'the most suggestive and the soundest that has been done yet' ('Savoy', p. 389). A. B. Walkley's reviews in *The Times* (he had been the drama critic of the *Speaker* in the 1890s) were done under the same pressure as those of MacCarthy, who could only admire his colleague's deft incisiveness and rare memory. Lytton Strachey, too, liked his criticism, especially his understanding of Racine. As a professional reviewer less sympathetic to Shaw, Walkley was more efficient than MacCarthy but his theories of the drama made his critical judgements less open and impartial. Shaw admired and mocked Walkley's critical expectations in the dedication of *Man and Superman*, but that did not keep Walkley from roundly declaring Shaw no dramatist in that play or in *Major Barbara*, which he found lacked any pretence of dramatic form (Walkley, *Drama*, p. 233). MacCarthy criticised Shaw's dramatic form too, but without denying its existence; because he knew considerably less about drama than Walkley, he may have been more receptive to Shaw's innovations. Walkley also dismissed Shaw's 'cheap German philosophic baggage' but did not go into any detail about it (p. 229). MacCarthy was aware of the sources of Shaw's transvalued vitalism in Schopenhauer and Nietzsche, but in his particular criticism of Shaw's ideas there was no need to refer to them.

MacCarthy could be as perceptive a reviewer as any of his critical colleagues at the Court. On occasion his reviews are less stimulating than Archer's, Beerbohm's, or Walkley's, and sometimes they are little more than summaries or digressions. His writing was not as well made as theirs, yet he could be more catholic and at times even more incisive. That is why his Court Theatre criticisms of Shaw's plays have endured. Shaw himself recognised their excellence. 'Certainly, as regards my own plays', he wrote to MacCarthy after *The Court Theatre* appeared,

> you were not only nearer the mark than other sharp shooters, you were actually in the same valley, whilst the others, even when they got on the targets, did so mostly by quite unintentional ricochets or vagaries of spent bullets. (Cecil, p. 98)

Nevertheless MacCarthy remained something of a critical schizophrenic in *The Court Theatre* and later. In a 1930 essay called 'The Ideal Spectator', MacCarthy divided himself and most other regular theatre-goers into two kinds of critics. D. M. No. 1 is hard to satisfy, finds most of the plays he sees artistically negligible, and so usually sleeps through them. D. M. No. 2 is a good-natured, impressionable man with a natural taste for the theatre; he does most of the reviewing, and when bothered by the insomnia of No. 1 he can produce an unfavourable notice[3] (*T*, pp. 9–10). In *The Court Theatre* these critics are roughly apportioned the criticism and commentary parts of the book. MacCarthy's critical dualism is not unique in Bloomsbury's criticism. In some respects it resembles Virginia Woolf's two ways of reading in 'How Should One Read a Book?', the first being as openly receptive as possible and the second as demandingly critical. Later MacCarthy's two critical identities would coalesce into the critical persona he would call 'Affable Hawk'.

6 Lytton Strachey and the Prose of Empire

'You don't know how superb one feels – writing a real book, with real chapters', Lytton Strachey wrote to Maynard Keynes in the summer of 1904 (MH/LS, p. 223). This last, still unpublished book of Bloomsbury's early Edwardian years is as important in its way to the Group's literary history as *The Court Theatre, Euphrosyne*, or *Where Angels Fear to Tread*. A list of Bloomsbury books centrally or peripherally about English imperialism would have to include Forster's *Howards End* and *A Passage to India*, his collections of stories and essays, as well as his Egyptian writings; a half-dozen of Leonard Woolf's works, among them his books about Ceylon and Africa; Virginia Woolf's *The Voyage Out, Mrs. Dalloway, The Years* and *Three Guineas*; Keynes's *Indian Currency and Finance*; and Strachey's *Eminent Victorians* and *Queen Victoria*. If the idea is extended to other forms of exploitation and control than national ones, imperialism could be seen as perhaps the central concern in Bloomsbury's criticism of English life. It is interesting for Bloomsbury's development, then, that the first sustained consideration of imperialism among the Group's writings was a fellowship dissertation by Lytton Strachey defending an eminent eighteenth-century English imperialist.

Strachey's vindication of Warren Hastings, the first Governor General of India, shows the Edwardian continuities and changes in his development as a writer. It began in 1901 as a long undergraduate essay for the Greaves prize, which it did not win. Strachey then expanded his essay into a fellowship dissertation on Hastings's dealings with Cheyt Sing, the Rajah of Benares, and submitted it, unsuccessfully, to Trinity College in September 1904.

He spent the next year extending the dissertation to include Hastings's struggle with the wife and mother of the Vizier of Oude who controlled his treasury. The revised dissertation, now well over 100,000 words, was resubmitted under the title *Warren Hastings, Cheyt Sing, and the Begums of Oude*, at the end of August 1905, but again it failed to win its author a Trinity fellowship. For the next five years Strachey worked desultorily at turning the dissertation into a book while reviewing, mainly for the *Spectator*. Then he abandoned his decade-old exercise in unironic imperial history.[1]

No writing of Bloomsbury's displays more distinctly the Victorian origins of the Group than Strachey's dissertation. His family had been importantly involved in Indian administration for four generations; the very name Lytton that he chose to use was a viceroy's. His father and his Uncle John, both knighted for their Indian work, had been known as 'the Strachey Raj'; there was no important office in the government of India that one or the other of them had not held, his uncle claimed in a book on Indian administration (B. Strachey, *Line*, pp. 156, 164). In another work Sir John Strachey had defended Hastings's war with the Rohillas; it followed the book written by his and the Viceroy Lord Lytton's close friend Sir James Fitzjames Stephen on Nuncomar and Impey; 'An episode in the great Warren Hastings story', Leslie Stephen called it (*Fitzjames Stephen*, p. 429). As an implicit defence of his family's tradition of Indian imperial service, Strachey's dissertation continued the work of his as well as Virginia Woolf's uncles.

Yet in both form and content, the dissertation was a dead-end for Strachey. During the Edwardian years Strachey's and Bloomsbury's attitudes markedly changed towards imperialism and the nationalism behind it that was leading to the First World War. Leonard Woolf's experiences in Ceylon and, to a lesser degree, Keynes's in the India Office disillusioned the Group about achievements of empire. Strachey's dissertation is also the least literary of his books. Little of it is inherently interesting as writing, even though a number of the figures he deals with were masters of English prose. Almost none of the rhetorical flair or iconoclastic wit to be found in his reviews of the time and especially in his other unpublished Cambridge writings is present in the dissertation. Nevertheless these Cambridge papers together with a few Indian reviews are part of the literary context necessary for understanding the place of Strachey's prolonged work on Hastings in his own development as a writer of history. Strachey's Cambridge papers were in various ways the antithesis of his Anglo-Indian thesis, but the result was not a synthesis.

II

In his undergraduate essay on Warren Hastings Lytton Strachey proposes to give a short, clear factual account of three episodes in Hastings's controversial career as Governor General. Only when this has been done, he maintains, can the examination of motives begin. Hastings's motives are never examined by Strachey, even in his dissertation, and this makes these writings very different from his later ones. Strachey's narrative is not just an account of the facts, however, for he also justifies Hastings's actions as he goes along. No doubt is left as to the nobility of Hastings's intentions or the greatness of his achievements. He is 'perhaps the best-abused personage in history', 'the one great figure of his time' (a time that included the founders of the United States), the man who saved the Empire. Because his aims are unquestioned, Hastings remains vaguely mysterious in all of Strachey's writings on him. At the end of the essay Strachey uninhibitedly idealises him as a superhuman being: 'he never descended to a fault or even to a foible; he was perfection as a statesman, a husband, a friend; he soared' (pST). One waits here for an irony that never comes.

Most of Strachey's undergraduate essay is spent on Hastings's involvement in the Rohilla War, his difficulties with Nuncomar, and the revolt of the Rajah of Benares. More briefly treated are Hastings's dealings with the Vizier and Begums of Oude, and then his impeachment. The Rohilla War and the Nuncomar affair were the subjects respectively of John Strachey's and Fitzjames Stephen's books; Hastings's difficulties with the Vizier and the Begums became the subjects of Strachey's dissertation. In the essay these different episodes are treated for the most part in narrative or descriptive summaries, with pauses for arguments against the prevailing view of Hastings. While describing Hastings's dealings with the Begums of Oude, for example, Strachey raises the question of what is illegal in a time of anarchy and he comments: 'It may be possible for some persons to hesitate in answering this question. For Hastings it was not, and the result is that the English are still in India' (pST). The view of Hastings as a ruthless imperialist was popularised by Macaulay in a famous essay based on James Mill's

biased history of the British in India. Strachey thought Macaulay's
rhetoric 'blatant'. Yet Macaulay has left his traces in the recurrent
contrasts of Strachey's essay. Hastings's career is a flash of notoriety
followed by nearly absolute oblivion. English rule in India is a
balance of native institutions and English administrative methods.
The incorruptible goodness of Hastings is opposed to the utter
malignity of his enemy Philip Francis. Hastings the man of deeds is
arraigned by Edmund Burke, the man of words. History itself splits
into facts and motives.

That Macaulay was a more important predecessor than, say Pater,
is apparent in the reviews that Strachey wrote for the *Independent
Review*. There are also touches in the essay, however, that anticipate
Strachey's development away from Macaulay into complex irony.
The death of Hastings that Strachey closes his essay with goes
considerably beyond facts or motives.

> He was eminently secret; and it is in keeping with the weird
> seclusion of his mind, that he drew his last breath in private. As
> he sank back upon the cushions he took in his hands a napkin
> and covered his face; the onlookers, moved by a common
> emotion, were awed as in the presence of some appalling
> mystery; and indeed, even to us, the vision of the women's
> fingers plucking so softly and delicately the handkerchief away,
> and revealing with all the shock of inevitability the silent fixity of
> the face, seems to give, by the very force of its intimate pettiness,
> a new and strange and terrible image of Death itself. (pST)

The essay on Warren Hastings is a remarkable performance by a
twenty-one-year-old undergraduate. Its hyperbolic finale prefigures
the creative biography that Strachey would later write.

III

The dissertation on Warren Hastings offers little that is as
imaginative as this.[2] According to a draft preface, its object is to
continue the research begun by Sir James Stephen and Sir John
Strachey by giving an accurate, complete account of Warren
Hastings's relations with Cheyt Sing and the Begums of Oude,
these being the episodes that figured most importantly in
Hastings's impeachment. Because the events are so controversial,

Strachey says he has had to include a great number of extracts from the records of the time in order to achieve his dual purpose.

> My aim has not been merely destructive; I have not simply attempted to expose the shortcomings of Mill; I have attempted to write an account, based upon the evidence of contemporary records, of the actual conduct, the actual motives, and the actual policy of Hastings in two important sections of his Indian career.
>
> (Redford, p. 47)

By the time of *Eminent Victorians* Strachey presented his historical intentions as neither imposing nor proposing, but exposing. The scope of his dissertation was wider and more diffuse. His examiners complained of its obscure style and poor organisation (MH/LS, p. 265). The masses of quotations in text and footnotes that Strachey needed to expose Mill and Macaulay interfere with the narrative asserting Hastings's innocence and greatness. In addition to its unassimilated evidence, the dissertation's two purposes do not cohere stylistically. Fairly straightforward accounts of what was happening are rather jarringly interspersed with elaborate characterisations, summaries, and denunciations.

The difficulties that Strachey had with the writing of his dissertation and the resulting incongruities of its styles were caused first of all by the extent and complexity of his material. But the difficulties were also a consequence, it appears from the introduction to his dissertation, of the various accounts of Warren Hastings's administration with which he had to work. This interesting introduction, published in 1980, appears to be a reworking by Strachey of the original preface when he was thinking of turning *Warren Hastings, Cheyt Sing, and the Begums of Oude* into a book. In order to see the significance of the introduction in Strachey's development as a writer of history, it is necessary to summarise the two parts of his fellowship dissertation.

The seven chapters on Cheyt Sing that make up the first submitted version of Strachey's dissertation treat the relations between the Rajah of Benares and Hastings's Bengal Government, relations that culminated in the insurrection and expulsion of Cheyt Sing in 1781. Strachey is at pains in the first Chapter to show how the illegitimate Cheyt Sing and his father were not hereditary potentates but robbers, tax collectors, and landholders who had only recently become rajahs, and he undermines their status in periodic prose. Chapter 2 discusses the dependence of Cheyt Sing on the sovereignty of the East India Company, the argument here being interrupted by tableaux that a recent critic of the dissertation found redolent of Macaulay (Redford, p. 46). In maintaining Cheyt Sing's dependence, Strachey also fiercely attacks James Mill's 'jumble of incoherent arguments, of unbridled insinuations, and of malignant perversions of fact' (Hastings, I 49). The third and fourth chapters concern Cheyt Sing's relations with the English governing Council in Calcutta, which became fatally divided when Hastings lost majority control of it to three new members from England, one of whom was Philip Francis.

The summary narrative becomes leaner as Strachey covers the developing Maratha War, Cheyt Sing's shuffling evasion of demands for troops or money, and the machinations of Francis that ended with Hastings shooting him in a duel. Hastings had said of Francis, 'I judge of his public conduct by my experience of his private, which I have found to be void of truth and honour', and Strachey observes 'after such words as these, a recourse to arms seems, even in the twentieth century, almost natural' (Hastings, I 123). The last three Chapters of Part 1 are about the revolt of Cheyt Sing. Page-long, single-spaced quotations of evidence are given as Strachey traces the dispute between the Rajah and the Governor General over the money due the Company for the Maratha Wars. Hastings fined Cheyt Sing fifty lakhs of current rupees or £500,000 in late eighteenth-century sterling (Marshall, p. x). The correspondence of Hastings and Cheyt Sing, his arrest, the subsequent insurrection and massacre, and Hastings's retreat from Benares are covered in Chapter 6; the quelling of the revolt and replacement of Cheyt Sing, and the treatment of his female relatives in Chapter 7. Strachey's narrative of Hastings's surprise withdrawal and the consequent rumours that British rule in India had ended is dramatically effective. The Latinate adjectives, parallel clauses, and rhetorical questions anticipate their ironical use in Strachey's mature style. (The natives remember, for example, 'the tumultuous flight of the great Governor. He had disappeared, he had fled into the night; and who could tell when he would return?' – I 197.)

The chapter following this narrative is interrupted by a lengthy defence of Hastings's treatment of Cheyt Sing's women that Mill had so criticised. Strachey hotly describes Mill's misrepresentations as 'the most disgraceful, the most wantonly malignant, and the most monstrous' of all his accusations; a phrase of Hastings's about the Ranee not escaping an examination concerning her treasure is contorted by Mill 'into an abominable license for indiscriminate plundering. Never was so terrible a charge based upon so frivolous a foundation' (Hastings, I 219–20). Compared with this, the peroration at the end of Part 1, on the vanquished weak and foolish Cheyt Sing, who nearly brought down the great Governor General, is calm.

The first version of Strachey's fellowship dissertation ended here. Two contemporary reactions to it may be compared. One is that of the economic historian William Cunningham of Trinity, the examiner inauspiciously chosen for the dissertation. (It was to the same Reverend Dr Cunningham that Strachey's 'First and Last Will and Testament' had left a treatise on syphilis, two years earlier! – *LS/LSH*, p. 108.) Strachey wrote to his mother that Cunningham's main objection was to his dissertation's lack of originality, for his view of Hastings's administration had already been established by his Uncle John and Fitzjames Stephen. Michael Holroyd adds that Cunningham also criticised the separation of the Cheyt Sing affair from that of the Begums of Oude, which made it less controversially important than the events Sir James and Sir John had investigated (*LS*, pp. 226–7). These criticisms led to Strachey's expanding his work for a second attempt at a Trinity fellowship. The other response to the dissertation was from Leonard Woolf, who was soon to be serving English imperialism in the East while Strachey was continuing to defend one of its founders. Woolf apparently read the dissertation before sailing for Ceylon and found it 'too enthralling, and not enough like a dissertation'; had it been less graceful, more laboured in its points, Strachey would obviously have been given a fellowship (*MH/LS*, p. 228). Woolf is not simply being sardonic here, for the writing in 'Warren Hastings and Cheyt Sing', uneven as it is, has in places a polish that some consider inimical to the scholarly transmission of truth.

Warren Hastings's relations with the Cheyt Sing were closely connected with the Vizier and Begums of Oude whose territory adjoined that of Benares in the North of India. This wealthy, maladministered district remained independent until England annexed it after the Mutiny in 1858. Hastings's troubles with Oude began with the new Vizier, Asuph-ud-dowla. A conflict developed in the governing Council between Hastings's and the majority's policies toward the independence of the Nabob's government, which itself was divided by a conflict between the Nabob and his mother and grandmother who controlled Oude's treasure. The role of these Begums in Cheyt Sing's revolt exacerbated the conflicts. Hastings finally imprisoned the Begums' eunuchs until he obtained the money owed to the East India Company and restored the Nabob's authority. For the managers of Hastings's impeachment in London after his return from India, this despoiling of the Begums was among his most outrageous crimes. Strachey's account of these matters in Part 2 of his dissertation, which is also divided into seven Chapters, forms a parallel narrative to Part 1. The first and second chapters concern the majority's policy toward Oude and Hastings's efforts to implement it. The third deals with his reforms in a treaty with Asuph-ud-dowla, who financially supported the war with Mysore that the English were fighting. Chapters 4 and 5 discuss the nature of the affidavits about the Begums' support of Cheyt Sing. The last two chapters are about the treatment of the Begums and their eunuchs by Hastings's agent, and then the Governor General's triumphant visit to Lucknow, the capital of Oude, after the Vizier's authority had been restored. Hastings had not been able to guarantee good government there, however, and with this point *Warren Hastings, Cheyt Sing, and the Begums of Oude* ends. There is no conclusion.

Again there are large infusions of quotation from the records into the narrative, but Strachey's indignation with the accounts of Hastings's enemies has somewhat abated. (On the question of the affidavits collected by Hastings's supporter, Judge Sir Elijah Impey, Strachey quotes the censure of Macaulay from Fitzjames Stephen's book on Nuncomar and Impey.) Hastings remains remotely superior but the portrait of the Vizier Asuph-ud-dowla in Part 2 is more detailed and sympathetic than that of Cheyt Sing in Part 1 – and also more like some of the minor characters in Strachey's later biographies. Beset by powerful women, the Vizier led a life 'of gluttony, of intoxication, of abominable vice' (Hastings II 6):

> His vacillating will, his hatred of business, his utter lack of ambition, combined to make him the most incompetent of rulers; and the enormous corpulence of his bodily frame appeared to symbolize a temperament which had fallen through sloth into a nerveless and incorrigible decay. (Redford, p. 51)

Strachey's somewhat wordy description and imprecise imagery is shown up by Macaulay's more muscular writing:

. . . Asuph-ud-Dowlah was one of the weakest and most vicious of even Eastern princes. His life was divided between torpid repose and the most odious forms of sensuality. In his court there was boundless waste, throughout his dominions wretchedness and disorder. (p. 488)

If Strachey's early prose is inferior to Macaulay's mature style, his sympathetic view of the Nabob is more paradoxical in portraying him as also pathetically honest and faithful, particularly to Hastings at the crucial juncture of the Mysore War. Strachey relishes the ironic conclusion that 'it would indeed be difficult to exaggerate the debt which the Company owed this incompetent debauchee' (II 64–5).

IV

Strachey failed once more to gain a fellowship with his expanded dissertation, which he had resubmitted at the beginning of September 1905. Instead of the lack of originality, now the writing and use of lengthy extracts were criticised (MH/*LS*, p. 265). It is not possible to tell whether, in reworking his unsuccessful dissertation for a book, Strachey intended to revise his method of presenting evidence to refute Mill and Macaulay. But in the introduction apparently composed later for *Warren Hastings, Cheyt Sing, and the Begums of Oude* he suggests that the problems of style and quotation resulted from the various historical attacks on Hastings's Indian administration that Strachey was trying directly or indirectly to refute.

After saying in the introduction that he is going to give an accurate, complete account of Hastings's involvements with the Rajah and the Begums, Strachey actually spends most of his time criticising the historical accounts of Hastings by Mill, Macaulay, and Burke.[3] His concern here is more literary, more historiographic, than historical. Strachey's interest in the nature of historical writing was a lifelong preoccupation, beginning with a November 1903 Cambridge paper entitled 'The Historian of the Future', and ending with his miniature portraits of six historians in 1931. In his Cambridge essay Strachey offers a theory of historical writing that antedates his dissertation and is therefore interesting to compare with the introduction he wrote afterwards. The paper was one of a number

of responses in Cambridge and beyond to the inaugural lecture that
J. B. Bury, Acton's successor as Regius Professor of History, had
given the year before. Bury had stressed that history was not a
handmaiden for the statesman or the moralist but a science in its
own right. According to the *DNB* his lecture was widely misunderstood; G. M. Trevelyan, for example, in an essay published in
the *Independent Review* a month after Strachey's paper (and later
revised as the title piece of *Clio, A Muse*) objected that the scientific
treatment of evidence was only one of the historian's functions; he
also needed to be imaginative in his speculations and literary in his
narrative. For Strachey, too, Clio is a muse not a scientist, but that is
not his main concern. 'The Historian of the Future' is the first
Bloomsbury text to use G. E. Moore's distinction between good as a
means and as an end. Writing just a month after the publication of
Principia Ethica, Strachey applies Moore's analysis to the meaning
and value of history. As a means to good ends histories are of little
worth because history does not repeat itself, but as goods in
themselves Strachey finds historical writing to be of great potential
value. History, he agrees with Bury, is about true past events
concerning man in society, but Strachey does not believe the
scientific method can be applied to individual minds. For them a
totally different 'artistic method' is required. Although this other
method is never defined, it can be surmised from the intrinsic value
of history, which according to Strachey depends on two conditions:
'first, the interest of the facts narrated, and secondly, the beauty of
the narration.' The great historians who fulfil these conditions – he
instances Thucydides, Tacitus, Gibbon, Michelet and, rather
surprisingly, Carlyle – are stars to be contemplated for their own
sake, not candles to illuminate the arid workshops of future
historians (pST).

　　History as an art belonged therefore in the realm of *Principia
Ethica*'s Ideal. Yet Strachey himself as a future historian in his
dissertation encountered serious difficulties over the interest of his
facts and the art of their narration – both his own and those of the
predecessors he was attempting to refute. And when he came to
write the introduction to *Warren Hastings, Cheyt Sing, and the Begums
of Oude* Strachey was mainly concerned with the imagination of
Macaulay, the style of Mill, the rhetoric of Burke, rather than their
misrepresentations of history.

　　No English historical figure had more great prose stylists
opposing him than Warren Hastings did. Hastings himself was a

powerful writer, as his great enemy Francis acknowledged. In a *Spectator* piece, 'The Prose Style of Men of Action', Strachey wrote of Hastings's 'swelling and romantic utterance' as conveying at times the mystery as well as the grandeur of the East' (p. 142).[4] Philip Francis, described by Strachey in his introduction as a Miltonic toad crouching by the ear of his Eve, Burke (*SS*, p. 228), is generally recognised now as the author of the Junius Letters, those master-pieces of political invective that defended the importance of public opinion. Leslie Stephen thought their satire inferior to Swift's and their rhetoric to Burke's, but the very comparisons imply their power (*History*, II 169). Edmund Burke was the prime parliamentary mover in Hastings's impeachment. Strachey alludes in his dissertation to Burke's characteristic depiction of Hastings as 'the head, the chief, and captain-general in iniquity – one in whom all the frauds, all the peculations, all the tyranny in India are embodied, disciplined, and arranged' (*Speeches*, IV 304). Such utterances of Burke's, Strachey describes in his introduction, stand out from the attacks of others on Hastings

> in virtue both of their hideous violence of language and their splendid elevation of thought. The scintillating wisdom, the passionate nobility, the gorgeous rhetoric, which characterize Burke's speeches against Hastings, have given them a place in literature which they would certainly have ill deserved if sanity, clarity, and accuracy were the sole tests of literary merit.
>
> (*SS*, p. 227)

In these antithetical characteristics lay Strachey's problem as a writer of history. Even more celebrated than Burke's speeches at Hastings's trial were Sheridan's. The playwright turned politician created a sensation with his defence of the Begums; phrases such as 'their treasures were their treasons' (Sheridan, p. 288) were remembered, rather than the involved explanations by Hastings and his defenders of the women's duplicity. Then there was Fox's oratory. Macaulay said the managers of Hastings's impeachment before the House of Lords 'contained an array of speakers such as perhaps had not appeared together since the great age of Athenian eloquence' (p. 529). To which must be added Macaulay's own eloquence, though not Mill's. James Mill's terrible prose was, nevertheless, another kind of rhetoric used against Hastings, according to Strachey. Its 'crabbed, cold, and dull' style – the very opposite of Macaulay's – creates the impression that Mill 'has sacrificed every grace of language and every audacity of thought for the sake of meticulous accuracy', when in fact his style's dryness 'is nothing more than the cloak for a multitude of errors'. Fitzjames Stephen accused Mill of bad faith, and Strachey speculates on the psychology of a historian who produced such distortions (*SS*, pp. 226, 230). On the other hand Strachey recognises that Macaulay's 'Warren Hastings' is a masterpiece – but of imagination, not history. His Hastings is a satanic villain of romance, Strachey claims, indulging in a little exaggeration of his own. Macaulay's Hastings quickly vanishes under the light of impartial inquiry but he will live in the memories of many readers 'until there arises a greater master of the art of writing, who will choose to invest the facts of Indian history with the glamour of literature, and make the truth more attractive than even fiction itself' (*SS*, pp. 225–6).

Strachey's introduction to *Warren Hastings, Cheyt Sing, and the Begums of Oude* thus finds, particularly in the writings of Burke, Mill, and Macaulay, an opposition between truth and art, between the facts narrated and the beauty of their narration. It must have been a dismaying recognition for a young man with an elaborately developed prose style, a Cambridge passion for reality, and a strong family interest in imperial history, who aspired, perhaps, to be the literary artist who would make truth more attractive than fiction. As a disciple of Moore, Strachey cared too much for truth to accept, as some postmodern critics have, the equation of history with fiction. He knew that 'in all history, the evidence must be "treated"', as he says in his introduction when describing the supposedly impartial style of Mill (*SS*, p. 230). Indeed, this was the chief problem with the writing of his dissertation; Strachey does not treat the evidence enough; he fails to integrate his lengthy quotations from the records into his explanations, narratives, and refutations. Yet the great prose 'treatments' by Junius, Burke, Sheridan, Fox, and Macaulay were too unhistorically fictitious.

Strachey did not go on very far with the revision of his dissertation after the introduction that is chiefly preoccupied with the historical rhetoric. Eventually he would resolve this dilemma of the literariness of history, absorbing the influence of Macaulay and others while maintaining his belief in the importance of truth, by becoming an ironist and limiting his historical scope to biography. (The writings of two other opposed eighteenth-century English prose-writers of genius would help him here: the irony of Gibbon's history and the moralised biographies of Johnson, who was also a friend and correspondent of Hastings.) In what Virginia Woolf called the new biography, Strachey would find the freedom to write descriptive and narrative prose about the past that was critical yet imaginative, even flamboyant, and whose elucidations of truth, unlike the historical misrepresentations of Hastings's great literary detractors, could be appreciated as belonging to the art of irony.

V

Beyond his difficulties with the interest of the facts to be narrated and the beautifully written narrations to be confuted, Strachey also had to contend in his dissertation with changing attitudes toward imperialism during the Edwardian period. These changes may also have interfered with the revisions of *Warren Hastings, Cheyt Sing, and the Begums of Oude* into a book. The Boer War had already disillusioned many in England about imperialism. Leonard Woolf in the late 1920s thought 1905 – the year Strachey resubmitted his dissertation – was the beginning of a new period of complete revolt against European imperialism, signalled by the Japanese defeat of the Russians (*IC*, p. 57). (The same year Virginia Woolf wrote of arguing for hours with Vanessa about various remote causes such as 'the Ethics of Empire' – *L*, I 192.) The essentially capitalistic purposes of this imperialism had already been analysed by J. A. Hobson in his very influential *Imperialism*, which Strachey could have read as articles in the *Speaker* as early as 1902. In Strachey's revised introduction, however, he was still writing with unironic enthusiasm of

> those wise and wondrous actions, those portentous revolutions, which, from the time of Clive to the time of Dalhousie, have gone to the making of our vast, our mysterious, our noble Empire of India! (*SS*, p. 231)

That Strachey considered his review of Lytton's letters for the *Independent Review* in 1907 a defence of imperialism against the New Liberals has been noted (see p. 24). The next year the *Spectator*, he praised so highly a book on Indian guides converted through English discipline from savage barbarism to noble virtue that James Strachey included it in the posthumous *Spectatorial Essays* as a reminder of how his brother remained under the ancestral spell of British India despite his later pacifism and anti-imperialism (*SE*, pp. 10, 46–9). Writing like this belongs to Kipling's India, not Forster's.

Lytton Strachey's final word on Hastings also appeared in the *Spectator* in 1910 as a review of selections from his state papers. It could almost serve as the missing conclusion to his dissertation. The opening quotation from Hastings is actually the same one he used at the end of his revised introduction. Strachey again laments that 'for some mysterious reason, one of the most enthralling and stupendous interludes in English history has been left untouched by English historians.' The biographies of Hastings are 'unscientific' (a word he would not have used in 'The Historian of the Future'). From Macaulay onwards, historians have concentrated on personalities rather than 'the great movements of peoples and policies' (a criticism that would be made of Strachey's own biographies). Again Hastings's actions in Oude are defended but without quite so much insistence on the blamelessness of the Governor General. Here are Strachey's last published words on Warren Hastings:

> His severities towards the Begums' Ministers were the necessary result of his determination to secure peace and order to a vast number of human beings, and it is to his honour that, having the intelligence to understand what his duty was, he possessed no less the courage to perform it. (*SE*, pp. 39, 45)

What Strachey's defence of imperialism seems to come down to here is the suppression of violence and confusion for the sake of security and stability. He does not mention what the cost was in the freedom of those for whose sake the suppressing and preserving were supposedly being carried out. In Strachey's public Edwardian writings the behaviour of the British in India is justified by the need for peace rather than the usual motives of power or profit or even civilisation (Thornton).

The ethical principles behind Strachey's justification of imperialism are apparent in the Apostle and other Cambridge papers that Strachey was also writing around the time of his dissertation. They reveal the values implicit in the dissertation and published reviews – values which were leading to a basic shift in Strachey's attitude towards imperialism. Though he may never have been completely free from the historical romance of the British raj, his view of late Victorian and early modern imperialism became quite grim. How remote the admiration for the consequences of Hastings's actions is from the ironic conclusion, half a dozen years later, to 'The End of General Gordon': 'At any rate, it had all ended very happily – in a glorious slaughter of twenty thousand Arabs, a vast addition to the British Empire, and a step in the Peerage for Sir Evelyn Baring' (*EV*, p. 309).

Gordon was no Hastings, to be sure, but before completing the history of Strachey's earlier Edwardian writings by looking at his unpublished Cambridge texts, it is tempting to speculate on what might have been. Had Strachey been less romantically a hero-worshipper when he wrote on Warren Hastings, had the consequences of imperialism been more revealed to him, had he been less trammelled by his own family's imperial history, then his treatment of Hastings might have developed some of the comic and tragic ironies of history and human behaviour that so fascinated him in his later biographies. The verdict of P. J. Marshall's thorough modern investigation of Hastings's trial, for instance, is that although Francis, Burke, Sheridan and the other instigators of Hastings's impeachment deserved to lose their case, by most standards Hastings sacrificed justice to the needs of the East India Company in his dealings with both Cheyt Sing and the Begums of Oude (pp. 87, 189). The conflict of the Company's despotism with the security of the native subjects was the central issue of the impeachment, according to Marshall, but the rhetoric of Sheridan and Burke considerably distorted the problems, while Hastings's self-justifications oversimplified them (pp. 183, 109). The seven-year trial was a cruel ordeal for Hastings but it did much damage to Burke too. And for all the bitterness of their opposition, both men had deep respect for native customs and culture, which is more than can be said of Mill and Macaulay's utilitarian ignorance of Indian religion and literature.

Strachey brings out none of these antinomies in his various accounts of Warren Hastings. The Governor General's personality and character remain impenetrable throughout. (If Strachey had chosen a picture of Hastings as he did for his eminent Victorians, it ought to have been Lawrence's wonderfully enigmatic portrait of Hastings in implacable old age.[5]) An intimation of how Strachey might have treated Hastings, if the time not been out of joint, may be found in the book yet another Strachey wrote on India and imperialism. The Labour Party politician and writer John Strachey, the son of Lytton's uncle St. Loe, carried this family tradition into the fifth generation with *The End of Empire*, first published in 1959. This is how he describes Hastings:

> Brilliant, scholarly, brave, arbitrary, financially lax (sometimes even to his own disadvantage), loving India, conquering India, enriching India, despoiling India, this strange man stands out as the first, and perhaps the only, fascinating figure amongst the long, stiff line of Governor-Generals who came and went over the next hundred and seventy-five years.

He was impeached for all the wrong reasons; he could not have been anything but an imperialist in his time, and was in fact genuinely concerned with the welfare of the Indians.

> What was unique in Hastings amongst Governor-Generals was not that he was a reformer, but that he was an intellectual. He was that rare and usually uncomfortable being, an intellectual functioning as a man of action. . . . His repute rests, I think, above all, on what he was *not*: on the fact that he was not an ordinary, straightforward, normal, hearty Englishman. . . . He was far more sympathetic to his Indian contemporaries than the virtuous but frigid noblemen who succeeded him. In old age Hastings said that he had loved India a little better than his own country. It may well have been true. A man may stay to love what he comes to rape. Above all, he loved not only India, as many a stolid nineteenth- and twentieth-century sahib was to do; he loved Indians. (pp. 46–8)

The influence of Bloomsbury from Lytton Strachey and Leonard Woolf to J. M. Keynes and E. M. Forster is not difficult to trace here.

VI

Strachey's prolonged Edwardian association with Cambridge during what Clive Bell has called his King's Period (*OF*, p. 27) resulted in various writings for discussion societies, for his friends or for himself. Like the other texts in this chapter, their literary significance is primarily to be seen in Strachey's development as a writer. They express ideas and emotions for the most part very different from those of the dissertation he was writing – which may further explain the unsatisfactoriness of *Warren Hastings, Cheyt Sing, and the Begums of Oude*. The conception of history in 'The Historian of the Future' is one example. Others are to be found in Apostle papers, a Sunday Essay on the ethics of the Gospels, a dialogue on gender roles, and a sequence of poems. As varied as these writings are in occasion and form, all except the paper on history and two important Apostle papers are preoccupied with love. Love had little to do with Strachey's treatment of Warren Hastings; 'the weird seclusion of his mind', as Strachey put it in his undergraduate essay, remains unvisited. Looking back from *Eminent Victorians* and his later works, one might see in Strachey's Edwardian Cambridge texts a divorce of the outer from the inner. His dissertation is almost exclusively concerned with the manifestations of Hastings's actions, whereas his essays for discussion societies are mostly about states of mind. Several of Strachey's earlier Edwardian Apostle papers continue the discussions by himself and others on what the Apostles should be and what they should value (*Victorian Bloomsbury* pp. 251–63). None is quite as outrageous as some of his undergraduate papers, nor as much concerned with aesthetics. One paper, written, like 'The Historian of the Future', shortly after the publication of *Principia Ethica*, argues that the Society is really a kind of religion, whose essence is identified as an abnormal sense of true values. These may be manifested, Strachey thinks, in the brothers' paradoxical ways of being holy by scoffing, of combining the sacred and the obscene, as his own private writings around this time were doing. All that the Apostles seem to share in their religion, Strachey believes, is an incapacity for phenomenal existence; they need to become more mystical, ecstatic, eternal (p/ST). Another Society paper a year later on the topic of whether absence makes the heart grow fonder discusses the Apostolic marriage of true minds in terms of the Scylla and Charybdis of love, which are boredom and lust. Marriage is theoretically eschewed for irregular associations at short intervals – though given the chance, Strachey admits, he would marry his beloved. (There are anticipations here of Forster's *The Longest Journey*.) The paper ends with the fillip that the sexes of the lovers are not really relevant to the discussion (*RIQ,* pp. 102–6). In a third earlier Edwardian Apostle essay, written at the end of 1905 and entitled 'Should We Take the Pledge?', Strachey considers whether love should be physical or not. He finds a confusion of good as a means with good as an end in the Christian doctrine that the spirit triumphs when physical love is renounced. The paper ends affirming and quoting the poetic arguments of the Dean of St Paul's, 'our brother Donne', in 'The Ecstasy' (*RIQ*, p.132).

Earlier in the year Strachey had delivered a more elaborate analysis of the moral teachings of Christ to the Sunday Essay Society. He wrote to Leonard Woolf that he wanted to call his paper 'The Ethical Teachings of Our Lord', but the outcry was too great (6.ii.05, LS/pT). 'The Ethics of the Gospels' is one of Strachey's better analytical papers. Its irony is cloaked by what appears to be a disinterested inquiry. The tone is calm, unexclamatory, as Strachey questions the commandments to love God (He does not exist), thy neighbour (it is unclear who he might be), and thine enemies (that subverts justice). Furthermore, these imperatives of indiscriminate love omit the most important kind of love in our lives, that for one or two other people. Of the unworldliness taught by Christ, Strachey objects that it excludes the love of beauty and scientific truth. The ethics of the Gospels, in other words, are found wanting by the ethics of Moore:

> To sum up, we find that, while the Gospels fail to recognise or to indicate clearly the most important and far-reaching of all ethical distinctions – that between good as an end and good as a means, they at the same time fail to draw any attention whatever to what are probably the two most important classes of goods with which we are acquainted – love or friendship, and the contemplation of beauty. (pST)

Furthermore, there is the example of Christ himself. Like Forster, Strachey found his personality unattractive, and thought the Gospels full not of pity but cruelty, fulminations, and the like. None of this was news to the Apostles, of course, who had decided years ago with Dickinson not to elect God, but in the Sunday Essay Society, Strachey's paper created a stir, and after being attacked, was repeated later by request (MH/*LSBG*, p. 67).

Love in a very different context is the subject of a short dialogue written in 1904. The literary significance of 'He, She, and It' is simply that it may be the earliest piece of feminist fiction in Bloomsbury's history. In the dialogue 'She' charges that the institution of marriage and the role of women in society is entirely regulated for the convenience of men. In order to discuss this 'from what politicians call a strictly non-party standpoint', the speakers change sex roles. Then speaking as a she, 'He' attacks the shameful education of women and their lack of the vote, while also expressing alarm at the prospect that with equality, women will become like men and both will therefore cease to love one another, because that occurs only between different minds (they have agreed not to discuss the love of bodies). When 'She' mentions that Jowett's Plato speaks of men in love with men, 'He' is delighted and suggests that this kind of love happens more easily between men and boys, women and girls. So the tacit homosexuality of the dialogue emerges at the end but not before some still quite recent-sounding feminist arguments have been aired (*RIQ*, pp. 92–7).

VII

The gulf in Lytton Strachey's earlier Edwardian writings between the administration of Warren Hastings and the ethics of the Cambridge Conversazione Society is crossed in two interesting, unpublished Apostle papers that also involve other members of Bloomsbury. The prose of these essays is more ambiguously ironic than those already mentioned on love and the Ideal. And they reach quite opposite conclusions from each other.

The first paper is undated but appears to have been written in the autumn of 1904. 'Shall we be Missionaries?' is the question posed, but Strachey does not intend to discuss it because the answer is so obviously negative. 'Our brother' Condorcet is quoted on the ferocious beasts that ignorant enthusiasts such as missionaries become – a quotation Strachey used again to describe Burke in the introduction to *Warren Hastings, Cheyt Sing, and the Begums of Oude*. After reacting comically to various moral, racial, economic, and patriotic straw arguments offered by distinguished or insignificant missionaries of empire (only Kipling is referred to) Strachey turns,

> for comfort & consolation to Moore's book. It is one of the characteristics of that work that it deludes you with hopes of being able to solve every problem, & finally informs you that the solution of every problem is already known. (pST)

Strachey develops then destroys an analogy between the empires of Rome and England, as he insists that the English in India are not the forerunners of a great civilisation but just policemen, railway-builders (like his father) or benevolent businessmen. He concludes there is no sufficient reason for England's conquering Europe or the Transvaal. Irony aside, this conclusion displays a noticeable diminishment of the imperial argument for civilisation that Strachey had followed elsewhere.

At this point in the paper something odd happens. A paragraph in Leonard Woolf's hand is inserted which disavows all the preceding arguments as the writer throws himself into the arms of *Principia Ethica.*[6] The only question to be asked, he insists, is whether the effects of one government will be better than another. If 'the total state of the world would be better if England ruled Germany & Russia & Constantinople & America & Spain & Portugal' then it should. The question of how one determines the total state of the world is left begging as the paper goes on – now in Strachey's hand again – to attack opponents of imperialism for their arguments that it interferes with Ideal good, which is described as 'a judicious mixture of Cambridge and McTaggart's heaven.' This Ideal is unattainable anyway, Strachey concludes facetiously because the loves of the anti-imperialist Little Englanders who advocate it end, simply, in copulation – like his Apostle papers (pST). 'Shall we be Missionaries?' is more evidence that the Bloomsbury Apostles did not always scorn the life of action for that of contemplation, but it also manifests a simplistic faith in the ability of their ethics to determine the best means to good ends. In some respects this over-confidence in the human ability of resolve questions of means inheres in the Group's writings on international relations, economics, art, literature, and feminism.

In February 1905, a week after his paper on the Gospels for the Sunday Essay Society, Strachey read another paper to the Apostles, this time completely accepting the contemplative Ideal. 'Shall we go the Whole Hog?' contradicts not simply his previous collaborative missionary paper but also the ethical assumptions of the dissertation he was reworking. The biographical backgrounds of this reversal relate again to Bloomsbury's developing associations at Cambridge, as described in *Victorian Bloomsbury,* for the paper was read at the first meeting of the Apostles after the election of the beautiful Arthur Hobhouse, whose Apostolic qualifications Duncan Grant, for one, claimed never to have grasped. Strachey, prevented from being his sponsor by Keynes, took the occasion to read Hobhouse a lecture on the difference between the phenomenal and the Apostolically 'Real', with examples from the brothers themselves. Calling himself a religious – though not missionary – maniac in the Apostolic sense that he had defined earlier as possessing an abnormal sense of true values, Strachey discusses how many of the older brothers of Society now believed 'that you are definitely improved if you do social work (whatever that may be) and go into Parliament, and govern niggers in Ceylon.' This was no longer Strachey's belief:

> The essence of the apostolic state is that it is both analytic & passionate, that it combines acute feelings with acute thoughts. It seems to me far the best kind of state possible, and I want to have as much of it as I possibly can. I refuse to be virtuous or to be powerful or to be active, if by being these things even for a moment I cease even for a moment to be apostolic.

Success in practical affairs is unApostolic. Then comes the surprising illustration: 'A great Greek scholar was lost to the world when Mr. Warren Hastings went to India' (pST). Instrumentally, it was a good thing he went, but not intrinsically. One must decide, in short, whether to be philanthropic and give lectures to working men (as Forster and other Apostles were doing) or talk with Moore (who had also given such lectures), write Russell's *The Principles of Mathematics*, and paint. The fact that there are false Apostolic images of these Ideal activities in places like the *Independent Review* is not relevant, says Strachey, though they were pertinent in his previous missionary paper. What matters is that one brother (Hobhouse), who only believes in the distinction between the real and the phenomenal because others do, is being misled by another (Keynes), whom Strachey brilliantly skewers with paradoxes: 'he is a hedonist and a follower of Moore; he is lascivious without lust; he is an Apostle without tears' (MH/*LS*, p. 252). Woolf administering imperialism in Ceylon and Keynes presiding over the Cambridge Union or writing a prize essay on the political doctrines of Edmund Burke (in which Hastings is unmentioned) were not going the whole Apostolic hog.[7] Only Moore, it seems, was (pST).

Keynes remained a close friend, however. When, a year later after being awarded first-class honours at Cambridge, Keynes was ranked second in the Civil Service examinations, Strachey wrote an epitaph describing him as

Both penetrating and polite,
A liberal and a sodomite,
An atheist and a statistician,
A man of sense, without ambition,
A man of business, without bustle,
A follower of Moore and Russell . . .
He got a first with modest pride;
He got a second, and he died.

(MH/*LS*, p. 291)

With his second place, Keynes joined the India Office rather than the Treasury. Among his duties as an imperial civil servant was to help edit the annual report on 'The Moral and Material Progress of India'. (He told Strachey that 'a special feature of this year's edition is to be an illustrated appendix on Sodomy' – Skidelsky, I 177.) When he reviewed one of these reports a few years later, Keynes criticised its reticence and the lack of information about famine, plagues, and Indian unrest but still found in the report enough material 'for a just appreciation of the steady advance in nearly all departments' of British Government in India (*CW*, XV 35). As yet Keynes appears no more disillusioned with imperialism than was Strachey or Woolf. Nevertheless, he stayed only two years in the India Office, before returning to King's College in 1908 with a successful fellowship dissertation, strongly influenced by Moore and Russell, on the theory of probability. Keynes remained interested in Indian economics, and his first book, published in 1913, was on Indian finance and currency.

VIII

Strachey continued to follow the work of Keynes and Woolf sympathetically though not uncritically. Hobhouse was eventually forgotten, but Strachey left a literary memorial of the triangular relations with him and Keynes in a loose sequence of nearly a dozen poems in March 1905. Titles like 'The Category' or 'The Exhumation' (published posthumously by MacCarthy – *M*, p. 43) show the influence now of Donne and the Metaphysicals instead of Swinburne and the late Victorian Romantics, as in *Euphrosyne*.[8] The poet offers himself two kinds of consolation: the infinite nature of his own undying love (the imagery of disinterrment, Egyptian and otherwise, abounds) and the awfulness of his love's other lover. In poems like 'The Two Triumphs' (also published posthumously in the *New Statesman* but without an indication of the triangle's uniform gender) the consolations appear in the poet's mystically resurrected love and the transient accidents of the other's kisses. 'The Resignation' urges in an original metaphor, 'Oh! let us smile, not laugh, and never miss/The daily circumcision of a kiss'. One of the poems is a series of similitudes comparing a Keynesian figure to, among other things, 'a safety bicycle with genitals' (pST). The prose invective of Strachey's Apostle paper is better than this.

Despite his avowals in 'Shall we go the Whole Hog?' Strachey went on working at *Warren Hastings, Cheyt Sing, and the Begums of Oude* and then turned for a while to phenomenal journalism. It would take ten years and the First World War before he was able to be both analytic and passionate about public affairs and personal relations in biographies that were written for their own sake as well as for the good they might do.

7 Virginia Woolf: Beginnings

I

Two deaths delimit the beginnings of Virginia Woolf[1] as a professional writer, her father's in February 1904 and her brother's in November 1906. After the breakdown that followed Leslie Stephen's death, Woolf began, late in 1904, to write essays and reviews in several periodicals. She did thirty-nine of them in 1905 while looking for a substantial historical subject on which to write a book. In 1906 she published another twenty-six pieces and wrote several stories not for publication before the fatal trip to Greece where Thoby Stephen contracted typhoid fever. In addition to all this writing, Woolf was also reading widely in English literature and history, studying Greek and Latin, keeping diaries and a reading notebook for her reviews, carrying on an active correspondence, and teaching several subjects at a working people's college.

Curiously, Woolf appears never to have written any verse during this time and earlier, though she read poetry and wrote criticism of it. Prose was her medium, as it was her father's, and prose fiction became her great opportunity to go beyond his work. Leslie Stephen had begun his London literary career at thirty as an reviewer and essayist under the auspices of his brother Fitzjames. When more than forty years later Virginia began hers at twenty-three, her first editors knew she was the daughter of the late Sir Leslie. Before examining the context of her first professional work, however, it is worth glancing at the unpublished work that she was writing in her early twenties before her father's death.

One of the most surprising aspects of both Forster's and Woolf's literary beginnings is their variousness. Like Forster, Woolf began quite early to write diaries, parodies, travel sketches, essays, short stories and novels, though they were not intended for publication. Her earliest Edwardian writings consist primarily of letters, two chapters of a novel, and a diary kept for three months in 1903.[2] The letters are more important biographically than as documents of literary history; amid their fluent self-conscious expressions of insecurity and affection, however, can be glimpsed an incipient satirist.

The two chapters of a novel, which has no title but a list of characters, are headed 'The Hero' and 'The Heroine'. The hero, Roger Brickdale, is a popular, well-to-do young gentleman of good looks and bad brains who has fallen in love with an aristocratic young woman, a duke's cousin named Hester Fitzjohn. Hester's family oppose the match, and in the ensuing conflict of love and class, the despairing, emotional Roger, who is counselled by an older Lady Esmonde, fears that Hester will realise all he has achieved is a certain popularity. The style is smooth and occasionally clichéd. The mannered Thackerayan novelist intrudes and ironises, but there is another nineteenth-century writer's influence at work here too, as Roger, Hester and the marble faun attest. Late in her diary Woolf recalled how absorbing the art of writing had been for her,

> ever since I was a little creature, scribbling a story in the manner of Hawthorne on the green plush sofa in the drawing room at St Ives while the grown ups dined. (*D*, V 192)

The novel fragment is of a later date than this, but the influence of Hawthorne's psychological romances persisted. The allusion to the marble faun occurs early in the hero's chapter:

> He was often, to his great disgust, taken for a foreigner; certainly he was very unlike an Englishman, but I hold to it that his greatest resemblance after all was to the marble head of Donatello's faun. . . . I say that he was *almost* a faun – but something took away from the perfect likeness. After a time one saw that the defect lay in the eyes. These were small, & though they had a very pleasant expression, it was not one that seemed to harmonize with the rest of [his] features. . . . He was but a tame faun after all. (p/S)

Later the lack of facial harmony is attributed to Roger's stupidity.

The idea of a good-looking, stupid and excitable hero is the most original part of Woolf's chapters – original in literary not biographical conception, for Roger Brickdale's appearance and situation resemble those of George Duckworth. Of George and Gerald Duckworth, Woolf exasperatedly predicted to Violet Dickinson in October 1903 'If ever I write a novel, those two shall go in large as life' (*L*, I 101). Sometime probably between 1902, when George Duckworth was briefly engaged to the Duke of Bedford's niece, and 1904 when he married another Lady, his half-sister put him into the beginning of a novel. George's emotional reaction to his broken engagement is described in Woolf's Memoir Club paper '22 Hyde Park Gate', which contains the following description:

> though he had the curls of a God and the ears of a faun he had unmistakably the eyes of a pig. So strange a compound can seldom have existed. And in the days I speak of, God, faun and pig were all in all alive, all in opposition, and in their conflicts producing the most astonishing eruptions. (*MB*, p. 166)

This devastating description descends from the earliest fragment of a Woolf novel that has been preserved.[3]

A briefer, less immaturely self-conscious fictionalised fragment that describes Woolf's important early friend Violet Dickinson has also survived from 1902. All six-foot-two of Virginia's closest early friend arrives for a country visit in the midst of a hunt. The mild comedy is followed with an articulate analysis of Violet's appearance, situation, and character as they might inadequately appear to the casual observer (QB/*VW*, I 82–3). Woolf returned to her friend as a subject for humorous biography a few years later.

The detached but hardly casual observer is the viewpoint of the thirty or so sketches that make up Virginia Woolf's 1903 diary. 'Between the ages of sixteen and twenty-one, speaking roughly, every writer keeps a large notebook devoted entirely to landscape', she wrote in a critical review of Kipling's notebooks in 1920 (*E*, III 238). Most of the half-dozen surviving early journals Woolf herself kept between the ages of fifteen and twenty-six have pages devoted to the description of landscape, but the journal she kept at twenty-one in 1903 intermixes them with descriptions of historical places, little essays of social observation, a portrait, accounts of reading, and so on. Formal titles and even a table of contents emphasise the individual subjects of these exercises, which begin in

London during the summer, continue around Salisbury, and conclude in the autumn back in London. This and other early journals served her, she said, as a written sketch-book where, as artists fill their pages with studies of drapery, legs, arms, noses 'so I take up my pen & trace here whatever shapes I happen to have in my head' (*EJ*, p. 187). The analogies between verbal and visual art that run throughout the literary history of Bloomsbury had part of their origin in what has been called the sisters' arts of Virginia and Vanessa (Gillespie).

Woolf's 1903 summer sketches are mostly social descriptions: a neighbouring dance heard in bed late at night (recalled later in *The Years*); some thoughts on social unsuccess; an Academy soirée of intolerant artists and philistines; an expedition to Hampton Court (anticipating *The Waves*); and an afternoon with barbarians – as Matthew Arnold called the aristocracy, though Woolf thinks they are better described as pagans because of their gods. There is a brief portrait of her Greek teacher Janet Case, who was to play, Woolf said later, so great a part in her visionary life before it was absorbed into her fiction (*D*, V 103). Case was less cultivated than her predecessor Clara Pater but more professional, and more sympathetic. She taught her pupil the proper use of the article ('which I had hitherto used with the greatest impropriety') and offered a moral view of Aeschylus's and Euripides's drama for her to think about (*EJ*, p. 183). One entry is about reading to do in the country, and it contains the seed of an important critical idea in Woolf's development. Reading history,

I think I see for a moment how our minds are all threaded together – how any live mind today is of the very same stuff as Plato's & Euripides. It is only a continuation & development of the same thing. It is this common mind that binds the whole world together; & all the world is mind. Then I read a poem say – & the same thing is repeated. I feel as though I had grasped the central meaning of the world, & all these poets & historians & philosophers were only following out paths branching from that centre in which I stand.

From this early notion of a 'common mind' through her mid-career conception of *The Common Reader* to her late mystical account in 'A Sketch of the Past' and fragmentary notes about Anon, Woolf was fascinated by the connections that could be made between writers and readers of the past, the present and the future. Her exploration of these interrelations became, if not less Platonic, at least less mentalistic under the impact of Moore's disciples. Yet from the beginning of her thoughts about tradition and individual talent, there was the crucial difference of her gender. In the same entry on reading she wrote,

> then I lay down the book & say – what right have I, a woman to read all these things that men have done? They would laugh if they saw me. (*EJ*, pp. 178–9)

Essential to her critical theory would be the defining of that right.

The sketches around Salisbury in her 1903 diary were written during a last family trip with the dying Leslie Stephen. There are some melancholy and humorous nature sketches with reflections on water meadows, downs (likened to long waves), fields, storms, and sheep, but descriptions of places predominate. A comparison of Salisbury Cathedral with Stonehenge finds the latter 'a more deeply impressive temple of Religion . . . ' (p. 200). The agnostic Leslie Stephen would perhaps have agreed. A second trip to Stonehenge is called a pilgrimage. Yet the Cathedral is beautiful, and so is a Norman abbey which reminds the diarist of Milton. There is also an essay on country reading; neither the unspontaneous intellectuality of *Roderick Hudson* nor the social brutality of *Tess of the d'Urbervilles* satisfies, but she likes Boswell in the Hebrides and is inspired to read all of Johnson. Back in London she writes of her room and walking in the park. The last essay-sketch, entitled 'The Serpentine', is a meditation on a newspaper account of a forty-five-year-old woman found drowned there. Her moving suicide note is transcribed as 'No father, no mother, no work. May God forgive me for what I have done tonight.' Woolf remarks how 'very few people go out of the world in silence; almost every dead man or woman who is picked up has written some word of apology or farewell or justification.' She could not get the words out of her head and writes a kind of soliloquy of the woman's imagined thoughts on how more completely one is alone when parents die than when husbands or children do (pp. 212–13). 'The Serpentine' closes Woolf's 1903 journal. Written as she was losing her second parent, it testifies to her own loneliness. The entry is also her earliest text on suicide. To the disinterested reader of Woolf's early writings, it should be clear that her most shattering experiences as a girl and young woman had much more to do with death in the family than sex.

II

'And I suppose you write?' he said, 'poems presumably?'
'Essays', she said.

(The Introduction', VW/*CSF*, p. 187)

After Leslie Stephen finally died, Virginia Woolf went with her family to Wales. There she grieved and wrote. Some of her letters have survived but not apparently the essays that were also written there.[4] In 1922 she remembered a vision of a book at this time:

> I was for knowing all that was to be known, & for writing a book – a book – but what book? That vision came to me more clearly at Manorbier aged 21, walking the down on the edge of the sea. (*D*, II 197)

Following a summer of madness, the desire to write a book – a work of history it seems rather than a novel – returned, partly at the prompting of her Quaker aunt, Caroline Emelia Stephen, with whom Woolf was recuperating at Cambridge while her sister and brothers moved to Bloomsbury. (Years earlier Leslie Stephen had written to his wife that he thought Virginia would be an author some day and history might be a good line for her to follow as he could give her some hints – *Mausoleum Book*, p. xxviii.) As part of her recovery she began to help the distinguished historian and family friend F. W. Maitland with his biography of her father by making extracts from her parents' correspondence for him; this involved her in Victorian anxieties of reticence on the part of Maitland and her half-sister's widower, Jack Hills. For relief, perhaps, she also wrote now lost comic lives of Caroline and another aunt. Around the same time she began sending some of her Manorbier essays to friends – and then to editors.

Christmas 1904 saw Woolf beginning another of her attempts at diary-keeping. Like her later diary, it is a flexible account of happenings and observations: a blade of grass with frost on it, the receipt of a cheque, a begging blind woman's quavering song (remembered in *Mrs. Dalloway*?), her old Hyde Park Gate room revisited (she could write the history of every scratch and mark on the wall), exhibitions and plays seen, people met, parties attended, letters received, books read, writing done. For five months she kept her diary on pages with printed dates, then renounced the whole thing because it had ceased to be spontaneous. Later on in the year she wrote a record of her Cornwall visit, and there would be other travel journals during the next few years, but it was not until 1915 that she again began to keep the quotidian record that became her great diary. As a daily account, the diary of 1904–5 appears at first glance to lack the literary interest of the apprentice sketches of 1903. For Woolf's literary history, however, this diary is more significant than her earlier exercises, and not only because it anticipates her later masterpiece. The form of this diary is interesting, but it is the contents that reveal how Woolf started her career as a writer. They exhibit the conditions of authorship in early twentieth-century London that influenced reviews, essays, and unpublished fiction of Virginia Woolf. The different types of periodicals she began writing for, the diverse kinds of books she was given to review, the expectations of her editors and their readers, the editing that her contributions were subjected to, the texts that were rejected, the money she was paid – all of these belong to her formative experiences as writer. The start of Virginia Woolf's literary career also illuminates the circumstances of authorship that were experienced differently by the men of Bloomsbury as well as other young modern writers of English literature, the origins of whose careers cannot be documented in the way Woolf's can. The diary entries from Christmas through May 1905, along with letters and the reading notebook Woolf also began to keep early in 1905 constitute the fullest record we have of a major modern writer's professional beginnings. To reconstruct this record, the early literary history of Bloomsbury needs to become almost microscopic in its focus on the writing and reading Woolf was doing month by month.

December

A quarter of a century after Virginia Woolf began to write for publication and be paid for it, she deprecatingly fictionalised the start of her career in the draft of a speech on professions for women. She asked her audience to imagine a girl sending off an article to an editor and requesting books to review. She was sent Mrs Humphry

Ward's fifty-sixth masterpiece because, the editor said, it did not matter what an uneducated or incompetent young woman said about the book. The review was published, and with the proceeds of £1 7s. 6d. she bought a Persian cat (*P*, p. xxix). (The only part of this account to survive in Woolf's revision of her speech was the cat; even the payment was changed to £1 10s. 6d. – *CE*, II 284–5.)

The actual story of Woolf's beginning as a professional writer, which goes back to October 1904, is significantly different. Her first editor was a woman, not a man. Mrs Arthur Lyttelton, widow of a bishop and mother of a friend of Violet Dickinson's, edited what were described as 'pages dealing principally with women's work and interests' in the *Guardian*, a Church of England paper.[5] Dickinson was convinced Woolf would be a great writer some day and forwarded to Mrs Lyttelton one of the Manorbier essays that Woolf had given her, though not the accompanying comments that reveal Woolf's early literary independence and professionalism:

> I dont in the least want Mrs L's candid criticism; I want her cheque! I know all about my merits and failings better than she can from the sight of one article. . . . I honestly think I can write better stuff than that wretched article you sent me. Why on earth does she take such trash? – But there is a knack of writing for newspapers which has to be learnt, and is quite independent of literary merits. (*L*, I 154–5)

Some sensible criticism seems to have offered anyway, and Woolf was encouraged to try a 1500-word essay, rather to her dismay. She wanted to do something longer and easier. Arnold Bennett had warned, a few years before, in *Journalism for Women* that Fleet Street was 'simply running with women who are writing fanciful essays and not selling them . . . ' (*VW/E*, I xi, xvii). (Bennett was the famous male writer, according to her draft speech on women's professions, that she had been able to criticise only after ridding herself of that inhibiting feminine ideal, the Angel in the House – *P*, p. xxxi.) Whether or not Woolf read Bennett's condescending guide, she thought she could place some of her essays, fanciful or not, through family connections, in the *Cornhill*, for example, that her father had so successfully edited, or possibly the *National Review* where Stephen's late memoirs had been published and whose editor was Leo Maxse, husband of the Stephen family's friend Kitty. In the meantime Woolf wondered if Mrs Lyttelton would let her

review for the *Guardian* (*L*, I 156). During a recuperative visit to
Yorkshire later in the month, Woolf tried a 1500-word essay on the
Brontës' home, which she said was written in less than two hours.
Also, she received for review from Lyttelton a novel by William
Dean Howells rather than Mrs Humphry Ward. The review was
written in half an hour (*L*, I 158, 161). These became her first two
publications. Three more reviews and another essay quickly fol-
lowed before the end of the year.

While she was doing her first *Guardian* pieces, Woolf continued to
think about writing a book. Caroline Stephen urged her not to sell
her soul for journalism's gold, but to do 'a solid historical work'
(*L*, I 166). To Nelly Cecil, perhaps her most helpful literary
correspondent after Dickinson, Woolf was describing herself as 'a
lady in search of a job at present – that is a good large ambitious
subject to which to devote the next ten years of my life'. She hated
'the critical attitude of mind' that had her dictating to authors
'when I couldn't, probably, do as well myself!' (*L*, I 168). The
adverbial qualification is revealing.

In their subjects, genres, and audience, the first half-dozen
anonymously published texts of Virginia Woolf illustrate what she
had to work with at the beginning of her career. The two essays she
wrote are both biographical in a way, though one is about a place
and the other a dog. 'Haworth, November 1904', the earliest piece
of writing that Woolf published, might be seen as a symbolic linking
of herself with another great English woman writer of lyrical prose
fiction, Emily Brontë, whom Vanessa used to think Virginia
resembled.[6] The link is not a simple one. The description of a
literary pilgrimage begins a little surprisingly by suggesting such
sentimental journeys should be condemned. They can be justified if
they add to our understanding of literature, the humorously severe
essayist decides and recommends, for example, that an examination
on Carlyle's work should be required of visitors to his house in
Chelsea, which Woolf had visited with her father. (Stephen's dry
accent is sometimes audible in the essay's style.) Haworth is visited
through Mrs Gaskell's life of Charlotte Brontë – a greater writer
than Emily, the essayist rather surprisingly thinks. The place of
pilgrimage is a parsonage, but the talk of literary shrines and relics
might make an attentive Anglo-Catholic reader a little uneasy about
what was appearing in the women's pages of her church paper.
Like Forster, the traveller has Sterne's sentimental journeys and
perhaps James's passionate pilgrims in mind. All ends appropri-

ately, however, with the Brontës' epitaph about the sting of sinful death and victory through Christ. The *Guardian*, of course, was an odd place for the daughter of a famous agnostic to begin writing, even anonymously, and one wonders what Vanessa, Thoby, and Thoby's Cambridge friends, who were beginning to drop into Gordon Square, might have said about it. But if Virginia Woolf's first editor was a churchwoman and the widow of a bishop, she was also a friend of the feminist reformer Josephine Butler and something of a feminist herself. In considering the significance of Woolf's first audience, it is important to realise she began by writing essentially for women; ambivalent as she remained about Lyttelton's literary taste and the interests and occupations of her readers, these readers conditioned her point of view as an essayist and reviewer in the *Guardian*. (Her most Christian *Guardian* piece, written around this time but published later, was a short sketch of a church that contrives, however, to mention nothing religious about it.)

Woolf's second published essay, an obituary notice of her old dog (*L*, I 164), may have resembled a little the lost comic lives of her aunts. Vanessa had urged her sister to write Shag's life after he had been run over (8.xii.04, VB/pNY). 'On a Faithful Friend' works nicely up until the end against its sentimental occasion by amusingly anthropomorphising him as a sociable, clubman type of dog; later when joined by a puppy, he departs as a kind of canine King Lear, returning blind and deaf to live happily until mercifully killed by a cab. The essay ends very feebly. Lyttelton wanted cuts made, her author was too amenable, and the result was a cobbled essay and a lesson in writing for editors. Next time she would try to make the cuts herself (*L*, I 169, 172). Woolf's beast fable may have been a touch too satirical for the *Guardian*, but among her early writings it most conspicuously anticipates her later work. From Shag to Flush, mock biography was a lifelong literary amusement.

The earliest of the reviews that Woolf did for the *Guardian* at the end of 1904, and the first text of hers to appear in print, was of the minor Howells novel *The Son of Royal Langbrith*. It seems the editor took some trouble to find her fledgling reviewer a good book (24.xi.04, VB/pNY). The first sentence of the first review suggests how well Lyttelton succeeded: 'Mr Howells is the exponent of the novel of thought as distinct from the novel of action.' Much of Woolf's subsequent energy as a novelist and critic would also be spent in distinguishing and evaluating these kinds of novels. It is an arresting fact of literary history that a future advocate of modern psychological realism should be given a work to review by one of its nineteenth-century American proponents, who was a colleague and friend of Henry James. Woolf would review many American books, though the country and the culture would remain more remote to the goddaughter of James Russell Lowell than it had been to his friend Leslie Stephen. Much of the review is taken up with summary because Woolf wants to criticise the plot's psychological improbability, but she ends praising the novel's shape and its 'reserved and expressive language'. These words could describe her own future fiction as well (*E*, I 3–5).

Two much briefer, dismissive reviews followed of an ephemeral London short-story collection that might better have been newspaper sketches, and of a melodramatic novel by George Gissing's brother that the reviewer mildly makes fun of through plot summary. (The heroine is conveyed 'to a convenient desert island somewhere near the Isle of Man' – *E*, I 41.[7]) Woolf's last review in December points forward again in a remarkable way. There were advantages in writing for a female editor and audience at the beginning of the twentieth century when the book to be reviewed was a man's pronouncements entitled *The Feminine Note in Fiction*. Woolf's first published text on the subject of women and fiction – a topic with which she would transform modern literary history – begins, after a brief, quietly negative description of the book, with questions that resonate throughout her criticism and feminist writing: 'Is it not too soon after all to criticise the "feminine note" in anything? And will not the adequate critic of women be a woman?' Counter-examples of Sappho and Austen refute the claim that women are seldom artists because they care more for detail than proportion, but the assertion that women have a genius for psychological analysis is noted and filed for future confirmation. The fear that women may be extinguishing the novel form is doubted because the classically educated writer will be able to shape her novel, whereas her predecessor has 'blurted out her message somewhat formlessly' (*E*, I 15–16). Woolf will say something similar a quarter of a century later in *A Room of One's Own*.

January

In the calendar of Bloomsbury's literary history, January 10, 1905, is a notable date. On that day Virginia Woolf recorded in her diary that she had received from the *Guardian* her first professional earnings of £2 7s. 6d.[8] Though she lived on income inherited from Leslie Stephen, her illness had been costly, and she made a New Year's resolution to earn pocket-money from writing (*L*, I 172). Along with the cheque came another book for review in the *Guardian*: an English woman's 'natural history of the American woman'. Woolf had trouble keeping her review within the 600-word limit set by Lyttelton. She thought the book was interesting despite its superficial method because it brought out the contrast between the English woman's private philanthropy and the American's organised charity. But where the book touched on the current controversy of votes for women, the reviewer attacked the author's fear that political motives would injure feminine moral sensibility. Woolf's words might have come from *Three Guineas* this time:

> But it is open to remark that the same might be said as emphatically of the male politician, and that the real question is whether the use made by women of political freedom is sufficiently valuable to justify the alleged injury. (*E*, I 47)

There were clearly advantages in writing for an audience of women.

At the beginning of her career in 1905 Woolf was also, appropriately enough, writing a brief memoir of her father for F. W. Maitland's biography. She was also going through more letters for Maitland and helping with the bibliography, all of which interfered with her plan of making some money from her writing. Maitland had asked for something about Stephen from his children several months before, and Vanessa had urged Virginia in a letter to do it because she understood him better than any of them (25.x.04, VB/pNY). Virginia wrote this 'note', as she called it, very carefully over a period of weeks, sketching affectionately her impressions of her father as a companion, reader, reciter, and teacher. There is nothing of her later ambivalence in this first of several portraits she would do of him; even his anti-critical attitude toward literature – which at this time she may have shared to some extent – is not unfavourably presented. The natural subjectivity of the first sentence draws the reader right in: 'My impression as a child always was that my father was not very much older than we were' (Maitland, p. 474). Woolf felt the prose of her note 'all cobblestone sentences, brisk & matter of fact, without an atom of beauty or swing about them', and she did not want the note published (*EJ*, pp. 226, 246). But Maitland thought the reminiscence really beautiful, as did others (VW/*L*, I 180, 259), and he began the last chapter of Stephen's biography with her account, which is identified only as coming from one of Stephen's daughters. Woolf had great respect for Maitland as a scholar and as a writer; his was high praise indeed.

In January Woolf also recorded in her diary that Dr Savage now considered her normal again. In January too she began teaching at Morley College and was glad to have an excuse for refusing Mrs Humphry Ward (whom she had been reading about in *The Feminine Note in Fiction*) when an invitation came from her to work at a settlement in Bloomsbury where Leslie Stephen had been a Vice President. From time to time in her diary and letters Woolf mentions the lectures she is writing for her small class of working women. The first one she gave was on prose; two later ones have survived together with a report on her teaching and will be discussed later.

Woolf's progress as a professional author in January can be measured by the periodicals for which she was hoping to write. Without Cambridge associations with journals like the *Independent Review*, she relied on family connections and friends like Violet Dickinson and Kitty Maxse. An article which is now lost on Boswell's letters was sent to the *Cornhill*; she knew it was too short but the editor, Reginald Smith, annoyed her by rejecting it with a printed slip (*L*, I 171). Leslie Stephen's daughter expected more consideration than that from the editor of his old magazine and head of the firm publishing the *DNB*. She showed some of her writing to Kitty and was quickly asked to write for Leo Maxse's *National Review*. Kitty also passed Woolf's writing on to the head of the foreign department of *The Times*, Valentine Chirol, to see if it were suitable for *The Times Literary Supplement*, for which he also reviewed. At its founding three years earlier, the editor, Bruce Richmond, had asked Leslie Stephen to contribute but he was unable to (QB/*VW*, I 104). By the end of the month, Woolf exulted in her diary that the great Mr Chirol had approved. Early in February she met Richmond and he asked if the *TLS* might send her books for review. (Richmond also asked if she would review for J. L. Garvin's *Outlook*, but there is no record of her having done so.) Thus began the most important professional connection of her career. Thirty years later she would recall to herself how much she learnt of her craft writing for 'the Major Journal' from Richmond – 'how to compress; how to enliven; & also was made to read with a pen & notebook seriously' (*D*, V 145).

On January 24th, the day before her twenty-third birthday, Woolf began her first reading notebook. She occasionally made notes from some background reading in it, but mostly it was for books she was reviewing. There is no record in it of the amazing reading she was doing on her own this month, though at the end of her 1905 diary she made a list of books read in January that included William Morris's life and early works, Pater's *The Renaissance*, Jefferies's *After London* (the only fiction listed), Layard on Nineveh, Galton on heredity, Mackail on Latin literature, the works of four English historians, and a biography of Stonewall Jackson (*EJ*, pp. 274–5). Her early notes on books she was to review over the next eighteen months intersperse summary and quotation with occasional commentary; their interest lies not in themselves but in how they show Woolf selecting among and organising her reading responses for a review. The first entry was devoted to another *Guardian* review, her fifth. Lyttelton, she noted in her diary, had liked her reviews so far, and she rather liked Lyttelton, a 'large & healthy, & broad minded, refreshing & inspiriting woman', whom she had met at tea (*EJ*, p. 228). The book was another American one, not a novel this time but a memoir by a Southern senator's wife of Washington and the South around the time of the Civil War. (Leslie Stephen had visited the United States during that war and attacked *The Times*'s support of the South.) Whatever the reason was that she was asked to do it, the review was the first of a genre she became very fond of, and about which she wrote some of her best essays. Women's memoirs particularly interested her, of course, and she praises *A Belle of the Fifties* for making the situation of aristocratic Southern women and their medieval plantation life so real.

At the end of the month Woolf took up the Maxses' invitation to contribute to the monthly conservative and imperialist *National Review*. In two days she wrote her longest piece for publication so far. The 2500-word essay 'Street Music' is a London dissertation, somewhat in the manner of Charles Lamb, on a notice posted in a Bloomsbury square, perhaps, that proclaims 'Street musicians are counted a nuisance' (*E*, I 27). This 'terse bit of musical criticism' leads the essayist through radical Romantic thoughts of art and society to the conclusion that street musicians ought to be accounted holy. What matters is the inspiration not the execution – the god within, who makes the musician the more dangerous that others of his tribe of artists because this deity can

> breathe madness into our brains, crack the walls of our temples, and drive us in loathing of our rhythmless lives to dance and circle for ever in obedience to his voice. (*E*, I 30)

The punning pagan imagery here is part of the hyperbole that is the essay's essential rhetorical figure. Through it, Woolf as essayist makes two aesthetic musical claims that bear on her and Bloomsbury's later work. One is that rhythm is the soul of music, as innate as our pulse, but we are taught to mask it with tune. The other finds music, especially rhythm, to be the art most closely allied to writing. Later in Bloomsbury's history Woolf would find closer analogies between writing and the spatial arts, but she remained convinced that style was a matter of rhythm (*L*, III 247).

Leo Maxse was charmed with 'Street Music', which was a relief. It would have been embarrassing to be rejected by a friend. (He did reject a piece in March by Vanessa who, encouraged perhaps by her sister's success, was trying unsuccessfully to publish some a criticism of Watts.) Woolf was delighted to be paid £5 for two mornings' work, but the editor's enthusiasm did not raise her doubtful estimate of the piece or perhaps the *National Review*; she wrote nothing more for it. Virginia was pleased, however, when Kitty wrote to say how much it had interested her friend Elizabeth of the German Garden (*L*, I 190). Did Elizabeth, one wonders, show the essay to her children's young English tutor in Germany? Forster might have found the form congenial, if a little derivative, but the invocation of a pagan past through art was figuring in his work at this time too; later the notion of rhythm would be fundamental to his theory of the novel.

February

During the second month of her 1905 diary Woolf recorded that she finished two more essays and two reviews, did more research for Maitland's biography, wrote a lecture for Morley College, and continued her Greek and Latin study. That writing and reading involved her with Henry James's *The Golden Bowl*, Aristotle's *Poetics*, the genre of the modern essay, and the comic sense in women.

James's latest novel may have seemed a reasonable sequel to Howells, to the editor of the *Guardian*'s women's pages, but the choice confronted her young reviewer with the most demanding fiction of the age. Perhaps to keep from being overwhelmed, she took *The Golden Bowl* quite critically. James was praised for having a point of view and conveying it with 'exquisite felicity of word or thought'. She found him one of the few novelists 'who attempt to picture people as they are; his work, therefore, always commands our respect and gratitude' (*E*, I 22). No contemporary novelist had a higher standard, none a greater consistency of achievement. And yet she found the plot was slight, the analysis hair-splitting, the theme ingenious, the characters ghostly, the style overburdened, the book overlong. (She mentions the novel's 550 pages three times.) If one did not know that the anonymous reviewer in the *Guardian* was to be one of James's great successors, her review would resemble others that complained of later James's difficult, expansively subtle fiction. Some of this kind of criticism would ultimately be made against the reviewer's future novels, which suggests that in 1905 Woolf was less ready for late James than Forster was. The psychological realism of her mature fiction would be more lyrical than analytic, but there is a clear continuity between Woolf and James in their methods of fiction and also in the scope with which they envision the life of women.

Woolf received *The Golden Bowl* on February 7. She read it and wrote her review in just one week, exclaiming in her diary 'never was there such a book to review.' The review was returned as too long, however. The *Guardian* had allowed her 2000 words for *A Belle of the South* but for *The Golden Bowl* she was permitted only one or two words for each of James's 550 pages because 'the worthy Parsonesses want to read about midwives'. In her diary and letters she complained that her cutting of the review by a third or a half had ruined it. (*EJ*, pp. 236–7; *L*, I 178). Even with her notes on the novel (which have been published in an appendix to Andrew McNeillie's indispensable edition of her essays) it is not possible to reconstruct the original review, and therefore an assessment of the first criticism Woolf published on her greatest Edwardian contemporary must remain to some degree uncertain.

The reading notes for *The Golden Bowl* do indicate, at any rate, how Woolf developed her reviews out of the summary, paraphrases, quotations, and comments that she made while doing her preparatory reading. Her conclusion in the *Guardian*, for instance, that the genius which could have dissolved the novel's fatiguing details into a word, is 'precisely what we do not find' occurs bluntly in her notes as 'a touch of genius would lighten the whole, but it dont come' (*E*, I 23–4, 386). The praise of James's point of view and the novel's close felicity of style are first stated in the notes, as is the criticism of his ghostly characterisation. Perhaps the principal difference in emphasis between the notes and the review is in the attention to the characters' relationships. Woolf said she had 'to cut out all the plot & a good deal else' (*EJ*, p. 237). A considerable portion of the notes is devoted to Maggie's relationship with her father and Charlotte Stant's with the Prince; almost all that survives of this in the review is the slightly paradoxical description of *The Golden Bowl* as 'a study in the evils of unselfishness . . . ' in which two women struggle for supremacy (*E*, I 23). Desmond MacCarthy in his more admiring review in the *Independent Review* several months later also praised James's realism but thought he valued the characters' relations more than the characters themselves (see p. 27).

The Golden Bowl 'deserved a good, and careful review', Woolf wrote to Dickinson, but Lyttelton had in effect kept her from doing it, and this increased her equivocal feelings about writing for women in a paper that 'takes up the line of a Governess, and maiden Lady, and high church Parson mixed . . . ' (*L*, I 178). As if to make up for it, her letter went on, Richmond had sent his first two books and was allowing her 1500 words in which to review them. Alas, they were bad books, the products of scissors not pens, and she had to contrive her first *TLS* review without saying much about them – a useful technique in the craft of reviewing. The title of the review – which like most reviews came probably from the editor – was 'Literary Geography'. It identifies a subject that Woolf had already written on for the *Guardian* and would return to many times in her later reviews and essays, before her own art and life became part of England's literary geography. As in her Brontë essay, Woolf continues to be a sceptical literary pilgrim of many distinctions. She distinguishes between the sentimental and scientific aims of literary excursions; between writers who exert spiritual sovereignty over places (like Scott, the Brontës, Meredith or Hardy) and those who do not (Thackeray and Dickens); between the importance of place in the writers' lives and in those of their characters. 'Literary

Geography' is a knowledgeable, clear-sighted review that insists 'a writer's country is a territory within his own brain . . . ' (*E*, I 35). The Thackeray part of the review was highly praised by Thackeray's daughter, Woolf's Aunt Anny Ritchie, who had found 'Street Music' charmingly young (31.iii.05, VB/pNY). Bruce Richmond thought Woolf's first contribution 'admirable' (*L*, I 182).

While reading *The Golden Bowl* for review, Woolf also wrote an essay on essays, fearing as she did so that her style might be infected by the master's. 'The Plague of Essays' is a reflexive protest against the proliferation of writing, especially essays, that Woolf suggests is the result of the spread of education and the improvement of penmanship: these have mechanically set the mind in motion even when it has nothing to say. Certain practitioners (none is mentioned) are inspired, she thinks, because the form fits their thought. The modern personal essay is, indeed, one of the few justifiably new literary forms, though it derives from Montaigne – 'the first of the moderns', she calls this hero of Bloomsbury writing – and reached its greatest brilliance with Charles Lamb, another hero. The essay is an essentially egoistical form, but the trouble is that most modern writers of it shrink from 'the terrible spectre of themselves', and thus their work lacks the simple sincerity that is the genre's cardinal virtue (*E* I 25–6).

This discussion of essays might be suitable for the *Outlook*, Woolf thought, but then she received a request, originating perhaps with Richmond, for a contribution to the weekly *Academy* that had taken over *Literature* from *The Times* when the *TLS* was started. She polished her essay carefully, hating the process – 'all niggly work, done with a cold brain' (*EJ*, p. 239) – but felt the result better than the one on music when she saw the proofs, and was excited at the prospect of it being the first piece of writing to appear over her name. (All her *Guardian* and *TLS* pieces were anonymous, and her signed *National Review* piece had not yet been published.) The *Academy & Literature* duly appeared on February 25th and its young contributor received another blood-boiling lesson in the ways of editors. The title was changed to 'The Decay of Essay-writing', half the essay was deleted, words were added, and this hotchpotch then credited to Virginia Stephen (*L*, I 180–1). Once more it is difficult to determine with certainty what Woolf was going to say about essays. She found the altered title meaningless (it alludes apparently to Oscar Wilde's 'The Decay of Lying'). Still, there is a certain superciliousness about her essay's attitude toward personal essays, which is ironic because her own text verges on being one. But the irony is unacknowledged, at least in its published form. When Woolf returned to the subject of the modern essay nearly twenty years later, she was more appreciative of her contemporaries' work – and also more forceful in her condemnation of the egoistic profusion of the genre.

How prolific Virginia Woolf was becoming, even at the very start of her career is shown by yet another essay she began for the *Guardian* just before the end of the February. She wanted to add to her quarterly income and yet take more pains with her writing. 'The Value of Laughter', which was her own title this time, announces a banal topic. The treatment is anything but that. Taking advantage, once more, of her medium, she offered her readership of women – governesses or parsons' wives though they might be – an early feminist analysis of the comic spirit. Humour, the essay begins, is a means between comedy and tragedy that men say is denied to women. As if to disprove the denial, the anonymous but obviously female essayist humorously describes the male gymnast trying to balance between the comic and the tragic but frequently toppling over one side or the other into buffoonery or 'the hard ground of serious commonplace, where, to do him justice, he is entirely at his ease'. How familiar this early note of masculine ridicule already sounds. The essay goes on to personify modern solemnity (our substitute for tragedy) as masculine and comedy as feminine. Though male humour is supposed to preserve one's balance, it is feminine laughter that preserves the sense of proportion and expresses the comic spirit. Women and children, their eyes not obscured with men's books, can see things for what they are, and their laughter shrivels up the excrescences of convention that obscure reality. No wonder the learned professions look with such disfavour on women. Laughter's value, then, is like that of a knife which 'both prunes and trains and gives symmetry and sincerity to our acts and to the spoken and the written word' (*E*, 158–60). Again, how early these familiar themes (not always accompanied with castration symbolism) are expressed in Woolf's writings. For Bloomsbury, too, laughter would be a weapon in the fight for more fairness and more beauty in everyday reality.

'The Value of Laughter' displays, furthermore, the impact of a critical work that Woolf had been enthusiastically translating toward the end of February. Along with her reviewing and essay-writing, the classes at Morley College, and an increasingly

active social life that began in the middle of this month to include
Thoby Stephen's Bloomsbury evenings for his Cambridge friends,
Woolf was keeping up her classics. At the end of January she started
translating Thucydides and, stimulated by him, wondered if she
might not write a melodrama. A week later after doing thirteen
foolscap pages of Greek she shifted for a few days to the Latin of
Virgil's *Georgics* that was stately, melodious, charming but without
Greek vitality for her. Then on February 21st, while trying to read
some fiction in Spanish, she started on Aristotle's *Poetics* 'which will
fit me for a reviewer!' (*EJ*, p. 240). As she read Aristotle in Greek
sometimes all morning for the next ten days, her excitement grew.
In fifty pages she discovered Aristotle had said the first and last
words on the subject, laying down the rudiments of both literature
and criticism simply, surely, unabstrusely yet subtly. She found the
Poetics 'singularly interesting & not at all abstruse . . . ' (p. 242). And
from the *Poetics* she went on to Sophocles in March. It may come as
a surprise to those convinced that Woolf's art of criticism is
essentially impressionistic that she read Aristotle with such close
attention; how many of her critics, one wonders, have read the
Poetics in Greek? 'The Value of Laughter', which was written while
she was translating Aristotle, begins with his distinction between
comedy and tragedy and goes on to invoke his ethical idea of the
mean as that which laughter preserves. There are other critical ideas
in the essay, as well, of course, and the essay as a whole is more
Meredithean than Aristotelian. There remains in Woolf's criticism,
however, an awareness of structure that reflects her early interest in
the *Poetics*.

March

March was a less successful month than February for Virginia
Woolf's career. The two principal texts she wrote for publication
were both rejected, and only four short reviews were published.
The month began with a house-warming in Gordon Square,
followed by the start of Thoby Stephen's Thursday evenings at
which his sisters met Bell, Strachey and other Cambridge friends
and established the basis for Bloomsbury. It was from Thoby that
Virginia first heard about the Zanzibar hoaxing of the Mayor of
Cambridge that Adrian had participated in; five years later she
would join Adrian and his friends in the more daring *Dreadnought*
Hoax (see pp. 222–3). There were no books to review, so Woolf

finished translating Aristotle and then began *Oedipus Tyrannus* as a sequel, while continuing to look up more articles for the bibliography of Maitland's life of her father. By the second week she had volumes to review from both the *Guardian* and the *TLS* (as it later came to be called). Her first review for the *TLS* was written quickly because once more there nothing to be said about W. E. Norris's imitation of Trollope except generalities. In all, Woolf would review six of Norris's seventy or so books, admiring always his competence and never his conventionality. A shorter review for the *Guardian* would not come right and took much longer. The book, a collection of stories about Irish peasants, she called nondescript in her diary but charming in the review, after effectively emphasising the poverty of their life. She grumbled in her diary after such hard reviewing that she would rather write anything else, except a dutiful letter. Another *TLS* review of a sentimental novel by A. J. Dawson required little brains, like most novels, except Henry James's, but her criticism of the book's dullness had to be watered down for *The Times*. The only interesting review that Woolf published in March was of an anti-feminist novel, again for the *Guardian*. The tone of the review and technique of its argument anticipate once more her later feminist writings. Elinor MacCartney Lane's *Nancy Stair* mixed fiction and history to tell in a lively but unimaginative way the story of a brilliant poet who meets Burns, realises how much more valuable real life is than poetry, and gives it all up for 'marriage and motherhood'. The reviewer observes: 'this is the eighteenth-century solution of the doubts of the nineteenth century', and in reply to the novelist's sentimental solution, asks prosaically if the world would not be considerably poorer had its great writers 'exchanged their books for children of flesh and blood' (*E*, I 40). She would have occasion later to reflect on the choice in her own life.

The day Woolf wrote her Lane review she recorded the purchase of some works by Robert Louis Stevenson and Walter Pater in order to continue her education as a critic that had begun with Aristotle. 'I want to study them – not to copy, I hope, but to see how the trick's done', she noted. Stevenson was a trick, 'but Pater something different & beyond' (*EJ*, p. 251). This acknowledgement of interest in the writer who some claim to be her primary predecessor, may have been partly the result of her struggle to review Edith Sichel's *Catherine de Medici and the French Reformation*. When Richmond sent her this 'great, fat book' earlier in the month (*L*, I 182), she explained she was not at home in medieval French. The review went ahead anyway, and it was hard going, partly because Richmond had specified no length. 'It is a satirical fact', she told her diary, 'that when I am allowed $^1/_2$ a column I can always fill 2 & when I am to have as much space as I like, I cant screw out words at any price' (*EJ*, p. 252). She worked at her review amid other writing, turning for background to the *Cambridge Modern History*, among other sources. Woolf was unsatisfied with the review, which she finished in a week, and expected Richmond to reject it, which he did. Though an excellent piece of work, he said, it was not sufficiently academic; Woolf agreed that a professional historian should have reviewed it. The review has not survived, but Woolf's reading notes indicate that though she was unable to correct Sichel's facts, she could fault the book's writing as repetitious, scrappy, and unimaginative in its treatment of an interesting woman and her times. Sichel, she said in her diary was 'a clever woman, hunting for a style' (*EJ*, p. 251). What Woolf did not know was that Edith Sichel was one of the few other women reviewing for the *TLS* at this time. Perhaps that is why Richmond sent her book to Woolf, and also why he had then to reject it as the work of an amateur historian.

But Sichel started Woolf thinking about history again. In the middle of her review she took a day off to write for herself rather than for an editor, and what she wrote was not fiction but some notions about history. Woolf may have been trying to articulate her dissatisfaction with Sichel's efforts to illuminate an age through vivid facts and impressions. It is a complaint that Lytton Strachey repeated often enough before finding his own way to make history interesting.

The one essay Woolf wrote in March was also rejected because of its point of view. She wrote for the *Academy & Literature* (they appear to have been quickly forgiven for butchering her last contribution) a piece probably called 'Magic Greek'. It may have grown out of her sense, after finishing Sophocles's play earlier in the month, that there was still a veil, perhaps an inevitable one, between her and the Greeks; possibly it also had some connection with the Greek myths and history she was now teaching her students at Morley College. The essay lacked finish, she believed, and titivation, as MacCarthy called it, was what she disliked in writing. But the essay was finally done and submitted to the *Academy & Literature* editor, who said he was entertained by the piece but found the whole performance too uncompromisingly against their view to be published by them. There is no way of telling now how much of 'Magic Greek' survived to be reformulated in the other essays such as 'On Not Knowing Greek' in the first *Common Reader*. Twice in March, then, the work of an educated man's daughter – as she would come in *Three Guineas* to call those like herself who had been declassed through the lack of education – had failed to satisfy the academic standards of the men who were her editors.

At the end of March Virginia and Adrian went to the Iberian peninsula for four weeks. It was Bloomsbury's first link with Spain, a country that would continue to attract them. Lyttelton had urged her to write some *Guardian* articles about her personal experiences there, and Woolf hoped to make some of her travelling expenses out of a Grub Street view of land and sea. Books for the trip were by Borrow, Hawthorne, Meredith, and the historian J. R. Green, plus a guide book and a Spanish grammar.

April

Her diary did not prosper during the trip and survived only for a few weeks after Woolf returning home. Some remarks about the sea and descriptions of people such as a Portuguese Jew or a boring professor are noted along with a record of places visited and travel arrangements endured, but that is about all. Adrian Stephen, her travelling companion, is not even mentioned by name. 'Every sight and sound sickened me with diary writing', she told the Memoir Club later (*MB*, p. 186). Nothing also seems to have been written for the *Guardian* in Spain; her sketch of an inn, first adumbrated in a letter to Dickinson, was written in London (*L*, I 187). And there is little in her letters or diary to suggest how her trip would be imaginatively transmuted into her first novel (QB/*VW*, I 104).

Back in London at the end of April, Woolf received the rejection from the *TLS* of her Sichel review, followed soon by some books about Spain on which she was now supposed to be an authority (*L*, I 189). Richmond wanted a general article, which 'means I suppose that I can be as silly & amateurish as I like – but I earn money anyhow' (*EJ*, p. 268). Other tasks awaited her. She began to write some Spanish sketches, while continuing her reading in English history, ostensibly for her Morley College classes. And Maitland was to send the manuscript of his biography, for the Stephens to look at and Virginia to type.

May

Virginia Woolf's Spanish review is neither silly nor amateurish. It shows that, when relaxed and unharried by scholarly facts, she could articulate a perception in a way that reveals a talent beyond the reviewer's art. The first half of 'Journeys in Spain' is a general discussion bearing on her own travel writings as well as her later critique of Edwardian materialist fiction. Explicitly invoking Sterne's *A Sentimental Journey* this time, Woolf distinguishes between books like Baedeker's, which concentrate on the journeying but whose asterisks are not to be trusted in matters of art, and those like Borrow's or James's, which convey the sentiment of travelling as well. Borrow, for instance, in *The Bible in Spain*, 'gives a clear portrait of both Borrow and of Spain, but it would be hard to say where Spain ends and Borrow begins'. Such an amalgamation is rare, and neither of the books she is reviewing achieve it. In the fat two volumes of the first book reviewed, 'the sentiment is out of all proportion to the journey' (*E*, I 45). Woolf felt her criticism too abrupt and modified it in proof; in her diary she wished she could be 'brave & frank in my reviews, instead of having to spin them out elaborately' (*EJ*, p. 270). The second book, 'slim and reticent . . . edits the country carefully', and is valuable for both traveller and reader (*E*, I 45). Its author was a young novelist and playwright named W. S. Maugham.

Early in May Woolf was also writing several Spanish sketches. One on the Protestant Cemetery in Lisbon where Fielding was buried was written as a possible piece for the *Academy & Literature* but not published there or anywhere else, apparently. Another on a Spanish Inn she preferred to send to Maxse's *National Review* rather than to the 'High Church parsonesses' at the *Guardian*, where it finally appeared anyway. No other Spanish texts seem to have survived.[9] 'An Andalusian Inn' is a comic account of a night in a primitive country inn. Its unidentified first-person plural point of view is clearly Woolfean, rather than Forsterian. There is some self-mockery from the naïvely confident, then timorous narrator and his or her companion, but the humour arises more from the baffling linguistic behaviour of foreigners than from the preposterous insularity of Forster's English abroad (*E*, I 49–52).

The Spanish writings that she did in May had not satisfied her very much. The only other review she wrote during the last month in which she recorded her beginnings as a professional was again for the *Guardian*. Lyttelton sent her a novel by Elizabeth Robins, the American actress of Ibsen and feminist, author also of the contemporary play *Votes for Women*, who had known Julia Stephen. Privately Woolf thought her clever but brutal (*L*, I 190), but in the review she praised *A Dark Lantern* as highly as any fiction she had reviewed so far, finding the novelist genuinely gifted and her work strong and sincere. Yet she criticised the novel's intensity, the melodramatic Brontëan hero, and the prolonged account of the heroine's nervous breakdown. This is the only reference in Woolf's writing at this time to what she had been through the previous year(*E*, I 42–3).

At the end of May Woolf renounced the diary, which she had not been keeping for weeks. After that it is not possible to follow her literary development from month to month. The diary had ceased to be a spontaneous exercise and therefore lost its value. But reflections on diaries were unnecessary: the months that she had kept it would find themselves mirrored there – 'if the sight is one that profits or pleases', she added ambivalently at the end (*EJ*, p. 273). In her later Memoir Club paper in the 1920s, Woolf observed that her diary ended just as it might have begun to be more interesting on the origins of Old Bloomsbury.[10] But for Bloomsbury's literary history, that mirror already reflects interestingly an image of the writer as young woman who could describe herself on a library application in May as a 'journalist who wants to read history' (*L*, I 190). Six months of journalism had taught her something about editors, and their periodicals, but little about the art of the essay or the review. That she had to learn from the work of Leslie Stephen, Aristotle and Pater, from her friends like Violet Dickinson, and from her sister and brothers and their Bloomsbury friends. As a 'journalist' Woolf had succeeded in reviewing for quite different audiences a series of books that ranged in fiction from imitation Trollope to late James. She had also written essays on her father, literary geography, dogs, street musicians, English churches, Spanish inns, laughter, and essays themselves. In these varied writings, which included lectures on various subjects for Morley College, she had shown a quite unusual facility and felicity in prose for a twenty-three-year-old, privately and self-educated woman, who was keenly aware of the restricted status of women in her class, could read Greek, Latin, and French, was widely familiar with English literature, and interested in learning enough history to write it. But of the writing of fiction, there is as yet no mention.

III

'By the way', Woolf wrote to Violet Dickinson around the time she gave up her diary, 'I am going to write history one of these days. I always did love it; if I could find the bit I want' (*L*, I 190). She was reading the historians J. R. Green and E. A. Freeman for her Morley College classes; Freeman she described in her diary as 'a good manly writer with no nonsense about him', which sounds more like something Leslie Stephen might have said than his daughter (*EJ*, p. 271). The history that Woolf began teaching at Morley College lasted only a term, however; then she was asked to do composition instead. 'Prose' was originally to have been her subject, according to her diary, but rather than lecturing on English literature earlier in 1905, she began talking to her working students about Venice, Florence and her trip to Italy last year. After teaching composition Woolf may have been a librarian at the College for a while before returning to English literature again. The college magazine reported 'Miss Stephen, daughter of the late Sir Leslie Stephen', leading a class on Keats, Shelley and Browning in the Autumn of 1907 (*Morley*, XVII 2). In letters, Woolf mocked both her students and herself as teacher, and at the end of 1907 she gave the whole thing up.

Two of Woolf's lectures at the College have been preserved among her papers along with the draft of a term report on her teaching dated July 1905.[11] These unpublished texts convey her early impressions of teaching, history, and hack work. The second of them may be her first public statement of what is now called literary theory. The first lecture Woolf mentions writing in February 1905, is on Benvenuto Cellini's autobiography. The informal, self-conscious tone of the lecture with its use of both first-person singular and second-person plural is quite unlike that of her reviews at this time (after 1901 there was no new edition of Symonds's translation of Cellini for many years). Woolf's friend Margaret Symonds Vaughan would have been pleased by the tribute to her father. His masterpiece of a translation is praised for its transparency – though the lecturer confesses she has no Italian. Woolf's account of Cellini is basically a summary of his violence and versatility. Of the artist as goldsmith and sculptor, Woolf has little to say; she thinks that he would be only a name today were it not for his autobiography, but she does not discuss its art either. Cellini remains for her a 'full blooded sensual man of genius' among the shadows of the renaissance (pS).

The other more interesting lecture is entitled 'The Dramatic in Life and Art'. Mainly in point form, it distinguishes between three 'processes': life, fiction, and drama. The tone again is very simple as the lecturer tries to work out some rudimentary ideas on literary matters. The basic idea being explored is that (in language only a lecturer could use) 'the liver: the novelist: the dramatist: [are] all reproducing thought and emotion in different shapes. . . . ' In real life the shapes result essentially from turning our thoughts and emotions into actions; in plays it is action rather than thought or emotion that has to be dramatised; but with fiction, where plot is less important, we can have 'the form of life without its details'. The drama may be external, with thought and emotion being determined by circumstances, or the reverse, which is preferable. Novelists, however, can work with complicated feelings and ideas without having to turn them into scenes on a stage; their characters can be more subtle – an opinion Woolf withdraws parenthetically as an exaggeration after recalling Hamlet. The only fiction alluded to is *Pendennis* (p/S).

Woolf's lecture is interesting for its effort to connect life, fiction and drama, as well as for its embryonic conception of fiction as an art concerned more with the shape of thought and feeling than with plotted actions. Clearly she had not yet read her Aristotle. Neither lecture is as finished a performance, say, as Forster's paper on pessimism in literature that he published in the *Working Men's College Journal* the next year. There is little in them to suggest Woolf's later mastery of the lecture form.

Virginia Woolf enjoyed the history she was teaching at Morley College in May. In a letter to Dickinson she wrote,

> Tomorrow also is my working women, for whom I have been making out a vivid account of the battle of Hastings. I hope to make their flesh creep! Aint it ridiculous – teaching working women about the ancient Britons! (*L*, I 191)

On the basis of this Quentin Bell has humorously suggested that Woolf was offering her students an *Orlando* version of history in which ancient Britons fight with Normans. But it is clear from her diary as well as the draft teaching report published as an appendix in Bell's biography that Woolf was thoroughly conversant with the standard English historians as her class worked their way 'through Early British, & Romans, & Angles Saxons & Danes, & Normans, till we were on the more substantial ground of the Plantagenet Kings' (QB/*VW*, I 106, 203). The draft report is revealing in other ways. Woolf writes of talking from notes instead of reading lectures, as she strove to make her own interest in history visible to her students:

> I used to ask myself how is it *possible* to make them feel the flesh & blood in these shadows? So thin is the present to them; must not the past remain a spectre always?   (I 203)

She tried to focus their interest on a scene. 'I find that scene making is my natural way of marking the past', she wrote – but that was at the end of her life when she was thinking about the origins of her writing (*MB*, p. 142). The conviction of history's importance runs through Woolf's literary beginnings, and she was unhappy in her report that she had to shift to the less valuable teaching of 'essay writing & the expression of ideas.' She had already expressed her hostility to the teaching of writing in the essay on essays that blamed the plague of the genre on the teaching of penmanship. The college's argument that her students can hear some lectures on the French Revolution (given by G. M. Trevelyan) is rather pointless, she thinks, for they 'have absolutely no power of receiving them as part of a whole, & applying them to their proper ends' (pp. 203–4). Evaluations based on wholes and ends had by now become familiar to her from Thoby Stephen's Bloomsbury evenings. Woolf's scepticism about academic institutions was also reinforced by her experiences at Morley College. Nevertheless, the college magazine reported in November 1905 that she had begun an English composition class which 'should prove useful, as we constantly hear of students with literary aspirations who wish to improve their style' (*Morley*, XV 19). Woolf supposed it 'the most useless class in the college' and her supervisor Mary Sheepshanks agreed (*L*, I 210).

One of the purposes of Woolf's draft report was to describe the students attending the course. Among them was 'the germ of a literary lady' who gave her teacher a vision of Grub Street that added to her dissatisfaction with reviewing, for the student also reviewed for a religious paper, but under rather different conditions:

> She was a writing machine to be set in motion by the editor. For some reason, unconnected with the author, the notice was to be

favourable or unfavourable; but to record this notice it was not necessary by any means to read the book; that indeed would be impossible, considering the number of reviews to be turned out. . . . Quotations picked out at random need only be linked together by a connecting word, & the column was filled out of someone else's pocket. (QB/*VW*, I 202)

IV

By June Woolf felt herself sinking in the literary world, as she rose in the philanthropic one of Morley College. Lyttelton and Richmond had sent no books to set her writing in motion. To further her plan of writing a sustained work of history, she read and annotated four volumes of medieval English history, but they did not reward the efforts she was making (*L*, I 202). A visit to her boring cousin, the Oxford historian H. A. L. Fisher did not help. She wrote one short review in June of a novel on farm life that found the work hampered by its fictional form and the necessity of telling a story; in proof she thought the review a little scornful, but felt no authors cared what the *Guardian*, with its preaching of charity, said about them (*L*, I 197). Lyttelton asked for another 'literary article' and Woolf chose not fiction or poetry as her subject this time but the domestic writings of an eminent Victorian's wife.

'The Letters of Jane Welsh Carlyle' was a hard essay to write. 'Six volumes of real genius' had to be 'boiled down into 1,500 words of solid prose!' (*L*, I 200). She found herself writing 'marvellous dry nonsense' trying to analyse Mrs Carlyle and asked Dickinson whether she preferred 'my fluent rounded style, or my curt and mordant style?' (*L*, I 197–8). But what she produced, after revisions to make it easier for her *Guardian* audience, was, she felt, 'an ugly angular piece of writing, all jagged edges.' At least it was not that paper's usual 'mild and mellifluous cant', despite Sydney-Turner's regular suggestions of proprieties for her prose (*L*, I 201–2). The attempt to define Jane Welsh Carlyle's style may have made Woolf stylistically self-conscious, but what she says in the *Guardian* bears on her own epistolary art. Much of the essay is a revealing early discussion of the genre and style of letters that Leslie Stephen had told her were the most wonderful in the language (VW/*L*, I 76).

Their biographical interest shadows the essay, as Woolf illustrates the hard life of the compassionate letter-writer, concluding on a Stephenesque note that 'under other conditions she might have written more; she could hardly have written better'. The letters themselves Woolf describes as unintrospective – written by a woman of wit, whose sarcasm was self-protective. Mrs Carlyle favoured in her letters 'the natural and simple style' that, in her own words, could not throw her soul 'into deliquium by any hundred horse-power of upholstery or of moral sublime'. Although Mrs Carlyle's diction is neither simple nor natural, Woolf finds in her 'a substantial common sense, a power of seeing things as they are, which gave the sting to her words. . . . ' Thomas Carlyle's own early letters to Jane Welsh were written, the recipient supposed, for his biographer. But hers, Woolf argues, are 'genuine letters in the sense that she had always some definite object in writing them at a particular moment to a particular person.' Their analysis of character – which both Carlyles practised in their writing – turns the insignificance of her 'mere letter-writing' into a creative and critical art of genius (*E*, I 54–7).

In August the four Stephens returned to Cornwall for nearly two months. Virginia wrote only one review there but she kept a diary of the holiday that reads like a source-book for *To the Lighthouse*. The review for the *Academy & Literature* (she was glad to do it for the sake of her bank balance) was of a book on celebrated late eighteenth- and early nineteenth-century 'women of wit and beauty'. All but one of them had faded, Woolf finds; they survive, if at all, as phantoms in vague Victorian memoirs. Not even their writings could preserve their fame. The exception is Mrs Norton, who endures in a work of literary art: Meredith's *Diana of the Crossways*. (Another possible exception to the forgotten women of the book was Mary Wortley Montagu, whom Strachey would praise in the *Albany Review* two years later.) 'Their Passing Hour' is a kind of review-ballad 'des dames du temps jadis', written near St Ives, where the life of another beautiful and compassionate woman was still remembered and would eventually be given literary immortality by the reviewer (*E*, I 61–3).

Virginia Woolf's Cornwall diary begins on 11 August as an essay on the train that, like a wizard, is to transport the diarist and her unidentified companions 'into another world, almost into another age.' Ten years had passed (it was actually eleven, as she remembers a little later) since they were at St Ives – the same interval of

time passed in *To the Lighthouse* – and like ghosts they returned
to their house, hoping to recover 'something tangible of their
substance' (*EJ*, pp. 281–2). They went sailing in the bay where Woolf
records seeing in the distance that symbol from another novel, a
black fin cutting the surface of water. Walking in the villages they
encountered people who remembered the Stephens, especially
Julia. A regatta, likened in the diary to an impressionist painting, is
visited to fulfil a tradition, and before they left the Stephens
watched pilchards being caught in the bay. After two dates,
chronology is abandoned for descriptive notes that serve the diarist
as landmarks of her journey. She concludes thinking of the lights of
London that will surround her tomorrow 'as the lighthouse gleams
now' (p. 299). Among the descriptions of the diary were misty
walks along the coast and inland. One recounts in some detail
returning at dusk as the lighthouse flashes; the mist and dark soon
obliterate the land, and the walkers' pilgrimage – a repeated word
in the diary – becomes an unearthly progress where halos of light
occasionally illuminate dark figures. Finally safe at home they miss,
as caged birds would, the air's 'vague immensity' (pp. 297–8).

While in Cornwall, Woolf was writing for her own pleasure, as
a relief from 'Guardian drudgery'. Half-mockingly to Dickinson,
she said she was planning two large books, one on the medieval
Paston letters and another describing Cornwall. She was trying 'to
write descriptions without adjectives' and wondered if she would
ever be able to write 'a really good book' (*L*, I 206, 208). It may have
been at this time that Woolf reworked her diary description of the
misty night walk into an essay for the *Guardian*, where it appeared
under the title 'A Walk by Night' at the end of the year.[12] The diary
entry's anticipations of the really good book she would write –
particularly the prose poetry in the middle 'Time Passes' part of *To
the Lighthouse* – are even clearer in the essay. A group of people are
walking home at dusk near the cliffs of Cornwall in the essay; the
lighthouse's golden light symbolically illuminates harsh rocks, and
the walkers quickly become engulfed in mist and darkness. Their
voices and conversation change, identities dissolve, the narrator's
mind swoons away from the body: 'both eyes and ears were fast
sealed, or, for the pressure on them was of something intangible,
had grown numb insensibly. . . . ' Sounds and lights appear like
apparitions in their strange pilgrimage before they are flooded with
silence and darkness again. The village finally reached is lonelier
than a ship at sea, 'anchored to the desolate earth and exposed

every night, alone, to the unfathomed waters of darkness.' Yet once accustomed to the misty night, the walkers find it very beautiful and peaceful, where the ghosts of solid things were about, and

> the eye might bathe and refresh itself in the depths of the night, without grating upon any harsh outline of reality; the earth with its infinity of detail was dissolved into ambiguous space.

Back in the narrow walls and glaring lights of their house, they 'were as birds lately winged that have been caught and caged' (*E*, I 80–2).

'A Walk by Night' suggests more than anything else in Woolf's early work some of the directions her lyrical fiction would take. Several features of the text are worth noting. One is the ambivalent attitude of the narrator to an experience that both liberates from harsh reality and isolates in unreality. The sharing of this experience by a group is also important here and in her later writing. Another characteristic is the essay's epistemological descriptiveness: the loss of sense-perception in the mist and dark seems to separate mind from body until the eye perceiving light again wakes the brain to reconstruct reality. Literal and metaphorical images of light and darkness, of air, land and water, combine as the mist dissolves the land and the night drowns the light. Certainly the descriptive writing here is adjectival, yet by writing of a walk instead of a scene, Woolf can do more with verbs and adverbs. There is, however, a Romantic allusiveness about the description. In a diary entry on an afternoon walk in a blinding mist, Woolf reflects how Lucy's fate could have been her own, and there is an echo of Wordsworth's 'A Slumber Did My Spirit Seal' in the image of sealed numbness experienced in 'A Walk by Night'.[13] Finally in this Cornwall evocation there is the sense of a strange pilgrimage among phantoms. But how the walk is a pilgrimage and what the phantoms are, the essay never discloses.

V

Back in London again in the autumn Woolf found herself with more reviewing to do than she thought quite moral, but there were bills to be paid. She shrugged off her aunt's advice to do serious work but tried to fit 'some Greek and good English in between' (*L*, I 210).

Thoby's Thursday evenings continued with the Cambridge friends Virginia was now calling 'the little poets' after the publication of *Euphrosyne* in August. Vanessa (to whom Clive had proposed and been rejected before the Cornwall vacation) was now planning the first exhibition of her Friday Club devoted to the visual arts.

By the end of 1905 Woolf had done fifteen more reviews, about a half a dozen each for the *Guardian* and the *TLS*, another essay-review for the *Academy & Literature*, and, more importantly, her first review for the *Speaker*, which had asked her to write on a Victorian critic. Most of the books reviewed were ephemeral novels to be disposed of in a few hundred words, yet they contributed to her developing ideas about modern fiction. Woolf is critical of the characterisation and plotting that seem to hamper several of the novelists. A work set in the dramatic eighteenth century is praised as a good adventure novel, though its characters are made mostly of powder (*E*, I 70). Occasionally Woolf seems to admire the skill of short-story writers over novelists; one of the few enduring writers she reviewed at this time was Mary Wilkins Freeman, whose well-written but disconnected novel *The Debtor* she thought might have been done better as another collection of her excellent stories (*E*, I 68–9). The absence of psychological subtlety or development is commented on more than once in the work of W. E. Norris, again, whose polished novels end where Henry James's begin (*E*, I 66). Critical as these reviews can be, they are not often dismissive. The reviewer is usually able to rescue something of value from wrecks of books. Her reading notes tend, unsurprisingly, to be more assertive than her published remarks; in the review of two Irish novels, for instance, a note that the Irish lose their poetry when they emigrate is turned into a question.

Some figures in Woolf's notebook show her dividing a column of the *Guardian* or the *TLS* into 300, 500, and 800 words, which suggests her reviews may have been assigned by column lengths. A third of a column was the space allotted for most of her fiction reviews at this time. The *Guardian* did give her a full column for a biographical review of David Moir, and another in which to summarise a charming book on the Sahara written in the anti-utilitarian spirit of Kinglake's *Eöthen*. But for Edith Wharton's *The House of Mirth*, Woolf had only three or four hundred words. Woolf's only review of one of the few notable women novelists writing in English mentions the subject and tragic seriousness of the novel then leaves its moral to the reader. A brief quotation from the novel about society's negative force eliminating 'everything beyond their own range of perception' (*E*, I 68) could describe English society in Forster's Edwardian fiction. What might Woolf have said if Lyttelton had allowed as much space for Wharton's remarkable first novel as she allowed for James's last? Again the conditions of reviewing need to be remembered in assessing Woolf's early reviews. She certainly remained aware of these limitations, complaining in letters of how her *Guardian* editor 'sticks her broad thumb into the middle of my delicate sentences and improves the moral tone', while the *TLS* hurried her into grinding out reviews like sausages (*L*, I 214, 211–12).

The *Academy & Literature* gave Woolf more space and time, but they seem to have typecast her as their reviewer of books about notable women of the past. In November she had to discuss Wilhelmina, the devoted sister of Frederick the Great. Woolf took twenty-two pages of reading notes for a summary narrative of the brutal upbringing, eccentric education, and unhappy career of a high-born, brilliant woman memoirist (*E*, I 87–91).

Woolf was pleased, then, to be asked, perhaps at the suggestion of Desmond MacCarthy, to write for the *Speaker*. For her first review they sent the lectures and essays of Leslie Stephen's old friend Canon Ainger. Woolf found his Victorian literary criticism more interesting to review than novels (*L*, I 214), and she was given one and a half columns in which to discuss it for a knowledgeable liberal audience. 'A Nineteenth-Century Critic' is the first public comment from Bloomsbury on Victorian literary values and a fitting conclusion to Woolf's first year as a published writer. Ainger revered literature; he was very cultured and sincere; he had charming sympathy for the sweet and true. This is Woolf's tribute. For the editor of Ainger's work the Victorian period was an age of great writers concerned with ideas. But for Woolf, 'the nineteenth century is already yesterday.' Tentatively she expressed for the first time the fundamental Bloomsbury criticism of their predecessors, whose ideas were essentially limited to one kind:

> The distinction of the writers of the nineteenth century, so far as we are now able to judge them, seems to be that the ideas which interested them were, roughly speaking, ethical rather than aesthetic.

The Cambridge Thursday evenings and the Friday Club meetings were having their effect. As if to demonstrate how early twentieth-century criticism would be aesthetic, Woolf singles out the defects inherent in the lecture form of Ainger's criticism. His points are directed to the ear not the eye; they are adapted to the least intelligent of his hearers, and recall that genre of the Canon's profession, the sermon. But Woolf's central objection to Ainger's criticism is that he unduly emphasises 'the personal element' with which the ethical is allied.[14] Ainger's chief purpose as a literary critic 'seems to be to institute an anxious inquiry into the state of the writer's morals' (*E*, I 83–5). The tone is respectful here, but there is a clear affinity with Strachey's debunking of Matthew Arnold a decade later. The criticism could also be levelled, of course, at some of the literary essays of the anonymous reviewer's father.

VI

In 1906 'the author's progress', as one of the books Woolf reviewed that year was called, involved less reviewing and more un-published writing of various kinds, including finally some fiction. The idea of writing a substantial historical work receded, as the range of her reviewing widened. Early in January she received from the editor of the *Guardian* himself seven volumes of poetry and poetic drama to review, this time for the main part of the paper rather than the women's pages. Her notice is more tactful than her notes. She appears to have had no hesitation in reviewing poetry, but she was clearly bored by the bathetic verse, flat characters, ('Miss Von Herder makes the fatal mistake of adding a tail to the ordinary mortal and thinking that she has created a mermaid' – *E*, I 99) and fragmentary dramatic structure of the poetic plays – a genre in which Lytton Strachey was still trying to write. Only one volume by a young woman leaves her hopeful.

For *The Times Literary Supplement* Woolf was reviewing mainly minor fiction, and her reviews serve to remind us just how many modern novels Woolf read before beginning to write one of her own. Titles like *A Supreme Moment, The Scholar's Daughter* or *The House of Shadows* sound promising for her development, but most of the eight novels reviewed were shallow in their plots and charac-ters, or so schematic they lacked human truth. Woolf's preference at this time was clearly for realistic contemporary fiction. The American Winston Churchill's historical novel *Coniston*, perhaps his best work, is criticised, for example, as a shabby affair in the shapeless old clothes of the previous generation (*E*, I 115–16). Mrs Hamilton Synge's *A Supreme Moment* interested her, however; its characters were indefinite yet the awakening of a middle-aged woman is memorably represented through understatements and omissions (I 92–3). *The House of Shadows* is a flawed but remarkable melodrama that depicts the victory of pain over the soul but is not psychological enough (I 93–4). Another novel's unconventional simplicity in skipping generations and telling ghost stories attracts her (I 110). A novelist's purpose, she says of Stanley Weyman's *Chippinge*, 'demands individual men and women who will fall in love with each other, and fight their dragons and live happily ever afterwards', but there are problems when the dragon is the Reform Bill; still the representation of a crowd is memorable (VW/ '*Chippinge*')[15]. More interesting, however, was Woolf's review of a remarkable first novel *Abbots Verney* by one R. Macaulay. The reviewer conjectures the initial conceals a woman novelist trying to pass as a male one; the actions, talk, and feelings of the characters in the novel all point to this. There are improbabilities in the plot, and the characters say a good many clever things aimed at shocking the commonplace; they sometimes forget, indeed, that they are taking part in a story requiring action and emotion. Nevertheless, the novel 'is undoubtedly a very able and interesting piece of work, and the failures are of the kind that promise success' ('*Abbots Verney*'). The promise was fulfilled, and Rose Macaulay became one of the contemporary women writers that Virginia Woolf would measure herself against from time to time.

The fiction reviews that Woolf was writing for the *TLS* were between 300 and 500 words each and grouped with others under the general heading of 'Fiction'. But for two books on the Lake District, one of them by Wordsworth, Richmond allowed her three times as much space for a separate article. Never having been to the Lakes, she concentrates on Wordsworth's descriptions of them in his *Guide to the Lakes*, admiring the book's 'tone of solemn enthusiasm'. She is amused at Wordsworth's condescending to suggest accommodation in the district, but much admires his ability to see minute natural details 'all as living parts of a vast and exquisitely ordered system.' The 'terse veracity of the poet's prose' completely contrasts with the other book under review which consists of a clergyman's irrelevant, if not impertinent, conceits on the Lakes (*E*, I 105–8).

Poets' prose was also the subject of Woolf's second *Speaker* review, which was now signed 'A. V. Stephen'. The poets are the Brownings, and the reviewer's tone is distinctly less respectful with them than with Wordsworth. 'If it were possible', she begins with a disenchanting metaphor, 'to condense into set phrases that mist of felt rather than spoken criticism which hangs round all the great names in literature', it is fairly certain that Elizabeth Barrett Browning would have to be judged 'a bad poet'. An interesting small selection of her letters with commentary by Percy Lubbock makes Woolf wonder if the same thing might not be done for her poetry. The famous Browning love letters are behind much of the distrust of her poetry, Woolf suggests, and then describes their effect on the guilty Victorian reader:

> The eavesdropper became so weary of those emphatic voices, protesting and asseverating, uttering commonplaces with dreadful distortion of the lips and drowning even the simple emotions in a twisted torrent of language, that he might surely consider that his fault was expiated as soon as committed.
>
> (*E*, I 101–2)

As with Ainger, Woolf is again critical of the Victorians in the *Speaker*, this time unanonymously and with humour. Yet she is not out to debunk Mrs Browning, who continued to interest her later as the author of a novel-poem and the owner of a remarkable dog. Her genius, she finds in her early and later life rather than her art – in the valiant way she coped with her father, her admirers, and her critics. Woolf likes Elizabeth Barrett Browning for saying that truth made her 'splutter' in poetry, but disagrees with the assumption that a scrupulous concern for literary form interferes with truth. A tacked-on discussion of a book on Browning's *Waring* suggests some editorial interference with Woolf's review.

The final *Speaker* review of Woolf's, printed anonymously, again in August 1906, was her first published comment on another subject of lifelong literary interest, the Elizabethans. Reading the accounts by Hakluyt and others of sixteenth-century voyages is likened by her to voyaging; there is need of a chart and Walter Raleigh (the professor not the Elizabethan) provides a luminous one in his introduction. But what delights the reviewer is not so much the adventures as the Elizabethan descriptions of them. 'Wherever the book is opened', she writes, 'one finds rough phrases to be tuned to such melody, that as you go along you may be your own poet' (*E*, I 123). The poetry of Elizabethan language made that time in history always fascinating for her and for Strachey.

Two more reviews for the *Speaker* by Woolf were never printed and are now lost, although the notes for them survive. One was of a collection of letters written to the Betham family by people like Coleridge and Lamb so garrulous and silly that they gave her a horror of writing letters (*L*, I 219–20). More to be regretted was a critique of Mrs Humphry Ward's latest novel that Woolf sent to the Speaker and then discovered they had already printed a review of it (by Edward Garnett) that was more vindictive than hers (*L*, I 219). In her notes Woolf called the art of *Fenwick's Career* crude and flimsy; its webs of pretty words did not 'make you feel the real things' (*RN*, p. 179).[16]

Woolf's last review for the *Academy & Literature* also appeared in the summer of 1906. The ironically titled 'Sweetness – Long Drawn Out' is also a significant early review not for its subject, which was the fictionalised biography of another eighteenth-century German noblewoman, but for Woolf's remarks on the book's mixture of fact and fiction. The review begins with an analogy between Joshua Reynolds's portraits of women and their biographies. These beautiful women appear better in paint than in words, and when the words are partly factual and partly imaginary 'we have a composite production, where the truth has the vagueness of fiction and the fiction is diluted with fact' (*E*, I 118). The spurious result of the author's research encumbers her characters instead of revealing them, and they turn into historical puppets. The German Pompadour, as the book title describes her, leaves a fragrance of rose leaves for her biographer; the reviewer thinks something more pungent might have remained in a shorter work, like a sonnet or an article.

VII

The last five contributions Virginia Woolf wrote for Mrs Lyttelton concerned the work of very different authors. One was about writing professionally. Her attitude toward the subject now and later in her career is consistent. She finds the subject of *The Author's Progress* ugly, yet to deny its interest would be an affectation. 'The root of the matter is that the confusion between art and trade must always be ugly, and that the confusion – since writing is sold as boots are sold – is inevitable' (*E*, I 117). Woolf wrote this in the *Guardian* while she was doing *TLS* reviews in the midst of what is called *The Times* Book War of 1906–8. During these years, some of Woolf's *TLS* reviews, among many others, carried an extraordinary editorial heading (later it was a footnote) urging readers not to buy the book being reviewed because The Publishers' Association would not supply it to *The Times*'s Book Club, which was a free circulating library. The newspaper said it was trying to break the monopolistic system of The Publisher's Association (which prohibited booksellers from selling a book below the net price) by offering books at discounts after their book club was through with them. The Publishers' Association replied that *The Times* was discounting books in an attempt to improve its declining circulation. It must have all been very educational for the future novelist, critic, and publisher to realise so early how writing was a commodity subject to economic conditions like any other.

A longer review of Woolf's for the *Guardian* was of an eighteenth-century bluestocking's biography. There is not much to be said about Elizabeth Carter, the reviewer observes, 'unless you possess a real gift for the interpretation of character. . . . ' The biographer does not have this, but the reviewer does, as she proceeds to demonstrate. 'The Bluest of the Blue' is an admiring, amusing sketch of a learned, and eccentric woman, energetic in mind and body, who (like her reviewer) walked as vigorously as she read. She tied a bell to her bed so that she could be woken early to study Greek, learned nine languages, and translated Epictetus. Not a witty woman but an instructing, oracular one who would 'utter common sense as though it were the inspired wisdom of the gods' (*E*, I 112–14). No wonder Woolf remembered Mrs Carter for over twenty years and then put her with her bell among the heroic precursors in *A Room of One's Own*.

The accomplishment of this review may have been recognised by Woolf's editor, for the next, and as it turned out last, three texts Woolf wrote before Mrs Lyttleton died early in 1907 were all literary essays. How Woolf came to write these anonymous 1500-word pieces on George Gissing, Thomas De Quincey, and Henry James is unknown; indeed two of them have only recently been identified as having been written by her.[17] Gissing's' The *Private Papers of Henry Ryecroft* had been published in 1903, the year of his death. Woolf alludes to subsequent editions but she is not writing a review as much as a meditation on a book about a writer who has the delightful and sufficient freedom of £300 a year and a cottage of his own in which to read and think. The essayist dismisses the question of how autobiographical the novel is, arguing that Henry Ryecroft 'needs no external support.' In a return to Leslie Stephen's critical values, she writes that the interest of the book for herself and other readers is not in its prose, humour, or mature knowledge, but rather in the impression it gives of a living, sincere human being. Henry Ryecroft has survived harsh poverty; he has heroically shed superfluities, paring his thoughts and emotions down to their pith. The essay ends with the triumphant result: 'a book, a pen, a cottage in the country, and the world is at your feet' (*E*, I 131–4). Gissing has clearly described an ideal that Woolf would make use of, again, in *A Room of One's Own*. Her respect for the moral if not the aesthetic power of Gissing's writing remained, and she wrote about him again several times, including an essay in the second *Common Reader*.

The essay on Thomas De Quincey, despite being titled 'The English Mail Coach', does not focus on one of his works but considers the extraordinary kind of writer he was. Once more the essay points forward to others Woolf would write, but in contrast to Gissing's terse, sincere style, it is De Quincey's lyrical prose that excites her admiration and made him an important influence on her style. The present age – 'meaning by that, of course, the opinions of two or three elderly people' – finds his prose immature, she remarks, thinking perhaps of the mixed evaluation accorded De Quincey by her father in *Hours in a Library*. (*Confessions of an English Opium Eater* was a favourite book of her mother – VW/*MB*, p. 86.) The question of influence appears more directly in the essay through a comparison of De Quincey's exuberant writing with the careful prose of the two English essayists Woolf had bought to study the previous year. Pater and Stevenson would have disposed of De Quincey's ecstasies, reorganised his structure, clipped and combed his sentences, but they could have added nothing to what he was expressing. That expression undoubtedly has its faults – it is too big and too long for her. De Quincey sees everything enlarged, and he is incorrigibly digressive. Yet with his huge spaces and organ-like sounds, he achieved effects that can delight the generous reader. And it is the reader around whom 'The English Mail Coach' is organised. A true book, the essay begins, 'dictates the mood and season in which it shall be read. . . . ' De Quincey's work, the essay

ends in imitation of his style, is to be read out-of-doors 'in some
sheltered garden where the view between hedges is of a vast plain
sunk beneath an ocean of air . . . ' (*E*, I 365–8). The responses of
readers became fundamental to Woolf's criticism as it developed,
and in a number of her essays – 'How Should One Read a Book?'
for example – the experience of reading interacts with the setting in
which it is happening. And in later essays on De Quincey, she will
show how much more important a predecessor in 'impassioned
prose' (as one of her essays on De Quincey was called) he was than
Pater.

In her third *Guardian* essay, written in Norfolk shortly before
travelling with her sister and brothers to Greece, Woolf turned
again to the writings of Henry James, this time his travel sketches.
'Portraits of Places' takes its title from an early collection of Henry
James's travel essays, a number of which were reprinted the
previous year in *English Hours*. Woolf had described James in her
notes for *The Golden Bowl* as a 'great landscape painter', and in her
TLS review of Spanish travel books she had placed his sentimental
journeys among the most delightful in English (*E*, I 385, 44). Here, in
an essay devoted to James's descriptions of England, she begins
lightly on the subject of place painting. The opening words (that she
thought would tell Dickinson she wrote the unsigned piece) make
an unqualified claim then qualify it: 'Nothing, it seems, should be
so easy as to paint the portrait of a place.' Outside the window, the
sitter reclines any time you want to scrutinise him; it is unnecessary
to bother about his soul or his sex, for indeed he probably is not
even a he. The inadequate results reveal, however, that a map will
tell you more about a place than its picture. Rather ambiguously, it
emerges that the essayist is talking about written not painted
scenes, but a faint ridicule of art remains. The whole tone of the
essay is one of amusement. James is, of course, the most perceptive
of travel writers and an amusing one too. He exposes his brain like
a film, and his American point of view (which was more pronounced in the earlier pieces reprinted in *English Hours*) keeps his eyes
focused on the complex historical psychology of the land. Woolf's
camera metaphor implies James's are photographs of places, yet she
also views his essays as self-portraits of an American. This makes
them even more diverting. Only an American could have described
young English women as possessing 'an intimate salubrity', the
intimacy being illustrated by the following conversation which
Woolf quotes from James's landscape of Warwickshire:

The young man stood facing her, slowly scratching his thigh, and shifting from one foot to the other. He had honest, stupid, blue eyes, and a simple smile that showed his handsome teeth. He was very well dressed. 'I suppose it's pretty big', said the beautiful young girl. 'Yes; it's pretty big', said the handsome young man. 'It's nicer when they are big', said his interlocutress, and for some time no further remark was made. (*E*, I 126)

The subject under discussion here – a boat – is unrevealed in Woolf's essay, and it is difficult to tell just how indecent she meant to make Henry James sound. Her editor, for one, seems not to have noticed the suggestiveness. (Years later when she wanted to call James's ghost stories lewd in the *TLS*, Richmond objected – *D*, II 151). Making fun of James's fastidious American sensibility was one of the ways Woolf and Bloomsbury coped with his influence.

VIII

'I have been writing all the mornings; not a word will ever be seen in print or by mortal eyes: except mine', Virginia Woolf teased Violet Dickinson early in January, 1906 (*L*, I 215). Some of the private writing she was doing around this time has survived, and the most noteworthy of the texts are, for the first time, fictional.

The non-fiction pieces consist of brief or fragmentary descriptions and several short essays (VW/pS). Some are undated and may have been written a little earlier or later. A page headed 'Sunday up the River' is a mildly melancholic description of the river playing amid trees and meadows until the sun sets and 'the mad and sad' unmoor their boats to drift in the moonlight. A few pages, also undated, on going up the river by a penny steamer are interesting for the contrast of the uproarious Strand that is crossed to reach the river, as at the beginning of *The Voyage Out*; London becomes unreal as one floats by churches, warehouses, and docked ships that look like beached whales. Another fragment written in July 1908, is about going to places like Greenwich or Hampton Court, where childhood memories make them forever juvenile and delightful. A short essay written in March 1906, explores the contrasts of the city, which is compared favourably with the country, as the essence of a garden is better perceived in a London square than at a celebrated country house. While visiting the Vaughans in April, Woolf probably wrote a satirical sketch of the Manchester Zoo to which she had taken the Vaughan children and then described in her diary (*EJ*, pp. 307–8). Ordinary things are described uncomprehendingly from a child-like point of view, like the animals, which appear dissipated. In May she wrote her ironic commentary on *Euphrosyne* (see p. 74). Undated and probably earlier is a little essay, somewhat in the manner of Lamb, on marginalia. The identities of various annotators are imagined: the indignant, the lachrymose, the public spirited correctors of misprints and grammar, the botanists who leave their specimens between the pages, and those (like Leslie Stephen) who write 'pooh' in the margins. Related to this essay is the early amusing fragment of a story in which a writer of literary textbooks starts to develop a relationship with an unknown woman through his corrections of her banal marginal comments in library books (*CSF*, pp. 327–330). The writer's speculations on the woman's situation look forward a little to the women imagined by Woolf's later narrators in 'An Unwritten Novel' and 'Mr. Bennett and Mrs. Brown'.

Two rather more mature texts date from June and July 1906. The first is a vision of Greece that begins with a map and goes on to speculate how disillusioning the place will be to the classically educated, with the monuments all ruined and the Greeks unable to understand their own classical language. At night, however, a image of 'the great statue of the Maiden Goddess' appears, as if to inspire the words of her lovers, Plato, Sophocles, Pericles. The vision lasts until the morning, when a farmer, after impiously cursing her, leaves a carrot on her altar because his priest had told him there is but one God. The shift here from disillusionment to the visionary and back to ordinary reality is a familiar pattern in Woolf's later writing. The other essay, a fragment, sets out to praise the Covent Garden Opera. Its slum and vegetable-market setting are part of this complex English structure that neither cynicism nor seriousness can adequately describe. The claim that it satisfied all classes is not presented very persuasively, and the piece ends in the midst of describing the indifference of the rich to the performances (pS).

The two earliest complete stories of Woolf's to survive are about the unreal existences of sisters. 'Phyllis and Rosamond', written first, is an omniscient contemporary narrative of two young women, the 'daughters at home' of 'official parents'. Their South Kensington or Belgravia life is disturbed by an encounter with the

Bloomsbury Group. The story is dated and set in June 1906, and one does not need to know that the ages of Phyllis and Rosamond are those of Vanessa and Virgina to recognise how autobiographical the story is. Woolf's biographer has described the story as though it were of a visit paid by the Miss Stephens of 1903 to the Miss Stephens of 1906. When asked by a Bloomsbury woman named Sylvia what they do, one of the 1903 Stephens replies they are 'slaves', which is how Desmond MacCarthy actually described Vanessa and Virginia when he saw them in London shortly after the turn of the century (QB/*VW*, ı 99, 103). The home life of Phyllis and Rosamond is determined by their mother's crude matchmaking; only occasionally can they escape their social duties to read Anatole France or Walter Pater. (Two other less frivolous, more insensitive sisters go to college and become like the professors they marry.) None of this is very convincingly narrated, though there are touches of wit. The interest of the story for Bloomsbury's literary history lies in its early fictional rendering of the Group setting, conversation, and values. Phyllis, for example, thinks that in Bloomsbury,

> one might grow up as one liked. There was room, and freedom, and in the roar and splendour of the Strand she read the live realities of the world from which her stucco and her pillars protected her so completely. (*CSF*, p. 24)

She enters, looking like a Romney portrait, into a smoky room of informally dressed people arguing intensely and technically about pictures, and she knows her gracious platitudes are useless amid their 'strange new point of view'. What astonished the sisters is the manner, not the subjects of conversation, for despite their upbringing, Phyllis and Rosamond are described as appreciating intellect and practising compassion. Candour and precision are expected even in discussing love, and 'reality' is the criterion of value. Phyllis is asked by Sylvia to explain exactly what she means when she says she is a slave, and is then questioned as to whether she is 'solid all the way through'. Finally when Sylvia enquires if she wants to marry, Phyllis speaks Bloomsbury truths desperately:

> We want so many things, that we can never see marriage alone as it really is or ought to be. It is always mixed up with so much else. It means freedom and friends and a house of our own, and

oh all the things you have already! Does that seem to you very
dreadful and very mercenary?

Sylvia replies unhelpfully, 'It does seem rather dreadful; but not
mercenary I think. I should write if I were you' (pp. 27–9). The
freedom of Bloomsbury comes too late for Phyllis and Rosamond,
and they return to their captivity.

The second, much shorter, story about the unreality of the sisters'
lives is more original and less feminist. Its autobiographical
significance is contained in a single letter of its title 'The Mysterious
Case of Miss V'. There are actually two Miss V's who have been
'gliding about London for some fifteen years'.They are so indistinct
in their city loneliness that their identities collapse into one Miss V
who seems 'to melt into some armchair or chest of drawers' at
parties. Miss V 'drops out of the closeknit chain of human life'
when the ministrations of the butcher, postman, and parson's wife
cease. The first-person narrator, whose tone is depressing, hilarious,
and satirical all at the same time, wakes up crying Miss V's name
one morning and is propelled into visiting her, only to discover that
she had died that morning. (A cancelled ending leaves her merely
alive – CSF, pp. 30–2, 295.) The slightly Kafkaesque existence of
Miss V remains undeveloped in Woolf's odd little fantasy of
identity and isolation.

A different experimental fragment of fiction, perhaps also written
around this time, is a description of an ordinary beautiful day in the
lives of two jungle monkeys who sound like Kipling's animals but
live like Woolf's characters in her experimental sketches (CSF, pp.
324–5). The most substantial story that Woolf wrote at the beginning of her career, however, was not fictional autobiography or
fantasy, but an imaginative rendering of the history she had been
reading, teaching and hoping to write for the past two years.

IX

Virginia Woolf had been keeping diaries again in 1906, one brief one
during her visit to Yorkshire and the Vaughans in April (which
included the Manchester Zoo visit) and another short one in
Norfolk during a month's stay in an Elizabethan manor house
called Blo'Norton Hall, a fairly extensive one while in Greece, and
then a few pages at the end of the year back in the New Forest.

Offering Madge Vaughan some literary advice about making a good book out of a diary, she wrote,

> suppose you went on day by day, writing out soberly and exactly, what you think, feel, see, hear and talk about, as you have done that one day, all things growing naturally out of each other as they do – wouldn't the result be something very true and remarkable? (*L*, I 220)

Woolf was not herself yet writing this kind of associative prose and would not be doing it until *Monday or Tuesday*. Her Yorkshire and Blo'Norton Hall diaries consist of fairly stiff, literarily self-conscious notes on scenes, walks, and local inhabitants. 'But words! words!' she exclaims after one descriptive attempt. 'You will find nothing to match the picture.' She took her Bloomsbury values with her to Yorkshire. A young schoolmaster and his Newnham wife put William Morris's words over their hearth and named their child after a George Meredith hero – a combining of life and literature that strikes Woolf as all wrong (*EJ*, pp. 304–5). Blo'Norton itself could not be described while under her eyes. The little essays of her diary are on its antiquity, which would so appeal to Americans, on its fen setting, and on nearby medieval towns and villages (*EJ*, pp. 309–16). Henry James had remarked in *English Hours*, which Woolf was writing on for the *Guardian* while in Norfolk, 'It is not too much to say that after spending twenty-four hours in a house that is six hundred years old you seem yourself to have live in it six hundred years' (p. 235). From this Jamesian germ, perhaps, and certainly from the medieval history she had been reading, which included the Paston letters, came quite a different sort of diary by Woolf – a fictive one kept by a young medieval woman named Joan Martyn and introduced by a historian named Rosamond (again) Merridew who had discovered it in a Norfolk Hall.

Miss Merridew's modern narrative is connected to Joan Martyn's journal in more than just an introductory way. Both women write about the nature of time, both are concerned with the relation of temporal reality to the imagination, both reflect on the situation of women in their times. The historian says frankly that she has given up marriage for pieces of parchment. She is a travelling antiquarian; but unlike the tale-teller and seller Joan writes of, she buys manuscripts. She researches manor rolls to illuminate the past. Critics complain that her digressions have nothing to do with medieval land tenure and are too imaginative for 'the sterner art of the Historian.' (The great expert on medieval English law at this time was Stephen's biographer F. W. Maitland.) To which Merridew replies 'unless you choose to draw all your inspiration from the *Paston Letters* you must be content to imagine merely, like any other story teller' (*CSF*, p. 35). Merridew puts aside these quarrels of historians over history versus art, yet in Joan Martyn's journal the split reappears in a different form. The antithesis preoccupied Woolf at the beginning of her career, as it did Lytton Strachey in his dissertation. The two parts of 'The Journal of Mistress Joan Martyn', as it has come to be called, reflect the alternatives of historical and imaginative writing that Woolf had been thinking about for the past two years. Both Rosamond Merridew and Joan Martyn are her personae

There are also hints in the story, which Woolf never revised, that Joan is a projection of Rosamond, whose ability to envision the reality of medieval brains from medieval bodies brought complaints from historians. The two parts of 'The Journal of Mistress Joan Martyn' are not interconnected enough, however, to make this relationship between historian and diarist quite plausible. Lack of revision seems to explain the incoherencies of dates in the story that has Joan born in 1495 but starting her journal in 1480. (A later Joan who dies of smallpox caught from her father may be a version of this Joan.) It is possible that the confusion in dates is that of the current incumbent, Jasper (or John) Martyn. Male/female contrasts of the introduction are pronounced. The unmarried historian is moved by farmer Martyn's unromantic concern for ancestral continuity; she sees her antiquarian zeal as trivial compared with such 'large substantial things' (p. 44). Still, the genealogies she is shown represent 'a husband depending . . . with a family of ten children and no wife' (p. 41), and Martyn fancies an ancestral stud book more than he does the journal of 'Grandmother Joan'.

Contrasts continue in the journal itself. Joan Martyn is no medieval feminist but she regrets having to marry a man almost her father's age. Her masterful mother's vision, in a time of civil war, of an ideal kingdom of well-ruled households makes Joan sigh for something strange and new, but war and the squalor of peasant life appal Joan. The literary visions that absorb her are from Lydgate's Troy or Tristram and Iseult. She wishes not to marry and, according to Jasper Martyn, died unmarried at thirty – one of the first in a series of young women and men to die prematurely in Woolf's fiction. Yet Mistress Martyn's life as she records it is not a sad or even very discontented one. If the times are frightening, Joan has her ardours, and these are described in the most luminous passages of her journal.

The structure of the journal consists of eight parts covering a cycle of seasons that begins and ends with winter. One thing grows naturally out of another, as Woolf told Vaughan it could in a diary narrative. Time too is the recurring context of Joan's thoughts. 'The state of the times' are the first words of the journal, but Joan believes from reading Lydgate that her world is not worse off than it has always been. Her morning prayer is that all 'who have the gift of the present' may use and enjoy it, and she does so through the imagined spatial experience of a moment in time:

> I like to fancy that I am pressing as closely as can be upon the massy wall of time, which is for ever lifting and pulling and letting fresh spaces of life in upon us. May it be mine to taste the moment before it has spread itself over the rest of the world!
>
> (p. 48)

She fears the future of a loveless marriage that will cloud this clear vision, and wishes she could remain innocently young in nature. The itinerant performer of romances, Master Richard, says his visions 'are to be seen by those who look', and one place to look further is in the fairy world of his book (p. 57).

The journal's reflexive regard for writing is its other central subject. At midsummer Joan attempts to describe the year's stopping, then tells herself 'figures are slippery things!' Trying to describe 'without metaphor' her feelings on a pilgrimage to Our Lady of Walsingham, she ends up writing,

> I saw them as solid globes of crystal; enclosing a round ball of coloured earth and air, in which tiny men and women laboured, as beneath the dome of the sky itself. (pp. 57–8)

At the shrine there is another moment followed by the perception of a regenerated world. It is perhaps the only particularly Christian religious experience in Woolf's writings:

> For one moment I submitted myself to her as I have never submitted to man or woman, and bruised my lips on the rough

stone of her garment. White light and heat streamed on my bare head; and when the ecstasy passed the country beneath flew out like a sudden banner unfurled. (p. 59)

In the last pages of Mistress Martyn's journal the theme of continuity emerges. Joan's father envies Joan her diary, but she has grown weary of it, 'for, truly, there is nothing in the pale of my days that needs telling . . . ' (p. 61). If she writes again it will not be of Norfolk but of romantic knights and ladies in strange lands. Nevertheless, the stories she most admires are those not of Master Richard's books but realistic strange tales of an ancient illiterate dame about sights seen, deeds done in her past:

I have always thought that such stories came partly out of the clouds, or why should they stir us more than any thing we can see for ourselves? It is certain that no written book can stand beside them. (p. 62)

Aside from *Orlando*, with which there are interesting affinities, 'The Journal of Mistress Joan Martyn' is the only sustained historical fiction Woolf wrote. (*Flush* is a fantasy of her father's world.) Both her and Forster's short historical writings were confined to essays. Though the journal is an imaginative rendering of a fifteenth-century Norfolk world, with careful traces of stilted syntax, archaic vocabulary ('massy', 'pale'), and medieval observations, much of the interest of the story lies in its depiction of two women, Rosamond Merridew and Joan Martyn, who are feeling their way out of diaries and histories and essays into more self-expressive, aesthetic modes of prose. (Even in the Paston Letters, whose world she would so imaginatively re-create at the opening of *The Common Reader*, Woolf would complain 'there is no writing for writing's sake' in them – *CR1*, p. 21). To write of the moment in and out of time and space, to describe crystal globes of feelings, to make up stories of strange and beautiful everyday life, freely to imagine lives of past, present, and future women as well as men, to share though fiction the gift of the present – all of this is both desired and done in the story.

Earlier in 1906, before any of her datable fiction had been written, Woolf had shown some experimental stories, now lost, to several of the older women who had been her literary confidantes. One of them, Madge Vaughan, apparently found the writings rather bloodless. It was really rather alarming, Woolf then complained to Dickinson, if one had to marry for the sake of one's style *(L,* I 228). To Vaughan she defended herself and her visionary world by reason of age, education, opportunity, and finally, reality:

> My present feeling is that this vague and dream like world, without love, or heart, or passion, or sex, is the world I really care about, and find interesting. For, though they are dreams to you, and I cant express them at all adequately, these things are perfectly real to me. *(L,* I 227)

'The Journal of Mistress Joan Martyn' shows Virginia Woolf trying to write imaginatively of her real dreamworld while striving to make it more human as well.

X

The journal of Miss Virginia Stephen that she kept in Greece and Turkey in 1906 focuses on describing her reactions to places. Reflections on manners or politics are avoided, she writes, because 'travellers deal far too much in such commodities, & my efforts to rid myself of certain preconceptions have taken my attention from the actual facts' of, say, the situation of women in these countries *(EJ,* p. 351). As with her Cornwall diary – and Greece reminds her of Cornwall – the identities of the narrator and her companions are taken for granted and never mentioned. So impersonal is the diary that a sickroom episode is mentioned only as the context for reading and analysing Prosper Mérimée's *Lettres à une inconnue.* (Bedbugs appear once but the dirtiness of Greece remains vague.) Guide-book prose is shunned while the diarist complains about the inadequacy of her own descriptions. She cannot lay her hands on the words she wants because the associations of Greece inhibit her.

> . . . When I consider Mycenae, . . . I might well leave a blank page. Where does the place begin – where stop – what does it not gather on its way? There never was a sight, I think, less manageable; it travels through all the chambers of the brain, wakes odd memories & imaginations; forecasts a remote future; retells a remote past. . . . (p. 331)

The taste of Homer was in her mouth. A vaguely Keatsean procession is imagined and abandoned because we can be sure only of the landscape, not the thoughts and feelings of the ancients. Can Constantinople be made plain on a sheet of paper? 'You must remember . . . ' not only mist and domes but turbaned men, veiled women, Arab horses, yellow dogs, praying crowds. The 'you' point of view here is the diarist as reader back in London, which also partly accounts for the lack of immediacy, of incident and detail (pp. 357–8). Her account of the Parthenon begins this way:

> The ravages are terrible, but in spite of them, the Parthenon is still radiant & young. Its columns spring up like fair round limbs, flushed with health. . . .
> Beautiful statues have a look not seen on living faces, or but rarely, as of serene immutability, here is a type that is enduring as the earth, nay will outlast all tangible things, for such beauty is of an essence that is immortal. And this expression on a face that is otherwise young & supple makes you breathe a higher air. It is like the kiss of dawn. (p. 322)

A little later, it is true, she will call the caryatides of the Erectheum fat maidens smiling at tranquil ease, glorying in their strength, but the description oscillates too often between self-consciousness and conventionality. Here she is again on the Parthenon:

> The yellow pillars – how shall I say? gathered, grouped, radiating there on the rock against the most violent sky, with staring ice blue, & then cinder black; crowds flying as if suppliants (really Greek schoolchildren). The Temple like a ship, so vibrant, taut, sailing, though still all these ages.

But that vivid description is from Woolf's diary a quarter of a century later when she came back to Greece and met at the Parthenon 'my own ghost . . . the girl of 23, with all her life to come . . . ' (*D*, IV 90–1).

The attitude toward foreigners in Woolf's 1906 diary is more critical than in Forster's and Leonard Woolf's writings around this time. A visit to an English estate (supervised by a young woman whom Desmond MacCarthy had fallen in love with and visited in 1902) elicits the view of an Englishman fifty years in Greece, 'how all Greeks lie, how all Greeks are dirty, ignorant, & unstable as water' (p. 339) – a view the diarist accepts. An almost casual, Forster-like murder of one Greek by another near the estate sustains the view, and later the vacant, respectable domestic life of a Greek mother and daughter in a hotel is depressingly described. But there is little or no criticism of the English in the diary. 'The modern town of Athens is like most foreign towns, so a British traveller may summarily conclude, . . . ' she writes without irony (p. 325), and later even the detestable Teutons are praised for their cleanliness.

The English in Greece are laughed at, however, in a story that Woolf quarried out of her visit to Greece.[18] Now entitled 'A Dialogue upon Mount Pentelicus', it recounts a dialogue between English tourists descending Mount Pentelicus that culminates in a vision of Greece quite different from the one she imagined the previous June in England. Woolf's biographer treats the dialogue as straight autobiography, and certainly the principal speakers are easily recognisable, one with his recent third in the Cambridge tripos and the other with his new MA, as Adrian and Thoby Stephen. However, the ironic narrator writes quite differently from the way Woolf does in her Greek diary; there a trip to Mount Pentelicus near Athens is recounted, but without dialogue, and the appearance of an ancient monk carrying brushwood is unremarkable. In the story the opening description of the tourists is reminiscent of the English-abroad stories Forster had been publishing in the *Independent Review*. The travellers deny they are tourists; Germans and French are tourists but the English are Greeks in the classical sense of the term. They meditate on the quarries for the Parthenon while the narrator comments that you must think not just of Plato at his marble casement but of the slaves who died to make it. This mix of modern and classical views is the substance of the story. The English feel the tremendous presences of antiquity around them and curse the barbarous natives who serve them and cannot comprehend their classical English Greek.

The Forsterian atmosphere of this story about the road from Mount Pentelicus increases as the party stop on a green ledge where large plane trees and a murmuring stream remind the narrator of Theocritus. The Greeks arrange themselves pictorially, as only they can, and the narrator introduces the dialogue with this apology:

Since dialogues are even more hard to write than to speak, and it is doubtful whether written dialogues have ever been spoken or spoken dialogues have ever been written, we will only rescue such fragments as concern our story. (*CSF*, p. 65)

Woolf renders the fragments largely through that later favourite narrative technique of hers, indirect discourse. Talk, description, and commentary blend. The dialogue ranges over such subjects as birds, foxes, Greek wine and cheese, Sophocles's metres, the role of women in the Greek state ('that was eloquent!' interjects that narrator) before finally settling on the ideal nature of the classical Greeks. They had rid themselves of the superfluous in their art and philosophy, according to the first speaker; they were ignorant of the right things – charity, religion, domesticity, scholarship and science – and concentrated on the beautiful and good, which was sufficient for them and ought to be for us. For support the speaker needs a quotation from Thomas Love Peacock, for this is a Peacockian not a Platonic dialogue, but he has unfortunately left the book behind. This ideal, the second speaker retorts, is only in the eye of the sentimental beholder who embalms all of beauty and wisdom in the writings, sculpture and landscape of ancient Greece.

A vigorous reply is interrupted as a large monk carrying firewood charges out of the hillside into the midst of this Bloomsbury symposium. It was not in their power, says the narrator, to see his ears as furry and his toes as hoofs – to turn him, that is, into an Edwardian Pan; the power of his gaze creates not panic among the English but a miraculous chain-of-being moment:

Thousands of little creatures moved about in the grass, and the earth turned solid for miles and miles beneath the feet. Nor did the atmosphere begin and end with that day and that horizon, but it stretched like a lucid green river on all sides immeasurably and the world swam in its girdle of eternity. Such was the light in the brown monk's eye, and to think of death or dust or destruction beneath its gaze was like placing a sheet of tissue paper in the fire. For it pierced through much, and went like an arrow drawing a golden chain through ages and races till the shapes of men and women and the sky and the trees rose up on either side of its passage and stretched in a solid and continuous avenue from one end of time to the other. (pp. 67–8)

The English could not have said where they stood in the ring of gold that bound them to Plato, Sophocles and others, and all the monk says is good evening in Greek.

XI

Back in London Woolf wrote to Violet Dickinson, who had been to Greece with the Stephens and was now ill with typhoid fever, that she had three or four silly novels to review.[19] This was written November 20th, the day Thoby Stephen died of the fever, and is part of the 'grim exercise in fiction' that she practised in her letters to Dickinson for nearly a month, pretending for Violet's sake that Thoby was getting better (QB/VW, I 110). The ironies in some of these letters are indeed quite grim. The dead Thoby is 'as well as possible. We aren't anxious'; he 'doesn't sleep very much, but otherwise he is all right'; 'Dear old Thoby is still on his back – but manages to be about as full of life in that position as most people are on their hind legs'; 'he still isn't allowed to move, but next week the feeding stage will begin'; 'Thoby wont get away for Xmas . . . ' (*L*, I 249, 253, 254, 258). Earlier in the month, Maitland's life of Stephen was published and it was while reading reviews of it that Dickinson learned the truth.

Leslie and Thoby Stephen's deaths came together in this way at the end of Woolf's beginnings. For months afterwards she wrote nothing for publication, though Thoby's death brought her first letters to Clive Bell and Lytton Strachey. Maitland himself died in December, and when she heard of it, Woolf wrote to Dickinson, summing up what she had been through emotionally during the past three years, 'O dear – the earth seems swept very bare – and the amount of pain that accumulates for some one to feel grows every day' (*L*, I 270).

8 Roger Fry and the Early Aesthetics of Bloomsbury

I

Apart from continuing associations with the Cambridge Apostles, Roger Fry was not much involved with the Bloomsbury Group as a critic or painter before 1910. Yet in the development of Bloomsbury's critical theory and practice, Fry's Edwardian writing was important. His authority as critic and theorist converted them to post-impressionism, and thus altered their painting and their writing. Fundamental to Bloomsbury's aesthetics is a complex analogy of visual and literary art, and that analogy is assumed in Fry's criticism. By 1906 Roger Fry had established himself in the columns of the *Athenaeum* as one of the leading art critics in England – and then threw over this career for another as a curator in America. (He was the only member of Bloomsbury to have resided in the United States.) Much of Fry's early art reviewing lies outside the literary history of Bloomsbury, yet some of the essays and reviews that he wrote have a place in the extended idea of literature assumed in this literary history.

When near the end of her career Virginia Woolf looked back to the start of Roger Fry's, she found more in his early pieces than simply his critical beginnings. Her description of his *Athenaeum* criticism summarises beautifully the value of his early writing.

Even to the common seer, to coin a counterpart to Dr Johnson's Common Reader . . . these old articles seem curiously alive, alert and on the spot. Further, they are very amusing. This is more remarkable, because writing was often drudgery, and drudgery is apt to leave its trace on the printed page. Nor was Roger Fry a born writer. Compared with Symonds or Pater he was an amateur, doing his best with a medium for which he had no instinctive affection. For that very reason perhaps he was saved some of their temptations. He was not led away to write prose poems, or to make the picture a text for a dissertation upon life. He wrote of pictures as if they were pictures, and nothing else. . . . Often in those early articles he makes shift with terms that belong to the literary critic, or to the musical critic. . . . It was to take him many years and much drudgery before he forged for himself a language that wound itself into the heart of the sensation. And yet in spite of these difficulties, perhaps because of them, it is plain even to the common seer, even in these old articles, that here is someone writing with a pressure of meaning behind him. (*RF*, pp. 105–6)

Woolf's notion of a common seer illuminates Fry's significance in Bloomsbury's literary history. But it should be noticed in her account of his work that the common seer's relation to Fry's art criticism is not just an extension of the common reader's to literary criticism. The differences, Virginia Woolf sees, have to do with style and theory. They bring up again the whole question of the Bloomsbury Group's Victorian sources.

   One of the several difficulties that recurrent claims for Walter Pater's pre-eminent influence on Virginia Woolf and Bloomsbury have to face is Roger Fry. Beyond Bloomsbury, Fry's criticism – early or late – has failed to attract the literary attention that Pater's, Symonds's, or even his contemporary Berenson's has. All figured in Fry's development, but as has been pointed out, Fry's values are really closer to Ruskin's than those of the aesthetes like Pater (Fishman, p. 109). William Morris was also important for Fry, but no English writer on art had a greater influence than Joshua Reynolds, who was also a painter-critic. Had Fry been a prose-poet, moralist, or connoisseur, his criticism would not have had the aesthetic impetus it did on Bloomsbury. Its literary significance comes partly from the aesthetic concentration and energy of Fry's critical practice, as Woolf indicates, and partly from the connections of art with literature in his early writings.

II

Fry began his public career as he ended it, in Cambridge lecturing on art.[1] His *Last Lectures* as the Slade Professor had their origins in a course of lectures he gave at the end of the nineteenth century on Venetian painting. It was while attending these that E. M. Forster thought he detected the coming Bloomsbury undertone of formalism (see *Victorian Bloomsbury*, pp. 242–3). Cambridge phil-osophy, as expounded by McTaggart and Dickinson, helped to insulate his aesthetics from Oxford aestheticism but not Idealism; the later influence of Russell, though not Moore, would do that. In Fry's first and least characteristic book, however, traces of Ruskin, Symonds and Pater have been detected along with Berenson's acknowledged influence (Spalding, *RF*, p. 64). While preparing his Venetian lectures Fry was invited to write a monograph on Bellini for a series that the poet and art historian Laurence Binyon was editing. *Giovanni Bellini* is erudite, but the style is airless, and the aesthetics Idealistic. Bellini is praised for mirroring nature by constructing 'a world of perfectly realised and concrete types, more complete than any one individual' (pp. 29–30). No Bloomsbury undertone sounds there. Writing later to Vanessa Bell, Fry remembered his study as 'all from a deplorably literary point of view' (25.v.26, VB/pKC).

Fry's Cambridge lectures were followed by a London series on Italian art. They were successful enough to be plagiarised, and this may have given Forster an idea for a story (see pp. 56–7). A few of the lectures were published as essays in the new *Monthly Review* edited by Henry Newbolt, whose poetry Leslie Stephen enjoyed declaiming. An old Cliftonian, like Fry, Newbolt asked him to be the review's first contributor. Macmillan then asked Fry to write about art in their *Guide to Italy*, and on the strength of his Bellini book the *Pilot* offered him the post of art critic in 1899. This led next year to his writing for the *Athenaeum* (RF/L, I 179). Fry's critical success was not followed by an artistic one, now or later. A series of woodcuts he did for R. C. Trevelyan's *Polyphemus & Other Poems* in 1901 did nothing to help their meagre sale.

Two of Fry's essays on Giotto for the *Monthly Review* are par-ticularly important in his and Bloomsbury's critical development, and a third on art and religion is an early modern discussion of a subject variously relevant to the Group's history. The Giotto texts, combined, reduced, and annotated, were the earliest writings Fry chose to collect. Their reappearance in *Vision and Design* discloses the measure of Fry's formalism at mid-career. He is still tempted in 1920 'to say of Giotto that he was the greatest artist that ever lived', or at the very least that 'he was the most prodigious phenomenon in the known history of art' (*VD*, p. 122). But his reasons for saying so had changed. In 1901 Fry describes in literary language Giotto's genius at reconciling the everyday life of his time with the universal myths of Christianity. Dante is alluded to, and Fry writes of the privilege Giotto shared with him of seeing life as a consistent, systematic whole (p. 116). Shakespeare and Dickens are also invoked to describe Giotto's ability 'to be at one and the same time in "Ercles" vein and Mrs Gamp's' – an ability that makes him 'the greatest story-teller in line, the supreme epic-painter of the world' (p. 103). Fry calls into question the distinction that Berenson and others had drawn in painting between literary illustration and artistic decoration, arguing that the imaginings of playwright, poet, and painter share much in common, though they are not identical (pp. 110–11). For all the early emphasis on Giotto's literariness, he is still seen as a marvellous translator of literary visions into the language of pictures. Fry emphasises his great skill at drawing and praises – in a favourite term now irremediably dated – his 'plastic' unity of design. But the assumption that Giotto's form depended for its value on the recognition of a dramatic idea was what Fry found so unsatisfactory when collecting his article in *Vision and Design*. He had come to feel by then that further analysis of our aesthetic experience before a picture could 'disentangle our reaction to pure form from our reaction to its implied associated ideas' (p. 92). At the end of his life Fry returned to some of the assumptions in his Giotto essay, to the extent of recognising that painting might have a dramatic or psychological as well as a formal appeal ('Double Nature'). The dialectic of vision and design in Fry's career is reflected in Bloomsbury's literary writings as well.

One reason that the style of Fry's Giotto articles differs from that of his Bellini book is that they began as lectures for common seers. (Only Ruskin, among Fry's nineteenth-century forerunners, lectured extensively on art.) The syntax can still be involved but the tone is more direct, easy, sometimes even humorous. His description of the donor in Italian art sounds rather like Forster:

> The donor having once found his way into pictures of sacred ceremonial remained, but he not infrequently found it difficult to comport himself becomingly amid celestial surroundings; as he became more important, and heaven itself became less so, he asserted himself with unseemly self-assurance, until at last his matter-of-fact countenance, rendered with prosaic fidelity, stares

out at the spectator in contemptuous indifference to the main
action of the composition, the illusion of which it effectually
destroys. (p. 112)

In another *Monthly Review* essay – the first of his writings to be
published in America – Bloomsbury notes are also audible as well
as some Victorian ones. Fry shows his early Idealism in the essay
entitled 'Art and Religion' when he writes 'personally I am
convinced that art only attains its full development when it sets
before itself the aim of presenting an ideal world, not merely
repeating an actual' (p. 126). What concerns Fry, however, is the
relation of religion to art, not vice versa. He expounds the
advantages for art of Christian mythology: its anthropomorphic
conception of the supernatural is so much more human than the
monsters of Egyptian or Buddhist art. (Fry sounds like Macaulay on
Indian literature here.) Speaking 'aesthetically and not doctrinally',
he finds that Christianity's polytheism relies on classical mythology's imperfect idealisation of nature, in sun-god Apollos and
earth-mother Demeters (that so attracted Forster). The pictorial
possibilities of the Mother and Child or the Annunciation are
considerable; still, Fry sees the greatest advantage for art in
Christianity to be one of content not form. Like Greek tragedy,
Christian painting and sculpture exploited a small number of
thoroughly familiar subjects; most importantly, its artists were
compelled to practice not a lyrical but an intensely dramatic art in
which the human figure symbolised spiritual states of mind. What
remains necessary for great religious art, Fry concludes, is not
metaphysical conviction but 'imaginative appropriateness'. Though
this may sound Arnoldian, Fry is perhaps nearer to Ruskin:
religious art could be rescued from the dishonest counterfeits
manufactured today, if the Church became a patron again – but
then maybe not, for 'eternal truths must not be distorted even to
make life beautiful once more' (pp. 137, 139).

Roger Fry had abandoned his Quaker faith under the ministrations of McTaggart. He never lost his invaluable, if at times
credulous, open-mindedness. All his life he was interested in
mind-over-body cures. (In 1899 he published an essay in the
Cornhill describing how a Mohammedan sect in North Africa
performed weekly miracles such as eating glass.) His receptivity as
an art critic was carefully qualified, however. What made Fry 'the

most stimulating of critics', wrote Virginia Woolf, was his 'rare combination – the capacity to accept impressions implicitly and then submit them to the test of reason . . . ' (*RF*, p. 86). That combination was one of Woolf's own critical ideals.

III

Before he became the art critic for the *Athenaeum*, Fry spent the better part of a year writing for the weekly *Pilot*. It had been started, like the *Monthly Review*, in 1900 but focused on ecclesiastical and general politics as well as on literary and scholarly subjects. The aesthetics of Fry's *Pilot* articles remained implicitly Idealistic. Discriminating between appearance and reality for common seers was his principal critical activity in reviews that range from Turner and Ruskin through the English impressionists to Sargent and the Royal Academy. In the very first review he confessed of Sargent's brilliant portrait of a Boer-War general that 'I cannot see the man for the likeness' ('New Gallery', p. 291). (This may have led to the suggestion in his next review that the Royal Academicians might be more usefully employed in South Africa.) Fry repeatedly criticised Sargent's work, and the first time he talked with Vanessa Bell, who had been taught by Sargent, they argued about him (Spalding, *VB*, p. 84). In another *Pilot* review that criticised Sickert and Steer, among others, for their fidelity to nature, Fry distinguishes for the first time between those paintings one looks at and those one looks through. Later Fry felt he had not sufficiently praised these artists (*VD*, pp. 201–2). Turner is praised in one review as an 'imaginative realist', who studied not just natural appearances, as Ruskin or the impressionists did, but saw through them to the reality beneath ('Turner', pp. 482–3). In his last *Pilot* review, Fry admired Ruskin's amazing skill at drawing – he wonders why he did not paint – but again found that Ruskin's veneration of nature and dislike of metaphysics 'prevented his ever realising the importance for aesthetics of the distinction between the real and the actual' ('Ruskin', p. 207). It was a favourite Apostolic distinction.

The *Athenaeum*, the great Victorian weekly which Fry started writing for early in 1901, had been associated with early Victorian Apostles almost from its inception in 1828. During the nineteenth century its contributors included Lamb, Landor, Carlyle, Browning, and Pater. At the end of the decade Clive Bell was one of its reviewers of books and then exhibitions. Apostles returned to write for the *Athenaeum* when it was absorbed by the *Nation* in the 1920s but the title disappeared when the *New Statesman* swallowed the *Nation and Athenaeum* in the 1930s. Back at the turn of the century, the *Athenaeum* was describing itself as a review of literature, science, fine art, music, and drama. Fry's predecessor F. G. Stephens had been its art critic for forty years. The short history of English art criticism can be illustrated in the columns of the *Athenaeum* where a former pre-Raphaelite (Stephens had been one of the Brethren) was followed by a future post-impressionist. In 1901 a new editor of the *Athenaeum* found Stephens's writing bad and paid Fry the literary tribute of bringing him from the *Pilot* as a replacement (Marchand, p. 91). Fry was allowed from two to four columns of some 700 words each in which to review anonymously, and more or less weekly, the leading art exhibitions and publications in England.[2]

Given the drudgery of steady reviewing, it is indeed surprising how much of what Fry wrote remains interesting for the common seer and occasionally for the common reader too. In his first notice, for example, of 'that great national amusement', the annual Royal Academy exhibition, Fry maintains that 'beauty should console us for the chaotic jumble of incongruous sensations which life presents', but he finds little consolation at the Academy ('Royal', p. 601). The sentimentality of much of the art Fry reviewed is described in metaphors of disease; so is the art nouveau of an Italian exhibition, where the critic finds himself painfully asserting with Mr Podsnap that 'other nations do – as they do'. Rembrandt puts the critic's aesthetic theories to the test in another review: all classical canons of proportion and design fail completely to account for the beauty of his 'squalid nudes' (Rembrandt, p. 229). Fry's appreciative yet qualified responses to both Watts and Whistler, the antithetical masters of English painting at this time, demonstrate the range of his own critical sensibility. He brilliantly describes Beardsley – in the only one of his *Athenaeum* reviews Fry reprinted in *Vision and Design* – as possessing

all the stigmata of the religious artist – the love of pure decoration, the patient elaboration and enrichment of surface, the predilection for flat tones and precision of contour, the want of the sense of mass and relief, the extravagant richness of invention.

Yet so affronted is Fry's puritanism by the corruption of Beardsley's drawings that he can see nothing 'funny or amusing or witty' in his art (*VD*, p. 164). Like the rest of Bloomsbury, Fry was both attracted and repelled by the genius of a greater English religious artist, William Blake. Describing some of his paintings (on this occasion for the *Burlington Magazine* in 1904 and reprinted again in *Vision and Design*), he described Blake's advent as that of an 'Assyrian spirit into the vapidly polite circles of eighteenth-century London.' Equally singular was the irony of the forms with which Blake's anti-Hellenic temperament worked:

> It was with the worn-out rags of an effete classical tradition long ago emptied of all meaning, and given over to turgid rhetorical display, that Blake had to piece together the visible garments of his majestic and profound ideas. (*VD*, pp. 149–50)

The ideas on the function of art criticism that Fry himself was working with are shown from time to time in his *Athenaeum* reviews. He wrote of the painter and critic Charles Ricketts's study of the Prado, to take another example, that here art history fulfilled its true end of increasing the understanding of great art. This has to be done for each generation, he went on in a passage quoted by Woolf as expressing the fundamental idea behind Fry's *Athenaeum* notices:

> Pater did it to some extent for the last. Each successive performance of this work of appreciation and interpretation is based upon fuller knowledge and approaches nearer to completeness and finality. (*RF*, p. 106)

The mention of Pater is revealing; even more so is the qualification by Fry that Woolf silently dropped from her quotation. In the review, the sentence referring to Pater continues,

> and Mr Ricketts, with far more intimate knowledge and greater familiarity with his subject, but without all Pater's gift of felicitous poetical surmises, has done it, in part again, for the present generation (Prado, p. 181).

In his own criticism Fry, too, strove to enhance the appreciation and interpretation of art for his generation; his work was also based on a greater knowledge of art than Pater's and lacked, too, his 'felicitous poetical surmises'. But Fry's rhetoric here leaves in some doubt how much this is a matter for regret.

The leading English art critic during the time Fry wrote for the *Athenaeum* was probably D. S. MacColl, who reviewed for the *Spectator* and then the *Saturday Review*. A few years older than Fry, he too was a painter and a curator. Fry admired his criticism of the Academy's notorious Chantry Bequest mismanagement, and praised highly his major work on nineteenth-century art, valuing MacColl's mental agility and literary resourcefulness as a critic, if not always his analogies. There remained a fundamental disagreement between the two critics, however. MacColl was a committed impressionist, and Fry spent almost as much time in the *Athenaeum* reproaching the impressionists as he did the Royal academicians. Fry's objections to impressionism were both artistic and scientific and cannot be adequately understood apart from the aesthetics on which he based his objections. Before discussing them, it is first necessary to mention Fry's response to another, more famous contemporary authority on art who influenced his aesthetics.

The intellectual climate of Bloomsbury can be defined partly by differences. The Group's moral and aesthetic values, their writings and paintings, occupations and dissipations, contrast almost completely with those of Bernard Berenson and his circle at I Tatti. Berenson himself detested what he called 'Gloomsbury', though he was variously associated with it. His stepdaughters became the sisters-in-law of the Stracheys and the Stephens. For a time before the formation of Bloomsbury, Berenson was even something of a mentor of Fry's, though he was but a year older. R. C. Trevelyan was a close friend of both men, and there were Quaker affinities between Fry and Berenson's wife Mary. The details of Berenson's eventual resentment of Fry are unimportant here. (In paranoid old age Berenson wrote, 'the most perfidiously hypocritical of my enemies, like Roger Fry, seldom published anything not inspired by the wish to assert himself against me' – Spalding, *RF*, p. 69.) What remains relevant for Bloomsbury's development is how Fry came under Berenson's sway and then moved away from it.

Fry and almost everyone else at the time were impressed by Berenson's late nineteenth-century studies of Italian painting and his learned perceptiveness in the lucrative game of attribution. Seeking as always to relate aesthetics to science, Fry was attracted by Berenson's use of Morelli's morphology, which he found to be a more systematic, if not scientific, way of determining who painted what in Renaissance Italy. Berenson's explanation of the psychology of aesthetic perception in terms of the tactile values of retinal impressions or the ideated sensations of touch and movement (in *The Florentine Painters* of 1896) assisted Fry to articulate his own responses, which culminated in 'An Essay in Aesthetics' more than a decade later.[3] Berenson's distinction between decoration and illustration (in *The Central Italian Painters* of 1897) also stimulated Fry to think further about the values of form versus content in pictures. It has also been suggested that Berenson's emphasis on 'the material and spiritual significance of forms', contributed to Clive Bell's famous doctrine of significant form (Berenson, p. 85; Spalding, *RF*, p. 68).

By 1902, according to Leo Stein, Berenson, considered Fry to be 'the only man writing decent criticism in England chiefly because he has managed to get my ideas straight instead of mangling them as all the rest . . . do'. Leo, the brother of Gertrude and a formidable aesthetician himself, agreed (Samuels, *Connoisseur*, p. 382). There was more to Fry's criticism than that, but the compliment beneath the conceit suggests how Fry had absorbed Berenson's work. In 1901 he reviewed a collection of Berenson's essays, agreeing with him that attributions stimulated and liberated aesthetic perceptions. (Mary Berenson wrote to say how pleased Bernard was, and how envious of Fry's literary style – Samuels, *Connoisseur*, p. 372). Fry continued to review Berenson in the *Athenaeum* and then in the *Burlington Magazine*, which they both had helped to found as the first serious art periodical in England. But eventually the magazine became a cause of dissension between them, as Berenson unfairly blamed Fry for what he took to be hostile articles in it.

Though Fry's notices of Berenson remained very favourable, they began to show the differences in critical temperament between the two men. Reviewing a revised edition of Berenson's study of Lotto, for instance, Fry found in it the culmination of Morelli's influence, which Berenson had gone beyond; he sought now for psychological causes of the artist's formal peculiarities, and Fry thought this took him beyond aesthetic values. In 1904 Fry belatedly devoted a two-part review to Berenson's magnum opus, *The Drawings of the Florentine Painters*. He felt helpless as a critic before the intricate questions Berenson raised, though he still managed to put forth a few of his own about the attributions. Most revealing for Fry's own style as a critic is the evaluation of Berenson's:

> Mr. Berenson writes vigorously and sometimes picturesquely, using similes which always arrest the attention, though the shock is not always agreeable. He writes, we think, with his mind fixed too exclusively upon the reader, whom he encourages with condescension, informs demonstratively, or, if necessary, compels into submissive agreement. . . . Affectations result from this attitude – useless inversions, conceits, and elaborate periphrases. . . . One is charmed, amazed, indignant, irritated, by turns, but boredom or a mere sleepy acquiescence is out of the question. ('Drawings', p. 771)

Fry focused his criticism more on the work of art than the reader. His prose from the *Athenaeum* onward is plainer, livelier, less self-conscious than Berenson's. Fry is writing as a critic and painter, not a connoisseur and an expert on the authenticity of old pictures. His passion for post-impressionism largely replaced his concern with Renaissance art, whereas Berenson was only mildly interested in modern painting. In many of these respects it is apparent that Berenson, far more than Fry, was Pater's successor – as Fry thought Berenson might be after reading Pater in 1898 (*L*, I 171–2).

IV

The 'pressure of meaning', that Virginia Woolf observed behind Roger Fry's *Athenaeum* criticism came from an emerging aesthetics that he would eventually articulate in 'An Essay in Aesthetics' for Desmond MacCarthy's *New Quarterly* in 1909. Fry's early responses to the old masters, the descriptions of them by Ruskin, Pater, and Symonds, as well as Berenson's psychology of aesthetic perception and his own Cambridge Idealism and scientific training all contributed to the process. This development can be seen in Fry's various criticisms of impressionism, which he recognised to be 'the only vital art of the day' (*VD*, p. 201) and whose philosophy he himself had once put forward at Cambridge (see *Victorian Bloomsbury*, p. 254). But when he matured, Fry had to contend with impressionism as a critic and a painter. The critical effort to formulate his dissatisfaction along with the discovery of Cézanne led to the post-impressionist aesthetics so important in the history of Bloomsbury. The Idealism implicit in Fry's objections to impressionism has been mentioned; he wanted painting to represent the reality behind the appearances of actuality. As an early Edwardian critic he was not content with the Paterian subjectivity of knowing one's impression as it really is.

In 1903 Gerald Duckworth's company published the first authoritative study of impressionism in English, Camille Mauclair's *The French Impressionists*. Other Duckworth publications on art soon followed, including Chesterton on Watts and Mauclair again on Rodin. For Gerald's half-sister Vanessa, Mauclair on impressionism was a revelation '̇that there was something besides the lovely quality of old paint to be aimed at, something fundamental and permanent and as discoverable now as in any other age' (Spalding, *VB*, p. 37). Clive Bell had read the book at Cambridge and been impressed (Edel, p. 102). For Roger Fry in the *Athenaeum*, however, the book (which he reviewed in translation and later again in the original) talked nonsense about the scientific dissociation of tones instead of concentrating on the impressionists' aesthetic merit. As in his early *Pilot* reviews, Fry complained about impressionism's limited adherence to actuality, to the truth of appearance, while ignoring all other ideals. Yet the book had an important moral for Fry, which was that all sincere modern art lay outside the current art establishment. Later reviewing an exhibition at the New English Art Club, Fry observed that while all the older painters were impressionists analysing nature 'into the component parts not of the thing seen but the appearance', the younger men such as Augustus John were going back to earlier traditions, 'penetrating through values to their causes in actual form and structure'. The review was quoted at length by Woolf in her biography (*RF*, pp. 114–15).

Fry also criticised impressionism in the one piece he wrote for his Cambridge friends' *Independent Review*. (Fry would probably have written more for it, had he not been the art critic of the *Athenaeum*.) Contradicting the Royal Academy's dismissal of impressionist art as 'mere technique', Fry argues this technique is just where these painters conspicuously fail. Invoking a distinction he had used earlier, Fry suggests their work can be enjoyed only by looking through the surface images of their canvasses to the objects themselves. He went on to make some interesting criticisms of machine-made art that point backwards to Morris and forwards to the Omega Workshops, but it was on the issue of the impressionists' technique that Fry was criticised from another quarter of Bloomsbury. One of the French impressionists that Fry had been noticing with approval in the *Athenaeum,* was Lytton Strachey's brother-in-law Simon Bussy. Bussy answered Fry in the *Independent Review* by pointing out the mere technique of painters like Rembrandt or Turner was not all that good, and besides, painting was not an imitation of nature but an attempt to show the invisible through the visible. Lytton wrote to his sister Dorothy Bussy that he thought the reply a thorough set-down of Fry (20.v.05, LS/pP). Later, however, and with his characteristic generosity of appreciation, Fry wrote to Bussy offering 'enthusiastic homage' to one of his paintings (*L,* I 309).

But it was the art of James McNeill Whistler that brought out most clearly Fry's earlier Edwardian objections to impressionism. In the history of English art criticism, Whistler's aesthetics and polemics make him the *fin-de-siècle* figure who was perhaps closest to Bloomsbury – but this proximity also serves to illustrate the clear differences between turn-of-the-century aestheticism and the post-impressionism of Bloomsbury a decade later. Whistler died in July 1903. In his *Athenaeum* obituary, Fry valued Whistler's art above his polemics; he approved of Whistler's attack on sentimental illustration in painting, but could not accept

> the astounding theory, enunciated in his 'Ten o'Clock', that pictorial art consists in the making of agreeable patterns, without taking account of the meaning for the imagination of the objects represented by them – that, indeed, the recognition of the objects was not part of the game. The forms presented were to have no meaning beyond their pure sensual quality. . . . As a working theory for an artist of extraordinary gifts it was unfortunate, since it cut away at a blow all those methods of appeal which depend on our complex relations to human beings and nature; it destroyed the humanity of art. ('Whistler', p. 133)

These, of course, are the kinds of objections that would be raised against Roger Fry and Clive Bell's aesthetics of significant form in 1914. And Fry himself, reviewing a book on Turner later in 1903, had agreed that Ruskin's analysis was aesthetically irrelevant because 'it is on the intrinsic quality of the artistic form, and not on its content, that we must fix our attention' (RF/Armstrong, p. 587).

Whistler's aesthetics may have made Fry appreciate Ruskin's point of view more.

Fry returned to Whistler in a 1905 *Quarterly Review* essay that compared him with G. F. Watts, who had died the year before. It is one of the stranger essays in the history of Bloomsbury – one which Fry did not choose to reprint. At a time when Vanessa Bell and even Virginia Woolf were discovering Whistler and ridding themselves of their Victorian aesthetic heritage represented by Watts (he had painted Leslie Stephen and inspired Julia Margaret Cameron's photographs), Fry was exalting him over Whistler. After the Stephen sisters attended an exhibition of Whistler's work in February 1905, Virginia acclaimed him 'a perfect artist' in her diary: 'Oh Lord, the lucid colour – the harmony – the perfect scheme. This is what matters in life' (*EJ*, pp. 241–2). Fry, in his April article, admitted that Whistler was more original, but Watts was a painter in the grand style. Though he subordinated his intellect to his emotions, though his allegories were sometimes hackneyed and his mysticism misty, it was unfair to say Watts's pictures were literary rather than painterly. 'He was surrounded by adulation enough to have killed a dozen ordinary geniuses', but he survived because, despite his idealism, he trusted the physical, the instinctual ('Watts and Whistler', pp. 617–18). (What fun Woolf would have with the adulation of Watts later in *Freshwater*.) Whistler, by contrast, almost sank his genius in taste – and taste, Fry writes Miltonically 'is, like asceticism, a negative and cloistered virtue . . . ' (p. 613). No artist shrank more from life than Whistler did. He was the insolent prophet of the religion of beauty:

> The world laughed; and the terrible irony of his situation lay in the fact that, on the main issue, a stupidly emotional world was right and the prophet wrong. For beauty cannot exist by itself; cut off from life and human realities it withers. . . . Whistler, like Oscar Wilde – who was in some ways a similar product of the same moment in modern life – wanted beauty to be self-contained and self-sufficing. (p. 609)

Both aesthetes were heroic in their insolence but Wilde learned humility, Whistler never. Fry goes so far in his criticism of Whistler as to find a gulf separating him from the great French impressionists, who 'nod recognition to Watts behind Whistler's back, for they are all interested in life, ironically, scientifically, or lyrically, as their temperaments incline'. The impressionists may protest that Watts was a *littérateur* but so are they for Fry, who finds Zola in Degas's paintings and Maupassant in Renoir's (p. 614).

It may be tempting to interpret Fry's comparison of Whistler and Watts as an illustration of the deviousness with which influences are acknowledged. Fry and Bloomsbury certainly owe much more to Whistler than Watts. Clive Bell's polemical style in *Art*, for example, has affinities with Whistler's in *The Gentle Art of Making Enemies*. Yet the criticism Fry is making defines quite clearly the difference between Whistler's aestheticism and Bloomsbury's. For the Group, beauty was extremely valuable, and aesthetic emotion disinterested as well, but these were never regarded as self-sufficing.

V

'I can't go on with the *Athenaeum*', Fry wrote to Mary Berenson in October 1904; 'these weekly snippets are ruining my mental digestion' (*L*, I 224). It was also interfering with his painting (Spalding, *RF*, p. 78). But he went on for another year before turning into a curator. One of his last reviews commented on a still life and a landscape by Cézanne. Fry had been sceptical about his genius yet these pictures had power, 'though the artist's appeal is limited, and touches none of the finer issues of the imaginative life . . . ' ('New Gallery', p. 56). Fry soon began to change his mind about Cézanne's limitations, but he never altered his opinion of the *Discourses* of Sir Joshua Reynolds that he had been writing about – perhaps as an aid to intellectual digestion – for an edition published in 1905. Fry, in a lecture at the end of his career, said that his highest ambition had been to carry on Reynolds's work 'in his spirit by bringing it into line with the artistic situation of our own day' (*FFBA*, p. 153).

Roger Fry on Joshua Reynolds is another significant text for the understanding of Bloomsbury's critical origins. It is, to begin with, a Cambridge-influenced text. Fry acknowledges the help of his Apostle brothers: the late Theodore Llewelyn Davies, to whom the edition is dedicated; Bertrand Russell, for help in philosophical matters (Fry cites his 'The Study of Mathematics'); and the biologist William Bateson for scientific advice. In aesthetics, Fry acknowledged George Santayana's 'admirable' *The Sense of Beauty* (1896), which attempted to base the study of art on Idealist psychology rather than on ethics or metaphysics. More importantly, Fry's reinterpretation of Reynolds's *Discourses* shows the eighteenth-century affinities of Bloomsbury that are sometimes forgotten in accounts of their Victorian and Romantic origins or in theories that view English literary modernism as entirely as post-romantic. Lytton Strachey's enthusiasm for the age of enlightenment is well known, but Clive Bell also admired neo-classic civilisation; E. M. Forster was also devoted to Gibbon and Voltaire, and then there is Virginia Woolf with her Sternean narrators and Johnsonian common readers. Fry as a critic, considered himself on the side of the classicists. His excitement over Cézanne came when he discovered the classical form of his painting; his dislike of academy art, as well as that of the impressionists, was partly an aversion to their romantic content.

After more than a century of criticism by Blake, Hazlitt, Ruskin, and others, Reynolds's *Discourses* were found by Fry to contain 'what is, perhaps, the truest account of the functions of art criticism that has ever been framed' ('Reynolds', p. 139). Among the Bloomsbury writers there was a disposition to connect critical theory with creative practice, and what Fry found congenial in Reynolds's lectures to students at the Royal Academy was, first of all, the applied aesthetics of a painter who followed the grand style of the old masters. As a latter-day painter-critic, Fry hoped to reconcile Reynolds's ideas and values with modern ones. He esteemed Reynolds's genially reasonable style, eclectic sympathies, and generosity of character. He felt the first president of that bastion of the establishment the Royal Academy ought to be revere 'by all who think that art is more than a relaxation from the serious cares of the money market' because Reynolds had criticised the subjectivity of taste proclaimed by Philistines (pp. 177, 348).

Fry's commentary on Reynolds is not simply a sympathetic appreciation. Despite Sir Joshua's restricted notions of beauty and unity in painting and his Humpty-Dumpty use of the word 'nature', Fry recognised in the *Discourses* a belief in the logic of sensations and emotions which he thought was still the basis for all aesthetics and criticism, though it was difficult to define (p. 139). That basis remains as vague in Fry's commentary as it is in Reynolds's lectures. For Reynolds, the proper function of art was to appeal through the senses to the imagination. In his commentary, Fry observed that as the discourses proceeded, Reynolds relied more on art's conformity to human rather than to external nature

(p. 347). Yet Fry rejected romantic inspiration as a proper source of art. He wrote in his introduction that after the bankruptcy of tradition in the nineteenth century, followed by an art of revolt that ended in the Whistlerian cult of genius, it was time to listen again to Reynolds – to seek some aesthetic principles beyond enthusiastic romantics and contemptuous sceptics (pp. xx–xxi). For Fry, Reynolds was a preparation, along with Berenson, Santayana, and Tolstoy (whom he may not yet have read) for an aesthetics beyond impressionism.

Later Fry went so far as to claim that Reynolds had been an advocate 'of plastic rather than literary art' (*FFBA*, p. 153). Yet his edition did bring out a feature of Reynolds's eighteenth-century aesthetics that was of great importance for his own and Bloomsbury's, and this was the unity, or at least the interrelation, of the arts. Reynolds's ruling idea in the *Discourses* was that success in art depended upon the industry of the artist's mind rather than his hands. His favourite aesthetic analogue for painting is the greater art of poetry. 'A Painter must compensate the natural deficiencies of his Art', he wrote; 'he has but one sentence to utter, but one moment to exhibit' (Reynolds, p. 76.). The Bloomsbury painters came to think of fiction, if not poetry, as an impurer art that tried in its temporal way to exhibit the timeless moments of visual art as best it could. Yet in his commentary Fry rather extends Reynolds's poetic comparisons by suggesting with Aristotle that painting like poetry was more philosophical than history (p. 47). Fry nevertheless thought Reynolds had left the musical element out of painting, and he tried to supply it indirectly with an epigraph that fits both Reynolds's ruling idea and his own still somewhat mentalistic view of art. Reynolds's last lecture ended with a paean to the divine Michelangelo. At the head of Fry's edition of the *Discourses* are some words of Michelangelo's that Fry may have preferred to Pater's more famous dictum about all art aspiring to the condition of music: 'Finally, good painting is a music and a melody which intellect only can appreciate, and that with difficulty.'

VI

What Vanessa Bell and her Friday Club, founded the same year as Fry published his edition of the *Discourses*, might have thought of his revival of Reynolds is unrecorded, but on the subject of impressionism there was certainly discussion. Virginia Woolf described a meeting of the committee to form the Friday Club as divided: one half 'shriek Whistler and French impressionists, and the other are stalwart British' (*L*, I 201). How many in Bloomsbury were reading what Berenson considered the only decent art criticism of art in England is also a question. Fry's friend Desmond MacCarthy probably was. MacCarthy gave a paper to the Friday Club early in 1906 that sparked a debate, Strachey wrote to Leonard Woolf, between adherents of Fry and less persuasive defenders of impressionism (2.ii.06, LS/pNY). (Woolf had been sent a copy of Fry's Reynolds by R. C. Trevelyan.) And Thoby Stephen read a paper to the club on decadence in modern art that quite likely developed out of his review of *Euphrosyne* (see pp. 73–4). Impressionism was also being discussed by the Apostles. Keynes wrote to Strachey how only he and Harry Norton voted for impressionist pictures in one of their discussions (31.v.06, JMK/pKC).

It was possibly around 1906 that Strachey also wrote an undated Apostle paper entitled 'Ought Art To Be Always Beautiful?' Strachey mediated between the fallacies of the impressionists who argued that representation was the important thing about art, not what was represented, and those of the classical school who maintained that art should be concerned with objects beautiful in themselves. The paper begins with a dream in which Strachey's great aunt criticises the ugliness of Degas's subjects; he attempts a defence but the dream ends as he begins to wonder if she was not really E. M. Forster in thin disguise! Forster does not reappear in the paper as Strachey goes on to argue that the impressionists' pictures are merely decorative forms, while the classical artists represent much that is not simply beautiful. The value of all great painting, music (the C Minor Symphony is mentioned again among the greatest works), and literature depends, he concludes, on the interest of their objects; beauty alone is not enough. The examples are mostly literary; Watts is mentioned but not Reynolds or Whistler (pST).

Strachey was never a formalist nor much of an art critic; however, he understood some of the issues involved. Vanessa Bell wrote to her sister that Strachey wanted the Friday Club to do for art what Granville Barker had done for drama, and she asked what that was (16.iv.06, VB/pNY). The connection is a suggestive one, pointing forward to what Fry and his Bloomsbury friends were to do. Even in the Group's earlier Edwardian years, however, there were some noticeable resemblances between the targets of MacCarthy's *Speaker* criticism and Fry's in the *Athenaeum*. The similarities between the technically elaborate Royal Academy exhibitions and the actor-manager extravaganzas have already been mentioned (see pp. 107–8). Neither MacCarthy nor Fry greatly admired the turn-of-the-century art of Wilde or Whistler. But the incipient Idealism of Fry's early critical theory was not philosophically grounded in McTaggart or Dickinson the way MacCarthy's was in Moore's ethics. It was almost a decade later that the relevance of *Principia Ethica* for Bloomsbury's aesthetics appeared in Clive Bell's *Art*.

While the older Fry was establishing himself as a critic, Bell in his twenties was desultorily studying history as a postgraduate student, first in London and then for a year in Paris, where he discovered his real vocation. 'Paris 1904' is the title of a Memoir Club paper he wrote about that year. Along with other memoirs by Duncan Grant of his years in Paris in 1906 and 1907, it gives a further glimpse of the aesthetic development that was so momentous for Bloomsbury's literary history. Grant, who had become a member of the Friday Club late in 1905, went to study in Paris, after a visionary voice had told him to go into the world and see what the impressionists were doing. His memoirs are not that pertinent to Bloomsbury's literary history, although there are various allusions in them to Balzac, Austen, Thackeray, Musset, Hardy, Proust – and Wyndham Lewis; Grant's café breakfasts with Lewis anticipate somewhat Bloomsbury's later encounters with the Enemy (DG/pHG).

In the Memoir Club recollections that Clive Bell gathered together in *Old Friends*, his Paris memoirs follow the Bloomsbury ones. Bell recalls in 'Paris 1904' that two painters he met that year were as influential on him as the Cambridge friends he had been describing in earlier chapters. Neither painter was French; Bell did not become friends with any French artists until after the post-impressionist exhibitions, by which time he had also mastered their language. It was the Canadian J. W. Morrice, in particular, but also the Irish Roderick O'Conor, and more briefly the English Gerald Kelly, who introduced Bell to the Paris of the impressionists. Bell, unlike Fry, had been passionately attracted to their work even before coming to Paris. Morrice was an excellent second-generation impressionist, Bell thought, and a remarkable character who taught him to enjoy Paris and understand pictures better. He advised Bell to look at Matisse's work, for example. (This recollection occasions a scornful digression by Bell on Berenson's poor taste in modern art.) Morrice's pleasure in beauty, which he relished in painting and music as well as in the sights and sounds of Paris, encouraged and developed Bell's own considerable capacities for enjoyment – and had an effect on Bloomsbury's linking the enjoyment with the creation of art. O'Conor, a grimmer, less Bohemian figure, was widely-read in French literature. His paintings were austere but incompletely realised; still, he had been a close friend of Gauguin's and was a follower of Cézanne. Through O'Conor and Morrice, Bell came in contact with post-impressionism before Fry or the rest of Bloomsbury. When the Stephens visited him on their way back from Italy in the Spring of 1904, however, the only studios they visited were Rodin's and Kelly's; but they met the formidable O'Conor, who was frightened by Virginia, according to Bell.

Gerald Kelly, a Cambridge man who knew a lot of English literature, could talk a little philosophy, became a successful portrait painter, and was 'about the best president the Royal Academy has given itself since Sir Joshua Reynolds', according to Bell (*OF*, p. 142). Under Kelly's guidance, Bell moved to Montparnasse, visited Montmarte, and encountered the artist exiles, writers and painters, who met in the *Chat Blanc* café. The only French artist of renown who occasionally came there was the patronising Rodin. But among the writers were Somerset Maugham, whom Bell did not remember meeting, and Arnold Bennett, whom he did. Bennett's consequence for Bloomsbury is considerable, and Bell's rather contemptuous recollections of encounters with him describe the earliest relations between Bloomsbury and the writer that Virginia Woolf would find representative of materialistic Edwardian novelists. In Bell's 1918 preface to *Pot-Boilers*, he says Bennett's critical journalism in *Books and Persons* was so much more readable that he almost gave up the project of reprinting his own. He persevered, nevertheless, because of the provincial in-discrimination that had led Bennett to praise Wells, Galsworthy, and George Moore (*PB*, pp. 1–3, 8–14). Bell and his friends were rather fond, he says in 'Paris 1904', of this ridiculous little man whom they would meet in his gimcrack flat and then go out to eat. They thought nothing of his writing, and Bell – comparing him with Eliot's lowly, self-assured clerk in *The Waste Land* – adds charac-teristically, 'I do not think much of it now' (p. 145). For his part, Arnold Bennett rather liked Clive Bell in Paris (Edel, p. 104).

Bennett's Parisian years also prepared him to be one of the very few English writers capable of appreciating post-impressionism, which makes Virginia Woolf's attack on him more complicated than it is sometimes seen to be.

Clive Bell figures discreetly in the unlikely recollections of another writer and English exile in Paris. Among Kelly's Cambridge friends, and soon to be his brother-in-law, was the notorious Aleister Crowley. Bell recalled dining with him at an expensive restaurant and then daringly visiting – Crowley thought at the risk of their lives – a workingman's eating-house. In his recollections, Crowley disguised all his acquaintances with letters of the alphabet, but a note in his *Confessions* identifies the man labelled 'I' as Heward Bell. (Heward was the third of Clive's given names.) Crowley writes:

> There also did he meet the well-known ethicist, I – fair as a boy, with boy's gold locks curling about his Grecian head; I – the pure and subtle-minded student, whose lively humour and sparkling sarcasm were as froth upon the deep and terrible waters of his polished irony. It was a pity that he drank. (pp. 360, 362)

The description of his hair tallies with other accounts of the young Bell, and the drinking may have been part of the alcoholic Morrice's influence at the time. But the most interesting aspect of the description is the classification of Bell as an 'ethicist'. He could hardly be called a moralist in that company, but was he spreading the gospel of *Principia Ethica*, published the previous autumn, to his Cambridge acquaintances in Paris? As early as 1904, perhaps, Clive Bell was beginning to bring Cambridge ethics and French art together in a way that would fundamentally affect Bloomsbury's aesthetics.

Part Two
Later Edwardian

Introduction

During what Virginia Woolf called the second chapter of Old Bloomsbury, E. M. Forster published three novels, the last of which established him as a major Edwardian writer. Lytton Strachey became Bloomsbury's most widely read critic through his anonymous reviews for the *Spectator*. Woolf herself was beginning to be noticed as a writer in both her unsigned *Times Literary Supplement* reviews and the signed ones she contributed, for a year, to the *Cornhill*. Clive Bell began to practise criticism in literary reviews for the prestigious *Athenaeum*. Desmond MacCarthy started a journal that would publish the best Edwardian essays of Strachey and Roger Fry. Fry left the Metropolitan Museum to become a full-time critic and painter, and J. M. Keynes left the India Office to teach and write economics at Cambridge. In Ceylon, Leonard Woolf became the youngest Assistant Government Agent on the island with responsibility for governing 100,000 people.

The bare outlines of these later Edwardian Bloomsbury careers do not convey the involved, sometimes intense, personal relations that were developing among the Stephen sisters, Strachey, Bell, and even Leonard Woolf. Not all of the Bloomsbury Group formed around Vanessa and Virginia after their brother's death, however. Another network of friendships contributing to the Group's development was beginning with Desmond and Mary MacCarthy, who were married in July 1906. (Mary's uncle had married Anny Thackeray Ritchie, who was thus Aunt Anny to both her and Virginia.) Desmond moved in many circles, and during Bloomsbury's later Edwardian years the MacCarthys were visited by a group of contributors to the *New Quarterly*, which Desmond began editing with the support of a wealthy, eccentric Cambridge friend. Strachey was to help with the quarterly, and later MacCarthy's close friend G. E. Moore edited an issue. A number of the other contributors such as Fry, Keynes, Dickinson, and Russell were also Apostles. MacCarthy also knew writers as diverse as James, Hardy, Beerbohm, Shaw, Wells, Belloc, and Baring, a number of whom were to be quite antipathetic to Bloomsbury's developing outlook.

The more central Bloomsbury marriage of Vanessa and Clive Bell took place in February 1907. They settled in Gordon Square, while Virginia and Adrian moved over to Fitzroy Square, where later in the year they began again the Thursday evenings at home Thoby had started two years before. Julian Bell's birth in 1908 intensified Clive's relationship with Virginia. The consequences of their flirtation were painful, complex, and long-lasting. 'My affair with Clive and Nessa . . . ', Virginia Woolf wrote in 1925, 'for some reason that turned more of a knife in me than anything else has ever done' (*L*, III 172). Her description of it as an affair with both Clive and Vanessa testifies to the emotional importance of her relations with her sister as well as her brother-in-law. Indeed, Vanessa thought Virginia's letters to her would read like love letters if they were published without replies (25.viii.08, VB/pNY). Something of the profound significance of Vanessa for her sister's writing at this time can also be seen in the family biography of her that Virginia wrote. Clive Bell's role in Bloomsbury is often underrated by those who view him primarily through Virginia's writings. In 1906, for example, she says she told him, 'You are all sensitive appreciations, Mr Bell; you have no character. You want bottom' (*L*, I 247). Bell's considerable importance for her writing appears in her letters, sometimes in their competing reviews, in the biography of Vanessa, in an unpublished dialogue with Clive, and in the unfinished autobiographical sketch of him by her. Clive wrote verse for Virginia, appreciated her skills as a reviewer, and – most importantly – gave her perceptive, encouraging criticism of the novel that she was beginning. After the publication of *The Voyage Out* (to be discussed in *Georgian Bloomsbury*), Virginia wrote to him 'you were the first person who ever thought I'd write well' (*L*, II 167).

Lytton Strachey's relationships with the Stephen sisters, Bell, Woolf, and Sydney-Turner all helped deepen the friendships of Bloomsbury after Thoby's death. Vanessa told Carrington after Strachey's own death how she had loved him 'ever since the time Thoby died & he came & was an inexpressible help & made me think of the things most worth thinking of' (25.i.32, VB/pT). Strachey also extended Bloomsbury's relations through his love for his cousin Duncan Grant, whom he helped bring into Bloomsbury. The Stephens and Bells met Grant when he was studying art in Paris in 1907. (They also met Arnold Bennett, according to his journal, and he was impressed how well Leslie Stephen's children bore the weight of their distinguished name.) The addition of another painter to the Group was welcome. Then in 1908, Grant fell in love with Keynes, who now became more involved with Bloomsbury. Clive's marriage led to occasional difficulties with Lytton, and his 'affair' with Virginia led to Lytton's remarkable proposal of marriage in February 1909, which she accepted for a day to the consternation and subsequent relief of them both. Vanessa had written to her husband the year before that she expected her sister to marry Lytton or at least be engaged to him within two years (29.xi.1908, VB/pKC). The subject of marriage with Virginia was discussed in the correspondence of Strachey and Leonard Woolf, who had met the Stephen sisters at Cambridge and visited them again in London before leaving for Ceylon. Just before Lytton's proposal Leonard wrote to him asking 'Do you think Virginia would have me?' He offered to take the next boat home if she would, but thought when he arrived he would probably just go and talk with Strachey instead. Lytton's response was to wonder why he had never been in love with Leonard (*L*, p. 145). Leonard's ambivalence on the subject changed in his letters after Lytton proposed to Virginia. In August Lytton was insisting that Leonard must marry her – though Virginia might go off at any minute with Duncan Grant perhaps. Leonard replied that, were it not for complications of virginity, marriage, and money, he would wire her a proposal (*L*, pp. 149–50). (Strachey's speculation about Duncan and Virginia was not a bad guess – only the sister and the time were wrong. Duncan, who was in love with Adrian for years, appears to have been attracted to all the Stephens; one of the various definitions of Bloomsbury is that of a group of women and men who were all in love with Duncan Grant.)

Strachey's influence on later Edwardian Bloomsbury also changed the nature of their manners. In a letter congratulating Clive Bell on his engagement, he formally proposed that the Group should now address one another by their Christian names. 'Henceforth between friends manners were to depend on feelings rather than conventions', Bell recalled (*OF*, p. 31). Virginia Woolf illustrated, for the Memoir Club, the difference between Bloomsbury's earlier monastic chapter and the later very different one in a famous scene. The age of Augustus John was beginning, as she sat with her sister in Gordon Square. Strachey entered, pointed to a stain on Vanessa's dress, and asked if it was semen.

With that one word all barriers of reticence and reserve went down. A flood of the sacred fluid seemed to overwhelm us. Sex permeated our conversation. The word bugger was never far from our lips. We discussed copulation with the same excitement and openness that we had discussed the nature of good.

(*MB*, pp. 195–6)

The changes in Bloomsbury's modes of address, topics of discussion, and vocabularies mark a shift in modern English literary sensibility that most published writing did not catch up with for more than half a century. One literary result of this shift in Bloomsbury was Strachey's showing his erotic verse to Vanessa and Virginia too, who sent her compliments and 'green blushes' (*L*, I 365). Private or unpublishable writings such as poems, plays, burlesques of one kind or another, and even a novel – Forster's *Maurice* – would circulate in Bloomsbury over the years.

Personal and literary relations in later Edwardian Bloomsbury were further intertwined through the Play-Reading Society that Clive Bell started late in 1907. Members included Saxon, Vanessa, Adrian, Lytton, and Virginia, according to the records kept by Clive (CB/pKC). They began with Restoration drama, namely Vanbrugh's *The Relapse, or Virtue in Danger*, because, as Lytton wrote to Leonard, 'Vanessa said that we'd better begin with the most indecent thing we could, so as to get it settled' (6.ii.08, LS/pNY). Over the next year, the Society read dramatic works by Ibsen, Jonson, Milton (*Samson Agonistes* followed by *Comus*), Browning, Dryden (three plays), Congreve (two), Swinburne, and Shakespeare. Then the readings lapsed for five years, and another form of literary entertainment began briefly. Bloomsbury Group members and their friends started a letter game early in 1909, that may have resulted from the Play-Reading Society. There is a Restoration air about some of the fictive correspondents' names: Strachey's was Vane Hatherley, and Virginia's Elinor Hadyng. The game has been described by Quentin Bell as an 'epistolary *bal masqué* in which the disguises served only to embolden the participants' (*VW*, I 142). Under the cover of fictitious letters, for instance, Lytton suspiciously probed Virginia and Clive's relationship. The letters of the game are more interesting as biographical than literary texts, but the game itself reveals the Group's cohesion and literary interests at this time and also their evolving sexual mores.

Bloomsbury's changing personal relations and sexual attitudes are reflected in several short or fragmentary diaries of the Group that were written around 1909. Brief entries in a 1910 diary of Lytton Strachey mention talking bawdy with Virginia and later record Bell's complaint about the 'collective affectation and dullness of set', with which Strachey did not agree (*LSH*, p. 120). In her 'Old Bloomsbury' Memoir Club paper, Virginia quoted from a 1909 diary, now apparently lost, to describe a visit to James Strachey's rooms in Cambridge, where she met Rupert Brooke among other people. The scene was different from the discussions of Moore's ethics that used to take place in earlier Edwardian Bloomsbury – and by now she had admiringly read Moore herself. She liked the atmosphere but found the company unsympathetic; they had nothing to say to each other and she became aware 'that not only my remarks but my presence was criticised. They wished for truth and doubted if I could speak it or be it.' Bloomsbury, in losing its monastic character, had become associated with a society of buggers, she realised, and while it had certain relaxing advantages if you were a woman, she could not show off; something always had to be suppressed. It was a very different world from the 'lustre and illusion' of Lady Ottoline Morrell's rooms in London, which Woolf described on the next page of her diary (*MB*, pp. 193–5). Ottoline began to be associated with Bloomsbury around this time, and is alluded to in the letter game. Invited to one of her parties with anyone she liked, Virginia took along Rupert Brooke (*MB*, p. 199). Vanessa facetiously told Lytton that Ottoline was drawing her sister into 'Sapphist circles' (30.v.09, LS/pBL). Virginia's acquaintance with Rupert indicates the beginning of Bloomsbury's association with another Cambridge circle forming around Brooke, who became an Apostle in 1908. Virginia would later dub them the Neo-Pagans. Older Bloomsbury Apostles such as Maynard Keynes and Lytton Strachey were involved to some extent through their brothers. The literary significance of the group for Bloomsbury was negligible, but a few enduring friendships were begun.

In June and July 1909, Adrian Stephen kept a diary while he and Virginia were living irritably together in Fitzroy Square. It shows how their Thursday evenings had turned into something more self-consciously humorous, ironical, and dissatisfying (QB/*VW*, I 146-7). Adrian's diary records the many musical and theatrical performances Bloomsbury was attending at this time; the enthusiasm for opera, especially Wagner, took him, Virginia, and Sydney-Turner to Bayreuth that year. The last entry of Adrian's diary on 16 July 1909 records that while he stayed home, Virginia and the Morrells went to see the Russian dancers. The arrival of the Ballet Russe with its fusion of modern music and post-impressionist art marks an important development from the nineteenth century in Bloomsbury's musical taste. Increasingly it was ballet rather than opera that they went to see and talked about.

Adrian also wrote much later an account of the famous hoaxing of the British Navy in February 1910. The joke had its origins in an undergraduate hoax played on the Mayor of Cambridge in 1905 by Adrian, his college friend Horace Cole, and others. Also part of the inspiration was the notorious Captain from Köpenick who captured a town hall by disguising himself as a Prussian officer and commandeering a platoon of soldiers. The *Dreadnought* Hoax occasioned newspaper stories and questions in Parliament. Though not initiated in Bloomsbury, it involved Adrian, Virginia, and Duncan Grant. The story is familiar of how the hoaxers dressed up as the Emperor of Abyssinia and his suite, sent a telegram from the head of the Foreign Office to the *Dreadnought* saying they were coming, and then were given a tour of the ship (duly interpreted to the Emperor through garbled Latin by Adrian) before returning triumphantly to London. Also well known is the sequel in which naval officers reclaimed their honour by administering symbolic spankings to Grant and Cole. In Adrian's account of the hoax, which the Hogarth Press published in 1936, he says he is telling the story, not because he is in any sense 'a literary person' but because he participated in both of Cole's hoaxes and is a truth-teller who finds it almost impossible to lie (pp. 19–20). This view of the literary imagination keeps his account quite simplified, and unfortunately that of his literary sister, which she read with hilarious effect to meetings of a Women's Institute and the Memoir Club during the Battle of Britain in 1940, is now largely lost. Yet it is Virginia's role in the hoax that now seems so interesting. Clive angered her by disapproving of the escapade, and Vanessa was appalled that her sister had participated in it, given the risks. Indeed, the term 'dreadnought' could be applied to the hoaxers as well as the object of their hoax. Afterwards, the Stephens' first cousin William Fisher, an officer on the ship who had failed to recognise either of his relatives, told Adrian severely that in the mess they were saying Virginia was a prostitute. In the fragment of her paper, Virginia's deadpan response to the affair was to note that the regulations concerning telegrams and official visits had been tightened up; she adds 'I am glad to think that I too have been of help to my country' (QB,*VW*, I 215).

The *Dreadnought* Hoax has a wider historical and literary context than just a remote Edwardian practical joke. It displays the Group's emerging anti-military outlook, which is closely related to an increasing disillusionment with imperialism – a disillusionment that Leonard Woolf expressed in the Ceylon fiction he wrote before the First World War. The *Dreadnought* was the biggest and most powerful battleship of the time; it was built in secrecy in 1906 and became the flagship of the Home Fleet and later the prototype of First World War One battleships (Ensor, pp. 363–4, 522–3). The Germans were envious and competitive – which explains Adrian's unease when Cole misheard his pseudonym and gave him a German one on the ship. The First World War shadows the retelling of the hoax, as Adrian notes that one of the charming officers showing them the ship died a few years later in the war. Today it is clearer just how much of a class joke the *Dreadnought* Hoax was (the navy's gentlemanly honour is much at stake) and also how racist, but then the imperial ignorance of the navy that permitted upper-middle-class ladies and gentleman to deceive them with blackface, costumes, and gibberish is all part of the hoax. For Virginia Woolf, the affair displayed the follies of the naval patriarchy. It is interesting that the month before the hoax she had started volunteer work for women's suffrage. When she retold the story of the ceremonial beatings in the story 'A Society' ten years later, Woolf emphasised the petty male class distinctions that were involved. It is not difficult to trace the line in her development that runs from the *Dreadnought* Hoax to *Three Guineas*. The hoax has also contributed to the myth of Virginia Woolf. E. M. Forster, in his 1942 lecture on her, speculated on how, disguised as the young Orlando, Virginia might have hoaxed the authorities of Cambridge into granting her a degree (2*CD*, p. 239).

Forster himself began to appear in Edwardian Bloomsbury toward the end of the decade, according to Virginia Woolf's Memoir Club recollections. He used to flit erratically through Old Blooms-bury like a butterfly with a bag, on his way to catch a train. Yet she listened to him 'with the deepest curiosity, for he was the only novelist I knew – except Henry James and George Meredith; the only one anyhow who wrote about people like ourselves' (*MB*, p. 198). She had heard of Forster from other Apostles, of course, and had reviewed both *The Longest Journey* and *A Room with a View* for the *TLS*. Leonard Woolf and Lytton Strachey had continued to complain about his novels in their correspondence. Not until Leonard's return from Ceylon did Forster became more closely involved with the Woolfs and the Bells, and by then he knew both Strachey and Fry well. Unlike all other members of the Group except MacCarthy, Forster was never in love with anyone in the Group, not even Duncan Grant. Aside from his mother, his deepest relationships were with men of other classes or races. In his later Edwardian novels about people like those in Bloomsbury, Forster took his ethics from G. E. Moore's Cambridge, particularly in *The Longest Journey* (as he later acknowledged) but also in the symbolism of *Howards End*. Yet the changes in names and subjects of conversation noted by Clive Bell and Virginia Woolf in their memoirs are not reflected in Forster's writing at this time. (His diary note on speaking to the Friday Club in 1910 refers, for example, to the favourable comments of 'Miss Stephen' – p/KC.) Though he was more successful as a writer than anyone else yet in Bloomsbury, Forster was still searching for literary forms in which he could write of the love relationships that interested him most. When he began to write fiction he told Lowes Dickinson he thought he was trying to invent realism; by his second novel he was trying at times to avoid it. The dissatisfaction of both E. M. Forster and Virginia Woolf with the realistic Edwardian novel is one of their important resemblances as Bloomsbury writers. The alternative of Henry James was before them, and it was during this time that Virginia Woolf, Forster, the Bells, MacCarthy, and even Keynes all met James. In Leonard Woolf's Ceylon writing, during the later Edwardian years of Bloomsbury and afterwards, James along with Flaubert was combining, not always originally, with Kipling and Conrad.

For Forster, however, James's fiction did not address directly enough 'the condition of England' that he wanted to write about, among other things, in his English novels. That condition included the severe economic disparity among classes, the campaign for woman's suffrage, the consequences of imperialism at home and abroad, and the growing military competition with Germany. Reflections of these concerns can be traced in Bloomsbury's later Edwardian writings. The *Dreadnought* Hoax would not have been out of place in *Howards End*. In dedicating *Civilization* to Virginia Woolf in 1928, Clive Bell wrote lightly of their lives before the war, 'You remember, Virginia, we were mostly socialists in those days.

We were concerned for the fate of humanity' (p. v). This could describe Forster too and his fiction during the Edwardian years as well as later, but he would not have implied it was something one outgrew. Virginia Woolf's writing – the novel she was beginning, the biographical and autobiographical forms she was experimenting with in her public and private work – did not have Forster's scope of interests, though she read his fiction with more understanding than either Strachey or Leonard Woolf. Nevertheless in her writing too she was beginning to anticipate that alteration in human character and personal relations, already visible perhaps in *Howards End*, that she liked to think began around the end of the Edwardian decade (*E*, III 421).

9 E. M. Forster's Refutation of Idealism

The fiction of E. M. Forster dominates Bloomsbury's later Edwardian literary history. He published three novels in four years. The last established his reputation as a novelist; the second revived his reputation more than two generations later in the cinema; the first, which was his favourite, has remained Forster's least read novel. Yet *The Longest Journey* is the first piece of fiction to be written about Bloomsbury's Cambridge origins, the first to use Moore's philosophy, the first to represent certain values of the Group.

Forster recognised that bits of the novel were 'tiresome and cranky', but he felt he had come nearer to saying what he wanted to in it than anywhere else (*HD*, p. 295). That may be the reason why he has been more forthcoming about the novel. In a Memoir Club paper of the 1920s Forster described how the novel's 'meagre theme (a man learns he has an illegitimate brother) and its meagre moral (we oughtn't to like one person specially)' were transformed by an encounter with a Wiltshire shepherd into one of those experiences that bequeath us

> something which philosophically may be also a glamour but which actually's tough. From this a book may spring. From the book, with the violence and persistency that only art possesses, a stream of emotion may beat back against and into the world.
>
> (*LJ*, pp. 305–6)

In a later lecture, Forster recalled that even before the Wiltshire inspiration he had taken his title from Shelley, started with the theme of an unknown illegitimate half-brother, and noted the novel's philosophy 'about reality and the need of accepting it' (*HD*,

p. 295). Finally in the introduction he wrote half a century after the novel was published, Forster indicated that the philosophy of *The Longest Journey* came from Cambridge,

> the Cambridge of G. E. Moore which I knew at the beginning of the century: the fearless uninfluential Cambridge that sought for reality and cared for truth. (*LJ*, p. lxviii)

The significance of Moore's philosophy, both his ethics and his epistemology, has not yet been widely accepted for *The Longest Journey*, yet the Cambridge context makes the novel among the most interesting of Bloomsbury's Edwardian works for literary history. When it is seen just how comprehensively organised a novel of ideas *The Longest Journey* is, and also how eccentrically modern its form is, the 'tiresome and cranky' bits can be read in a different way. Forster's introduction to *The Longest Journey* sets forth the thoughts and emotions that he says co-operated or collided to bring him nearer 'that junction of mind with heart where the creative impulse sparks.' In addition to the theme of a man who discovers he has an illegitimate brother, he distinguishes six subsequent ideas that confused or enriched his original one:

> There was the metaphysical idea of Reality ('the cow is there'): there was the ethical idea that reality must be faced (Rickie won't face Stephen); there was the idea, or ideal, of the British Public School; there was the title, exhorting us in the words of Shelley not to love one person only; there was Cambridge; there was Wiltshire. (*LJ*, pp. lxvi–ii)

These ideas, taken in the order Forster lists them, offer a very good way of organising the literary historical description of a complex novel in which, as Virginia Woolf said, 'everything is accentuated' (*CE*, I 344).

II

Forster's original idea for *The Longest Journey* is that staple of fiction, the birth mystery, complete with the problems of love and money that attend the quest for personal and social identity. The idea first appears in Forster's writing the year before *Where Angels Fear to*

Tread was published, when he noted down in his diary the plot for a novel involving a Cambridge youth and his Italian half-brother. Rickie and Ansell are foreshadowed in the plot, as are Agnes, Herbert Pembroke, and Mrs Failing. Discord over the revelation of the brother's identity occurs in an uncle's Italian household, and is resolved with the intervention of a Cambridge friend; the half-brothers die in a fire, and the hero's posthumous book is successful. Two months after recording this plot, Forster mentioned in his diary meeting a young, lame Wiltshire shepherd in the Figsbury Rings (*LJ*, pp. xlviii–l). This was 'the genius loci' who, indirectly and complicatedly, provided the only inspiration Forster says he ever experienced for a novel (*CSS*, p. vi) Forster's introduction does not mention the lameness of the shepherd who fructified his 'meagre conception of the half-brothers, and gave Stephen Wonham, the bastard, his home', yet the imaginative transference of the disability to Rickie shows how Forster further reworked his source material to give it greater significance (*LJ*, p. lxvii).

The shepherd who vivified Forster's plot comes from fiction as well as from Wiltshire. Forster has testified to the influence of Samuel Butler's *Erewhon* on his literary ideas and forms (*2CD*, pp. 212–15). The sequel, *Erewhon Revisited* (1901), is narrated by a man who wishes for a brother and then discovers he has an unknown half-brother – his father's son this time, though the mother's situation is not unlike that of Mrs Elliot. The unknown brother lives in Erewhon and his occupations are like Stephen's; he is a ranger. In *Erewhon Revisited* the question is whether the illegitimate brother George will accept his father, not whether brother will accept brother. Still, the general resemblance of George to Stephen is revealing. (Forster said the name 'Wonham' came from a place, but it also sounds a little like 'Erewhon'.) Butler's iconoclasm was influential on Bloomsbury and on Forster. In *The Longest Journey* it can be seen in the ideas of Rickie and Stephen as well as Ansell and Mr Failing, as opposed to the high-minded conventions of the Pembrokes and Mrs Failing that are part of the idealism repudiated in *The Longest Journey*.

But the significance of brotherhood in the novel extends far beyond anything suggested by Erewhon characters or Wiltshire shepherds. The meanings of the word start with the novel's one-word dedication 'Fratribus' and include everything from love and friendship to Mr Failing's notions about the brotherhood of man, or what it means to have Herbert Pembroke for a brother-in-law. The distinction between friendship and homoerotic love is not easy to draw in the novel, as the following passage shows. It begins with Rickie's thoughts about friendship then merges indistinguishably with those of the narrator:

> He was thinking of the irony of friendship – so strong it is, and so fragile. We fly together, like straws in an eddy, to part in the open stream. Nature has no use for us: she has cut her stuff differently. Dutiful sons, loving husbands, responsible fathers – these are what she wants, and if we are friends it must be in our spare time. Abram and Sarai were sorrowful, yet their seed became as sand of the sea, and distracts the politics of Europe at this moment. But a few verses of poetry is all that survives of David and Jonathan.
>
> 'I wish we were labelled', said Rickie. He wished . . . there was a society, a kind of friendship office, where the marriage of true minds could be registered. (*LJ*, p. 64)

The remarkably current allusion here to the politics of Europe refers to the rehabilitation of Alfred Dreyfus that finally took place in 1906 as Forster was writing his novel. But when the context of the allusion is taken together with the fact that Ansell is Jewish, the references to male friendship 'passing the love of women' is reinforced. (Ansell's name was that of the garden boy who was Forster's first friend; he had already commemorated him in the unpublished story 'Ansell' – see pp. 54–5[1]). And Rickie gets his wish. The male friend he loves best bears the label of half-brother. How homosexually symbolic Forster wanted to make this brotherly love is a question in the novel, but at times the symbolism seems unavoidable, as with the Oedipal limp that ought to have kept Rickie from procreating.

The 'Fratribus' dedication of *The Longest Journey* includes, of course, the Apostles, which Forster joined in 1901 and whose members addressed one another as brothers. Various of Forster's brothers recognised the opening of the novel as an Apostolic symposium. Forster's mentor Lowes Dickinson had dedicated his *A Modern Symposium* to the Society in 1905, while Forster was beginning work on *The Longest Journey*. He wrote to Dickinson, '"arguments", to me, are only fascinating when they are of the nature of gestures, and illustrate the people who produce them'; and he praised Dickinson for doing this in *The Modern Symposium*

(*L*, I 84). It is also what Forster was trying to do in *The Longest Journey*, but to understand the gestures and the characters they illustrate, the arguments being used have to be comprehended – and this takes us to G. E. Moore's Cambridge rather than Dickinson's.

III

The uses of philosophy in *The Longest Journey* are various. Characters are judged by the attitudes they have toward philosophy. Herbert Pembroke cannot see what it is for; the Elliots can, and they offer Rickie's mother stony 'views', 'emotional standpoints', and 'attitudes towards life', which they call philosophy, instead of the bread of facts that she hungers for (pp. 234–5). Ansell's father, on being assured that philosophy lies behind everything because 'it tries to discover what is good and true', knows that money or social position are less important, and therefore urges his son to take it up seriously (pp. 29–30). Stephen feels he has to get himself fixed up philosophically before starting life properly and follows the ideas of an agnostic American materialist until the Demeter of Cnidus, celebrated by Forster in his second essay for the *Independent Review* (see pp. 31–3), helps him realise the spirituality of nature. But it is 'the metaphysical idea of Reality ("the cow is there")' that initially represents philosophy in the novel through ideas and symbols associated with Rickie and Ansell – ideas and symbols that came from the Cambridge that Forster knew at the turn of the century.

Forster has been quoted by several interviewers as saying he never read G. E. Moore. (He also said he never read Freud or Jung.) But what he wrote on the subject indicates he did not need to:

> I did not receive Moore's influence direct – I was not up to that and have never read *Principia Ethica*. It came to me at a remove, through those who knew the Master. The seed fell on fertile, if inferior, soil, and I began to think for myself. . . .
>
> ('How I Lost', p. 263)

The Apostles H. O. Meredith and A. R. Ainsworth were the friends who taught him most about Moore, Forster explained in an interview.[2] So successful were they that Leonard Woolf included Forster among those in Bloomsbury who were 'permanently inoculated with Moore and Moorism' (*BA*, p. 24). In a piece on Woolf's autobiography, which Forster wrote about the same time as his late introduction to *The Longest Journey*, he described his own relation to the Apostles in a way that illuminates the philosophical values and the form of his novel:

> What they were after was not the Truth of the mystic or the ter-uth of the preacher but truth with a small 't'. They tried to find out more. They believed in the intellect rather than in intuition, and they proceeded by argument and discussion. I hovered on the edge of the group myself. I seldom understood what they were saying, and was mainly interested in the way they said it. I did, however, grasp that truth isn't capturable, or even eternal, but something that could and should be pursued. And this moderate discovery helped me. ('Looking Back')

Bloomsbury's and Forster's Moorist inoculation was both epistemological and ethical, as has been shown in *Victorian Bloomsbury*. The opening philosophical discussion in *The Longest Journey* about the existence of objects – 'do they exist only when there is someone to look at them? or have they a real existence of their own' (*LJ*, p. 3) – is on same general topic as that of a famous paper of Moore's entitled 'The Refutation of Idealism'. It appeared in *Mind* (the journal Ansell's sister waves around complaining about its criticism of her brother) in October 1903, which was the month of the publication of *Principia Ethica*. It was apparently around this time that Forster began to formulate his conception of Cambridge in *The Longest Journey* (PNF/*EMF*, I 104).[3]

G. E. Moore's 'The Refutation of Idealism' attempts to refute Berkeley's assertion that *esse est percipi* (to be is to be perceived), which Moore takes as the basis of the modern Idealism[4] prevalent in Cambridge and Oxford at the turn of the century. Moore showed that the *est* of the famous formula was fallaciously ambiguous. In another paper a few months later, Moore criticised Kant's transcendental Idealism by arguing that Kant had confused the cause of our knowing with the truth of what we know. In so far as he claimed matter consisted of mind, Kant's Idealism was as wrong as Berkeley's. Moore's general position here is that of philosophical Realism. He is not an Idealist because he finds no reason for denying the existence of objects apart from our consciousness of them, and he is not a Materialist because he can see no reason for denying the existence of our consciousness apart from the objects of which we are conscious. Something of the significance of Moore's refutation for Forster's fiction is described by Bertrand Russell in an autobiographical passage that might have come from *The Longest Journey*:

> With a sense of escaping from prison, we allowed ourselves to think that grass is green, that the sun and stars would exist if no one was aware of them, and also that there is a pluralistic timeless world of Platonic ideas. The world, which had been thin and logical, suddenly became rich and varied and solid.
>
> ('Mental Development', I 12)

Stewart Ansell is, with some inconsistencies, also a philosophical Realist in *The Longest Journey*, Stephen is for a while a Materialist, and Rickie's waverings between Idealism and Realism mark the crucial stages of his development. But little of Moore's actual argument finds its way into the book. Ansell, like Moore, demands exact meanings and relentlessly pursues metaphors, but in the opening scene Ansell's opponent is obviously right when he says Ansell has not proved the existence of cows by lighting matches and asserting 'the cow is there.' (Ansell's matches are the beginning of the light imagery that is associated throughout the novel with reality as well as love.) Moore did not try to prove the existence of external objects, of course; he simply denied that they could be disproved. The question to be asked about material things, he wrote at the end of 'The Refutation of Idealism',

> is thus not: What reason have we for supposing that anything exists *corresponding* to our sensations? but: What reason have we for supposing that material things do *not* exist, since *their* existence has precisely the same evidence as that of our sensations? ('Refutation', p. 30)

Ansell indirectly concerns himself with Moore's question when he denies the reality of Agnes Pembroke, but this takes us from what Forster called the metaphysical idea behind his novel to the ethical one. 'The Refutation of Idealism' is an essay in epistemology only, a piece of negative analysis, as its title implies, but implicit in it is the seeking for reality and caring for truth that Forster so admired in Moore. Forster's Apostolic brothers, including Moore – brothers to whom *The Longest Journey* is dedicated – would have agreed with Rickie when he insists at first, after learning he has a half-brother, that Stephen 'must be told such a real thing' (p. 136). The epigraph to *Principia Ethica*, Bishop Butler's 'Everything is what it is, and not another thing' – expresses very well the passionate importance of knowing what is real, what is true, in *The Longest Journey*.

IV

While Forster was at work on his novel in the autumn of 1905, G. E. Moore completed a longer, more difficult epistemological paper entitled 'The Nature and Reality of Objects of Perception'. In it, he sought to link the question of how we know anything other than our own perceptions exist, with how we know there are other people with perceptions like our own. It was this paper that converted Keynes (see p. 84). Forster would not have read Moore's paper, but placing *The Longest Journey* in the context of his philosophy illuminates the way Forster's novel seems imaginatively to transmute the epistemological concerns of Moore's refutations of idealism into ethical ones. The word *idealism* and its cognates appear and reappear under various guises in the novel. Idealisms that deny the objective existence of other people, of other societies, of nature, and of time can all be seen to be 'refuted' in the course of the narrative. The idealising of people in life and art is also rejected. Victorian altruism, especially in its institutional form, is repudiated too, though the importance of the Ideal is maintained. Finally the novel agrees with Shelley in criticising the modern Romantic ideal of monogamous love. The use of Shelley is explicit in *The Longest Journey*. Except for the later introduction, the use of Moore remains implicit.

The first of the idealisms refuted in *The Longest Journey* are described in Forster's introduction as 'the ethical idea that reality must be faced (Rickie won't face Stephen)'. At one time or another in *The Longest Journey* all the important characters, except maybe Stephen Wonham, behave like epistemological Idealists in denying the reality of people whose existence, for one reason or another, they do not wish to acknowledge. The reasons are metaphysical, moral, psychological, social, and sexual. Rickie's father, wife, aunt, and brother-in-law all practise that a kind of class-Idealism that recognises the lives of inferiors only when they impinge upon the consciousnesses of their superiors. These superiors are vulgar Idealists, in the sense of Mr Failing's distinction between vulgarity which conceals something and coarseness which reveals it (p. 207). (Ansell at times behaves like a coarse Idealist.) *'Procul este, profani'* ('Hence, you uninitiated') is their motto and no-trespassing sign (pp. 18, 209). The consequences of their Idealism extend from aesthetic snubs to gross social injustices.

Moore's analyses in 'The Refutation of Idealism', 'Kant's Idealism', and 'The Nature and Reality of Objects of Perception' have little to do with Forster's moral transpositions of them. Moore nowhere suggests that Idealists behave worse than Realists or Materialists. How Forster fashioned moral symbols out of epistemological arguments appears most clearly in the case of Rickie Elliot. Initially Rickie tries to love everyone, which is a kind of denial of human individuality, as Ansell implies. At certain times – which he calls symbolic moments – Rickie realises the importance of facing reality, as when he insists that Agnes should mind the reality of Gerald's death. But after refusing to acknowledge Stephen's identity, Rickie finds the world becoming unreal. A cloud of unreality hangs over his life, and his depression is expressed in the little joke 'that the cow was not really there' (p. 176). Later the partial acceptance of Stephen makes him feel happily real again, he says to his incredulous aunt,

'Because, as we used to say at Cambridge, the cow is there. The world is real again. This is a room, that a window, outside is the night – '
'Go on.'
He pointed to the floor. 'The day is straight below, shining through other windows into other rooms.' (p. 277)

The use of rooms as symbols of other existences here and in Forster's next novel will be continued in Virginia Woolf's writings and Bloomsbury's paintings. After Stephen breaks his promise not to get drunk (drunkenness is wrong for Rickie because it entails forgetting one's existence – p. 265), Rickie concludes it is a pretence to treat people as real. His end, which follows immediately afterwards, is ironical: he sacrifices his own life for a brother whose reality he has just denied. Mrs Failing, consistent to the end, pretends that Rickie had once been alive as she buries him. It is part of the novel's pathos that her pretending may be more justified than Rickie's pretence.

One of the reasons why Rickie has so much difficulty with metaphysical and ethical ideas of reality is his imagination. Moore's refutations of Idealism say little about the existence of imagined objects. Rickie's difficulty as a person is how to meet the full objective reality of other people without ignoring or idealising them, but his problem as a writer is how to make his imaginative conceptions fully real. Epistemological Idealism has been part of literary theory at least since Romanticism, for it offers a reality to imagined creations beyond the external world's perceived actualities. Idealism has therefore a special attraction for the writer in *The Longest Journey*. As an author, however, Rickie is involved in another meaning of the word 'idealism' that recurs in Forster's novel. It has often been noted that Rickie's stories, like those of his creator, represent idealisations of nature, such as dryads. Just after Rickie hears that Ansell is writing a dissertation about things being real, he is told by an editor that he should try to get inside life because his stories do not 'convince' (p. 143) – just as Forster had been told his tales did not 'compel' (see p. 59). Rickie's last long story, written after he has left his Idealistic Sawston marriage, differs from those included in the posthumous *Pan Pipes*; Rickie describes it as being 'about a man and a woman who meet and are happy'. 'Somewhat of a *tour de force*, I conclude', says Mrs Failing (p. 277). Perhaps the work was to be called *A Room with a View*.

To understand that *The Longest Journey* is a novel about appearance and reality, it is, of course, not necessary to know anything about Moore's refutation of Idealism. But some familiarity with Moore's philosophy can bring out certain interrelated aspects of this novel and avoid various misinterpretations of the text. This may be illustrated with the ideas and behaviour of Stewart Ansell. Throughout the novel, Ansell's comments on Rickie's attempts to cope with reality are essential to his friend's education. He points out how Rickie's imaginative idealising of people prevents him from judging their real worth. But *The Longest Journey* suggests that Ansell's notions of reality may also need some modifying. His quasi-Apostolic distinction between two kinds of phenomena – 'those which have a real existence, such as the cow', and 'those which are the subjective product of a diseased imagination, and which, to our destruction, we invest with the semblance of reality'

(p. 17) – have often been taken by critics as authorial. The distinction is a kind of answer to Moore's question, quoted above, about the reasons we have for supposing that anything corresponding to our sensations does not exist. Agnes's condescending disruption of the symposium that is discussing the existence of objects (Rickie has forgotten about *her* existence) brings Ansell to deride his friend's dangerous idealising propensities in the novel by treating Agnes as if she exists only in diseased imaginations like Rickie's. That is not exactly what Moore had in mind. Ansell's fellowship dissertations, the first one of which was 'about things being real' (p. 143), both fail at Cambridge. The reason given is that he has read too much Hegel, and it was Hegel's Idealism, as represented at Cambridge chiefly by McTaggart, that Moore and Russell's Realistic philosophical revolution replaced at the turn of the century. Furthermore, Ansell's distinction between kinds of phenomena is undercut by Forster at the opening of Chapter III of *The Longest Journey*, where it is noted that Ansell did not apply it to those for whom *he* had a special affection:

> Mr. Ansell, a provincial draper of moderate prosperity, ought by rights to have been classed not with the cow, but with those phenomena that are not really there. But his son, with pardonable illogicality, excepted him. He never suspected that his father might be the subjective product of a diseased imagination. From his earliest years he had taken him for granted, as a most undeniable and lovable fact. (p. 29)

The issue here is not Ansell's illogicality or even the fallacy of giving ethical answers to epistemological questions. *The Longest Journey* does that throughout for its own aesthetic and ethical purposes. Among them is Forster's point that although our love for people may lead us to our idealising of them, we endanger our own existence, our own loves, when we refuse to acknowledge the independent existence of those for whom we do not care. Honest, intelligent, and moral, Ansell realises this better than most of the characters in the novel, but he too is flawed with Idealism. His perceptions are also altered by love, which partly accounts for his jealous antagonism towards Agnes. The connection between love and perception recurs even more significantly in the novel with Forster's use of Shelley.

Ansell's mandalas are symbols of his incipient Idealism. The first occasion he draws one in the novel is just after he has denied Agnes's existence to Rickie, who then asks about the reality of the drawing and is told only the undrawable, unperceivable middle is real. Later in the British Museum, when Ansell is pursuing the unattainable truth that Forster came to understand through the Apostles, his sense of reality receives a shock: he learns that Rickie, and that figment of Rickie's imagination Agnes, are to have an undoubtedly real baby. Ansell has been drawing another mandala in the margin of his dissertation while discussing Rickie and explaining to their friend Widdrington that the way to fight Agnes is with poetry, not philosophy. She should be opposed not with distinctions about the perception of phenomena, but with what he calls the poetic 'Spirit of Life', which is a phrase 'unknown to their philosophy' (p. 181). (This is another of the places where Forster appears to change the philosophical ground of his novel, this time by etherialising it.) After the news, Ansell admits, among the carved Greek gods and goddesses, which he dislikes, that there are spirits or powers of life 'he could not cope with, nor, as yet, understand' (p. 182). In the very next chapter Rickie thinks of a mandala as a symbol of continuity, with the inner circle or square standing for the son in whom he will forget himself. But the baby is a daughter and afflicted with the hereditary lameness of the Elliots that should have prevented Rickie from having children. Rickie has attempted to idealise the future as he idealised the past.

Ansell's sense of reality is finally corrected and completed by Stephen Wonham – a correction sometimes disregarded by interpretations of Ansell as a Forsterian spokesman 'whose position, humanly speaking, is absolutely sound' (Furbank, 'Philosophy' p. 46). In one of his Idealistic phases, Ansell ignores Stephen when first addressed by him; afterwards he describes their ensuing fight as 'a momentary contact with reality' (*LJ*, p. 222). Stephen's view of reality is quite simple:

> He only held the creed of 'here am I and there are you', and therefore class distinctions were trivial things to him, and life no decorous scheme, but a personal combat or a personal truce.
>
> (p. 244)

Stephen's creed seems closer to Forster's than Ansell's or Rickie's in its moral denial of Idealism and acceptance of the independent reality of others. But it too needs to be widened. When Stephen repeats the creed to Rickie and adds from his philosophy of atheistic materialism 'the rest is cant', the authorial narrator disagrees and says that Stephen will come to realise this in time. (At the conclusion of a cancelled Chapter of fantasy in which he runs mad in the woods, Stephen 'the materialist, the semi-bounder, the foe to poetry and wonder' is converted to a world 'which could not be measured or touched ' – *LJ*, p. 338.[5]) The epilogue to *The Longest Journey* intimates that Ansell and Stephen are continuing to educate each other in the metaphysical and ethical implications of philosophical Realism.

V

In his introduction to *The Longest Journey* E. M. Forster explicitly endorses Ansell's refutation of the Idealism manifested in Sawston's 'Idea or Ideal, of the British Public School' (pp. lxvii–iii). Moore's Bloomsbury disciples connected his refutation of epistemological Idealism with a general repudiation of Victorian altruism. A similar repudiation was taking place in the works of writers like Samuel Butler as well as George Bernard Shaw, whose attacks on idealism Leonard Woolf found so congenial at Cambridge (*S*, pp. 164–5). These discarded Victorian ideals need to be distinguished in *The Longest Journey* and in Bloomsbury, from 'The Ideal' of personal relations and aesthetic enjoyments that is in propounded the last chapter of *Principia Ethica*. The ultimate standards of love and beauty are brought to bear on the whole nineteenth-century structure of altruistic duties and virtues, which are seen as valuable means only in so far as they lead to the ideal end.

Epistemological and altruistic meanings of idealism converge at Sawston, a setting near London that Forster had already used in *Nottingham Lace* and *Where Angels Fear to Tread*. Sawston School's ideals are patriotism, athletics, learning, and religion. Herbert Pembroke's promulgating of them to educate rich boys (instead of the poorer ones the school was originally designed to serve) is justified by his conviction – shared with others of his class and profession – that the school is a miniature, not fully real, copy or anticipation of the great world. The boys themselves are not taken as completely real human beings – hence the cruel treatment of Warden. Teaching is done through personal influence rather than through the personal intercourse that Rickie prefers. In the 1930s Forster briefly revived Herbert Pembroke in a review of some school memoirs whose vinegary tone Forster liked; it was a needful change, he says in his review, 'after so much oil' (*LJ*, p. 292). Forster's tone towards the pretensions of Sawston in the second part of *The Longest Journey* is also vinegary.

Ansell at Cambridge denounces to Rickie the idea or ideal of the public school because it lies about the reality of other worlds, just as Idealists like Mrs Failing in the novel lie about the reality of other people:

> There is no great world at all, only a little earth . . . full of tiny societies, and Cambridge is one of them. All the societies are narrow, but some are good and some are bad. . . . The good societies say, 'I tell you to do this because I am Cambridge'. The bad ones say, 'I tell you to do this because I am the great world'. . . . They lie. And fools like you listen to them, and believe that they are a thing which does not exist and never has existed, and confuse 'great', which has no meaning whatever, with 'good' which means salvation. (pp. 62–3)

Bad societies such as Pembroke's Sawston are, in short, like the second class of Ansell's phenomena: products of diseased imaginations which invest them with the semblance of reality.

The good, which means salvation in *The Longest Journey*, is a matter of facing reality not divinity. 'Will it really profit us so much if we save our souls and lose the whole world?' the narrator asks rhetorically in the little essay on spiritual coinage at the end of the Sawston section (p. 227). The notion of a divine coinage appears in Plato's *Republic* and was quoted by Lowes Dickinson in *The Greek View of Life* (Thomson, p. 284), but Forster's questioning rejection of it, together with his emphasis on physical joys, comes from Lytton Strachey's review of Blake in the *Independent Review* when Forster was writing his novel (see p. 20). It is one of the many things in *The Longest Journey* that make it such a Bloomsbury novel. There is even a character named Widdrington with Stracheyesque gestures who does historical research in the British Museum to confute Sawston's values by showing that 'family life is more real than national life' (p. 178).[6] As for fighting Sawston with Ansell, however, Widdrington will only emit plaintive cries against Rickie's wife.

Agnes thinks she and Rickie are saved when Mrs Failing conceals

Stephen's identity from everyone except them. But they are really lost. True salvation comes when Rickie throws his life away to save Stephen, in whose reality he says he no longer believes. The final chapter shows Stephen demonstrating to Herbert Pembroke the difference between the natural world and the unreality of public school Idealism. Echoing what Ansell has presumably taught him, Stephen seizes Pembroke and forces him to look at nature: ' . . . that's the world, and there's no miniature world. There's one world, Pembroke, and you can't tidy men out of it' (p. 286).

The plurality of real societies and people is connected in *The Longest Journey* to another idea – one that is as important as that adapted from Moore's 'The Refutation of Idealism'. This brings us finally to Shelley.

VI

The title of *The Longest Journey*, 'exhorting us in the words of Shelley not to love only one person' *(LJ*, p. lxvii) encompasses an Idealism of love that Forster's novel fictively refutes. Rickie reads the passage out loud to himself the day after his ride with Stephen, during which he fell asleep and dreamt of the world dissolving as he and Agnes rose to the throne of God, and from which he awoke in a valley full of men. Immediately after reading Shelley's lines, which he used to think very good but now finds a little inhuman, Rickie is told by Mrs Failing that Stephen is his half-brother. With Agnes's essential help he then proceeds to ignore his brother's real identity. Shelley's words (words the monogamous Leslie Stephen despised – *Victorian Bloomsbury*, p. 41) are a commentary on Rickie's relationship to both Agnes and Stephen:

> I never was attached to that great sect
> Whose doctrine is that each one should select
> Out of the world a mistress or a friend,
> And all the rest, though fair and wise, commend
> To cold oblivion – though it is the code
> Of modern morals, and the beaten road
> Which those poor slaves with weary footsteps tread
> Who travel to their home among the dead
> By the broad highway of the world – and so
> With one sad friend, perhaps a jealous foe,

The dreariest and the longest journey go.[7]

(*LJ*, pp. 126–7)

When these lines of 'Epipsychidion' are read in the context of Moore's 'The Refutation of Idealism', the crucial connection between reality and love in *The Longest Journey* emerges. The monogamous ideal of modern morals results in the practice of an Idealism that denies the independent human reality of all but the loved or jealous one. Like cows when unperceived, all but the friend or foe are commended to the 'cold oblivion' of non-existence. The longest journey is thus a trip into subjective unreality. After Rickie's denial of Stephen and marriage to Agnes, he becomes attached to the sect and undertakes this journey. Mists and fog arise around him, and the world becomes unreal. He prays at Sawston 'to be delivered from the shadow of unreality that had begun to darken the world'. In the end even Agnes, 'like the world she had created for him, was unreal' (pp. 152, 188).

Moore pointed out in 'The Refutation of Idealism' that if the object of an Idealist's sensation really were inseparable from his experience, he could never be aware of himself, let alone anything else that was real, and the result is solipsism (pp. 28–9). Shelley's lines describe a solipsism *à deux* that ultimately makes the solipsists themselves unreal in *The Longest Journey*. After Rickie has begun to accept Stephen, he describes the journey he had into unreality:

Two years ago I behaved badly to you, up at the Rings. No, even a few days before that. We went for a ride, and I thought too much of other matters, and did not try to understand you. Then came the Rings, and in the evening, when you called up to me most kindly, I never answered. But the ride was the beginning. Ever since then I have taken the world at second-hand. I have bothered less and less to look it in the face – until not only you, but every one else has turned unreal. Never Ansell: he kept away, and somehow saved himself. But everyone else. (*LJ*, pp. 254–5)

The way Forster has combined philosophy and poetry is not as paradoxical as might at first seem. It does sound odd to maintain that in *The Longest Journey* Forster is using Moore's analytic refutation of Idealism to support the poetic ideas of an altruistic Platonist like Shelley. But Moore was attempting to refute modern not Platonic Idealism, and the dualism he assumes is present in both 'Epipsychidion' and *The Longest Journey*. (Rickie speaks of going behind right and wrong, of standing behind things at last – pp. 249, 278.) Moore, who was no sceptic, concludes in 'The Refutation of Idealism' that the only reasonable alternative to Idealism or agnosticism was either absolute scepticism or belief in matter and spirit (p. 30). The spiritual love of 'Epipsychidion' is described in metaphors of sexual passion; in the novel love's dualism appears in the account of Rickie's unhappy fate. Orderly people, the novelist asserts at the opening of Chapter VII, say love 'can be fallen into by two methods: (1) through the desires; (2) through the imagination.' The English add that the first is the inferior method, and the omniscient narrator comments that the second breeds tragedy (*LJ*, p. 61). Rickie Elliot's love-tragedy is a consequence of both: his inadequate love through desire is symbolised by his deformity, while the inadequacy of his spiritual loving commits him to the code of modern morals. He must limp through the longest journey.

The idealism of Romantic passion that *The Longest Journey* 'refutes' may also be found in the novel's Arthurian, Wagnerian allusiveness. Agnes is associated with the Rhine maidens, Mrs Failing's house with the Perilous Chapel, Stephen with Siegfried in earlier drafts of the novel, and Rickie with both the questing Perceval and the wounded Fisher King. *The Longest Journey* has been read in terms of these often ironic allusions (*LJ*, p. xiii), but half-way into the novel they cease at Sawston. An imagery of stars, especially the constellation of Orion, is maintained throughout the book, however, as are references to mythological sculpture, particularly the Cnidian Demeter. Perhaps the shedding of Wagner's Romanticism is a mark of Rickie's unsteady progress toward reality in love and life.

In Shelley's 'Epipsychidion' the loved one who helps the poet avoid the longest journey with his one other love is described as a sister and twin as well as a spouse. In this respect, Stephen is more Shelleyan than Rickie. He eventually has a brother to love yet 'love for one person was never to be the greatest thing he knew' (p. 242). He wants to marry eventually ('Does it disgust you?' he asks Rickie) because something outside of himself makes him wish to, and the narrator intervenes to comment on the nature of romantic love and qualify the title passage from Shelley:

Romantic love is greater than this. There are men and women –

we know it from history – who have been born into the world for each other, and for no one else, who have accomplished the longest journey locked in each other's arms. But romantic love is also the code of modern morals, and, for this reason, popular. Eternal union, eternal ownership – these are tempting baits for the average man. (pp. 271–2)

Agnes is an average woman, yet she is also the kind of person, we are told, who loved only once. In that love she was more real for Rickie than in any love she had for him; Stephen alone invokes it in her again. Rickie is not the average man, still his physical and spiritual shortcomings allow him to succumb to the ideal of modern morals until rescued by Ansell and Stephen. After accepting Stephen's real identity, however, Rickie idealises him again and begins another longest journey.

The Longest Journey, to repeat, connects epistemology and love, Moore and Shelley, by refuting the Idealism of Romantic love in which the lovers become oblivious to the reality of other people. The balancing of Shelley's anti-Idealism with Moore's may have been what Forster meant when he remarked of his novel to Russell 'hardly anyone had gone into what seemed an obvious and symmetrical field, so I determined to try' (PNF/*EMF*, I 151). The basis for true loving in *The Longest Journey* depends upon the ethical facing of reality that Forster imaginatively derives from Moore's refutation and applies to the kind of class-bound Idealism which ignores the existence of inferiors. But the precise nature of that loving remains ambiguous in Forster, and perhaps, in Shelley and Moore as well. The brotherly loves of Rickie, Ansell, and Stephen are erotically tinged in *The Longest Journey*, like the Platonic love of 'Epipsychidion'. Moore's various essays on the refutation of Idealism have nothing to do with love, but the Ideal in *Principia Ethica* does. The association of homoerotic and spiritual love in *The Symposium* was not forgotten by those Apostles whose Socrates was Moore.

VII

The Cambridge section of *The Longest Journey* occupies more than half the novel. As one of the 'ideas' that confused or enriched original inspiration, this Cambridge, it is worth re-emphasising, was identified by Forster as the Cambridge of G. E. Moore. Forster describes Ansell in his introduction as 'the undergraduate high-priest of that local shrine' that was Cambridge (p. lxviii), and it has been variously asserted that he was modelled on the two Apostle friends that Forster says helped him to understand Moore's philosophy, one of whom later became Moore's brother-in-law (Wilkinson, p. 18; PNF/*EMF*, I 77)[8]. Ansell's career resembles Moore's in some respects but not in others. He is a Victorian undergraduate about the time Moore was – before Moore had disproved the subjective status of cows, that is (*LJ*, p. 70). The first fellowship dissertations of both failed, Moore's perhaps because he had read too much Bradley and not enough Kant (Regan, p. 90). Ansell's demanding to know exactly what Rickie means in criticising Cambridge, together with his unremitting analysis of metaphors (pp. 62–3) displays traces of Moore's impact, as does the criticism of Rickie's attempts to love everybody and his incipient monism (pp. 19, 80). Despite Ansell's failure at Cambridge and lapses into Idealism (he reads a paper on Schopenhauer to a Cambridge discussion society) Forster clearly endorses his fearless, uninfluential Cambridge values of seeking truth and caring for reality – in contrast to those of the Pembrokes at Sawston, who value mere success.

Cambridge is described as Rickie's 'only true home' (p. lxviii), yet even there 'he was frightened at reality; he was frightened at the splendours and horrors of the world' (p. 59). Trying to love everyone, he fails to distinguish between the real worth of individuals, as Ansell and Stephen later show him. When Rickie falls in love with Agnes (or perhaps Agnes and Gerald), Ansell warns him he has now substituted her for humanity in his quest to hang all the world's beauty on one peg:

> You are not a person who ought to marry at all. You are unfitted in body: that we once discussed. You are also unfitted in soul: you want and you need to like many people, and a man of that sort ought not to marry. 'You never were attached to that great sect' who can like one person only, and if you try to enter it you will find destruction. (p. 81)

This is the novel's first allusion to Shelley's lines, and they have been interpreted as expressing a central Apostolic antithesis in *The Longest Journey* that can be found in King's and Trinity College states of mind (PNF/*EMF*, I 107).[9] Shelley's lines that begin the stanza following the one that Rickie reads in the Cadbury Rings are also relevant to the differences between the tough-minded intellectual pursuits of Trinity and the tender-minded moral concerns of King's:

> True Love in this differs from gold and clay,
> That to divide is not to take away.
> ('Epipsychidion', ll. 160–1)

Shelley's idea here was popular among the Apostles (at his wedding, Roger Fry reminded Dickinson of it – VW/*RF*, p. 96), and it is akin to Moore's discussion of organic wholes. Forster developed the point later in several essays, including the well-known 'Notes on the English Character' (*AH*, p. 6). In *The Longest Journey*, however, the antithesis between Trinity intolerance and King's tolerance is not borne out in the disagreements between Ansell and Rickie. Rickie's tragedy is not so much that he softly refuses to hate people but that they become unreal for him after he joins 'the great sect'. The lines of 'Epipsychidion' in which Shelley restates the consequences of loving just one person apply in the novel not to the critical Ansell but the Idealistic Rickie:

> Narrow
> The heart that loves, the brain that contemplates,
> The life that wears, the spirit that creates
> One object, and one form, and builds thereby
> A sepulchre for its eternity.
> (ll. 169–74)

The Cambridge aspects of *The Longest Journey* were, of course, what most interested and irritated Forster's friends in the Apostles and Bloomsbury. Indeed the novel may be the first representation of the Society in fiction, but before looking at the book's reception, one final idea whirling around Forster must be considered.

VIII

The 'idea' of Wiltshire that Forster listed among the sources of inspiration for *The Longest Journey* includes the refuting of Idealism through an affirmation of the beautiful objective reality of nature. The cow is the basic rural and female symbol in the novel for the reality that exists whether it is acknowledged or not. Throughout the text, the existence or non-existence of people for Rickie is tied to the reality or unreality of the natural world. Rickie begins the longest journey into unreality while riding with Stephen; as he dreams of ascending to God with Agnes, the lark stops singing, and the earth dissolves. He awakes in a valley full of men. After the second, complementary ride with Stephen near the end of the novel, Rickie believes that 'the earth had confirmed him' (p. 278). As Forster put it in an earlier draft,

> one by one Stephen had stripped him of his illusions, until the world was again real. Ansell had tried, but he was sentimental, he was Cambridge, and could but evoke the reality they had found in that beautiful past. This man belonged to the present.
>
> (*LJ*, p. 378)

At last Rickie is able to distinguish between the appearance of convention and the reality of people, nature, and love. For a little while before his pathetic lapse, he is able to reject Mrs Failing's Idealism, which relies on convention and leads her into dishonesty and injustice because, as Rickie says to her earlier, she has forgotten what people are like. Her indifference to the lives of others is hardened by her hatred of the ways of the earth that have afflicted the Elliots (and perhaps in some respects the Forsters too, for Cadover and its chief occupant were partly based on the household of Forster's uncle – *LJ*, p. lxx).

Wiltshire stands for the ways of the earth in *The Longest Journey*. The three places that name the novel's three sections represent for Rickie and his creator types of existence, but they constitute no Christian trinity or Hegelian triad. Wiltshire takes nothing from Sawston.[10] Stephen and Ansell are together at the end educating each other, Ansell perhaps having his Idealistic tendencies corrected further and Stephen his Materialistic ones, as he comes to realise that the dead past exists as well as the unrealised future. Stephen's handling of Herbert Pembroke also reveals what he has learned from Ansell. But Rickie fails finally to accept the reality of other people and of nature; he breaks Mrs Failing's conventional coffee cup of experience with Stephen's Wiltshire chalk but he cannot accept his half-brother's drunkenness. Stephen had scoffed at

Rickie's Forsterian fable in which a girl turned into a tree is identified by Agnes as 'getting in touch with nature' (p. 119). *The Longest Journey* is not entirely free of this kind of allegorising. Stephen the natural son is in touch with instinct, Ansell with intellect, Rickie with imagination. (Perhaps this was the 'obvious and symmetrical field' that Forster told Russell he had attempted – PNF/*EMF*, I 151). The three friends all need one another but there is only a partial synthesis of natural beauty, rational truth, and creative art at the novel's end. Stephen, Ansell, and Rickie are also associated with time: Stephen tries to live in the simple present, Ansell studies the thought of the past, and Rickie becomes a successful author only posthumously. The ending of the novel also suggests that the bastard Stephen, like the child of Helen Schlegel and Leonard Bast in *Howards End*, is the legitimate inheritor of a renewed rural England of the future.

The assertion of nature's objective existence is thus finally an avowal of the reality of time in *The Longest Journey*. Throughout the novel, natural and temporal symbolism go together. Rickie retells his past to his Apostolic brothers in the Madingley dell and then finds out more about it in the Rings, by a tree of knowledge, where he is literally encircled by the ancient past. (The Rings and dell can also be seen as mandalas whose centres are the past rather than the future.) Rickie's subsequent inability to face the reality of his past is, in addition, a denial of human and natural realities. He proclaims the importance of accepting the symbolic moment – so important to Bloomsbury's fiction – and is able to do so with Agnes and Gerald but not with Stephen (p. 136). Rickie also refuses to confront the reality of the future until the child he should never have had dies.

One of the means Forster uses to convey the reality of time in his text is a classical symbolism that becomes schematic in places. The Roman road intersecting the railroad, for example, represents a past violated by the present – a present that is destroying the future when children are killed at the level-crossing. Throughout his Edwardian fiction, Forster's regard for human continuity appears as an inescapable aspect of nature. All the major characters of *The Longest Journey* have to learn to accept this continuity, to recognise that the past really has existed and that the future really will exist. The novel's river symbolism is one of the ways in which the realities of time and change are related with nature and with love, as in the scene where Stephen and Rickie float burning paper under the bridge. Sometimes this symbolism is understated, as when

Ansell leans against the pedestal of the Athenian river god Ilissus after hearing Agnes is pregnant, or when Rickie thinks how friends 'fly together, like straws in an eddy, to part in the open stream' (p. 64). When Ansell returns to his dissertation in the British Museum, he walks past the pillar of a temple devoted to the goddess of chaste as well as pregnant women (the pillar – a favourite of Forster's – depicts Hermes and Death taking Alcestis to the underworld) and also past the Cnidian Demeter. Ansell's antipathy to these sculptures reveals his inadequate response to nature and to art. Forster uses the Demeter effectively in the novel to foreshadow the relation of Stephen and Rickie. This most beautiful of Greek earth mothers with her gifts of corn and tears, as Forster wrote in 'Cnidus', has a broken nose, which mars her ideal beauty; Rickie's mother is also flawed. The Demeter's knees are smashed, just as Rickie's legs will be when he rescues Stephen – Stephen the atheist and Materialist who nevertheless hangs a picture of the sculpture in his room. Again, love, nature, art, and their continuity are symbolised by the 'stone lady'. The phrase is that of Stephen's daughter who, we are told in the last line of the book, has been named after the mother of Rickie and Stephen. The past has come to signify something more to Stephen than death.

Past and future realities that the novel's characters connect, as they journey by the broad highway of the world or by other paths, are an essential aspect of the refutation of Idealism in *The Longest Journey*. The philosophical background for the book's emphasis on the reality of time – of natural change, including death – and the ethical importance of facing this reality is again to be found once more in Forster's Cambridge. Time was famously denied there in the early years of the twentieth century by the Hegelian McTaggart, who dominated the Apostles before the advent of Moore. McTaggart's argument was first published in *Mind* in 1908, the year after *The Longest Journey*, but it was familiar to his students and friends long before that. McTaggart's abstruse logic (see *Victorian Bloomsbury*, pp. 190–1) is irrelevant to Forster's novel, but it is worth mentioning that in Forster's original note for *The Longest Journey*, the character who became Ansell is described as a 'brainy uncouth undergraduate soaked with idea of mutability' (*LJ*, p. xlviii). Throughout the novel various characters' lives are shaped by unexpected deaths.

The acceptance of both the reality of the dead past and of the future reality of one's own death is yet another indication of how

Moore's philosophy suggested to Forster ideas about the sense perception, brotherhood, metaphysics, ethics, education, love, truth, and nature. These ideas are presented, as his remarks to Dickinson suggest, not as arguments so much as gestures illustrating the kind of characters he was creating in his novel. But they also have in *The Longest Journey* 'something which philosophically may be also a glamour but which actually's tough', as he told the Memoir Club his experience in Wiltshire had become (*LJ*, p. 306). And as he indicated in his late introduction to the novel, that philosophical glamour and toughness comes from the philosopher who has been described as Bloomsbury's prophet.[11]

IX

Despite its context in Moore's philosophy and its expression of Bloomsbury's values, *The Longest Journey* had a mixed reception in the Group, partly because Forster says in his introduction he went wrong in 'the spirit of anti-literature' (p. lxvi). Critics all note where they think the novel goes wrong – usually in the abrupt deaths of numerous characters – but often without much consideration of just what Forster was trying to achieve. His intentions are worth noting first, before discussing the response to his novel in Bloomsbury and its reception and influence elsewhere.

In a letter to a critic whom Forster thought understood exactly what he was trying to do, he wrote again of how he

> *insisted* on doing things wrong there. It wasn't incompetence; it was a perversity the origins of which I can no longer trace. But for this, it would have been my best piece of work, I am sure.
>
> (EMF/*L*, II 131)

The biographical origins of this perversity may be found in his uncertainty over the sexual significance of brotherly love in *The Longest Journey*. Forster felt that he had put more of himself into Rickie, and also into Philip in *Where Angels Fear to Tread*, than any of his other characters (Interview, p. 33). Rickie and Philip's priggishness may well be a form of self-criticism. (In one interview Forster said he could kick Rickie – *LJ*, p. lxi). How much wish-fulfilment may have gone into the sentimental characterisation of

Stephen is indicated by Forster in a very late diary entry after revisiting the Figsbury Rings:

> I was filled with thankfulness and security and glad that I had given myself so much back. . . . I shall lie in Stephen's arms instead of his child. (PNF/*EMF*, II, 319)

To the Memoir Club, again, Forster described Stephen as a 'theoretic figure . . . so dead, because he is constructed from without', yet in another sense 'so alive because the material out of which he was constructed is living' (*LJ*, p. 305). Forster explained further to another sympathetic critic that Stephen had never been shown as understanding or fond of Rickie, 'so that, in the end chapter, he lies as a somewhat empty hulk on that hillside' (*L*, II 267). Rickie, however, is shown from within as well as from without, and some readers have not observed these shifts, attributing, for example, Rickie's purple view of Gerald and Agnes's love to his creator.

Forster's remarks, although made after the fact of creation, convey a greater self-consciousness in the art of fiction than he is usually credited with. The plotting that manipulates death so arbitrarily, the novel's sometimes overt and sometimes quite subtle symbolism, even the narrator's intrusive omniscience – all can be read as resistance to conventions of Victorian and Edwardian fiction that much of *The Longest Journey* appears to accept. The modernist, Flaubertian conception of the novel as an unsentimental work of art was not his, Forster told Dickinson (PNF/*EMF*, p. 148). In this sense Forster did not want his novel to be objective, convincing. His manifestations of 'the spirit of anti-literature' call attention to the artificiality rather than the art of fiction. In the 1920s, after he had written his last novel, Forster made clear his idea of the novelist's business. It was to adjust and conciliate the characters (he insisted on calling them people) with the other aspects of fiction, to give his human beings 'a good run and to achieve something else at the same time' (*AN*, pp. 73, 116). Matters like plot or point of view were subordinated to an expanding openness in the treatment of human beings.

In *The Longest Journey* Forster cheerfully, even comically sacrifices the means of narrative consistency and plausibility for the ends that are his characters. Their spiritual progress and interactions matter most to him. In describing this moral development through an epistemological symbolism, Forster repudiates the ideal of realistic psychological fiction. The various internal and external, limited and omniscient points of view are utterly unJamesian. For example, when Rickie announces to friends in the second chapter that he wants to talk of his past and Ansell says go ahead, if it is boring they have books, the author-narrator remarks in a playful paradox, 'the reader who has no book will be obliged to listen to it' (p. 21). Elsewhere the intrusions can be quite serious, as when Rickie's decline is announced and defended (p. 193). The most unusual interruption of the narration follows the climactic revelation of Stephen's parentage at the conclusion of the Sawston section. Chapter XXVIII is simply a brief, disconnected essay about spiritual coinage. The mystery of Stephen's origin is, of course, carefully concealed by the narrator but other features of the story are treated quite casually. Asked once by a worried interviewer about the famous opening of Chapter V ('Gerald died that afternoon. He was broken up in the football match'.) Forster replied simply, 'it had to be passed by', and he conceded it may have been passed by the wrong way (Interview, p. 29). But this forsaking the plausibilities of plot is more interesting than, say, his using a schoolboy's pulled ears and missent letters to bring Rickie and Stephen together again. The surprise caused by Forster's disregarding the verisimilitudes of death suggests he went wrong quite creatively here.

But Virginia Woolf for one did not think so. In her 1927 essay on Forster's novels, she was still baffled and amused by the accentuation of everything in the book, which lead to her conclusion that for all his gifts Forster lacked the most essential one for a novelist: 'the power of combination – the single vision' (*CE*, I 344–5). Woolf's judgement may have been coloured by her disagreements at this time with Forster's theories of fiction in *Aspects of the Novel* (Rosenbaum, *Aspects*). Certainly her own elegaic novel of a young Cambridge man was very different, but singleness of vision is not a quality of *Jacob's Room* either. But Woolf had also reviewed *The Longest Journey* earlier for *The Times Literary Supplement* – a review that is the first published document in the fascinating and complex literary relationship of Woolf and Forster, and also the first of what would be a long series of Bloomsbury reviews of Bloomsbury.[12] In her brief review, which Forster probably never knew was by Virginia Woolf, she found *The Longest Journey* very entertaining, 'so very clever and so very well pleased with its own ingenuity.' She emphasises the satire of the novel, likening its author to 'some sharp wholesome insect' which fastens itself on the life and ideals of the suburbs. Cambridge is different, where the concern is with the existence of objects and the reality of circles in squares. Forster is an expert in 'the art of stinging', yet the method can be dangerous, and sometimes the seriousness of the book is impaired by the shrillness of its comedy. Agnes Pembroke is considered a successful creation, but not Mrs Failing – a judgement not shared by some later critics. The Cambridge, Sawston, and Wiltshire stages of Rickie's life are skilfully developed, yet Forster's facility leaves his reviewer gasping and groping for connections in the novel, as she thinks he intended her to be. The development of this young Apostolic novelist interested Woolf deeply, and she asks at the end of the review the same question she had felt at the end of his first novel: 'What will be the next?' (*EMFCH*, pp. 67–8).

The Bloomsbury Apostles were understandably less detached in their assessments of *The Longest Journey* than the *TLS* reviewer. Roger Fry, still tinged with aesthetic Idealism, was fascinated, and despite the book's imperfections found some things wonderfully said and an atmosphere all Forster's own. He said it reminded him of Gorky (*L*, I 285). Desmond MacCarthy thought there were very bad things in the novel but felt Forster had at least 'hit off those miserable muffs the Cambridge Apostles pretty well', (PNF/*EMF*, I 150). Years later he wrote to Moore, who was re-reading Forster, that he should try 'that odd story' *The Longest Journey*, which was vivid and interesting yet unconvincing. 'Do you remember the amusing beginning', he asked, 'which was evidently suggested by a discussion in the Society?' (17.vii.48, Moore, Cambridge papers).

The younger Apostles rather disparaged Forster's fictional representation of the Society and its philosophy. Keynes read the book with 'very great interest and a good deal of bewilderment as well as admiration'. Forster, he thought, had filled his mind with cranky and disagreeable characters; he got a lot out of them but appeared to Keynes unintentionally to caricature the Society quite cruelly (PNF/*EMF*, I 150). Strachey referred to the novel in a revealing Apostle paper on mysticism that he read a month after the book's publication. Strachey maintained in 'Do two & two make five?' that believing in mystical Platonic reality beyond common-sense Aristotelian appearance was justified but unprovable: one is bored by the seeming of teacups and suffragists, then suddenly revelations of happiness and beauty occur. The nebulosity of mysticism made it impossible to establish, agnosticism was no solution, and unfortunately the success of works of art like *The Longest Journey* with its symbolic moments depends upon the truth of mysticism because only in the greatest works of art is mysticism's truth irrelevant. (Strachey also noted, as Forster and Virginia Woolf would show later in their novels, that mystical revelations could also be horrible: 'one suddenly discovers that twice two, so far from making five, makes three' – p/ST). The tone of Strachey's paper is quite mild, but earlier in the month he wrote to Duncan Grant that the book was 'dreary fandango' based on the author, on H. O. Meredith and even, he recognised, on himself (PNF/*EMF*, I 150). Strachey was 'not one to countenance fanciful transferences', Forster remarked in his late introduction when describing how he once tried to test the fictive magic of the Cadbury Rings while staying nearby with Strachey (*LJ*, pp. lxvii–iii). In a letter to Leonard Woolf, Strachey was even harsher on the novel: it was infinitely fouler than *Where Angels Fear to Tread* in its morals, sentimentality, and melodrama – 'but there are even further depths of fatuity & filth' (2.v.07, LS/pNY). Woolf, struggling with the unreal realities of Ceylon, agreed the novel was 'an astonishing & irritating production'; yet his dislike was qualified in ways he would show in the short story based on Forster that he wrote a little later (see pp. 403–4):

> I thought on every other page that he was really going to bring something off, but it all fades away into dim humour & the dimmer ghosts of unrealities. It might have been so magnificent & is a mere formless meandering. The fact is I don't think he knows what reality is, & as for experience the poor man does not realize that practically it does not exist. Yet his mind interests me, its curious way of touching on things in the rather precise & charming way in which his hand (I remember) used to touch things vaguely. (LW/*L*, p. 130)

Strachey wrote back that he had leapt with joy at the idea of Forster's not realising that experience practically did not exist (1.viii.07, LS/pNY).

Why, apart from some envy, were Strachey and Leonard Woolf so hostile to *The Longest Journey*? What they saw as aesthetic flaws do not account for their reaction. They make no comment on the criticism of Idealism, monogamous love, or public schools; even the homoeroticism of what Strachey liked to call the higher sodomy at

Cambridge is unmentioned. Perhaps Strachey and Woolf were convinced these Apostolic mysteries could not be fictionalised by a novelist unable to read Moore. Whatever the reasons, it is interesting that Bertrand Russell liked the novel and congratulated Forster on it. (Like Rickie, Russell regarded Cambridge as his only home – *Autobiography*, I 74). Forster was gratified and wrote to Russell of the symmetry he had attempted to represent, and of his own displeasure with, among other things, all the corpses in the book (PNF/*EMF*, I 151).

X

The reviewers outside Bloomsbury were also more encouraging. Blackwood had again been Forster's publisher, though for the last time, and Forster found him tiresome in the matter of proof changes (*LJ*, p. lv). (Blackwood was also among the publishers who refused to supply books during *The Times* Book War, and readers of Woolf's review in the *TLS* were urged not to buy the novel.) The reviews criticised the corpses and the jerkiness of the narrative, but most of the early critics thought the author of *Where Angels Fear To Tread* – he was so described on the title page of *The Longest Journey* – had written a very clever, even brilliant book. The *Morning Post* review, written, Forster believed, by William Beveridge, future author of the Beveridge report, amused him by calculating the sudden-death rate in the novel at 44 per cent, children excluded (*EMFCH*, pp. 78–80). The longest, most perceptive reviews were those by Edward Garnett and C. F. G. Masterman, and both found the novel elusive. Garnett, writing anonymously in the new *Nation* which had just replaced the *Speaker*, found originality and subtlety in a novel that was 'both philosophical and witty, spiritual and full of humorous by-play'. He recognised the influence of George Meredith, praised the characterisation of Mrs Failing as well as Stephen, and understood the sham Idealism of the worldly Pembrokes (*EMFCH*, pp. 68–71). Masterman (who helped edit the *Independent Review*) felt Meredith's influence in a novel that he found not great but astonishingly clever, and he was aware of the philosophical concerns of an author 'determined to face the world of real things' (*EMFCH*, pp. 73–6). Garnett and Masterman's reviews appear in some ways more appropriate to the complex concerns of *The Longest Journey* than those of later critics, perhaps because the reviewers were closer to Forster's milieu. An anonymous reviewer wrote sympathetically in the *Independent Review*, but described Ansell as 'a diabolical young fool' (*EMFCH*, pp. 85–6). There were, of course, hostile notices. One reviewer, like Uncle Willie in the novel (*LJ*, p. 141), could not follow the plot, which another managed to summarise without mentioning Stephen or Ansell. St. Loe Strachey's *Spectator* (where Lytton would soon be reviewing with unhappy regularity) found Forster had talent and humour but these were overlaid with 'an "abnormal," almost brutal, cynicism'; the reviewer then proceeded cynically to dismiss the Cambridge values of the novel (*EMFCH*, pp. 91–4).

In assessing the general response to the novel at the end of 1907, Forster, though encouraged, felt he had vexed his readers when he could have pleased them, and he was not anxious to widen the gulf between himself and others (*LJ*, p. lix). The next novel he was now finally finishing, which he would publish in 1908, pleased him more. Forster said that *The Longest Journey* did not sell but a second impression of 500 copies was called for two months after Blackwood's original printing of approximately 1500 (*LJ*, p. lxx; Kirkpatrick, *EMF*, p. 7). This was as good as the sales of *Where Angels Fear to Tread*. (There were no American editions of either until the 1920s.) Forster also said *The Longest Journey* was remaindered, and his malicious Uncle Willie, in revenge perhaps for the crack about his reading abilities in the book, bought copies at sixpence apiece – it had been published at six shillings – 'and sent them to those of my relations whom they were most likely to upset' (*LJ*, p. lxx).

Later critics have been more severe on *The Longest Journey* than the reviewers. F. R. Leavis saw disastrous weaknesses in it, John Harvey found an essential failure in the representation of reality, and even critical admirers like James McConkey complain of the shifting narration. But in the novel all the world's a stage, not just part of it, as the narrator reminds the spectatorial Ansell (*LJ*, p. 218), and that world includes the narrating-dramatist. Archetypal readings of the novel, such as John Magnus's or George Thomson's, synthesise overt and remote symbols in the novel but without considering its complexities of narration. *The Longest Journey* still seems to be Forster's least regarded novel, along with the posthumous *Maurice*, whose Cambridge and country settings of homosexual love contrastingly reveal how intricate and subtle the earlier novel was, for all its apparent artlessness. Only Lionel

Trilling appears to have considered *The Longest Journey* as Forster's most brilliant, if disintegrative, novel. Unaware of Moore's significance, Trilling perceived the importance of Shelley for the novel, and his placing of *The Longest Journey* in the *Bildungsroman* tradition partly explains why, despite the critics, *The Longest Journey* has been perhaps the most influential of Forster's three early novels.

Forster's portrait of the artist as a young man owes something not just to Samuel Butler's *Erewhon* books but also to *The Way of All Flesh*, which appeared in 1903, the year of *Principia Ethica* and *The Ambassadors*. Another modern novel that he may well have heard about at the Countess von Arnim's was Thomas Mann's *Buddenbrooks* (1901). Important in a very different way was Rudyard Kipling's widely read collection of stories about schoolboy iconoclasts turned imperial idealists. The antitheses of Forster and Kipling are not confined to India, and the damage that *The Longest Journey* did to the reputation of *Stalky & Co.*, which was published in 1899, has been noted (J. Stewart, p. 264). Joyce's *Portrait of the Artist as a Young Man* does not seem to have been influenced by Forster's novel, but there are resemblances between 'The Dead' and *The Longest Journey*. D. H. Lawrence responded to Forster's writings more than to anyone's in Bloomsbury, and there are parallels and echoes of *The Longest Journey* in *Sons and Lovers*, *Women in Love* and elsewhere.[13] Trilling has noted the similarities between the club-footed heroes in Somerset Maugham's naturalistic *Of Human Bondage* (1915) and *The Longest Journey*; the sexuality of both is somewhat ambivalent and this is reflected in their painful relations with women (Trilling, p. 79). Maugham's masochistic failed artist hero is named Philip, and he talks about art and the nature of reality with his friends (there is even a Miss Förster in a German pension).

Forster's exposure of 'the idea, or ideal, of the British public school' resonates throughout Edwardian and Georgian writing. Novels like Compton Mackenzie's *Sinister Street* (1913) and Alec Waugh's *The Loom of Youth* (1917), though more romantic in their school visions than Forster's, continue the criticism of public school pretensions. Mackenzie's attitude toward St Paul's can be compared to Leonard Woolf's sterner, later view in *Sowing*. In Bloomsbury's writings, however, the subject was most devastatingly treated in Strachey's eminent-Victorian treatment of Dr Arnold. Forster returned to schools briefly in several of his essays and reviews, one of which concludes wittily with a mock speech for schoolboys that should have been delivered to those in *The Longest Journey*:

> From this platform of middle age, this throne of experience, this altar of wisdom, this scaffold of character, this beacon of hope, this threshold of decay, my last words to you are: There's a better time coming. ('Breaking Up')

It was not only as a school novel that *The Longest Journey* has remained an influential Bloomsbury text, conveying not philosophical arguments so much as a philosophic point of view. The novel's whole symbolic dismissal of epistemological and altruistic idealisms in both miniature and great worlds has continued to attract and amuse readers. Julian Bell's unsuccessful fellowship dissertation for King's, entitled 'The Good and All That', begins with a discussion of Forster's cow; it is picked up again in an article on perception entitled 'The Cow' by Forster and Bloomsbury's friend Charles Mauron that was published in Eliot's *Criterion* in 1933. (Mauron's French translation of *The Longest Journey* was published in 1952.) Farther from Bloomsbury the implications of Berkeley's philosophic myth became the subject of light verse. The famous Oxford limericks about God in the quad have a tree at the centre, like the Cadbury Rings. And part of Richard Wilbur's brief, ironic poem 'Epistemology' derives quite directly from *The Longest Journey*:

> We milk the cow of the world, and as we do
> We whisper in her ear, 'You are not true.'

Asked about the poem by Elizabeth Heine when she was editing *The Longest Journey*, Wilbur replied that as a student in New England it was possible, 'without explicit reference to the novel, to express a philosophic attitude by saying "The cow is there"' (*LJ*, p. 406). And the novelist Cynthia Ozick, who later found the homosexuality of *Maurice* debased the humanism of Forster, once made a pilgrimage to King's College to stand outside his door unable to knock, asking herself 'Are they talking of cows?' (pp. 8, 12).

The influence of *The Longest Journey* is, in the last analysis, inseparable from Forster's narrative style in the novel. The hardest task of modern criticism, wrote Cyril Connolly, 'is to find out who were the true innovators'. Forster was one, he thought, in novels like *The Longest Journey* and *Howards End* because there he established

> a point of view, a technique, and an attitude to the reader that were to be followed for the next thirty years by the psychological novelists. . . . Forster wrote for men and women, chiefly women, of a larger though still cultured public, and evolved a more radically simplified, disintegrated, and colloquial form of art.
>
> (*Enemies*, p. 39)

The surprising, amusing flexibility of form in *The Longest Journey* would come to be appreciated in Forster's later novels as well. But whether his readers were chiefly women is open to question. The problem of representing homosexuality in *The Longest Journey* concerned Forster's followers such as Christopher Isherwood. In Stephen Spender's 1929 novel *The Temple* (reworked and published finally 1988) a character modelled on Isherwood complains that the novelistic problem Forster never solved in *The Longest Journey* is what happens after two men go to bed with each other.

Another male novelist who has born witness to a different impact of *The Longest Journey* on his art is Norman Mailer. He singled it out as one of the novels he learned most from technically; the abrupt death of Gerald and its effect on other characters had quite an extraordinary effect on him:

> It taught me that personality was more fluid, more dramatic and startling, more inexact than I had thought. I was brought up on the idea that when you wrote a novel you tried to build a character who could be handled and walked around like a piece of sculpture. (Mailer, Interview)

After the shock of Forster's novel, Mailer found he could no longer create fictional characters from the third-person point of view (pp. 264–5).

It is unlikely that *The Longest Journey* will again become a widely read book of Forster's. Forster insisted repeatedly that the novel should not be dramatised (Parker, p. 424), and as yet no one has tried to base a film on it. For the historian of English literature, however, it will remain, as Connolly said, one of the vital books in the modern movement.

10 Desmond MacCarthy and the *New Quarterly,* Clive Bell and the *Athenaeum*

I

The Cambridge origins of Bloomsbury reflected in *The Longest Journey* appear as well in the quarterly that Desmond MacCarthy also began editing in 1907. The *New Quarterly* lasted less than three years, but in its pages there are essays by Lytton Strachey, Roger Fry, J. M. Keynes, and MacCarthy himself, together with contributions by the four Apostles who shaped Bloomsbury's philosophical education at Cambridge: Dickinson, McTaggart, Russell, and Moore. Along with the *Independent Review* and the *Speaker,* MacCarthy's quarterly illustrates the development of Bloomsbury as a literary group during the Edwardian period, despite the presence of well-known Edwardian writers with little or no Bloomsbury connection – and the absence of Bloomsbury writers such as Forster, who submitted one article, Virginia Woolf, who had not established herself as an essayist yet, and Clive Bell, whose critical career only began in 1909.

The most important Bloomsbury texts that MacCarthy published in the *New Quarterly* were by Lytton Strachey and Roger Fry. MacCarthy had written to Strachey late in January 1907 asking him to help edit the magazine and offering him around £100 a year plus £2 per 1000 words for writing whatever he chose. 'I think we are worth that', MacCarthy went on, 'or at least you are and I *intend* to

259

be' (27.i.07, LS/pBL). The *New Quarterly* or perhaps *London Quarterly* was to appear in July, Strachey told Duncan Grant, adding that MacCarthy was 'a very wild editor, but he's cheerful and seems to believe in me.' J. M. Dent was to publish the quarterly free 'in order MacCarthy thinks to get the reputation of dealing with first-class gents' (MH/*LS*, p. 337). By July the *New Quarterly* had not yet appeared. In the meantime Strachey's cousin St. Loe Strachey offered him a position on the *Spectator* where he been doing some occasional reviewing; for £150 a year he was to contribute a weekly review. (Strachey, unlike Forster, MacCarthy, and Virginia Woolf, had no independent income.) That stipend plus the £100 from the *New Quarterly* would now give him a livelihood, he wrote Keynes, mentioning also that his brother James thought he had sold himself to 'the Mammon of Unrighteousness'; he hoped and prayed, however, that he had only become friends with it (MH/*LS*, p. 361). In September MacCarthy informed Strachey his duties would begin in October and asked for a list of potential subscribers as well as Strachey's contribution to the first issue; this finally appeared in November, a month after Strachey had begun writing regularly for the *Spectator*. Three more pieces were contributed by Strachey to the *New Quarterly* before it ceased in May 1910. Strachey also helped with the proofs but how much other editorial work he finally did for MacCarthy is uncertain.

Desmond MacCarthy's quarterly and St. Loe Strachey's weekly appealed to quite different kinds of Edwardian reader, as did the *Athenaeum*, for which Clive Bell wrote monthly or fortnightly book reviews from 1909 through 1912. Bell had known MacCarthy since 1901 but he had done no reviewing until his involvement with the *Athenaeum*. The readers of that distinguished, unpolitical paper differed from both those of the short-lived *New Quarterly* and those of the influential, imperialistic *Spectator*. In some respects the *Athenaeum* was closer to *The Times Literary Supplement*, except that the range of its reviewing – as Roger Fry's earlier Edwardian art reviews show – was not specifically literary. The Bloomsbury contributions to the *New Quarterly*, Bell's reviews for the *Athenaeum*, and Lytton Strachey's for the *Spectator*, which are the subjects of this and the next chapter, all reveal, together with Forster and Virginia Woolf's earlier and later Edwardian writings, the diverse conditions of periodical publication that are an important but largely unfamiliar part of the Bloomsbury's literary history in the first decade of the twentieth century.

II

The backing for the *New Quarterly* came out of Cambridge again. At Eton and then Trinity, MacCarthy had been good friends with G. A. Paley, a wealthy, eccentric young Suffolk squire and descendant of the illustrious Utilitarian archdeacon who wrote *Evidences of Christianity and Natural Theology*. MacCarthy passes silently over the *New Quarterly* years in his apprenticeship memoirs[1] but Mary MacCarthy in her fragmentary sequel to *A Nineteenth-Century Childhood* describes how she and Desmond moved into a farmhouse on Paley's estate after their marriage in the summer of 1906. The rent was free and MacCarthy was given £400 a year to edit the quarterly (Cecil, p. 92). Various contributors such as Strachey, Moore or Russell stayed the weekend with them; few were aesthetic enthusiasts, she felt, and all seemed to have a tragic or pessimistic point of view (Mary MacCarthy, Papers). Desmond continued to write for the *Speaker* while he set about organising the new magazine. When in March 1907 the *Nation* replaced the *Speaker* and no place was found for its drama critic, MacCarthy became a full-time editor, while reviewing occasionally for the *Independent* or *Albany Review*. He finished his *Court Theatre* book, continued to think about his novel, and was also collaborating on a memoir of Bertrand Russell's grandmother.

The first issue of the *New Quarterly* (its title somewhat misleadingly suggesting a successor to the old yet still influential Tory *Quarterly*) was published by Dent in November 1907. The cover of the magazine described it as 'A Review of Science & Literature' and proclaimed Desmond MacCarthy as editor. Characteristically, there was no editorial statement of aims or principles. The lead article on the perception of sound was by Lord Rayleigh, Nobel prize-winner, President of the Royal Society – and a relative of Paley's. Another fellow of the Royal Society, who happened to be Rayleigh's son, wrote on astronomy. Russell contributed his early Platonic 'The Study of Mathematics' (rejected by the *Independent Review*). An article by Paley which MacCarthy helped write criticised the political implications of biological theories. Sandwiched between these scientific discussions were essays by G. L. Strachey, Max Beerbohm, Arthur Symons, and T. Sturge Moore. The issue concluded with excerpts from the unpublished notebooks of Samuel Butler. It was an auspicious start. The combining of scientific with literary discussions gave the short-lived *New Quarterly* a distinctive character among Edwardian periodicals. Its concern with modern British philosophical thought interested Bloomsbury, of course, and is one of the characteristics that distinguishes the Group from most other English modernists.

The *New Quarterly* continued to publish essays in science and philosophy as well as literary criticism. Discussions on a variety of scientific subjects occupied as much as a third of each issue. Only two really political articles appeared, and both showed the Liberal slant of the quarterly. One was a criticism of socialism by Paley that elicited a reply by H. G. Wells rejecting Paley's arguments for a more conciliatory and practical socialism. The other was by J. M. Keynes defending the Liberal Government's 1909 budget by arguing it would not affect England's foreign investments, as claimed. On the literary side of the quarterly there was another essay by Beerbohm, one each by Austin Dobson, Hilaire Belloc and G. K. Chesterton, some reminiscences of Turgenev by Anne Thackeray Ritchie, two pieces on Russian literature by Maurice Baring, and two on French literature by T. Sturge Moore. Modern German literature received some attention too, and there were essays about drama, including Granville Barker on repertory theatre, and MacCarthy himself on play-censorship. Passages from Butler's notebooks appeared in five more issues. There were also poems by Belloc and Hardy, some Carlyle letters on Saint-Simonianism, a translation of Virgil with discussion by the future Poet Laureate Robert Bridges, and two Chekhov stories. Three articles were written by MacCarthy's Warre-Cornish in-laws. Many of the other contributors were Apostles. Oscar Browning and A. W. Verrall contributed (as did Mrs Verrall on psychical research), Dickinson wrote on immortality, McTaggart on mysticism, Moore on Hume, and Russell on mathematics and then ethics. From Bloomsbury came three more essays by Strachey, Fry's important 'Essay on Aesthetics', which appeared in April 1909, and Keynes's essay in February 1910. The May 1910 issue included both Lytton Strachey on Rousseau, which he had written in 1907, and his sister Marjorie on Marivaux. (Comparing him with Henry James, among others, she tried to do for Marivaux what her brother had done earlier for Racine.) Then abruptly the *New Quarterly* stopped. Articles in proof for a planned September issue were abandoned, Russell's discussion of ethics was left incomplete, and Butler's notebooks uncontinued.

Some twenty years later when MacCarthy was starting his

second magazine, *Life and Letters*, Virginia Woolf wrote of how the *New Quarterly* 'died so thin, at the wrong time of year too, it made one cry to see it; and this was to make Desmond's fortune' (*L*, III 459). MacCarthy had reluctantly agreed early in 1910 to go to South Africa with Paley; he was to give some lectures there and also help Paley write an unnecessary book on social questions. MacCarthy asked G. E. Moore to edit the magazine in his absence, rather than Strachey, who had now stopped reviewing regularly for the *Spectator*. Strachey was furious when he discovered that an old essay of his entitled 'The Rousseau Affair' was included in the final issue of the *New Quarterly*; he wrote to MacCarthy asking 'what is going to happen to that appalling paper?' and demanding £5 for his work (MH/LS, p. 368). Moore warned MacCarthy in May that something would have to be done to get more articles for the next issue, the May number having already been reduced to 128 pages (DM/pM; Moore, Cambridge papers). In the beginning, contributions had apparently been commissioned as well as invited, but later the quarterly became dependent upon what was submitted. (Moore paid one pressing contributor a guinea a page, which was about what MacCarthy proposed to pay Strachey and himself; Keynes however received only £4 for his 6000 words.) Perhaps Paley grew tired of subsidising the venture; perhaps he objected to what Strachey perceived as MacCarthy's 'wild' editing. When the *New Quarterly* first appeared, Strachey wrote to Leonard Woolf that it was really founded on a lie because Paley was an idiot who wanted to run a magazine, and MacCarthy was willing to do it for him (19.x.07, LS/pNY). With the failure of the *New Quarterly*, MacCarthy returned to miscellaneous journalism and odd literary jobs, but did no more magazine editing until the 1920s.

III

With the exception of Lytton Strachey's essays on Beddoes and Racine, which are among his best critical performances, the *New Quarterly* is disappointing as a literary periodical, particularly when compared with two of its near contemporaries that lasted much longer. A. R. Orage started a new series of the *New Age* in May 1907, and he soon had Chesterton, Wells, and Shaw involved polemically in its pages; a little later Arnold Bennett, alias Jacob Tonson, began his widely read column there. In a few years Orage would be publishing the stories of Katherine Mansfield (Carswell, pp. 39–41, 59ff.). A year after the *New Quarterly* started, Ford Madox Ford began the *English Review* with a first issue that contained James's 'The Jolly Corner', a long Hardy poem, reminiscences by Conrad, stories by Galsworthy and Tolstoy, and the first instalment of Wells's *Tono-Bungay*. Later he published Forster's 'Other Kingdom'. Ford's generous payments soon put the magazine in a financial crisis, however (Mizener, pp. 154ff.). Orage's Fabian weekly and Ford's literary monthly were very different magazines from MacCarthy's quarterly review of science and literature, yet it was unfortunate for the editor that he was unable to attract work from Henry James or Bernard Shaw, to take two examples. James replied charmingly to MacCarthy's request for a critical essay but could provide nothing; Shaw retorted that if MacCarthy had read what he had already written on the topic of censorship he would not have asked for more, and then went on to offer high praise for *The Court Theatre* book and express his considerable interest in the Butler notebooks (DM/pM.) E. M. Forster, who subscribed to the quarterly, sent not a story but an essay, on the writings of the fifteenth-century Florentine humanist Poggio, whose *Facetiae* were stories collected from a club of humanists. It had not been 'compelling' enough for the sinless Americans, he told R. C. Trevelyan (17.vi.07, Trevelyan, Papers) nor apparently for MacCarthy either. Forster's essay never appeared in the *New Quarterly* or anywhere else. Nor did anything by the Trevelyan brothers.

The work that MacCarthy did attract, such as Max Beerbohm's essay on the hearth fires or law-court drama, Belloc on an English road, or Chesterton on swearing, while all characteristic of their authors' skill and charm, are not among their most memorable productions. Thomas Hardy's brief 'The House of Hospitalities' is also a representative rather than a remarkable poem. Robert Bridges's contributions were translations rather than original poetry. Ritchie on Turgenev is less appealing than some of her Victorian literary reminiscences. Sturge Moore on Baudelaire is appreciative but unoriginal (what did his brother think of his calling Nietzsche the last of the great German philosophers?), and his two-part article on Flaubert and the critics is just a digest of opinion. Dobson and Symons's critical essays are similarly unremarkable. The attention of the *New Quarterly* to Russian literature was more interesting. Maurice Baring described two plays of Chekhov – who had yet to be produced in Britain – and also his developing reputation as a short-story writer, which was furthered by translations (not yet by Constance Garnett) of two moving stories of narrow desire and futile love, 'The Gooseberry Garden' and 'About Love'. Baring, who also wrote on Gogol for the quarterly, was a friend of Mary MacCarthy's family. His knowledge of Russian literature contributed to the early modern English awareness of it, including Bloomsbury's and especially the Woolfs'.

Bloomsbury and others also read the six instalments of notes and an essay from Samuel Butler's unpublished notebooks that were printed in the *New Quarterly* and which added significantly to Butler's Edwardian reputation, following the posthumous publication of *The Way of All Flesh* in 1903. Among the notes in the *New Quarterly*, some of which are very entertaining, can be found examples of Butler's characteristic concerns with immortality and unconscious memory as well as an epitome of *Life and Habit* and some further ideas for *Erewhon Revisited*. MacCarthy had known Butler and been influenced by him. Butler's future biographer showed MacCarthy the notebooks, and the publication of extracts in the *New Quarterly* encouraged the bringing out an edition of the notebooks in 1912 (Butler, *Note-Books*, p. vii). The importance of Butler for Bloomsbury and especially Forster has been noted. Virginia Woolf thought the *Note-Books* and *The Way of All Flesh* were Butler's most remarkable works, though his insisting on his own views makes his novel stagnant at times. She predicted Butler's notebooks would be disappointingly influential on other keepers of the form who lacked the viewpoint essential for the maintaining of a good notebook (*E*, II 37–8). This could not be said of Woolf's own diaries, and Butler's example may have encouraged her to be less subjective, more opinionated in them. Strachey wrote to her that he too found Butler's notebooks amusing but regretted their lack of personal panache; the ideas about evolution, so influential on Shaw, he regarded as rubbish (*LVWLS*, p. 47).

The *New Quarterly* is really more interesting for its philosophical contributions than its literary ones. The essays of the Cambridge philosophers that MacCarthy persuaded to address a wider audience, recapitulate a number of the basic ideas of early twentieth-century British philosophy that moulded Bloomsbury's assumptions about ethics, perception, truth, and mysticism. It was Russell's Platonic paean to the study of mathematics in the first issue that made Strachey wish to have 'He knew Moore and Russell' engraved on his tombstone (*Victorian Bloomsbury*, p. 199).

The last two issues of the quarterly contained half of Russell's 'Ethics', which begins with a footnote referring the reader to *Principia Ethica* for a fuller discussion of what follows. Russell had originally written the piece for a manifesto on Moore's philosophy. If Bloomsbury needed a review of Moore's principles, here it was in Russell's discussions of the subject matter of ethics as well as the meaning of good and bad, right and wrong.[2] MacCarthy wanted Moore himself to write on William James's recently published *Pragmatism* but he had agreed to do it instead for the Aristotelian Society. (The Apostle and economist Ralph Hawtrey criticised James instead, with Moore's approval – DM/pM.) What Moore did write for MacCarthy, protracted painfully for over a year, he told Leonard Woolf (*S*, pp. 141–2), was an essay on the philosophy of Hume. 'It's not easy to understand; it's childish; it's awkward; and all the points are very badly made', he wrote to MacCarthy, hoping something else would be found in place of it (Regan, p. 286). 'Hume's Philosophy' is a difficult text, but some of its arguments resemble those in his earlier refutations of Idealism; here they are directed at Hume's scepticism. Moore argues influentially, as Susan Stebbing says, 'that probable knowledge is not less *knowledge* than *demonstrative* knowledge . . . ' (p. 526). Moore is enough of a empiricist at the end of his article, however, to confess his uncertainty as to whether anything exists beyond our observation that is not based on experience ('Hume', p. 165).

Dickinson on immortality and McTaggart on mysticism were more conclusive than Moore and more accessible to the general reader of the *New Quarterly*. Dickinson's lecture 'Is Immortality Desirable?' desires an individual immortality beyond the remembrance that Samuel Butler counted upon. Citing the investigations of the Society for Psychical Research, Dickinson claims it is merely prejudice to say we cannot know there is life after death, and ends urging people to take the pursuit of this knowledge seriously.[3] McTaggart's analysis of mysticism, also very general, is more rigorous and interesting for Bloomsbury. His central distinction is between mystical unity and the mystical intuition of that unity. Belief in gods is not essential for either. An assertion of mystical unity in the universe could be combined with a recognition of diversity. Similarly, the mystical intuiting of that unity is not inconsistent with an awareness of diversity that ordinary experience discloses. The value of mysticism for McTaggart is ultimate and unarguable, like Moore's *summum bonum* of love and beauty. Even for those who find the reality of differentiation inescapable, the contemplation of mystical unity can bring great happiness. McTaggart does not commit himself further than this in 'Mysticism'. But in lucidly maintaining that the high good of mystical intuition did not have to be monistic or theistic, McTaggart was describing in the pages of the *New Quarterly* a conviction Bloomsbury could, and at times in their writing did, accept. (Virginia Woolf, for example, found his 'mystic Heqelianism' interesting in the 1930s – *L*, VI 6). Other aspects of McTaggart's mystical Idealism remained less appealing to Bloomsbury (see *Victorian Bloomsbury*, pp. 189–92).

Philosophically, however, the most important essay for the Bloomsbury Group in the *New Quarterly* was on aesthetics. Roger Fry's 'An Essay in Aesthetics' is as much a part of Cambridge philosophy as the essays written by philosophers who were his Apostolic brothers, only now the influence of Russell and Moore appears more clearly. The Idealistic traces of his *Athenaeum* texts are gone. Fry's departure point in his succinct and persuasive essay is the inadequacy of mimetic theories as an explanation of the graphic arts.[4] His aim, he says, is to arrive at some conclusions that will account for our feelings about visual art and also allow us to relate them to the other arts. This regard for the interrelation of the arts made Fry's theories all the more relevant for Bloomsbury's writers and their literary history.

The basic premise of Fry's and Bloomsbury's aesthetics is the distinction he makes in his essay between actual and imaginative life. Though there is no moral responsibility in the latter (*pace* Ruskin), art does exercise our spiritual faculties, for it is the chief organ of the imaginative life, which is stimulated and controlled by art's clarification of perception and expression of pure, free emotion. The question of aesthetic emotion is central to Fry's *New Quarterly* essay, which further suggests its relevance to literary, rather than just graphic-art theory. It was Fry and Bell's idea of aesthetic emotion that I. A. Richards later attacked in *Principles of Literary Criticism*. Fry's argument that 'art appreciates emotion in and for itself' comes with major modifications from Tolstoy's *What Is Art?* (*VD*, pp. 19–20). Fry was later to date the beginning of fruitful aesthetics with that work – especially Tolstoy's suggestion that art had no essential connection with natural beauty and his recognition that art is the communication of emotion (*VD*, p. 205). From Tolstoy, Fry develops his own theories that art orders and varies our perceptions, as he now recognises impressionist painters had done. But disinterested contemplation is not all there is to aesthetic judgement. We also experience a kind of sympathy with the artist who has expressed something latent within us. The recognition of his purpose is part of aesthetic judgement, but not much about this important qualification of formalism would be said later in Fry and Bell's aesthetics. In discussing how art can order and vary our perceptions, Fry distinguishes the sensuous charm of beauty from its role in unity of design, where ugliness may in fact be represented, as in Rembrandt and Degas. Earlier Fry had criticised the puritanical view that narrowly equated the imaginative with the sensual life, but in some ways he himself was never completely free of that association. After describing how pictorial art may have a balanced or successive unity, Fry elucidates the ways emotion can be expressed by the pictorial elements of design that he identifies as rhythm, mass, space, light and shade, colour, and possibly the use of inclined planes. Most of these elements 'are connected with essential conditions of our physical existence', which unlike Reynolds, Fry now finds to be art's great advantage over poetry (pp. 24–5). In response to the devil's advocate who asks if Fry is not bringing imitation of nature back into aesthetics, he replies that nature, which can of course be beautiful, does not give order and variety to our perceptions or elicit the emotional elements of design in the way art does. Fry's conclusion is that likeness to nature may finally be dispensed with as a test for art. Except for pictures where 'the emotional idea' depends on likeness or completeness, all we need to do is consider 'whether the emotional elements inherent in natural form are adequately discovered' (p. 27).

The impact of Fry's aesthetic theory in the April 1909 issue of *New Quarterly* would be fully felt at the end of the next year with the first post-impressionist exhibition. In 1909 Fry did give a series of unpublished lectures based on his theory in which he classified works of art according to the emotional states in which they place us. These he described in literary terms of epic, dramatic, lyric, and comedic (RF/pKC). The emphasis on the aesthetic emotion of the spectator and the interconnectedness of the arts would continue to distinguish Bloomsbury's aesthetics. Fry's 'Essay in Aesthetics' was available, however, only in MacCarthy's magazine until it was finally reprinted more than a decade later in *Vision and Design*.

IV

Three of Lytton Strachey's four contributions in the *New Quarterly* also remained unavailable until he collected them in 1922, and the fourth he never reprinted. The critical essays signed G. L. Strachey are similar to those Strachey wrote for the *Independent Review* but quite different from the weekly reviews he was writing anonymously and pseudonymously for the *Spectator*. They also differ from the works of biographical irony he would later publish under the name Lytton Strachey. Three of Strachey's *New Quarterly* pieces are about widely different kinds of poetry from the past which, Strachey argues, deserves more critical appreciation by modern readers. Among Bloomsbury's writing there is comparatively little poetic criticism; the best of it was written by Strachey.

After Rayleigh on sound, Beerbohm on fire, and Russell on mathematics in the inaugural issue of the *New Quarterly* came Strachey on 'The Last Elizabethan', who turns out to be the nineteenth-century Romantic, Thomas Lovell Beddoes. Lady Strachey had long admired his poems. A new edition of them is the occasion for her son's essay (which now commends Gosse for earlier editions of the poems and letters that corrected their errors). Beddoes's fondness for blank verse, Gothic melodrama, and a nineteen-year-old baker had their autobiographical appeal for Strachey, who wondered why the poet's eccentric but very English life had not attracted more interest. 'For one reader who cares to concern himself with the intrinsic merit of a piece of writing' – he observed prophetically for his own career and influence – 'there are a thousand who are ready to explore with eager sympathy the history of the writer . . . ' (*BC*, p. 227). Strachey wrote to Keynes that he was convinced Beddoes belonged to their 'sect' (the use of this Shelleyan term a few months after the publication of *The Longest Journey* is interesting), and he had tried to make this plain to 'the perspicacious reader' (Merle, p. 799) – presumably by writing that the poet lived 'in close companionship' with a young nice-looking baker (*BC*, pp. 236–7). In Strachey's essay, the intrinsic value of the last Elizabethan's writing justifies the interest in his life. Beddoes's poetry leads Strachey into a dichotomy of thought and expression. Beddoes learned early the magic secret of dramatic blank verse, which is phrasing. That metre is a djinn that turns poetic thought into either toads and fishes or flying carpets of the imagination, according to whether the poet is its slave or master.

But Beddoes never learned effective dramatic characterisation or construction. His plots unravel, his characters ignore ordinary existence in 'puzzling over eternity and dissecting the attributes of death' (p. 245). No more criticism of life is to be found in his poetry than in that class of writers like Spenser, Keats, and Milton 'who are great merely because of their art'. Strachey is quick to support the inclusion of Milton on the authority of Stephen, who remarked that all of what Milton had to say in *Paradise Lost* could have been put into a few pages of prose – Fitzjames Stephen, that is, not his brother Leslie. Poems like Wordsworth's *The Excursion* and Pope's *Satires* are different; their thought could survive their expression. The classification is not an evaluative one. The styles are simply different, like peaches and roses, and 'Beddoes is among the roses' (p. 246). (In his next, essay, Strachey compared Racine with roses and Shelley and Virgil with salmon, but then deleted the analogy when the piece was republished – Sanders, 'Revisions', p. 232.)

Simplistic comparisons and Arabian Nights imagery in a critical style Strachey knew to be flamboyant leave the reader rather uncertain of the Strachey's critical aim. The essay opens mockingly on 'Apollo's pew-renters' who risk destruction should the god descend to question the Poet Laureate (who was Alfred Austin) about the state of poetry worship. In places, Strachey moves from quoting Beddoes to describing his work in the style of Sir Thomas Browne. There is something ridiculous about Beddoes's career, yet Strachey is serious about the excellence of the poetry, and some of his quotations from it are impressive. 'The Last Elizabethan' is an enjoyable piece of writing, even if its irony sometimes unfocuses the case being made for Beddoes's recognition.

'The Poetry of Racine' in the third issue of the *New Quarterly* is a much more effective piece of criticism, as Strachey must have realised when he placed it first in his collected essays of 1922. The title was changed simply to 'Racine', perhaps because the essay discusses Racine's drama as well as his poetry. Strachey's critical purpose with Racine is the same as with Beddoes: to enlarge 'the glorious boundaries of art' (*BC*, p. 6), and it remained one of the principal aims of Bloomsbury criticism. Here Strachey is more persuasive, less ironic with the greater writer because he has a critic to confute. John C. Bailey is now quite forgotten, but to young Bloomsbury he was a leading figure in the critical establishment – 'one of the most distinguished literary critics of the first quarter of our century', G. M. Trevelyan thought (Bailey, *Letters*, p. 7). He set the standard for editors like his sister-in-law Mrs Lyttelton, who considered it an honour to publish his work – thus causing Virginia Woolf not so innocently to wonder just what Lyttelton thought of hers (*L*, I 167). In 1906, Bailey published in *The Claims of French Poetry* nine studies of 'the greater French' poets, who did not include Racine (or Baudelaire for that matter). A chapter entitled 'English Taste and French Drama' explains why Racine could not be included, and this gave Strachey his opportunity. Bailey had been reviewed anonymously by Strachey in the *Spectator* in 1907; the review praised his 'rare interpretative gift' but objected to his treatment of Racine (*SE*, p. 114). Strachey now developed his objections fully in the *New Quarterly* the next year. 'The Poetry of Racine' begins discursively on a French painting of Homer surrounded by all the great poets of the world except Shakespeare, who was allowed in at the edge only after protests. This pictorial symbol of the unaccountability of French and English taste unfortunately illustrated the mutual artistic ignorance of the two cultures more than Strachey intended, for he mistakenly attributed it to David instead of Ingres. He corrected the mistake in *Books and Characters* and also changed a comparison of Racine from painting – Tintoretto and Hooch – to music – Mozart and Wagner (Sanders, 'Revisions', p 231). Bloomsbury and the Friday Club had not done much yet for Strachey's art education by 1908.

The first aspect Strachey examines of the divergent French and English evaluations of Racine has to do with the dramatic form of his work. English readers like Bailey fail to appreciate the greatness of Racine's style because they do not realise his is a classical drama of concentrated spiritual crisis. The unities of his restricted form function theatrically, Strachey now argues from his experience as a play-reviewer for the *Spectator*. Bailey's inability to appreciate the dramatic effectiveness of Racine's poetry has a deeper origin in literary theory, however. Using Matthew Arnold's touchstone technique, Bailey objects to the absence of 'a wide view of humanity' in Racine's poetry. Strachey replies, as he does in 'The Last Elizabethan', that Milton lacks this too, and he throws in Dante as well to expose the limited Victorian view of humanity that Bailey seems to accept. But the force of Strachey's objection is directed at Bailey's whole *a priori* Arnoldian method that tries, almost scientifically, to isolate the elements of poetry and then seeks for them in particular poems:

Mr. Bailey's attempts to discover, by quotations from Shake-speare, Sophocles, and Goethe, the qualities without which no poet can be great, and his condemnation of Racine because he is without them, is a fallacy in criticism. There is only one way to judge a poet, as Wordsworth, with that paradoxical sobriety so characteristic of him, has pointed out – and that is, by loving him.

(*BC*, p. 12)

The rhetorical use of Wordsworth to counter Arnold brings in an amorous element in criticism not much regarded today, but it was something that Leslie Stephen could have accepted and that Forster advocated much later when he wrote that only love could establish a completely satisfactory *raison d'être* for criticism (*2CD*, p. 118).

From objections to Bailey's fallacious critical method, which ignores Moorean organic unities, Strachey moves to particular questions of French versus English style. The Saxon, Latin, and even Hebrew history of the English language has produced an art of writing 'under the dominion of the emphatic, the extraordinary, and the bold', whereas French exalts 'the beauties of restraint, of clarity, of refinement, and of precision . . . ' (pp. 12–13). Though the antithesis is Macaulayan, Strachey's quotations from Racine make it difficult to pass off the poet's elegance as frigidity. And when Bailey complains of the unmysterious finiteness of Racine's style, Strachey turns on this kind of criticism and does not spare the Romantics this time as he attacks 'the craving, which has seized upon our poetry and our criticism ever since the triumph of Wordsworth and Coleridge at the beginning of the last century, for metaphysical stimulants' (p. 18). Bailey's pages are filled with allusions to mystery, infinity, and eternity, to the secret of life and the nature of ultimate reality – none of which is to be found in Racine. Racine has mystery, nonetheless, and for Strachey it is far more valuable, more consoling than any metaphysical view of life. Racine's mystery is the human mind; his greatness as a writer is the expression he gives of its states. 'There was never a greater artist', Strachey wrote to Virginia Woolf, 'and he writes about the only thing worth writing about, in my opinion, – the human heart!' (*LVWLS*, pp. 12–13).

'Racine' is one of Strachey's best pieces of criticism. MacCarthy said it was the making of the magazine's third issue, which included work by Dobson and Baring (12.vii.08, LS/pBL). Arguing for the English appreciation of Racine's greatness, Strachey strives to extend their boundaries of art by urging critical attention to states of mind rather than metaphysics in Racine's work. This attention, derived from Moore's philosophy, characterises much of Bloomsbury's literary criticism. Strachey's critical style in his essay is more lucid, less ornate and ironic than in his piece on Beddoes. The criticism of Bailey is fairly mild and quite straightforward. Only occasionally is there a glimpse of the irony to come in Strachey's work, as when he ticks Bailey off for thinking Johnson's *Irene* is in couplets, or counters the complaint that Racine's alexandrines are monotonous:

> To his lovers, to those who have found their way into the secret places of his art, his lines are impregnated with a peculiar beauty, and the last perfection of style. Over them, the most insignificant of his verses can throw a deep enchantment, like the faintest wavings of a magician's wand. (p. 24)

The trite eroticism of this imagery does little for the appreciation of Racine, yet Bailey was persuaded by Strachey's arguments and wrote to tell him so when the Racine article was reprinted in *Books and Characters*.[5]

In the next issue of the *New Quarterly*, Strachey attempted to extend the English reader's horizons of poetry in a more modernist direction. 'An Anthology' begins with contradictions: the anthology in question may be the best poetry of this generation, even though it has been written for ten centuries and many readers have never heard of it. In a gibe at Idealism, Strachey says these contradictions are as easy to synthesise as Hegel's because the poems are verse translations from the Chinese by H. A. Giles, Professor of Chinese at Cambridge, done several years ago, and which may now be hard to obtain. (By not mentioning the book's title in his essay Strachey made them a little harder.) *Chinese Poetry in English Verse* is classical in spirit but not Greek, Strachey thinks. The poetry lacks the epigrammatic finality of the Greek Anthology; its authors are

> poets of reflection, preoccupied with patient beauties and the subtle relationships of simple things. Thus from one point of view, they are singularly modern. . . . (*CC*, p. 153)

The modern poet that such writers as Li Po, in his 'trance of exquisite inebriation' remind Strachey of is Verlaine. The Chinese poets 'know the art of being quiet in verse' (pp. 152–3); their love poetry is more concerned with the memories than the expectations of love. Its lovers are always friends. The 'mastery of the tones and depths of affection' in such poetry is what most moves him. Yet there is something cruel as well in this art of personal relations: 'one longs somehow or other, to shake it; and one feels that, if one did, one would shake it into ice' (pp. 155–6).

At the end of Strachey's essay a further French analogy occurs, this time to Versailles, in a poem described as 'perhaps . . . too modern to be included in Professor Giles's anthology':

> Here in the ancient park I wait alone.
> The dried-up fountains sleep in beds of stone;
> The paths are still; and up the sweeping sward
> No lovely lady passes, no gay lord.
>
> Why do I linger? Ah! perchance I'll find
> Some solace for the desolated mind
> In yon green grotto, down the towering glade,
> Where the bronze Cupid glimmers in the shade.
>
> (p. 157)

Even if the reader misses the ambiguous 'perhaps' introducing the poem, the unoriental Cupid discloses that here is another work by the reviewer who once published a Chinese epitaph in the *Cambridge Review* under the pseudonym of Se Lig – his inverted first name, which was also that of the Professor of Chinese at Cambridge.[6]

Lytton Strachey's discovery of Chinese poetry preceded the translations of Arthur Waley, who praised Giles's work for combining 'rhyme and literalness with wonderful dexterity' (p. 35), and Ezra Pound, who also used some of Giles's translations. T. S. Eliot has called Pound 'the inventor of Chinese poetry for our time' (Pound, *Essays*, p. xvi). Bloomsbury thought Waley had a share in that invention but both Waley and Pound realised what Strachey with his fondness for French poetry did not – that free verse was needed to render the modernity of Chinese lyrics. In Giles's (and Strachey's) rhymes they remain *fin de siècle*. This may have been why, after Pound's *Cathay* and Waley's *One Hundred and Seventy Chinese Poems*, Strachey did not reprint his review.[7]

Strachey's annoyance over MacCarthy's publishing 'The Rousseau Affair' in the last issue of the *New Quarterly* did not keep him from reprinting that with minor changes in *Books and Characters*. His only biographical contribution to the magazine, the piece was basically a review of some recently discovered memoirs having to do with Rousseau's quarrels. Strachey rejects the interpretation that Rousseau was right after all and people like Diderot wrong because it is not common sense. He offers instead an explanation of these contradictory accounts that perhaps explains more of his own development as a biographer than it does Rousseau's life. Modernism is again his theme, this time in behaviour. Rousseau was misunderstood by his contemporaries, as Leonard Woolf had noted earlier in the *Independent Review*, because he belonged not to the Enlightenment but

to the new world of self-consciousness, and doubt, and hesitation, of mysterious melancholy and quiet intimate delights, of long reflexions amid the solitudes of Nature, of infinite introspections amid the solitudes of the heart. (*BC*, p. 204)

He was, in other words, like the translated Chinese poets and the reviewer himself, a Romantic and a modern.

V

Desmond MacCarthy contributed two articles of his own to the *New Quarterly* while editing it after a fashion and supposedly working at several other literary projects as well. The first drew on his experience as theatre critic for the *Speaker*, a position he would occupy again on the *New Statesman* in a few years. 'The Censorship of Plays' was virtually a review of the 1909 parliamentary select committee report, which MacCarthy regards as a verdict condemning the practice. In the first of a number of Bloomsbury public protests against censorship in England, he discusses parts of the testimony in detail (how, for example, the censor had prevented a production of *Oedipus Rex*) while also presenting some of the familiar arguments against censoring plays – such as the inconsistency in censoring theatres but not music halls. MacCarthy supports the moderate recommendations that allow for both licensed and unlicensed drama, even conceding such conditions that licensed plays may not 'do violence to the sentiment of religious reverence' or 'impair friendly relations with any Foreign

Power' (p. 612). Nothing was done about the report, however, and licensing of plays continued for another half century.

MacCarthy's other piece displayed an interest in the writing of biography that Strachey, Forster, and Virginia Woolf shared. John Donne was his subject, and for years afterward MacCarthy would refer to the life of Donne he was writing. The *New Quarterly* essay is all of the project that was published. It begins as a meditation, somewhat in the manner of Sir Thomas Browne, on Donne's extraordinary tomb in St Paul's; then with the acknowledged help of Edmund Gosse's life, which he intends to supplant, MacCarthy develops the thesis that Donne was, like Beddoes in Strachey's earlier article, a belated Elizabethan out of joint with his Jacobean times. At first MacCarthy calls his essay a biographical study, but at the end he says it is on Donne's poetry. Dropping his critic's mask 'of only liking what he thinks he should admire', MacCarthy admits he rather likes Donne's conceits ('Donne' p. 277). Here too he is following Gosse, anticipating the modern enthusiasm for the metaphysicals in opposition to Leslie Stephen's representative Victorian view, also cited by MacCarthy, that Donne's poetry was indigestible. MacCarthy has his reservations about 'the Chinese concentration' of Donne's poetry and 'the wailing rhetoric' of his sermons (pp. 276, 289) but he recognises the connection with Browning who helped make Donne available to modernists.

MacCarthy's novel made little progress while he was editing the *New Quarterly*, and he told Virginia Woolf at the end of 1909 before going to Africa with Paley that it had become ridiculous (VW/L, I 415). All that MacCarthy seems to have published from his African trip was a brief contrast of the impressions made on 'an imaginative historian' by the characteristic houses of Paul Kruger and Cecil Rhodes (*P*, pp. 204–8). And after much delay and repeated expressions of impatience from Bertrand Russell, the commissioned memoir of Lady John Russell, co-edited with her daughter Agatha Russell but largely written by MacCarthy, finally appeared at the end of 1910. Interspersed with selections from her diaries and correspondence, the memoir is smoothly written for the general reader, who the editors hope may find 'his notions of past politics vivified and refreshed' by the passionate interest in them that the prime minister's wife expressed in her letters and diaries (p. 2). MacCarthy was hampered in his efforts to make the memoir more interesting by his co-editor's piety and avoidance of analysis. G. M. Trevelyan wished there was more of MacCarthy in it, but praised the book and told Desmond that he had the makings of a prime biographer (Cecil, pp. 97–8). It was also toward the end of 1910 that Roger Fry, whose aesthetics essay he had published the previous year, involved MacCarthy significantly in the first post-impressionist exhibition.

VI

Clive Bell, who would make his reputation as a critic and theorist of post-impressionist art, had not yet begun to write critical journalism at the time MacCarthy began the *New Quarterly*. As the son of a squire whose wealth came from coal, he had independent means and did not need to write for his living. During Bloomsbury's later Edwardian years when he thought the Group 'mostly socialists', Bell had planned a *magnum opus* that would give

> a picture of contemporary art, thought, and social organisation by tracing the history of those manifestations of civility from earliest times to the present – to 1909 say.

It was to be called the *New Renaissance* – a contrasting allusion to Walter Pater's old one, among other things. A little wiser by 1911, Bell realised the topic was unmanageable, and under the inspiration of the two post-impressionist exhibitions he turned his projected *opus* into the books he would write over the next fifteen or twenty years (*C*, pp. v–vii).

Before 1909, Bell's surviving papers indicate that he continued to write a little poetry like that in *Euphrosyne*, while also beginning to accept the vocation of a critic. As he told Virginia Woolf in August 1908, 'I am condemned all my life, I think, to enjoy through an interpreter; but then as the interpreter is art one must not complain too much' (Spalding, *VB*, pp. 74–5). He started practising criticism by reviewing not art but French literature. Bell wrote to Strachey asking if he knew any publication that would send him books to review (6.v.07, 30.i.08, LS/pBL). Later he sent an article on Mérimée's *Lettres à une inconnue* to Strachey, who was not impressed. Bell also recommended Mérimée's letters to Virginia Woolf, who practised reviewing them herself in Greece. Lytton Strachey and Virginia Woolf were Bell's chief literary guides in Bloomsbury at this time. Always an appreciator, he thought they both had genius and told them so. Bell also tried reviewing the early novels of the little known Edouard Estaunié – whom he found the most interesting of young French novelists in 1907. Applying Moore's ethics to an examination of Estaunié's Catholic novels, Bell proclaims that purpose in life can be found in cultivating the mind and emotions for the utmost enjoyment of beauty and love – which says more about Bell than about Moore or Estaunié (CB/pTC). Despite his early efforts with French literature, the only prose that Bell appears to have published before starting to write for the *Athenaeum* was an anonymous 1906 review of G. M. Trevelyan's *The Poetry and Philosophy of George Meredith* in the *Cambridge Review*. Trevelyan, who had been a fellow at Trinity when Bell was there, was too enthusiastic a critic for his reviewer; he had little sense of art, like Meredith himself, who also lacked feeling for the beauty of language. Bell did not much care for Meredith's poetry, and the philosophy he found extraneous to literary criticism. *Modern Love* was, nevertheless, brilliant, and required no explanation, whereas a poem like 'Of Love and the Valley' (Leslie Stephen loved to recite it) was a 'bank-holiday pageant'. Meredith had written five or six good novels, and in the familiar Cambridge tripos metaphor, Bell allowed him a good second, but not a first like Balzac or Flaubert. Of Trevelyan's exposition of Meredith's philosophy, Bell complained that it was 'wholly unimportant' whether Meredith was an agnostic, and he asked,

> how long are we to wait before critics and commentators shall recognise the irrelevancy, the impropriety, the indecency, of publishing their opinions on the 'moral teaching' and 'messages' of painters and poets? ('Strenuous', pp. 432–3)[8]

There is an incipient formalism here and elsewhere in Bloomsbury's increasing complaint about the present state of criticism. Yet like others in Bloomsbury, Bell fluctuated in his opinion of Meredith. When reviewing Meredith's posthumous fragment *Celt or Saxon* four years later in the *Athenaeum*, he praised its 'brilliant wit, profound insight, and superb passages of lyric prose' ('Meredith').

The *Athenaeum* that Clive Bell began reviewing for in January 1909, was still being edited by Vernon Rendell, who had invited Roger Fry to be the paper's art critic earlier in the decade. Bell reviewed no art for the *Athenaeum* until after the first post-impressionist exhibition, when he then made the transition in its pages from literary to art critic. The thirty odd literary reviews Bell wrote in 1909 and 1910 were of a miscellaneous nature: biography and autobiography, a little poetry and fiction, most of it from the past century, and several seventeenth-century plays. There were a few lead reviews and a number of brief notices. Bell's critical demeanour is that of a gentleman of letters, classically educated of course, and quite conversant with English literary history and French culture. Although there is an occasional whiff of the humorous polemic in *Art* and later books, for the most part the reviewer's tone was moderated by the editor's convictions, as Bell explained later in the preface to a collection of his pieces. Like the journalism of Fry, MacCarthy, Strachey, the Woolfs, and Forster, Bell's reviews were shaped, willingly or unwillingly, consciously or unconsciously, by the paper for which he was writing. He and his colleagues on the *Athenaeum* naturally wrote what they thought and felt, he explained later in the preface to *Pot-Boilers*, but

> we all hoped that our thoughts and feelings would not be too dissimilar from those of our presiding genius, Athene the wise, our eponymous goddess; because, if they were, her high-priest, albeit one of the most charming and accomplished people in Fleet Street or thereabouts, stood ready with the inexorable blue pencil to smite once and smite no more. (p. 4).

Bell's relationship with the editor was good enough for Rendell to ask him to edit the *Athenaeum* for several weeks in 1910, which involved writing some brief obituaries for the paper. Bell nevertheless found his reviews, especially the earlier ones, sometimes smitten in the name of concision: the rhythm of his clauses, the balance of sentences, the shape of paragraphs, even the development of arguments were altered. He tried but without much success, he felt, to repair the damage when reprinting some of the pieces in 1918 (*PB*, pp. 4–6).

The conception of literary criticism in Bell's early *Athenaeum* writing first appears in reviews of books on Keats and Shelley. Francis Thompson's posthumous study of Shelley is placed alongside works of Plato, Dryden, Coleridge, and Shelley himself as a profound appreciation by one poet of another because Thompson tries to see the world as Shelley saw it and conveys his vision with a lightness and perspicacity (which the rhapsodic excerpts in Bell's review do not really illustrate). A Keats biography recognises the essential Romantic quality as intuition, defined revealingly by Bell as 'a mysterious gift for discovering beauty and a magic touch for its elucidation'. ('*Keats*', p. 8). That could describe Bell's own critical hopes in writing on art. Bell's first lead review in the *Athenaeum* at the end of 1909 of a Shelley biography by Arthur Clutton-Brock celebrates the poet for being 'our mythopoeist' instead of a complacent anthropomorphist like Wordsworth:

> he has peopled earth and sky with beings of exquisite beauty; and his highest achievement is to have expressed his sense of them in such a way that, as we read, we catch something of his sympathy and understanding. ('*Shelley*', pp. 753–4).

Bell finds in the work of Clutton-Brock (who was one of the principal reviewers for *The Times Literary Supplement*) a new kind of biography that attempts with partial success to connect men's existences with their achievements. Bell is more tolerant of Victorian biography here than his sister-in-law was in her review of Sterne a few months before in the *TLS* (see p. 345). But he nicely observes that in such an excellent series as the English Men of Letters it is amazing how much the writers resemble one another.

Another review of a book on autobiography by Anna Robeson Burr is dismissed by Bell because it does not distinguish good from bad autobiographies. Burr thought candour essential; Bell disagrees. Ranging from Augustine to Gibbon and Rousseau to Mill, he argues that good autobiography must be personal, though not necessarily sincere, for one could write an excellent fictitious autobiography. He then discriminates between objective autobiographies such as memoirs and subjective ones like letters. Several volumes of letters were the subject of *Athenaeum* reviews by Bell. He reviewed James Boswell's letters to William Temple, stressing Boswell's powers of self-revelation as well as his amours, and criticising the editor for merely appending a new introduction to the old unsatisfactory edition. (The review is padded with quotations, but Bell reprinted it anyway in *Pot-Boilers*.) Reviews of the Carlyles' love letters along with a book on Thomas's first love were also reprinted, but with a difference. In 1909, Bell thought anything published about the Carlyles of interest. Thomas was no great letter-writer; Jane had a genuine epistolary gift, yet Bell was less enthusiastic about her than Woolf or Strachey in their reviews (see pp. 168–9, 299). When Bell reprinted his reviews in 1918, he admitted her letters had genius but ranked them below Mérimée's, Sévigné's, Walpole's, and Byron's. As for Thomas Carlyle, he was dismissed, in a section added to *Pot-Boilers*, as a thoughtful, obsolete journalist, not a great nineteenth-century figure like Darwin, Swinburne or Mill (pp. 86–9, 94). (Strachey's view of eminent as opposed to truly great Victorians may have influenced this revision.) Also included in *Pot-Boilers* was a review of Trelawny's letters that brought a compliment from Virginia Woolf that distinguished Bell's assertive criticism from her own: 'you are much sturdier on your legs than you were; you stride over the ground, and plant words firmly, in a way I admire. My tendency would be to insinuate' (*L*, I 445).

Bell's emerging attitude toward the Victorians in the *Athenaeum*, where some of the most famous of them had been published, is apparent in a review of *Nineteenth Century Teachers and Other Essays* by Julia Wedgwood, whose *Moral Ideal* Forster had helped revise. The title essay of the volume discusses Maurice, Carlyle, and Ruskin, but not Bentham or Mill, and this leads the reviewer into a disquisition on nineteenth-century thought via G. E. Moore. Bell describes the basic division between utilitarian and intuitional Victorian ethics as a split between what he calls the Intellectual and Emotional Schools. Wedgwood's great teachers like Maurice and Carlyle were confused and confusing emotionalists. Bell illustrates this in Maurice (with Wedgwood's help) and in Carlyle, whose Right is Might theory can also means Might is Right. But intellectualists were not completely correct either, as Moore demonstrated in his refutation of Mill's hedonism . Bell's moral is implicit: modern ethics must, like *Principia Ethica*, be grounded in both reason and intuition, thought and feeling. This basic dualism runs throughout Bell's Edwardian criticism and his later aesthetic doctrines of significant form and aesthetic emotion. For instance, in an *Athenaeum* review of Max Beerbohm's essays (including the two that MacCarthy had published in the *New Quarterly*) Bell writes that there are two kinds of humour, intellectual and emotional; what makes Beerbohm an imaginative humorist is his intellectual style and emotional sensitivity. By contrast, the prose and poetry of Mary Coleridge fails to grasp ideas. In her 'shrinking fastidiousness' she is a characteristic representative of Kensington culture: 'her life is an exquisite preoccupation with the surface of truth and the heart of unreality' (*PB*, pp. 47–9). Bloomsbury's criterion of reality invoked in this ironic way will recur in Bell's criticism. The review opens

with the statement, 'the greatest art is, in a sense, impersonal', and
goes on to suggest Miss Coleridge's poetry, though charming, was
the opposite. Bell appears to be echoing here Strachey's earlier and
more sympathetic review of her poems, which begins, 'The greatest
poetry is always impersonal' ('Late', p. 19). (Fry would later
complain that Bell's writing borrowed his ideas.)

Gathered Leaves from the Prose of Mary E. Coleridge appeared as the
lead review of the *Athenaeum*, and it upset her friends including
Edith Sichel who had contributed a memoir. Bell liked Sichel's
writing no more than Virginia Woolf had years before (see p. 161),
and criticised it for being too heavy, literary, and professional. In
reprinting the review after Sichel's death, Bell added an apologetic
footnote citing Voltaire on the regard we owe the living and the
truth we owe the dead. He revised the review in various places,
making it stronger, if anything. He changed, for example, 'her
equipment was not really strong' to 'fundamentally she was feeble'
(p. 45). But Bell noted in the foreword to *Pot-Boilers* that he was
attempting, in some of his revisions, to restore what had been
changed by the *Athenaeum*'s editor:

> Re-reading these articles – some of which were written nine or
> ten years ago – I come on such phrases as 'this is a notable
> achievement', 'his equipment was not really strong', and I
> wonder, of course, what the devil I did say. No doubt it was
> something definite and particular, for in those days I was a most
> conscientious writer.' (p. 5)

Clive Bell's critical theory in his *Athenaeum* reviews was a form of
intentionalism that he would never have accepted later in his art
criticism. 'The first object of the literary critic', he says in reviewing
G. K. Chesterton on George Bernard Shaw, 'is to discover the effect
that the writer wished to produce; the second, to consider his
achievement from as many standpoints as possible.' Bell wants to
dissociate the journalist's single point of view from that of the man
of letters who tries 'to base his criticism on general principles, is
philosophic in the old and admirable sense.' The complete
confidence with which the reviewer disposes of both Chesterton
and Shaw matches the utter assurance of those two writers, and
may be one of the reasons the review was not reprinted. Shaw is an
inferior playwright, Bell thinks; he lacks the dramatic form and
sense of someone like Congreve, yet 'few men, in our time, have

done more for truth', which makes his work permanently valuable. Chesterton with his dislike of aesthetic criticism is a journalistic critic, seeking to reveal and refute Shaw's purposes. Bell defines aesthetes as those who incorrectly hold beauty to be the sole good end; they are wrong, but they come closer to the ethical truth than Chesterton or Shaw. According to the philosophic reviewer of the *Athenaeum*, both writers commit the 'common error of confusing means with ends' ('*Shaw*' pp. 291–2). For Bell as for MacCarthy, Moore's principles offered a basis for criticising Shaw and other moderns.

Though he deprecated the prose of Chesterton and Shaw, Bell still found evidence that 'the expected renaissance of imaginative prose-writing in England is already upon us', as he put in a 1910 review of some stories by L. P. Jacks, whose writing Virginia Woolf later admired ('*Mad Shepherds*'). This is the only allusion in Bell's reviews to the New Renaissance book he had been planning. The works of J. M. Synge that he reviewed very favourably the next year would have given him further indications of a prose renaissance, as of course would Woolf's reviews, essays, and drafts of *The Voyage Out* that he had read. Bell's comments on Woolf's novel-in-progress – which became his most important Edwardian literary criticism – will be discussed in the Georgian history of Bloomsbury's writing. About their reviewing, Bell wrote to his sister-in-law that he had received compliments on his *Athenaeum* work but they fell a little flat after those he had heard on her *TLS* Boswell and Carlyle reviews from London acquaintances who did not even know she had written them. 'It's the devil having a lion in the family', he admitted (11.iv.09, CB/pS). More proof of the modern revival of imaginative prose was E. M. Forster. Bell reviewed *Howards End* briefly but illuminatingly in the *Athenaeum*; it confirmed Forster's place among the few living writers who counted for him, but the review is also best considered in the context of that novel's literary history (see pp. 474–5).

Few signs of a new literary renaissance were to be found in the little poetry Bell reviewed for the *Athenaeum*, and none in the light verse he himself had continued to write since *Euphrosyne*. Their singing-times were over, he told Lytton Strachey in a sestina, even if the season of the lover could make the poetic embers blaze (CB/pTC). Several of Bell's poems were written for Virginia Woolf. One in a letter to her describes a minor poet who 'fathoms life by still appealing/To lyric lust from common feeling' (CB/pS).

Another written in December 1909 to accompany a gift is entitled
'To A. V. S. with a Book'. The first stanza develops the thought that
'Books are the quiet monitors of the mind' allowing us to 'meditate
wise thoughts and passionate lays.' In the second, the idea that
books are the last symbols of dead minds surviving on the lips and
in the hearts of the living causes the poet to draw nearer to A. V. S.
with his book. Books become 'the heart's memorial' in the last
stanza; they measure self-knowledge, yearnings, agonies, and this
brings the speaker to ask his most dear recipient by her English
firelight if she remembers the Italian sunlight where he is, and can

> Recall the pregnant hours, the gay delights,
> The pain, the tears maybe, the ravished heights,
> The golden moments my cold lines commend,
> The days, in memory of which I send
> A book?
>
> (*Poems*, pp. 10–11)

It is not a very original poem, but Clive liked it well enough to
include in both his collections of verse, perhaps as a literary
memorial of his and Virginia's Edwardian love.

11 Lytton Strachey and the *Spectator*

The *Spectator*, for which Lytton Strachey wrote a weekly review from August 1907 until April 1909, was unlike any other paper that Bloomsbury wrote for regularly. Except for the reminiscence of its name, the *Spectator* had no connection with Addison and Steele's famous periodical; it descended instead from a nineteenth-century Benthamite paper. By the early twentieth century its politics were Independent Liberal, the liberalism being old rather than new like that of the *Independent Review* or the *Speaker*. Politically, St. Loe Strachey, the paper's editor and proprietor, felt he lacked party influence because his tenets ran athwart Liberal and Tory lines (Amy Strachey, pp. 150–1). He advocated free-trade and imperialism but opposed Irish home rule. Almost all his causes were lost ones. Yet the *Spectator* was considered to be the most widely read political paper in the country. James Strachey, who worked for St. Loe later, estimated its circulation around 20,000 copies – triple that of any of its competitors. Every vicarage in the country was said to subscribe (LS/SE, p. 7).[1] Thus Lytton Strachey's anonymous *Spectator* reviews circulated more widely than Fry's *Athenaeum* art criticism or Bell's literary reviews, MacCarthy's *Speaker* theatre notices or Virginia Woolf's *TLS* reviews.

There was a price for the readership. To the tedium of weekly reviewing were added the expectations of Lytton's cousin St. Loe. An editor's first duty, according to that experienced Bloomsbury journalist Leonard Woolf, was to 'impress upon his paper an indelible character, a journalistic aroma':

the way in which a real or 'good' editor pervades his paper is very remarkable; when you write for him his unseen presence broods over your pen or typewriter and unconsciously your thoughts and your words are infected by him. You become a ventriloquist's puppet. (*BA*, p. 131)

It is not easy to think of Leonard Woolf, Lytton Strachey, Virginia Woolf, Roger Fry or Clive Bell as editors' dummies, but all had their early writings shaped to some degree by their editors' expectations. Strachey felt, according to his brother James, that he had a secret collaborator when writing for the *Spectator*. St. Loe went over every contributor's work, deleting, adding, rewriting. To keep this to a minimum, Lytton adopted what James calls 'the method of pre-censorship, and this he did so successfully that editorial intrusions were rarely needed'. This may be why Lytton never reprinted any of his *Spectator* work (LS/*SE*, pp. 8–9).

St. Loe Strachey's journalistic aroma appears to have been compounded of his eclectic political convictions, an amiable volubility, and a vicarage mode of particularly pompous, respectable pronouncement dubbed by his cousins as 'Spectatorial' (LS/*SE*, p. 7). He remembered Lytton Strachey as the one reviewer whose work he never altered, (MH/*LSBG*, p. 118), although James found indications in Lytton's own copies of his reviews of St. Loe's 'protective additions' (LS/*SE*, p. 9). St. Loe considered Lytton his most competent reviewer – almost as good, he thought, as Lord Cromer, whom Lytton would deride in *Eminent Victorians* (St. Loe Strachey, p. 372). In Lytton Strachey's reviews, there is little evidence, aside from the pre-censorship, that he took much trouble either to understand or to offend St. Loe's Spectatorial point of view. Lytton's dissertation indicates how his imperial attitudes were essentially those of his family, and *Spectator* reviews such as the one on the Indian frontier Guides could only have delighted the editor (see pp. 129–30). St. Loe's enthusiasm for Elizabethan drama and Donne as well as Pope and the Romantics accorded well with his younger cousin's tastes, and while it is unclear who selected books for review, the *Spectator* provided Lytton with opportunities to review works about these authors or editions of their writings. St. Loe also timorously allowed Lytton a little theatre reviewing in his paper.

The *Spectator* was subtitled 'A Weekly Review of Politics, Literature, Theology, and Art'. The art reviewer was another Strachey, St. Loe's brother Henry, but little art was actually noticed.

Lytton wrote two unformalistic pieces of art criticism, apparently with Duncan Grant's help, and Grant himself seems to have written several, possibly with Lytton's help.[2] Most of the books discussed were not literary. Groups of short reviews were published, including a section devoted to novels, and there was a weekly poem, but Lytton's two columns or so – each about eight hundred words – constituted the principal literary review of the issue. Occasionally two of his reviews appeared in the same number. His main subject was English poetry from the sixteenth century to the present. Though Shakespeare figured more than anyone else, there were also several reviews of other Elizabethans as well as of Milton and Wordsworth. A number of Strachey's reviews were devoted to works of history, biography, including those of some eminent Victorians. French literature was the subject of several columns, and some reviews were devoted to books on places Strachey knew – Rothiemurchus, Cambridge, even Bloomsbury (which to his delight he found included in a book on provincial places). More than a dozen of Strachey's *Spectator* texts were theatre notices. He reviewed no fiction until his brother arranged later for two Dostoevsky reviews, but his scope as an Edwardian reviewer of literature is even wider than Virginia Woolf's. As a literary critic, however, Strachey did not develop much beyond his Edwardian criticism. The early *New Quarterly* essay on Racine may have been his most influential piece of criticism. To Leonard Woolf afterwards, Strachey dismissed his *Spectator* writings as 'balderdash' (21.viii.09, LS/pNY), but these weekly reviews were always interestingly written. For literary history, the value of the nearly one hundred reviews Lytton wrote under the vigilant Spectatorial eye of St. Loe lies for the most part in the early Bloomsbury critical attitudes they articulate and in their intimations of Strachey's progress as a biographer and ironist.

II

In the course of his *Spectator* reviews Lytton Strachey makes various observations on critics that disclose a general, if not wholly consistent, view of the functions of criticism. He finds in a rare great critic like Dryden, 'the qualities peculiarly essential to criticism –

sympathy, discrimination, breadth of outlook, and power of exposition', to which was added 'the crowning grace of an exquisite prose style' (*SE*, p. 127).[3] Strachey's own practice hardly attains these ideals, but they are what he admired and aimed for in criticism. And criticism, he thought, could have creative power in an age like Corneille's, Dryden's, or Wordsworth's. In a review of Swinburne, Strachey divides most critics and other people into Platonists or Aristotelians, according to whether they are bold intuitional judges or patiently sympathetic analysts. Johnson, whom Strachey continues to admire and deplore, is the great Platonic judge, a life critic instead of a literary one, whose pronouncements on Shakespeare (edited by yet another Strachey cousin, Walter Raleigh) throw more light on the critic than the playwright. Hence the modernist title of Strachey's review: 'Shakespeare on Johnson'. Johnson had a breadth of outlook and a masterful style, but for all his understanding of Shakespeare's poetry, Strachey thinks he might as well have been discussing some prose translation of a foreign classic. Strachey himself in his earlier *Spectator* reviews, appears more Aristotelian – more sympathetic than judgemental, though not completely so. However, the endless critical analyses of Aristotelians bring out the Platonist in him. Reviewing James Thomson's poetry, Strachey argues that 'the first duty of the critic is to point out to his readers what is best worth reading in an author', something Thomson's scholastic editor failed to do (*SE*, pp. 153, 157). Similarly, the dramatic critic must ask what the central interest of a play is, his true business being 'to discuss, not the story of the play, but its subject – which is an entirely different matter' ('Three New Plays', p. 899). Strachey sounds somewhat like a Leavis in the theatre here. Yet he can also be quite uncritical about literary analysis. Sidney Lee's Shakespearean theories lead Strachey to flaunt anti-critical metaphors in concluding 'it is better to scatter incense than to construct theories' ('Lee on Shakespeare', p. 888). A lexicon to Milton makes him mix his metaphors: 'the most accurate net of scholarship is of too coarse a grain to catch his "winged imaginations"' ('Milton's Words', p. 992). Still, Strachey can be appreciative of works by scholars such as Ker, Greg, Lounsbury, Spingarn, and Brooke.

Appreciation is finally more congenial to Strachey as a reviewer than evaluation or analysis. This may partially explain why he did not continue as a critic. Another reason may be that his aesthetic convictions were already developed; expounding and reconfirming them in reviews could be tiresome. A review of Coleridge's *Biographia Literaria* is quite revealing here. Though he thought him a fine critic, Strachey judges Coleridge, as Johnson (and Moore) might have:

> he speculated too much and thought too little. His mind was constitutionally incapable of the hard and continued effort, the scrupulous precision, the systematic method, without which no reasoning, however brilliant, can be of enduring value.

The value of the *Biographia Literaria* lies in its variety of information not in its German metaphysics. The work is excellent as talk and even good as criticism when it analyses Wordsworth's theories, but Coleridge failed even here to realise the greatness of Wordsworth's Preface to the *Lyrical Ballads* when it maintained 'the immense aesthetic value possessed by extreme simplicity' (*SE*, pp. 166, 170).

Informing Strachey's opinions of Coleridge and Wordsworth and his responses to Johnson and Dryden are convictions about the nature of aesthetics. Analytic precision and method, simplicity and clarity in exposition, and breadth of understanding in theory of value were all involved. One of Strachey's early *Spectator* reviews was devoted to a book by Gosse's scourge, the hapless Churton Collins. Leonard Woolf had attacked his work at Cambridge, but Strachey is more sympathetic, except on the crucial point of Collins's confusion of means with ends. Strachey's review, entitled 'The Value of Poetry', ends with words that anticipate again the wording in Strachey's manifesto-preface to *Eminent Victorians* a dozen years later:

> For it is not by its uses that poetry is to be justified or condemned. Its beauty and its goodness, like the beauty of a landscape or the goodness of a human being, have a value of their own, a value which does not depend on their effects. We love poems, as we love the fields and the trees and the rivers of England, and as we love our friends, not for the pleasure which they may bring us, nor even for the good which they may do us, but for themselves. (p. 95)

St. Loe Strachey's direct or indirect influence may have been responsible for the English illustration here. Even so, he allowed his reviewer to preach a fundamental principle of *Principia Ethica* to the vicarages of England. Keynes wrote to Strachey complaining that as usual the review stopped just as the argument was getting underway, but he supposed it was asking too much for a complete exposition of Moore's philosophy 'as applied to criticism in the columns of the Spectator' (29.vii.06, JMK/pKC).

In several other places in his *Spectator* reviews, Strachey distinctly applies Cambridge philosophy to literary criticism. The blinding of Gloucester in *King Lear* is justified (along the lines of Strachey's Apostle papers on aesthetics) not in itself but for its effect on the play as a whole. Shakespeare's authorship is defended with Hume's common-sense argument against miracles that general testimony is invalid when the fact testified to is incredible; the true miracle of Shakespeare's plays is not that Shakespeare wrote them but that anyone did ('The Shakespeare Problem', p. 185). A late theatre review distinguishes between wit and humour, suggesting the former is intellectual while the latter may be one of those indefinable, unanalysable qualities. Therefore 'a point of view or a state of mind is humorous in precisely the same simple manner in which a proposition is true or a billiard-ball is red' ('Follies', p. 262). Moore's philosophy is apparent as well in Strachey's critical opinion of what is real and what is not in literature and on the stage.

Strachey invidiously compares realism with reality in a few reviews that indicate how early Bloomsbury's misgivings about Edwardian literary realism developed. Sometimes he enjoys defending unrealistic works like pastorals from a scholarly apologist:

> Their characters. . . . belong to a universe which is very different from ours – a universe where there are very few proprieties and no reputations, where the only conventions are the conventions of art, where one can transgress without doing ill, where one can preach without being a bore, where there is nothing to do but to make love, and where everything comes right in the end. To discover in the airy population of Arcadia the weight and the solidity of the material world is to commit a fallacy in perception.
> (*SE*, pp. 80–1)

The prose is supple and the literary criticism sound, but some of the severer Apostles would have probably wanted to know just what exactly was meant by 'a fallacy in perception'. In another review, Strachey found medieval writers profound in their representation of feeling, simple in their psychology, and remote from modern realism in the childlike relishing of realistic description for its own sake, rather than for its aesthetic purposes in the work of great nineteenth-century realists such as Balzac and Flaubert ('Mediaeval Studies', pp. 786–7).

Strachey reviewed nothing relating to these or other novelists, however. His only substantial discussion of fiction during the time he was writing his weekly columns for the *Spectator* came in the revealing introduction he was commissioned to write in 1908 for *A Simple Story* by the late-eighteenth century English novelist and playwright Elizabeth Inchbald. Raleigh obtained this commission for him from the Oxford University Press and Strachey selected the book.[4] Mrs Inchbald's undeserved obscurity is Strachey's opening theme. He deplores the comprehensive distractions that have so little to do with the art of even great novels. Inchbald was influenced by Richardson, to be sure, but her indifference to realistic detail connects her work more closely to Racine's tragedies, and this fascinates Strachey. She is a stylist in fiction but with a clumsy style that she uses to convey her matter rather than as an ornament in itself, like Thackeray. For all Inchbald's artificiality and thinness,

> she can invest, if not with realism, with something greater than realism – with the sense of reality itself – the pains, the triumphs, and the agitations of the human heart. (*CC*, p. 138)

Strachey's own style here is a little clumsy. His discussion of *A Simple Story* ignores, as Virginia Woolf's would not have, the split structure of the novel's two parts as well as the moral afterthought that the painful events of the story could have been avoided had the heroine and her daughter received proper educations. Strachey's introduction, much of which simply recounts Inchbald's biography, is nevertheless an early Bloomsbury appreciation of the art of psychological fiction. And while it had no influence on the satiric novel Strachey was attempting to write, *A Simple Story* may have helped stimulate the epistolary-novel game that was going on in Bloomsbury around this time.[5]

III

It was in the contemporary theatre that Lytton Strachey found a literary art which managed to be both unrealistic and unreal. St. Loe's *Spectator* did not review drama, but several months after he began to write regularly for it, Lytton was allowed to introduce some. An editorial note attached to the first review disclaimed responsibility for the opinions of the reviewer, who was now given pseudonymity in place of anonymity. Strachey guarded himself with the pen-name Ignotus, which identifies the writer as unknown and perhaps unknowing. Lytton Strachey did not become known as a dramatic critic, nor did his efforts to become a playwright during this time receive any encouragement from the current theatrical scene. He did not find there what, in one of his art reviews, he saw in Hogarth's 'The Green Room at Drury Lane': the feeling of 'all the good things of civilization, – tranquillity, and easy talk, and familiar friendship, and smiles, and the happiness of love' ('Old Masters', p. 62).

Strachey's dozen or so Ignotus reviews resemble MacCarthy's *Speaker* notices in their criticisms of the current acting, directing, and writing of drama, except that there was no Court Theatre to offer hope. Strachey would not review Ibsen's *The Wild Duck*, for how, he asked a friend, could he explain its great dramatic effect when he hardly understood the language? (16.viii.08, LS/pKC). Galsworthy he did review, but unfavourably. Only in comedy was there any relief. Good serious drama for Ignotus ought to produce 'the effect of absolute reality'; farce was its opposite, and light comedy somewhere in between ('Lady Epping', pp. 673–4). Strachey found the plays of H. H. Davies more enjoyable than those of Shaw, Pinero, Barrie, and Maugham. (In a letter to Grant, Strachey parodied Wilde's *A Woman of No Importance* – not a play the *Spectator* was likely to review – as being about buggery – MH/*LS*, pp. 357–8.) In his review of Davies, Strachey agrees that the basis of comedy is ethical, and he argues, through a graphic-art comparison, that the comic writer 'is as much concerned with the value of persons as the artist is concerned with that of tones; in either case a misjudgment of values ruins the picture' ('Mollusc', p. 867). Strachey often has recourse to art metaphors in his *Spectator* criticism. The analogy in his review of Davies's play is one that will exercise Bloomsbury aesthetics later in its efforts to find a formalistic basis for literary criticism. Strachey's criticism cannot be described as formalistic, but his attempt to connect literature with painting or sculpture is a distinctive attribute of Bloomsbury's critical writing.

In addition to a Moorean theory of value, Strachey's basic critical assumptions are historically grounded, though the ground is sometimes indistinct. In a *Spectator* review entitled 'Tragedy Old and New', Strachey distinguishes between the classic Sophoclean drama of concentration and crisis, and the romantic Shakespearean one of gradual panoramic development. The novel has taken over the romantic method, in his view, while the classical has evolved into modern theatre, as epitomised by the actor-manager Beerbohm Tree. Strachey's criticism of Tree has been disputed (MH/*LSBG*, pp. 112–13) but his objections are the same as Desmond MacCarthy's in the *Speaker*. Both deplored the exaggerated emphasis on pageantry, the pantomimic acting, the rant. In his first review of Tree's acting Strachey puzzled over the paradox of a bad successful actor who is more concerned with the audience than the play. (The comic actor-manager Charles Hawtrey was another for whom the play was not the thing; Strachey's review of Hawtrey does not even mention Somerset Maugham, the author of the play in which Hawtrey was appearing.) When Tree did Shakespeare, Strachey said, he turned him into a debased modern form of classic drama that stressed the climaxes of scenes and ignored the anti-climaxes that gives them their dramatic reality. This 'same sacrifice of the truly artistic and the real to the false and the over-emphatic' occurs in Tree's and other actors' exaggerated declamation of Shakespeare's verse (*SE*, p. 186). But Strachey does not want to agree with Charles Lamb, another critic he thought great, when Lamb says that Shakespeare is better read than acted. After three centuries Shakespeare still remains a vital force on the stage for Strachey, who believes literary critics have an obligation not to abandon his work to the crudities of actor-managers.

One modern English actor did understand Hamlet's advice to the players, and that is Harley Granville Barker. With Vedrenne he presented a series of performances at the Savoy Theatre that gave Ignotus some sense of what the Court Theatre days had been like, even if it did not persuade him that some kind of national theatre was needed. Strachey argued against it in his review of a book, published by Duckworth, in which William Archer and Barker put forth a scheme for such an institution. Strachey's purely Blooms-bury arguments may have also appealed to the editor of the

Spectator. They begin with La Fontaine's fable about the sleek, collared dog and the thin, free wolf. Where the authors cite Matthew Arnold on the need for the government to concern itself with the theatre, Strachey counters with Milton's 'the State shall be my governors, but not my critics'. The French example of Molière is not encouraging, and moreover Molière is not Shakespeare. Another of the authors' examples, the British Museum, deals with dead science and art, not the drama, which, in a piece of awful rhetoric Strachey describes as 'a living creature, winged and wondrous, hovering inexplicably over magical flowers and amenable to no laws but that of fancy.' More effective is Strachey's argument against what Renan called 'l'art administratif'. What is most alarming in the proposals, however, are the suggested sources for trustees – Oxford and Cambridge, the London County Council and, even worse, the Royal Academy. 'After all', Strachey concludes, 'has our experience of academies been so fortunate as to make us look forward to another with eager hope?' A repertory theatre, especially one run by Archer and Barker, would be wonderful, but 'there must be no trustees' (*SE*, p. 215–7).[6] A decade after the death of Strachey and Fry, and several years after Virginia Woolf's, J. M. Keynes became centrally involved in what turned into the Arts Council. Would they have deplored this institutionalisation of art as well?

One of the best pieces Strachey wrote on drama for the *Spectator* was not a theatre notice but a book review. It preceded his drama reviews, and may have helped persuade St. Loe of his cousin's abilities as a theatre critic. The review of a translation of Molière, introduced by Saintsbury, prepares for Strachey's *New Quarterly* piece on Racine the next year. In contrast to Racine, the English have always loved Molière, but Strachey regrets that the imprecision of the translation fails to convey Molière's ability to 'call up with a common sentence a whole universe of reverberating suggestion and pervasive irony' (*SE*, p. 123). Molière's art combines classical and romantic; he can be as witty as Voltaire, as vitally humane as Shakespeare, Cervantes, Balzac, and Scott (a roster Strachey would possibly have revised later). Saintsbury said Molière was the master of the laugh; Strachey asks if he was not also the master of the smile. What gives his characters value is not their laughableness but their psychology. The psychology of *The Misanthrope* approaches the tragic, from which classical tradition had kept Molière, as Strachey had said in the *Independent Review*.

IV

English poetry from the Renaissance through the Romantics to the
moderns was Lytton Strachey's speciality as a *Spectator* reviewer.
His Elizabethan reviews are the earliest published texts that reveal
Bloomsbury's enthusiasm for the period. But Elizabethanism for
Strachey is a force not a period – the greatest force in the literature
to be found everywhere from Chaucer through Beddoes even down
to Kipling. The fundamental characteristic of the Elizabethans was
'an extraordinary capacity for expressing with immense vigour and
endless variety the breadth and depth of human life' ('Poet on
Poets', p. 502). Still, they did not write about the real world; their
inner spirit belonged to 'a world of strange imagination and
mysterious romance' ('Elizabethan Drama', p. 976). Strachey's
favourite metaphor for Elizabethan writers is exploration.
Christopher Marlowe was their Columbus discovering or
rediscovering English tragedy, blank verse, and the heroic couplet,
while the greatest poem of the age, *The Faerie Queen* – 'a less brac-
ing poem was never written' – was retrospectively elaborating
languorous ease ('Age of Spenser', p. 458). Strachey also protests
against the misinterpretation of Elizabethan imitativeness as lacking
in emotion, and he denies that Shakespeare's sonnets, for instance,
are literary exercises devoid of feeling, as Sidney Lee had claimed
(*SE*, p. 75). The Elizabethans were literary explorers of strange
states of mind. Early and late, Strachey was fascinated with their
interest in abnormality. Shakespeare's greatness, he argued in his
first literary review for the *Spectator*, was to be found in the poetry
and the psychology of his plays, not in their puerile plots: 'the
contrast is complete between the simplicity of his situations and the
subtlety of his characters'. In their fiction and their criticism
Virginia Woolf and E. M. Forster will reaffirm this unAristotelian
distinction. Strachey remains critical of interpretations by Swinburne and Lamb of Shakespeare that pay less attention to the
dramatis than to the *personae* of his plays. Nor would he allow
Shakespeare to be judged by fallacious Flaubertian or Stevensonian
standards of classical finish. Inspiration was the poet's inexplicable
guide, Strachey says, and quotes several times Arnold's 'We ask
and ask; thou smilest and are still,/Out-topping knowledge'
('Praise', pp. 881–2). Lytton Strachey's impatience with 'the
artificialities of criticism' (*SE*, p. 75) reappears on various occasions
in his *Spectator* writings. He is fond of using the vague, atemporal

antithesis of classic and romantic, but the distinction is not evaluative. Strachey fully admires Shakespeare and Racine, Pope and Wordsworth; he is a catholic critic arguing against inappropriate standards in the judging of various writers. Milton he admired for poetic rhetoric and compared, as others have, his conscious, consummate art with Milton's conception of Shakespeare as a natural genius warbling wild wood-notes. Strachey's Milton lacks Donne's 'intellectual subtlety', Pope's 'psychological intensity', and Wordsworth's 'spiritual tenderness'. He is, to use the dichotomy Strachey applies to Beddoes, a poet of style rather than matter. Milton is also a great literary egotist, but Strachey cites Coleridge's words that 'the egotism of such a man is a revelation of spirit' (*SE*, pp. 107–8).

A Cambridge production of Milton's *Comus* that included Rupert Brooke and other friends was reviewed by Strachey for the *Spectator* in 1908. He found the undramatic sententiousness of the masque when dramatised became 'a play of prigs' ('Comus', p. 94), whose morality was not unlike that of Samuel Richardson's novels. The performance was saved by the beautiful delivery of Milton's blank verse, so different from the ranting of Shakespeare on the London stage. Finally, on the occasion of the tercentenary of Milton's birth in December 1908, Strachey wrote a *Spectator* article that sums up in Macaulayian antitheses Bloomsbury's ambivalence toward their own nineteenth-century Puritan heritage.

> Milton is the least dramatic of great poets, and the least tender. . . . He is gay in his earliest poems, but nowhere else. In his middle and later life he had lost the sense of joyousness; . . . he gave himself up altogether to the difficult, the sublime, and the severe. Thus he represents in the highest degree the strength and the weakness of Puritanism – its grandeur and its narrowness, its noble sincerity and its coldness of heart.

An adult Puritan, but a child of the Renaissance, Milton was torn between what Strachey calls his passions of egoism and sensibility. These account for his attitude toward women: he was too masculine, too susceptible, too angry, too disdainful ('John Milton', pp. 933–4). He was not, in short, as Virginia Woolf would say, androgynous enough.

Strachey's criticism of Milton in the *Spectator* anticipates certain modernist attitudes of Eliot and others, including Woolf. But Strachey and Bloomsbury did not view the history of English literature in terms of decline or fall after the middle ages, the seventeenth century, or whenever. Strachey could appreciate Andrew Marvell's greatness as a poet more than Augustine Birrell, whose Man-of-Letters volume he reviewed. In Dryden, Strachey recognised a great critic. Pope he believed misunderstood because of the failure to appreciate his passionate nature or the inspired artistry of his poetic form – a couplet, after all, is no more rigid than a fugue. But neither his nature nor his art made Pope as good an editor of Shakespeare as Theobald. James Thomson's 'The Castle of Indolence' was better than 'The Seasons', no matter what scholastic editors say, for Thomson was a rhetorician not a landscape painter like the great Wordsworth. Strachey's enthusiasm for Wordsworth, which was not manifested at Cambridge by himself or his Bloomsbury friends, is again expressed, as so much of Strachey's literary and biographical criticism, in paradoxes. Wordsworth was the first poet to articulate 'the beauties of extreme simplicity' and also a master of grandiloquence (*SE*, pp. 160–1). He is as new-fashioned as Rousseau, as old-fashioned as a Patriarch; he is 'the first of the Romantics and the last of the Romans' ('Wordsworth', p. 461). Strachey preferred Wordsworth's egotism and love of freedom to Milton's. No Romantics other than Wordsworth and Coleridge were reviewed by Strachey in the *Spectator* but passing references indicate he liked them all except, curiously, Byron.

Bloomsbury's relation to the Romantic poets is complex, as Strachey's reviews demonstrate. Though the Group's aestheticism is Romantic in origin, this connection is occasionally obscured by Bloomsbury's fondness for eighteenth-century writing and their fatigue with much Victorian and Edwardian Romantic poetry. Strachey reviewed no Victorian poets in the *Spectator* except William Barnes, as edited by Thomas Hardy. Barnes's Dorset poetry was much admired by St. Loe Strachey, and Lytton praised its use of dialect in terms of means, ends, simplicity, and reality again. Modern poetry, on the other hand, was the subject of three Strachey reviews, all of which illuminate his and Bloomsbury's Edwardian opinion of it. Reviewing an anthology of modern poetry in 1908, Strachey found that while it communicated delight, as Cowley said poetry should, it did not suggest 'what is most beautiful and wise and good', as Wordsworth said it should. The reason was a lack of inspiration and originality; poets today are heirs of an effete Romantic tradition. Where, the reviewer asks, will be found 'the new great poet who shall free us from the bondage of Wordsworth, just as Wordsworth himself freed his contemporaries from the bondage of Pope?' ('Modern Poetry', p. 623). Ten years later, Bloomsbury began to think it might be T. S. Eliot. Strachey's review illustrated his own Romantic bondage by using Wordsworth to define poetry's purpose. In the narrow verse of Dobson and Housman, Strachey sees some originality but finds Kipling to be the only poet writing about anything like real Edwardian life. Modern verse plays, a collection of which Strachey also reviewed for the *Spectator*, were almost contradictions in terms. 'The essential fact about drama is that it deals with realities; no one nowadays writes poetry unless he wishes to escape from realities, . . . ' Therefore if the drama is good, the verse will have failed, and if the verse is good, the drama will be feeble ('New Plays', p. 998). These strictures on modern poetry and poetic drama reveal not only the dissatisfaction but the dilemma of any would-be poet and dramatist, including the reviewer.

In the faults and merits of William Butler Yeats's early poetry Strachey found 'the material for a criticism of the whole romantic school.' Reviewing two volumes of Yeats's collected early lyrical and narrative poems in 1908, which included *The Wanderings of Oisin*, *The Wind Among the Reeds*, and *In the Seven Woods*, Strachey found Yeats instructive. 'His poetry might almost be defined as romance in process of decomposition, . . . ' he wrote ('Yeats', p. 588). The basis of his criticism identifies the limits of Bloomsbury's attachment to Romanticism. Strachey's devotion to Wordsworth and Coleridge together with his misgivings about Blake indicates that he admired a reasonable Romanticism. A review around this time on Boileau complains about 'the vague and wandering spirit' that has seized so much poetry of the present day; the 'Art Poétique', of Verlaine, whom Strachey admired, is as narrow in its way as Boileau's was, and if the reviewer had to choose, it would be Boileau's 'rien n'est beau que le vrai', not Verlaine's 'l'impossible' ('Boileau', p. 736). (Roger Fry, with his growing interest in Mallarmé, would probably not have agreed.) In Yeats's volumes, Lytton – though one must allow for the possibility of an inter-polation by St. Loe – finds 'an object lesson of the bad results which may follow when reason is left out of account in the making of poetry'. The narrative poems, while better than his plays, are unreasonable in their incoherence. Although his best poetry is lyrical, its dreaminess lacks the force, the unforgettableness of Coleridge, for example. But it hardly matters that his lyrics, like the rest of his work, are weak in clear thinking and construction because such poems as 'The Lake Isle of Innisfree', from which Strachey quotes, illustrate that Yeats 'possesses the true lyrical gift; he can write with spontaneity, with melody, with haunting charm'. It was difficult to think of another contemporary writer offering such evidence of inspiration ('Yeats', p. 588–9).

V

Lytton Strachey's gradual development as a biographer is reflected in his *Spectator* reviews of biographies, histories, letters, essays, and satires. His first *Spectator* review, written in January 1904 while he was still at Cambridge, is of a biography of James I's granddaughter, the mother of George I. The review ironically finds this ancestor of Queen Victoria (and friend of Descartes and Leibniz) so coarse that her correspondence will 'make a modern reader hold his nose' (*SE*, p. 26). Another very short early review of an excellent monograph on Newman refers to his designation as 'the great pervert', which sounds odd to contemporary ears. (The sexual meaning of pervert dates from Havelock Ellis's use in 1897, according to the *OED*; Forster used the word in the same ambiguous sense as Strachey when beginning his sketches for *A Room with a View* – EMF/LN, p. 6.) A late review of the Carlyles' love letters, the last regular one Strachey wrote for the *Spectator*, agrees with Virginia Woolf and Leslie Stephen, but not Clive Bell, that she was an epistolary genius while he, so earnestly Scotch and literary, forgot 'the first business of a letter-writer, – that of putting his correspondent into a good temper'. The real interest of the letters is therefore psychological ('Carlyle Letters', pp. 577–8). Another late Strachey review of Canning's letters ends with an admiring description of the strange and bright Regency world, so different from what was to follow. Beyond these dim anticipations of *Eminent Victorians*, the only review that clearly foreshadows Strachey's later biographies is of a book that E. V. Lucas devoted to the fatuous Swan of Litchfield, Anna Seward, whose circle consisted 'for the most part of second-rate celebrities and third-rate poets'. Lucas's 'light-hearted intrepidity' as a biographer carries him successfully 'through the desert of Miss Seward's writings' from which he brings back delightful curiosities. The review includes a sketch of the author of *Sandford and Merton* that would not be out of place among the miniature portraits of Strachey's last book. Lucas might be seen as one of Strachey's predecessors but his biographical game is really too easy. Strachey himself cannot resist a parting shot at Seward's writing and life, summing up their results with Antony's 'The evil that men do lives after them;/The good is oft interred with their bones' (*SE*, pp. 28–33).

Some assumptions of the biographies to come are manifest in Strachey's 1908 review of books on the Italian Renaissance. The review opens, like *Eminent Victorians*, with a comment on the mass of material and the innumerable ways of exploring it. Strachey proceeds to criticise one of the works for its moralistic Victorian account of the Dukes of Urbino that does not attempt to 'understand their motives and to realise the actual conditions of their lives.' Another biography 'fails to produce a really vital impression' of Lorenzo the Magnificent. The reviewer wonders at the end if these lives of action can be properly memorialised only in bronze, marble, or paint ('Italian Renaissance', pp. 838–9). In the same fashion a biography of the actor Henry Irving is superficial and unreal because it is all external; nothing of Irving's expression of thought and feeling is given. A boring volume on the age of Louis XIV, written by some of his Trinity teachers for the *Cambridge Modern History*, fails to be interesting as minutely detailed or broadly general history (*SE*, pp. 115–120). And the author of a book on Napoleon was 'far more occupied with the collection and verification of his facts than with the arrangement of them', a complaint Strachey will repeat. A remark in the review sounds the ridiculing note that Strachey's critics will deplore: 'Really, it is difficult to decide which was the more remarkable thing about Napoleon, – his generalship or his lack of humour' ('Napoleon', pp. 1100–1).

The reviews of biography and history that Strachey wrote for the *Spectator* cannot be discounted simply as the envious carpings of a critic whose dissertation on Warren Hastings had failed to win him a fellowship. One of the books Strachey reviewed was by the sociologist and historian Guglielmo Ferrero, whom Strachey and Bell among others thought brilliant. Ferrero's interpretation of Cleopatra's motives in a volume of his history of Rome stimulated

Strachey to disagree about Antony. Characteristically and traditionally Strachey argues that Antony was not a blunderer but a passion-blinded hero whose world was well lost for love. More significantly, Ferrero elicited from his reviewer a statement of belief in the art of history on which Strachey's practice of a biographer would rest.

. . . The first duty of a great historian is to be an artist. The function of art in history is something much more profound that mere decoration; to regard it, as some writers persist in regarding it, as if it were the jam put round the pill of fact by cunning historians is to fall into grievous error; a truer analogy would be to compare it to the process of fermentation which converts a raw mass of grape-juice into a subtle and splendid wine. Uninterpreted truth is as useless as buried gold; and art is the great interpreter. It alone can unify a vast multitude of facts into a significant whole, clarifying, accentuating, suppressing, and lighting up the dark places with the torch of the imagination. More than that, it can throw over the historian's materials the glamour of a personal revelation, and display before the reader great issues and catastrophes as they appear, not to his own short sight, but to the penetrating vision of the most soaring of human spirits. That is the crowning glory of the greatest history – that of Thucydides, for instance, or Tacitus, or Gibbon; it brings us into communion with an immense intelligence, and it achieves this result through the power of art. Indeed, every history worthy of the name is, in its own way, as personal as poetry, and its value ultimately depends upon the force and the quality of the character behind it. (*SE*, pp. 13–14)

The grounds on which Strachey's work would be praised and damned are present here: his imaginative interpretation unifying lives into significant wholes as a personal expression, through literary art, of the human spirit and the artist's character. All of which is expressed in lucid, fluent, sometimes impassioned, sometimes clichéd, periodic prose.

Strachey's concern with prose style in his dissertation is continued in his *Spectator* reviews. A piece that may well be a collaborative effort with St. Loe praises the prose of men and women such as Raleigh, Elizabeth, Cromwell, Lincoln, Clive, and Hastings, whom the cousins might have agreed in admiring, and then deprecates the styles of mere writers, which Lytton would not have done. The prose of another man of action, Francis Bacon, was admired so much by Lytton in a *Spectator* review that St. Loe edited in qualifications and repudiations after some of his reviewer's quotations.[7] Bacon is called a great lawyer, statesman, philosopher, as well as a consummate writer of English, equal to Browne, Bunyan, Swift, Gibbon, and Burke (whose rhetorical violence Strachey criticised elsewhere in the *Spectator*). He is 'a supreme master of the sententious style', a great colourist in prose like Sir Thomas Browne, but differing from him in his combination of thought with colour. The concentration of meaning, the 'happy valiancy' of Bacon's phrases, the universal comprehension of his mind, compress 'into his immortal pages nothing more nor less than the spirit of the world itself' (*SE*, pp. 82–7). This extravagant praise of Bacon as a man and writer is in complete contrast with Strachey's treatment in *Elizabeth and Essex* twenty years later, and even differs from the character he would draw in the play *Essex* that he would soon write. Perhaps Strachey delighted in praising a writer's essays that were so different from the sermons of the *Spectator*'s numerous clerical readers.

Closer to Strachey's style than Bacon's was that of Clarendon, who alone, Strachey thought, may have succeeded in English literature 'as a prose portrait-painter' – though he fell short of the great French artists like Saint-Simon or La Bruyère (*SE*, p. 133). (In *Eminent Victorians* he will cite Fontenelle and Condorcet instead.) Johnson too was a master: 'what a contrast there is between the sober and polished sentences of the *Lives of the Poets* and the rough brilliance of the talk in Boswell!' ('Henley', p. 197). Swift's prose Strachey found unemphatic but powerful:

> The only ornament in his writing is the rhythm, so that, compared with the decorative and imaginative prose of such a writer as Sir Thomas Browne, it resembles the naked body of an athlete besides some Prince in gorgeous raiment. (*SE*, p. 144)

The imagery of this passage, like the earlier description of Ferrero's art of history, discloses how remote Strachey's writing is from Swift's unadorned, Browne's ornate, Bacon's sententious, or

Johnson's forceful style. The prose of a predecessor Strachey's most resembles is that of Macaulay.

Strachey described Macaulay's style this way in the *Spectator*:

> As a thinker Macaulay was neither original nor profound; but he possessed a compensating gift – he had the power of expressing the most ordinary thoughts in the most striking ways. Platitudes are, after all, the current coin of artists, critics, and philosophers; without them all commerce of the mind would come to a standstill; and a great debt is owing to those who, like Macaulay, have the faculty of minting fresh and clear and shining platitudes in inexhaustible abundance. Macaulay brought to the making of platitude more fire and zest than most writers can summon up for their subtlest and most surprising thoughts, with the result that there are few paradoxes so brilliant and pleasing as his commonplaces. (*SE*, p. 172)

The analysis is not original or profound either, but it does illustrate what is being said. In its minting imagery and clear, complex sentences Strachey expresses a paradoxical platitude. This kind of writing can be tiresome in reviews that insist on the value of literary art. It would be years before Strachey found in biography a public form of writing in which he could use his ripe prose effectively – that is ironically. In some of his *Spectator* reviews, however, the humour of Strachey's figurative language sometimes seems uncertain in its intention. A Shakespeare review uses culinary imagery to describe critics' interpretations; another on light verse begins by calling it 'the millinery of literature' ('Light Verse', p. 304). Occasionally, Strachey does turn a commonplace comparison into an original one, as when he describes Shakespeare's sonnets as a country where '"airy tongues that syllable men's names" lure the unwary traveller at every turn into paths already white with the bones of innumerable commentators' (*SE*, p. 71). More consequential than some of his other critical imagery are the recurrent analogues to visual art in Strachey's reviews that connect his criticism both to Bloomsbury and the eighteenth century.

Lytton Strachey realised when writing for the *Independent Review* that his flamboyant style was a problem. But St. Loe seems to have liked it and went so far as to offer his cousin the editorship of the *Spectator* early in 1908. Lytton told James that he had refused the position because literature not politics was his business (MH/*LS*,

p. 369). Would he have also turned down the editorship of an essentially literary paper at this time? When Strachey started writing for MacCarthy and the *New Quarterly*, he wrote to Dorothy Bussy that he thought he would still have time for masterpieces in the intervals (MH/*LS*, p. 336). He also considered writing a biography of his father after his death in February 1908, but decided not to, explaining again to James that it would have meant writing the history of nineteenth-century India (MH/*LS*, p. 372). He continued to write poems, Apostle papers, and plays while he was reviewing and began, more surprisingly, a comic political novel. But the weekly reviewing told on him, as it had on Fry. Some of the late reviews in the spring of 1909, such as the one on Swift, appear wearily digressive. Strachey could hardly hope as an anonymous *Spectator* reviewer to make a reputation as a critic, even if he had wanted to. The range of his literary taste was impressive, and it was supported by aesthetic and ethical principles derived from Moore. He could write fluently, plausibly, amusingly, but he was not an original critic. The significance of many of his *Spectator* texts depends upon the context of his and Bloomsbury's literary development.

VI

Midway in his career as a *Spectator* reviewer, Lytton Strachey told Virginia Woolf that he wanted 'to write a novel about a Lord Chancellor and his naughty son', but he could not think of a plot, and then there was the problem of the British public. Woolf wrote back 'plots don't matter and as for passion and style and immortality, what more do you want?' A few months later Strachey described how he lay in bed making up scabrous conversations for his lord chancellor novel: it was to have every sphere of life, including a prime minister, a don's wife, amazing footmen, prostitutes – 'but it's impossible to get any of it together'. Tantalised again, Woolf complained facetiously (in the midst of an early draft of *The Voyage Out*) that after his versatile genius 'a painstaking woman who wishes to treat of life as she finds it, and to give voice to some of the perplexities of her sex, in plain English, has no chance at all' (*LVWLS*, pp. 19–20, 28–9). Among Strachey's papers are four chapters of a satirical novel, titled *Lord Pettigrew*, whose topicality indicates they were begun around 1908–9. No lord chancellors, naughty sons, prime ministers or prostitutes appear in them, but there are lords enough, for the novel focuses on the aristocratic reaction to the Liberal triumph of 1906 and Lloyd George's subsequent budget (defended by Keynes in the *New Quarterly*) that was to finance social reform through taxes on land, inheritance, and income. Mixed in with these political issues are sexual ones. Lord Pettigrew is a distinguished middle-aged English gentleman with an unfortunate squint who arrives for a visit to a ducal estate and receives a farcical billet-doux from a noble lady, and then a sclerotic set speech from her husband about the duty of the Lords to throw out the budget – which was eventually done, provoking a constitutional crisis and two elections in 1910. (Strachey had been studying a *Times* booklet on the debates in the House of Lords over the budget – MH/LS, p. 401.) A chapter is devoted to a tea-party of political opinions and sexual motives; the ladies castigate suffragettes and post-impressionist paintings among other things. In the last chapter the empty life of the woman whose husband is heir to the dukedom is recapitulated, and there is a description of the duke's great house in another set piece. The house has matured through the centuries – the nineteenth century had done the best it could, which was to leave the place alone – and has become, like Knole in *Orlando*, a thing 'of grandeur and grace . . . as near perfection as it is given to any of man's works to be' (*RIQ*, p. 60).[8]

Some notes left by Strachey list more characters, further scenes in various locations in the house and on the estate, as well as other social and political topics for discussion. But the four chapters of *Lord Pettigrew* do not suggest how he could have brought them together. Speeches and dialogue are unintegrated with the descriptions of characters and settings. Strachey's only surviving attempt at a novel suggests he was still more attracted to the drama. At times it even reads like a play with extensive stage directions – perhaps a farcical comedy of the kind Strachey had been reviewing for the *Spectator*. In novel form, however, the dramatis personae all appear as caricatures. *Lord Pettigrew* is occasionally amusing and its political content may reflect Strachey's involvement with the *Spectator* at this time. (One lord dismisses people who write long letters to that paper.) It shows that Strachey was hardly indifferent to the political issues of the day.

Lord Pettigrew was not the kind of masterpiece Strachey hoped he would have time for in the intervals of regular reviewing. Neither was the imitation Elizabethan tragedy he wrote for a Stratford competition in 1909, after leaving the *Spectator*. *Essex: A Tragedy* again displays Strachey's early enthusiasm for Elizabethanism that is apparent in his *Spectator* and *New Quarterly* reviews, but the play's chief interest now is its relevance to the last full-length work that Strachey wrote nearly twenty years later. *Essex* dramatises approximately the last quarter of *Elizabeth and Essex, A Tragic History*. The play suffers from the same lack of dramatic construction and characterisation that Strachey perceived in the work of Beddoes, and there is none of Beddoes's exploratory Elizabethan genius that so delighted Strachey in the *New Quarterly*. The blank verse of *Essex* consists largely of undramatic set speeches. Strachey imitates a languorous Elizabethan love song nicely, but its context – Elizabeth is dressing with her ladies in the morning just before Essex bursts in – is inappropriate. Something of the queen's shrewd vacillation and Essex's impetuosity are caught, but mostly from words, not dramatised actions. The Essex of *Essex* has more brains that the one in *Elizabeth and Essex*. Mr Secretary Cecil is, with his asides, more nervously ineffectual in the play, and there are ladies in love with both himself and Essex who do not appear in the later work. Francis Bacon, the betrayer of his friend for his country, is clearly the ancestor of the character in the biography but has little relationship to the great artist in prose that Strachey had celebrated, the year before in the *Spectator*. And *Essex* uses the sentimental ring legend that Strachey dismisses in *Elizabeth and Essex*. Unlike the biography, of course, the play is quite unFreudian in viewpoint. And it is the author's point of view so integral to Strachey's biographies that is missing from his plays. Again, as with *Lord Pettigrew*, there are difficulties in connecting personal relations and public events. The problems that beset his earlier plays remain in *Essex*.

Essex did not aim at being a great work of art, Strachey wrote to his mother, who wondered how he would fill up the acts (Merle, p. 415). It did not win the competition. Strachey's various *Spectator* complaints that Elizabethan tragedy was a defunct form and that recent poetic drama escaped from the realities of life can obviously be applied to *Essex*. When Strachey did try a modern theme, as in *Lord Pettigrew*, he chose to write comedy not tragedy. Nevertheless, the play is an accomplished imitation. Strachey had learned the phrasing that he said was the secret of blank verse when writing of

Beddoes. Essex, for example, appeals to Elizabeth to make peace with Ireland and war with Spain, instead of the other way round:

> Spain shall gasp and reel.
> Her loaded argosies shall plumb the seas
> To dazzle gaping fishes, while wealth undreamed
> Shall flow in newer channels, and amaze
> Our unaccustomed shores. Then shall we see
> Strange visions of unending merchandise
> Heaped on our galleys, where grisambered isles,
> Surrendering all their marvels, fill the seas
> With radiant ivory and translucent pearl.
> Then Thames's bank shall glow with Indian gold,
> And richest spices waft their odours far
> Over our English fields. Then men shall say
> 'Spain was'; and on their ears shall beat the roar
> Of our imperial realm, whose awful power
> Shall far outmatch the wonder of old Rome,
> And through illimitable ages crown
> The names of England and Elizabeth.

'Marry the rogue speaks well', says Elizabeth, unconverted by Essex's imperialism (pST).[9]

The poetry that Strachey continued to write while reviewing for the *Spectator* also resembles his earlier work. None of it is modern in the sense he defined in his reviews of recent poetry. As a writer of verse, Strachey too is a late Romantic escaping current realities. The language is occasionally archaic but rarely Edwardian. A poem entitled 'Knowledge', written in 1907 and sent to Leonard Woolf, was published posthumously by Desmond MacCarthy, who noted the Elizabethan and Jacobean influences and observed how Strachey loved in poetry 'the golden moments of emotion that shoot up and spatter the skies – though he always kept his eye on the falling stick' (DM/M, pp. 41–2). The knowledge in question includes 'the guttural voice of lust/Moaning upon, the boundaries of thought . . . ' (lines that could describe the heroine's dreams in Virginia Woolf's first novel). Romantic poetry is a primary source for Strachey's inspiration in poems like 'The Haschish', which floats somewhere between 'Kubla Khan', 'The Lotus-Eaters', 'The Garden of Proserpine', and 'The Lake Isle of Innisfree'. Mostly, however, Strachey wrote lust poems. They are at least original in the sexually

descriptive uses to which he puts the form and diction of the
metaphysicals and the romantics. Sometimes there is an ironic
twist, as in a poem that celebrates the loved one's body in hopes of
forgetting his face. In 'To Bazzi' Strachey's exuberant erotic fantasy
culminates in the exotic, and is as close as Strachey comes to
modern verse.

> To turn ecstatic from the imagined bliss
> Of Laura's vision or of Dante's swoon,
> To press a peacock twixt your amorous thighs,
> Or feel upon your lips grow warm and rise
> The emerald penis of a gay baboon!
>
> (pST)

VII

'Art and Indecency' is the title of Strachey's best paper on literary
theory, and it bears directly on his verse and other writings. Clearly
derived again from Moore's epistemology and ethics, it could not
have been published in the *Spectator* or even in the *New Quarterly.*
Strachey read the paper to the Cambridge Heretics discussion
society in 1921 (three years before Virginia Woolf delivered 'Mr.
Bennett and Mrs. Brown' to them), but it is based on a series of
Apostle papers that he wrote on the relation of ethics and
aesthetics. Strachey raised the subject in his first outrageous Apostle
paper of 1902 (see *Victorian Bloomsbury,* pp. 256–7). He returned to it
in a paper on the fallacies of impressionists who were convinced
that art always ought to be beautiful (see p. 211). In another Apostle
paper of 1907 entitled 'Was Diotima Right?' he recalled to the
Apostles how they had rejected his original claim that anything
could be beautiful in its right relations because he had not
distinguished between 'real' and other kinds of relations (his
illustration in 1902 had been defecation). Whatever we mean by
reality, Strachey insists that it is involved in art and love. The
universe is queerer than we realise, and Diotima's Platonic vision
that 'what is most beautiful and best *is* the really real thing . . . '
may be right after all. One thing is certain for Strachey: beauty is of
life's essence, not merely an inferior appendage to it, as
anti-aesthetes like Raleigh kept insisting. The peroration urges the
Apostles 'to really live' and quotes a sonorous passage ending 'to

live indeed is to be again ourselves.' Its author was not Pater but 'our brother Browne' (LS/pST). 'Art and Indecency' itself is a reworking of an earlier, more imprudent Apostle paper entitled 'Will It Come Right in the End?'[10] That paper distorts Moore's principles by arguing that only feelings are good or bad in themselves, and the difference between them is indescribable. Aesthetic wholes are complex, so is conduct, and neither should be interfered with. Swinburne's poems are the chief literary example, but Strachey's conclusion goes considerably beyond them:

> The only hope of our ever getting a really beautiful and vigorous and charming civilization is to allow the whole world to fuck and bugger and abuse themselves in public and generally misbehave to their hearts' content. (*RIQ*, p. 80)

One can judge something of the Apostles' reaction to Strachey's Wildean exaggerations here by the concession he makes at the beginning of the later 'Art and Indecency'. He now admits that art can have ethical consequences, but observes how impossible it is to generalise about art's moral effects, for 'many clergymen who have read Catullus with impunity have been, it is reported, completely demoralised by Mrs Humphry Ward' (*RIQ*, p. 84). Art for art's sake, then, is a false doctrine when it maintains ethics is irrelevant to art, for in addition to art's ethical consequences, there are also ethical elements in it. But art for art's sake is true when it maintains that aesthetic wholes with ethical parts must still be judged only by aesthetic standards. Strachey then considers the views of three quite different classes of people on the relations of art and indecency. First are the Prudes, the censors and bowdlerisers, who were so formidable in the golden age of Victoria but now have begun to compromise. Next are what Strachey, alluding maybe to the naturalistic fallacy in *Principia Ethica*, calls the Naturalists. (In 'Will It Come Right in the End?' Edward Carpenter was the humourless example of this class which never titters about sex, and St. Loe Strachey an exemplar of the Prudes in his *Spectator* attack on H. G. Wells's advocacy of free love from *In the Days of the Comet*.) Indecency simply does not exist for the Naturalists. They affirm 'it is as absurd to attach ethical qualities to . . . the emission of seminal fluid from a penis as it would be to attach them to the emission of mucous fluid from a nose' (p. 86). The third group, the Bawdy, realise that indecency has to do with states of mind, not states of body. The extreme Bawdy position, which with Strachey happily identified himself in an earlier Apostolic version of his paper, is now criticised because indecency can sometimes ruin a work of art. The extreme prudish position is equally unsatisfactory. The solution is a middle course that recognises works of art are Moorean organic wholes, not sums; their parts in isolation may be bad or insignificant, yet of the greatest value when combined aesthetically into complex wholes. In so far as Lytton Strachey can be said to have an aesthetic theory, 'Art and Indecency' expresses it. While only implicitly formalistic, it is nevertheless a distinctively Bloomsbury theory of art – but one that Strachey had little scope to express in the pages of the *Spectator*.[11]

12 E. M. Forster: Rooms and Views

The moral and aesthetic inadequacies of art for art's sake that Lytton Strachey explored in his later Edwardian Apostle papers also figure in E. M. Forster's third novel. While Strachey was still writing weekly reviews for the *Spectator*, a note arrived from Forster in November 1908, asking if he could arrange for *A Room with a View* to be reviewed (LS/pBL). A review duly appeared in the *Spectator*, and it was much more favourable than the notice of *The Longest Journey* had been. The anonymous reviewer found *A Room with a View* by far the best of Forster's three novels, one in which an earlier disfiguring cynicism had been replaced by 'a kindlier tolerance' (*EMFCH*, p. 118). Some critics still find *A Room with a View* the best of Forster's early novels, but most readers would probably agree with Forster's judgement, half a century later, that though not his favourite novel, 'it may fairly be called the nicest' (*RV*, p. 210).

'Nicest' is faint praise for Forster, his editor Oliver Stallybrass has observed (*RV*, p. xiv), and it is consistent with the disparagement Forster expressed during the rewriting, and then reception of *A Room with a View* in 1907–8. At the end of 1907, on the eve of his twenty-ninth birthday, Forster noted in his diary, 'Shall scarcely write another "Longest Journey", for it vexed people and I can with sincerity please them' (PNF, *EMF*, I 159). It was harder to please himself. He had begun the work as early as 1901, written and rewritten drafts or sketches of the Italian part by 1902, and then done a version of the English half in 1903 before breaking off to write his first two published novels. Returning to what he called his 'Lucy' novel after *The Longest Journey*, Forster was depressed by it. He wrote to R. C. Trevelyan that it was 'bright and merry', and he liked the story, but would not and could not finish it in the same early style for unexplained moral reasons. To his diary he complained that it was 'so thin'. Later during the rewriting and proofing he called the novel 'toshy . . . inoffensive', 'bilge', 'slight, unambitious, and uninteresting . . . '. In response to E. J. Dent's strictures, however, he insisted that the novel 'does, sincerely or insincerely, commend an attitude'. It came off as far as it went, 'which is a damned little way', but the characters of Lucy and Beebe interested him a good deal. Charlotte Bartlett he made the subject of a parody of Wordsworth's 'Lucy' poem 'A Slumber Did My Spirit Seal' and then sent a postcard in her name to Trevelyan. Earlier he had told Nathaniel Wedd that the characters seemed more alive to him in an external way than in his other novels and that the book 'will probably gratify the home circle, but not those whose opinions I value most' (*RV*, pp. viii, xii–xiv).

Two of those opinions have survived from Bloomsbury, and both are revealing. Leonard Woolf, who had been investigating a squalid murder in Ceylon, wrote characteristically to Strachey that the book 'which appears to me really rather good & sometimes thoroughly amusing is absolutely muddled, isn't it?' Turning Mr Emerson's key term 'muddle' against the novel, Woolf went on,

> Isn't it dominated by a spectral Moore? He [Forster] still seems to think death is real & sightseeing unreal; I think I shall have to write to him & explain once more that it doesn't exist, that after all the smell of cheese is as real as the smell of a corpse. There is a curious twilight & pseudo mystery over his books which irritate me into this: to be petty & to like bad things may be bad but he always seems to hint mysteriously that they are unreal.
>
> (LW/L, pp. 141–2)

Despite his severities, Woolf did perceive continuities between *A Room with a View* and *The Longest Journey* in their concerns with reality and unreality.

A more interesting public response to *A Room with a View* from Bloomsbury was Virginia Woolf's short, anonymous review in *The Times Literary Supplement*. Woolf uses Forster's symbolism of rooms and views to comment on how Forster makes the reader care for Lucy's development and wait expectantly for her to separate truth from falsehood and burst then forth with her own beliefs instead of other peoples'. But then comes the qualification. At the end of her review of *The Longest Journey*, Woolf had asked what Forster would do next. She found the novel that followed clever, funny, and occasionally beautiful, yet by the end of the book,

> the view is smaller than we expected. The disappointment is not due to any change of scene, but to some belittlement, which seems to cramp the souls of the actors. Lucy's conversion becomes a thing of trifling moment, and the views of George and his father no longer spring from the original fountain.[1]

(E, I 221–2)

In her review of Forster's work in 1927, Virginia Woolf virtually ignored the novel.

Forster was right, then, in his anticipation; A Room with a View did not really gratify those in Bloomsbury whose opinions he would come to value most. What Virginia and Leonard Woolf praised and what they were disappointed with, may be seen by looking at the novel's structure, the story's progression, and how Forster changed them from the early versions that have survived. Particularly relevant for Bloomsbury's literary history are the attitudes in the novel about art and reality, love and truth, religion and the situation of women. These are some of the things Virginia Woolf is alluding to in her review when she writes of recognising in Forster's novel 'that odd sense of freedom which books give us when they seem to represent the world as we see it' (p. 221). The odd sense of freedom that A Room with a View gave Woolf also helped her to become a novelist. Her most enlightening commentary on A Room with a View would ultimately be The Voyage Out.

II

Virginia Woolf's review begins 'Mr E. M. Forster's title A Room with a View is symbolical, of course.' In The Longest Journey and also Where Angels Fear to Tread rooms, windows, and views can symbolise individuals' consciousnesses. In Woolf's work from Jacob's Room and Mrs. Dalloway through To the Lighthouse to A Room of One's Own and beyond, a room and its view belong to the fundamental symbolism of her art. Often it is a private room that stands for a way of life and also an awareness of the individual rooms and views of others. In a room and its view can be seen the basic dualism of Bloomsbury's Moorean epistemology that distinguishes between the acts of perception and the objects perceived. This dualism figures prominently in Bloomsbury painting, as in that of many modern artists, so much is modern life lived in separate rooms. *A Room with a View* is more about views than rooms, however. Rooms are largely noticed for the shutters or curtains that conceal or reveal the view. The climactic chapters of the novel – the murder, kiss, and bathing scenes – all take place out of rooms. What matters most in the novel are the changing or unchanging outlooks of the occupants of rooms.

In *A Room with a View*, Forster plays on both the physical and mental senses of 'view'. The various physical meanings pertain to views of nature and art. In pensions, churches, squares, houses, hills, and woods the appearance of people and their settings are viewed directly, or through painting and sculpture. The mental views in the novel extend from attitudes about manners and morals to philosophical and religious ideas. *A Room with a View* – the only novel of Forster's to be divided into two parts – doubles around viewing and hiding, inner awareness and outer concealment, truth and muddled lies. Light and darkness provide the basic imagery. And the focus of all this perception and deception is passion. That is the 'message' frowned to Lucy by the dying Italian whose life-blood spoils her art photographs of Botticelli's *Venus*, other nude 'pities', the della Robbia babies, and Giotto's *Saint John*. Only the instinctual Phaeton driving the carriage interprets the message that made Lucy faint and George realise with a frown that life was worth living and Lucy worth loving (*RV*, pp. 41–5, 69). The murder is another of the scenes of panic and emptiness that occur in Forster's novels. It takes place in a square with cave-like entrances and a throbbing phallic tower; the time is twilight, 'the hour of unreality . . . when unfamiliar things are real' (pp. 40–1).

Leonard Woolf, in his irritation over Moore's spectral influence, thought Forster was contrasting the view of an real murder with the unrealities of sightseeing. Yet reality in the novel is most closely associated with love. 'When love comes, that is reality', Mr Emerson teaches George and then Lucy (p. 196). Love not work saves George from Carlyle's Centre of Indifference, which is represented by the large question mark in his room. Love is the only answer to the pessimism of Housman's stanza that Mr Emerson quotes in Santa Croce – an answer that is given in the poem (*RV*, p. 26; Housman, p. 49). Love, says the novel's narrator, is 'the most real thing that we shall ever meet'. Lucy's struggle 'lay not between love and duty. Perhaps there never is such a contest. It lay between the real and the pretended . . . ' (p. 161). If *A Room with a View* can be said to commend an attitude, as Forster thought it did, this is the attitude.

The conflict of the real with the pretended applies also to art and religion in the novel. After *Howards End* it is easier to realise that in *A Room with a View* Forster also wants to connect art with life, to see it as an enhancement and not a substitute for human existence. Strachey had criticised aestheticism for its disregarding the ethical in art. Forster's third novel develops the satire of aestheticism in *Where Angels Fear to Tread*, associating it with a kind of modern medieval asceticism that values art above love. Ruskin, Baedeker, and Berenson are all laughed at along with the pretentious Florentine culture of English and American exiles there. (One of the exiles, an American of the rarest type, writes on Gemisthus Pletho, like the author of *A Room with a View*.) The 'tactile values' of Berenson, whom Forster had been reading with disapproval in 1907 (*RV*, p. 222), take on various amusing meanings in a novel where the kissing of a cheek is fraught with significance. Lucy prefers the della Robbia's Renaissance babies to Giotto's saints – but she understands Beethoven, and when she plays, 'by touch, not by sound alone, did she come to her desire' (p. 30). The charming, celibate Mr Beebe waits for the exciting time when Lucy shall live as she plays, but turns into an inhuman black column when he learns she has been transformed by her love for George Emerson (pp. 31, 203). Gothic Cecil treats Lucy as a Leonardesque work of art rather than a living woman. He connects her with views; she connects him with rooms (p. 106). The Michelangelesque George ends her engagement, undertaken in the eighth or 'Medieval' chapter. After much concealment and lying comes marriage. The last chapter is entitled 'The End of the Middle Ages' (p. 205).

Mr Beebe's change is sexually as well as religiously motivated. The narrator informs us that he is 'from rather profound reasons, somewhat chilly in his attitude towards the other sex'. He never heard of a broken engagement without some pleasure. His belief in celibacy is described as 'very subtle and quite undogmatic', yet he thinks that helping to confirm Lucy in her virginity is also a help to religion (pp. 32, 187). Beebe's participation in the homoerotic comedy of the bathing scene, with its 'call to the blood and to the relaxed will' (p. 133) – a scene as memorable as that of the murder, to which it is subtly linked – suggests that his celibacy may be of the kind described in Apostolic Cambridge as 'the higher sodomy'. When Lucy finally confesses her love for George, Beebe tells Emerson that his son no longer interests him. (Beebe's interest is much stronger in an earlier draft of the novel where he flirts with George.) The religious dimension of Beebe's celibacy is nevertheless an important aspect of the anti-clericalism of *A Room with a View*, which first appears in the condescension of the Reverend Mr Eager. Eager lectures on St Francis and the brotherhood of man in a chapel of Santa Croce while in the next chapel that brotherhood is exemplified by the also allusively named Mr Emerson. Eager's remarks on Giotto's unrepresentational form and praise of his spiritual significance shows he has not read Roger Fry on Giotto's aesthetic values. (He has read Berenson but dismisses Giotto's tactile values.) Fry's high praise for Giotto's Santa Croce fresco *The Ascension of St John*, its design and colour, is also unknown to Emerson, who describes it as a fat blue saint sailing to heaven like an air-balloon (p. 23). (*The Ascension of St John* was one of Lucy's bloodied photographs, and both Lucy and George keep reproductions of Giotto in their rooms in England.) George's father preaches to Lucy a Forsterian form of self-reliance that owes something to Samuel Butler and possibly to Edward Carpenter as well as to Ralph Waldo Emerson. Lucy Honeychurch's name describes a worship of sweetness and light very different from Eager's Christianity and even the amusing Beebe's. Mr Emerson is described as profoundly religious; he differs from Beebe 'chiefly by his acknowledgment of passion' (p. 199). Beebe, for instance, thinks Scott's song from *The Bride of Lammermoor* wise and beautiful. Echoes of that novel turn up again from *Where Angels Fear to Tread* in various places, as in the heroine's first name, which Charlotte Bartlett likes to translate into 'Lucia'.[2] The novel's song, a gift from Cecil, calls for a vacant heart and hand and eye in order to 'Easy live and quiet die'. ('Why throw up the sponge?' Freddy asks pertinently – p. 189.)

The vacancy of hearts, hands, and eyes in art, religion, and life are variously exposed in *A Room with a View*. The one character in the novel compared to a great artist is Charlotte Bartlett:

> She had worked like a great artist; for a time – indeed, for years – she had been meaningless, but at the end there was presented to the girl the complete picture of a cheerless, loveless world. . . .
>
> (p. 78)

Lucy and George learn finally that Charlotte's artistry was in the service of their love. She appeared to them 'brown against the view' of the violets and Florence (p. 68). (Symbolically, the colour violet has traditionally signified the love of truth and also the truth of love – Brewer, p. 1130.) Only at the end of the novel do they surmise how their love must have appeared to her. Charlotte's apparent change that leads her to arrange a meeting of Lucy and Mr Emerson so she can confess her love for George eventually makes the couple aware at the novel's close of an even more mysterious love than theirs.[3] (The change is foreshadowed in the strange image of Charlotte's bird-like head silently demolishing an invisible object while Lucy lies to George about her love.) Charlotte's transformation is not as surprising as Beebe's because her point of view is almost never displayed. She descends from Jane Austen as well as from an aunt of Forster's. Charlotte Bartlett is one of the best comic characters in Forster, triumphantly martyred in an unselfishness that 'had entirely usurped the functions of enthusiasm' (p. 65). Her effectiveness in *A Room with a View* derives partly from Forster's external treatment of her. When Beebe has tea with her (with all his experience of maiden ladies, he still finds her baffling), the reader hears and sees her from the clergyman's point of view. Not until the very end of the book does one know how aware she is of what she has been so successfully doing. 'It is impossible to penetrate into the minds of elderly people', the narrator explains (p. 147).

Forster has no difficulty entering Lucy's and Mr Beebe's minds, the two characters who interested him most. Cecil's unspoken or unshown thoughts and feelings are also given directly from time to time. George's never are, though he was modelled originally on Forster's friend H. O. Meredith, to whom this most Meredithean of Forster novels is dedicated.[4] *A Room with a View*, as the title makes manifest, is a novel about points of view. The most important are those of Lucy and the narrator. They need to be described further in this Bloomsbury novel of love, art, and truth.

III

The education of Lucy Honeychurch is not rendered from her point of view alone, as Henry James might have done in his later novels. *A Room with a View* is even not a Forsterian *Portrait of a Lady* in the way *Where Angels Fear to Tread* can be read as his version of *The Ambassadors*. There are some similarities in the Italian scenes and the emphasis on art; Cecil may be a descendant of the Italianate American aesthete Gilbert Osmond and George Emerson related to Isabelle Archer's would-be rescuer Goodwood, but Lucy's is a romantic comedy not a moral tragedy. The influence of George Meredith's *The Egoist* in Part Two of *A Room with a View* seems stronger than anything of James's. Cecil, like the egoist Willoughby Patterne, tries to mould in a country house his incipiently feminist fiancée, while she is increasingly attracted to an independent-thinking young man (whom Meredith modelled partly on Leslie Stephen).

In the Italian part of *A Room with a View*, Lucy is always present. The narrator does not concentrate on her consciousness, but her inner, unexpressed thoughts and feelings are, except for Beebe's, the only ones are described, and Beebe's are focused on Lucy and her playing. George Emerson has a view, his father says at the beginning of the novel; Mr Emerson has got one too, but all that readers know of these views is what the Emersons, various other characters and the narrator say about them. The Emersons' consciousnesses are not depicted. The stabbing scene, for example, where Lucy is alone, is described from her angle of vision; almost all we know of George's reactions to the event and to Lucy, are what he says and does.

Part Two of *A Room with a View* opens with a change in view and point of view. The season is late summer rather than early spring; autumn winds seem to blow away the engagement at the end. Instead of Florence and its environs, there is Meredith's 'fluffy and lush' Surrey, as Forster later described it (*AN* p. 62). This is a very different landscape from that of the Wiltshire of *The Longest Journey* or the Hertfordshire of *Howards End*. English nature does not replace Italian art, for there are books and music scattered about at Windy Corner (as there are hills and flowers around the art of Florence), yet in Part Two all the beautiful views are of nature, not art. Florence, said Forster in a late summary of the novel, functions as an awakener and then a consummation of Lucy's and George's love (*HD*, p. 291). Surrey's views, according to George, are just air and distance. His father, however, says they are wholes, like crowds – greater than the sums of their parts; men may be divided into those who forget views and those (like Wordsworth) who recollect these wholes in small rooms (*RV*, pp. 158–9). Then there are ladies like the Alans whom Mr Beebe pleasantly describes as seeking 'the Pension Keats', with rooms and magic views in faery lands forlorn (p. 177).

The change in narrative point of view from Part One to Part Two of *A Room with a View* is marked by the absence of Lucy for the first time in the novel. The omniscient narrator, who accompanies her everywhere in Florence, confines himself now to setting the scene and then dramatising it, until Cecil Vyse enters and we begin to see the Honeychurches and their society from Cecil's superior view. (Forster thought later he resembled Philip Herriton a little in *Where Angels Fear to Tread* (Interview, p. 33), and in *Howards End* he is described as a friend of Tibby Schlegel's.) When Charlotte and George re-enter the story, the narrator begins to represent Lucy's point of view again, although he does not disclose the nature of her nightmare in Mrs Vyse's flat. The wonderful bathing scene is omnisciently narrated and dramatised. Lucy's response to the prancing nudity of her lover, her brother, and her priest is unrendered. The change in narrative focus from the Italian to the English halves of the novel accords with Lucy's concealment and deception. Veils and scales encumber her vision; figurative and literal images of night spread during the dark ages of her engagement. When Lucy starts to lie, the narrator refocuses on her consciousness, but there are still scenes, such as Mr Beebe and Charlotte at tea, where she is not present. Cecil's supercilious attitude towards Lucy's milieu is presented from his point of view, but the night scene in which she breaks off their engagement is largely one of dramatised dialogue and stage directions. Some description of the thoughts and feelings of the ascetic Cecil, and then of Lucy, are provided as she watches him impressively leaving his love: she decides she will never marry, and thinks of George also going into darkness, before she puts out the light, leaving the narrator in the dark to sum up her benighted state.

Lucy's sentimental education is impeded by both men and women in *A Room with a View*. To Cecil's asceticism, Beebe's celibacy and the Emersons' gaucherie are added Charlotte's gentility, Lavish's vulgarity, and Mrs Honeychurch's conventionality. Lucy's struggle to understand her own feelings and those of others may not be as exciting or heroic as Beebe hopes it will be when her music and life connect, yet she is still a latter-day heroine in the tradition of Shakespeare and George Eliot (Forster would have added Austen and Meredith) that Henry James makes a plea for and associates his own novel with in his late preface to *The Portrait of a Lady*. The preface appeared in the New York Edition of James's work in 1908, the year Forster met him and finished *A Room with a View*.[5] Lucy Honeychurch is one of the 'much smaller female fry', James writes of, yet she also is a bearer of human affection; in her intelligence and presumption she too 'matters' (James, *Criticism*, pp. 1077–8). What matters in her progress is not only love but also truth that can distinguish real from pretended affection. James said his subject was his heroine's consciousness – her relation to herself. This is not Forster's subject, but he certainly would have agreed with James, that the windows in the house of fiction were not to be reckoned (p. 1075). Forster represents his heroine in relation to herself sometimes, but not as much as he shows her relation to the narrator. Lucy's love of George, for example, is not really represented from her viewpoint. Her coming to realise the truth is dramatised mainly in the deceptions of others and herself. In her music, she chooses to play Schumann not Beethoven at the Vyses's well-appointed flat, Gluck and Mozart at Windy Corner, as well as Scott's song after the end of her engagement. Her feelings about the music she plays are not revealed. The reader and Mr Beebe never behold her mingling life and art heroically. Her lying is hardly that. In the novel's only scene of married love, when the couple are back in their room overlooking the river and hills of Florence in springtime, Lucy is darning her husband's socks, and George finally has to carry her over to the window. As Virginia Woolf said, the view is smaller than expected.

At the end of *A Room with a View* Lucy and George join the great monogamous sect and go the longest journey that Forster had attacked in his previous novel. True, she does not marry the Idealist Cecil, and George does allude to Shelley's ideas when he remarks that 'liking one person is an extra reason for liking another', which pleases Lucy and alarms Charlotte (p. 74). (In an epilogue to the novel written fifty years later, Forster fancies that during the Second World War George did not remain 'chaste'. Any later love life of Lucy's is unmentioned– (*RV* p. 211.) But there is little else in the novel to suggest Lucy's fate was much different from the Victorian heroine's that Forster had described in his 1906 Working Men's College lecture 'Pessimism in Literature' (see pp. 53–4). 'How can the novelist of today end his novel with a marriage?' Forster had asked, contrasting the Victorian heroine – for whom there was no new development or emotion after marriage – with the modern suffragette, who regards marriage as just the beginning. Modern writers, whether pessimists or not, were seeking a more permanent end to novels or plays; they found this, Forster thought, in separation. *The Wings of the Dove* with its demonstration of 'the sadness of personal relations' was his example. (*AE*, pp. 132, 135–8). At the end of his early drafts for *A Room with a View*, Forster kills off George in the same abrupt manner that he disposed of Gerald in *The Longest Journey*. The story ends impermanently, without Lucy's reaction. This is not the kind of separation Forster had called for in his lecture. Yet what makes the final happy ending in *A Room with a View* incongruous in the light of Forster's lecture as well as *The Longest Journey* is the feminism of the novel. Lucy's uncertain progress as a liberated woman begins with her and the narrator's restlessness over Charlotte's conception of the medieval Victorian lady. At the opening of the murder chapter Lucy wants to drop the role of Eternal Woman and live 'as her transitory self'; by the end, she is regretting George's lack of chivalry (pp. 39–40, 44). Back at Windy Corner, where her mother rails at female scribblers, suffragettes, and women who take jobs away from men (pp, 139, 193), Lucy realises Italy has offered her own soul to her, and she reaches the Bloomsbury stage 'where personal intercourse would alone satisfy her'. She has become a rebel who desired not the wider drawing-room view that Cecil was prepared to offer her, 'but equality beside the man she loved' (p. 110). (Cecil does not believe in London educations for women; Beebe does not believe in the equality of the sexes, though Mr Emerson does – pp. 122, 126). The connection of feminism with the criticism of modern medievalism recurs in Cecil's feudal views of protecting a woman rather than offering her the 'comradeship' for which Lucy yearns (p. 154). She feels Cecil stifles her with books, art, and glorious music as he hides her from more glorious people (p. 172). George admits a pre-Lawrentian desire to govern women, which men must fight out with them before they can re-enter the Garden of Eden, but he also wants Lucy to have her own thoughts even when in his arms (pp. 166–7). She never appears as George's free, equal comrade, however. It is difficult to avoid the suspicion that there is something ironic in the novel's representation of feminism. Miss Lavish is personally and artistically an inauthentic feminist. The honest and admirable Mrs Honeychurch is an anti-feminist. Cecil recognises Lucy as 'the new woman' only when she is lying about the reason for leaving him. Lucy rages at Cecil and again at Mr Emerson over the old idea that women break off engagements for the love of other men rather than for sake of liberty. Yet is not this just what she does? (pp. 172–3, 201).

IV

Despite Virginia Woolf's disappointment at the triviality of Lucy's conversion and the belittlement of other characters, she experienced in *A Room with a View* the sense of freedom that came from the representation of the world as she too saw it in 1908. To a considerable degree this representation is the narrator's. Narrative point of view in *A Room with a View* resembles that of Forster's earlier novels, stories, and essays. The moral tone of the selectively omniscient authorial voice is similar: humour, compassion, exhortation, and judgement mingle in its observations and descriptions. Sometimes the views of the narrator extend those of the characters, and sometimes he shows their blindness. There is little wondering over what characters are feeling or thinking, as in Virginia Woolf's work. *A Room with a View* could not be titled *Lucy's Room* any more appropriately than it could be called *The Portrait of a Lady*. At times the narrator's views of Lucy are hardly distinguishable from her own, as the free indirect discourse modulates among them. Still, the narrative voice in *A Room with a View* is not quite as audible or essayistic as in Forster's earlier novels. *A Room with a View* is more scenic, its narrator less a storyteller and more of dramatist. It was the first of Forster's works to be turned into a play, and the most successful of the films that have been made from his novels. His reviewer in the *Spectator* thought Forster might now try his hand at a play – which indeed he did while revising his novel.

Yet the narrative techniques of *A Room with a View* are less innovative than in *The Longest Journey*. Books are made fun of in *A Room with a View*, and they in turn make fun of the characters, but the spirit of anti-literature that nudged Forster in the writing of *The Longest Journey* left him alone more in the next novel. Cecil, who thinks modern books bad, invokes Meredith's Comic Muse, proclaiming that the causes of comedy and truth are one. The Muse obliges and undoes his engagement, with the help of a bad modern

book by Miss Lavish, whose pseudonym is Prank. To keep up with
Cecil, Lucy now reads only serious literature. Mr Beebe's literary
culture is out of date – he has never heard of *A Shropshire Lad* or *The
Way of All Flesh*, whose author is apparently a friend of Mr
Emerson's. (Perhaps Mr Emerson's son was named after George,
the ranger in *Erewhon Revisited*, whose situation as the illegitimate
lost son and half-brother resembles Stephen's in *The Longest
Journey*.)

Forster does continue the narrator's overt use of sculptured myth
that is also a feature of *The Longest Journey*. The narrator remarks of
the violent or suffering statues in the Piazza Signoria that in their
presence, as well as in nature's solitude, 'might a hero meet a
goddess, or a heroine a god' (p. 57). The most famous statue in the
Piazza, which Lucy could not have missed – a reproduction of
Michelangelo's *David* – is palpably absent, however, even though
George is described as Michelangelesque. In the next chapter the
Italian driver and his 'sister' are called Phaeton and Persephone.
The analogy to the reckless George and the half-alive Lucy is not
spelled out. Another god present at the outing is the lesser Pan
'who presides over social contretemps and unsuccessful picnics' in
Forster's stories (p. 69).

There is one deliberately unrealistic, self-conscious feature of *A
Room with a View* in which the authorial narrator's control is
asserted more explicitly than in any of Forster's other novels, and
that is the chapter titles. No other novel of Forster's uses them.[6]
With their addition to the final draft, Forster may have resolved
the moral difficulties, mentioned to Trevelyan, of the style in which
he had begun the novel. The titles, and of course the changed
ending, make *A Room with a View* a less serious novel than that
prefigured in the early sketches. The chapter headings constitute
an amusing, ironic, authorial commentary on the narrative, much
in the manner of *The Egoist* – authorial because in the titles the
distinction between author and narrator disappears. In Part One
the headings deride Baedekerless touring; music, violets, and
euphemistic stomach-talk at the Pension; and an outing in which
the English characters are ambiguously driven by Italians to see a
view. Chapter titles in Part Two tell of Lucy's progress from
'Medieval' to 'The End of the Middle Ages'. The duality of the
novel is again apparent in headings that announce the outer and
inner disasters of Lucy's life. Four of the chapters flatly describe
as 'lying', the evasive, self-deceptive attempts of Lucy to justify her

behaviour. Two crucial chapters of the novel are titled merely with numbers: the stabbing scene in Part One and the bathing scene in Part Two. Both are calls to the blood, which George hears and responds to with love for Lucy. Both are also scenes in which the narrator is actively present, conveying Lucy's reactions in the Piazza Signoria and describing the cavorting nudes in the Sacred Lake where, for example, clothes proclaim their importance for enterprise and are mocked by Mr Emerson and then the narrator à la Thoreau and Carlyle (pp. 125, 131). Nakedness in Italian art and English life is also being associated in the fourth and twelfth chapters, as is the scenic and metaphorical water imagery that flows through the novel.

On one or two occasions in *A Room with a View* the authorial narrator addresses his audience directly. He intervenes to explain Lucy's muddlement and to challenge readers to explain it to her (p. 142). And at the opening of the last chapter he describes rather floridly the Greek world visited by the Alans with their digestive bread before taking himself and the readers back to Italy where Lucy and George are. Elsewhere the narrator relies sometimes heavily on the Emersons to express moral ideas in the novel. Mr Emerson especially provides authorial views that the narrators sometimes offer in Forster's earlier fictions. Ansell to a certain extent and then Mr Failing function this way in *The Longest Journey*; the role is more subtly given to Mrs Wilcox and Mrs Moore in the later novels. It is Mr Emerson who urges Lucy to let herself go, but warns of the horror of muddle (pp. 26, 201). (Emerson also describes his son's pessimism by quoting from Housman and alluding to Carlyle; we learn later George has been reading Schopenhauer and Nietzsche in German.) By the end of *A Room with a View*, Mr Emerson's sententiousness is less effective than his more dramatised wisdom in Part One. In Florence Mr Beebe comments ironically on the difficulty of understanding people like the Emersons 'who speak the truth' (p. 7). No one has much trouble understanding Mr Emerson in Summer Street. Nonetheless, Mr Emerson's concluding insistence that 'we fight for more that Love or Pleasure: there is Truth. Truth counts, Truth does count' (p. 204) is an unmistakable expression of Bloomsbury values (though the Group did not tend to capitalise them). Lucy's recollection that 'he had made her see the whole of everything at once' is again Moorean as well as Arnoldian, and it clearly anticipates the concerns of *Howards End* (p. 204).

V

Forster's concern in *A Room with a View* for truthful love and beauty does not seem to have been part of his original conception of the novel. The moral symbolism of viewing, the conflict between pretence and reality, are not developed much in the surviving drafts of the Parts One and Two of what has been published as *The Lucy Novels*. There is no indication in what have been called the *Old* and *New Lucy* novels, for example, of the final symbolic title. (*Windy Corner* was one early title.) These sets of drafts, written before *Where Angels Fear to Tread*, do not directly correspond to each other. *Old Lucy*, written in 1901–2, is an early version of the Italian half of *A Room with a View; New Lucy*, begun a year later, is a version of the English part but continues a rather different story from that of *Old Lucy*, one that is closer to Part One of the published book. *Old Lucy* is twice as long as what survives of *New Lucy*, whereas Part One of *A Room with a View* is shorter than Part Two. The differences between each of these drafts and the novel that Forster rewrote from them after *The Longest Journey*, suggest his development as a Bloomsbury novelist in several ways.

The Lucy Novels are accurately described by their editor as sketches. The story they tell must be pieced together. Lucy's spiritual development remains the focus, but her relations with Charlotte Bartlett and George, who is called Arthur or Tancred, are changed. There is no Mr Emerson or Mr Beebe, but they are faintly foreshadowed in the figures of a solemn young man preparing for the priesthood and a dyspeptic travelling salesman who reduces the pension to hysteria with his visceral table-talk. A projected concert to raise money for the English Church at Florence occupies much of Lucy and her Pension's attention; scandal spread by Charlotte leads to a row and the abandonment of the concert at which Lucy was to be an accompanist. Arthur, who is trying to be a painter, seeks to connect art and life, but a stabbing that he witnesses shows the remoteness of painting to human reality and he gives up art. (He clearly needed to talk with Leonard Woolf about kinds of reality.) Lucy separates from Charlotte, who is hoping Arthur will propose and be refused. Lucy goes to Rome alone after visiting a piazza where she hopes for a sign but has only a strangely unreal view. Her Italian train travel is the occasion for some good Forster farce, none of which is really relevant to her development. *Old Lucy* ends with the narrator choosing to leave his

heroine not at a crisis in her life but simply overlooking a sunny
view of Rome.

Descriptive bits of English and Italian behaviour in *Old Lucy* were
used by Forster in *Where Angels Fear to Tread* (Herritons turn up
twice); others appear to be notes for essays on Italian boys or
sacristans. The alternation between pension life and Florentine
scenes in Santa Croce and elsewhere is retained in *A Room with a
View* along with a some anti-clericalism. (Mr Eager wants money to
pay for frescoes in his church that he hopes will bear kinship with
Giotto's – hence the concert, which is also to bring English music to
the Italians.) But Lucy, Charlotte, and Arthur/Tancred are all rather
different characters. Charlotte is less sympathetic, less evasively
mysterious, and her relations with Lucy are described more
comically, as in the scene where they divide their clothes while the
narrator invokes *Sartor Resartus*. Lucy plays no Beethoven and, as
far as one can tell from the sketches, remains unkissed, though
scenes described as 'The Catastrophe' and 'The Revelation' were
planned. Lucy's desire is for freedom, but she comes to see bondage
is inevitable. The narrator informs us she has not yet realised we
have the power to choose and change our bonds. There are no
feminist allusions here yet; the women's movement had not
impinged much on Forster's consciousness by 1902. He writes that
Lucy 'was of the sex which fills the auditorium of great deeds, . . . '
and which is lead by reason to great goals separate from those of
men (*LN*, p. 46).[7] Even Miss Lavish, among the least altered of the
secondary characters, is less emancipated in *Old Lucy*.

The change in Arthur's character indicates that the main
difference between *Old Lucy* and *A Room with a View* may be the
drafts' accentuation of art rather than love. Truth does not count as
much in the early sketches; views are not as concealed, feelings not
as suppressed. Arthur's preoccupation with the meaning of life
seems to be more a matter of aesthetics than passion. The stabbing
scene shows the difference most clearly. It has no apparent
connection with Arthur and Lucy's relationship, for Lucy is not
even present. There are, however, homoerotic implications. The
beautiful, nearly naked, bleeding youth affects Arthur strangely:

> By some subtle connection, the sight of the young Italian's perfect
> form lying on the fountain brim had led him to disbelieve his
> own capacity for rendering beauty. That indeed was an aesthetic
> connection, intelligible if unexpected, but there was also a

stronger connection of a more subtle kind. He longed to be more emotional and more sympathetic: to see more, and more largely, of the splendid people with whom he should live so short a time. Art was not helping him: it was always supposed to help, but it was not helping. (p. 37)

A tea-party of male aesthetes that Arthur attends completes his disillusionment. The attribution game is played there – 'a sorry inhumane business'. While the 'viewy young men' debate over pictures, Arthur prefers to contemplate the sunset, feeling 'the professors of the beautiful had severed themselves irrevocably from all beauty' (pp. 31–3). There are no allusions to Berenson, but Stallybrass points out there may be some relation to Roger Fry. In 1901, Forster mentioned in his diary, Fry's attribution of a Piero della Francesca painting to Baldovinetti, and the same names appear in *Old Lucy* (pp. 32–4).

The emphasis of *Old Lucy* on the connection of art and life is apparent in the relationship of Arthur and Lucy. In one early sketch, Lucy takes Ruskin's *Mornings in Florence* to Santa Croce instead of a Baedeker; the exasperating fulminations of 'the great purist' are summarised for her by the narrator. She prefers attending to the people not the art of the Church until Arthur turns up and offers some genuine instruction (pp. 23–6). But a beggar-woman distracts her and she leaves without seeing Giotto's frescoes. (Forster may not yet have read Fry on Giotto in the *Monthly Review*.) There is some satire of pension art: several concert programs display 'a figure of St George, treading nervously upon a very slippery dragon' (p. 44). A discussion with Lucy of the 'crime' of unself-ishness turns into a commentary by Arthur on *King Lear* as well as Tolstoy's *What Is Art?* which Arthur began to read, then threw away before he got to Italy. According to Arthur, Tolstoy asserts the true purpose of art is to promote not beauty but brotherhood. Lucy replies if she believed that she would never be an artist, and Arthur agrees (pp. 45–7). The attitude toward Tolstoy's book in *Old Lucy* remains unclear. Arthur apparently abandons art because it does not help him with human sympathy. The importance of *What Is Art?* for Roger Fry has been noted (see pp. 267–8). What impression it made on Forster at the beginning of the century (it was translated into English in 1898) is hard to determine from *Old Lucy*, but the sketches do reveal Forster's early fictional interest in aesthetics.

What remains clever and funny in *Old Lucy*, to use two of Virginia Woolf's terms of praise, is the comedy of pension life. It seems appropriate that a manuscript page – describing how 'two little old ladies, one white and the other brown' timidly discuss Florence's sights with Lucy at dinner until the sprawling Arthur kicks one of them – should have been sold by Forster on some occasion to Virginia Woolf for the sum of 2*s*. 6*d*. (*LN*, pp. xii, 20–1).

VI

New Lucy, like *Old Lucy*, is a collection of parts, not a whole. Forster began thinking of it at the end of 1903 as a new novel with some characters continued from *Old Lucy*. There were to be Italian and English halves, but only the latter survives. More than with *Old Lucy*, the sketches show Forster still working out the main lines of his story. Different incidents in the sketches precipitate Lucy's awareness that she loves George. She faints when excerpts from Lavish's book are read out loud, she becomes angry when Charlotte threatens to reveal the secret of the Florentine kiss (Charlotte appears black, not brown, against the view there – *LN*, p. 120), and she is rather literally thrown into love with George by a carriage accident. Mr Emerson dies in one outline (he bequeaths Lucy a copy of *Don Quixote*) but is around later to offer congratulations on her exercise of women's rights through her proposal to his son. This is the only feminist reference in the sketches. Beyond his approval, Mr Emerson offers no wisdom as in the revised novel. The satire of contemporary fiction continues from *Old Lucy*. Lavish's novel is described as a story of 'hazy idealism' against which snapshots were pasted (pp. 96–7). Lucy's mother, not yet an anti-feminist in her literary taste, will tolerate 'no seafaring tales, nothing historical, and nothing that Mrs Humphry Ward has written or is likely to write' (p. 94) – a remark worthy of Vanessa Bell.

Charlotte remains unredeemably unpleasant. Lucy correctly calls her a sneak. Beebe is less charmingly cogent. His character and relation to George Emerson are quite noticeably different. He is obviously attracted by George and tells him in the woods: 'you are what the cads call irresistible'. The narrator notes during the silence that follows this remark how 'Mr Beebe prepared to be classed among the cads'; but then George outrages him by delightedly surmising that he himself is loved by Lucy (pp. 108–9). Beebe is opposed to marriages for love, calls George 'intellectually diseased' (p. 118), and assists in delaying Lucy and George's elopement, with fatal consequences. His role at the end differs sharply from that of *A Room with a View*, as he repents of his sin against youth.

Another significant shift between *New Lucy* and *A Room with a View* is that Lucy does not originally lie. 'Concealment is impossible' she says after the carriage accident, which shows the distance still between this version and the concern for truth in *A Room with a View*. The first scene of *New Lucy* opens with her saying 'I can see nothing', as she looks for a book in the lending library (p. 93); Forster does not yet develop the imagery of viewing and concealing beyond remarks like George's 'I find all big views alike' (p. 97). Lucy's character is described in terms a little like Maurice's later; she 'becomes quickened by experience rather than sensitive by nature. One of those difficult people who have developed through Music'. And 'except when she forgets herself' she is unemotionally proper (p. 91). Lucy is still practising unselfishness, as in *Old Lucy*. Cecil's character is amplified in just one scene. Lucy breaks her engagement by letter, and in reply Cecil spitefully deceives her by exaggerating a financial loss he has suffered, which implausibly leads her to put off the elopement with George. Beebe perceives the lie – the only one in *New Lucy*. The unhappy ending of George fatally riding his bicycle into a fallen tree, does not convey the sense of pessimistic separation that Forster in his Working Men's College lecture said modern writers wanted, because his death is merely accidental. Lucy's reaction to it lies outside the ending of the story.

Turning *New Lucy* into *A Room with a View*, Forster brought out more consistently the comic potential that a tragic ending would impair. No bathing scene takes place in *New Lucy*, for instance. Cecil is developed more, and George less, although his love for Lucy is given more expression than in *A Room with a View*. In the sketches, Lucy is educated by George's teaching instead of his father's. When Beebe preaches about 'the eternal sanctity of an engagement', George answers in good Bloomsbury fashion that there are 'plenty of sanctities, but none of them are eternal' (p. 111). At the end of *New Lucy*, Beebe's condescending criticism of George is put down by Lucy with,

'You know how you teach us on Sundays to cultivate a moral

sense and distinguish between right and wrong? Well George is
teaching me to distinguish between pleasure & pain'.

(p. 128)

In this crucial distinction between nineteenth-century intuitional
and Utilitarian ethics, Forster significantly aligns his hero and
heroine with the latter to indicate the physical as well as mental
reality of their love. Forster was writing *New Lucy* just after the
publication of *Principia Ethica*, which combined moral intuition with
consequentialist calculations, and argued that the ends of moral
action were more complex than pleasure and pain. This may be
why Lucy's fine rebuke did not survive revision. *The Lucy Novels*
were written before Forster had absorbed the influence of G. E.
Moore or Samuel Butler, which may also partly account for the
continuing influence of George Meredith as well as Carlyle. In
rewriting *A Room with a View* from the Lucy sketches, Forster
changed his focus from the sterility of aestheticism and the crimes
of unselfishness to a young woman's more contemporary pursuit of
truth in love and art.

VII

The later Edwardian setting of *A Room with a View* is often
mentioned by the novel's critics. Virginia Woolf glanced back at it as
a typical pre-First World War novel in her famous 1940 lecture 'The
Leaning Tower' (*CE*, II 167). Forster himself emphasised the text's
datedness in retrospective epilogue written in 1958, which he called
'A View without a Room'. The reversal of the title reflects the
further experiences of George and Lucy as briefly imagined by
Forster. They settle down in Highgate and begin to prosper but
have to move after the First World War and undertake the search of
Howards End for a home. As a conscientious objector George loses
his government job and gets no help with housing; Windy Corner is
sold by Lucy's brother to support his family. George, of course,
fights in the Second World War, is wounded and captured in Italy
while Lucy is bombed out of their London flat. George still finds the
Italians sympathetic sometimes and has not been chaste; in Florence
he looks for the Pension Bertolini, as his creator had done, but has
to tell his homeless wife that though the view was still there, he
could not find the room. He visits the Piazza Signoria; after two

world wars, the stabbing there that brought Lucy and George together is described as 'a trifling murder'. As for the other characters, Cousin Charlotte leaves everything to Lucy and George, as the author expected her to, even if his readers did not. Cecil, having gone into propaganda during the First World War, persuades the military in Forster's Alexandria that Beethoven could still be played because the composer was really a Belgian. And old Mr Emerson dies 'still looking out and confident that Love and Truth would see humanity through in the end (*RV*, pp. 210–12). Of Mr Beebe nothing more is said.

Forster's fanciful return to his novel half a century after its completion brings out the novel's niceness by viewing the future more disillusionedly than Mr Emerson does. In this epilogue, if not in *A Room with a View* itself, there is something of the separation that Forster had once thought modern novels should represent.

Rose Macaulay, who wrote the first book-length study of Forster's work, commissioned by the Woolfs for their press in 1938, considered her author in 'a very small minority' for not liking *A Room with a View* very much (p. 97). She also articulated one of the plot's historical improbabilities that had been commented on by early reviewers and later critics. 'Were Edwardian young ladies so sensitive, their honour so quaint?' she asked (p. 96). An early serious review of *A Room with a View* by the critic R. A. Scott-James objected to the belated satire of Victorian proprieties and accused Forster of tilting at windmills, while admitting the novel's brilliance. Other reviews were mixed, some praising the book's enjoyableness – like the *Spectator* review (which may have been by Edward Garnett[8]) or the *Nation* where Masterman thought the title could be applied to all of Forster's work. The *Athenaeum*, on the other hand, found the book too flat (*EMFCH*, pp. 101–20). Subsequent critics have continued to debate the structure, genre, and sexuality of the novel. In the Thirties, Frank Swinnerton found 'the book as a whole, though often delicious in phrase and satire, will not, in its composition, bear looking into' (p. 395). F. R. Leavis reviewing Macaulay found she had pointed out the novel's 'curious spinsterish inadequacy in the immediate presentation of love'; yet Leavis liked the book better than *The Longest Journey* or *Howards End*, finding it charming and 'extremely original' (*Pursuit*, p. 263). E. K. Brown's study of rhythm in Forster's art distinguished between the unrelenting symbolism of views and the richer expanding symbols of water in the novel, and Richard Ellmann saw

the obvious thematic organisation around the symbols of the title
and the sudden secular alteration of Lucy's self-perception as characteristic of Edwardian fiction. More recent critics have stressed the
non-realistic elements in the novel and its ambivalent views of
sexuality; one or two of them consider it a masterpiece.

The critical consensus that *A Room with a View* was Forster's
nicest novel does not seem to have emerged before *A Passage to
India*. An American edition was not published until after the success
of *Howards End*, and it was the second of Forster's novels to be
translated into French, after *A Passage to India*, by Charles Mauron
who unsymbolically entitled it *Avec vue sur l'Arno* (1947). In
England *A Room with a View* sold better than either of Forster's
earlier novels. It was the first of Forster's works to be published by
Edward Arnold, who then remained the English publisher of his
books. In October 1908, Arnold issued a first edition of 2000 copies
– 500 more than Blackwood's had done – and in January of 1909 he
printed a further 500 and wrote to Forster congratulating him on his
sales (Kirkpatrick, *EMF*, p. 10; Lago, p. 17). *A Room with a View* has
continued to be one of Forster's most popular novels, and after
Howards End and *A Passage to India* has probably been the most
influential. The influence of the English half of it on D. H.
Lawrence's first novel, *The White Peacock*, which Forster thought one
of Lawrence's finest novels, has been noted a number of times.
There is a handsome young taciturn farmer named George, a
piano-playing heroine named Lettie who gives up George for a
more sophisticated, upper middle-class mate; the narrator named
Cyril is half in love with George, and there is even a homoerotic
bathing scene in the woods.[9] In 1915 Lawrence, wrote to Forster
about class, insisting it was now time 'to look all round, round the
whole ring of the horizon – not just out of a room with a view; it is
time to gather again a conception of the Whole . . . ' (*Letters*,
II 265–6) – which is part of what Mr Emerson taught to Lucy (*RV*,
p. 204). Forster's book stayed in Lawrence's mind, however, and
two years later he began a novel that only apparently Leavis, in a
passing criticism of Forster's callowness, has noticed was influenced by the Italian half of *A Room with a View* (Leavis, *Lawrence*,
p. 32). *Aaron's Rod*, published in 1922, ends where *A Room with a
View* begins, in Florence. Aaron the runaway flautist arrives with
two effete English friends, stays a night at 'Bertolini's Hotel' before
going off to a pension like Forster's Bertolini. In the Piazza Signoria
he has an intense, vitalising perception in the rain with the great

wet naked male statues that include the *David* this time. The English that Aaron mingles with in Florence are artists and aesthetes, not tourists, clerics, or even Italians very much. After being seduced by a Jamesian American Marchesa, Aaron has his flute smashed in a scene of violence; an anarchist bomb explodes in a cafe, leaving a bleeding man on the floor. Aaron's broken rod, like Lucy's bloody photographs, is then dropped into the Arno. The novel ends with a country excursion and a conversation in which Aaron is told by his friend Rawdon Lilly that he must learn submission. Lawrence's creative transposition of Lucy's Florence into Aaron's retains the associations of the English in Florence with art, love, violence, and truth.

A Room with a View has remained in modern literary consciousness. It may have some connection with an obscure work of Gertrude Stein's, called *Lucy Church Amiably* and subtitled 'A Novel of Romantic beauty and nature and which looks like an Engraving'.[10] Noël Coward helped to popularise the novel's title in a 1928 revue song that found in a room with a view and you a paradise where no one gave advice and there were no beseeching preachers. Bloomsbury's continuing interest in the novel is suggested by J. M. Keynes, who recommended it rather exuberantly, in a 1936 broadcast, as a pleasant novel to be read along with Austen's *Emma* and Hardy's *Tess of the d'Urbervilles* (*CW*, XXVIII 330). There are also allusions to *A Room with a View* in English poetry of the Thirties. (Sturge Moore had once singled it out as the novel that Yeats should read to see Forster's quality – *EMFCH*, p. 168.) W. H. Auden dedicated a sonnet from China to Forster and includes Lucy among the characters who 'are delighted/To join the jolly ranks of the benighted' (p. 157). The allusion is to the description of Lucy after she has lied to Cecil in breaking off her engagement:

> She gave up trying to understand herself and joined the vast armies of the benighted, who follow neither the heart nor the brain, and march to their destiny by catchwords. The armies are full of pleasant and pious folk. But they have yielded to the only enemy that matters – the enemy within. They have sinned against passion and truth, and vain will be their strife after virtue.
>
> (*RN*, p. 174)

The passage glosses a good deal of Auden's poetry.

Forster's slightly disenchanted 'A View without a Room' did not foresee, of course, how, thirty years later, a film would make *A Room with a View* one of his most widely-known works. The scenic form of much of the narrative, especially in the second part, lends itself to dramatic treatment, and in 1951 Stephen Tait and Kenneth Allott turned the novel into a play that was first performed at Keynes's Cambridge Arts Theatre. Later their script was adapted for television. It may be the success of the film of *A Room with a View* that retrospectively makes the play claustrophobic to some extent. The drama is confined entirely to rooms; there are no views or outside scenes. The characters are simpler, and a good part of the novel's irony has disappeared along with the narrator's voice. The action of the play follows the novel fairly closely, except at the end when Lucy tells everyone she lied; no return to Italy occurs. A new screenplay by Ruth Prawer Jhabvala was used for the Merchant–Ivory film, which introduced several scenes with Forster's Chapter titles and thus retained something of the novel's comic narrative style. With one important exception, the novel is followed more closely than is usually the case in such translations from fiction to film, and this may be why it has been the most successful of the five movies that have so far been made of Forster's novels. The bathing scene is triumphantly rendered, for example, as is the stabbing scene and its setting in the Piazza Signoria. The exception is the simpler portrayal of a smooth Mr Beebe, who never renounces Lucy or George; he lacks even the complexity he retains in Tait and Allott's play. The nicest of Forster's novels thus became an even nicer movie.

VIII

While rewriting *A Room with a View* in 1907, Forster quickly did a one-act farce ridiculing the current fuss over the Deceased Wife's Sister's bill. Such marriages had been prohibited since 1835, and it was not until 1907 that the law was finally changed despite the opposition of churchmen. (When Forster's great uncle had ignored the ban, his sister Marianne Thornton left her home, as Forster tells in her biography.) The characters in 'The Deceased Wife's Husband' include a widowed clergyman, Revd Goodybrick, who steals from a child atheist, and a church supporter named Mr Flather, who defrauds agnostic widows. Goodybrick has hurried to obey the law and marry his deceased wife's sister. Flather rebukes him, but

Goodybrick's defence is that he hates his new wife. She then turns up, and the men commit suicide after discovering they have been bigamously married to the same deceased wife. The deceased wife's sister decides that she must marry her deceased husband's brother but is arrested by an outraged policeman, who has now seen everything but still knows that England will never allow women such equality under the law. The play is more Gilbertian than Shavian, and shows how satirically anti-clerical Forster could be when he let himself go (EMF/pKC; PNF/*EMF,* I 157–8).

The same month that *A Room with a View* was published, Forster read a paper to the Weybridge Literary Society on Kipling's poems in which he returned to the criticism of art for art's sake. Its followers undervalued Kipling, he found, while those believing in the equally dangerous doctrine of art for life's sake over-praised him. Kipling's great merit was his vitality; he may be vulgar but he is never dull. A poem like 'The "Mary Gloster"' Forster thought great because it was inspired by love. India gave Kipling the gift of mysticism, yet his conception of the unseen is a little too Anglo-Saxon for Forster, whose interest in India was growing with his love for his Indian friend Syed Ross Masood. Indeed the discussion of Kipling is relevant in a number of ways to Forster's subsequent writings on India. Already in 1908 the paper left some of Forster's audience trembling with rage, he told Edward Garnett (29.xi.08, pT).

More significantly relevant to *A Room with a View* is the justly well-known story Forster published a year after the novel. 'The Machine Stops' has been called the first fully developed anti-utopia of twentieth-century literature (Hillegas, p. 82). While some studies of Forster have found the story unconvincing, other discussions of modern writing by critics like V. S. Pritchett or Irving Howe have called it a classic and the most successful of Forster's short fictions. As unlikely an enthusiast as Edith Sitwell wrote Forster in 1928, when 'The Machine Stops' was collected as the opening story in *The Eternal Moment,* 'I believe it is the most tremendous short story of our generation' (*EMFCH,* p. 339). And Lowes Dickinson, who did not much like Forster's stories – he did not think their realism and values connected very well – was pleased to find Forster turning the prophecies of Wells and Shaw inside out (EMF/*GLD,* p. 180). At the time it was written, however, Forster recalled that on the whole 'The Machine Stops' was judged unfavourably. He remembered reading it to some friends, 'and the sole comment was "Too long"'

(Conklin, p. 84). Still searching for new magazine outlets, he sent the story to Ford Madox Hueffer for the prestigious *English Review* with a letter reminding the editor he had written one or two novels and that they had once met at lunch with Edward Garnett (13.12.08, pNY). Hueffer's critical acumen seems to have deserted him on this occasion, and the *English Review* printed the more typically Forsterian 'Other Kingdom' instead. Forster finally placed his story in the short-lived *Oxford and Cambridge Review*[11]

The relation of 'The Machine Stops' to the central symbol of *A Room with a View* appears in the story's opening sentences:

> Imagine, if you can, a small room, hexagonal in shape, like the cell of a bee. It is lighted neither by window nor by lamp, yet it is filled with a soft radiance. There are no apertures for ventilation, yet the air is fresh. There are no musical instruments, and yet, at the moment when my meditation opens, this room is throbbing with melodious sounds. (*EM*, p. 1)

'The Machine Stops' is the story of a room without a view. Forster said in the introduction to his *Collected Short Stories* that it was a reaction – he originally wrote a 'counterblast' – to one of H. G. Wells's heavens (*CSS*, p. vii[12]). In various ways this story of hell resembles Wells's *The Time Machine* of 1895. Forster's machine does not transcend time, it obliterates the sense of space. The physical dimensions of life in 'The Machine Stops' have all been reduced to isolated individuals in their viewless cells. Bodily contact among them exists only for purposes of procreation. If one has the misfortune to travel in the world outside the machine, visual experience is shunned. If love is of the body, as Mr Emerson insisted, then theirs is a loveless existence. Vashti is an aesthete; her only occupation is lecturing on music, which it also seems is her only aesthetic experience. Like her friends, she lives for ideas alone, not impressions. Their dystopia is an ironic hell for Idealists in which only ideas really matter; space is annihilated and physical perceptions minimised by totalitarian technology. Personal relations have all become blurred, says Vashti's rebellious son Kuno (p. 37). The opening and closing images of the story are those of a hive of solitary bees. Their lives are controlled by a worm-like mending apparatus and invisible committees, including the Central Committee (a prescient term in 1908). The scientific facilitation of life is necessarily political, of course, (a failed great rebellion is alluded too) and finally religious too as the machine becomes an end-in-itself to be worshipped, until it stops. Though apocalyptic, Forster's story is also amusing in the imaginativeness of its technology and the adaptability of the victims.

The essayist-narrator calls 'The Machine Stops' a meditation, but the central part is a first-person narrative, rather like Wells's *The Time Machine*. A meditation better describes the connection of Forster's text to Wells's, rather than reaction or counterblast because both works are actually anti-utopian. (In 1907, Forster did read Wells's amorous utopia *In the Days of the Comet* but made little use of it, and he may have borrowed some features of some of Wells's earlier utopias such as *A Modern Utopia*.) Wells's leisured, degenerate upperworlders and cannibalistic underground engineers have been developed by Forster into the effete underworld dwellers like Vashti and the anonymous committees of the machine, plus a few natives of the mist who manage to survive outside the world of the machine. Vashti, like Wells's pallid, worm-coloured Morlocks, is a 'lump of flesh . . . white as a fungus' (*EM*, p. 1). The dilapidated world of the Wells's Eloi is reflected in the memorable entropy of Forster's stopping machine, where the mending-apparatus itself requires mending.

The Time Machine is also a political parable of class stratification in which the pleasure-seeking rich turn into the cattle of the workers they drove underground. The great future that Wells's Time Traveller dreamt of 'had not been simply a triumph over nature, but a triumph over nature and the fellow-man' (Wells, p. 302). That is also true of 'The Machine Stops', even though Forster does not discuss how the machine evolved. He is more concerned with representing the discord of the mechanical and the natural – both human and non-human. (Kuno's maxim is the sophist's 'man is the measure' – pp. 28–9). Here he followed not Wells, whose story is unsatirical, but Samuel Butler. Forster reread *Erewhon* while finishing *A Room with a View* in 1907. He thought its remaking of the human race tremendous, and wrote to R. C. Trevelyan in words that Kuno might have used: 'it will help us among the planets when we are dead' (*RV*, p. 236). Vashti's bible, the Book of the Machine, is an ironic allusion to The Book of the Machines in *Erewhon*, which warns of the dangers inherent in the development of mechanical consciousness. Bondage to machines increases as they prey on human materialistic desires; to preserve the spiritual, the Erewhonians ban all machines made in the last 271 years.

E. M. Forster created in 'The Machine Stops' another fictive critique of Idealism that looks backward to Wells and Butler, but also forward to Huxley, Orwell, and their many successors. In his own career, its nightmare viewlessness comes just after the dream of *A Room with a View*. And its punishment of 'homelessness' (fatal exile in the upper world for revolts like Kuno's) as well as the final catastrophe that makes all the machine's inhabitants homeless immediately precedes *Howards End*, the novel Forster wrote about the quest for an English home.

13 Virginia Woolf and the Proper Writing of Lives

I

Three different kinds of writing figure in Virginia Woolf's literary history from the death of her brother toward the end of 1906 until 'human character changed' in December 1910. She continued to review fiction regularly for *The Times Literary Supplement*, but more of her reviews – including six longer essay-reviews in the *Cornhill* – had to do now with biography and autobiography. She began experimenting herself with various forms of life-writing. And she began a novel.

Woolf took six years to finish *The Voyage Out*. Only one of the three extensive versions that have survived was partially written in the Edwardian years. An account of the novel must therefore wait until she finally finished it in 1913, although there will be earlier references to the composition what she called her 'work of the Fancy and the Affections' (*L*, I 331).

Compared with the effort of writing *The Voyage Out*, Woolf told Violet Dickinson in 1908, 'my reviews dont count at all' (*L*, I 375). Most of her critics agree and ignore them. Yet these reviews display her development as a professional writer. More of them after 1908 were about biographies, letters, and diaries, rather than novels. After her own novel, Woolf's most imaginative work during these years was the writing of lives – Violet Dickinson's, Vanessa Bell's, an imaginary novelist's, and more directly in letters and diaries, her own. She discussed the theory and practice of biography and autobiography in her reviews and essays, and these discussions are as important for understanding Woolf's art as the more personal writings that she did not publish. In addition to revealing her literary preoccupations at a time when her work was beginning to attract attention, the reviews and essays also continue to reflect the editorial conditions under which she, Forster, Strachey, MacCarthy, and Clive Bell were writing.

'The only work I do is for The Times', Woolf wrote to Madge Vaughan in November 1908, explaining why she could not review her reprinted guidebook to Perugia (*L*, I 373). She had been writing for the *Cornhill* this year as well, but that was practically all. The much wider audience of *The Times Literary Supplement* had replaced the churchwomen of the *Guardian*, where Woolf did one more survey-review of poetic drama and then stopped. Leo Maxse sought for subjects or suggestions for *National Review* pieces but none were apparently found or offered (*L*, I 309). Nothing more appeared in the *Academy & Literature* either, and the *Speaker* was gone. Of MacCarthy's *New Quarterly*, there is no mention, nor of the Stracheyan *Spectator*. When George Meredith died in 1909 Woolf wished vainly that the editor of the *Quarterly*, with whom she had had some discussions, would ask her to explain him (*L*, I 396). *TLS* did ask but not for another twenty years, when her and Bloomsbury's enthusiasm for him had withered away.

Woolf's last *Guardian* review appeared at the beginning of 1908.[1] She wanted to be writing fiction and reading Pindar but set herself to survey seven volumes of poetic drama (*L*, I 307, 309). The review, which does not tie the plays together much, began with William Butler Yeats's *Deirdre*. In the first published comment on her great contemporary, Woolf found nothing in this violent play to break 'the strange and melancholy peace which Mr. Yeats casts about his work like a mantle.' His characters are not the passionate beings a great poet might have created, but Yeats was certainly a true poet with melodic stanzas and exquisite lines that have the ability, as another play does not, of penetrating 'to those regions of the brain where so many delicate ideas lie furled that words wake more images than they bring.' The other plays are variously criticised for their flaws in characterisation. One, on 'our great romance' reclaimed for us by the pre-Raphaelites, unfortunately presents King Arthur as 'an amiable imperialist'. Jack London's vigorous play *Scorn of Women*, set in Dawson City, was interesting, but the reader might need a glossary, she thought, and illustrated this by referring to characters described as 'dog punchers' ('Some Poetical Plays').

By May of 1908, Virginia Woolf told Dickinson she was refusing to review any more novels for *The Times*, and they sent her philosophy instead (*L*, I 331). She had read twenty-one works of mostly mediocre fiction for them in 1907 – Forster's *The Longest Journey* was among the few conspicuous exceptions – and another eight by May of the next year, which included *A Room with a View*.[2] Several of the books were essentially travel novels, one being a somewhat interesting English-Italian work by an author who unfortunately seldom dropped his unForsterian pose 'of the grave observer pondering wide issues' (*E*, I 135). But novels of manners and historical romances constituted most of the fiction Woolf was asked to review in about 500 words apiece. Unqualified praise she almost never gives, but though critical – at times indeed devastating – Woolf also found something to praise in most of the books she reviewed. A novel by M. P. Willcocks that she liked was no masterpiece but 'it is among the books that are, like other living things; we have no need to test the degree of life' ('*Wingless Victory*'). The believableness of fiction, especially the characters, but also the story, is a recurrent criterion for judgement. She frequently criticises the historical romances she had to read because their plots or pageantry drained the characters of any psychological interest. Sincerity is valued, particularly when combined with the observation of simple things, yet conviction was not enough to make characters plausible. The lack of subtlety, even irony in some of the books, could be wearying. One novel she rather liked was a chaotic satire on nerve specialists, asylums, and the like (medical satire was in the air – Shaw's *The Doctor's Dilemma* had played at the Court Theatre the previous year). From her own considerable experience with doctors, Woolf found *The New Religion* more entertaining than profitable (*E*, I 148–9). An absence of vitality is felt in a number of the competent novels she criticised. The conventionality of yet another able W. E. Norris book is noted with disappointment. A novel with the moral that the income necessary to live in society should not be forgone for love, has 'the effect of a solicitor's statement', with its monotonous good sense and excellent arithmetic ('*Outrageous Fortune*'). Woolf felt she had damned a novel that mixed Scottish history and fiction but it went into a second edition (*L*, I 295). Its incredibly prolific author, who wrote under the pseudonym of Marjorie Bowen, among others, produced another historical novel the next year which Woolf again criticised for its lack of psychology and 'perfectly frank and crude delight in what we may call the pageantry of the time' ('*Sword Decides*'). Scott had shown that history did not necessarily impose limitations on fiction, but lesser writers, Woolf found, produced historical novels in which politics annihilates private life. There are, however, restrictions in the genre whose spell for imaginative writers puzzles Woolf's reviews. Plot summaries occupy considerable space in these reviews, and Woolf is not hostile to all historical romances. An imperialist adventure novel about Africa is about as exciting as a nightmare, yet in another romance she admires how the author keeps the concoction on the boil, flavouring the mixture whenever it starts to cool; despite the sacrifice of probability, the romantic atmosphere 'infects us with its delightfully irresponsible spirit, and we are well content' ('*Red Neighbour*'). She regrets that another fictionalised eighteenth-century autobiography will have fewer readers than its excellent, unaffected prose deserves.

The wide reading behind Virginia Woolf's judgements of modern fiction in the *TLS* appears in allusions to greater writers than those under review. She finds, for example, a form of Ruskin's pathetic fallacy in novelists who insist that peasants must be as elementary as their settings. 'The malign breath of Mr. Meredith's influence' blights a clever book, whose self-consciousness is not justified by the self it illuminates' ('*Disciples*'). In another, a house haunted by comic and tragic drama lacks 'the mystic beauty which Hawthorne . . . could draw from the supernatural' ('*Feast of Bacchus*'). Several of the works of fiction sent to Woolf for review were collections of stories. Some religious ones by R. H. Benson impress with their sincerity and intelligence yet do not arouse the feelings of those who cherish the supernatural, perhaps because the author is a too much of an agnostic. A book of stories about timeless, violent episodes contrasts unfavourably with the subdued, emotional contexts that Henry James's tales illuminated. One well-crafted collection by Anthony Hope with its clean, well-mannered but exceedingly commonplace English people was a safe investment for the reader. Woolf is fiercer about an epistolary fiction by the woman known to readers as Elizabeth of the German garden – though not as fierce as she intended to be. She had hoped to scourge the fine noblewoman, 'chatter and trash' but the *TLS* cut and tamed her review (*L*, I 295). She was still allowed to find the novel a shallow, slipshod collection of personal impressions; its belittlement of Christina Rossetti's song 'When I am dead, my dearest', which Woolf thought a great poem, is neatly belittled in turn by the reviewer. But it was pointless to criticise, the book's charming frankness and vivacious verbosity were bound to be popular (*E*, I 136–7). That is the edited review's last point, and no reading notes for it or other reviews done around this time have apparently survived to suggest what else she might have said. Did Woolf sense in the novel of Elizabeth von Arnim (who had been interested in her essay on street music several years before – see pp. 153–4) a kind of literary degeneration to which her own writing might be susceptible?

The philosophy which Woolf said *The Times* had sent her when she declined to review any more novels may have been the personal account of Buddhism by an English civil servant who discovered Buddhism in Burma around the time Leonard Woolf met it in Ceylon. Fielding Hall's *The Inward Light* left an impression 'of singular peace, but also of singular monotony' on his reviewer, and she asks if such a faith is as high 'as that which believes that it is right to develop your powers to the uttermost?' (*E*, I 173). (A fictive symposium of Hall's she reviewed in 1909, and liked the questioning of everything, but she wondered if his gentle monism was not the source of his popularity.) A few months later Woolf would begin reading modern philosophy in earnest with Moore's *Principia Ethica*.

Among the reasons why Woolf did not want to review any more novels for *The Times Literary Supplement* in 1908 – *A Room with a View* would be a significant exception to her refusal – was, of course, the quality of the novels she was being sent. She dealt with inferior works in issues of the *TLS* that also carried reviews by others of Conrad's *The Secret Agent*, Galsworthy's *The Country House*, and the third volume of Hueffer's *The Fifth Queen*. The effect that the novels she was reviewing may have had on the novel she was trying to write was perhaps another reason. Over the next three years, Woolf's reviewing for the *TLS* shifted largely to biography and autobiography. The arrangement of its reviews possibly prompted the change. The supplement was much smaller then compared to now; eight pages was the usual length, which swelled with advertisements and notices to twelve or sixteen pages during the publishing seasons. Reviews were classified under general headings, the main one being *Literature*, which always appeared first and included practically everything – poetry, biography, history, classics, older novels – except drama and current fiction. There was always a *Literature* section, and often one called *Fiction*. Others dealing with drama, philosophy, music, chess, even science; notes and correspondence appeared from time to time as well. By declining to review more novels, Woolf advanced, as it were, from the fiction to the literature category of the *TLS*. This shift is a significant one for Bloomsbury's literary history, for it allowed Virginia Woolf to write for a wide, literate audience on major Victorian forms of writing that she along with Strachey and Forster would practise and modify. She could not yet see her way clear in fiction. That would take fifteen years and three novels. From her own emerging point of view as a modernist and a feminist – but with her father's *Studies of a Biographer* and *Dictionary of National Biography* on her shelves – she began to write professionally about biography and autobiography in *The Times Literary Supplement* and at greater length, for a year, in her father's old magazine, the *Cornhill*, while she was also experimenting with these forms herself. Perhaps the most illuminating connections in Woolf's later Edwardian writings are between her biographical criticism and practice. They show she did not consider the lines between biography, autobiography, and fiction as fixed; in *Melymbrosia*, as she began to call her first novel, the three were already being intermixed. An examination of her early reviews of life-writing offers the basis for a careful understanding of the literary origins of Virginia Woolf's fictive and non-fictive narratives.

II

A central premise of Virginia Woolf's reviews in the literature section of the *TLS* is the poor state of biographical art. The causes seem to be not just aesthetic but moral and psychological. She concludes her review of an unmemorable nineteenth-century family's prolix memoirs with a protest against

> the strange methods of modern English biography: you are presented with a great bundle of papers, and bidden, substantially, to make a book for yourself. To arrange or to criticize, to make people live as they lived, is considered unnecessary, or perhaps disrespectful. We feel that there is a spirit in letters which we must not allow to perish, but we are too timid to set it free.
>
> (*E*, I 242)

The felt spirit of letters in her reviews is at times self-consciously modern. Editors, biographers, historians should know at least the rudiments of literary art. In that art our contemporary regard for both the inner and the outer life should also be reflected. 'It is undeniable that the records of good people preserved on faded paper to which your own name is attached have a charm and possibly a value', she writes with mild irony of another fragment of family history, but there is the additional danger that the gain in charm is a loss of truth (*'Rachel Gurney'*).

The need for art as well as truth in biography is all the more so when the subject is himself an artist. (Woolf kept to the masculine pronoun in her reviews and other writings.) The issues are put clearly in the first lead review Virginia Woolf wrote for the *TLS*. She was allowed three-and-a-half columns to review the standard life of one of her favourite authors, Laurence Sterne. (The size of Woolf's non-fiction reviews in the *TLS* ran anywhere from half a column to four of them at this time, a column being about 1000 words.) The material of Wilbur Cross's biography was excellent, yet the book revealed how low the art of biography had sunk. In an extended introduction to her review Woolf attacks the distinction Cross and others draw between a respectable interest in a man's work and a baser curiosity about his life. Her justification of genuinely literary biography that treats of literature while being well-made itself is aesthetic in the fullest sense:

> A writer is a writer from his cradle; in his dealing with the world, in his affections, in his attitude to the thousand small things that happen between dawn and sunset, he shows the same point of view as that which he elaborates afterwards with a pen in his hand. It is more fragmentary and incoherent, but it is also more intense. To this, which one may call the aesthetic interest of his character, there are added the various interest of circumstance. . . . The weakness of modern biographers seems to lie not in their failure to realise that both elements are present in the life of a writer, but in their determination to separate them. It is easier for them to draw distinctions than to see things whole.

As a consequence 'we have lives that are all ceremony and work; and lives that are all chatter and scandal.' Biography that is primarily personal becomes stigmatised, and would-be authors are driven to write novels, which have greater freedom because 'the dull parts can be skipped, and the excitements intensified'. Yet there is a loss of reality, 'for the aesthetic effect of truth is only to be

equalled by the imagination of genius' (*E*, I 280–1). With her concern for wholeness and truth here, Woolf appears to favour
biography as an art-form over fiction. In the discussion that follows,
she illustrates briefly how with Sterne 'we must combine a life of
extraordinary flightiness and oddity with the infinite painstaking
and self-consciousness of an artist' (*E*, I 286). She discusses Sterne as
an artist and a man, and judges him a great stylist and a humorist
(less sublime than Meredith, less ridiculous than Thackeray[3])
whose zest could sometimes end in a sentimentality which she does
not hesitate occasionally to call hypocritical, as Leslie Stephen had
done before her and with far less sympathy in *Studies of a Biographer*.
Woolf would not acclaim the modern inwardness of a work like *A
Sentimental Journey* for another twenty years.

Writers' lives are the subjects of the majority of the reviews that
Woolf was writing for the *TLS* toward the end of the Edwardian period. Her texts are informed by two closely interrelated
assumptions: that the lives ought to be well written and that they
should convey something of the reality of their existences, which in
the case of writers meant a consideration of their work. Art and
reality were more important than 'the hard framework of date and
fact' to which modern biography had become so attached (*E*, I 139).
That assertion is made in a 1907 piece on the only historical
biography she reviewed at this time, Fulke Greville's life of Sir
Philip Sidney. The challenge of writing such a biography was
Sidney's fame; it resulted from qualities which are 'beautiful in their
sum and in their harmony rather than in the supremacy of any
single one of them' (*E*, I 140). But that also is the achievement of
Sidney's friend, a poet and dramatist who carved him a plaited
monument in prose that delighted Woolf. In another illustrative
metaphor of her own she describes Greville as 'often closely
throttled in the embraces of a sinuous metaphor' (I 142). The
biography is a Renaissance achievement, of course, which is one of
the reasons she liked it so much; another may have been the theme
of a promising young man's early death. Sidney is viewed more as
a man of action than a writer by Greville, yet it was the
biographer's prose, not any factual framework, that created a figure
still warm to the touch.

A writer whose public career was more important to himself and
his contemporaries than the literary one we now value is the subject
of the lead article for the *TLS* by Woolf in December 1909. She was
allowed four columns in which to discuss a recent biography of

Richard Brinsley Sheridan. Walter Sichel's biography is an exception to the decayed art of writing lives; its full treatment of Sheridan's contradictory humanity rescues him from the legend of a gorgeous but intoxicated insect who 'wrote three standard plays, was famous for his debts, his wit, and his speech at the trial of Warren Hastings' (*E*, I 303). Sichel has restored Sheridan to his own charming, inconsistent human shape, which Woolf sketches in her review. She focuses more on the human tragedy he acted than on the celebrated comedies he wrote. Mention is made of the early loves and duels; the plays are also briefly discussed and found inferior to Congreve's and Villiers's. (She had been reading Congreve, Vanbrugh, and others, but not Sheridan, in Bloomsbury's Play-Reading Society.) Recounting his career as a politician and reformer, Woolf is more sympathetic than Strachey had been in his dissertation. Sheridan's tragedy is not to be found in any particular event but in human nature, and 'there is something ludicrous in the stupidity of fate which never fits the fortune to the desert and blunts our pain in wonder' (*E*, I 311).

Sheridan's life shows that the achievement of writers is not proportional to the interest we take in their biographies. A good biographer's life of a minor writer, like Thomas Hood, may tell us more of his times than the lives of Keats or De Quincey. Woolf was reviewing an edition of Hood's poems together with his biography, and she takes the opportunity to argue that his life is reflected in his work. In another of the striking metaphors that makes her writing more than just reviewing, she describes how 'the sharp blade of his own circumstance is always wearing through' in his best poetry, and that is why we want his biography (*E*, I 163). It gives us the necessary relationship between his exuberant puns and his personal tragedy, which the poetry does not. The biography of a virtually unknown Italian writer whom Samuel Johnson liked to argue with shows us a literary world of conversational strife and of contradictions that went beyond words. Baretti's 'life was full and vigorous; as for his works, he wished that every page lay at the bottom of the sea' (*E*, I 276). That is where the review leaves us.

Even bad writers' lives can be intriguing. Woolf's review evaluates E. V. Lucas's life of Anna Seward in the *TLS* somewhat differently than Strachey's did in the *Spectator*. Both reviews have fun with the Swan of Lichfield, but Woolf probes beyond what Strachey calls Lucas's 'light-hearted intrepidity' (see p. 300). 'We laugh till we are bored', she says, because Seward and her friends do not interest us 'more than any other tedious and prolix people much at the mercy of their pens.' The fault seems to be Lucas's, who is a caricaturist instead of a historian or satirist. He never gives us the reality behind his parodies. Seward's letters (Scott said he received them 'with despair') 'half cover and half express a genuine attitude towards life' and that 'is what Mr Lucas for all his vivacity fails to show' (*E*, I 152–3).

Virginia Woolf is closer to Lytton Strachey in her reviews of nineteenth-century writers' biographies. A book entitled *Mrs Gaskell, Haunts, Homes, and Stories* brings out a Bloomsbury irritation with mid-Victorian writers, in this case novelists, that will be heard again:

> Nothing would persuade them to concentrate. Able by nature to spin sentence after sentence melodiously, they seem to have left out nothing that they knew how to say. Our ambition, on the other hand, is to put in nothing that need not be there. What we want to be there is the brain and the view of life; the autumnal woods, the history of the whale fishery, and the decline of stage coaching we omit entirely.

Related to the lack of concentration was a lack of personality. 'The tuft of heather that Charlotte Brontë saw was her tuft; Mrs Gaskell's world was a large place, but it was everybody's world' (*E*, I 341–2). Woolf's criticism, written in the autumn of 1910, is becoming more modernist. Her exasperation is partly the result of the biographer's enthusiasm; a pure Gaskell heroine praised in print by Aunt Anny depresses the reviewer 'like an old acquaintance' (*E*, I 343). Her criticism is also clearly a product of the kind of fiction she was struggling to write at this time. Woolf finishes her review, however, by turning its evaluation upside down: one reads Mrs Gaskell's books with delight because they offer us the run of her fictive world. Whether anyone still reads Maria Edgeworth is another question, and one the author of an illustrated biography of her life and times fails to ask. Woolf laughs a little sourly over the simplistic visual impressions 'of turbans and chariots with nothing inside them' (*E*, I 316) and laments the lost opportunity of finding out what Edgeworth's contemporaries were really like.

Generational differences whet another of Woolf's *TLS* reviews of nineteenth-century authors. Like those on Sterne and Sheridan, it is really a biographical essay – one of three she wrote in 1909 – which with her two essays on opera, mark a stage in her development as a contributor to *The Times* and its literary supplement. The occasion for her lead review was the appearance of a centenary biography of Oliver Wendell Holmes. For the reviewer, the main interest 'of these centenary celebrations is that they provide an opportunity for one generation to speak its mind of another with a candour and perhaps with an insight which contemporaries may hardly possess' (*E*, I 296). The chief opportunity Holmes's biography offers is not the book itself, Woolf scarcely mentions it, but a reconsideration of *The Autocrat of the Breakfast Table*. The situation of its author is different from the Victorians. The international criticism of American literature is a delicate matter, as Henry James has shown. In certain respects Holmes is more completely American than Hawthorne or Lowell, she realises; yet her sketch of his development from a Calvinist child to a doctor and writer is not especially delicate. She notes his 'pathetic desire' to connect, like Hawthorne, his childhood memories with American history, and she finds in his mature style 'the typical American defect of over-ingenuity and an uneasy love of decoration; as though they had not yet learnt the art of sitting still' (*E*, I 294, 297). The spell of *The Autocrat* has dissipated, for reasons the reviewer admits are personal:

> It is one of the first books that one reads for oneself. . . . The miraculous ease with which the talk flows on, the richness of simile and anecdote, the humour and the pathos, the astonishingly maturity of the style, and, above all, some quality less easy to define . . . make it impossible to think of the Autocrat save as an elderly relative who has pressed half-sovereigns into one's palm and at the same time flattered one's self-esteem. (*E*, I 297)

Woolf might almost be talking here of James Russell Lowell, Holmes's friend and Leslie Stephen's, who stood as a kind of god-father to her and used to give her sixpences. In Stephen's own review of an earlier biography of Holmes in *Studies of a Biographer*, the differences in generation emerge. Stephen too declares his personal interest. He is very sympathetic to Holmes's rejection of his puritan heritage and finds his writing paralleled in the work of Addison, Goldsmith, and, most obviously, Lamb. Holmes would endure as a writer, Stephen believes (*Studies*, II 160–95). His modern daughter knows better. She sees the shallowness of the Doctor's humour that valued sanity above all. Healthiness, charity, tolerance, living to the utmost – it all reads, she concludes in another remark with personal resonance 'like a medical prescription, and one does not want health alone' (*E*, I 299). Woolf is beginning here to work autobiography more into her criticism.

III

The mediocrity of recent biography is not a concern in the lives and letters of nineteenth-century poets that were the subjects of three reviews by Virginia Woolf in *The Times Literary Supplement* during 1908 and 1909. The reason is that the lives are reflected through the letters themselves, without the mediation of biographers. The value of these letters for her is contingent on the writers' talents, on the aesthetic interest of their characters (as she said in her Sterne review) and on the circumstances of their lives. Christina Rossetti's letters, for example, tell no secrets and are unremarkable in their wit; they remain interesting, however, because their author was a true artist who conveyed the same spirit in her exquisite poetry as in her letters, where it was obscured by 'the furniture of existence'. Rossetti's letters are slight and trivial, they contain nothing that 'can make private letters the most intimate form of literature that exists', yet she always treats her subject, writes well, and is almost heroic in defence of her real but limited gift (*E*, I 225). The letters therefore return us to the poems; for that alone they are worthwhile. (Woolf reformulated her qualified admiration for Rossetti at greater length and with more humour and criticism in the second *Common Reader*.) A good edition of Shelley's early letters to Elizabeth Hitchener, an older schoolmistress, make a faded world live again as they exhibit, in the reviewer's acute metaphors, an 'incongruous alliance between the rushing poet, whose wings grew stronger every day, and the painstaking but closely tethered woman.'[4] Something of the poet's odd 'lack of humanity' is brought out too, but this review finds little to say about the letters' relations to Shelley's poetry (*E*, I 175–6). The emphasis is more on a past world, which Woolf filled out from the standard biography of Shelley.

A month later Virginia Woolf was praising three volumes of Wordsworth's letters for different reasons. Wordsworth disliked writing letters and said nothing in them that was unnecessary – no epigrams and little literary criticism. The mass of correspondence from his long life is as impressively authentic as one of his poetic sheepfolds. In his letters there is 'no gulf between the stuff of daily life and the stuff of poetry, save that one is the raw material of the other. . . . ' A lonely, austere, even pathetic figure emerges but one who never lost the ability to live, as he said, 'in the midst of the realities of things' (*E*, I 186), which is what Woolf wanted and tried to do in her own life and writings. She thinks the daily life of Wordsworth's letters has something of the quality that affects us in his best poems. Woolf did not write much on Wordsworth, who was so important for Leslie Stephen, just the earlier review of his Lake District guide and a later essay on his sister and their relationship, which she also mentions here. But like Strachey, who reviewed the same letters earlier for the *Spectator*, she admired the man and the poet, and respected his literary life more than Shelley's or Christina Rossetti's.

Reviews by Virginia Woolf early in 1909, of the letters of James Boswell and then of the young Carlyles for *The Times Literary Supplement* offer further occasions for Bloomsbury comparisons because Lytton Strachey reviewed the Carlyle letters in the *Spectator* and Clive Bell did both Boswell and Carlyle for the *Athenaeum*. Of Boswell, Woolf wrote in her two-column review of his letters to William Temple, 'when a man has had the eyes of Carlyle and Macaulay fixed upon him it may well seem that there is nothing fresh to be said' (*E*, I 249), and she is echoing here Leslie Stephen's conclusion in his *DNB* article on Boswell that 'Macaulay's graphic description of his absurdities, and Carlyle's more penetrating appreciation of his higher qualities, contain all that can be said'. But Woolf's review demonstrates the insufficiency of this view, observing that Macaulay's fun-house-mirror image of Boswell is quite unlike Carlyle's description of the ill-assorted but true hero-worshipper, and Carlyle's is the view she prefers. She praises the rare quality of Boswell's vanity and his vitality, and finds in the contemplation of contemporary heroes an exuberant sense of life. Inseparable from these qualities was his literary capability:

> He was not anxious merely to display all his emotions, but he was anxious to make them tell. He left out much that other people put in, and directly that he had a pen in his hand he became a natural artist. (*E*, I 251)

Again, it is not personality or circumstances that finally matters in autobiography or biography but the literary art that can express ●

them. As for what Boswell actually felt, we can never finally know: 'when we try to say what the secret is, then we understand why Boswell was a genius'. The *TLS* picked up the term from this final sentence and headed the review 'The Genius of Boswell'.

Woolf thought her own review 'rather good' (*L*, I 379). It is certainly better than Bell's a few weeks later, which was critical of the editing by Thomas Seccombe. Woolf liked the editor's introduction and said nothing about the editing, perhaps because the publishers had preferred Seccombe to herself. Woolf had suggested the idea for an edition of Boswell's letters (they had been the subject of one of her earliest efforts, which the *Cornhill* rejected – see p. 152) to Strachey, who passed the idea on to the publishers Sidgwick & Jackson. Sidgwick asked Strachey to edit them, offering merely five guineas and an early deadline; Strachey refused and recommended Woolf. Sidgwick instead chose Seccombe, an assistant of Sidney Lee's on the *DNB*, but sent copies to Strachey and Woolf (*LVWLS*, pp. 15–16; LS/pBL). Perhaps Boswell's epistolary vigour was thought unsuitable for a young lady's introduction.

Woolf's review of the Carlyles's letters preceded Strachey's and Bell's. Strachey had found *The Love Letters of Thomas Carlyle and Jane Welsh* interesting as psychological rather than literary texts; Bell had been more sympathetic to Mrs Carlyle as a letter-writer than to her husband. Woolf's opinion, expressed earlier in her *Guardian* essay was closer to her father's high praise of them (see pp. 168–9, 280, 299). She begins, as she did in her earlier review, by expressing relief that assigning credit or blame to the Carlyles has become irrelevant. Her summary of their courtship brings out the psychological interest and also, through quotation, the letters' literary quality. The sacrifice Jane Welsh hesitated to make in marrying Thomas Carlyle is described along with their moving expressions of love for each other. Woolf quotes Welsh: 'Are you believing? I could easily convince you with my eyes and my kisses; but ink-words are so ineloquent'; the reviewer then asks how she shall explain the tragedy that their relationship turned into, when 'ink-words' are all she has too (*E*, I 260–1). The unsayableness of Boswell's genius, the ineloquent ink-words of the Carlyles is a repeated note in Woolf's reviewing at this time. (It is heard earlier in a review of a young, early nineteenth-century German woman's letters; her soldier-fiancé was executed by the French, and in her grief, like most people, 'she found language a rude implement' – '*Letters of a Betrothed*').

The lives of women not known as writers – especially aristocratic women – are also the subjects of a number of Woolf's later Edwardian reviews in the *TLS* as well as the *Cornhill*. This is not surprising. The *TLS* had been sending her books by and about women, even before she stopped reviewing novels for them, and many of the unliterary figures commemorated in these books came from the upper classes. Woolf found the memorials of Marie Antoinette's last days piteous. A conscientious biography of a masterful eighteenth-century Methodist countess brings her to echo Strachey's question about Blake that Forster had used in *The Longest Journey*. (Woolf was probably reading the novel for her review three weeks later.) She admires this masterful woman 'who did not lose the world while she kept her soul in all austerity' ('*Lady Huntingdon*'). Most of the nineteen Scotswomen grouped together in a biography (one was a Grant) were aristocrats but their male biographer is fortunately not a pious worshipper of them; the brutality of Scottish life is not concealed, nor are the minds of some of the women, though it is asserted that the genius of Scotswomen was not creative or speculative. Their modesty interfered perhaps, and this leads Woolf to an early statement of a favourite feminist theme: the anonymity of women's creativity. It was exemplified in Scottish ballads and may have prevented the publication of memoirs which made 'the raciest reading in the world' (*E*, I 213). The charm of a Scottish professor's widow is rarer than aristocratic memoirs, for it shows 'how the lettered people lived at their ease' ('*Mrs Sellar*'). A short review of a charming nineteenth-century Scottish 'cookery book' allays the anxiety of the compiler's knighted husband that readers will think his wife a mere house- wife. Cooking 'is a genuine art after all, calling not only for skill, but for virtues of character' (*E*, I 301). The situation of women in India is the subject for an early book by Cornelia Sorabji reviewed by Woolf, who condescends to her about her English but not the extraordinary pictures she exhibits

of infants who are brides, and children who are widows, of secluded rooms where terrible superstitions prevail, and barbaric households, ruled by despotic Queens, where the entrance of the husband brings awe. ('*Between the Twilights*', p. 191)

Sorabji's book, she thinks, is an indication of the independent critical spirit that is awakening among Indian women.

In biographies of Queen Elizabeth and Lady Hester Stanhope that came under her review in the *TLS*, Virginia Woolf found the interest to lie both in the lives of these remarkable women and in the writing of these lives. A work narrating the girlhood of Elizabeth in contemporary letters, which include her own, stirs Woolf's lifelong fondness for that age beyond the eighteenth century. Elizabeth liked a style 'chaste in its propriety and beautiful in perspicuity', as did her reviewer; both were admirers of metaphor. Amidst the disagreements about her character by Froude and others, Woolf tentatively constructs from these letters and her own fantasy, perhaps, a picture of Elizabeth as a priggish, precocious girl, isolated from her sex by her station and her scholarly education, but managing by the age of twenty-five to become a 'seasoned woman' and the Queen of England (*E*, I 321–2).

'A silly new book' on Lady Hester Stanhope (*L*, I 418) sent Woolf and her readers back to the six volumes of absorbing memoirs by Lady Hester's physician on which the book was based. The central impression of the review is taken from the *DNB* and stated in the opening sentence: 'The writers in the *Dictionary of National Biography* have a pleasant habit of summing up a life, before they write it, in one word, thus – "Stanhope, Lady Hester Lucy (1770–1839), eccentric"'. (The article was by Thomas Seccombe and gave her birth date as 1776.) The trouble with this latest book on a woman Woolf in her final sentence calls 'the last of the great English aristocrats' is that the author smooths away the aristocratic eccentricities, as if she were not writing a book but conducting a tea-party:

> It would be polite there to remark 'Lady Hester is very fond of cats,' but in private, and writing is private, one should allow oneself to luxuriate in the fact that she kept forty-eight of them, choosing them for the harmony of their stars with her own, joining in a deep bass voice with their music at night, and accusing her doctor of a lumpish, cold, effeminate disposition if he found the noise intolerable. (*E*, I 325)

Buried in the comedy of this description is a serious point about the privateness of writing and its implications. Woolf's review was written in 1910, and it shows her growing mastery of style. And as in Woolf's later feminist work, the high humour here expresses a deeply-felt feminism. A comparison of Woolf's review with a miniature portrait of Lady Hester that Lytton Strachey wrote in 1919, a year after *Eminent Victorians*, brings out Woolf's emphasis on Stanhope's life as a woman. Strachey begins with her family background – symbolised by the Pitt nose which in Hester was 'altogether in the air' (*BC*, p. 281). His rapid, marvelling narrative brings out the hilarious eccentricity of the woman and the responses of the mysterious East to her, but there is little damning analysis here, as in *Eminent Victorians*. We are left simply with the ironic incomprehensibility of astonishing human beings like the Pitts and their noses.

For Virginia Woolf, Lady Hester's eccentricity verged on lunacy because she was a woman of extraordinary ability and no occupation – a noblewoman, the niece and companion of Prime Minister Pitt, who was prevented, as a woman, from being anything but eccentric:

> her powers fermented within her; she detested her sex, as though in revenge for the limitations with which ordinary women cramp remarkable ones; and drove herself as near madness as one can go by feeding a measureless ambition upon phantoms. (I 326)

Her thirty years' exile in the East made her a sensation there but her life was melancholy. 'Talk, since nothing ever happened, became the solace of her life' (I 328), and her doctor's memoirs are made out of that talk, from which she quotes various passages. Reading the memoirs, she wrote Clive Bell, 'one gradually sees shapes and thinks oneself in the middle of a world' (*L*, I 416). That world must have made her think of her own. While working on her review on Stanhope, Woolf wrote to Janet Case volunteering to work for women's suffrage.

IV

Self-writing was a fundamental subject for Virginia Woolf – which lends some literary justification to the endless fascination of her biography for some readers. The extent to which her novels can be so described has been debated in criticism almost from the beginning of her career. With the publication of Woolf's complete diaries, letters, and essays, it has become evident how much of her creative energy went into reflection on the nature and art of writing about oneself in forms other than fiction. Woolf's later Edwardian reviews of journals, travel writings, essay collections, and narratives of various kinds reveal her interest in autobiographical texts as clearly, if differently, as her reviews of the biographies and letters of writers do.

The only eminent author's journals she reviewed in *The Times Literary Supplement* were Emerson's. (Leslie Stephen had written a qualified appreciation of him in *Studies of a Biographer*.) In her review Woolf forsook the delicacy of international criticism James cautioned. She generalises easily about Emerson's situation – how he was 'born among the half-taught people in a new land'; his Harvard is a bleak contrast with Oxford – where prejudice saved Shelley from 'complacent self-improvement' – or Cambridge, where even Wordsworth got drunk. Yet Emerson's 'bland and impersonal spirit' kept the reflections in his journal from being smug, though not from being priggish. Disagreeing with his theory that words become one with things in good writing, Woolf formulates an ideal of style that she will approach in her own diaries:

> Emerson did not see that one can write with phrases as well as with words. His sentences are made up of hard fragments each of which has been matched separately with the vision in his head. It is far rarer to find sentences which, lacking emphasis because the joins are perfect and the words common, yet grow together so that you cannot dismember them, and are steeped in meaning and suggestion.

The implications of style extend beyond the merely literary. Americans such as Emerson conceive of man, as schoolmasters do; they view him as consisting of distinct qualities to be developed separately, rather than for their contribution to the whole individual. At the end of the essay, remembering perhaps James's warning, Woolf asks whether Emerson is too simple or we are too worn, then admires the beauty if not the understanding of his view (*E*, I 335–9).

The moral and social importance of style, of being able to represent exactly a complex human or natural reality remains a concern of Woolf's reviews even when they are not about well-known writers. The authors of a book on Venice fail with their accumulated phrases 'to see the single object clearly', and therefore it is difficult to determine what purpose their book serves (*'Venice'*). For Woolf, in another review, four medieval German travel narratives that mix the ordinary and the legendary in a dreary and brutal age are not interpreted enough by their editor. Here and elsewhere, Woolf appears to find more in the book than its author or editor has, and the charm of these narratives provides her with material for a thousand speculations. Even the lowly travel diary makes its literary demands, she says in another review:

> Every one who writes at all writes a diary of impressions when he travels abroad. The scene is so new, so original, and so charmingly arranged as though on purpose to be looked at and written about, that the figures curve round a visionary pen, and the lips form words instinctively. . . . It is not necessary to be profound, to compare situations, or to forecast the future in order to interest; all that is required of you is to see truly, and to describe as closely as may be. (*E*, 1 200–1)

'A visionary pen' (Clive Bell delighted in the phrase – 30.vii.08, VW/pS) and the habit of close description are practically extinct among middle-aged natives, however, although foreigners can sometimes do it for us, as Woolf finds in two sketch-books of London, one German, the other French. They also remind her how isolated English culture is; she mentions the ideas of three men that have swept the continent but failed to disturb the English: Tolstoy, whose *Anna Karenina* she had been reading in French, Ibsen, whose *Master Builder* she had also read, and more surprisingly, Nietzsche, whose *Thus Spake Zarathustra* she may have read.[5]

Exact specificity of observation is what Woolf seeks, often vainly, in the self-writings she is reviewing. A diary by the minor Victorian poet William Allingham she finds interesting for its reminiscences of Carlyle and others (including her father); the brief spontaneous notes of his childhood make her glad his formal autobiography was never finished. An account of French country life by an English woman inhabiting a chateau fails to make its rather thin matter into a whole. The reader must separate out the extraneous and repetitious, as the reviewer does in an evocation of French landscape at the start of her review (*E*, 1 222). Two large volumes of a diary written by a lady-in-waiting to the Prince Regent's pathetic wife are described, in another review, as those of 'a correct and kindly woman, with a diffuse taste for sentiment of all kinds', whose memoirs become insipid when she has nothing on which to concentrate. The historical atmosphere of the diary is watery, except when something particular is described, such as the meeting with an eccentric painter named Blake, whose talk interested her despite the sneers of another painter called Lawrence (*E*, I 197–8). And a seventeenth-century aristocrat's memoirs, excessively edited by one of her descendants, convey a family history with which the reader may set the whole landscape humming, even though 'the lack of meditation in proportion to so much action' in the book washes it in one shade. The simplicity and candour of Lady Fanshawe's memoirs – she had eighteen children in twenty-one years and survived a civil war – are also likened to a bird's song, for which five appendices and 350 pages of notes seemed inappropriate (*E*, I 144, 146). This judgement and a very free translation of the lady's tombstone brought twelve more pages of remonstrance from Fanshawe's editor but praise from the *TLS* (*L*, I 302). This was the only occasion on which Woolf's free use of quotation and translation was questioned. Andrew McNeillie's notes to his edition of Woolf's essays document the amount of creative, interpretive, telescoped, and sometimes just plain inaccurate quotation to be found in her reviews. Most of the examples are trivial but occasionally the meaning is quite changed, as with Emerson, who is incorrectly quoted as saying he studied nature with a 'classical' instead of 'chastised' enthusiasm' (*E*, I 336, 339).

The charm of Anne Thackeray Ritchie's quasi-autobiographical *Blackstick Papers*, which Woolf was sent by *The Times Literary Supplement* for a brief review in 1908, is not largely visionary. That the author was almost a relation of the anonymous reviewer does not seem to have mattered. Like Thackeray's fairy, after whom they are named, the essays with their great charm, their suggestions of eighteenth-century prose style, their 'flitting mockery', perceive more in common things than we do (*E*, I 228). Most of the papers had been published in the *Cornhill*. Their charm dates, and the style flows too easily now, but echoes of the mockery can still sometimes be heard in the niece's prose. Aunt Anny's old-fashioned essays were preferred over those of Mary Christie, another late Victorian woman of letters, reviewed earlier by Woolf, who pursued Thackeray and George Eliot with religious questions and wrote criticism with 'great vigour and a kind of wholesome shrewdness, like a capable housemaid with a broom. She loves literature while she rates it . . . ' (*'Mary Christie'*).

The essays of a woman who was a closer contemporary of Woolf's were the subjects of *TLS* reviews in 1908 and 1909 that suggest other limitations on the visionary pen in impressionistic hands. Virginia Woolf first met Vernon Lee, as Violet Paget called herself, when the 'dashing authoress' in a coat and skirt presented Leslie Stephen with her books at Talland House. Virginia reviewed a travel book of hers in 1908, then met her the next year in Florence where Lee appears to have fallen in love with Vanessa (*L*, II 550). Another review of her work by Woolf, this time of some essays on aesthetics, appeared in the *TLS* in 1909, and much later she based a fictive reminiscence on her. The review of Lee's *The Sentimental Traveller: Notes on Places* begins with an exasperated question: 'Have we not heard a little too much lately about this pervasive *Genius Loci?'* – which happens to be the title of a collection of travel essays Vernon Lee published a decade before. The review continues hostilely,

Her method . . . is purely impressionist, for if she were to concentrate her mind upon the task of seeing any object as exactly as it can be seen there would be no time for these egotistical diversions.

With all her curiosity, candour, sensitiveness, Lee 'lacks the exquisite taste and penetrating clearness of sight' that make the essays of Charles Lamb or Henry James works of art. 'The question as to what exactly distinguishes the truth from the falsehood in such a work is a delicate one', but Vernon Lee's 'slipshod thinking' stumbles on truth by accident (*E*, I 157–8). To Dickinson Virginia Woolf complained how Lee so plausibly 'turns all good writing to vapour, with her fluency and insipidity', and she blacklisted her along with Mrs Humphry Ward (*L*, I 320).

'Art and Life', as the second review of Vernon Lee was called, is one of Woolf's few excursions into aesthetics, and it came after her reading of G. E. Moore. The reviewer's tone is calmer but the complaint about the emotional quality of Vernon Lee's prose recurs. Much of the text is taken up with summarising Lee's objections to art for art's sake theories which make no connections between the beauties of art and life. Plato is invoked in a transcendental way by the author, which gives the reviewer an opportunity to observe that whereas Plato's dialectic sometimes ends with myth or rhapsody, Vernon Lee begins there, without having first argued her way to it. Lee tries to be logical at times, but without sufficiently defining her terms. Doubtful as her conclusions may be, she has read her Plato, Ruskin, and Pater with perhaps an infectious enthusiasm (*E*, I 277–9).

Vernon Lee's aesthetics of empathy is sometimes associated with Clive Bell's, but Woolf's review indicates the remoteness of Lee as an aesthetician and stylist from Bloomsbury. The criticism of her egotistical insensitivity to precise description suggests that Woolf valued Matthew Arnold's critical aim to see the object as it really is more than Walter Pater's knowing one's impression as it really is. Critics who take Woolf as a Paterian sometimes make her sound a little like T. S. Eliot's Fresca, who is described in a draft of *The Waste Land* as having been 'born upon a soapy sea Of Symonds – Walter Pater – Vernon Lee' (p. 27). In the 1930s, Woolf wrote an ironic portrait of a waste land figure who was reminiscing about Vernon Lee; the speaker lives in a Florence of the spirit where those who love beauty reside, and though having never spoken to her, 'in a sense, the true sense, I who love beauty always feel, I knew Vernon Lee' (*CSF*, pp. 245–6). For a woman writer who did know her, Lee seems to have stood for a kind of writing into which Woolf was perhaps aware she might decline. When she was trying to work out her modernist directions in fiction in 1919, Woolf reflected on the kind of diary she wanted to keep; Vernon Lee and the dangers of the visionary pen came to mind again:

> What sort of diary should I like mine to be? Something loose knit, & yet not slovenly, so elastic that it will embrace any thing, solemn, slight or beautiful that comes into my mind. . . . But looseness quickly becomes slovenly. A little effort is needed to face a character or an incident which needs to be recorded. Nor can one let the pen write without guidance; for fear of becoming slack & untidy like Vernon Lee. Her ligaments are too loose for my taste. (*D*, I 266)

A few months after reviewing Lee in 1909, Woolf was sent some essays of Oscar Wilde's friend Robert Ross for review in the *TLS*, and she again measured her distance, and Bloomsbury's from *fin-de-siècle* aestheticism. The essays were enjoyable, particularly Ross's 'delightful habit of discussing the living as though they were the dead.' Ross led her to reflect on literary history, how it seems to fall into chapters when we look back, but in the present we can detect no movements, only books being written from separate points of view. The classifications of literary history are to be made nervously from a distance; and Ross perceives that there is a current movement going on. Naturally she does not agree with him always or even understand some of his allusions to the contemporary scene, which make his reviewer feel like an outsider. For despite his modernity, Ross and his style belong to the past – with *The Yellow Book*, Beardsley, Wilde, and 'the pale shade of Walter Pater in their midst, controlling their revels' ('*Masques and Phases*').

V

Virginia Woolf's later Edwardian reviews for *The Times Literary Supplement* show how far she had come in the five years since she described herself as 'a journalist who wants to read history' (*L*, I 190). Only two of her reviews during this period were of historical, as distinct from biographical, works, and they show why history now dissatisfied her. In four volumes of a monumental history of Venice's golden age and decadence, for example, she finds the fascinating paradox of outer political decline coinciding with inner cultural splendour. She goes on to suggest eighteenth-century Venice attained an unreal beauty in literature and art that was unimagined in its renaissance, which was not the standard historical view. The growing modernist basis of Woolf's criticism of historical writing is apparent in her 1910 review of a pictorial German book on nineteenth-century fashions. She opens with a dismissal of traditional history as the early Victorians conceived it:

When one has read no history for a time the sad-coloured volumes are really surprising. That so much energy should have been wasted in the effort to believe in something spectral fills one with pity. Wars and ministries and legislation – unexampled prosperity and unbridled corruption tumbling the nation headlong to decay – what a strange delusion it all is! – invented presumably by gentlemen in tall hats in the Forties who wished to dignify mankind. Our point of view they ignore entirely.

The thoughts, feelings, morals of contemporaries have nothing to do with trade or politics, and the review concludes

> only great artists, giving their minds to nothing else, represent their age. . . . History is not a history of ourselves, but of our disguises. The poets and the novelists are the only people from whom we cannot hide.

As if to demonstrate this, the future novelist offers a description of the relation of men and women's disguises in the previous century. The humour and style here reveals how far Virginia Woolf had matured as a writer in half a decade's reviewing:

> Fashion dealt more discreetly with men, and chiefly haunted their legs. Nevertheless, there was a sympathy between the sexes. When her skirts ballooned, his trousers swelled; when she dwindled away, he wore stays; when her hair was Gothic, his was romantic; when she dragged a train, his cloak swept the ground. About 1820 his waistcoat was more uncontrollable than any garment of hers; five times within eight months it changed its shape. . . . The only parts of men that survived the stark years of the Thirties and Forties were the hat and the beard; they still felt the sway of political changes. The democratic spirit required felt hats that drooped; in 1848 they dissolved about the ears; stiffening again as reaction set in. The same principle ruled the beard; to be clean shaven was a sign of unflinching respectability; a ragged beard, or even a beard alone, showed that one's opinions were out of control. (*E*, I 330–4)

What might be called the memorials of history – the letters, diaries, essays, travel writings, confessions, reminiscences of the past – became Woolf's preferred historical reading. She would continue to enjoy historians who were also artists, like Gibbon, Macaulay, and Michelet, but contemporary historians, such as her cousin Herbert Fisher or even the Apostle G. M. Trevelyan, she would only use. They belonged too much to the intellectual, academic patriarchy.

Woolf's desire to write beyond the confines of *TLS* reviews is indicated in two essays she did for *The Times* itself rather than its literary supplement. The essay-reviews she was contributing to the *Cornhill* in 1909 may have led to this writing. She hoped to write more than two but no more were published (*L*, I 392). The two anonymous essays lack the wit, pace, and cohesion of her best Edwardian prose, however; there is a straining in them, a self-consciousness of essayist's limitations. The subject of both essays is the opera, which interested Bloomsbury before their post-impressionist days, before the revelation of modern ballet. The first essay discusses the possibilities for the coming London operatic season. The choice she finds most interesting is between Gluck's *Armide* and Wagner's *Die Walküre*. (In *A Room with a View*, Lucy plays music from *Armide* while Cecil asks for *Parsifal*.) The questions revolve around the relation of music to the emotions it expresses; Gluck's music conveys a perfect whole, whereas Wagner's expresses emotion more emphatically, sweeping us away at moments but dropping us into disillusionment at others. Various kinds of Wagnerians then attract the essayist's attention: the Romantic ones in cloaks who take the cheap seats, and pace on the Embankment after the opera, the scholarly ones who detect 'motives' in their scores to instruct 'humble female relatives', and the enthusiasts who find in Wagner's art the highest development of music. Also mentioned is *Lucia di Lammermoor* with Madame Tetrazzini, who had inspired Forster in *Where Angels Fear to Tread*. Abandoning any attempt to convey a general idea of the nature of opera, the essayist leaves us again with the image of Covent Garden in her earlier unpublished essay (see p. 182) where the rich mingle absurdly with vegetables in slums (*E*, I 269–72).

'I told many lies in Covent Garden Opera house,' Woolf exaggerated years later to Barbara Bagenal. 'My life was largely spent there. And we used to write the names of operas in books.' She wondered if her early admiration of Wagner had been in deference of Saxon Sydney-Turner, a Wagner devotee (*L*, III 56). Virginia travelled to Bayreuth for the Wagner Festival in 1909 with Saxon and her brother Adrian; there she wrote her second essay on opera for *The Times*. She focuses again on responses to the music rather than the music, which involves her in aesthetic questions that will preoccupy Bloomsbury. The essay begins by noting the rudimentary state of musical criticism: it has no tradition, no standards, no Aristotle. The writer who cannot go the root of the matter and is unsatisfied with critical evasions may be justified in trying 'to give his impressions as an amateur'. The title of the essay is 'Impressions at Bayreuth'. Brief attention is devoted to the audience before the essayist turns to the difficulties of *Parsifal*. Listening to it, 'one feels vaguely for a crisis that never comes, . . . ' yet an indescribable impression is produced as Wagner unifies human and unearthly emotion so that the transition from words to music is now hardly noticeable. Wagner's mastery of technique is likened to Shakespeare's. '*Parsifal* seems poured out in a smooth stream at white heat; its shape is solid and entire. . . . It is the only work which has no incongruous associations' (*E,* I 289–90). Woolf wrote to Vanessa Bell that *Parsifal* brought her close to tears, as 'it slides from music to words almost imperceptibly', and she had been 'niggling at the effect all the morning without much success' for her essay (*L,* I 406–7). *Lohengrin* is dismissed as an opera of tinsel and sham compared with *Parsifal.* Questions occur as to whether the music or words of Wagner give rise to the impressions he creates; but only a scientific writer, perhaps, can discriminate among the sources of our aesthetic impressions. Music's power over us may come from its indefinite articulation, which can generalise and also enclose private emotion – again as in Shakespeare, when he creates a symbolic character like the nurse in *Romeo and Juliet.* (Woolf's notebook shows she had been reading Shakespeare's tragedies along with A. C. Bradley's commentary – *RN,* pp. 149–50.) With relief, the essayist abandons the attempt to render musical experience in words, and resumes, with pleasure, the old literary tools to describe the pleasantness of the scene. The essay ends with a quick series of criticisms – supplied probably by Saxon and Adrian – of the orchestra, the singers, and the audible prompter.

Four years later, Virginia attended with Leonard what she said would be her last performance of the Ring cycle:

> My eyes are bruised, my ears dulled, my brain a mere pudding of pulp – O the noise and the heat, and the bawling sentimentality, which used to carry me away, and now leaves me sitting perfectly still. Everyone seems to have come to this opinion, though some pretend to believe still. (*L,* II 26).

VI

The six review-essays that Virginia Woolf wrote for the *Cornhill* in 1908 are more pertinent to her growth as a writer than *The Times* essays on opera. All are about the writing of lives, and four of them review the memoirs or journals of well-known women. Again the circumstances of publication are relevant to the literary history of

Woolf's contributions. Her essays appeared in a section of the magazine called 'The Book on the Table' that she and her friend Nelly Cecil had persuaded the editor Reginald Smith to start. Other sections of the magazine were devoted to general literature and fiction. The *Cornhill* allowed Woolf more space than the *TLS* usually did – up to 4000 words for one of her essays; more importantly, the essays were all signed. Yet Woolf's attitude toward her editor was less benign than her feelings for Bruce Richmond. Leslie Stephen had been editor of the monthly *Cornhill*, as had his father-in-law Thackeray before him, and was still remembered in the magazine. (A reminiscence of his 'Sunday Tramps' appeared in the January 1908 issue.) Reginald Smith was a publisher, not a writer. Woolf and Cecil, who also wrote six reviews in the same section of the *Cornhill*, liked to think of him as a grocer (*L*, I 353), though he was a graduate of Eton and King's and had been a barrister. According to the *Dictionary of National Biography*, whose publisher he became, 'Smith's salient characteristic was consideration for the sensitive race of authors.' This was not to be Woolf's experience in dealing with him. She mocked in Bloomsbury his compliments that she would make her mark in reviewing if only she would put her heart and mind into it, or that her reviews would not have that originality the *Cornhill* loved if she had read more (*L*, I 327, 360). Woolf admitted posing as an illiterate young woman who wrote her reviews with great difficulty, and Smith apparently had no idea of the extraordinary range of her reading.

Another problem with reviewing in the *Cornhill* was publicly running in tandem with Lady Robert Cecil, as she is described in the magazine's table of contents (her reviews were signed Eleanor Cecil, however). Woolf's fondness for Nelly is shown in the comic life she wrote of Violet Dickinson, also a close friend of Cecil's. But there were difficulties with her writing and her aristocratic views of art and morality. The year before Cecil had written a fierce review of May Sinclair's *The Helpmate* for Maxse's *National Review*, and Woolf felt, in characteristic Bloomsbury fashion, that the review failed to explain why morality was essential to art (*L*, I 317). After one of Cecil's *Cornhill* reviews criticised Galsworthy, Woolf complained to Vanessa, 'she means to be honest, and to blurt out the truth without thought for style – but the result is mere rant' (*L*, I 360).

Essays published over the name of Virginia Stephen in a prestigious journal associated with her father, and encountering a certain editorial resistance from Smith, as well as some competition from Cecil, all left marks on Woolf's *Cornhill* texts. How the books were selected or apportioned is unclear. (One wishes Woolf rather than Cecil had reviewed Gosse's *Father and Son*.) Some of the books reviewed were proposed by Woolf herself, but others such as the biographies of John Delane, former editor of *The Times*, and Theodore Roosevelt, were requested by Smith. With both of these uncongenial subjects, Woolf insinuated criticisms of the powerful worlds in which these men had triumphed. Delane was a vigorous sportsman who became editor of *The Times* at twenty-three. He was strong, dispassionate, 'with a capacity for shooting words straight if need be, and for distorting them at will, which is the despair of lady novelists who seek to reproduce it'. The gibe at the end of the sentence cuts both ways. Woolf takes a remark of Delane's tutor that he was 'part and parcel of his horse' and applies it to his career at *The Times*. The paper's independence, authority and anonymity were all his. Delane's ability to trace the growth of a rumour into opinion and then fact is described as Hawthornesque. Yet he was a philistine, unconscious of beauty, for example. At the end, his dispassion became indifference, and he took up farming 'perhaps to enjoy an easier intercourse with these dumb things than with human beings'. But it would be unwise, Woolf cautions, 'to colour too sadly that colossal erection of courage and devotion which he called "the Paper"' (*E*, I 188–93).

To describe *The Times* as a 'colossal erection' conveys a meaning today not perhaps present in 1908, though its sexual connotation can be found in Shakespeare. Smith gave his reviewer detailed instructions on how to review the two-volume life of Delane; he approved of the finished piece, which she thought a bad sign, and then infuriated her by cutting and adding to the review (*L*, I 330, 332). Why Smith wanted Woolf to review Delane's biography in the first place is a question. Did he remember Leslie Stephen's 1865 pamphlet attacking *The Times* for its views – Delane's views, that is – of the American Civil War? There is no allusion in her review, however, to the Southern partisanship of *The Times* that Leslie Stephen had called a public crime.

After Smith's editing of her review, Woolf threatened to resign as a *Cornhill* writer, she told Cecil, yet two months later she was back with a review on Theodore Roosevelt in the White House. She boasted to Violet Dickinson that the subtlety of her insinuations 'is so serpentine that no Smith in Europe will see how I jeer the

President to derision, seeming to approve the while' (*L*, I 337). Her article on Delane was more a biographical sketch than a book review of his biography, which she never mentions. With Roosevelt she plays the biography off against its subject. William Bayard Hale claims to be presenting a cinematic record in *A Week in the White House with Theodore Roosevelt*, but his reviewer knows words are not like eyes; they must interpret what is seen. The general impression Hale conveys of Roosevelt is that of an efficient, stifling machine, and the reviewer questions the state of American civilisation 'when the whole range of human speculation is made food for such mechanical measures'. Roosevelt's power of sympathy, so admired by his observer, is for the simplest forms of life – 'he is intoxicated by a crowd; he might do homage to the glow in a dog's eye'. Woolf recognises Hale's rhapsodic admiration authorises his own self-content: next to the fire of the president's genius 'your limbs grow warm and your brain becomes passive.' Yet even in America 'there must be some who dream, who meditate, who enjoy rare and lovely emotions' (*E*, I 207–9).

An Englishman like Delane, an American like Roosevelt – how different they were from a great French actress, a mistress of Louis XIV, and two nineteenth-century English noblewomen that are the subjects of Woolf's other *Cornhill* essays in 1908. Nevertheless, in these essays too, similar standards of value appear – standards by which these lives and the art that presents them are judged. Woolf's first contribution to the *Cornhill* was an essay on Sarah Bernhardt's memoirs, *My Double Life*, which came as close as any book Woolf had yet reviewed to defeating her. The doubleness of the memoirist watching her performing self, calls for an unusually complex interest and review. The life represented in Bernhardt's memoirs is likened to barely connected brightly coloured beads. Woolf uses anecdotes to illustrate the actress's highly concentrated, very literal mind and her 'alien art of letters' that is often crude, sometimes strange and brilliant, sometimes grotesque and painful. Images swarm as Woolf tries to sum up the effect of Bernhardt's revelation. She makes and at the same time questions a distinction fundamental to her later fiction: 'Where after all', Woolf asks, 'does dream end and where does life begin?' How should we distinguish between the perfumed 'undulating crimson vapours', the high-pitched French voices, the chafing applause that surround the reader of these memoirs and ordinary existence, which the book's 'thin stream of interest' fails to submerge? Is daily life the great falsehood, or is the belief that each of us is the centre of innumerable rays which it is our business to reflect back, as Sarah Bernhardt did? She at any rate will sparkle while we 'lie dissipated among the floods' (*E*, I 164–70). The final triumph of personality in Bernhardt's memoirs is not boredom but exhaustion, says the reviewer, describing perhaps her experience of reviewing *My Double Life*.

Compared with Bernhardt's, the life of Louise de La Vallière seems quite simple. For Woolf, the main problem was how 'to contrive some decent way of alluding to her relations with Louis', she wrote to Sydney-Turner, 'I think R. Smith will strike out the word "mistress" and substitute "unfortunate attachment."' Should she just leave it out, she asked Nelly Cecil (*L*, I 352–3). That is what she did. 'Louise de la Vallière' is based on a French biography which is quoted but never discussed, as Woolf retells La Vallière's life in 2500 words. The reviewer is practising biography here, and doing it well. This is the setting for Louis's attraction to Louise:

> The summer of 1661 was known in after years for its splendour. June, in spite of some storms, was more lovely even than May; and the Court was at Fontainebleau. To imagine what happened when the sun rose, on a cloudless summer morning, and promised brilliant hours till dusk, and then a warm summer night among the trees, one must conceive the untried vigour of men of twenty and of women of eighteen, set free from all constraint, and inspired by love and fine weather. They drove out to bathe in the morning and came back in the cool of the day on horseback; they wandered in the woods after dinner, at first to the sound of violins, which faded away as the couples drew further and further into the shadows, losing themselves till the dawn had risen.

Woolf succinctly narrates how the unassuming Louise de La Vallière was used as cover for the King's attraction to his sister-in-law, with the result that he fell in love with her instead, and she with him, until Madame de Montespan came along; La Vallière then became a front in truth for that affair. The King inflicted this 'most exquisite of punishments' for years before finally allowing her to enter a convent (*E*, I 215–9).

The quality of women's lives as well as the art with which they are conveyed in autobiography are once again important considerations of Woolf's review-essays for the *Cornhill* on the memoirs of Lady Dorothy Nevill and Elizabeth Lady Holland. But the ladies are hardly comparable. Lady Dorothy's two volumes of aristocratic Victorian reminiscences are dismissed in a quietly savage review. The brilliant ball of the opening paragraph dissipates as Nevill is unable to reproduce its conversation. One is forced, Woolf remarks acidly, to people Buckingham Palace with characters from Mrs Humphry Ward (who began serialising a novel in the *Cornhill* next year). The solidity of Nevill's world in all its audacity appears in the country life of the leisured aristocracy, especially in the author's

> sublimely insolent disrespect for art that vitiates the whole of the structure, for, surely, it is fatal if you are an aristocrat not to honour the only people who have imagination enough to believe in your beauty. (*E*, I 182)

That passage gives the key to the structure of Woolf's own essay, which opens with an imaginative representation of aristocratic life that the reality in Nevill's memoirs ruins. Later Woolf collected in the first *Common Reader* a review of Nevill's biography that likened the author's existence to a species of bird life.

The journals of the great Elizabeth Lady Holland and a book on the Holland House Circle of which she was the centre were the subjects of the last and longest *Cornhill* essay that Woolf published in December 1908 (though it was not the last text she wrote for Reginald Smith). The character of Holland and the nature of her diaries form another double interest for the reviewer. Her dominating personality – she could listen 'to the cleverest talk in England until she was bored', and then cry out '"Enough of this Macaulay!"' (*E*, I 230, another telescoped misquotation) – was largely formed by her first marriage at fifteen to a violent, philistine member of parliament, whom she dragged around Italy and then divorced in order to marry the cultured Lord Holland. Lady Holland's character, as Woolf discloses it, is a function of her diary, which she began in Italy 'to propitiate her own eye' and 'to assure herself she was doing her duty with all her faculties. . . . ' Elizabeth is imagined to be uneasy with such a version of herself, and she 'would soon dissociate herself entirely from her reflections.' Thus her diaries were saved from the usual self-conscious fate, for 'she could be as impersonal as a boy of ten and as intelligent as a politician' (*E*, I 231–2). With her brilliant success as a hostess, her diary fills up with anecdotes and political news, 'and it is very seldom that she raises her eyes for a moment to consider what it is all about' (*E*, I 235). When she does once, it is the advantage of her husband that she hopes to forward. The scenes of her diary show her insolent, masterful, whimsical strength of character, but she had little political influence. And what the reviewer misses in the way of introspection is made up for by the 'numbers of likenesses she struck off, and with what assurance! . . . She took in the whole sweep of the world, and imprinted it with her own broad mark', which was sometimes off the mark. Wordsworth, for instance, she regarded as superior to his writings (*E*, I 237).

Woolf's final judgement of Lady Holland returns to the imagery of portraiture. She is, as in a picture by Leslie, 'a hard woman perhaps, but undoubtedly a strong and courageous one' (*E*, I 238). Another portrait is thus added to the gallery of women in Woolf's later Edwardian reviews. Few of them were triumphant but several were heroic, if eccentric. Some were vain, some silly, some creative. And most were fundamentally disadvantaged by the historical circumstances of their gender.

VII

'The Book on the Table' by Lady Robert Cecil and Virginia Stephen lasted only a year in the *Cornhill*. In 1909, Woolf did a final review-essay for the magazine of Miss Linsett's authorised biography of her friend, the now forgotten Victorian novelist and sibyl Frances Willatt (1823–84). The biographer and her subject are both found wanting, Linsett for her life-and-letters tricks and lack of understanding, Willatt for her ill-imagined, badly written books and prophetic pretensions. Woolf's own biographer sought for Willatt and Linsett in the catalogues of the British Museum and the Library of Congress but found no trace of them (QB/*VW*, I 153). They exist only in the ironic pages of Virginia Woolf. 'Memoirs of a Novelist', as she entitled her piece, is a work of fiction that satirises the lives of nineteenth-century women and the things they write. Through the form of an essay on an imaginary novelist's biography, Woolf attempted to combine the criticism and biography she had been writing with the fiction that she wanted to do. It was to be the first of a series for the *Cornhill*. Smith had been asking her for a year now to write a series of articles, she told Clive Bell, 'upon Men and Women, as I see them in their biographies' (*L*, I 356). What Woolf saw in these books is momentarily suggested in a letter to Nelly Cecil, whose *Cornhill* review of the official biography of Dorothea Beale she liked. After looking at the biography, she wrote,

> O what inflictions people are with their dreary phrases! I sometimes think no crime is so bad – the suffocation of life – But it is authorised, on the contrary, and if you had to bring up a child you could not avoid the Miss Beales and Miss Busses. But to explain what I mean would take too long, and I never can explain it. (*L*, I 354)

Clive Bell found 'Memoirs of a Novelist' very clever as well as imaginative, which pleased her; he thought she may have discovered a new medium but he also had some misgivings (27.x.09, CB/pS; VW/*L*, I 412). So did the editor of the *Cornhill*, and he felt compelled to reject the piece because his contributor had impaled a bumble-bee upon a pin instead of a butterfly, and with a humour that had more vinegar than salt in it. He had never turned her down before, he said apologetically, forgetting the unceremonious refusal of her contribution on Boswell's letters in 1906, but he was concerned about what the series would be like (VW/pS). Woolf never wrote for the *Cornhill* again; her fictive essay remained unpublished, although the generic mixture of 'Memoirs of a Novelist' is among the most interesting of Virginia Woolf's later Edwardian experiments in the writing of lives. Throughout her career she sought for new ways to write biography and criticism, the unfinished sketches for *Anon* being her last efforts in this direction. 'Memoirs of a Novelist' is also one of the most characteristic Bloomsbury texts to be written in their Edwardian years. The writing of fiction in non-fictional forms, the protest against Victorian biography, and the criticism of certain kinds of novels would all become familiar features of Bloomsbury's writing.

Imaginary portraits were not new in 1909; Woolf was certainly familiar with Pater's unsatirical ones (Beerbohm's were later). The originality of 'Memoirs of a Novelist' lies rather in her use of the critical essay as a form for fiction. Through this form, the critic plays the imaginary novelist off against her biographer, complaining that readers will confuse Miss Willatt with her remains in the slipshod, two-volume life by Miss Linsett. Its droning platitudes, evasions, and digressions ('a short sketch of the history of Bloomsbury may not be amiss' it says, for example) suggest to the critic that the novelist was not what she seemed:

> the sight of that large selfish face, with the capable forehead and the surly but intelligent eyes discredits all the commonplaces on the opposite page; she looks quite capable of having deceived Miss Linsett. (*CSF*, p. 74)

'Nervous prudery and the dreary literary conventions' keep Willatt's most interesting experiences a biographical blank (p. 73). Her development into a novelist and then a prophetess is unreflected in Linsett's chapters, which are organised around changes of address. A mere thirty-six pages cover the first seventeen years of her upbringing, but her dying is cooed over interminably because death gave the biographer an emotion.

In some respects 'Memoirs of a Novelist' is another of Woolf's comic biographies, only this time the subject is completely imaginary and literary. A family anecdote tells how as a girl Frances walked into a pigsty reading and had her book eaten out of her hand; later she reads an entire church history by a chink of light in bed. 'She was not generally considered handsome', her brother recalls, 'although she had (at the time of which I speak) a nearly perfect arm'. From history, according to her biographer, 'she got a general notion of pride, avarice and bigotry; in the Waverley novels she read about love' (pp. 71–2). But what makes 'Memoirs of a Novelist' a further development in Woolf's playing with biographical forms is the use of a critic's point of view to rid the imaginary novelist of her biographer's disguises. Woolf adapts the genre of the review-essay for a two-pronged satire that impales the novelist with her biographer. The critic reconstructs 'a restless and discontented woman, who sought her own happiness rather than other people's.' She turned to writing, and this allows Woolf's persona to generalise on realism and nineteenth-century women's fiction in a way that anticipates *A Room of One's Own*:

> After all, merely to sit with your eyes open fills the brain, and perhaps in emptying it, one may come across something illuminating. George Eliot and Charlotte Brontë between them must share the parentage of many novels at this period, for they

disclosed the secret that the precious stuff of which books are made lies all about one, in drawing-rooms and kitchens where women live, and accumulates with every tick of the clock. (p. 75)

Willatt had a different theory of fiction. She considered it indecent to represent her own experience, so she created Arabian lovers and set them in a South American utopia. Willatt also had scruples about good writing:

There was something shifty, she thought, in choosing one's expressions; the straightforward way to write was the best, speaking out everything in one's mind, like a child at its mother's knee, and trusting that, as a reward, some meaning would be included. (p. 76)

Her best writing was done for self-justification; she then went on to prophecy, growing very fat and discoursing on the soul to trembling women in Bloomsbury. With her talent for obscurity, she offered her disciples a 'draught, vague and sweet as chloroform, which confused outlines and made daily life dance before the eyes with hints of a vista beyond' (p. 77). (There may be some private allusion here to Caroline Emelia Stephen, who had recently died.)

'Memoirs of a Novelist' finishes inconsequentially. While part of the irony, this ending also dulls it. No conclusion is drawn by the critic after uncovering a more intelligent, but hardly more commendable writer beneath the biographer's subterfuges. The review-essay's form, which conventionally has a firm conclusion, is not carried through, and this may explain some of Smith's dissatisfaction with it. Woolf will be variously criticised later for not sustaining her satire. Yet the text remains an important one for the connections of biography and criticism with fiction, of women with writing, and of Victorian with modern Bloomsbury. Among Woolf's friends who read 'Miss Willatt' at this time was probably Lytton Strachey.[6]

In another of her unpublished, later Edwardian biographical texts, Woolf mixed fact and satirical fiction for a parodic biography of the type she had written years earlier. 'Friendships Gallery' is like a sequel to her 1902 sketch of Violet Dickinson. It is told by a sincere, if self-conscious biographer 'anxious to use only those words that cannot be avoided' (p. 275). As comic exaggeration develops, the author protests too much that 'this Biography is no novel but a sober chronicle' (p. 279). An introductory chapter goes from the birth of 'the long baby' to her first ball and season. Encounters with Christian aunts, German governesses, and great ladies are narrated along with absurd, benevolent acts. The biographer is tempted to analyse Violet as a modern novelist might, but becomes rather autobiographical in describing 'the flight of her mind, rising like a cloud of bees, when a question was dropped into it', or wondering 'did she reason or only instincticise?' (p. 282). (Woolf will use the metaphor of the mind's flight again in her diaries.) A second chapter or portrait in the gallery describes magic gardens, especially Nelly Cecil's at Hatfield House. That idyllic setting looks forward to the comic biography Woolf would call *Orlando*. A vision of unForsterian fauns pursuing naked maidens fails to distract Violet from the gardener and the drains. She is inspired to build her own cottage – an event that G. M. Trevelyan, fresh from his championing of Meredith, is expected to find very significant of a new spirit some day in his work on the social life of the nineteenth century.[7] 'The Comic Spirit laughed meanwhile' (p. 284). The capricious biographer keeps pitching into pitfalls or constructing paragraphs that conceal the subject rather than reveal it. But finally it is possible to report that Violet talked of such subjects as 'modern English prose; how it is written by women' (p. 291) and fallaciously confused morals and aesthetics. At the end, however, it is necessary to admit that Violet was somehow wrongly right, and the biographer concludes equivocally that 'the life of Miss Violet Dickinson is one of the most singular as well as the most prolific and least notorious that was lived in our age' (p. 292). A third disconnected chapter is a fantasy set in Tokyo that tells of disastrous sea-monsters, holy birds, religious propitiations, and the saving of everything by two sacred, fish-borne princesses resembling Dickinson and Cecil (who had stopped in Japan on a world cruise in 1905). Woolf rarely wrote this kind of mythic tale again.

'Friendships Gallery' is private writing that satirically celebrates her friendships with Dickinson and Cecil. After typing it with a violet ribbon and binding it in violet leather for Violet Dickinson, Woolf tried to get it back, asking her not to show what she called 'The Life, or Myth' to anyone (*L*, I 304, 314). But she herself let Vanessa and Clive Bell read it along with other manuscripts the next year, commenting 'it is rather thin and hasty, and as you will see, I have had to refrain and conventionalise where I might have been pointed. Even so', she added, 'Violet thinks it a little harsh – such is the vanity of the modest' (*L*, I 336). Vanessa thought it brilliant (11.iv.09, VB/pB). Bloomsbury and Woolf's early literary mentors were growing farther apart.

VIII

The life-writing done by Woolf in Bloomsbury's later Edwardian years combined other genres than the fiction, criticism, and fantasy. One of her most remarkable pieces of writing was done in the form of a family biography that is also a species of autobiography. Before concluding with this moving text, we should glance at the other autobiographical writings – the letters, notebooks, and especially diaries – that Woolf was writing from 1907 to 1910.

The potential literary value of a form such as the letter for Virginia Woolf and others in Bloomsbury is reflected in the Group's short-lived literary game of composing an epistolary novel. Woolf's slight contribution is inferior to her actual correspondence. But her best letters during these years are about writing and reading (as is indicated by their frequent use in this literary history). Though often self-conscious, these letters can still be very amusing. Her frequently quoted account for Violet Dickinson of a encounter with Henry James while staying near Rye in 1907 displays a talent for mimetic mockery:

> Henry James fixed me with his staring blank eye – it is like a childs marble – and said 'My dear Virginia, they tell me – they tell me – they tell me – that you – as indeed being your fathers daughter nay your grandfathers grandchild – the descendant I may say of a century – of a century – of quill pens and ink – ink – ink pots, yes, yes, yes, they tell me – ahm m m – that you, that you, that you *write* in short.' This went on in the public street, while we waited, as farmers wait for the hen to lay an egg – do they? – nervous, polite, and now on this foot now on that. I felt like a condemned person, who sees the knife drop and stick and drop again. Never did any woman hate 'writing' as much as I do.
>
> (*L*, I 306)

(James for his part described Virginia as sitting on a near hilltop writing reviews for *The Times* (*Letters*, IV 504). Her reputation was clearly growing.) To Dickinson, again in another letter, Woolf describes Oxford intellectuals with a striking simile that is then reflexively commented on:

> The atmosphere of Oxford is quite the chilliest and least human known to me; you see brains floating like so many sea anemonies, nor have they shape or colour. They are bloodless, with great veins on them (This reads like a school childs exercise – so precise and true is it.) (*L*, I 319–20)

Different cerebral imagery is used to describe to Clive and Vanessa her reading of G. E. Moore:

> I split my head over Moore every night, feeling ideas travelling to the remotest part of my brain, and setting up a feeble disturbance, hardly to be called thought. It is almost a physical feeling, as though some little coil of brain unvisited by any blood so far, and pale as wax, had got a little life into it at last; but had not strength to keep it. I have a very clear notion which parts of my brain think.

She was not 'so dumb foundered' by the time she finished *Principia Ethica*,

> but the more I understand, the more I admire. He is so humane in spite of his desire to know the truth; and I believe I can disagree with him, over one matter. (*L*, I 357, 364)

But what it was she does not say.

As a correspondent, Virginia Woolf was still shy about personal relations with almost everyone except Vanessa Bell and Violet Dickinson. Her most affectionate letters are to Vanessa, prompting her to respond once that Virginia's read like love letters, and if published without the replies, readers might think 'we had a most amorous intercourse' (25.viii.08, VB/pNY). The Bells were now her most stimulating correspondents, and the letters to Clive, particularly about *The Voyage Out*, express most clearly her literary ideas at this stage in her career. What literary criticism of Bloomsbury there is in her correspondence remains quite tentative, however. To Lytton Strachey she offers 'green blushes' by way of compliment for his erotic poems, while to Clive she criticises their lack of fresh diction (*L*, I 365, 344). Her comments to Clive on his letters reflect on the aims of her own: they were a little too 'reminiscent', too deliberate; he should let his style gallop more (*L*, I 361–2).

No very substantial reading notebooks or any diary in which she recorded her professional progress, survive from Woolf's later Edwardian years. There are no indications of what she was being paid for her reviewing, and money is never mentioned in the letters she writes about her work. Woolf may have kept no notes for her reviews beyond the few that remained among her papers (*RN*, pp. 150–1). She did make notes while reading Swinburne, Crabbe, some Restoration comedy, and Molière, the letters of Cowper and Keats, Tolstoy's *Anna Karenina*, and Shakespeare's tragedies with Bradley's commentary, (*RN*, pp. 149–52). In another notebook of Latin and Greek reading, she expresses admiration for the sense of completion in the *Odyssey*, and partly translates Socrates's beautiful speech on love in the *Symposium*, which she described as 'an entire expression of something often hinted at in his dialogues' (*RN*, 166–9; pS).

Several short diaries that Woolf kept have survived from her later Edwardian years. A single entry on New Forest after Thoby Stephen's death remarks that without Celtic mysticism it is too tamely Saxon (*EJ*, pp. 363–4). Another entry briefly describes a trip to Golders Green on the newly opened underground. During a summer holiday at Playden, near Rye (where she met Henry James), Woolf recorded how she was vexed with the desire to describe Sussex, and what imagination it would take to comprehend a Sussex labourer's life. Earlier she attempted a meta-account of an expedition that 'a conscientious annalist' might describe (*EJ*, p. 370). A later sunset view of Rye and Winchelsea stresses their colours and shapes; the flashes of a lighthouse are compared with the opening and shutting of an eye, an image she would use again. The next entry begins with a criticism of her diary, 'the wildness of its statements – the carelessness of its descriptions – the repetitions of its adjectives, . . . ' but she feels if conditions were imposed, it would never get written (p. 375). A stay near Wells Cathedral leads to reflections on Christianity (it is tolerable in its senility) and children playing. Back at Manorbier again she returns to descriptions of landscape and weather.

Virginia Woolf briefly continued her 1906 Greek diary while travelling in Italy in 1908 and 1909. There is more critical description of the English in Italy than there was in Greece. She practises reviewing again on books she has been reading during the trip. The diarist's travelling companions – in Italy she was with the Bells – remain unidentified, though their influence on the recurrent discussions of art is evident. Observations on the relation of painting to writing and then some reflexive thoughts on the functions of description make these self-conscious texts more interesting for literary rather than their autobiographical or topographical insights. The entries are much more concerned with practising and reflecting upon travel-writing rather than travelling. 'There are many ways of writing such diaries as these' is the opening sentence of the diary Woolf begun in Milan in September 1908. She goes on to note how she distrusts both description and the narrative arrangement of daily adventures. And she hopes to write 'not only with an eye, but with the mind; discover real things beneath the show' – or failing this, to honestly record matter for later writing or remembering (*EJ*, p. 384). The second diary opens in Florence in April 1909, with worries about 'empty and ladylike writing' and her habit of making descriptive writing too definite. That is not the fault many readers have found in her prose, but when she proceeds to explain how easy it is to write description, she anticipates a recurrent criticism of her own writing that also worried her:

> One seizes some broad aspect, as of water or colour, & makes a note of it. This single quality gives the tone of the piece. As a matter of fact the subject is probably infinitely subtle, no more amenable to impressionist treatment than the human character. What one records is really the state of one's own mind.
>
> (pp. 395–6)

The descriptions of places, books, people and pictures that follow these modernist preliminaries are usually more formal than the rapid sketching she would develop so distinctively in her mature diaries. Pictures of unEnglish landscapes form slowly for her. She sees Milan in water-colours and contrasts the casually organised worship in a Siena cathedral to the military-like procedures of an English service. The next entry abruptly shifts to Thomas Hardy's *Two in a Tower*, and generalises impressionistically on him as a novelist: he forces his characters into the plot, and thinks of letters and dates instead of the stars and the love that his novel was to be about; this keeps him from writing classics, despite 'his intense original stare at things' (p. 387). A later digression on *Harry Richmond* also finds George Meredith, for all his brilliance, an unsatisfying creator of characters, who deceives himself over the stupidity of the reading public that underestimated him for so long. These judgements are bolder than those to be found in her reviews around this time, and that may have been their value as critical practice.

Pension life has its place in the diary too. Woolf constructs the history of one futile old lady who belongs to the world of *Where Angels Fear to Tread* and *A Room with a View*. She appears to have spent her life in testing pensions; unenthusiastically she fills her 'torpid case with food and wine,' for 'the life of a lodger is one of perpetual hostility' (p. 389). But the portrait is bleaker than those in Forster. In Perugia the daughters of an Englishwoman are described, the plain one industriously reading while the pretty one 'with great curves of red & white flesh on her bones' dreams of marriage and children (p. 390).

The literary interest of these diaries lies in such descriptive phrases and the reflections on the nature of writing they sometimes engender. Some notes on a fresco by Perugino are particularly striking.

> I conceive that he saw . . . all beauty was contained in the momentary appearance of human beings. He saw it sealed as it were; all its worth in it; not a hint of fear or future. His fresco seems to me infinitely silent; as though beauty had swum up to the top and stayed there, above everything else, speech, paths leading on, relation of brain to brain, don't exist.

Its interdependent parts come together through related lines and colours that express the artist's mental view of beauty. As a writer Woolf feels she also wants to express beauty or symmetry but of life and the world in action and perhaps conflict.

> If there is action in painting it is only to exhibit lines; but with the end of beauty in view. Isn't there a different kind of beauty? No conflict.
>
> I attain a different kind of beauty, achieve a symmetry by means of infinite discords, showing all the traces of the mind's passage through the world; achieve in the end, some kind of whole made

of shivering fragments; to me this seems the natural process; the flight of the mind. Do they really reach the same thing?

(pp. 392–3)[8]

The aesthetic questions that Woolf raises here about painting and literature, conceptions of beauty and the aim of writing, discord and unity, action and thought, will be perennial ones for her. 'The flight of the mind', which she had used in 'Friendships Gallery', she employs again at the end of her life to describe what she wants to capture in criticism as well as fiction (*D*, V 298). Her early diary also expresses misgivings about the value of criticism. Pension talk about masterpieces exhibits the talkers not the paintings, which endure unaltered the viewers' crawling over them.

The next year in Florence, Woolf continued her Italian diary briefly. She begins by describing the city of the Brownings and Ruskin, then becomes too self-conscious to go on:

the discomfort of writing here is intense – constrains my style to be tense, in the form of lapidary inscriptions.

Walking on San Miniato the other evening, it occurred to me that the thing was running into classic prose before my eyes. I positively saw the long smooth sentence running like a ribbon along the road – casting graceful loops around the beggar woman & the dusky child – & curving freely over the bare slopes of hills.

After the enigmatic exclamation 'London!', the diary moves to unflattering sketches of Anglo-Italian and English celebrities (she met Berenson and a mistress of Meredith's) and the entries begin to sound like those of her later dairies:

Among the guests was a lean, attentuated woman, who had a face like that of a transfixed hare – the lower part was drawn out in anguish, while the eyes appealed piteously. This was Mrs. Meynell, the writer, who somehow made one dislike the notion of women who write. (pp. 396–8)

For another paragraph Woolf continues her unsparing reflections.

She gives up writing about Florence – it is too marked, emphatic – and goes on to characterise two other women whom she met in Florence, one young and morbid, the other a charming old lady who wrote devout books and versified Father Damien's life into English. Her writing, Woolf expects, 'is graceful, & fresh, with no originality or much power', and on the theme of style again her travel diary stops (p. 401).

The trip to Florence was not apparently a success; Virginia quarrelled with Vanessa and Clive, then returned alone to London (QB/ *VW*, I 143–4). 'I was unhappy that summer, & bitter in all my judgements,' she remembered much later (*D*, III 243). This may be part of the context for a kind of introductory appendix to her Italian diary that is devoted to a character sketch of her brother-in-law. Virginia's shifting relationship with Clive is reflected in a number of the things she was writing around this time, including her novel and the biography of Vanessa. Using only his first name and addressing a familiar 'you', her sketch of Clive sets out to show how his character was formed by his birth and education. School made him aware that he differed from his country family, which allowed no art to disturb them. He became precocious, turned to reading for personal triumphs and also protection against them, yet remained gentle and willing to talk with whomever he could find. Convinced he was among the clever elect, Clive sought for ways to use his knowledge, became involved with an older woman and discovered he could quite easily write her verses. That is as far as the sketch goes, but some notes for it indicate a further emphasis on the self-consciousness of his differences, gifts, and good manners (*EJ*, pp. 383–4). The tone for the most part is non-committal; there is some praise and some ridicule. To a certain degree the account reflects Virginia's earlier views of Peter Bell (as Bloomsbury had nicknamed him after Wordsworth's odd poem) when he was courting Vanessa.

But these early attitudes and the sketch in Woolf's diary are very different from the fragmentary 'Dialogue on a Hill' that Woolf appears to have written in Cornwall in 1908. An intelligent woman and man, pastorally named Eugenia and Charmides, commune in the dialogue on an equal basis during a beautiful Cornish day but in a relationship that 'forbids any motive of another kind to have its effect upon their words'. The atmosphere of the dialogue is much closer than the sketch to Clive Bell's love poem 'To A. V. S. with a Book' (see p. 284). Quite different reactions are produced in

Charmides and Eugenia by a miserable old woman, however;
he asks more self-centredly if they will ever become like that, while
she wonders what kind of life brought the woman to this pass (*CSF*,
p. 326).

The attempt to render Clive's character was an attempt at family biography that is also a form of autobiography. Two short
Edwardian examples of this kind of writing were published by
Virginia Woolf – the account of Leslie Stephen in Maitland's
biography, and an obituary of Caroline Emelia Stephen requested
by the *Guardian* and published in April 1909. It was her final
contribution to the paper that had first printed her work. To Nelly
Cecil, Woolf complained that she was unable to say what she felt in
the obituary and saw no need for 'respectful lamentations' (*L*, I 390).
The anonymous obituary implies a personal acquaintance with the
deceased, but that is all. Her books and Evangelical background are
mentioned, her education 'after the fashion of the time, by masters
and governesses', the long illness of her mother that permanently
injured her own health, and then Stephen's discovery of Quaker
faith that inspired everything she did and was the secret of her
influence – for 'she was no solitary mystic' but one with a gift for
expression and robust practicality. Her life at the end 'had about it
the harmony of a large design' (*E*, I 268–9). It is an admirably
concise, respectful, and reticent tribute from an ambivalent niece.
'The Quaker', as Woolf liked to dub her aunt, may have left Woolf
some of her independence and Quaker mysticism (*Victorian
Bloomsbury*, p. 23) along with a legacy of £2500, the significance of
which will be suggested in *A Room of One's Own*. But something of
what Woolf would really liked to have said about her aunt is
disclosed in her letters. She disagreed 'entirely with her whole
system of toleration and resignation, and general benignity, which
does seem to me so woolly'; yet on one visit, the Quaker 'poured
forth all her spiritual experiences, and then descended and became
a very wise and witty old lady' (*L*, I 146, 229). Another time Woolf
described her as 'about as tough an old heathen as they make' (*L*, I
285–6). Later, Woolf mocked her again letters: 'the Quaker has
written me a "spout of pure joy, from my entrails" O Childhood! O
Motherhood! O Lamb of Light! O Babe of Purity! O! O! O!' Of
Stephen's *Light Arising: Thoughts on the Central Radiance* she wrote
acidulously to Dickinson after receiving the book, 'It is a gloomy
work I know, all gray abstractions, and tremulous ecstasies, and
shows a beautiful spirit' (*L*, I 320, 331).

IX

Virginia Woolf's most remarkable early work of family life-writing is the autobiographical biography that she wrote of her sister in 1908. Though not written for publication, it is a formally constructed beginning of a family biography composed ostensibly for the subject's newborn child. The first thing to be said, however, about the work published as 'Reminiscences' in *Moments of Being* is that it should not be called 'Reminiscences'. The text that Woolf typed and corrected bears no title at all.[9] To classify this writing as reminiscences obscures the work's generic originality and misconstrues its emphasis and tone. Woolf is not reminiscing. She is telling a nephew the early family history of his mother, and Woolf comes into it primarily as the authorial narrator. In this way she avoided, temporarily, one of the difficulties of memoir-writers. 'They leave out the person to whom things happened', as she much later wrote at the beginning of her very different memoir, 'A Sketch of the Past':

> The reason is that it is so difficult to describe any human being. So they say: 'This is what happened'; but they do not say what the person was like to whom it happened. (*MB*, p. 65)

In that late memoir Woolf put herself in by combining her past memories into the present form of a diary (see *Victorian Bloomsbury*, pp. 80–1). In the editorially mistitled 'Reminiscences', however, she made herself into a biographer who is describing not her own memories but the past lives of her sister, her step-sister, and their mother. She is trying to show what they were like. The model here is clearly the *Mausoleum Book* that Leslie Stephen addressed to his wife's children after her death; he thought of his account originally as a kind of letter and explicitly refrained from personal disclosure in it (pp. 3, 7). Virginia's biography of Vanessa finally does turn into autobiography when author begins to be centrally involved in her subject's life, and at that point the text stops.

Virginia Woolf began her biography of Vanessa Bell after her sister started to write her own reminiscences, as she called them, in August 1907. After about a dozen pages Vanessa stopped; to Virginia she wrote 'my biography is not fit to read – why not write yours?' and inquired if she had finished Violet Dickinson's life yet? (6.viii.07, VB/pNY). What Woolf did instead was pick up her sister's biography and write it for Julian Bell, who had been born in February 1908. This time it was not a comic fantasy like Dickinson's in 'Friendships Gallery', but a thoroughly serious account. Its form presented quite different problems of focus, as she confessed in a letter to Clive while finishing the first two chapters:

> It might have been so good! As it is, I am too near, and too far; and it seems to be blurred, and I ask myself why write it at all? seeing I shall never recapture what you have, by your side this minute. (*L*, I 325)

One of the periodic images of Vanessa's biography is the relation of reality to art, and the comparison here may imply the father of Julian was being addressed along with his son. (The typescript bears some pencilled marks and comments of Clive's, mainly having to do with Virginia's punctuation, but occasionally querying a phrase or praising an image.) Continuing on elliptically about the problems of focus and impersonality that she was struggling with, Woolf touches on the main preoccupation of her late Edwardian reviews, essays, and biographical writings and connects it with one of her later literary aims:

> I should like to write a very subtle work on the proper writing of lives. What it is that you can write – and what writing is. It comes over me that I know nothing of the art; but blunder in a rash way after motive, and human character; and that I suppose is the uncritical British method; for I should choose my writing to be judged as a chiselled block, unconnected with my hand entirely.
> (*L*, I 325)

This desire of authors for objectivity or detachment is a familiar characteristic of modernism, with origins in Flaubert, Ibsen, James and others. As much as Eliot and Joyce, Woolf aspired to literary impersonality. It can be seen as an aspect of Bloomsbury's formalism, appearing even in Forster's essays (the Woolfs published his *Anonymity* pamphlet in 1925). That Woolf should be thinking about impersonality while writing autobiographical biography is significant, but that is not the only writing she was thinking about at this time. Earlier in her letter to Clive, she wrote,

> I dreamt last night that I was showing father the manuscript of

my novel; and he snorted, and dropped it on to a table, and I was very melancholy, and read it this morning, and thought it bad.

(L, I 325)

The proper, impersonal writing of lives was a matter for the arts of fiction and non-fiction.

Virginia's narrative of Vanessa's life begins and ends with Vanessa herself, though most of it is about two other women. Vanessa's Stephenesque honesty of mind and passion for art are noted practically from the nursery on: 'She might not see all, but she would not see what was not there.' It was Vanessa, for example, who disturbed her sister's contentment with seasonal moments that had 'power to flood the brain in a second' by being more aware of what the older Duckworth children were allowed to do. Trying to see her clearly, Virginia uses an appropriately pictorial image to convey

how our lives are pieces in a pattern and to judge one truly you must consider how this side is squeezed and that indented and a third expanded and none are really isolated. *(MB,* pp. 29–30)

In these opening pages Woolf is clearly present as a narrator. But she withdraws when what starts out as a portrait of the artist as young woman turns into elegiac pictures of her mother and half-sister. Death the spoiler of what had been so fair becomes the real subject. Vanessa's development is checked by the disastrous death of Julia Stephen, whose own life was ruined by the death of her young first husband until she married the widower Leslie Stephen, whose wife had also died young. Stella Duckworth's death after a few months of marriage is the last of the early deaths recorded. In the background of Woolf's text, however, is the death of Thoby Stephen two years before. Thoby is largely absent from Virginia's account, and Adrian is virtually unmentioned. The focus is on the lives, or rather the deaths of beautiful women; men come into it as they relate to them. Again there is a resemblance here to the *Mausoleum Book,* which after an autobiographical prelude focuses on Stephen's first wife, to a lesser extent on her sister, and then on Julia.

The portrait of 'your grandmother' fills out Chapter 1 of Vanessa's biography. The first of three that Woolf did of her mother, it is the most accomplished short biography she had yet written.

Vanessa agreed Virginia had given the best idea of what their mother had been like (20.iv.08, VB/pNY). Neither Maitland's 'conventional phrases' in his life of Leslie, nor his own 'noble lamentations' in the *Mausoleum Book* gave 'any semblance of a woman whom you can love', says the biographer herself (*MB*, p. 36). One reason was the lack of Julia's recorded words. The contrast with her husband, whose voluminous writings were always available, will occur again in the 'A Sketch of the Past'. Biography's limits here are those noted in some of Virginia's Edwardian reviews. (A footnote connects her mother's lost words with Mrs Carlyle's that she had mentioned in the reviews of her letters.) With only a few recalled phrases or scenes, Julia's daughter manages to represent the idea of a beautiful, sorrowful, vigorous, and practical woman, mother of seven children and the centre of 'that interminable and incongruous procession which is the life of a large family. . . . ' She exhausted herself in sympathetic philanthropy, for 'she was no aesthetic spectator, collecting impressions for her own amusement', says the narrator in an unspoken contrast with herself and Vanessa (p. 35). The vigour of their mother is conveyed in the rapidity of Virginia's 'flying narrative' and in images like 'she flung aside her religion' after her first husband's death (pp. 30, 32). An implicit literary analogy is used to trace Julia's change from 'the golden enchantments of Tennysonian sentiment' to her love for an agnostic man, whose keen intellect was 'always voyaging, as she must have thought, alone in ice-bound seas.' The allusion to Wordsworth's famous *Prelude* description of Newton's mind (' . . . for ever/Voyaging through strange seas of Thought alone' – III 62–3) suggests Julia's change to Leslie's Wordsworthian belief in the power of sorrow to quicken the feelings that were left (pp. 32, 35, 37, 46). Leslie is also viewed as Hardy had described him in 'The Schreckhorn': a mountain peak, of which Julia was humbly proud. In even more conventional imagery Virginia writes of the rosy mists of her mother's first rapture being replaced by a new love pure as starlight. The marriage was 'truly equal', 'ceaselessly valiant', and their life 'triumphant'. The equality is also compared to birdsong in which 'the high consonance, the flute voices of two birds in tune, was only reached by rich, rapid scales of discord and incongruity' – as in Perugino's fresco. And though it seemed now to the narrator and her subject that Julia might have compromised too much and Leslie been too exacting (both could be ruthless) theirs was nevertheless a life, 'consistently aiming at high things' (pp. 32–7). The altruistic tone and some imagery seem at odds here with the more modern pace of the narrative.

Vanessa was fifteen when the family experienced 'the greatest disaster that could happen'. As for the biographer, who reappears at the end of the chapter, she still sees Julia on more occasions than can be counted, 'closer than any of the living are, lighting our random lives as with a burning torch, infinitely noble and delightful to her children' (p. 40). Not until she transmuted that torch into a fictional lighthouse nearly twenty years later, did Woolf cease to be obsessed by her mother's presence (p. 80). A short transitional Chapter 2 then takes Vanessa's biography from her mother's death through her father's 'Oriental gloom' (p. 40) to the marble image of Stella Duckworth, whose Greek beauty was of a later, more decadent style than her mother's. The biographer returns desperately, she says, to the metaphor of marble for Stella's statuesque appearance and almost morbidly dependent affection for her mother, whom she now had to replace in the family. The third chapter gives the rest of Stella's brief life. Vanessa begins to come more into the story. George and even Gerald Duckworth also now offered the Stephen children more emotional relationships; the sentimental George could be an unwitting brute, she says a little later, but there is little suggestion here or in 'A Sketch of the Past' that anything really incestuous may have occurred. It is true that Woolf was writing Vanessa's biography, not her own, but one might expect in this private writing some less reticent indication of George's conduct; on Gerald's behaviour Woolf is completely silent. The view of Leslie Stephen is also meeker than in the later memoir, but there is still bitterness. His grief did not quicken their feelings for the living:

> but hideous as it was, obscured both living and dead; and for long did unpardonable mischief by substituting for the shape of a true and most vivid mother, nothing better than an unlovable phantom. (p. 45)

Yet there are passing moments of happiness with him. The Stephen children approached a more equitable relationship with their father than the devoted Stella was able to maintain. But the chief male in Chapter 3 is Stella's stout-skulled lover Jack Hills, who treats his future father-in-law as an encyclopedia to be kept on the shelf.

Vanessa had great respect for Hills; Virginia did not. His 'canine qualities glowing with their utmost expressiveness' are contrasted with those of Stella, who had 'one of those beautiful feminine natures which are quite without wishes of their own' (pp. 47–9). The lover's wishes prevailed over the father's, the family responded clamorously, the social world of the Stephens impinged, and they were married. Woolf's narrative flies over these events with great dexterity. (Stella and Jack gave her the first vision 'of love between man and woman' but she says this only in 'A Sketch of the Past' – p. 105.) Again disaster intervened; Stella fell ill, and death ends another chapter. 'Even now it seems incredible', says the biographer, bringing the past into the present (p. 53).

The last chapter focuses again on the life of 'your mother', whose development is now forced by her relationships with her father, George, and the grieving Jack Hills. 'She was but just eighteen, and when she should have been free and tentative, she was required to be definite and exact' (p. 54). More than anyone else in the family, Vanessa was desolated by Stella's death. But she had greater agility and determination than Stella, as she demonstrated in her contact with the men in her life. Vanessa was acclaimed by friends of the family as the inheritor of her mother's and half-sister's beauty. They spoke as if life were a melodramatic novel in which the new heroine was to be 'beautiful on the surface, but fatally insipid within'. Vanessa's biographer observes that if sometimes their life appeared as a work of art, 'more often it revealed a shapeless catastrophe, from which there could be no recovery' (p. 55). The representation of shapeless catastrophe depends, of course, on the shaping art with which Virginia writes her sister's life. After Stella's death, for example, Leslie Stephen is described as a some type of monster: 'there were signs at once which woke us to a sort of frenzy, that he was quite prepared to take Vanessa for his next victim'. She stood up to his irrational rages over household expenses and became very angry herself.

> We made him the type of all that we hated in our lives; he was the tyrant of inconceivable selfishness, who had replaced the beauty and merriment of the dead with ugliness and gloom.
>
> (p. 56)

Writing just four years after her father's death, Virginia admits that they were unjust in their bitterness, but still there was truth in their complaints. He was too old, they were too young. Death had spoiled all. The theme will be taken up more circumstantially and less guiltily thirty years later in 'A Sketch of the Past'. That a shift in point of view has now taken place in Woolf's narrative is parenthetically admitted. In the future, Vanessa Bell's son is told, 'this "we" must stand for your mother and me' (p. 57). Together they now suffered the stupidly virtuous, emotionally irresponsible behaviour of George Duckworth that foretold the sundering of their family. Together the sisters tried to console the grieving Jack Hills. Two unusual images associated with him here suggest an increased literary self-awareness in Woolf's auto-biographical biography. The first is a small, silent, enduring, fruitless tree in the garden that symbolises his sorrow to the biographer. The second image is a full-blown metaphysical allusion, complete with scientific reference. The sisters accompanied Hills to his home:

> we were to soothe the first shock of his home-coming, or to know something which we could not know else; for when you examine feelings with the intense microscope that sorrow lends, it is amazing how they stretch, like the finest goldbeater's skin, over immense tracts of substance. And we, poor children that we were, conceived it to be our duty evermore to go searching for these atoms, wherever they might lie sprinkled about the surface, the great mountains and oceans, of the world. It is pitiable to remember the hours we spent in such minute speculations.
>
> (pp. 58–9)

The fragments of Hills's torn life were thus to be atomically repaired. Goldbeater's skin, according to the *OED*, is animal membrane used to separate leaves of gold foil during beating, and also to cover wounds. The second meaning applies more directly here, but the first is relevant too and echoes John Donne's comparison of the lovers' separation as 'gold to airy thinness beat' in the poem relevantly titled 'A Valediction Forbidding Mourning'. From this extraordinary comparison Woolf turns to the difficulties that arose from this healing work. Hills began to take unwitting satisfaction in being with Vanessa, and Virginia started to feel jealous. She treasonably complained of Jack 'in the old way' – presumably about his canine qualities – and was met with silence by Vanessa. The 'we' of the last chapter of Vanessa's biography has now become an 'I' and a 'she'. And with Vanessa's silence, Virginia's life of her sister ends.

When Vanessa read the first two chapters of her biography she wrote to Virginia of the awful gloom that their early lives had, and how good the picture of their mother was; she now looked forward with interest to Virginia's description of the relations between herself and Jack Hills (20.iv.08, VB/pNY). But it was not until 'A Sketch of the Past' that Virginia wrote of how George and others (but not her father, who was free of such cant) were upset over the prospect of Vanessa illegally marrying her deceased half-sister's husband. Virginia was asked to intercede, and when she did, Vanessa bitterly accused her of taking their side. Virginia stops her early life of Vanessa before the hurt and confusion that resulted from this episode. The painful relations of the sisters on the subject of a man who might have been Vanessa's husband was too immediate a personal problem as well.

By focusing on Vanessa's life, Virginia was able to write about her own family experiences and thus prepare for the metamorphosis of them into her novels, the first of which she was simultaneously writing. 'The proper writing of lives' was, at this stage in her career, a concern that cuts across her fiction, reviews, essays, and autobiographical writings. By continuing Vanessa's memoirs for her, as it were, she created an original form, and also continued a tradition of Bloomsbury family biography. The biography of Vanessa enabled Virginia to distance herself enough to describe death in the family so effectively – women's death. In the oft-cited phrase, she is thinking back through her mothers in this autobiographical biography. Woolf went on to say in *A Room of One's Own*, however, that the androgynous writer's mind 'can think back through its fathers or through its mothers . . . ' (pp. 114, 146). She would do both in her last great memoir.

14 Leonard Woolf's Ceylon Writings

While Virginia Woolf was writing reviews and experimenting with forms of biography, while Lytton Strachey was also reviewing and trying to become a historian or a playwright, while Roger Fry and Desmond MacCarthy were establishing themselves as critics, and E. M. Forster was becoming recognised as an Edwardian novelist, Leonard Woolf was labouring in the Far East as an imperial civil servant. His seven years away from Bloomsbury resulted in a variety of writings – letters, official diaries, short stories, a novel, and, fifty years later, an autobiography. These works of and about Ceylon have more than just tangential relations to Bloomsbury. When examined together and in the context of the Group's literary history, they display a family resemblance to Bloomsbury's writings that extends from the Cambridge philosophy to the literature of imperialism.

The novel *The Village in the Jungle*, published in 1913, is still read for its Bloomsbury and Ceylon associations, yet it is *Growing: An Autobiography of the Years 1904–1911*, published in 1961, that is now the best known of Woolf's Ceylon writings and may be the most enduring. Its synoptic account of Woolf's experiences is based upon letters and diaries that he wrote in Ceylon. *Growing* also uses, and comments upon the fiction that Woolf set there. For these reasons it is helpful to reverse chronology here and use *Growing* as a literary frame in which to examine Woolf's various visions of Ceylon. The emphasis this way falls more revealingly on the spirit of place that animates these writings and conditions the development they describe.

Critical discussion of Leonard Woolf's Ceylon writings has been largely thematic because the settings of these works are so much their subjects. In all of the Ceylon writings what Woolf called his 'education as an anti-imperialist' is being conducted or described (*G*, p. 133). Considering these texts together, however, brings out the literary significance of their different genres. Biography, travel writing, imperial history, natural history, social psychology, political theory, literary commentary, all are mediated quite differently in these works through the forms, sometimes combined, of letter, diary, story, novel, and memoir. *Growing*, to start with, is not, despite its author's assertions, a candidly straightforwardly record of seven years in the Ceylon Civil Service. Rather it is an account moulded by a theory of autobiography. Woolf disclaims any simple truth-telling in his foreword. He has tried to tell all the truth, relying on memory as well as contemporary letters and diaries, but he has of course failed because of the ravages of time, and the unconscious on memory. In response to a criticism that *Sowing* was simplistic in its descriptions of the writer's reactions, Woolf stops in the middle of *Growing* to explain the purpose of autobiography:

> If one has the temerity to write an autobiography, then one is under an obligation not to conceal. The only point in an auto-biography is to give, as far as one can, in the most simple, clear, and truthful way, a picture, first of one's own personality and of the people whom one has known, and secondly of the society and age in which one has lived. To do this entails revealing as simply as possible one's own simplicity, absurdity, trivialities, nastiness. (*G*, p. 148)

The changes rung on the word *simple* here should not obscure the art of *Growing*. For all his partiality to Voltaire, Woolf's auto-biography here and elsewhere is partly inspired by Rousseau's artful *Confessions*. And between Rousseau's and Leonard Woolf's autobiographies lie the unsimple self-records of Mill, Ruskin, Adams, James, and Gosse, among others, in English alone. What matters, however, is not the adequacy of Leonard Woolf's theory of autobiography but its effect on his own work. *Growing*, as well as *Sowing, Beginning Again, Downhill All the Way* (where the double aim of the theory is repeated – p. 40) and *The Journey Not the Arrival Matters*, are memoirs of people Woolf has known and events he has experienced. These accounts are leavened with a mixture of self-justification and confessional frankness, and although simpli-fication and oversimplification recur in them, their truth-telling (slightly qualified by some disguised names) leaves the impression that the simplification is never a conscious concealment. Leonard Woolf's grouping together of one's personality and acquaintances in his notion of autobiography and then separating them from society and the age is a familiar Bloomsbury distinction. It is implicit in the epigraph of a French song that Woolf uses again as a refrain in the epilogue to *Growing* where he recounts his resignation:

Reprenez votre Paris;
J'aime mieux ma mie, o gué,
J'aime mieux ma mie!

The love for which his colonial Paris was well lost, came after he had returned on leave to London, but the disjunction of self and personal relations from society and the times persists throughout his Ceylon writing. It begins during the first chapter of *Growing* which is entitled 'The Voyage Out'.

II

In using the same title for his first chapter as Virginia Woolf had for her first novel, Leonard Woolf invokes the Bloomsbury context of his autobiography.[1] Life on a P. & O. steamer was very different from family life on the *Euphrosyne*. The truth-claims of the autobiographer are also very different from those of the novelist. The difficulties of telling the truth begin with the opening sentence where Leonard Woolf gets the month in which he sailed wrong (it was November not October 1904), and in the second paragraph he exaggerates, to ninety, the beautiful seventy-volume Baskerville edition of Voltaire (on whom he had published his first essay in the *Independent Review*) that he was taking to Ceylon along with a wire-haired fox-terrier and some green flannel collars. These mistakes would be insignificant except for Woolf's scrupulous efforts to be truthful, and they direct attention to the psychology that preoccupies the narrator at the beginning of *Growing*.

Sailing out to Ceylon is a traumatic rebirth at twenty-four; only his Voltaire and his dog accompanied Woolf from the old life. He paradoxically learns from his fellow passengers 'first how to get on with ordinary persons, and secondly that there are practically no

ordinary persons . . . ' (p. 12). As an example he cites an army
captain whom he persuades to stop beating his bed-wetting child.
Freud's *A Child is being Beaten* is referred to, though Leonard Woolf
had of course read none of his works in 1904. The captain,
surprisingly, has the makings of a companionable intellectual, but
not his hostile wife. Several pages later a quotation is given from
Jokes and their Relation to the Unconscious to explain the resentment of
a socially inferior business man who plays a humiliating practical
joke on Woolf and a fellow civil servant. In both instances the
psychological interest is inseparable from their social setting. The
four classes of British on the ship were a microcosm of imperial
society in both Ceylon and India: civil servants on top, officers next,
then planters, and at the bottom business men. This is the
'suburban' social structure immortalised in Kipling's stories (p. 17).
As *Growing* proceeds, the Freudian perspective combines with
epistemological thoughts about the nature of reality, while Woolf's
observations of colonial society become part of the wider scene of
imperialism. *Growing* is not, however, a therapeutic work of
self-analysis; Freud explains only the behaviour of others, not the
writer's.

The allusions to Freud in 'The Voyage Out' chapter exhibit
multiple temporality of *Growing*. The ageing narrator is telling the
pre-Freudian experiences of himself when twenty-four. In an earlier,
slightly fictionalised Memoir Club version of an episode in *Growing*
entitled 'Memoirs of an Elderly Man', Leonard Woolf maintained
that his elderly 'I' was 'an entirely different person' from the young
'I' of the story (p. 77).[2] If not entirely different in *Growing*, the
autobiographer needs, nevertheless, to be distinguished from the
central character of his narrative. In order to emphasise Woolf's
dual identity in *Growing*, the elderly autobiographer will sometimes be referred to here as 'Leonard Woolf', while the young
imperialist in early twentieth-century Ceylon who is the subject of
his autobiography will be called 'L. S. Woolf' – the name he used in
his early writings.

The second chapter of *Growing*, entitled 'Jaffna', occupies nearly
half the book. Set mainly in that northern town, it describes the
initiation of L. S. Woolf into the Ceylon Civil Service. The narrative
moves smoothly between descriptions of his shifting states of mind
and the exotic, meanly governed East. His sensory experience of
Colombo is rendered in the chapter's first paragraph, for instance,
and then reflected upon in the second:

There was something extraordinarily real and at the same time unreal in the sights and sounds and smells . . . in those first hours and days, and this curious mixture of intense reality and unreality applied to all my seven years in Ceylon. (p. 21)

The use of evaluative Apostolic terms having to do with the nature of reality has already been noted in the letters that Woolf wrote to Strachey about E. M. Forster's early novels. The terms recur almost obsessively in the Ceylon writings as Leonard Woolf relates how as a young man he sought to connect his Cambridge education with the colonial one that followed it. Woolf's reflections on the realities and unrealities of imperialism are attempts to understand its worth. But there was more to his brooding than the ethical principles of G. E. Moore. He had intervened in a Strachey Apostle paper around 1905 to argue from *Principia Ethica* that England ought perhaps to rule the world (see p. 136), and later wrote to Strachey of using Moore successfully in public business (11.ii.05, LS/pBL).[3] But in accounting later in *Growing* for the bitter rage and lamentation of his letters to Strachey, Leonard Woolf supposes 'that at the back of my mind, and in its depths, I wanted to be a writer' (*G*, p. 172). He found himself instead back at school, as it were, an intelligent cadet concealing again his intellect and fearfulness beneath the carapace of a promising civil servant. This literary ambition is not much discussed by Leonard Woolf in his autobiographies, perhaps because it was eventually channelled into the writing of literary and political criticism. Yet the incipient, frustrated author that L. S. Woolf felt himself to be, illuminates his concern with the reality of his experience in Ceylon. Literature conditions his perceptions and descriptions there of himself, his acquaintances, their society and their times. In this and other aspects, *Growing* is the most literary of Leonard Woolf's autobiographies.

The mixture of intense reality and unreality that began in Colombo is frequently symbolised by Leonard Woolf in imagery of dreams and especially plays that he says were 'the psychological background or climate of my whole life in Ceylon.' In these images he is both the excited dreamer or actor and a somewhat cynically amused spectator (pp. 21–2). Against the crudely exotic scenery of jungle and sea, a cast of stereotypical literary characters played out the decline of British imperialism. 'All the English out here', Woolf wrote to Strachey, 'are continually saying things of which, if you saw them in a novel, you would say, "people don't say those sort of things"' (*L*, p. 81). The characters derived from Austen, Dickens, Flaubert, James, Hardy, Conrad, and, above all, Kipling. 'I could never make up my mind', Leonard Woolf wrote in *Growing*,

> whether Kipling had moulded his characters accurately in the image of Anglo-Indian society or whether we were moulding our characters accurately in the image of a Kipling story. (p. 46)

L. S. Woolf did not know that he was at the fag-end of empire, though Leonard Woolf does. There are no allusions to the Boer War or to the Russo-Japanese one which occurred during his first year in Ceylon and signalled to subject peoples throughout the world that the white race was not invincible. Later Leonard Woolf dated the period of complete revolt against European imperialism from 1905 (*IC*, p. 57).[4] As 'a very innocent, unconscious imperialist', who cared about the Dreyfus affair at Cambridge but little else in politics, L. S. Woolf, like others in Bloomsbury, came to understand the dilemmas of imperialism only gradually (*G*, p. 25).

Woolf experienced very early what he later understood, along with Forster, as the central dilemma of British imperialism: the isolation of the imperialist. This was increased by the personal isolation that L. S. Woolf endured in Ceylon as a Cambridge Apostle and a Jew. The account in *Growing* of his introduction to Jaffna society describes his former self as a quiet, formidable, slightly eccentric young man, who was good at games, very hard-working, and arrogant. Never mentioned, despite the allusions to Dreyfus and Kipling, whose Indian stories are anti-Semitic, is how the colonial enclave responded to L. S. Woolf as an assimilated Jew. (His official duties, for example, required his occasional attendance at church.) Letters to Moore and Strachey before he came out to Ceylon reveal that among the reasons he joined the civil service rather than becoming a school master were Moore's ethics, the pay, and his uncertainty of how Christians would welcome him as a teacher of their children. Jews, of course, have been involved in British imperialism from Disraeli to Israel; in 1904, one was even Governor of Hong Kong, where Woolf might have been sent instead of Ceylon. Yet Woolf's silence on his Jewish identity in Ceylon seems odd. Only occasionally in letters to Strachey does he obliquely refer to it. To the end of his life he insisted, as he wrote to the novelist Dan Jacobson, that he could recall no instance in

Ceylon when being a Jew had the slightest influence on his career or social life (*L*, p. 566). Some of L. S. Woolf's isolation in Ceylon was welcome. He enjoyed the romantic, passion-purging solitudes of the sea and jungle and describes them again and again in *Growing* and *The Village in the Jungle*. Ceylon had long been regarded as a paradisal island. Serendip was one of its early names, and at Mannar, Woolf visited the enormous mounds that are supposed to be the graves of Adam and Eve (*G*, p. 121). Edenic associations recur in his Ceylon writings. Related to them is Woolf's lifelong fondness for animals whose 'strange minds, fears, affections' make nonsense of all anthropocentric philosophies and religions (pp. 100–1). (Again an aspect of Leonard Woolf's identity seems relevant here: his very name echoed an animal's; Virginia and Leonard liked to call themselves 'the Wolves', as did their friends; and a wolf's head was the device of the Hogarth Press.) Yet the isolation of the imperialists was ultimately disastrous, not just for the people they were governing but for themselves.

Here the literary sources of Leonard Woolf's experience in Ceylon expand from Kipling to James, Conrad and perhaps Maugham, whose Eastern stories did not begin to appear until the 1920s. It may seem surprising how little Woolf writes of the non-white population in his pictures and stories of Jaffna's imperial and suburban society, though he was engaged in governing and being served by them. But this only reflects, after all, the social reality of his time at Jaffna. It would be different in Hambantota.

III

E. M. Forster in his review of *Growing* found that the central thread of Woolf's conversion to anti-imperialism frequently disappeared; the book was best read, he thought,

> as a series of episodes, fugitive dramas, bitter semi-comedies, *aperçus*, wisecracks, and most particularly for its descriptions of the horrors and the lovelinesses of untamed nature. ('Sahib')

Certainly *Growing* is an episodic autobiography, but the chapter on Jaffna might also be described in terms of plot, setting, and character. The setting is a distended village surrounded by a flat, dry landscape of scrub jungle, sand, and sea. The isolated enclave of white characters governing the Tamils there is made up of people such as a choleric captain or foul-mouthed police superintendent out of Kipling, an outrageous government agent's wife from Austen, a futile magistrate imagined by Conrad, a subtle Jamesian government agent, and finally the fatalistic Hardyesque Ceylonese. Sometimes the literary sources of these characters are explicitly identified by Leonard Woolf and sometimes just implied through the representation of them. The plot of 'Jaffna' essentially consists of Woolf's anti-imperial education, but here the traditional categories of fiction disappear in the narration's temporal and generic mixture. Old Leonard Woolf's account is based to some extent on young L. S. Woolf's correspondence with Strachey, as is acknowledged in the Foreword to *Growing*. But in using these letters a difficulty arises which the author attributes to the combining of genres. The tone of the autobiography is quite equable, while his letters to Strachey are not. Twice in *Growing* Leonard Woolf explains the glooms and rages of his correspondence resulted partly from L. S. Woolf's feelings of failure in leaving Bloomsbury, and partly from the nature of letters. The letter-writer, he believes, wants

> to reproduce as vividly as possible – to make the reader feel as deeply as possible – a mood, only one of the many moods which chase one another all day and all night long through our minds and bodies. Even to ourselves we habitually exaggerate the splendours and miseries of our life and forget in the boredom of Wednesday the ecstasy of Tuesday – and vice versa. (p. 62)

This description of shifting moods in *Growing* also resembles the life of Monday or Tuesday as described in the shifting, ordinary and extraordinary moods of Virginia Woolf's famous sketches. Strachey, for his part, wondered if any future readers of their letters would find their gloominess justifiable (LW/L, p. 112).

The differences in tone between the narrative of *Growing* and the letters to Strachey, Sydney-Turner and others are of subject as well as mood and viewpoint. L. S. Woolf's correspondence brings out that aspect of autobiography that Leonard Woolf said was to give a simple, truthful picture of one's personality and acquaintances, rather than the social and historical dimensions of his experience, in which for example Strachey, immersed in the history of Indian imperialism, would have been interested. Yet more important than the generic difference, is the disparity in time between the autobiography and the letters written from Ceylon. Leonard Woolf thought that even in the letters to Strachey 'one sees between the lines interest, fascination, even cheerfulness breaking through' (*G*, p. 62). This judgement may be tinged a little by the sentimentality with which age regards youth. Again there is a literary analogue, this time in Conrad. In the final chapter of his last volume of autobiography, Woolf describes revisiting Sri Lanka in 1960, just before he wrote *Growing*, and he quotes from Marlow's paean at the end of 'Youth' to the good old time of youth at sea as an expression of his own nostalgic, even lachrymose memories of Ceylon (*JNAM*, p. 198).

When L. S. Woolf first arrived at Jaffna, however, the first work he was given to do bored him so that he demanded something more interesting from his acquiescent superior, W. T. Southorn. Southorn was also his housemate and later brother-in-law, marrying Bella Sidney Woolf who had stayed for a time with Leonard at Kandy. Leonard Woolf says very little about his brother-in-law, who eventually became Governor of Gambia, or for that matter about his sister, who lived for years in Ceylon and published two books about it.[5] (Bella had some success as a children's author and offered Leonard £40 from the proceeds of a serial she was to do so that he could read for the Bar instead of going to Ceylon – LW/L, p. 50.) The new work that Woolf was given at Jaffna, which is described in letters to Strachey, involved arbitrating a dispute between priests, inspecting a leaking ship carrying government salt, and taking depositions from sick or dying men in squalid hospitals. Though always on the side of law and order, and against the brutalities of life in its natural state, Woolf writes of his disillusionment with the methods of justice in Ceylon – a theme he will take up in *The Village in the Jungle*. (After one sordid deposition, he told Strachey he was thinking of writing an anonymous article on 'Modern Humanitarianism in the East' for the *Independent Review* – *G*, pp. 77–8.) Still these scenes are not really real to him; they are merely part of the 'futile fullness' of his days. True reality consists of things such as a view of native rowers outlined against the white sea like praying ghosts or what Strachey writes about in his letters from England (p. 59). In some of Woolf's letters to Strachey which are not quoted in *Growing*, he apologises for being degradingly interested in his work (the work ethic is one thing Woolf might have agreed with Kipling about). One letter gets him a scolding from Strachey, who has been excited by his imperialist reading (10.viii.05, LS/pT). To Keynes, Woolf wrote 'I lead a life of strenuous unreality relieved by flashes of degradation' (*L*, p. 107). Moods of despair in Ceylon, transient or not, come through strongly in other unquoted letters to Strachey and Sydney-Turner. Receiving *Euphrosyne* and the early novels of Forster increased his disillusionment. In the letter to Strachey commenting on *Where Angels Fear to Tread*, he quoted Sir Thomas Browne:

> . . . If one were really supreme, one would be always happy, happy 'in the ecstasy of being ever', but the worst & deserved unhappiness is to know what supremacy is & to know that you aren't supreme. (28.x.05, LS/pBL)

The next year he announced to Sydney-Turner that he had finally solved the problem of happiness, which was the Victorian one of perpetual work requiring no thought (26.iii.06, LW/pH).

When Southorn was transferred in 1905, Woolf moved in with a police magistrate named Dutton, whom he interrupts his narrative to characterise more fully than anyone else in *Growing* except his last superior at Jaffna. The sketch of Dutton, which Leonard Woolf faintly fictionalised and published in 'Memoirs of an Elderly Man', reads like the background of a Conrad story, with Woolf in the role of Marlow. He meditates on Dutton's psychology, his inferior social standing and education, his sexual *naïveté*; fragments of his incomprehensible, pathetic life are presented, as Woolf becomes more involved in them. There are also touches of Forster in the character sketch. Leonard Woolf remarks that Dutton always reminded him of Leonard Bast in *Howards End* (*G*, p. 63), which shows the temporal shifts of the narrative here, since the novel was not published until 1910. (There are also reminiscences of the landscape in *A Passage to India*.) Dutton's pitiful, perhaps impotent marriage to a missionary results in another wife's hostility to Woolf, who had introduced them. Dutton's reams of fairy poetry are unlike anything Bast ever wrote, however; indeed, his whole absurd career as a police magistrate could have happened only in the colonies.

Dutton's possible impotence is one of the few places in *Growing* where some of the sexual significance of British imperialism is mentioned. Readers of *Sowing* who may have remembered Woolf's promise (p. 81) to relate in a later chapter how he lost his virginity at the age of twenty-five in Jaffna, might be forgiven for missing the account in *Growing*. In its entirety, it consists of his smiling at a Eurasian girl and being asked by a boy if he wants her to come to his bungalow that night: 'I very foolishly said yes, and she came and spent the night with me'. As magistrate, Dutton later encountered the girl in court and found her quite pure, to the considerable amusement of the Jaffnese. This trial is Leonard Woolf's excuse for mentioning the girl at all (pp. 67–8). As L. S. Woolf commented to Strachey, the pleasure of debauchery had been 'grossly exaggerated' (*L*, p. 102).

A later encounter with a prostitute also described in a letter to Strachey is connected with Forster. Shortly before leaving Jaffna, Woolf wrote that only two things interested him at the moment: women, in the form of a prostitute he had been offered but was too dejected to do anything about except leave her money, and Forster's mind which he had been encountering in *The Longest Journey*. The association of a prostitute and Forster's novel mentioned in this letter may have led to the story about sex in Ceylon that Woolf wrote with two others around this time or shortly afterwards. Collected together under the title *Stories of the East* in 1921, these texts relate variously to his Jaffna experiences, though none is mentioned in his autobiography. Looking at them before going on with *Growing*, one can see how Woolf selectively used his various writings about Ceylon in his autobiography.

IV

Stories of the East was hand-printed for the Hogarth Press by the Woolfs. On its handsome yellow cover by Carrington a red tiger walks between palm trees by a row of flowers while other flowers and pineapples float round (see Plate II). According to a flyer from the Hogarth Press, the collection contained three stories of Ceylon that are 'studies in uncompromising realism'. There are no tigers in the stories, or even any pineapples (and one of the stories is set in India). Yet in a way the cover is representative of the stories' realism, which is quite compromised throughout.

The first of the stories, 'A Tale Told by Moonlight', tells of an English author's love for a Ceylonese prostitute. In the heavily Conradian frame of the story of a middle-aged group of men musing by a moonlit river about love, a cynic called Jessop then tells a story to show that writers are responsible for sentimentalising the rare real

Plate II Carrington: Wrappers, Leonard Woolf, *Stories of the East* (1921)

thing that is love. In the tale an etiolated English novelist by the name of Reynolds visits a Colombo brothel and becomes infatuated with a Sinhalese called Celestinahami; he tries suicide but cannot figure out how to load the pistol, whereupon his friend Jessop, who took him to the brothel as a lesson in real life, points out that the girl can be bought for a modest sum. The happy couple retire to a seaside bungalow, and the infatuation shifts from Reynolds, who discovers Celestinahami has nothing behind her beautiful eyes, to the girl, whose animal-like worship for the novelist drives him away and her to suicide.

Hackneyed, sentimental and without any of Conrad's complex irony, the story is another comment on the relation of literature to life that Woolf kept returning to in his letters to Strachey, especially those on Forster's novels. Its main interest for the literary history of Bloomsbury lies in the narrator's view of the novelist. Jessop had been to school and college with Reynolds, whom he describes as

> a thin feeble looking chap, very nervous, with a pale face and long pale hands. He was bullied a good deal at school; he was what they call a smug. I knew him rather well; there seemed to me to be something in him somewhere, some power of feeling under the nervousness and shyness. I can't say it ever came out, but he interested me.

Jessop went East, while Reynolds stayed home and wrote novels.

> I read them; very romantic they were too, the usual ideas of men and women and love. But they were clever in many ways, especially psychologically, as it was called. He was a success, he made money.
> I used to get letters from him about once in three months. . . . He knew a good deal about how other people think, the little tricks and mannerisms of life and novels, but he didn't know how they felt; I expect he had never felt anything himself, except fear and shyness: he hadn't really ever known a man, and he had certainly never know a woman. (*SE*, pp. 9–10)

The resemblance of Reynolds to E. M. Forster in these descriptions has been noted by Elizabeth Heine (EMF/*HD*, p. xv). Jessop is distanced from Woolf in the tale by the narrator, yet 'A Tale Told by

Moonlight' can be seen as a fictive extension of his commentary on Forster's early novels in the letters to Strachey and Sydney-Turner. Jessop refers to one of Reynolds's psychological novels that preaches the facing of facts and then living life to the uttermost. Whether this is an allusion to *The Longest Journey* or not, the comment in the story about Reynolds's mind interesting the narrator echoes the conclusion of Woolf's letter about that novel (see p. 253). Like the letters about Forster, the tale is dismissive but still grudgingly admiring of Reynolds. He is described a little confusingly as someone who had perhaps never felt anything yet possessed 'the real thing', which is the 'rare power to feel' (p. 16). Reynolds's power of feeling also seems related to Woolf's arguing for the primary importance of imagination in his correspondence with Strachey about realism in literature and elsewhere (29.ix.07, LS/pBL). Yet the clichéd love of Reynolds and Celestinahami is psychologically so unrealistic that it is difficult to find much consistency between L. S. Woolf's theory and practice of realism. And it was Forster, of course, rather than Kipling or Conrad or Woolf, who wrote a great novel of British imperial and sexual relations.

The third of the *Stories of the East* is a slight, non-realistic satire of two Ceylonese Brahmans who lose caste, one by fishing and the other by digging a well; generations later their descendants are still enduring the consequences. (It was at Mannar, near India, that Woolf wrote ironically to Strachey about the 'stupendousness' of the British Empire, where thousands of rupees are spent to irrigate a waste land whose high caste inhabitants would rather starve than carry earth on their heads, 'and really no one knows or cares a damn whether anything is done at all' – 29.vii.06, LS/pBL.)

'Pearls and Swine', the second story and most interesting of the three, takes place at the pearl fishery so memorably described in the Jaffna chapter of *Growing*. After convalescing from typhoid fever, L. S. Woolf was asked to help administer the triennial gathering of oysters on the northwest coast of Ceylon. (Woolf's hospitalisation exemplifies the racial isolation of colonialism in Ceylon, for his Tamil nurse refused even to touch him and he had to take his own temperature; however, his American doctor was more successful than the English ones attending Thoby Stephen, who died of typhoid a year later in London.)

The pearl fishery is illustrated with more photographs than anything else in *Growing*. It was a pure exercise in economic imperialism. Five whites supervised twenty to thirty thousand Asians diving for oysters and then auctioned off two-thirds of the divers' catch for the government. The oysters rotted for days before their pearls were collected. The stink, heat, flies, and endless hours of choosing the government's share, arbitrating Tamil–Arab disputes, and guarding against fire and looting in the temporary town were all part of a six-weeks' ordeal that still fascinated him. Woolf's complete recovery from typhoid at the fishery is one of his several rebirths in *Growing*. He clearly enjoyed controlling thousands of noisy Arabs with only a walking stick and a loud voice. Much could be said against the bleak colonial rule of Ceylon, he observes in the midst of his narrative, but adds 'one of the good things about it, however, was the extraordinary absence of the use of force in everyday life and government' (p. 92). This is one of the few direct remarks Woolf makes on the Jaffna part of his anti-imperial education, and it marks the distance between his Ceylon and Sri Lanka today. How British rule kept the potential racial violence of the island under control is shown a little more in the Hambantota chapter, where the dismalness of colonialism is also more manifest.

In a letter to Strachey quoted in *Growing*, toward the end of his pearl fishery account, L. S. Woolf contrasts the Arab divers, whom he admittedly prefers, with the Tamils. Their humanity and morale appeal more to this Semitic imperialist than the separateness and squabbles of the Dravidians. And as if to illustrate the difference, Woolf closes the fishery episode with the description of a dead Arab diver that he says he wrote forty years ago. The diver is brought to the shore, his feet sticking out starkly over the shoulders of the four men carrying him; the dead man's brother sits in the sand covered with sackcloth:

I heard him weeping. It was very silent, very cold and still on the shore in the early dawn. A tall figure stepped forward, it was the Arab sheik, the leader of the boat. He laid his hand on the head of the weeping man and spoke to him calmly, eloquently, compassionately. I didn't understand Arabic, but I could understand what he was saying. The dead man had lived, had worked, had died. He had died working, without suffering, as men should desire to die. He had left a son behind him. The speech went on calmly, eloquently, I heard continually the word Khallas – all is finished. I watched the figures outlined against the grey sky – the long lean outline of the corpse with the toes sticking up so straight and stark, the crouching huddled figure of the weeping man, and the tall, upright sheik standing by his side. They were motionless, sombre, mysterious, part of the grey sea, of the grey sky. (p. 96)

As dawn suddenly breaks, the figures move down the shore with the body, and the protruding feet are mentioned again in a concluding refrain. The alliterative, repetitive prose that Woolf quotes from himself is more poetic than anything else in the prevailing plain style of *Growing*. There is no indication, however, that the description comes from fiction, where it is one of two contrasting accounts of deaths at the end of the story 'Pearls and Swine'.[6]

At the beginning of Woolf's fictional dramatic monologue about the pearl fishery, we have again one of Conrad's narrators, recently back from the East, telling of a group of men in the smoking room of a Cornwall resort hotel. In response to the ignorant imperialist views of a stockjobber and an archdeacon, another narrator – a commissioner with thirty years in India, the last of them in charge of a district as large as England – offers a story that illustrates their opinions through characters at a pearl fishery, which is located in India to disguise its autobiographical source, perhaps. The various views expressed in 'Pearls and Swine' are worth describing because the tale is Woolf's most outspoken pre-war text on imperialism.

The stockjobber's attitude is that there has been too much namby-pamby liberalism in the East; the people must be given schools, roads, medicine and so forth, but also should be strongly ruled in a way that shows whose race is master there. Much as he deplores violence, the liberal archdeacon agrees that it is impossible to impose civilisation on India without some disturbance, for things may have been going a little too fast. As the superior race we must guide their feet, through missionary societies and the idealistic young men who go out there to rule. In the tale the archdeacon's representative is a confident young man, just out from England, who is prepared to run India by the book. The experience of the fishery reduces him to tears and nausea; assisting in the process is the allegorical alcoholic Mr White, failed planter, pearl-dealer, etc. White expresses the stockjobber's imperial notions, when the delirium tremens allows him to. White's screaming dissolution at the end of the story is heavily contrasted with the dignified ceremony that follows an Arab diver's death, the description of which Leonard Woolf used again in *Growing*.

The origins of White's character are partly autobiographical, partly literary. He may have been suggested by the swindler Woolf mentions encountering at the end of 'Jaffna'. The *louche* white man 'gone under' is a commonplace in Eastern fiction, but the characterisation in 'Pearls and Swine' seems to have a particular and significant source. In his delirious death throes, White retells the history of his life and shocks the commissioner by 'the cold, civilised, corrupted cruelty' of what he had done to the natives:

> His remorse was the most horrible thing . . . the remorse of fear – fear of punishment, of what was coming, of death, of the horrors, real horrors and phantom horrors of madness. (p. 40)

White's life and death obviously derive from Kurtz's end in 'Heart of Darkness'.

Woolf's factual and fictive versions of the pearl fishery converge in the description of the Arab's funeral. A background comparison of the Arabs and the Tamils in the autobiography replaces the tale's foreground contrast of Arabs and whites. In the quoted description of *Growing*, the narrator of the story is merged with the reminiscing, eighty-year-old former public man of *Growing*, whose views of imperialism must have altered considerably from the commissioner's. (There may be a little of L. S. Woolf in the young assistant as well.) Perhaps this is why Leonard Woolf does not mention the source of his description.[7] By 1960 the pearls and the swine of imperialism had changed considerably. Though the commissioner's views are not given in the story – he just exposes the ignorant racism of the others – he gives the impression of a pragmatic imperialist, doing the best job he can under the circumstances, without glorifying it through theories of white supremacy or inquiring much into the circumstances themselves. Two Tamil proverbs flank his narrative; the first ridicules the ignorance of the business man and the clergyman, and the last says all is dark to a cat with its head in a pot – which leaves the pessimism of the tale inconclusive. 'Pearls and Swine' is finally not so much a critique of imperialism as of some of its assumptions. Even the narrator of *Growing* makes no suggestion that the pearl fishery might have been managed more fairly and efficiently.

Despite its melodramatic touches, 'Pearls and Swine' is certainly more successful in its realism than 'A Tale Told by Moonlight'. Again there is a connection with Forster, this time a comment by him on Woolf's fiction. 'Pearls and Swine' is apparently the story Woolf sent Forster for advice in 1912. Forster suggested that the story be sent to the *English Review* (no longer being edited by Ford) as a magazine that would pay for excrement and erections in fiction. He made some criticisms of the title, long introduction, double point of view, and tone of the story, which reminded him a little of the scold in Kipling. He also praised the description of the two deaths at the end but said the story left him peevish, as Conrad did, and wondered why Woolf wanted to stay in England. On reconsideration Forster did not think it mattered if one European scolded another and judged the story with its background of wild beauty 'very fine'. He considered Leonard Woolf a good writer and offered his critical services any time (EMF/pNY, LW/pS). 'Pearls and Swine' was not published in the *English Review* or any other magazine, it seems, but some of Forster's suggestions may have been adopted. That Leonard Woolf even turned to Forster for criticism suggests a change in his canons of realism.[8]

V

Autobiographical fact and realistic fiction mix more complexly at Hambantota, where the third part of *Growing* is set. Before going there as Assistant Government Agent, L. S. Woolf had been transferred to Kandy in the luxuriant high country of central Ceylon. Woolf had returned to Jaffna from the pearl fishery to find the new Government Agent F. H. Price in charge. Next to Dutton, the portrait of Price is the fullest in *Growing*, and it seems influenced more by James now than Conrad. Price is characterised as a highly intelligent, slightly mad snob whose complete lack of imagination prevented his maturing into 'the world of reality' (*G*, p. 116). Price was also lazily dependent upon and quite fond of his hard-working, equally intelligent office assistant. Woolf described to Strachey how Price kept him from being made Assistant Government Agent at Mannar, where for a month he had thoroughly enjoyed being the acting agent and only white man in 400 square miles. Price manipulated a delay in this appointment and then offered him the opportunity of accepting it, knowing he would not without Price's approval.

He took his own way, quite wonderfully, for it showed that he had grasped my position absolutely. . . . I was fascinated by watching his method. My whole object now is to force him to ask me the reason for my present coldness: but I think he is too wily.

(*L*, pp. 126–7; LS/pBL)

Woolf admired Price with reservations and shared his passion for games or he would not have played these Jamesian charades with him. From Price he says he learned two valuable lessons in administration. One was to answer, on the day they arrive, all letters that can be immediately answered. The other was 'never to use two words where you can express your meaning clearly in one' (*L*, p. 107). Price himself seemed able to use one word where anyone else would need ten (except perhaps Leslie Stephen who gave Virginia Woolf similar lessons in writing – VW/*CE*, IV 80). Woolf's concise prose appears first in his official Hambantota diaries, and this style may have hindered his success as a civil servant. Plain speaking seldom leads to places of high thinking in bureaucracies

Something else in Woolf's make-up may have responded to Price's harsh administrative methods. After discussing how he forced his clerks to implement Price's rule about correspondence, Leonard Woolf makes an assessment of his own unpopular reputation as 'a strict and ruthless civil servant' (p. 109). Some Tamils liked his scrupulous administrative methods but in his two years at Jaffna the Tamil Association twice asked the government to dismiss him. Once was for supposedly striking a lawyer with his whip while riding in town with Price. The false accusation shocked him, he says in *Growing*, and a twinge of doubt entered his imperial soul as to whether he and his administrative kind belonged on horseback at all in Jaffna (*G*, pp. 113–14). The twinge of doubt became an ache of uncertainty after Hambantota.

In Kandy, Woolf's education as an anti-imperialist is described again in somewhat discontinuous psychological and social ways. Going to Kandy is another rebirth, and Freud is evoked once more, this time for his theory of how the civilised child must renounce instinctive desire. A new carapace was needed in an environment where landscape, race, religion, and colonial society were all new. Life in the high-country jungle was now, in the words of Charles Elton's poem, 'full of trees and changing leaves'. These words haunted Woolf in Ceylon, and make *Growing* oddly echo *To the Lighthouse* at times (pp. 27–8, 132). The Europeanised planter society reminded him unpleasantly of Kipling's Anglo-Indian characters, but the Sinhalese were friendlier than the Tamils, and their Buddhism more congenial than Hinduism. It was much more satisfying to rule the feudal Kandyans than administer the endlessly irritating Jaffnese.

Writing to Strachey after visiting a Kandyan village in the rain where he was greeted as a feudal chief with a torchlight procession and prostrations of loyalty by the villagers, Woolf remarked that the non-Europeanising of nations was the only way to govern the East, where each race was to be left 'as it was before Adam'. The imperialist attitudes of L. S. and Leonard Woolf are quite skilfully balanced here and elsewhere in the Kandy and Hambantota chapters of his autobiography. Leonard Woolf has been reproached by some critics for enjoying his imperial work too much. Certainly the young man liked feudalism from the top, but the old narrator of *Growing* finds the remark about races before Adam 'a curious and somewhat exaggerated idea', and he goes on to describe the widening split in L. S. Woolf's imperialism:

> . . . as time went on, I became more and more ambivalent, politically schizophrenic, an anti-imperialist who enjoyed the fleshpots of imperialism, loved the subject peoples and their way of life, and knew from the inside how evil the system was beneath the surface for ordinary men and women. (pp. 157–9)

Even in the fleshpots, reality, or rather unreality, kept intruding. How cynical it was of history to make him, a sophisticated graduate of St Paul's and Trinity, the representative of 'Edward VII by the Grace of God in the village of Urugala on September 14th, 1907' (p. 158). As a consequence of 'the inveterate empiricism of British imperialism', this twenty-six-year-old representative, whose sexual experience seems to have amounted to one night with a Jaffna prostitute and another encounter in Colombo described only as 'curious' (p. 154), found himself holding legal inquiries into such fascinating marriage and divorce customs of the Kandyans as polyandry (p. 164).

The unrealities of imperialism recur in the Kiplingesque postures of the civil servants, soldiers, and planters at Kandy. Woolf's relationship with a planter's daughter, to whom he gives the name Rachel, also made him act like an Anglo-Indian out of *Plain Tales from the Hills*. (His relationship with Rachel carried over to his

Hambantota years but the spirit of place more than time provides the narrative basis of *Growing*.) In the rather digressive 'Kandy' chapter Rachel becomes the occasion for some observations on the mind of women that bear on Bloomsbury. In Woolf's letters to Strachey there are recurrent strains of general misanthropy and particular misogyny: women are indecent, and the colonial ones in Ceylon 'are all whores or hags or missionaries or all three . . . ' (*L*, p. 74). It is not surprising to find him agreeing with Strachey that it did not matter whether women had the vote or not because of his growing disbelief in democracy – a disbelief fostered by the hypocrisy of imperialism that told the inhabitants they are equals yet treated them as inferiors (p. 125).

Later in his letters L. S. Woolf finds women nicer, 'but they have just the feelings bare, they don't I think have the contortions of introspection afterwards. . . . They are merely played on' (29.xii.07, LS/pBL). The old autobiographer, however, writes of his attraction not just to the bodies but the minds of women because they seem to him 'gentler, more sensitive, more civilized'. He is not thinking here, he says, only of extraordinary women like Cleopatra (what could Woolf know of her mind?) or writers like Jane Welsh Carlyle, Jane Austen, and Virginia Woolf. Ordinary, even stupid, vain, tiresome women too have this quality of the female mind, which may be partly the result of their upbringing; it is a quality that gives him romantic and sentimental pleasure (*G*, pp. 151–2). Leonard Woolf's account of his relationship with Rachel in the lush hills of Kandy is somewhat different from the description to be found in a depressed letter of L. S. Woolf to Strachey that announces he is done for as regards England and happiness. He tells Strachey that he is in love with Rachel (though this is denied in *Growing*); he has no intention of marrying her, and wonders if he's really only in love with intrigue and her cow-like eyes. The letter ends, like so many to Strachey, with a cry of despair: 'God, the futility & mania of existence sickens me' (*L*, p. 134).

The Kipling world of Kandy could also become theatrically unreal in episodes like those of viewing of the Buddha's tooth or arranging a Kandy dance performance to impress the Acting Governor's paramour – which resulted, Woolf was convinced, in his promotion to Hambantota as the youngest Assistant Government Agent in Ceylon. The viewing of the sacred Buddha's tooth is presented almost in the form of a tableau. The actors were the Acting or 'pseudo-Government Agent' L. S. Woolf (*G*, p. 140); the visiting Empress Eugénie, relict of Napoleon III, and her little make-believe court; the Acting Governor of Ceylon, Sir Hugh Clifford; the tooth's guardian, an extraordinarily costumed Ratema-hatmaya; and the three-inch tooth itself, which looked more like a devil's canine than a god's. Despite his irreverence, Woolf is quite sympathetic to Buddhism in *Growing* and *The Village in the Jungle*. Its theology or metaphysics he thought a dream, but still preferable to the repellent polytheism of Hinduism, whose symbolism he came to understand later but whose followers and superstitions he never liked. The monotheism of Muhammadanism, while it bore a family resemblance to Judaism, was too formalistic and too harsh with heretics. Buddhism was gentle, humane, contemplative, unworldly, and its priests wise or amusing (pp. 159–64). Woolf is offering here an irreligious Bloomsbury view of these religions, though it was not Forster's in his Indian writings.

Extreme reality, in contrast to the Buddha's tooth and its beholders, characterised the executions L. S. Woolf had to preside over at Kandy. These are described in bloody detail as part of the truthful picture of Edwardian colonial administration in Ceylon, and also as an illustration of the barbarity of capital punishment (as it is in George Orwell's similar but more eloquent account of a colonial hanging). The description in *Growing* closely follows an account of four hangings in a letter to Strachey, where the conclusions drawn are quite different. The letter begins with questioning the supremacy of Lady Mary Wortley Montagu that Strachey had asserted in the *Independent Review* (see p. 23) because supremacy, like experience in Forster's novels, does not really exist until created by some transforming mind or imagination. That 'saddest and most beautiful book' *Madame Bovary* is quoted to demonstrate 'the beginning and end of realism', and then comes the account of the hangings, which concludes:

> I don't know why I have written all this to you except that whenever I stand waiting for the moment to give the signal [for the drop], you & Turner & the room of Trinity come to my mind & the discussion in which Turner enraged us so by saying that he would not turn his head if anyone said there was a heap of corpses in the corner by the gyproom [college servants' pantry]. I don't think I should any more. (*L*, pp. 132–3)

The Apostolic discussion with Strachey about the nature of

reality in life and literature continues back and forward in letters, Strachey arguing for the creation of beautiful realities of Racine, Watteau, Mozart, or at least Molière, and Woolf preferring the realities of whores and hangings in novels. The topic is a fundamental and familiar Bloomsbury one. How fiction can better represent reality will become, in the 1920s, the substance of Virginia Woolf's critique of Edwardian novelists. Beneath Strachey's and Woolf's divergent artistic tastes remains a basic agreement about the character and value of reality. As in G. E. Moore's philosophy, it consists of states of mind in which consciousness and external nature are organically connected. Yet differences between Woolf and Bloomsbury are beginning to emerge here. 'My seven years in the Ceylon Civil Service turned me from an aesthetic into a political animal', Woolf wrote in *The Journey Not the Arrival Matters* (p. 153). That process is made manifest in three very different kinds of texts that Woolf wrote about the place in Ceylon he went to after Kandy.

VI

L. S. Woolf was rather pathetically grateful, Hugh Clifford recalled when reviewing *The Village in the Jungle* (p. 850), to be put in charge of hundred thousand Sinhalese in an isolated district of a thousand square miles. 'The district is a curious one', Leonard Woolf noted in an introduction to the American edition of his novel on Ceylon. The dense jungle of the northeast is broken only occasionally with small villages or their remains, while in the fertile western part there are numerous pleasant villages. 'But as you go east, it becomes drier and drier, and the whole of the eastern part is a vast sea of jungle. In that sea of jungle on the coast is the "town" of Hambantota' ('Introduction', p. 5). L. S. Woolf's gratitude for his appointment was partly the result of satisfied ambition, and Leonard Woolf admits to being very ambitious in Ceylon, if not in Bloomsbury (*G*, p. 178). The situation of Hambantota was also attractive to him, for unlike Jaffna or Kandy there was no white suburban society to be endured. He lived a life of what he calls 'social solitude', never feeling lonely (pp. 177–8). Work with the villagers absorbed all his attention and energy. Relations with other whites were almost entirely official, and the nearest one, aside from a Belgian missionary, was an irrigation engineer twenty miles away. Big-game hunters who came occasionally for permits made Woolf even more unrelenting to white men (p. 176). The only exceptions seem to have been the missionary, whom he rarely saw, and a fearless Boer game warden, whose stubbornness and competence he admired. They oddly appear and are named in photographs of the office staff that Leonard Woolf includes in *Growing*; the other two or three dozen non-whites remain unidentified in picture or text, which adds to the sense of social solitude in the chapter. Apart from an occasional references to messengers or servants such as the 'dog-boy', Woolf never mentions the extensive personal staff he had at Hambantota.

Woolf was also grateful for Hambantota's setting of actual sea and the sea of jungle that bordered it. The residency was at the sea, and throughout his time at Hambantota, Woolf woke and slept to the great stamping sound that echoes throughout Virginia Woolf's *The Waves*. The jungle almost obsessed him. L. S. Woolf's deep, romantic love of nature which is manifest in his passion for animals and his later devotion to gardening, was excited and disturbed by the jungle's beauty and cruelty. In a 1917 essay ironically entitled 'The Gentleness of Nature', which he reprinted as the concluding piece in his collected essays, Woolf contrasted the tamed nature of Sussex even in winter with her melancholy ruthlessness in the villages and jungles of Ceylon. All his examples are of incidents described in his various Ceylon writings, including *The Village in the Jungle*.

That novel, the only work of his Ceylon fiction that Woolf refers to in his autobiography, may also explain why the Hambantota section of *Growing* is less allusively and descriptively literary than 'Jaffna' or 'Kandy'. In this chapter Woolf was treating a place and time that he had already embodied in a literary text. He was also writing of an earlier self that was becoming, as he said, a more political and less aesthetic animal. 'Hambantota' effectively completes, without really synthesising, the autobiography's tri-part structure, which like other Bloomsbury works is more analogous to musical form than Hegelian logic. Woolf uses a kind of sonata form to develop the themes of the jungle and its villagers that he had written about earlier not only in his novel but also in his official diaries. These diaries, together with some letters to Bloomsbury, are the basis for the recollections in the Hambantota chapter, and they need to be considered for their own sake as writing. Working backwards again from the synoptic autobiography, we can see more comprehensively how the anti-imperialist education traced in

Growing is represented in the very different earlier genres of official diary and novel.

'Hambantota' appears on the surface to be as episodic a chapter of *Growing* as 'Jaffna' and 'Kandy'. Teeth-clicking leopards, leaping jackals, fighting elephants, the fright from being lost overnight, various hunting stories and other jungle experiences are related in an anecdotal fashion that makes his anti-imperial education seem rather disjointed. Woolf was not just an 'aesthetic sportsman' in the famous Game Sanctuary of the Southern Province – an occupation Woolf recommends later in a *TLS* review on sport in Ceylon – but an actual hunter, though a bad shot (presumably because of his tremor). In memory, the jungle's fascination has overgrown the ruins of an empire builder's career, but the career is quite visibly there in third part of *Growing*. It had its distinct European and non-European sides, and Woolf was really interested only in the non-European one (pp. 178–9). His critique of imperialism is confined largely to the non-European side, which explains to some extent why the books and pamphlets he wrote as a Fabian and Labour Party critic of imperialism have little relevance to his writings on Ceylon. Still, it is somewhat surprising that Woolf has so little to say about the economic bases of his role as Assistant Government Agent. The recurrent official activities that he discusses in *Growing* primarily concern salt collection, cattle plague, and land disputes; he says little about road taxes or cultivation permits, though his *Diaries in Ceylon* show him to have also been more preoccupied with them than with one-time activities described at greater length in *Growing* such as supervising a famous religious pilgrimage or taking the 1911 census.

When Woolf writes that he 'did not want to be a successful imperialist', he is referring to the European aspect of his career (p. 180). On the Sinhalese side, he worked with a double impulse: to make his district as prosperous and as efficient as possible. Prosperity meant diminishing poverty and disease, increasing agriculture through irrigation, opening more schools, but his mania for doing these things efficiently made him ruthless to the Sinhalese and to himself. Fifty years later he analysed the means and ends of his work. Humanly, socially, and aesthetically Woolf says he liked the Sinhalese and wanted to improve their lives for their own sake, but his pursuit of efficient means unfortunately became an end in itself (pp. 180–1). How L. S. Woolf came to realise this and to see the essential flaw in Ceylonese imperialism is the not-always-apparent narrative line of 'Hambantota'.

L. S. Woolf's quest for efficiency was demonstrated in one of his central activities at Hambantota, which was supervising the lucrative government salt industry. But in describing his eventually successful struggles with the weather and the contractors to collect more salt at less cost, Leonard Woolf never explains the relation of this work to the prosperity of the Sinhalese. (Nor is there any allusion to Gandhi's historic passive defiance of the Indian salt tax in 1930.) In fact the collection and expenditure of taxes is nowhere discussed in *Growing*, though Woolf's letters reveal one of the reasons he joined the Ceylon Civil Service was the good pay. Where the dilemmas of imperialism do clearly emerge in Leonard Woolf's autobiography, is with the horrible cattle plague called rinderpest. Here the purposes and passions of the Assistant Government Agent – his desire for the well being of the Sinhalese, his striving for efficient government, his love of animals, and his fascination with the jungle – all came together. Cattle and buffalo were essential to the district's economy; without them there could be no effective ploughing or transport. The only way to control the highly infectious plague in Ceylon in 1909 was to isolate the infected animals, some of whom were wild, and get the villagers to restrict the movements of the uninfected ones. To enforce this almost impossible task, L. S. Woolf found it necessary every once in a while to shoot stray cows, and this of course outraged the villagers.

It was on the occasion of one of these shootings that Woolf heard the disturbing, depressing sound of communal hostility:

> I knew the villagers did not believe what I said to them; to them I was part of the white man's machine, which they did not understand. I stood to them in the relation of God to his victims: I was issuing from on high orders to their village which seemed to them arbitrary and resulted in the shooting of their cows. I drove away in dejection, for I have no more desire to be God than one of his victims. (p. 191)

(Woolf's religious scepticism appears to be infecting his imperialism here.) That evening he had an interview with the chief headman to discuss the problems of the plague. The extraordinary symbolic setting and the conversation are presented in 'Hambantota' as the conclusion of 'a moral tale about imperialism' (p. 193). They can also be seen as the completion of L. S. Woolf's education as an anti-imperialist. The symbol dominating this interview, and another one later in *Growing*, is Halley's comet. Walking out over a headland with the English-educated district headman, Woolf was irritated by the spectacle of the blazing comet; from a human point of view, he found it futile and silly. The headman's astrological view was quite the opposite. He believed the constellations determined life and character, which depressed the already irritated Assistant Government Agent. Rinderpest and the comet lead to this imperialist tale's moral, and that is 'the absurdity of a people of one civilisation and mode of life trying to impose its rule upon an entirely different civilisation and mode of life' (p. 193). Casting this conclusion in the metaphor of a moral tale is a way of seeing imperialism again in literary terms, and the unmentioned symbolism of the comet adds to it. Sometime later (*Growing* is vague about the time, but the *Diaries in Ceylon* seem to indicate it was about a year afterward) L. S. Woolf had another interview with a village headman while Halley's comet streamed across the sky. He was told that the people did not like the comet and that it was part of an evil age, the evils in question being taxes of various kind, the limiting of chena-cultivation and a strict Assistant Government Agent (pp. 232–3).

Comets traditionally have been symbols 'importing change of times and states' (Shakespeare, *1 Henry VI*, I. i. 2). (Between the two twentieth-century advents of Halley's comet in 1910 and 1986 there has certainly been a change in the times and states of Ceylon and the British Empire.) Woolf had been born, he says at the end of *Growing*, 'in an age of imperialism and I disapproved of imperialism and felt sure that its days were already numbered' (pp. 247–8). His anticipation of imperialism's demise may be why the comet irritated him, for Woolf appears to connect the absurdity of one people trying to govern those of a different civilisation with the ridiculous futility of a cosmos that has comets in it. Yet Woolf does not regret the change, only perhaps the futility of his role in the story of imperialism.

When Leonard Woolf returned to Sri Lanka at the age of eighty, he was confronted by an eighty-six-year-old former chief headman who insisted on asking him if he still thought his actions in another rinderpest episode fifty years before were fair. L. S. Woolf had shot a stray infected buffalo and then levied fines against its owner and the headman of the village, who turned out to be the same person. The old chief headman, who had to help pay the fines, demanded to know whether the former Assistant Government Agent still believed it was fair to fine the man twice. In *Growing*, Leonard Woolf says he could not be quite sure that it was fair. Toward the end of his last volume of autobiography, however, Woolf retells the story at greater length in the context of his revisiting Sri Lanka, and comes to a more definite and significant conclusion. That conclusion is his last autobiographical word on the anti-imperial education he received in Ceylon half a century before.[9] In response to the Headman's 'Was it just, Sir? Was it just?' Leonard Woolf replies 'Yes' but continues to feel ambivalent about it. He still has no doubts about the justice of the decision or the moral principles underlying it. But about the insistent question he was profoundly depressed, for the headman

> had as good a right to his code of conduct as I had, and there was no real answer to his question: 'Was it just, Sir, was it just?' I thought it was, but I was not prepared to spend my life doing justice to people who thought that my justice was injustice.

This 'ambivalence with regard to law and order and justice in an imperial society' was finally one of the principal reasons why he resigned from imperialism (*JNAM*, pp. 207–8).

Leonard Woolf's conclusion as to the injustice of imperialism is really more political than economic. (If he read J. A. Hobson's economic analysis in *Imperialism*, which appeared in 1902, he never mentions it in his Ceylon writings.) Woolf objects not so much to the exploitative taxes and control of Sinhalese agriculture as to the imposing of a foreign government and culture upon them. There were some good things about imperialism, Woolf still finds on revisiting Sri Lanka, but the worst aspect of British rule there was its 'democratic hypocrisy':

> Contrary to what we professed, we never did anything to prepare the way for self-government or responsible government. Our manners, officially and socially, were often deplorable and nearly always arrogant. (*JNAM*, p. 196)

Like Forster, Leonard Woolf is finally led to condemn undemocratic imperialism in *Growing* for what it does to human relations. The twinge of doubt felt at Jaffna, the ambivalence of being an imperial patriarch in Kandy and a god in Hambantota, had become, fifty years later, a conviction well stated by John Stuart Mill a hundred years before and quoted by Hobson at the turn of the century: 'Such a thing as the government of one people by another does not and cannot exist' (Hobson, p. 326). This remains an issue today in the civil war of Sri Lanka that has followed imperialism in Ceylon.

VII

Woolf's letters to Strachey from Hambantota are less revealing than those from Kandy or Jaffna. He wrote fewer of them as he buried himself and his past in his work, and he had another source for the last chapter of *Growing*: the official diaries that the Assistant Government Agent was required to keep. Only one letter describing the contrast between Cambridge and Hambantota is used in *Growing*, yet in it and others the rage and lamentation of his correspondence continues. In another to Sydney-Turner he begins 'I feel desolate & the horror of desolation . . . ' (*L*, p. 140). Despite the burial of his past, Woolf's letters still show a interest in Bloomsbury. To Strachey, Woolf sends a sordid account of a villager's murdered wife, and then brings in *A Room with a View* to ask if the corpse's awful smell would count as real to Forster (*L*, pp. 141–2). Some of the letters from Hambantota included short poems. One is on a Tamil prostitute; in another the poet's ghostly self embraces a girl on the sand, as L. S. Woolf had at Jaffna (*G*, p. 102). A comic, prescient topic of the letters to and from Strachey is their discussion, in the wake of Clive Bell's marriage to Vanessa, of the trinity of Trinity's prospects with Virginia. Strachey first mentions early in 1909 the possibility that he might marry her; this produces a not entirely mock proposal from Woolf, who wonders if she may not end up marrying Sydney-Turner instead. Strachey urges in variously ironic letters that Woolf should marry her (LW/*L*, pp. 147–9). Leonard responds in one letter that he is obsessed by copulation and wants a romantic prostitute, and in the next that he knows 'the one thing to do would be to marry Virginia' (11.vii.09, LS/pBL; *L*, pp. 149–50). In this manner were the personal relations of Bloomsbury carried on even in Ceylon.

L. S. Woolf's diary-keeping in Ceylon had little in common with his future wife's practice. *Diaries in Ceylon*, the title given them when they were published in the *Ceylon Historical Review* and then by the Hogarth Press after his visit to Sri Lanka in 1960, is an official record of daily activity and monthly expenditure that was read regularly by Woolf's superiors in Colombo. Along with reports, correspondence, and later telegrams, the diaries had been the principal means of written communication in Ceylon between the central government and its agents since the beginning of the nineteenth century. Leonard Woolf believed they were the kind of document that would reveal 'the iniquities of the ancient imperialists' regime' (*JNAM*, p. 200). As a detailed account of his work in the Hambantota District, Woolf's diaries also reveal the anti-imperial progress of L. S. Woolf that is traced in *Growing*. A number of incidents recorded in the diaries are retold in his autobiography, and material from them was reshaped for *The Village in the Jungle* as well. *Diaries in Ceylon* is therefore also a significant document in the literary history of Bloomsbury.

It is a curious text, this government document written in the most private of literary genres. It has the chronologically arranged miscellaneous content of a diary but without its usual reflexive form. The diarist is writing for the Colonial Secretary, not himself. Numbered marginal glosses on the subjects of the entries are provided. The usual contents of these colonial diaries consist of descriptions or observations of activities, happenings, and conditions in the district (*DC*, pp. xxxii–iii[10]). In Woolf's diaries the emphasis is on activities; he reports happenings and conditions, of course, but usually in the context of what he is doing on a given day. When they were first published in Sri Lanka, Leonard Woolf added a preface saying the diaries showed 'the work which I did there and to some extent its impact upon me', for he was moved and fascinated by the lives and psychology of the villagers in their beautiful, menacing jungle (pp. lxxvii–viii). In comparison with *Growing*, the work shown in the diaries is much more varied and circumstantial, though they do not include court records of the magistrate's work that he was also performing. Details of the salt collection, rinderpest, and land disputes occupy many of the entries, but so do the problems of chena-permits, the road tax, and irrigation works that are not much discussed in the autobiography. L. S. Woolf opposed government policy on the restriction of chena-cultivation (a primitive method of agriculture in which virgin plots of jungle called chenas are burnt, cleared, sowed for a few crops, until exhausted, and then abandoned). He argued that more should be allowed for villages that would otherwise become extinct and their inhabitants more undernourished (p. 117). Shorter-term human welfare was more immediately important than the longer-term welfare of the land for Woolf, but not apparently for his superiors. Little is said about chenas in *Growing*, but in *The Village in the Jungle* they are represented as the basis of life itself. In the matter of the road tax (six days of work a year on the roads for those unable to pay one rupee – p. lxx) the Assistant Government Agent pointed out in his diary the iniquity of a tax which was a burden only to those who did not benefit from it; he then collected it rigorously on the principle that bad laws should be enforced and then changed rather than unenforced and unchanged. A considerable amount of time was spent by Woolf interviewing, excusing, or fining those who did not perform the work. Complaints about the Assistant Government Agent's severity were referred to him from Colombo during his first year at Hambantota but the next year Woolf could point out beneficial results of his enforcement (p. 218). The Government Agent in whose province the district of Hambantota was, also complained about his Assistant's schemes for the collection of salt, which was the chief source of revenue; again, however, Woolf can point out in his diary that more money was collected in 1910 than ever before (p. 218). Opium sales, another government source of income not mentioned in *Growing*, are also discussed in the diaries and their methods criticised.

In the relative mellowness of his old age Leonard Woolf could say he had 'rather absent-mindedly' and 'light-heartedly' helped to govern the Empire in his youth (*JNAM*, pp. 193, 195). His letters home to Bloomsbury do not show a light-hearted colonial administrator, and the *Diaries in Ceylon* do not reveal an absent-minded one. The Sinhalese are pictured in the diaries as delighting, exasperating, and depressing the Assistant Government Agent. To pass a dull Sunday afternoon, they try to have him shoot a harmless wild buffalo, somewhat in the manner that Orwell's Burmese wanted him shoot an elephant. Disputes have to be adjudicated such as the man who found the price of a shave increase half-way through the job, or the group of working women who were allowed to wear jackets only around their necks. Futile attempts to teach the villagers to use modern ploughs, or getting the headmen to count their people brings forth execrations of stupidity from His Majesty's representative. But there are also moving descriptions of the villagers' often miserable existences. An abandoned child dies wretchedly of pneumonia because her family thought she had measles, which were considered too dangerous to treat. If there is anything absent-minded in the administration described by the *Diaries in Ceylon*, it has to do with L. S. Woolf's unexamined imperial assumptions. He does not yet question the right of himself and his kind to support themselves by governing in ways they thought best. The recurring criticisms of the Government and its agents in the diaries show that he will.

Leonard Woolf thought he took great interest in writing his diary 'fully and frankly' (*JNAM*, p. 200). Entries are sometimes rather short, however, and the style almost laconic. The prose lesson that Price taught him at Jaffna had been well learned. Once in his diaries, he quotes from those of a mid-nineteenth century predecessor who had described in a flowing, rhetorical manner a decline of irrigation that was similar to that his successor was noting. Woolf observes,

> It looks as if the only thing to have changed . . . during the last 60 years is the style of the A.G.A.'s diary – and that decidedly for the worse. (*DC*, p. 88)

Some observations, particularly of the jungle animals, are reported in the diaries. There is an amusing description of rear-end collision with an elephant, for example, and Woolf permits himself an occasional dry personal comment. Apropos the salt collection, he remarks that a month at the pearl fishery made it impossible for him ever again to enjoy an oyster, and he wonders if three months at Hambantota will produce the same effect with regard to salt (p. 29). The insufferable conditions under which he had to supervise the Kataragama pilgrimage that figures prominently in *Growing* and *The Village in the Jungle*, cause him to hope that its god 'sees to it that the supervisor of the pilgrims acquires some little merit from this pilgrimage' (p. 166). Difficulties with the quality of the headmen which he has to appoint leads to a feminist threat: 'The next time I shall have occasion to dismiss a headman in the Midwalakada I shall recommend the appointment of a woman' (p. 64). The occasion seems not to have arisen.

If they were not always full, the diaries were certainly frank. Disagreements with the Government Agent are noted by Woolf and objections registered to the Agent's comments on his Assistant's views. One entry complains about the Government's being 'so unmercifully swindled over the acquisition of land' (p. 239). In the last entry but one before going on leave in 1911, Woolf observes that 'the more trouble one takes over a thing, the less satisfactory as a rule is the result', and applies it to the time he wasted on two schemes that the Government Agent told him to go ahead and report on, with the predictable result that his report was considered incomplete. This is followed by an ironic hexameter of Virgil's on the difficulty of getting out of hell, which had been so easy to enter. Leonard Woolf cut this entry from his published diaries, but he reprinted in *Growing* a reprimand from the Governor instructing the Assistant Government Agent 'to comment with more restraint and discretion upon the orders of his Superior Officer' (*G*, p. 224).[11] Such were the constraints on public diary-keeping.

VIII

Diaries in Ceylon is the immediate background text for *The Village in the Jungle*, as *Growing* is the remote foreground. The diaries describe in their documentary way the world of the novel, including some of its happenings, while the autobiography retrospectively evaluates the experience that led to its writing. Looking at the novel in the contexts of both the diaries and the autobiography brings out more clearly the naturalism of the work and its subtext about imperialism.

When Woolf returned to England he remained fascinated by the Sinhalese and their jungle villages. As he wrote in the third volume of his autobiography:

> They continued to obsess me in London, in Putney or Blooms-bury, and in Cambridge. *The Village in the Jungle* was a novel in which I tried somehow or other vicariously to live their lives. It was also, in some curious way, the symbol of the anti-imperialism which had been growing upon me more and more in my last years in Ceylon. (*BA*, p. 47)

The echo of the title of *Growing* here emphasises the disillusioning education that the novelist had undergone as a civil servant. His vicarious intentions illuminate the naturalistic form of his book in which the lives of the villagers are mercilessly determined by a feudal jungle environment but dimly comprehended by the Western imperialist governing them. In a blurb written for a Hogarth

Press reprint of the novel, its author and now publisher summarised the novel as a story of 'a jungle man and his two daughters; the theme of their story is a struggle against man, fate and nature'.

To create a sense of the village of Beddagama's inevitable fate, Woolf abandons the Conradian narrators of 'A Tale Told by Moonlight' and 'Pearls and Swine' for a dispassionately omniscient point of view expressed through a very simple prose style. The novel opens with an undramatised narrator. No commenting Forsterian voice or Jamesian presenter of reflecting consciousnesses, this detached recorder's origins might be found in Flaubert, Maupassant, or Zola. The 'I' is soon replaced with a 'you' in the representation of the actions, sayings, and feelings of the primitively unintrospective villagers; then he disappears entirely from the book.

The detached fictive illusion in *The Village in the Jungle* is qualified in two ways, however. One is the brief factual footnotes of translation or explanation. From them the reader learns in what country the village and its jungle are set. Originally Leonard Woolf had given a subtitle to the novel indicating its Ceylon locale, but his publisher, Edward Arnold, rejected it (LW/pS). The notes may have been done at the publisher's suggestion.[12] They add to the verisimilitude of *The Village in the Jungle*, but also tend, along with certain explanatory passages (such as those on marriage customs at the beginning of Chapter 4) to dispel the novelistic representation of jungle village life by giving to the novel the informative air of a travel book.

The other qualification of the novel's naturalistic detachment begins with the talk of the hunter Silindu, whose fate is the centre of the novel. This is how he first describes the animal life of the jungle to his baby daughter:

Yesterday, little toad, I lay under a domba-tree by the side of a track, my gun in my hand, waiting for what might pass. The devils are very angry in the jungle, for there has been no rain now for these three months. . . . I saw on the opposite side of the track, lying under a domba-tree, a leopardess waiting for what might pass. I put down my gun, and, 'Sister,' I said, 'is the belly empty?' For her coat was mangy, and the belly caught up below, as though with pain. 'Yakko, he-devil,' she answered, 'three days now I have killed but one thin grey monkey, and there are two cubs in the cave to be fed'.

Wild pigs come, the leopard catches a piglet and climbs a tree.

The old sow, who had borne the little pig in Yakkini's mouth, put her forefeet against the trunk of the tree, and looked up, and said, 'Come down, Yakkini; she-devil, thief. Are you afraid of an old, tuskless sow? Come down.' But the leopardess laughed, and bit the little pig in the back behind the head until it died, and she called down to the old sow, 'Go your way, mother. There are two cubs at home in the cave, and they are very hungry. Every year I drop but one or two cubs in the cave, but the whole jungle swarms with your spawn.' (*VJ*, pp. 18–21)

The style of this child's story reappears in *The Village in the Jungle* when Silindu, his children, or other childlike villagers talk to the animals or listen to tales of the inhabitants with whom they share their jungle. The hearing and telling of folk tales is one of the villagers' few pleasures, but they usually concern Buddha and are droned out in a kind of chant. (When later Woolf reviewed a translated collection of Ceylon folk tales for the *TLS*, he thought them too monotonously literal for readers who did not know Sinhalese.) Silindu's narratives are different. With them Woolf again appears to be viewing Ceylon life through the imagination of Kipling, as expressed this time in *The Jungle Books*.[13] The main difference is that baby animals do not scream and die in Kipling. Native peoples were usually viewed by imperialists as children, and the euphemism 'non-adult races' appears even in Leonard Woolf's later anti-imperialist writings. Under the influence of the Mowgli stories Woolf conveys the impression of the villagers' immaturity in *The Village in the Jungle*. It is an irony of Bloomsbury's literary history that Woolf should criticise the realism of Forster and then turn in his Eastern writings to Kipling's child-in-the-jungle Indian stories for some, though not all, of his inspiration. (Kipling's influence is stronger on another, even more famous imperialist jungle book published a year after Leonard Woolf's: Edgar Rice Burroughs's *Tarzan of the Apes*.) The closeness of the village to the brute animal life of the jungle is reasserted at the end of the novel with the horrible entry of the boar into the hut of Silindu's helpless daughter in the deserted village. This is not the kind of thing

Kipling depicts in 'Letting in the Jungle'. Woolf's stylised presentation of the villagers' dialogue, whose syntax and diction (especially forms of exclamation and address) read like awkwardly literal translations, can also be found in Kipling and much other realistic and romantic fiction. In *The Village in the Jungle* the technique is effectively used to convey the characters' primitive states of mind that so fascinated their author.

Fear, hunger, thirst, savagery permeate the jungle of Woolf's novel. An opening anecdote, based on an event recorded in *Diaries in Ceylon*, describes the fate of a hunter who did not fear the jungle and was 'without understanding or feeling for things as they really are' (p. 2). Silindu, however, feels the nature of the jungle's reality more than others and finally understands its evil from talking to a Buddhist beggar:

> Always the killing, killing, killing; everything afraid: the deer and the pig and the jackal after them, and the leopard himself. Always evil there. No peace, no rest – it was rest I wanted.   (p. 269)

Village life is not much different. The novel's state of nature is Hobbes's, not Rousseau's. Hunger, poor food, and disease are added to hatred, spells, lies, exploitation, and killing. The characters are likened to animals. Even the Assistant Government Agent looks out at the dark-eyed villagers with cat's eyes. Silindu, who is sometimes compared to a leopard, comes to think of himself as a wounded, dangerous buffalo; his daughters are described as leopard cubs, buffalo calves, and deer; one of them nurses her child together with a baby fawn. Marks of a bear's teeth and claws are visible on the face of the doctor-medicine man vederala.

As a hunter Silindu is set apart from the other conforming cultivators of the village. He is controlled by his debt to the headman and his fear of the vederala's spells, yet he has an individuality that his author admires. The way Silindu raises his motherless twin daughters to be familiar with the jungle defies the rigid sexual roles of village life. When the headman's brother-in-law Babun chooses one of them, Punchi Menika, for a wife instead of a rich girl from another village, Silindu and his family incur more enmity. The initial refusal of the vederala by the other daughter, Hinnihami, brings a spell on Silindu, and she must sacrifice herself sexually after the pilgrimage to save him, though she will not live with the vederala. The desire of the townman Fernando for Punchi

Menika then brings disaster on her family, for the headman and much of the village are in debt to him. Her husband and father are framed as thieves, and after Babun is sent to prison and thus to his death, Silindu the hunter becomes a murderer. In all of these events the independent Silindu and his daughters are brought into economic, sexual, and religious conflict with the society of their village.

Two independent, motherless daughters figure centrally in both of Leonard Woolf's novels. While *The Village in the Jungle* is obviously not autobiographical in the same way as *The Wise Virgins*, it is still a Bloomsbury novel. The values that for Bloomsbury were inherent in reality and individuality appear in the struggles of Silindu and his daughters with the social conditions of their existence, but these values are as incidental to the fate of the good and the bad characters in the novel as the Buddhism is that consoles Silindu. Only the jungle endures. Yet despite Woolf's ingrained pessimism, the depressing fate of the village in the jungle is not all that vicariously engages his attention. To see more clearly what is encompassed in this naturalistic, Kiplingesque travel-novel that its author thought was also a kind of anti-imperialist symbol, it is useful to turn back to a few entries of *Diaries in Ceylon* and look forward again to the Hambantota chapter of *Growing*.

IX

One memorable event, the Kataragama Pilgrimage, is to be found in all three of the extended texts that describe so differently L. S. Woolf's experiences as an Assistant Government Agent. His diary entries on the supervision of the pilgrimage are quite short, however. The hardships endured by the pilgrims because of a drought is commented on and later the temple authorities are criticised for not providing some kind of accommodation for the pilgrims who are consequently subject to pneumonia and fever. Still, only two children out of the 4000 or so pilgrims died. Though Woolf's accommodation was good, he suffered from heat, noise, and insects. The religious mixture of the festival fascinated him, and in all three accounts he tells the pleasant myth of how this Hindu divinity decided to migrate. He called on some Tamils to carry him from his jungle hill across the river to Kataragama, but they were busy getting salt; some passing Sinhalese then helped with the move, and as a consequence he became a Sinhalese as well as a Tamil deity. The festival was clearly a fertility ritual, however; every night the god is taken from his temple to a goddess's, and back again in a procession Woolf likens to a juggernaut. After fourteen days of this it all ends with the water of the river being symbolically divided.

The account of the pilgrimage in *Growing* is much longer. Supervising it was the kind of imperialist work Woolf seems to have found most interesting, despite the appalling physical conditions that he describes in the quotation from his diary that ends with the hope of acquiring some religious merit. Merit as an imperialist he thinks he earned by recommending accommodations be built for the pilgrims by the temple authorities, and when he returned in 1960 he found they had, though the festival itself had been modernised and cheapened like Lisieux and other European shrines. In some ways Woolf's experience of the Kataragama festival was like the pearl fishery, the purpose here being a combination of spiritual profit and miraculous health cure. (The fear of epidemic led the Government to supervise these mass pilgrimages.) As with the pearl fishery, Woolf marvels at the self-confidence of British imperialism that put a young Englishman in charge of 4000 pilgrims from Ceylon and India, with only a medical officer and the village headman to help him. What intrigued the young L. S. Woolf in 1910 was not just the history of the god and the character of his festival, but the psychology of his worshippers. During one night of the festival, for example, he was kept awake by a blind child whose parents were torturing it so that the god might hear the screams and cure it. (Woolf quotes Tennyson's 'in the night with no language but a cry' to describe the plight of the child – G, p. 228.) He had the child examined by the medical officer, but neither the god nor science could restore its sight. 'These strange, alien psychological encounters' are what fascinated Woolf with their 'mixture of pathos and absurdity, of love and cruelty, in such horrible and grotesque incidents' (p. 229). And once again in his autobiography he is describing something he had previously depicted in fiction.

The account of the Kataragama pilgrimage in *The Village in the Jungle* is only faintly disguised, but it differs considerably from the later description in *Growing* because, unlike the account of the pearl fishery in 'Pearls and Swine', the view of events is the participants' not the supervisor's. There is no white presence in the long fifth chapter that tells of the exhausting pilgrimage of Silindu, his sister, two daughters, a son-in-law, and countless thousands of Sinhalese and Tamils to the Beragama festival. The story of the Tamil god whom the Sinhalese carried from the hill to their village is presented here as a tale that villagers might tell one another, only with a conclusion that stresses the significance of his origin:

> The god, therefore, is of the jungle; a great devil, beneficent when approached in the right manner and season, whose power lies for miles upon the desolate jungle surrounding his temple and hill.

His power heals, makes fertile, punishes false oaths and 'can aid us against the devils which perpetually beset us' (*VJ*, p. 106).

Along the way of the pilgrimage there is the traditional interpolated story for travellers, which the pilgrims prefer to the readings of a holy man. This time it is a traditional folk tale from the life of Buddha as narrated by Karlinahami, Silindu's sister, surrogate mother of his daughters, and village story-teller. The story recounts the trials to which the wife of the Buddha is subjected before being accepted. Told on a pilgrimage that will end with the sacrifice of Hinnihami to the vederala, the story brings out once more the particularly wretched situation of women in the novel. They lack even the little freedom the men have. Women are completely dependent economically on the feudal structure of the village; they cannot be hunters (or even headpersons, despite the threats of eccentric government agents); and their sexual choices are mostly ignored or opposed.[14]

The Village in the Jungle is not a feminist novel. Village life is a marginal existence for everyone, but it is plainly portrayed by Woolf as worse for the women, who are also more sensitive than the men in the book. In the Hambantota chapter of *Growing* there is a lovely photograph of two young women 'fetching water from the tank of a village in the jungle' (facing p. 176), but the scene is too idyllic for the women to be illustrations of Hinnihami and Punchi Menika. The alien religious psychology that intrigued Leonard Woolf in *Growing* is represented in the novel through Hinnihami's ecstatic response to the god at the festival.

> She formulated no prayer to him, she spoke no words of supplication: only in excitement and exaltation of entreaty she cried out the name of the god. (p. 109)

Though Hinnihami and Silindu are deceived by the conniving Hindu holy man, so different from the Buddhist one encountered earlier, she turns her sacrifice at this fertility festival into a kind of triumph. The god says she must be given to the vederala, according to the Hindu, and she is when the festival ends with the cutting of the waters. But afterwards she turns the god on the vederala in a nice bit of jungle casuistry. If he tries to make her live with him, she threatens to become a devil herself and strangle him while he sleeps because

> the god did not say I was to live with you. There is no giving of food or clothing. I was given that the devil might leave my father. Was the god disobeyed? I was given to you, you dog; the devil has flown; the god heard us there at Beragama; he will not allow you again to do evil. (p. 127)

The pilgrimage and festival of *The Village in the Jungle* serve quite different purposes than the Gokul Ashtami festival that Forster wrote about in his travel letters (published later in *The Hill of Devi*) and then used as an approach to reconciliation at the end of *A Passage to India*. Hinnihami's religiously inspired independence ends when her child dies and her pet fawn is stoned as a scapegoat by the villagers. The worlds of the novels are very different. Years before *A Passage to India* was finished, Forster concluded in a review of a book on Hindu villages in Bengal that 'Indian village life still waits for the writer who will do for it what Mr. L. S. Woolf has done for village life in Ceylon' (*AE*, p. 206). It is interesting, nevertheless, that both Forster and Woolf use religious festivals in their novels as sources of value and consolation for the characters, if not the authors. In these ceremonies could be found states of mind valuable for their own sakes. Religious experience is not part of the Ideal in Moore's *Principia Ethica* because God is not real. In Bloomsbury novels where characters believe in the reality of their deities, however, religious experience, along with love and the response to beauty, can be supremely valuable.

A comparison of *The Village and the Jungle* with *A Passage to India* brings back the question of the 'curious way' in which Leonard Woolf said his novel was a symbol of the anti-imperialism that had been growing on him in Hambantota (*BA*, p. 47). The symbolism is curious because it is inexplicit. Only in the inability of the novel's Assistant Government Agent to uncover what has been happening in the village of Beddagama is the simple failure of colonial justice made manifest. Among the sources of the novel in *Diaries in Ceylon*, however, there can be found an oblique commentary on the anti-imperialist symbolism that is implicit in the world of *The Village in the Jungle*.

A number of fictive incidents and descriptions in *The Village and the Jungle* have their factual counterparts in *Diaries in Ceylon*. The name and future of Beddagama may have been suggested by Beddawewa, a village decimated by malaria that Woolf inspected (*DC*, p. 215). The fate of the fearless hunter mentioned at the opening of the novel resembles that of a missing game-watcher in the diaries, whose name is given to the vederala (*DC*, pp. 167–8, 234). The fictive Hinnihami's fawn and the real Boer game-warden's pet bear are both cruelly killed by villagers or townspeople. Descriptions of drought and the animals snuffing the air in the Game Sanctuary are very similar to passages in the novel, only in the diaries they are accompanied with suggestions for improving water holes (*VJ*, pp. 8–9; *DC*, pp. 45–6). And Silindu's murders are interestingly like and unlike those Woolf had to investigate when an irrigation headman shot an acting headman in the back, in the jungle and then killed the headman's father in his garden before giving himself up to the Mudaliyar, or collector of rates (*DC*, pp. 210–1). Silindu is not an irrigation headman, and his victims are only a village headman and the townsman to whom all are in debt, but the way they are murdered is similar, and Silindu also gives himself up to the Mudaliyar. No cause for the murders is given in the diaries, however, while those behind Silindu's 'cold-blooded' killing are part of the novel's anti-imperialist symbolic action.

The Government Agent who was L. S. Woolf's immediate superior in Ceylon complained that his Assistant was 'continually writing to say that the villagers must have chenas or they will starve'. The Assistant denied this, for practically no one starved in Ceylon; what he did argue was that if chenas were not allowed, a number of villages in the district would become extinct, 'which will undoubtedly be accompanied by a considerable amount of distress' (*DC*, p. 117). Woolf had tried to point out, first, that the current policy of trying to conserve land by preventing villagers from burning off scrub jungle and then cultivating the land every ten years meant, in effect, the extinction of villages. Secondly, the method of paying in advance for permission to chena when deemed necessary 'throws the villager who is poor and is supposed to be helped into the hands of the well-to-do or it makes it impossible for him to chena at all' (*DC*, pp. 86–7). And that, of course, is Silindu's situation in Beddagama, a village that becomes extinct because of the government's chena policy.

The mainspring of village life in the novel is debt (*VJ*, p. 30). Silindu owes money to the headman and the money-lenders in town; the headman himself is in debt to them. And the only source of income is in the chenas, except for a hunter like Silindu who can sell the meat that he shoots – if he has paid the gun tax. The life of the village, explains the narrator, depends on chena-cultivation.

> he villagers owned no jungle themselves; it belonged to the Crown, and no one might fell a tree or clear a chena in it without a permit from the Government. It was through these permits that the headman had his hold upon the villagers. Applications for one had to be made through him. . . .   (pp. 33–4)

The headman also had the power to pay the road tax for villagers; his refusal to do this for Silindu shows his enmity and also the injustice of a tax Woolf had also criticised in his diaries. Finally, the denial of a chena permit because Punchi Menika rejected the townman makes Silindu and his family desperate; in a month they will either starve or have to leave the village. Silindu tries to appeal to the Assistant Government Agent, but he is away. Then comes the faked theft, the trial, and the murders.

The Assistant Government Agent, whom Silindu recognises as another hunter, correctly blames murders on 'not letting one another alone', which he finds along with the behaviour of some headmen as the causes of crime and trouble in his district (p. 248), but this good liberal perception hardly meets the situation of the villagers in their jungle. Behind it is the chena policy that gives the headman such power and makes the villagers so helpless. The consequences of that policy in *The Village in the Jungle* symbolises the failure of imperialism. There are other government policies criticised in *Diaries in Ceylon* that are relevant to the novel – the inadequate distribution of quinine, for example, that might have prevented the deaths of the children from fever – but the principal one is the management of chenas.

The Colonial Secretary who appointed L. S. Woolf as Assistant Government Agent and read his official diaries (he issued the reprimand for the tone of their prose) also reviewed *The Village in the Jungle* for *Blackwood's Magazine* in 1913. Hugh Clifford had twenty years experience as a colonial administrator in Malaysia; he was a friend of Conrad's, and an author in his own right. He praised the novel unstintingly, calling it

> the most faithful, the most true, and the most *understanding* presentment of Oriental peasant life that has ever been placed before Western readers by a European. (p. 850)

For Clifford the novel was a revelation; it showed him the truth of Henry Thomas Buckle's ideas in the East. *The Village in the Jungle* illustrated Buckle's theory of history by showing to Clifford the essential 'unmanageability' of the jungle, and explaining to him the inertia in the otherwise energetic Malaysian character.

That a literary Colonial Secretary of Ceylon, having read Woolf's diaries, could take his novel as a representation of the inability of villagers to manage the jungle, suggests how impervious the institution of imperialism was to criticism. For if the jungle is unmanageable, what are the British doing trying to manage it? The jungle is unmanageable in *The Village in the Jungle*, but the government does little to alleviate this in the novel; if anything, the imperialists make it more unmanageable. 'Who killed imperialism?' Leonard Woolf asked in his next volume of autobiography in the context of the 1915 Ceylon riots between Buddhists and Muslims that the British put down brutally. (He had written about the great injustice of the government's actions and had then participated, at the request of some Ceylonese, in a futile appeal to the Colonial Under-Secretary of State named Hewins.) And he answered 'I, said the imperialist, with my imperialism – and my Hewinses and my refusals' (*BA*, p. 231). To which he could have added Cliffords and later Lugards.

The anti-imperialism of *The Village in the Jungle* is clarified by Woolf's *Diaries in Ceylon*. Writing the novel back in England in 1911 and 1912 was a crucial stage in Woolf's evaluation of his imperial experience. The book he wrote was not what might have been expected – not the kind of ironic, pessimistic novel on the English in the East that George Orwell, for example, wrote in *Burmese Days*. (When he heard of Forster's first novel, Woolf told Strachey he was going to write a novel on the social intrigue of the English at Jaffna to be called *A Crown Colony*; much later he told William Plomer that he had begun a novel called *The Empire-Builder* but did not get past

the first scene of a boy uprooting a stone – 16.ix.05, LS/pBL; *L*,
p. 568.) And if Woolf is thought to have been naïve about imperialism when he went out to Ceylon in 1904, what shall one say
about Orwell, of all writers, going out to Burma nearly twenty years
and a world war later to be an imperial policeman? Yet Orwell also
said 'in all novels about the East the scenery is the real subject-
matter' (*Road*, p. 110). That is true in a way of Woolf's novel, and
Forster's too. But *The Village in the Jungle* is not only about the
jungle, however; it is also about villagers and how their lives are
circumscribed by the jungle and their rulers.

X

Leonard Woolf dated the end of his youth on the day he sailed from
Ceylon. The voyage back to Bloomsbury in the summer of 1911 was
like all return journeys, he thought, rather depressing (*BA*, p. 15).
Back in England he found he was still 'a native of Trinity and
King's, a Cambridge intellectual' (p. 20). But his experience had
made a difference; a permanent carapace had formed. The unreality
in London of what he had so often regarded as the unreal world of
Ceylon made him again, he felt, a split personality, a detached actor,
'once more acting a part in the same complicated play in front of a
new backcloth and with different actors and a different audience'
(p. 16).

In the autumn he began to write *The Village in the Jungle*, and to
fall in love with Virginia Stephen. Leonard determined that if she
would not marry him, he would return to Ceylon, but only if he
could continue to work with the Sinhalese and not the white sahib
side of imperialism. Characteristically, he still hoped to make his
area the most efficient and prosperous in Asia. Yet he was aware at
the back of his mind that this was all fantasy. He now knew he
disapproved of imperialism; moreover, its days were numbered (*G*,
pp. 247–8). The Colonial Service were true to their gentlemanly
code when Woolf asked for an extended leave without explaining the reasons, and they continued to behave so up until his
resignation. The reasons were that he did not want to be a colonial
governor, he disliked imperialism, and he wanted to marry
Virginia; if she would not have him he wanted to stay in
Hambantota as Assistant Government Agent. But none of this he
felt could be explained to the Secretary for the Colonies any more

than he could send him the refrain running in his head from the French poem about giving up Paris for love, which he had used as the epigraph for *Growing*.

The *Village in the Jungle* is dedicated to Virginia Woolf with these lines:

To V. W.

I've given you all the little, that I've to give;
You've given me all, that for me is all there is;
So now I just give back what you have given –
If there is anything to give in this.

Clive Bell told Mary MacCarthy the quatrain was 'the most economical statement possible of a complicated truth' and it made him think of Moore (1912, CB/pKC). But the epigraph of *Growing* might have done better. At any rate Virginia thought the novel 'amazingly good' when she read it, and so did Forster (VW/*L*, II 12, 44). Forster advised Leonard to send it to his own publishers; he did and it was accepted (LW/'Coming' p. 35). The only detailed response from Bloomsbury that has survived to *The Village in the Jungle* is in a letter from Lytton Strachey. Leonard had turned to him earlier for advice about publishing it, and Lytton's response is a fitting conclusion to their Ceylon correspondence. He did not really care for the subject, but taking it as given, he was certain the book was a great success.

> The two main aims of general atmospheric description and psychological drawing seem to me carried out completely. The restraint of it all is, I think, very supreme. The fewness of the epithets is wonderful.

It was better than Zola; only the plot toward the end might be a little thin. The fawn incident he liked very much, and thought the power of the headmen horrible. The psychology, he repeated, was masterly, and he hoped that Leonard Woolf would now attempt some whites in fiction. The letter ends: 'Whites! Whites! Whites!' (21.iv.13, LW/pS). Strachey's criticism is as sound as any the novel has received; he recognised the importance of setting and characters' states of mind, the naturalistic restraint of the presentation, and the significance of the headmen's power in the critique of imperialism. Neither he nor Bloomsbury would be as complimentary when Leonard Woolf did turn to whites in his next novel.

Outside of Bloomsbury, the book was well received. To their surprise, Edward Arnold sold out the first edition and had to reprint twice in 1913. They had expected poor sales, anticipated no foreign interest in the book (it was translated into Tamil, Sinhalese, and other languages) and deprecated the author's wanting to retain his copyright (*L*, p. 180). Woolf was not happy with the royalties or Arnold's business methods, (*LW/BA*, pp. 88–9). Their editorial methods were not much better; in addition to deleting the subtitle of the novel, they insisted on some bowdlerisation and then misnumbered the chapters so that there are two chapter nines in the first edition (LW/pS).

Though widely praised, *The Village in the Jungle* was not enjoyed by some modernists.[15] Forster lent his copy to D. H. Lawrence in 1915 when he was struggling with *Women in Love*, but he did not much like it. 'It was interesting', he wrote to Forster, 'but not *very* good – nothing much behind it' (*Letters*, II 291).[16] Lawrence did not much like Ceylon either when he later visited it. T. S. Eliot, who thought some of the *Stories of the East* very good, was also disappointed in the novel (*Letters*, I 434). On the other hand Wallace Stevens, who loved Ceylon and was interested in Bloomsbury's work, felt the novel 'exceedingly well written', full of Ceylon pictures and ideas, though it dealt with 'an isolated class' (*Letters*, p. 332).

But perhaps the most revealing response to *The Village in the Jungle* after Hugh Clifford's was that of Arnold Toynbee. He quoted from it at some length in *A Study of History* to illustrate the decline of a civilisation. Stevens's isolated class Toynbee found to be heroes, their story an epic 'which surpasses the tale told by the ruins of Angkor Wat' (II 7–9). Toynbee's is a more complex historical determinism than Buckle's, as applied earlier by Clifford, yet the conclusions are really the same: inert or heroic in their jungle, the villagers appear unaffected by the empire to which they belong.

Leonard Woolf along with Bloomsbury did not have much use for the philosophy of history. He was convinced, as he wrote in *Empire and Commerce in Africa* – his next major work on imperialism – that 'in history there is no logic of events and no logic of facts, there is only a logic of men's beliefs and ideals' (p. 8). His seven years in Ceylon combined with beliefs and ideals derived from Moore's philosophy and then modified by the Group of which he was a member, to focus his writing on what he would call 'communal psychology'. *Stories of the East* and *The Village in the Jungle* can also be read as representations of very different kinds of communal psychology. *Diaries in Ceylon* documents the actions, beliefs, and ideals of L. S. Woolf as an imperial civil servant in a colonial community, while *Growing*, as well as *Sowing* and their sequels are autobiographies that trace, among other things, the evolving communal psychology of Leonard Woolf in London, Cambridge, Ceylon, and finally the community known as Bloomsbury.

15 E. M. Forster: Ends and Means

I

Leonard Woolf returned to a Bloomsbury changed by 'marriage and death and division' (Swinburne, 'Dolores', ll. 159–60). England had also altered, and that alteration has been given perhaps its most enduring literary representation in a Bloomsbury novel: E. M. Forster's *Howards End*. Flitting through Edwardian Bloomsbury on his way to catch a train, as Virginia Woolf remembered him, Forster was usually on his way to Weybridge in Surrey (*MB*, p. 198). It was there that he wrote his fourth novel about people like himself, Virginia Woolf, and their friends. The last words of *Howards End* are 'WEYBRIDGE, 1908–1910'. They appropriately emphasise the significance of place and time in that work. (It is the only one of Forster's novels to be so commemorated.) *Howards End* is a novel of a particular place and historical time as none of his others are. The title designates a symbolic farmhouse. There, if anywhere, the heroine Margaret Schlegel believes, in a passage invoking the novel's famous epigraph,

> one might see life steadily and see it whole, group in one vision its transitoriness and its eternal youth, connect – connect without bitterness until all men are brothers. (*HE*, p. 266)

Howards End is the most autobiographical of Forster's fictive settings. At fifteen he wrote, in surprisingly mature, lucid prose, a memoir of the Hertfordshire farmhouse Rooksnest that he had lived in since he was four and now hated to leave. Rooksnest does not correspond to Howards End in all details (Forster's memoir provides a plan) but the resemblance is close. A family named Howard used to live there, and another family resembling the

Wilcoxes lived nearby.[1] Later Forster wrote of how Rooksnest was a source of passion and irrationality for him, only some of which he felt had been used up in *Howards End*. 'The house is my childhood and safety', he wrote. 'The three attics preserve me.' (PNF/*EMF* I 16). They also limited him; in his last book he said Rooksnest had given him an atavistic 'middle-class slant', which friends who never had or wanted such a home subsequently corrected (*MT*, pp. 270–1).

The time of *Howards End* is not of Forster's childhood, however. It is set in the decade when it was written, and that period is a considerable part of the work's subject. The Edwardian scene of *Howards End* can still be seen as autobiographical, however, for the novel has been widely read as a book about Bloomsbury. In a review of Virginia Woolf's *Three Guineas*, Graham Greene once asked if she were not a character invented by Forster, and as evidence he offered a description of the Schlegel sisters' convictions (*VWCH*, p. 406; *HE*, p. 25). Forster in a letter to Lowes Dickinson said that he had in mind Dickinson's London home and his three sisters, whom he had fused into two when creating the Schlegels (*HE*, pp. viii–ix). This intention has not prevented critics from identifying the Schlegels' household with that of the Stephens. Which sister resembles which is left vague in one account, but the 'dyspeptic and difficile' Tibby gets linked with the magnificent Thoby (*HE*, p. 28; Stone, p. 239). (No one has yet tried to connect Leonard Woolf to Leonard Bast, though *Howards End* is an interesting influence on *The Wise Virgins*.)

The sources of *Howards End*, in and outside of Bloomsbury are more involved and illuminating than such autobiographical equivalences suppose. Forster's novel is nevertheless about people, some of whom are like Leslie Stephen's children and their friends. Because *Howards End* has often been restrictively associated with Forster's childhood and his Bloomsbury connections, it is useful to look first at the novel's varied origins before turning to the remarkable art with which the ideal named in the title is integrated with the imperative of the novel's epigraph.

II

Howards End has been described as 'the most consummate representation of Bloomsbury attitudes and values in literary art'

(McDowell, "Fresh Woods", p. 320). Whether it is more consummate than, say, Virginia Woolf's *The Waves* could be argued, but certainly *Howards End* appears to be the most widely read embodiment of Bloomsbury values – values distinguishing between ends and means, wholes and pieces, the inner life and the outer. The prevailing beliefs in *Howards End* are liberal, feminist, and anti-imperialist. Forster calls the Schlegels 'gentlefolk', a term he also applied to Bloomsbury (*HE*, p. 43; *The Bloomsbury Group*, p. 26). But readers like Greene have, with some justice, taken the 'politico-economical-aesthetic atmosphere' of their home as a satirical representation of Bloomsbury (*HE*, p. 54). Margaret, 'zigzagging with her friends over Thought and Art', gives a quite inappropriate luncheon party for Mrs Wilcox (pp. 71, 74). Later at their women's Chelsea discussion club – which had little in common with Bloomsbury's mixed and more serious Friday Club – a paper on how to dispose of one's money sows the seeds of Helen's futile financial treatment of Leonard Bast (pp. 123–6). (The club's mock-Apostolic discussion will be echoed ten years later by Virginia Woolf in her story, 'A Society'.) As for Henry Wilcox, Helen compares him to art-grabbing supermen like Pierpont Morgan who lack self-awareness (p. 232). Forster would have heard about Morgan's antics from Roger Fry, who had been suffering from them at the Metropolitan Museum of Art. (There are allusions as well to the New English Art Club, of which Fry had been a prominent member, to the work of Ricketts, whom Fry had discussed with approval in the *Athenaeum*, and to the art of Rothenstein whom Fry had also recently praised in the *Nation*.)

The Schlegel sisters have also been related by critics to diverse novels with sisters in them, but Forster's identification of the Schlegels with the Dickinsons and, of course, with the German Schlegel brothers is more interesting. In the manuscripts of *Howards End* Forster described the father as 'a distant relation of the great critic' (*HEMSS*, p. 26:6[2]). It may be tempting to deconstruct the narration of *Howards End* with Friedrich Schlegel's ideas of romantic irony that are sometimes apparent in the narrator's comments, but Forster perhaps had other Schlegel theories in mind.[3] The background of the Schlegel family in *Howards End* introduces a different international theme from the Jamesian ones in *Where Angels Fear to Tread* and *A Room with a View*. In the German allusions, Forster made use of his experiences as a tutor to the von Arnim children, while also referring to the growing apprehension of

Prussian militarism. The Schlegel name may also suggest Lowes Dickinson's attraction to German Romanticism. Dickinson resembles Tibby more than Thoby Stephen did, though neither shared Tibby's distaste for personal relations. Forster noted in his biography of Dickinson that 'everything linked up' in him (*GLD*, p. 102), and this is a quality shared by the narrator in *Howards End* with Margaret Schlegel.

The relevance of Lowes Dickinson's character and work in the literary history of Bloomsbury has been discussed in *Victorian Bloomsbury* (pp. 176–86). His pre-war liberal socialist critique of Edwardian social anarchy is reflected in the lives of the Wilcoxes and Basts as well as the Schlegels. More specifically, certain of Dickinson's writings that were published alongside Forster's in the *Independent Review*, appear to have left their traces in *Howards End*. Two of his articles attacking the tyranny of motoring are echoed in the novel (*HE*, p. xi). A dialogue, following a Queen's Hall concert of Beethoven's Fifth, on the question of whether music means anything beyond itself appeared under the title 'Noise that You Pay for' in the same August 1904 issue that carried Forster's 'The Story of a Panic'. The setting, topic, even the word 'noise' to describe music all recur in the novel. (The painter in Dickinson's dialogue sounds like Roger Fry; Moore had also briefly discussed in *Principia Ethica* the cognitive element in appreciating Beethoven's Fifth.) But another *Independent Review* essay that Forster read also mentioned Beethoven's symphony and the famous drum passage that Tibby Schlegel urges all to concentrate on. As has been noted, Lytton Strachey's review of Blake describes the drum transition between the third and fourth movements as foretelling the annihilation of worlds, rather than of a new world as in Dickinson's dialogue (see pp. 20–1). There are Stracheyan aspects about Tibby Schlegel. Both Lytton and Tibby were dyspeptic, difficult, even unmasculine, though Strachey was certainly not frigid in personal relations. Still, if one is seeking for the Schlegels in Bloomsbury, the Stracheys are as good a place to look as the Stephens.

It was also Lytton Strachey who, in the course of an Apostle paper on mysticism and *The Longest Journey*, proposed taking an ordinary man to hear the Fifth Symphony (see p. 252). This suggests a wider social context for the origins of *Howards End* than the families of Forster's Cambridge friends. The relevance of Forster's teaching at the Working Men's College to *Howards End* has been recognised by P. N. Furbank (*EMF*, I 173–5). But also contributing to the novel's social, and political atmosphere were the writings of men like Dickinson and Strachey in the periodical that gave Forster his start as a writer and made him feel a new age had begun. *Howards End* can been seen to mark a literary end of the cultural and political milieu of Edwardian Bloomsbury that received its first published expression in the pages of the *Independent Review*. The serialisation in the first issue, for instance, of Hilaire Belloc's ironic novel *Mr. Burden*, in which the white man's burden of the title character is used by imperialist speculators, may have helped Forster with his conception of Henry Wilcox. In a late lecture on the three generations he had lived through, Forster described Belloc's book as a destructive popular satire on colonial exploitation, one that cleared the way for something new (pKC). Dickinson, of course, was a member of the editorial committee of the *Independent Review*, as was C. F. G. Masterman, who had reviewed Forster's previous three novels so encouragingly. At the end of the Edwardian decade Masterman published an influential book of essays entitled *The Condition of England*. In *Howards End* Henry Wilcox tells Helen Schlegel firmly 'there is no Social Question' (p. 188), and much of the novel's action shows how wrong he is. Some of Masterman's essays on the misery of the multitudinous poor, on 'The Conquerors' as he called capitalists like Wilcox, and on the deteriorating countryside, were first published in the *Nation* the year Forster began *Howards End*. Back in 1902, Masterman had written a collection of impressionistic essays on slum life entitled *From the Abyss: Of Its Inhabitants by One of Them*. The year before, in a more famous book, an American reported his experiences in the abyss at the time of Edward VII's coronation. Jack London's *The People of the Abyss* uses both the poetry and statistics that the narrator says in *Howards End* are necessary to approach the very poor (p. 43). The abyss of these books is what threatens Leonard Bast; its odours disturb the Schlegels, and Helen locates Beethoven's goblins there.

Beyond its origins in Bloomsbury, Cambridge, the *Independent Review*, and books on England's condition, *Howards End* has been connected by critics with a number of literary houses. Intertextual relations have been found with varying degrees of plausibility with Austen's *Mansfield Park*, Scott's *Waverley*, Dickens's *Bleak House*, Meredith's *Diana of the Crossways*, James's *The Spoils of Poynton*, Galsworthy's *A Man of Property*, and Wells's *Tono-Bungay*, just as the influence of *Howards End* has been detected in such works as Shaw's *Heartbreak House*, Ford's *Parade's End*, Waugh's *Unconditional Surrender*, and Cary's *To Be a Pilgrim*.[4] A nearer source for the converted farmhouse of Howards End in Hertfordshire is be found not in a country-house novel – Howards End is not a country house – but in an essay by Charles Lamb whose title and refrain are 'Mackery End, in Hertfordshire'. Like Howards End, Mackery End was a yeoman's farmhouse where a great-aunt of Lamb's Elia lived in 'hearty, homely, loving Hertfordshire' (p. 91). It was the oldest thing Elia remembered and became for him a phantom place that he talked of all his life. (In other essays Lamb recollected an empty Hertfordshire country house where his grandmother was house-keeper.) Lamb's memories appear to confirm Forster's at Rooksnest, and his essay helped Forster give literary form to the memories of his childhood home.

III

At the start of the pivotal Chapter 19 in *Howards End* the narrator tells us that a foreigner who wanted to see England should be taken to the summit of the Purbeck Downs on the south coast and shown how the system of England's landscape appears to spread out below. (Forster is fond of revelations on hills.) Later in the chapter, Margaret tells the appalled Helen of her coming marriage to Henry – a marriage that is to connect the primary antitheses of the novel. After the sisters quarrel Helen turns to the view, and the paragraph modulates into a description of the pulsing landscape as the sun and tide transform it. The paragraph and chapter conclude by posing the novel's fundamental questions:

> What did it mean? For what end are her fair complexities, her changes of soil, her sinuous coast? Does she belong to those who have moulded her and made her feared by other lands, or to those who have added nothing to her power, but have somehow seen her, seen the whole island at once, lying as a jewel in a silver sea, sailing as a ship of souls, with all the brave world's fleet accompanying her towards eternity? (p. 172)

The prose here has been both admired as beautifully descriptive and attacked as poetically sentimental. But the passage is partly a reflection of Helen's feelings towards her sister's engagement. The styles of *Howards End* will be discussed in the context of the authorial narrator's shifting attitudes towards his characters. What needs to be emphasised here are the crucial questions about the end of England.

Time and place come together in *Howards End* with the question of England's end. The meanings of *end* in the novel are various, and the absence of an apostrophe augments their ambiguities.[5] Literally, Howards End – like Mackery End in Lamb's essay – is the outlying property, beyond a village, once owned by the Howards. Symbolically, a farmhouse like Howards End is the purpose of England, the end-result of its 'fair complexities'. *Howards End*, like *The Longest Journey*, is concerned with the continuance of England, as Forster said late in life (*HD*, p. 294). These concerns raise questions in the novel about the meaning of England and to whom it belongs – the possessive Wilcoxes or the contemplative Schlegels. (The lowly Basts do not yet come into these questions.) The rhetoric of the passage quoted above suggests England belongs to the Schlegels, which leads to other meanings of the title and its lack of a possessive apostrophe: *Howards End* is not a possession, the end of *Howards End* is unpossessed, and so forth. Related to the question of England's destiny is the significance of Howards End as a beautiful and peaceful pastoral ideal of great value where life is fully worthwhile. The Schlegels' London home stood for culture without mistaking this for an end (p. 254). Howards End with its sheltering wych-elm symbolises a union of nature and art that is an end in itself. '*Howards End* is a hunt for a home', Forster wrote in the 1958 epilogue to *A Room with a View* (*RV*, p. 211). From rooms with views in his third novel, he went on to write of houses and their settings. The Schlegel sisters, Henry Wilcox, and Leonard Bast all hunt for homes in the novel. All end at Howards End. The last meaning of 'end' is ominously temporal. It is the place where not only the Howards but their successors the Wilcoxes and even the Schlegels have their ending. (Both Henry and Helen announce they are 'ended' at the close of the novel – pp. 331, 335). Howards End may thus be the end of any wholly and steadily connected English life.

Given these meanings of the novel's title-symbol, it is not surprising some readers have found the ending of *Howards End* equivocal. The meadow has been cut to the very end, and the hay crop is the biggest ever. Margaret is to inherit Howards End, which will eventually belong to the son of her sister and Leonard Bast. But the red urban rust creeps closer. Henry is a broken man; Leonard is dead. Margaret has a husband but wants no children; Helen has a child but wants no husband. Love and continuity are apparently incompatible. The ending of *Howards End* certainly illustrates better than *A Room with a View* the note of separation on which Forster thought modern literature should pessimistically conclude (*AE*, pp. 136–7). But is this the end, the meaning, of England's fair complexities? How consistent is the indeterminate ending of separations with the humour of *Howards End*? Comic encounters of the middle classes make up a considerable amount of the novel's action. And the novel's epigraph does not obviously project a depressing end. It reminds us that Howards End is a novel of means as well as ends.

Howards End is the only one of Forster's novels that he provided with an epigraph. The imperative '"Only connect . . . "' beneath the teleological title appears to say, among other things, that the ideal represented by Howards End is to be attained through connecting. The emphatic adverb, quotation marks, and ellipsis have their ambiguities too, however. 'Only' may say that all one needs to do is connect but there is also the possibility that connecting is the only thing left to do. The attributive quotation marks and ellipses refer to the use of the phrase in what is called Margaret's 'sermon'. But the quotation marks qualify the epigraph's authorial status, and the trailing ellipsis leaves a sense of incompletion and uncertainty. For many readers the epigraph affirms the novel's distilled wisdom outside the frame of the story. The wisdom is expressed in Margaret Schlegel's message to Henry Wilcox:

> Only connect! That was the whole of her sermon. Only connect the prose and the passion, and both will be exalted, and human love will be seen at its highest. Live in fragments no longer. Only connect, and the beast and the monk robbed of the isolation that is life to either, will die. (pp. 183–4)

Margaret's sermon is delivered to Henry after their engagement. It fails in its purpose, however, just as her attempts to make Helen understand her engagement fail. Henry obtusely and Helen intensely persist in living fragmented lives. Not until later at Howards End, does Margaret realise that here the pieces of Edwardian life might be wholly and steadily seen. The significance of the allusion to Matthew Arnold's sonnet on Sophocles is filled out in the fuller context of the poem:

> But be his
> My special thanks, whose even-balanc'd soul,
> From first youth tested up to extreme old age,
> Business could not make dull, nor Passion wild:
> Who saw life steadily and saw it whole . . . [6]
>
> ('To a Friend')

In *Howards End* Forster connects much more than steady, dull Wilcox business and wild, holistic Schlegel passion. The novel teems with antitheses, some schematically juxtaposed, others subtly implicit. These oppositions need to be considered if the scope of Forster's novel is to be fully appreciated.

Among the widest connections to be made in *Howards End* are those between means themselves and their ends. Nothing in the novel makes it a more characteristically Bloomsbury work than this theme, for the two fundamental questions on which G. E. Moore's and Bloomsbury's ethical principles rest are questions about means and ends (*Victorian Bloomsbury* – pp. 227ff.). Means are ultimately justified for Bloomsbury by the intrinsic value of the ends to which they are directed. The general criticism of modern life made in the Group's writings is that too much attention is devoted to means, while ends are ignored or confused with their means. (This is the basis, for example, of MacCarthy's criticism of Shaw.) 'It is impossible to see modern life steadily and see it whole', Margaret realises; she chooses to see it whole, while Henry looks at it steadily (*HE*, p. 158). The values of the Wilcoxes fail to aim at worthwhile ends such as those found in personal relations and the appreciation of nature and art. The Germans are interested, however inadequately, in the good, the beautiful, and the true, while the average Englishman concerns himself only with 'the respectable, the pretty, the adequate' (p. 167). The Wilcoxes are imperialists who plunder Africa of rubber, and never ask where the tyres of their cars are taking them or what their machines are doing to the English countryside. But the Schlegels are too preoccupied with valuing ends to care much about any steady means of realising them, though Margaret is something of an exception to this. In their leisured lives of culture they just discuss the economic struggles of others. Along with their upper middle-class friends and relatives, the Schlegels take for granted the means that make the pursuit of civilised ends possible. As for Leonard Bast, his impoverished means condition his sentimental ends.

The means of money is 'the second most important thing in the world', Margaret lectures her discussion group; it is 'the warp of civilization, whatever the woof might be' (p. 125). The woof, the end, is not necessarily love, which is presumably the most important thing. Earlier Margaret had told her aunt that 'the lowest abyss is not the absence of love, but the absence of coin'. Mrs Munt correctly suspects socialism when Margaret insists that the world's soul is economic and that their class's thoughts are conditioned by their money (pp. 58–9). (Margaret's forthrightness about money and the evasions of her businessman-fiancé is a source of comedy later in the novel.) But it is Helen who makes the remarkable connection of money and death in *Howards End*.

Forster thought while finishing *Howards End* that he was grinding it 'into a contrast between money & death – the latter is truly an ally of the personal against the mechanical' (p. xi). Money and Death, not Life and Death (all capitalised) are the eternal enemies, Helen tells Leonard after she and the Basts have confronted Henry and Margaret in Shropshire. Death explains the emptiness of money: as our inevitable end it shows the futility of being concerned only with means. Death is the ultimate imperialist, and this upsets the mechanically inclined Wilcoxes. 'Death destroys a man', Helen continues with a paradox that will console Leonard Bast before he dies, but 'the idea of Death saves him' (pp. 235–6). This leads to another fundamental connection in *Howards End* between the seen and the unseen.

IV

Helen pleads for the Invisible over the Visible (in Germanic caps again). She believed, as she told Margaret after her engagement, that the popular view was exactly wrong; it is not spiritual matters that are mysteriously unreal but visible things like money, the body, husbands, and houses. Margaret is not sure.

All vistas close in the unseen – no one doubts it – but Helen closed them rather too quickly for her taste. At every turn of speech one was confronted with reality and the absolute. Perhaps Margaret grew too old for metaphysics, perhaps Henry was weaning her from them, but she felt that there was something a little unbalanced in the mind that so readily sheds the visible. The businessman who assumes that this life is everything, and the mystic who asserts that is nothing, fail, on this side and on that, to hit the truth.

Margaret and the narrator balance the visible with the invisible, the natural and the supernatural, keeping proportion by excursions into each realm (p. 192). Margaret, for example, reads theosophy, a word Henry cannot even pronounce. But she knows it is only a half-way house, perhaps in the wrong direction (pp. 150, 258). Forster wrote to A. C. Benson that the supernatural element in the novel was not supposed to be 'compulsory', but he was afraid only those readers who 'take' it would get through the book easily (*L*, I 119). Bloomsbury would not have taken it easily, though they would certainly have shared Margaret's impatience with her sister's metaphysical absolute. And Bloomsbury would have agreed with the complaint that England's mythology had never got beyond Pan's pipes (*HE*, p. 264). By the end of the Edwardian decade Pan was dead even for Forster. Earlier in the novel the narrator remarks 'of Pan and the elemental forces the public has heard a little too much – they seem Victorian, while London is Georgian . . . ' (p. 106). (The Ballet Russe demonstrated this for Forster; Nijinski in *L'Après-midi d'un faune* was 'a humorous and alarming animal free from the sentimentality of my stories' – PNF/*EMF*, I 255.) Instead of Pan in *Howards End* there are goblins, apocalyptic parables, and pigs' teeth in the wych-elm. All of this may illustrate the limits of English mythology but there is also the omniscience of Ruth Wilcox, the prophetic knowledge of Miss Avery, and the mythic scene of harvest and inheritance in the last chapter of the novel.

Seen and unseen in *Howards End* are closely interconnected with past and present time, and with inner and outer experience. The landscape of Howards End (especially the Danish tumuli, described as 'tombs of warriors, breasts of the spring' – p. 305) express the past, as the Cadbury Rings and Roman road do in *The Longest Journey*. The reality of time is a preoccupation of both English novels. Seeing life whole at *Howards End* for Margaret means connecting 'its transitoriness and its eternal youth' (p. 266). But the message of the house and wych-elm 'was not of eternity, but of hope this side of the grave' (p. 203). The salvation symbolised by the farmhouse consists of the past sanctifying the present; the present, with wild heart-throb, declaring that there would after all be a future, with laughter and the voices of children. (p. 296)

Forster's concern with temporal reality and mortality throughout his fiction is moral and secular. Helen's argument about the saving idea of death (which Forster took from Michelangelo) exemplifies it. In the end, death is attractive to Leonard. And though he gives up the cultural past, including the books of George Meredith and others that once nourished him, he never confuses or forgets his personal past, as Meredith in *Modern Love* said he should not (*HE*, p. 315). The contrast with Henry Wilcox is sharp. He cannot connect his own past with the present and has no use for history or culture, unlike Ruth who worships the past. Henry concentrates his business mind on the five minutes of the past and five minutes of the future that constitute the present. He never thinks of death, and yet is no pagan philosopher seizing the day (p. 245). His present is not the peaceful, pastoral murmur of '"now" and "now"' that passes understanding (p. 312). The allusion here is as non-Christian as the teleology of *Howards End*.

As fundamental as means and ends to *Howards End* is the dualism of the inner and the outer. In Forster's novels the divisions between interior, personal life and exterior public existence are primarily moral and social ones. Early in *Howards End* the Schlegel sisters worry that theirs is a subjective existence of sloppy personal relations, whereas the Wilcoxes lead outer lives with real grit in them. But Margaret and Helen care deeply about politics. 'They desired that public life should mirror whatever is good in the life within', just as the 'private life holds out the mirror to infinity' and even hints, for Margaret, at a personality beyond daily vision (pp. 25, 79). All of which leaves the sisters inattentive to the imperial matters that exercise Henry and his friends. At the end of *Howards End*, the affection between Margaret and Helen shows that 'the inner life had paid' (p. 296). The Wilcoxes can be affectionate too – Henry is described as having 'strong but furtive passions' (p. 240) – but their unselfconscious inner darkness, their inability to understand themselves, to say 'I', inhibits their personal relations. It also gives them a power that Helen, who has been reading Nietzsche, fears might take over the world (pp. 231–2). Communication in the Wilcox world is often a matter of 'telegrams and anger' (p. 25). The Schlegels write letters and sympathise.

Howards End is a novel not about the superiority of private life over public, however, but about their necessary connections. Personal relations are not enough. (At university Tibby Schlegel, who has had too much of them in his upbringing, says that the importance of personal relations has been greatly exaggerated by specialists, the university in question being Oxford – p. 250.) Personal relationships must be grounded in an outer natural world. Urban life puts too great a strain on them (p. 258). 'Panic and emptiness' (p. 31) threaten those who live the inner or the outer life too exclusively. Margaret, the narrator suggests, is able to connect more than both Helen, who isolates, and Henry, who concentrates. Then there is Leonard Bast who fails in both worlds 'as one of the thousands who have lost the life of the body and failed to reach the life of the spirit' (p. 113). He will not gain his soul, Margaret insists in her discussion club, until he has gained something of the world (p. 125). (Echoed again here is the epigram from Strachey's Blake review that Forster had used in *The Longest Journey* – see p. 239.)

Inner–outer dichotomies in *Howards End* are given another revealing formulation by Forster in terms of love and truth. Caught at Oniton between Helen and Henry, Margaret realises how wide the gulf is between the loving of men like Henry as they are, and the yearning with her sister for the truth of what these men ought to be.

> Love and Truth – their warfare seems eternal. Perhaps the whole visible world rests on it, and, if they were one, life itself, like the spirits when Prospero was reconciled to his brother, might vanish into air, into thin air. (p. 227)

The inner reality of love can be connected with outer ideal truth but not harmonised. Irreconcilable differences remain. Such divisions in the novel manifest the irreducible pluralism of life. To see life whole does not mean seeing it monistically. '"Only connect . . . "' the epigraph says, not only synthesise. When the pregnant Helen hides from Margaret in a London that becomes 'a caricature of infinity', her sister believes that

> she had accomplished a hideous act of renunciation and returned to the One. Margaret's own faith held firm. She knew that the human soul will be merged, if it be merged at all, with the stars and the sea. (p. 277)

She fears the consequences of Helen's love of the absolute: that love is why the absolutely ruined Leonard so appealed to her sister (p. 314). Ironically, as a consequence of that appeal, the pregnant Helen is literally in the process of becoming two. The conclusion in the last chapter that Margaret draws for Helen, who worries that she cannot love as Margaret loves, is that

> people are far more different than is pretended. All over the world men and women are worrying because they cannot develop as they are supposed to develop. . . . Develop what you have; love your child. I do not love children. . . . Others go further still, and move outside humanity altogether. . . . Don't you see that all this leads to comfort in the end? It is part of the battle against sameness. Differences – eternal differences, planted by God in a single family, so that there may always be colour; sorrow perhaps, but colour in the daily gray. (pp. 335–6)

The eternal differences of *Howards End* make connecting more complex than the simple imperative of the epigraph seems initially to promise. How connections are made is as important as what is being connected. To connect in the novel is not simply to merge, for conflicts are also kinds of connections. To connect is to reflect, relate, associate, impact upon, or oppose the discontiguous, the separated, or the fragmentary. Connecting opens doors, makes bridges, crosses borders; it eliminates some distinctions, preserves or develops others. Seeing life steadily and whole means, among other things, perceiving its values in Moore's organic wholes whose connected parts may signify more or less than their totals (*Victorian Bloomsbury*, pp. 228, 230). The epigraph of *Principia Ethica* – Bishop Butler's 'Everything is what it is and not another thing' – is completed in the epigraph of *Howards End*.

'"Only connect . . . "' is also, of course, a reflexive statement of how to read modern texts. The quest for connection defines much modernist literature. Forster had been reading French symbolist poetry the year he began the novel (PNF/*EMF*, I 167), and works like Baudelaire's 'Correspondances' are in the novel's background. The art of connectivity in *Howards End* is metaphorical and metonymic, symbolic and realistic. The scope of its symbolic conjunctions extends from sex to metaphysics. Symbols such as the Mrs Wilcox's wisp of hay or the Schlegel sword and books that kill Bast may appear unduly explicit, but others like Beethoven's goblins of panic and emptiness are more complex. It is the imaginative Helen who hears the Fifth Symphony so programmatically (Margaret rejects the Wagnerian muddling of the arts) but the narrator then takes over the symbolism and connects the goblin footfalls with the abyss that threatens Leonard Bast, whose surname suggests his lack of status. Doors sometimes function symbolically in *Howards End* like windows in *A Room with a View*: they open for, or shut against, Bast until he feels them opening and shutting in his own body (p. 317). Other symbols are only partially explicable. An example is the use of glass; married couples seem isolated by glass, and the glass fragments of loved ones' framed photographs cut fingers. The title symbol of the farmhouse and its wych-elm stand for England itself. Howards End in Hertfordshire is the centre that proportion attains after excursions into the realms of London, the Purbeck Downs, Housman's Shrewsbury, even Germany – but again, connection is not a synthesis. City and country are related, but not united. At Christmas in London Margaret feels 'the grotesque impact of the unseen upon the seen' in a satanic city (pp. 79, 82). (In an essay on London written in the Thirties Forster recalled that, like Blake, he used to denounce the town when living in Hertfordshire but had come to agree with T. S. Eliot that London was a 'muddle which need not be unpleasant' – 2CD, p. 352.)

Travel is one of the principal forms of symbolic connection in the novel. Margaret wants to help Henry, who is described as an incomplete ascetic; she wants him to connect his arches of beast and monk into 'the rainbow bridge that should connect the prose in us with the passion.' The narrator's prose then undercuts Margaret's passion with a change of travel metaphors: 'it was hard going in the roads of Mr Wilcox's soul' (p. 183). The Wilcoxes are connected with destructive automobiles. Railway stock is a source of the Schlegels' income. ('Home Rails' do not do as well as 'Foreign Things', however – p. 11.) Edwardian England is becoming 'the civilization of luggage', says the narrator (p. 146). Behind all the comings and goings, the telegrams and anger (a characteristic symbolist association by Forster of objects with feelings) may lie some other familiar lines of Matthew Arnold's poetry that describe 'This strange disease of modern life,/With its sick hurry, its divided aims . . . ' (Arnold, p. 147). Figurative ship and water images are frequent in *Howards End*. The island of England is a ship of souls (p. 172). The question of her end depends upon whose hands are on the ropes. For Leonard Bast struggling to keep his head out of the gray waters, it is the Schlegels; but for the Schlegels, it is the Wilcoxes who control the ropes. The Schlegels' London life is very watery. They live in a backwater; the tides of the city lap at them on their islands of income. Ruth Wilcox tells Margaret they are all in the same boat, and then dies like a seafarer 'who can greet with an equal eye the deep that he is entering, and the shore that he must leave' (p. 100). Afterwards, her husband and son sail past her wish to bequeath Howards End to Margaret, as Ulysses's sailors sailed by the Sirens (p. 99). Margaret feels 'the vessel of life itself slipping past her' with Wilcoxes on board, and after Oniton, Helen has the look, Tibby thinks, 'of a sailor who has lost everything at sea' (pp. 147, 247).

Yet Forster is doing more in *Howards End* than connecting – both literally and figuratively – means with ends, the visible with the invisible, present and past, outer and inner, truth and love. He is also showing how the differences between these needed connections are manifest in the socio-economic inequalities of the novel's Edwardian world – and how they reveal the necessity for what may be the most important connections of all in *Howards End*, those of class and gender.

V

In 1939 E. M. Forster wrote a paper for a political discussion group in which he looked back to the Edwardian period as a liberal time of hope without faith that exalted personal relations and refused to divide the community into masculine and feminine. Would they had also refused to divide it into rich and poor, he added ('Three Generations', pKC). The rich and poor of *Howards End* reflect the author's middle-class slant. Middle-class inequalities are the ones the novel connects. The very poor are unthinkable, we are ironically told at the beginning of the chapter on Leonard Bast's home life, except by poets and statisticians (as if poetry was much concerned with the very poor in 1910). Even with Leonard and Jacky the limits of the novelist's knowledge or imagination are apparent. The books of C. F. G. Masterman and Jack London show how indescribable for a novelist with Forster's experience and gifts was the abyss of the London lower classes that yawns for the Basts. Also missing from *Howards End* are the aristocracy and the plutocracy. There are no references, as in Strachey's fragment of country-house fiction, to the crisis of Lloyd George's budget and the House of Lords. The means and ends of aspiring and established 'gentlefolk' are the subject of Forster's English novels (*HE*, p. 43).

Middle-class connections in *Howards End* occur through the upper-middle-class Schlegel sisters' flawed relationships with middle-middle- and lower-middle-class men. Inequalities remain, nevertheless, for both Leonard and Henry fail to connect. Leonard cannot connect the prose of an insurance clerk's existence with the passion of the romantic wanderer. The fault, it is suggested by the Forsterian narrator, is economic and cultural. Bast is undernourished in body and mind; he has the heart of a man, but it is symbolically diseased. The descendant of agricultural labourers, he along with his wife is now trapped in London and must maintain gentility as a member of the black-coated urban proletariat without sufficient means to do so. His precarious economic status is dependent upon the vagaries of capitalism. After losing his job, Bast is thrown back on the family that Forster sees as the basis of society in the novel. (Three extended families essentially comprise the social system of *Howards End*.) In the end he is culturally unemployed as well, for he discovers that even the literary walks in the woods depend on money. Without it, the bailiff takes the books.

Leonard Bast's cultural progress through *Howards End* begins with a concert and the loss of a shabby umbrella. His recovery of it reminds the Schlegels that beneath the superstructure of their wealth he wanders like a goblin of panic and emptiness from Beethoven's C Minor Symphony (p. 42). At home with Jacky, literature and art in the shape of Ruskin's *The Stones of Venice* and G. F. Watts's pictures fail Leonard.[7] His 'half-baked mind' hopes for a lucky cultural conversion, but it is not to be found in reading Ruskin's extraordinary Venetian description, which is parodied in a baroque sentence on the obscurity of the Basts' flat and its absence of ventilation. There is no connecting Ruskin's passionate prose with Leonard's style. '"My flat is dark as well as stuffy." Those were the words for him' he realises (p. 47). Matthew Arnold fails him too:

Oh, it was no good, this continual aspiration. Some are born cultured; the rest had better go in for whatever comes easy. To see life steadily and to see it whole was not for the likes of him.

(p. 52)

This qualification of one of the central connections in *Howards End* suggests that Forster's un-Victorian novel is less Arnoldian than some critics have found it. Certainly Ruskin appears to be irrelevant to Leonard's world. Forster's chapter on his home life ends rather bitterly with an anachronistic observation by Ruskin on the essential indifference of nature's power and beauty to Leonard's misery.

In trying to talk with the Schlegels later of his adventurous night walk, Bast mentions Meredith and Stevenson, Lucas and Jefferies, 'Borrow, Thoreau, and sorrow', the narrator continues, 'and the outburst ended in a swamp of books' (anticipating the shower of books under which he will die under). Bast had mistaken the means that the books of these writers are, for the ends they point to (p. 118). Culture, once again, is a means not an end. Forster makes the same point differently in 'The Celestial Omnibus', where the boy, not the cultural snob Bons, is crowned with 'telos' (*CO*, p. 83).

How are the material and spiritual inequalities of lower-middle-class lives like Leonard Bast's to be compassed? Margaret, who is the first to take an interest in Leonard, comes to think brotherhood might be attainable through connection in places like Howards End. To her, Hertfordshire promises 'the comradeship, not passionate, that is our highest gift as a nation'. She believes the county would vote Liberal if left to itself (pp. 265–6). The implication is that middle-class Conservatives like Henry Wilcox do not leave the county alone, as the 'gentle conservatism' of Ruth Wilcox did (p. 91). Domination and indifference rather than comradeship are the attitude of male Wilcoxes toward others in the country, the city, or the empire. The particular association here of the Liberal Party with comradeship and rural life is as close as Forster comes in *Howards End* to a political view of Edwardian inequalities, and his attitude can be traced back to the Cambridge liberalism of Dickinson, Masterman, and the *Independent Review*.

Comradeship is necessary for the transcending of not only class inequalities but those of gender in a narrative that represents the consequences of women connecting with men. *Howards End* is Forster's most feminist work, and not only because its leading characters are two suffragist sisters. The wise woman Ruth Wilcox is glad not to have a vote, which dismays the Schlegels; yet she is not content, like the wife of an imperialist in the novel, simply to influence her husband. The first Mrs Wilcox's 'idea of politics' is expressed in the conviction 'that if the mothers of various nations could meet there would be no more wars' (p. 88) – a radical idea from what has recently been identified as social feminism (Black). Certainly Margaret Schlegel's marital aspirations are more feminist, if less sexual, than Lucy Honeychurch's in *A Room with a View*. (But in both novels the consequences of Lucy's and Helen's being kissed seem quite old-fashionedly un-Edwardian.) Margaret has a reputation as an emancipated woman; she hopes women's not working will be as shocking in the future as their not marrying was in the past (pp. 144, 108). When Henry Wilcox refuses to connect his affair with Jacky and Helen's with Leonard, Margaret denounces him as criminally muddled (p. 305). Henry is right that the cases are quite different – but the difference, Margaret points out, is between infidelity of a man and the unchastity of a woman. Henry's medieval moral education makes him unable to understand the distinction (p. 256).

Margaret's condemnation of Henry's sexism was an attempt, the narrator says later, to adjust for once

the lopsidedness of the world. It was spoken not only to her husband, but to thousands of men like him – a protest against the inner darkness in high places that comes with a commercial age.
(p. 329)

The linking of sexual inequality here with men who see inner life darkly and outer life commercially displays the feminist significance of personal, cultural, and socio-economic connections and disconnections that *Howards End* represents.

The feminism of Forster's fourth novel manifests itself clearly in the way gender and class differences are symbolically related. Margaret seeks to connect her woman's experience of cultural wholes with the Wilcoxes's concentration on the fragmenting world of business. Helen was the first to be attracted by the male energy of the Wilcoxes; she enjoyed being told the Schlegel fetishes of suffrage, socialism, and the arts were nonsense, until Paul's panic had shown her the emptiness beneath Wilcox matter-of-factness. The tenuous, omniscient Ruth Wilcox, who had linked her yeoman and Quaker heritage with the Wilcoxes in order to save Howards End, is from another world, and she wants a Schlegel to inherit Howards End, not a Wilcox. Margaret nevertheless realises the Schlegel household is 'irrevocably feminine'. All they can do, she says, is to see that it isn't effeminate. Just as another house that I can mention, but won't, sounded irrevocably masculine and all its inmates can do to see that it isn't brutal. (p. 41)

Margaret wishes that her brother Tibby cared more for masculine life and had some of the Wilcox charm. (He has a good friend from *A Room with a View*, but it is Cecil Vyse – p. 108.) Though Tibby possesses more brains and character than his counterpart Charles Wilcox, he responds to an upbringing of feminine personal relations with frigidity, and passes from boyhood directly into middle age, the narrator tells us (p. 276).

It is Margaret once again who acknowledges the male economic basis of her artistic and intellectual leisure when she tells her sister after her engagement to Henry, 'more and more do I refuse to draw my income and sneer at those who guarantee it' (p. 172). Henry Wilcox had saved Howards End for the last of the Howards, whom Miss Avery thought should have married a soldier. There is no military class in *Howards End*; the tombs of the Danish warriors near Howards End are reminders of a past to which all the Wilcoxes except Ruth are oblivious. Commercial imperialists like the Wilcoxes are the nearest thing to soldiers in *Howards End*, and though they may protect, they are not conservers. (Imperial civil servants in Leonard Woolf's Ceylon despised commercial imperialists, yet their own government's policy of chena-conservation could be destructive.) Henry's is a siege mentality; he is described as reconstructing his fortress after set-backs. The imperialists of *Howards End* are called destroyers; they scatter dust and money as they ride over the countryside, harbingers of the urban blight that Forster terms cosmopolitanism (p. 320). Henry's imperial adventures overseas are explicitly connected with his betrayal of his wife and the sexual exploitation of Jacky (in the colony of Cyprus, birthplace of Aphrodite). The father of the Schlegels had been a disillusioned soldier who gave up German conquest for an English imperialism of the air (p. 26). His sword is used by Charles Wilcox to kill a clerk.

Women cannot win real battles, Margaret believes, 'having no muscles, only nerves' (p. 256). Her influence over Henry is exerted by 'the methods of the harem' (p. 227). Yet in the crisis of Helen's pregnancy,

a new feeling came over her: she was fighting for women against

men. She did not care about rights, but if men came into
Howards End it should be over her body. (p. 287)

Earlier she had said she, had no use for justice or duty (p. 225).
What counts ethically for Forster, his heroine, and Bloomsbury are
not notions of duty and right, but good or bad moral consequences.
And Margaret wins – 'she, who had never expected to conquer
anyone, had charged straight through these Wilcoxes and broken
up their lives' (p. 339). She had told Henry he must see the
connection between Helen's situation and his own even if it killed
him, and it almost does. Howards End will be inherited by her, as
Ruth wished, and then by the heir of the Schlegels and the Basts.
Women have won the battle of the sexes in *Howards End*. England's
fair complexities, in so far as they are symbolised by the house and
land, belong for the time being to those who add nothing to her
power but are able to see her whole (p. 172).

The price of the Schlegels' victory over the Wilcoxes appears to be
not so much a feminisation of the novel, as some male critics have
felt, but a general devaluing of heterosexual experience itself.
'"Only connect . . . "' functions as a sexual imperative in the plot of
Howards End, and we are told 'it is those that cannot connect who
hasten to cast the first stone' (p. 309). But the pleasures of sexuality
are minimised. Human beings are 'personalities capable of
sustained relations, not mere opportunities for electrical discharge',
the narrator says condescendingly about Helen's infatuation with
Paul, while also conceding such emotion can shake open the doors
of heaven (pp. 22–3). Henry's proposal thrills Margaret because 'her
personality had been touched' for the first time:

> She had often 'loved', too, but only so far as the facts of sex
> demanded: mere yearnings for the masculine, to be dismissed for
> what they were worth, with a smile. (p. 162)

Some readers in the Twenties and Thirties would interpret the
epigraph of *Howards End* homosexually, but it is simplistic to locate
the source of the work's attitudes toward sexual relations between
men and women in its author's sexual inclinations. There is a more
overt and convincing Bloomsbury basis for the criticism of middle-
class sexuality of *Howards End*, and it is located in the connection
Forster makes between heterosexuality and the inequality of gender
in Edwardian England.

After her engagement, Margaret experiences the segregation of the sexes practised by the Wilcox class as she travels with Henry and his friends to the wedding of Henry's daughter.

'Male and female created He them'; the journey to Shrewsbury confirmed this questionable statement, and the long glass saloon that moved so easily and felt so comfortable, became a forcing-house for the idea of sex. (p. 208)

Margaret hopes 'the tenderness that kills the monk and the beast at a single blow' will ultimately change Henry (p. 218). But after being prevented by Charles Wilcox from helping when a little girl's cat is run over in Shropshire, she asks herself

are the sexes really races, each with its own code of morality, and their mutual love a mere device of Nature's to keep things going? . . . She knew that out of Nature's device we have built a magic that will win us immortality. Far more mysterious than the call of sex to sex is the tenderness that we throw into that call; far wider is the gulf between us and the farmyard than between the farmyard and the garbage that nourishes it. We are evolving in ways that Science cannot measure, to ends that Theology dares not contemplate. (pp. 237–8).

The narrator, who has taken over from Margaret here, mentions again a little apocalyptic myth that he sketched after her engagement. In it, man will eventually be granted immortality by the gods at the world's end because the jewel of Love he produced is gathered by Fate from the slime. (Love is male in this story and cannot understand the infinitude of Fate, who is female.) With a characteristic Forsterian touch, this jejune myth – a reminder perhaps that England lacks a mythology – is subverted by a comic allegory of matrimony as a voyage between the rocks of Property and Propriety, in which the winds of Family Pride and the ground-swell of Theology are calmed by cold, creeping lawyers and the pouring of half-guineas on the troubled waters (p. 173). Nevertheless, love has been associated with slime, and sex with garbage. When Forster's mother and others were shocked by *Howards End* with its illegitimate child, colonial sex, and ruined women and men, Forster complained in his diary that he never written anything less erotic, and he was right (*HE*, p. xiii). He had also written little that was less Edwardian. Helen views Jacky Bast as a Victorian cliché – the fallen woman ruined by the likes of Henry Wilcox, who must now maritally entrap a young men like Leonard or follow prostitution to the workhouse and the lunatic asylum (p. 249).

The human evolution that Margaret foresees beyond the formulations of science or theology is referred to again when she questions the nature of Helen's personal relations. Helen

> could pity, or sacrifice herself, or have instincts, but had she ever loved in the noblest way, where man and woman, having lost themselves in sex, desire to lose sex itself in comradeship?
>
> (p. 309)

The desire to lose sex, the celebration of 'comradeship, not passionate', as England's greatest gift, is a rather ascetic end in *Howards End* – one that leaves the monks of prose more fit than the beasts of passion. It is symbolised by the wych-elm and Howards End itself. The tree bending over the house

> was neither warrior, nor lover, nor god; in none of these roles do the English excel. It was a comrade, bending over the house. . . . House and tree transcended any simile of sex. (p. 203)

Are the inequalities of gender also to be attained, then, with the transcending of heterosexuality in *Howards End*? The ambivalent ending provides no clear answer. Differences certainly remain, if not inequalities – the valuable differences of individuality that Margaret insists upon to Helen.

Although gender inequality may be transcended along with sex in *Howards End*, gender stereotyping is not. It would be rather surprising if it were in 1910. The separate worlds of male business and female culture endure. After Jacky's exposure of Henry Wilcox,

Margaret is eventually able to respond with love, and the narrator hazards a generalisation:

> When men like us, it is for our better qualities, and however tender their liking we dare not be unworthy of it, or they will quietly let us go. But unworthiness stimulates woman. It brings out her deeper nature, for good or for evil. (p. 240)

(The nuances of Forster's style are worth noting here in the identification of the narrator and reader with men, and then the comparison of the plurality of 'men' with the abstract singularity of 'woman'.) The narrator notes earlier how 'the female mind, though cruelly practical in daily life, cannot bear to hear ideals belittled . . . ' (p. 125). The tender comradeship into which heterosexuality should develop does not resemble the androgynous man-womanliness or woman-manliness notion sketched by Virginia Woolf in *A Room of One's Own*. Couples here transcend their sexuality rather than harmonising its opposites within themselves.

The most valuable personal relationship in *Howards End* is between two sisters. Theirs is the inner life that pays. Tibby Schlegel remains frigid and effeminate. As a man he is able to be more unconventional than his sisters; but without sympathy his attitude can produce no art and only a little culture (pp. 306–7). The notion of comradeship retains its masculine connotations in *Howards End*. (Forster had also been reading Whitman while writing the novel.) Even Margaret, in the passage that directly invokes the epigraph, thinks one is to connect 'until all men are brothers' (p. 266). Yet unlike *The Longest Journey*, which it so resembles in the concern for the pastoral future of England and the criticism of monogamy, *Howards End* represents no serious emotional relationships between men. Forster would attempt no more novels without these.

In his more hedonistic old age, Forster became impatient with the sexual attitudes of *Howards End*. He agreed in his *Commonplace Book* in 1958 that although it was his best novel (as Trilling may have persuaded him), he had just discovered he did not like a single character in it:

> Perhaps the house in *H. E.*, for which I once did care, took the place of people and now that I no longer care for it their barrenness has become evident. I feel pride in the achievement,

but cannot love it, and occasionally the swish of the skirts and the non-sexual embraces irritate.   (*CB*, p. 203–4)

VI

The spectrum of moral and social issues in *Howards End* helped to make it Forster's most widely read Edwardian novel, but its appeal also depended, of course, on the literary art with which Forster represented these concerns. Critics of the work have objected, however, to its implausible coincidences, intrusive narration, schematic symbolism, and unconvincing characterisation. Sometimes Forster agreed with them. He had trouble with the construction of *Howards End*. It was not, like his previous three books, an education novel. The first half of the book develops the Schlegel sisters' often comic encounters with the Wilcoxes and the Basts. But after Margaret's union with Henry, and then Helen's with Leonard, the relationship of the sisters that gives the first part so much of its interest recedes. Forster wrote to Edward Garnett amusingly – given the title and the treatment of sex – that he fancied the novel 'suffers from paralysis in its hindquarters' (Jefferson, p. 103). Garnett continued to be one of Forster's most perceptive and sympathetic critics; he praised *Howards End* highly for its philosophic criticism of the middle classes, but also thought the work lacked the inevitability of great art. Its plot was too ingeniously accidental, the characters too strained, and too much had been sacrificed to the moral (*EMFCH*, pp. 139–42). Forster found the criticism just and said he hoped to profit by it:

> It is devilish difficult to criticise society & create human beings. Unless one has a big mind, one aim or the other fails before the book is finished. I must pray for a big mind, but it is uphill work – ! (*L*, I 117)

Forster may never have attained a big mind, but he always had an artistic one. Garnett's criteria apply chiefly to realistic novels, and Forster was not always trying to write that kind of fiction. (A few years afterwards Garnett would have similar difficulty appreciating what Lawrence was doing in *The Rainbow*.) Virginia Woolf's assessment of Forster's work in the Twenties found a wavering double vision in it, and later critics have even argued that

Forster was not really writing novels but something like romances. *Howards End* does make use of the symbols, motifs, coincidences, and stereotypes of romance, but much of his fiction still belongs to the tradition of novelistic realism that Forster saw himself continuing from Jane Austen. Yet there are anti-novelistic elements in *Howards End*. From its offhand first sentence ('One may as well begin with Helen's letters to her sister') down to the death of Leonard Bast in a subordinate clause ('They laid Leonard, who was dead, on the gravel . . . ' – *HE*, p, 321) Forster plays down the story aspect of his novel. Indeed, the tone of the opening sentence is like the lecturer's drooping voice in *Aspects of the Novel*, which says regretfully, 'Yes – oh dear yes – the novel tells a story' (p. 17). In *Howards End* that voice is sometimes the narrator's.

Readers of *Howards End* remain aware of the novel's fictitiousness because the narrator keeps reminding them he is telling a story that is both comic and serious in its criticism of modern life. The narrator also continues making remarks on contingencies in the novel that are beyond his creation or control. Touches like the ellipses in Helen's first letter when clothes are mentioned contribute to the novel's verisimilitude. Forster's outlook is close to his narrator's, just as the narrator's is close to Margaret Schlegel's. (Margaret and Helen, though sisters, are not the composite Indian goddess that Leonard first takes them for – *HE*, p. 137.) Forster said once that in Margaret he was trying to connect up all the fragments he was born with (*M*, p. viii). He renders admiringly in the novel the 'profound vivacity' of her 'continual and sincere response to all that she encountered in her path through life' (*HE*, p. 7). Yet the narrator is not simply to be identified with the heroine of *Howards End* or its author.

The mediating narrator is essential in *Howards End* to its connections, its modernity, its charm. Although Forster dispenses with melodramatic suspense, the novel still has its conventions of surprise. The narrator does not tell all that the author knows about the story. Ruth Wilcox's death (it takes a while to find out whose funeral is being described in Chapter 11) is a little like the sudden ones in *The Longest Journey*. Leonard's demise is explicitly anticipated at the openings of Chapters 38 and 40, while Helen's pregnancy, though also foreshadowed, is carefully concealed. As a modern narrator, Forster's story-teller is not omniscient; he knows enough about his characters, however, to make moral judgements that challenge comparison with those of the reader. After the narrator's presence is established by the casualness of the opening sentence, the chapter then proceeds as if *Howards End* were going to be an epistolary novel. Throughout the text the narrator comments, sometimes personally, other times impersonally, on the progress of the story and the behaviour of its characters. Following Margaret's engagement to Mr Wilcox, for instance, the narrator announces he must now call him Henry (p. 174). While this intrusion may weaken the will of readers to believe by distancing them from the story, it also contributes to the detachment needed for an appreciation of the novel's humour. The narrator's tone and changing points of view – unlike the Wilcoxes he can say 'I' when he wants to – modernise a story that offers such traditional novelistic fare as a concealed bequest, a ruined woman, an illegitimate child, and a murder.

One of the ways the narrator maintains his independence in *Howards End* is through discourse with the reader. In Chapter 2, for example, the narrator comments on Margaret's view that King's Cross Station suggests infinity; he hopes this will not put off readers, and asks them to remember 'that it is not Margaret who is telling you about it . . . ' (p. 9). A little later the narrator again distinguishes between Helen's unquoted account of what happened with Paul Wilcox and his own more sympathetic words (p. 22). At the beginning of the chapter on Leonard's home life, the reader is addressed less familiarly; the pronouns shift from first-person singular to the plural when the narrator announces 'We are not concerned with the very poor' (*HE*, p. 43). A few pages later Jacky's photograph brings him back to the singular:

> Take my word for it, that smile was simply stunning, and it is only you and I who will be fastidious and complain that true joy begins in the eyes, and that the eyes of Jacky did not accord with her smile, but were anxious and hungry. (p. 46)

The narrator's association with the reader, who of course has no one else's word to take for it, begins in sardonic fastidiousness, but continues in moral compassion for the character.

A more fundamental intervention occurs with the Wilcoxes' denial of Ruth's dying wish. 'It is rather a moment when the commentator should step forward', the narrator proclaims. 'Ought the Wilcoxes to have offered their home to Margaret? I think not.' Various reasons are given, the main one being that Ruth was seeking a spiritual heir; the house for her was a spirit, and spiritual things cannot be bequeathed. (Henry's willing of Howards End 'absolutely' to Margaret at the end of the novel is presumably just a material bequest.) The Wilcoxes were wrong to ignore her personal appeal, but their agenda approach to human affairs protects them from the pain of seeing things whole (pp. 96–7). Later the narrator returns to the impersonal third-person to parody Henry Wilcox's steady view of life:

> Henry treated a marriage like a funeral, item by item, never raising his eyes to the whole, and 'Death where is thy sting? Love where is thy victory?' one would exclaim at the close. (p. 217)

The narrative art of *Howards End* appears thoroughly modern in the casual but serious, ironic, and self-conscious attitudes expressed toward the characters and story. Nevertheless, Forster's own expressed dissatisfaction with aspects of his novels brings up the question of just how thorough a literary artist he was – a question that is often conflated with a quite different one about how aware Forster was of what he was doing. 'People will not realize how little conscious one is of these things', he said in a late interview, and suggested critics should take a course 'on writers *not* thinking things out . . . ' (Interview, p. 34). Whatever he may or may not have been thinking about when he created *Howards End* and then *A Passage to India*, there is now abundant published evidence of the painstaking art with which Forster wrote and rewrote these works. Oliver Stallybrass's edition of the manuscripts of *Howards End* transcribes the extensive changes Forster made in revising the novel, which he completed in July, 1910.[8] (The changes Forster made in the novel's typescript and proofs have been lost, but a few working notes and fragments from earlier stages survive.) There is no space here to discuss in detail the changes Forster made between manuscript and book, but some of the revisions, particularly the deletions, should be mentioned, for they show Forster working out the matter of *Howards End*.

The original idea for his novel that Forster noted in his diary focused on 'the spiritual cleavage' between the Schlegel and Wilcox families, as manifested first with Helen's engagement and later with Margaret's after Mrs Wilcox's death. Despite Mr Wilcox's affair with a prostitute, Margaret wrongly marries him, and he goes to the bad because in his dread of ideas he cannot stand being understood

(*HE*, p. vii). Absent from this conception is any notion of Leonard Bast. Bast figures prominently but uncertainly in later working notes; also in those preliminary notes Margaret refuses the legacy of Howards End but is eventually settled there with a child. Forster had not settled on the form of the legacy and remained dissatisfied with his solution. (Years later he wrote to J. R. Ackerley that Miss Avery should have communicated Ruth's dying wish to the Wilcoxes – 4.i.65, EMF/pT.) Jacky appears with Leonard in the notes, as does Helen, who becomes involved with Leonard. Charles trying to horsewhip Leonard is killed by him, while Leonard's end is unclear; he may commit suicide, and Helen too might die (*HEMSS*, p. 355). In the manuscript drafts of the novel, however, almost all the features of the final story have been determined, though Helen's relationships are somewhat different; she confides in Ruth Wilcox, and later tells Margaret that Leonard had talked to her about his marriage (pp. 24:26, 145:14). Henry Wilcox's exposure by Jacky appears originally to have been planned for Swanage rather than Oniton, where Forster drew on Housman associations. (This change that may account for deleted passages describing Swanage – *HEMSS*, pp. xii, 184:31, 190:5.) Forster also cancelled several pages that sketched out Leonard's development after Oniton and had him wanting to take an immense walk or experience the sea, then obtaining some temporary employment while continuing to conceal his love for Helen (*HEMSS*, pp. 322–6).

The general style of the completed novel is basically unchanged from the manuscripts. Forster does not connect his prose any more or less with passion than in the drafts. His revisions reveal no trace of the feeling he expressed in a letter, while writing *Howards End* in 1909, that he had lost his inspiration and been unable to replace it with 'solidity', or that he seemed to be writing more now for an audience (*HE*, p. xii).

There are also no substantial alterations in the conception of the characters. Forster did change a number of passages that describe or comment upon the Schlegels. Originally, the source of their mother's money, on which they live, comes from the potteries, as in an Arnold Bennett novel (*HEMSS*, p. 98:1). Forster reduced this income by half in his revisions (p. 59:10–1). Tibby Schlegel is the occasion for a digression on the mysteries of young boys' growth in their teens that is autobiographically resonant:

The voices of devils distract him, the voices of men frighten him, literature and art, for which he longs, are unscaleable mountains of names. . . . He needs human aid. One does know that much.

(p. 103:33)

The crucial relationship of Margaret and Helen is essentially unaltered. In one deleted passage, Margaret insists that people cannot be idealised (p. 54:5). Her speech anticipates a later one on the eternal differences between people, and also looks back to the concerns of *The Longest Journey*. The culminating description of the sisters' love when they are together at Howards End, waiting for Wilcox's siege to begin, reads quite differently. Forster originally wrote:

> Wife who was never to be a mother, mother who was not a wife – they could not be parted by such things or by any things. The Schlegels had received their reward.

This was reduced to 'the inner life had paid', which ties in with their earlier valuing of personal relations (p. 296:18). (In an earlier passage on the security of their inner lives together, Forster cancelled Helen's description of them 'as safe as houses', which is a little too ironical, given the uncertain fates of houses in *Howards End* – p. 192:34.)

A number of revisions in the manuscripts of *Howards End* pertain to the views and qualities of Margaret Schlegel. Her generous enumeration of Henry Wilcox's virtues to Helen – 'Manliness. Frankness. Tolerance. Cleanness of mind and body. Very great kindness. Common sense.' – is cut but not her earlier criticisms of his obtuseness (p. 171:18). A paragraph toward the end of the novel on her love for Henry and how it may have lead her to presume beyond her abilities is also omitted (p. 329:29). Other deletions emphasise the preference of Margaret and the narrator for the country over the city. Howards End represents home versus cosmopolitanism for her (p. 219:24). An allusion to the novel's title – 'She knew that London is not the end, that the human soul will never be sucked down into civilisation . . . ' – is removed from Margaret's thoughts on Helen's monistic renunciation (p. 277:34). London stands for culture and movement, Howards End for poetry and rest, the narrator comments in another deleted paragraph (p. 264:31). In still another he describes the Wilcoxes's kingdom of the future – 'the future of the next five minutes' – as one of airplanes and telegrams (p. 246:29). The conflict between imperial preference and free trade is made more explicit in the drafts of the novel, with Margaret at one point declaring herself a free trader (p. 209:24).

More significantly, Margaret's sexual attitudes were revised in a number of instances. A physical attraction to Tibby's tutor was deleted (p. 70:34). Margaret remains more independent than most women, it is asserted, because 'she did not ignore the claims of the body' (p. 171:23). A conversation with Helen in which there are rare, rewarding moments of inner life is contrasted with those attained more frequently in Eastern asceticism at the cost of denying the body (p. 192:34). A cancelled phrase describes how Margaret's anger at Henry's betrayal of his wife is overcome by a love that 'bore her down and melted her logic like ice' (p. 240:7). With less consistency, Margaret is described in another deletion as 'dizzy with terror and shame' at the discovery of Helen's pregnancy (p. 287:4). Throughout these revisions there appears to be a general toning down of sexuality. Margaret's original protest against the forcing house of sexual segregation was less vague in manuscript:

Man in the smoking room – woman in the drawing room – do meet for a moment in the bedroom. Strip civilization of its cant, and was it reduced to this?

In his revision, Forster deleted the first sentence and modified the second to 'Strip human intercourse of the proprieties, and is it reduced to this?' (p. 237:30). References to the kisses of Margaret and Henry and the embraces of Helen and Leonard are deleted several times. Henry and Margaret are originally described as 'the lovers', which is changed to 'our hero and heroine' (p. 254:31); an ambiguous description of Leonard's manhood rising in irritation with the Schlegels is changed to a rising gorge (p. 139:2).

Revisions in point of view indicate the care Forster took with his narrator's interventions in the writing of *Howards End*. The opening of Chapter 6 about not being concerned with the very poor originally began with a description of the class distance between Wickham Place and Leonard Bast's Vauxhall flat (p. 43:1). A dismissive comment on Leonard's conversation, which is being transcribed 'for what it is worth', was dropped (p. 44:38), and the characterisation of Leonard somewhat softened. Twice Forster removed references that established relationships between the characters and reader beyond that of the narrator with the reader. Originally, Forster wrote that Margaret would probably not want the reader told her views of King's Cross Station (p. 9:36). Later the narrator describes as questionable Margaret's claim that a vivid emotion like Helen's love for Paul can completely die; omitted is the interjection 'and the reader is permitted to agree with her if he chooses' (p. 55:15). The narrator describes himself rather grandly as the Wilcoxes's 'chronicler' in the scene where they discuss Ruth's bequest of Howards End, but in the revision he becomes a mere 'commentator' (p. 96:24). A significant late comment on the Schlegel sisters' development suggests Margaret has succeeded with hers and then indicates again the story's independence from the narrator by adding, 'Whether Helen has succeeded one cannot say'. Originally, it was an 'I' who could not say; 'one' returns us to the one who begins telling the story of *Howards End* (275.38).

Forster's revisions show him taking pains with literary and artistic allusions and the names of his characters. An allusion to the place of the writer Hilaire Belloc was changed to the artist William Rothenstein at Margaret's luncheon party, for example (p. 71:29). Forster changed Leonard Bast's more symbolic name from Edward Cunningham. Mrs Munt (the name of a governess at Rooksnest) was originally named Mrs Yool, and Henry Wilcox had the affable name Harry for a while. Helen's child, nameless in the finished version, is once significantly called 'little Howard' in the manuscript (p. 339.22). Several references to Shakespeare are deleted from the manuscripts as well two allusions to Blake, one of which adapts the last stanza of his poem 'My spectre round me night & day' to express the central truth of love in Margaret's life (p. 101:27). A parlourmaid has her facetious literary name changed to Milton from Shakespeare. In general, however, there was a muffling of some of the comedy in the revisions of *Howards End*. A small but significant example of this may be the change of Beethoven's gnomes to more sinister goblins. A more extended illustration is Forster's cutting of an amusing disquisition on Mrs Munt's choice of headgear to wear on her journey to Howards End at the beginning of the novel. Descriptions of ridiculous hats worn by Dolly Wilcox and Leonard Bast survived in revisions. Mrs Munt's hat did not:

Her remark 'I think a hat, not a bonnet' opens a vista of subtleties. A bonnet implies decision. For one thing it cannot be taken off. It is suitable for weddings, ultimatums, and funerals. Whereas a hat, however monumental, denotes the open mind, and sympathy with youth. Though inclined to the bonnet, Mrs Munt had also to consider the wishes of her niece. She must not be too monitory. She must choose the hat. And the hat that she assumed, though black on the whole, gleamed iridescently in its more secret parts as if to reassure the Wilcoxes and to hint that the paths of Helen and Paul might yet be bright with flowers.

(p. 8:33)

While the tone here is appropriate for Mrs Munt, it does not fit the Schlegel/Wilcox story that *Howards End* tells.

Because the principal manuscript of *Howards End* lacks a title page, it is therefore not possible to determine now when Forster decided to call his book *Howards End* or at what point he decided to give it an epigraph. '"Only connect . . . "' may have been added later, perhaps in response to comments on the novel by Forster's publisher. Forster had sent Edward Arnold a synopsis and 'a rough draft' of thirty chapters in March 1910. He received some criticism concerning an unconvincing episode – probably Helen's liaison with Bast – which he agreed with, but as it 'had worked itself into the plot inextricably' he said it could not be changed. Forster also refused to reduce the length of his novel, mentioning the various complaints made of his earlier novels that they were too short (*HE*, pp. xii–xiii). Yet some of the revisions Forster subsequently made in his manuscript may have been in response to his publisher's criticisms. Arnold's was the first known response to a novel that would become so widely read and discussed. The reception of *Howards End* is, along with its origins, structure, ideas, and composition, an important aspect of the novel's literary history – and also of the Group's because *Howards End* has been read so often over the past eighty years as a preeminently Bloomsbury work.

VII

Howards End was published on 18 October, 1910 at six shillings a copy. The demand for it, Edward Arnold explained the next month in an advertisement in *The Times Literary Supplement*, was 'phenomenal'. The first printing of 2500 copies was quickly sold out, and the novel reprinted three times the next month. By 1913, nearly 10,000 copies of the book had been sold. (*A Room with A View*, published two years before, had sold only a little more than 2000 copies by that time.) The success of *Howards End* marked a important change in Forster's career, as the early sales and reviews reveal. Yet when compared to a novel like Jeffery Farnol's *The Broad Highway* – a Regency story of the open road, also published in 1910, that sold over 100,000 copies – Forster's sales appear rather small. It is worth remembering throughout the Group's literary history, how limited the sales of even Bloomsbury's most widely read books were, compared to best-sellers such as Farnol's. It is a mistake, nevertheless, to conclude, as one historian does, that Forster had little early commercial success (Hudson, p. 315). With a royalty of 25 per cent, Forster thought he was making 'preposterous sums' out of *Howards End*, as he wrote to his friend Malcolm Darling in India (10.ii.1911, p/T), and he began to think of a trip there. The popularity of *Howards End* led to its being the first of Forster's books published in the United States. After tampering with the text (Forster was able to prevent the editorial addition of chapter titles) Putnam's published it in January 1911 and then reprinted it three times in three months.[9]

The early reviews of *Howards End* (most of them, including the *TLS*, misspelled the title) criticised the story and also complained sometimes about the characters, but almost all agreed that Forster had written a remarkable book and become a notable novelist. The anonymous *TLS* reviewer was not Virginia Woolf but Percy Lubbock, whose Jamesian *The Craft of Fiction* would push Woolf and Forster to develop their own theories of the novel in the Twenties. Lubbock found Forster had finally got his method under control in *Howards End*, and the result was 'a very remarkable and original book'; he admired the plot, characters, power of generalisation, and especially the vein of poetry, which was still a refinement belonging to realism rather than romance (*EMFCH*, pp. 125–6). The *Manchester Guardian* praised Forster's 'feminine brilliance of perception', and the *Morning Leader* described him as 'an author of distinction and exceptional ability' (pp. 123, 128). The *Standard* did not like the novel's form, which seemed to emphasise nothing and fling the characters about indifferently; nevertheless it announced that Forster's niche was now secure. Similarly, the *Pall Mall Gazette*, while objecting to the opening, to the dialogue that led nowhere, and to the colourless treatment of episodes, admitted that Forster now counted for something. Some later critics would recognise these defects as artistic virtues. The *Daily Telegraph* hailed Forster as 'one of the great novelists', not as great as Meredith, but still 'one of our glories' (p. 131), and the *Spectator* (the reviewer was not Lytton Strachey) complained of the plotting and the lack of authorial self-effacement but still found Forster a vivid interpreter of the clash between culture and materialism. In the *Nation* Edward Garnett, as was noted, praised Forster's original treatment of the middle-class manners and morals without concluding that *Howards End* was great art. R. A. Scott-James in the *Daily News* saw Forster as a bridge between Galsworthy and Conrad and in a long review proclaimed *Howards End* the best novel of the year (pp. 135–9). The *Saturday Review* said the word 'Forsterian' was now demanded, and even *Punch* liked the Wilcoxes (PNF/*EMF*, I 188). Not all these reviews were favourable, but all had praise for the book. The conservative *Morning Post*, for example, thought the cryptic epigraph rather like instructions to the electricity company (*EMFCH*, p. 149). The American reviews were puzzled and a little bored by *Howards End*.

The competition for 'novel of the year' was not very fierce in 1910. Forster had to contend with novels by the likes of William De Morgan, Edgar Wallace, May Sinclair, E. F. Benson, Hilaire Belloc, Elinor Glyn, Zane Grey, and P. G. Wodehouse, not to mention collections of stories by Henry James, Edith Wharton, and Rudyard Kipling. There were no novels by Conrad or Ford that year but there were H. G. Wells's *The History of Mr Polly* and Arnold Bennett's *Clayhanger*. A review of *Howards End* in the *World* objected a little to the way it was overshadowing *Clayhanger*, and Bennett himself acknowledged in his *New Age* commentary that no other novel had been so discussed by the elite as Forster's. He added sardonically that it was not, of course, Forster's best novel because an author's most popular work never is. Bennett concluded that if Forster continued to produce a novel a year, remained discreet and mysterious, refrained completely from certain unspecified themes, and avoided his marked tendencies to humour, he would be England's most fashionable novelist in ten years. 'The responsibilities lying on him at this crisis of his career are terrific,' he concluded, 'and he is so young too!' Such advice contributed to the creative block that Forster began to suffer from with the success of *Howards End*. Desmond MacCarthy remembered Bennett asking with exasperation and astonishment, after *Howards End*, 'What's 'ee—doing? Why doesn't 'ee—follow it up? He's on the map' (*EMFCH*, pp. 154–6, 400).

The inhibiting popularity of *Howards End* did not change Forster's opinion of the novel, and he wrote no later introduction, notes or epilogue for it. In his diary at the end of 1910 he called the book 'over-praised', and wished he was still obscure (PNF/*EMF*, I 191). Some of his later dissatisfaction with the novel's non-sexual embraces, as he called them, may have had its origin in the attitudes of some early readers towards the work's treatment of sex. One reason his mother's shocked response bothered him, as he said again in his diary, was that 'the shocking part is also inartistic, and so I cannot comfort myself by a superior standpoint' (*HE*, p. xiii). Other members of Forster's family appear to have been more tolerant, but Mrs Forster's opinions had some distinguished literary company in the prudish reaction of Edmund Gosse. Gosse had admired Forster's earlier novels, but when Edward Marsh sent him *Howards End* he found the last hundred pages a great disappointment, delighted as he had been by the earlier parts of the novel. He believed Forster had apparently listened to those who wanted more story, coarser morals, a more coruscating style. The resulting work 'taken as a whole, is sensational and dirty and affected.' Gosse asked what Marsh thought 'of the new craze for introducing into fiction the high-bred maiden who has a baby', and he urged Marsh to use his influence on the author, to 'redeem him from the slough of affectation and false sentiment into which he has fallen' when he should have been concentrating on the creation of characters like Aunt Juley instead of lunatics out of *Jane Eyre* (Charteris, pp. 323–4). (Told of the letter years later, Forster reproached Marsh for having failed to influence him – PNF/*EMF*, I 190.) Another friend of Gosse's reported that he had described *Howards End* as 'a vile, obscene, decadent book . . . ' and damned Forster for having 'prostituted charming gifts to a sickening lust for popularity'. Gosse's biographer speculates that he may have been reacting to the similarities between Leonard Bast's aspirations and his own more successful ones (Thwaite, p. 442). Certainly Gosse would not have liked the disparagement of the authors Bast read and followed, especially Robert Louis Stevenson (as Gosse later made clear in dismissing Leonard Woolf for his criticism of Stevenson). Gosse's antipathy for Bloomsbury was matched by theirs for him; he well represented the literary establishment that Forster, Strachey, and the Woolfs despised.

Bloomsbury's enthusiasm for *Howards End* in 1910 did not equal that of the elite noted by Bennett. There is no reference to the novel in Leonard Woolf and Lytton Strachey's correspondence, which had almost ceased by that time. When Woolf mentioned *Howards End* later in a review of *A Passage to India*, he said it had renewed the promise of his first novel without fulfilling it, and, like all Forster's earlier novels, never quite came off ('Arch', p. 354). Desmond MacCarthy's published comments on *Howards End* in the Thirties were very general too. He found Forster's peculiar balance of qualities more feminine than masculine, and emphasised his moral message that 'you must *connect*, connect what you have felt, what you have read, what you have thought with your practical judgements. . . . ' Men tend to disconnect, whereas 'the feminine impulse, . . . whether on account of woman's education or her fundamental nature, is to see life more as a continuum' (*EMFCH*, p. 403). (Late in life, MacCarthy wrote to Moore that he remained unconvinced by Helen and Leonard's affair as well as the novel's ending – 17.7.48, Moore, Cambridge papers.)

Virginia Woolf, who had been ill since March of 1910, did not write about *Howards End* until her essay on Forster in 1927. But there was one short, revealing Bloomsbury review by Clive Bell in the *Athenaeum*. Bell, who did not normally review fiction for that paper, began by stating that Forster was now assured of 'a place amongst the handful of living writers who count.' He criticised the protagonists for being points of view, not characters, finding both Margaret's marriage and Helen's seduction unconvincing, and he thought the moral was wrong. He did not object (in 1910 at any rate) to didacticism in literary art but he could not admit 'that what is bad ought to be loved, or that the finer feelings are not too high a price even for enlarged sympathies.' The Wilcoxes represented everything that is worst – an opinion that was shared later in Bloomsbury by Strachey and Carrington (who read *Howards End* in 1920 and also wanted to know why a cat had to be run over and Leonard killed – LS/pBL). The criticism of the Wilcoxes would be repeated by D. H. Lawrence and others later. Bell also sounded an unmistakable note of the Group in what he found of greatest value in *Howards End*:

> The great thing in the book is the sisters' affection for each other; personal relationships, except those between lovers, have never, we venture to say, been made more beautiful or more real.

Added to this was the delicacy and clarity with which Forster revealed 'those subtle states of mind and elusive but significant traits that are apt to escape even the most acute observation' (*EMFCH*, p. 151). It might be asked of this criticism how consistent such moving states and mind and personal relationships are with characters that were merely points of view, but Bell did recognise in Margaret's and Helen's relationship a love often unmentioned in the subsequent extensive commentary that has been written on *Howards End*. He was, of course, in a good position to appreciate the love of sisters.

When Virginia Woolf wrote her essay on Forster's novels, she quoted from *Howards End* to describe sympathetically Forster's general belief that the private life matters, and that its prose and passion must be connected. She found all the qualities necessary for a masterpiece in the novel: real characters, a masterly story, an intelligent atmosphere with no humbug, exquisite comedy, faultless observation. It was, she said, an 'elaborate and highly skilful book, with its immense technical accomplishment and also its penetration, its wisdom, and its beauty' – and yet the novel was a failure because these qualities were not fused into a forceful work of art. Forster's was a baffling balance of gifts:

> The poet is twitched away by the satirist; the comedian is tapped on the shoulder by the moralist; he never loses himself or forgets himself for long in sheer delight in the beauty or the interest of things as they are.

In the big scenes, Woolf found a disillusioning insubstantiality that she thought had little to do with any feminine impulse. She wished, however foolishly, that Forster had kept to comedy and left the problem of the universe alone. She found *Where Angels Fear to Tread* a slighter, but more beautifully harmonious book, where the comic freedom of Tibby and Mrs. Munt remains more vivid, than the closely watched Schlegel sisters and Leonard Bast (*CE*, I 348–50).

Virginia Woolf's criticism of *Howards End* may have been influenced by her disagreement with Forster's diminishment of the art of fiction and its historical contexts in the popular lectures he had recently given on the novel at Cambridge in 1927 – lectures in which Forster classified Woolf as a fantasist on the basis of one story (*AN*, p. 12). The Bloomsbury debate over the nature of fiction belongs to a later period of their literary history (Rosenbaum,

Aspects) but it appears in Woolf's description of Forster as falling between the stools of novelists who are preachers and teachers, like Tolstoy and Dickens, and those who are pure literary artists, like Jane Austen, Ivan Turgenev – and presumably the reviewer herself. Woolf's critical judgement of *Howards End* in her essay on Forster should not be taken as her only response to the novel, however. There are traces of *Howards End* to be found the structure and subject of *To the Lighthouse*, with its connected antitheses, its family life in the country, the continuing presence of a dead woman, and a housecleaner called Mrs Bast. *To the Lighthouse* and 'The Novels of E. M. Forster' were both published in 1927.

VIII

The influence of *Howards End*, early and late, has been enormous outside of Bloomsbury. '"Only connect . . . "' appears in the *OED* as an allusive phrase, with citations from the novel. The earliest example of its use after the novel is in a 1911 letter of Rupert Brooke's, in which he explains to a friend how, in joining up Puritan and hedonist, 'we have (once more) only connected' (*Letters*, p. 302). Though the prose and the politics of *Howards End* were Edwardian, they have been viewed as characteristically Georgian in their impact. The influence of Forster's style has been discovered in the softness of Georgian lyrics (Stead, pp. 85–6). For Georgian poets, the pastoral values and urban criticism of the novel were congenial and later they found, in its references to Germany and imperialism, an anticipation of the Great War. Anti-Georgian poets also alluded to *Howards End*. A voice in the most memorable literary expression of post-First-World-War fragmentation laments his incapacity to follow the epigraph's prescription: 'I can connect Nothing with nothing' (*The Waste Land*, ll. 301–2). *Howards End* continued to be influential long after the condition of England it represented had worsened. Goronwy Rees, discussing the influence of Moore's Cambridge ethics on Oxford as expressed in Forster's novels, wrote of the epigraph to *Howards End*,

> it could be said that those two words, so seductive in their simplicity, so misleading in their ambiguity, had more influence in shaping the emotional attitudes of the English governing class

between the two world wars than any other single phrase in the English language. (p. 95)

Homosexuality and communism (neither of which is much in evidence in the novel) were essential elements in this extraordinary influence, according to Rees, who conflates the epigraph with Forster's later, now even more famous comment about betraying one's country rather than one's friend. '"Only connect . . ."' does seem to have been used as gay code, but the contexts of both epigraph and comment are often ignored.[10]

For literary history, however, it is among the writers and critics of fiction that a more complex and enduring influence of *Howards End* may be found. The response of D. H. Lawrence, for example, is again revealing for both Forster's art and his own. When Lawrence first read *Howards End* in 1911, he thought it 'exceedingly good', but while finishing *The Rainbow* in 1915 he was not so sure. 'I don't know where you've got to after *Howards End*', he wrote to Forster – and after *Sons and Lovers* he may have been asking himself a similar question (*L*, I 278, II 266). Lawrence's family chronicle of the Brangwen sisters in *The Rainbow* and its sequel *Women in Love* is very different in everything from class setting to moral philosophy from the story of the Schlegel sisters. But in retrospect, Margaret's 'rainbow bridge that should connect the prose in us with the passion' – without which 'we are meaningless fragments, half monks half beasts, unconnected arches that have never joined into a man' (*HE*, p. 183) – sounds rather Lawrentian. It has been suggested that Roger Fry's drawing of a rainbow-bridge for the end-papers of *The Celestial Omnibus* (a copy of which Forster presented to Lawrence in 1915) may have contributed to Lawrence's conception of the rainbow in his novel (Delany, 'Lawrence' pp. 59–60). Forster had also sent a copy of *Howards End* to the Lawrences after an unsatisfactory visit to them in 1915. Frieda thought it a beautiful book but had doubts about how broken Henry Wilcox really was at the end; Lawrence told Forster later he had made a deadly mistake in glorifying business people like the Wilcoxes (*L*, II 277, IV 301). It may have been during the 1915 visit that Forster, after listening to Lawrence attack his work, finally asked if there was anything in it Lawrence liked: '"Yes", he said, Leonard Bast. "That was courageous"' (EMF/'Conversation', p. 54).

Katherine Mansfield was also critical of *Howards End*, and funnier about it too. In her 1917 journal she mockingly associates Forster with Tibby Schlegel, who is described in the novel as warming the teapot 'almost too deftly' (*HE*, p. 40). Forster, she thinks, never gets beyond warming the teapot: 'He's a rare fine hand at that. Feel this teapot. Is it not beautifully warm? Yes, but there ain't going to be no tea.' She went on to offer a much cited modern interpretation of Helen's affair with Leonard that had so offended Forster's mother and Gosse:

> And I can never be perfectly certain whether Helen was got with child by Leonard Bast or by his fatal forgotten umbrella. All things considered, I think it must have been the umbrella.
>
> (*EMFCH*, p. 162)

As with Virginia Woolf's criticism, however, Katherine Mansfield's spontaneous journal thoughts often differ from her more considered public judgements. When Mansfield reviewed the Hogarth Press's publication of *The Story of the Siren* ten years after *Howards End*, she remarked that Forster had most successfully conveyed his inner sense of vision in that novel. But like Woolf again she was teased by Forster's not exerting his full imaginative power: 'How is it that the writer is content to do less than explore his own delectable country?' Perhaps it was his sensitivity and sense of humour that kept him from committing himself completely and so he drifts along (*EMFCH*, pp. 184–5).

After the publication of *A Passage to India*, the ironies and indirections of Forster's art of the novel began to be more appreciated. An illuminating example of Forster's influence here – having again to do with tea – occurs in Christopher Isherwood's *Lions and Shadows*, subtitled *An Education in the Twenties*, which was published by the Hogarth Press in 1938. Isherwood quotes the revelation that a character based on Edward Upward has while reading *Howards End*:

> Forster's the only one who understands what the modern novel ought to be. . . . Our frightful mistake was that we believed in tragedy: the point is, tragedy's quite impossible nowadays. . . . We ought to aim at being essentially comic writers . . . The whole of Forster's technique is based on the tea-table: instead of trying to screw all his scenes up to the highest possible pitch, he tones them down until they sound like mothers'-meeting gossip . . . In fact, there's actually *less* emphasis laid on the big scenes than on

the unimportant ones: that's what's so utterly terrific. It's the completely new kind of accentuation – like a person talking a different language. . . . (pp. 173–4)

According to Furbank the term 'tea-tabling' began to circulate as a critical description of Forster's method in fiction (PNF / *EMF*, II 177). Upward and Isherwood are essentially defining the nature of Forster's influence in the Thirties, but their recognition of his unique accentuation can serve to refocus the criticism of his art. What had been seen as defects in narration - defects admitted by Forster himself - may be re-read as forms of deflationary irony. Some of the theory for this accentuation is to be found in *Aspects of the Novel*.

Yet Forster is not simply a comic novelist. There are aesthetic as well as moral boundaries to the irony in *Howards End*, as Isherwood, Upward, and Spender – who described Forster later as writing 'elegies for England' – all knew. So did Auden:

> . . . still you speak to us,
> Insisting that the inner life can pay.
>
> . . . .
> . . . reason is denied and love ignored,
> But, as we swear our lie, Miss Avery
> Comes out into the garden with a sword.
> ('Sonnets from China', *Collected Poems*, p. 157)

The same year as *Lions and Shadows* was published, Cyril Connolly brought out his inquiry into how to write a book that would last ten years. The treatment of Forster in *Enemies of Promise* accords with Isherwood and Upward's appreciation. Forster has lasted because of his unemphatic, plain art of prose. He avoided what Connolly christens 'the Mandarin style', beloved of artists and humbugs who 'would make the written word as unlike as possible to the spoken one' (pp. 24–5). Forster's style has not been imitated, but it has been influential, he thinks, on the prose of Mansfield, and others, including Woolf before she developed a new Bloomsbury Mandarin way of writing. Connolly analyses Forster's prose in the scene where the Wilcoxes disallow Ruth's dying bequest of the house to Margaret Schlegel:

Extreme simplicity, the absence of relative and conjunctive

clauses, an everyday choice of words . . . constitute a . . . revolutionary break from the Mandarin style. . . . Twenty-two short sentences follow. How remote it is from James, Meredith, Conrad, Walter Pater, whom one cannot imagine interpolating themselves into a novel to ask a question, and answer 'I think not'!

Forster is a true innovator, Connolly maintains:

Novels like *The Longest Journey* and *Howards End* established a point of view, a technique, and an attitude to the reader that were to be followed for the next thirty years by the psychological novelists. (pp. 37–9)

A generation later in his hundred great books of *The Modern Movement* Connolly preferred the romance and passion of *The Longest Journey* over the larger, more patriotic and subtle *Howards End* (p. 28).

Christopher Isherwood and Cyril Connolly attempted to define the originality of Forster for subsequent writers.[11] But the attitudes of many readers towards *Howards End* were shaped more, perhaps, by I. A. Richards, F. R. Leavis, and Lionel Trilling, three widely influential academic critics writing about Forster in the Twenties, Thirties, and Forties, who were all concerned with Forster's values as a writer. They were not the only ones writing on Forster at the time, of course. Leonard and Virginia Woolf commissioned Rose Macaulay to write the first full-length study of Forster, which was published in 1938, the same year as Isherwood's and Connolly's books. Macaulay's account of *Howards End* is mainly taken up with describing the reality of the characters and summarising their story. (Morton Dauwen Zabel commented in a review that the book might have been written by Margaret Schlegel.) Macaulay does offer some shrewd observations, such as her reaction to Margaret's comment that only on English farms like Howards End can one connect until life is seen steadily and whole:

Untrue, of course. Nowhere is there less connection, more bitterness, less brotherliness, less vision of life steady and life whole, than there may be in the quiet country places; and life, death, partings and yearnings are as sharply and deeply felt in towns, as in villages, since in both it depends on the sensibility of the feeler. (p. 125)

I. A. Richards's perceptive yet somehow grudging short essay on Forster's work was written for an American journal in 1927. Richards notes Forster's odd novelistic methods that many reviewers had thought just failures of technique. Forster's particular point of view has to be recognised in order to understand why, despite his literary skill as an observer, Forster at times throws over verisimilitude. Although Richards sees no doctrine in Forster's work (he was perhaps too thoroughly familiar with Forster's Cambridge background, having studied under Moore himself), he still finds that 'Forster's peculiar quality as a novelist is his fiercely critical sense of values' (p. 162). Like Virginia Woolf, Richards compares Forster to Ibsen. He thinks Forster's real audience is youth; as we get older, we care less for truth, and this partially explains why some readers have deserted him. Yet Richards also finds Forster obsessed with the continuance of life, which, together with class conflict, is the theme of *Howards End* - 'the book that still best represents the several sides of Mr. Forster's worth' (p. 164). The future author of *Practical Criticism* then engages in a little close analysis of the vision of England at the end of the central Chapter 19, and discovers the prose to be vague and affected. Richards praises very highly, however, the characterisation of Leonard Bast's home-life with Jacky. Fifty years later, Richards added a brief apologia to his essay, explaining that he had been to India before writing it, and found the English rulers there managing to achieve something, and this explained why there was no discussion of *A Passage to India* in his critique. Also realising that he appears to be one of the deserting readers mentioned in his essay, Richards unequivocally acknowledges that for more than a decade he had been deeply devoted to *The Longest Journey* and *Howards End*. He had let them shape his outlook and life, and 'nothing in this essay should be read as reneging that great debt' (p. 159).

Critics of Forster's pre-war novels often divide into those who are most moved by his English novels and those who prefer the ones partly set in Italy. The split is clearly present in the differing judgements of Richards and Leavis. The occasion for F. R. Leavis's *Scrutiny* assessment of Forster, which he collected in *The Common Pursuit*, was Rose Macaulay's book. She is quickly dismissed, though Leavis keeps alluding sarcastically to her description of Forster as 'a born novelist'. Leavis's rather paradoxical aim is to define 'the oddly limited and uncertain quality' of Forster's 'real and very fine distinction'(*Pursuit* p. 261). Like Richards he is critically troubled by Forster's work, but he assumes, without much discussion, that *A Passage to India* is classic Forster, not *Howards End*. Of the earlier novels, Leavis holds that the Italian are the most successful, *The Longest Journey* and *Howards End* being flawed with immaturity. The crudity of plotting in *Howards End* shocks him into calling Margaret's marriage to Henry 'a kind of *trahison des clercs*.' The crudity Leavis perceives here depends to some degree on his finding in the end of the novel a serene 'promise of a happy future' (p. 269). Leavis's essay is, of course, very critical of Forster's Bloomsbury milieu, but he recognises, in 1938, the value of a 'liberal culture' in Forster, however imperfectly the Schlegels represent it. At the end of the essay Forster is saluted as someone 'that in these days, we should peculiarly honour' (p. 277). Leavis's honouring of Forster seems just that – peculiar.

E. M. Forster said Lionel Trilling was the critic to whom he was most indebted (*HD*, p. 294). Trilling's 1943 study in a series entitled 'Makers of Modern Literature' certainly made Forster into a widely known writer in the United States.[12] One recent anthologiser canonises Trilling as *the* critic of Forster and suggests facetiously that he might have written his novels if Forster had not already done so (Bloom, p. 1). But Trilling, in a later preface to his study, admitted the 'primitive simplicity' of its criticism. His judgement that '*Howards End* is undoubtedly Forster's masterpiece' (p. 114) has been widely doubted, finally even by Trilling himself (*HE*, p. xvi). In his original judgement Trilling was following Richards, and like Richards he had personal reasons for his opinion. Trilling explained in his 1964 preface that in writing on Forster he had an implicit polemical purpose, which was to attack the current state of American literature. (From his opening chapter on 'Forster and the Liberal Imagination', Trilling borrowed the title for his well-known collection of essays.) Hence the higher evaluation of a novel about the liberal imagination over one on the essential futility of that imagination in a place like India. As part of his polemic Trilling includes a substantial digression on the recent history of the intellectual class. After viewing the class conflict in *Howards End* through Plato's *Republic*, he concludes by connecting Margaret and Helen with the heroines of Goethe's *Faust*. Forster disavowed the

Faust allusions but agreed with Trilling's description of the novel's symbolic significance:

> *Howards End* is a novel about England's fate. . . . England herself appears in the novel in palpable form, for the story moves by symbols and not only all of its characters but also an elm, a marriage, a symphony, and a scholar's library stand for things beyond themselves. The symbol for England is the house whose name gives the title to the book. Like the plots of so many English novels, the plot of *Howards End* is about the rights of property. . . . It asks the question, 'Who shall inherit England?' (p. 118)

Trilling understands too that the novel's answer to the question is not a completely hopeful one.

Richards is referred to a number of times by Trilling, who agrees, for example, with his criticism of Forster's purple prose,[13] but disagreeing that Forster's real audience is youth. Trilling also mentions the criticism of Connolly and Isherwood as well as Woolf and Macaulay, the last two being grouped together as admiring critics of Forster who 'perceive the delicacy but not the cogency of his mind' (p. 8). Trilling combined them for reasons of gender, perhaps, but Woolf's view of Forster's double vision, in *Howards End* goes considerably beyond Macaulay's interest in the characters, and she raises issues of literary form that Trilling never really meets. Leavis's article is included in Trilling's bibliography but not discussed. Leavis in a *Scrutiny* review of Trilling's study found it uncritically American in the lack of concern with Forster's inferior Bloomsbury milieu. Trilling was not as disconcerted by Leonard Bast's unreality as an Englishman would have been – though Richards, for one, was certainly not, and neither apparently was Lawrence. As for Trilling's judgement of *Howards End* as Forster's masterpiece, Leavis counters that it seems to him 'the most patently *manqué*, as it is the most ambitious of the "pre-war" novels' ('Meet', p. 309).

The largely academic criticism that followed after Richards, Leavis, and Trilling has not gone that far in devaluing *Howards End*, though few critics have preferred it to *A Passage to India*. Trilling's new preface described the criticism of Forster in the twenty years since his book as going beyond him 'in complexity or ingenuity of perception and interpretation' (p. 6). This can also be said for the next quarter of a century's extensive writings on Forster. After

Trilling the criticism of Forster's Edwardian fiction has developed in two general ways. One has been the closer textual analysis of symbolism, structure, irony, style, tone, and voice in the fiction. *Howards End* has also been illuminatingly viewed through Forster's later *Aspects of the Novel*, especially his discussions of rhythm and prophecy. Mythic archetypes were found, and attempts made to read *Howards End* as a romance rather than a novel.[14] Stylistic analysis confirmed that the antitheses of the novel were to be found embedded in Forster's prose, and the narrator's voice has been distinguished from both the author's or his characters and related instead to the reader. More recent critics have been deliberately viewing *Howards End* unsteadily and unwholly – the product not of Forster's uncertain art but his mastery in depicting the abyss to which our goblin-haunted language inevitably returns us.

These various types of explication have often been combined over the past half century with increasing attention to the historical contexts in which his work was written and needs to be read. Trilling's emphasis on Forster's liberalism has been extended to considerations of the ideology of *Howards End*. The novel has been discussed as a reflection of Edwardian England's condition; the dilemmas of liberalism of the book have been explored, and its classes and contradictions given Marxist interpretations, some sympathetic, some not. Other ideological analyses have offered feminist interpretations to counter the criticism that *Howards End* feminises culture. There has been some psychoanalytical inter pretation of *Howards End*, and the Bloomsbury background of the novel's values has occasionally been considered from theoretical rather than historical perspectives. Several surveys of Edwardian novels have attempted rather invidious comparisons of Forster's first four novels with contemporary works of James, Conrad, and Ford, or Bennett, Galsworthy, and Wells. *Howards End* is not generally regarded as a difficult modernist text, but critical dis agreement persists over its symbolism, style, plotting, characters, narration, comedy, and closure. In a 1977 monograph devoted entirely to *Howards End*, Peter Widdowson argues persuasively 'that it is precisely in the tensions, irresolutions and ambiguities of the novel that its strength resides' (p. 12). For Widdowson, Virginia Woolf's 1927 essay on Forster is 'still the most brilliant and suggestive of short studies of Forster' (p. 123), and it is in Woolf's criticism that the basic paradox of the literary history of *Howards End* is most clearly articulated. 'Elaboration, skill, wisdom, penetration, beauty – they are all there', she said of *Howards End*, but found 'they lack fusion; they lack cohesion; the book as a whole lacks force' (*CE*, I 348). Nevertheless, this unfused, unforceful work has been the most compelling of the novels that Forster set in England, and Isherwood with others found in the absence of Forster's force an artfulness suitable to the times. The elaborate skill as well as the penetrating wisdom and beauty of *Howards End* – however variously defined – continues to exert a considerable aesthetic and moral inspiration. Two final and very different illustrations from a novelist and a journalist of this influence should suffice. On the occasion of Forster's ninetieth birthday in 1969, Elizabeth Bowen wrote 'I can think, also, of no English novelist who has influenced me more. . . . He considerably affected my view of life, and, as I was to discover, my *way* of writing' (p. 12). And the year after Forster's death, Bernard Levin paid homage in him *The Times* as the man who had exerted a greater influence on his own mind and convictions than anyone else; as a schoolboy, he heard a teacher read the passage on Beethoven's Fifth: 'in a sense my life ever since has been a passage through E. M. Forster' (p. 5).

Future critics of *Howards End* will continue to debate and evaluate its connections and disconnections, but unless their criticism is also able to describe the novel's art and wisdom, their interpretations may well be irrelevant.

IX

While he was writing *Howards End*, Forster suddenly started to write a play again. He had been asked after *A Room with a View* to do a play for a repertory theatre, and he began a historical drama about the fourteenth-century Swedish Saint Bridget's efforts to inspire the Queen of Naples to return the Papacy from Avignon to Rome. Forster was planning a tragedy but the first-act encounter of the northern Saint and her family, with the southern Queen and her court, is more reminiscent of his Italian novels. The supernatural enters the second act with the death of a child but then the play breaks off (pKCC; PNF/*EMF*, I 178). *Howards End* itself was dramatised in the 1960s but not very successfully. 'A major novel had been made a minor play', Ackerley, who had helped with the script, wrote to Forster (p. 318). It was never published, but another Merchant–Ivory film of the novel, again adapted by Ruth Prawer Jhabvala, was released in 1992. Because of the novel's greater scope and more ascetic view of heterosexual relations, the film varies much more from the novel than their version of *A Room with a View* does. There is little talk of connecting in the film, and Howards End itself loses most of its symbolic significance, as do Ruth Wilcox and Beethoven. The narrator's absence is felt here more than in the other films based on Forster's novels. The differences between the Schlegels' personal relations and the Wilcox world of telegrams and anger, is blurred in their similar contrast with the existence of the Basts. Thus, while the film follows the novel's plot fairly closely, including the inconclusive ending, and is visually very effective, it seems emptied of much of the complex interrelations of ends and means in Forster's work.[15]

Forster did complete two short texts soon after finishing *Howards End* that are illuminating glosses on the novel's concerns. One looks backward to the Victorians, the other forward to Georgian Bloomsbury. 'Mr. Walsh's Secret History of the Victorian Movement', published in the King's College magazine, *Basileon*, in 1911, comically considers a domestic manual of thirty years ago. 'The audience it assumes regarded comfort as everything, personal relations as nothing, passion and beauty as nothing'. Walsh seems happy only when writing of inanimate things like food and furniture. His section on what to do after the birth of a baby 'is refined to the point of obscurity.' The attitudes expressed toward the poor appal Forster. But Walsh would have been appalled by 'that idea of comradeship, which we are gaining through intellectual unrest, that idea of society as a whole and a fluid whole which permeates the literature of today. . . . ' *Howards End*, with its hope of comradeship is an example of that literature. Nevertheless, the success of Walsh's manual makes Forster wonder if Victorianism may not be an era but 'a spirit biding its time' (*AE*, pp. 109–116).

Forster's more important, forward-looking text began as a paper for the Apostles and was then rewritten for the Vanessa Bell's Friday Club, which had a wider and more intellectual membership than the one to which the Schlegel sisters belonged. The still unpublished manuscript, entitled 'The Feminine Note in Literature', appears to be a not completely coherent mixture of the two versions. At its previous meeting the Apostles had apparently been discussing John Stuart Mill's *The Subjection of Women*, which Forster introduces into his Friday Club version as well. Unlike Mill, whom he characterises as a philosopher and lawyer who wanted things tidied up, Forster intends to be self-conscious, undignified, colloquial, even illogical, 'giving proof of our double vision' – but he hopes he is neither chivalrous nor insulting. With Mill Forster disagrees that there is no feminine note in literature as such; he then tries to provide 'an attenuated answer' as to what that note might be. Forster does not think the differences between men and women's literature are just those of subject-matter. Nor does he believe with Ethel Smyth that the artistic creations of women and men are indistinguishable. Women have had a miserable time; their literature is still relatively new and cannot be expected yet 'to tell us the good only through the beautiful'. From this Platonic aesthetic, Forster criticises women's fiction, finding only Jane Austen's comedy of the first rank. But the situation may well change, as Mill predicts, when women have their rights. Then their literary triumphs may follow those they have now had in science and classical studies. 'If only women novelists could add to their solidity a sense of poetry', he continues, anticipating Virginia Woolf's fiction and criticism, 'there is no point they might not reach.' Women writers have shown intermittent lyric feelings, but none has yet written a good long poem, or even a novel that treats space as well as Thomas Hardy has or time as well as Arnold Bennett. Forster insists in a passage that he then cancelled that the emotional quality of women's books must connect, somehow, with sex.

Sexual connection was part of the impetus behind 'The Feminine Note in Literature'. In a diary entry made shortly after finishing *Howards End*, Forster said he wanted to work out the sexual bias of literary criticism and perhaps literature itself – to determine, for example, the influence on writing of the sort of person with whom the writer would like to sleep. Nothing of this rather promising notion appears in his paper, but it anticipates his own development as a novelist through the fragmentary *Arctic Summer* he would write next and on to *Maurice*. Forster's conclusion in 'The Feminine Note in Literature' is related, however, to the view of sex roles expressed in his *Howards End*, where the narrator comments on the admiration of men for our worthy qualities and the pity of woman for our unworthy ones. Forster developed an aspect of this idea in his paper by maintaining that the characters of women's fiction try not to be good, so much as to be worthy of other characters. Consequently, 'men, though they may misunderstand women, somehow have created heroines. Women, though they may understand themselves, have somehow created prigs.' For Forster, then, the feminine note in literature was not the impulse to see life connectedly, that MacCarthy thought rather feminine in Forster's fiction. It was rather a 'preoccupation with personal worthiness' – a preoccupation that has limited women's literature. As illustrations, Forster juxtaposes the protagonists of George Eliot's *Romola* and Charlotte Brontë's *Villette* with those in Conrad's *Lord Jim* and Meredith's *The Egoist*. From these literary observations, Forster draws what he realises is an ethical conclusion that, with its stereotyping of gender, is not much more than a footnote to Mill (pKC).

For the literary history of Bloomsbury 'The Feminine Note in Literature' is more significant than that. There was no discussion of his ideas at the Friday Club, but Forster recorded in his diary that 'Miss Stephen, said the paper was the best there had been, which pleases me' (pKC). Miss Stephen at this time, was trying to complete the kind of novel Forster had called for, one in which the solidity of prose would be connected with poetry. His paper showed her again the lack of contemporary models for such an endeavour. Mill had said the best novelists were women, but his examples were all French. As an English woman novelist, Virginia Woolf could look back only to George Eliot, whose last novel had appeared a generation ago. Not in the fiction of Mrs Humphry Ward, or Meredith, Hardy, Conrad, or Bennett (James is significantly absent from Forster's paper) would she find useful models. Her closest predecessor in fiction was actually the paper's author.

Forster read his paper to Bloomsbury's Friday Club in December 1910 – the time fixed famously by Virginia Woolf for a change in human character. The shift she perceived in the personal relations of married couples to their children, their servants, and themselves is already visible in *Howards End*. A month after its publication, the first post-impressionist exhibition opened. Roger Fry was among those who heard Forster give his paper at the Friday Club a few weeks later. The changes that Fry's exhibition brought about in the Group's novels, stories, biographies, essays, and reviews will be described in the literary history of Georgian Bloomsbury.

Notes

NOTES TO CHAPTER 1: INDEPENDENT REVIEWERS

1. In the course of his tribute Pollock noted Stephen's strong, ironic humour and compared his *The Science of Ethics* with Moore's brilliant dialectic, concluding that what Stephen really examined in his work was 'the art of living together'. Pollock's article appeared in the June 1904 issue which also contained Forster's 'The Road from Colonus'.
2. For the background of the New Liberalism see Peter Clark's *Liberals and Social Democrats*. Forster's connections with this liberalism and the *Independent Review* have been usefully discussed by Crews and Howarth.
3. Frederic Spotts in his edition of Woolf's letters attribtutes to Woolf an unsigned review of Churton Collins in the *Spectator* on 5 November 1904 (*L*, p. 38) but that review, which is completely different from the undergraduate paper Woolf wrote on Collins's book, was actually done by J. E. G. Montmorency. (I am grateful to the *Spectator*'s Librarian Mr Charles Seaton for this identification.)
4. The essay is misdated 1906 by Strachey in *Books and Characters*.
5. The tone of Strachey's essay is further shown by a fake quotation Strachey used to illustrate how badly Voltaire was capable of writing: 'Vous comprenez, seigneur, que je ne comprehends pas.' The quotation was invented by Lytton's sister Marjorie (MH/*LHBG*, p. 79). Marjorie Strachey also reviewed for the *Independent Review* a French version of *King Lear* playing in Paris in March, 1906. She concluded that it managed to make Lear look like Père Goriot. After reading the review in Ceylon, Leonard Woolf wrote to Sydney-Turner that 'the supremacy of the Strache [*sic*] family probably is that it is the only one in England of which every member understands Lear' (26.iii.06, pH).
6. Strachey's sketch is slightly different from the history of prose he suggested in an earlier review of Dover Wilson's book on Lyly for the *Speaker* at Desmond MacCarthy's suggestion. There Strachey had traced Johnson's sententious antitheses back to Lyly in disputing Wilson's claim that Lyly's prose was superior to Sidney's in the *Arcadia*, which he thought was the true inspiration of Elizabethan prose. Strachey admired Wilson's book, however, but thought his scientific approach, like Gosse's impressionistic one towards Browne, had failed to catch the narrow classical spirit of Euphues's style.
7. Strachey reworded Lamb's question at the end of the quotation; it originally read 'do these things go out with life?' (Lamb, p. 35).

NOTES TO CHAPTER 2: E. M. FORSTER'S EARLIER SHORT WRITINGS

1. Forster's short texts have been extensively commented upon, but most books on Forster ignore the circumstances of their publication and bundle them into fiction and non-fiction chapters that obscure the generic complexity of these writings. Apart from specific references to particularly enlightening or wrong-headed commentary, I have not attempted to note my debt to the extensive critical literature on the work of Forster and Woolf beyond the bibliography to this volume. For guides to the criticism of Forster see the Critical Heritage volume that reprints various reviews and criticisms of his work, (*EMFCH*), the monumental, extensively annotated secondary bibliography of Forster by McDowell that covers Forster criticism up to 1975, and the useful, more selective discussions in Summers's guide to research that brings the criticism up to 1990.

2. Judith Herz has describes the differences between Forster's and Strachey's biographical styles but her conclusion that Forster shared little more than an idiom and tone underestimates the deep similarities in moral outlook that the two writers share, as is clear from the writers they most respected. Strachey did not share Forster's fondness for Montaigne (Virginia Woolf did) but he admired Gibbon and Voltaire as much if not more than Forster did. Herz also says that Forster's essays in the *Independent Review* preceded Strachey's properly 'Stracheyesque' ones, but this is doubtful, as the accounts in Chapter 1 of Strachey's 1904 *Independent Review* texts indicate (Herz, 'Narratives', pp. 77–93). The similarities of Forster's and Strachey's *Independent Review* biographies appear more distinctively when compared, for example, with the essays and reviews of Lowes Dickinson in the same periodical. Dickinson's fearless review of Oscar Wilde's *De Profundis* appeared in the same issue as 'Voltaire's Tragedies' and 'Cardan'; neither Strachey nor Forster would have written an account of Wilde as a martyred artist in Dickinson's outspoken, unironic way.

3. A sentence cut when 'Cardan' was republished illustrated the logic of the Counter-Reformation with modern authors: ' . . . it would deal tenderly with Mr. George Meredith, though it would be relentless towards Mr. Bernard Shaw' (*Independent Review*, v (April 1905) 373–4).

4. K. W. Gransden oddly finds 'The Celestial Omnibus' interesting because he thinks it 'irreproachably anti-Bloomsbury' in favouring innocence and self-effacement against experience and self-assertion. Gransden seems to identify Mr Bons with Bloomsbury in his scepticism and lack of reverence that Lawrence found wanting in Bloomsbury (p. 14). To what extent Forster perceived these qualities in Bloomsbury in 1908 is a question; he seems to have missed them in 1912, at any rate, when he asked Roger Fry to illustrate the end-papers of *The Celestial Omnibus* four years later. But there can be little doubt that Gransden has misunderstood Forster's characterization of Mr Bons, whose reverence – his honouring Dante's book as an end and not a means – leads right to his destruction. Summers's interpretation of

the story as a Christian parody is more germane but leaves out the play with Moore's principles (*Forster*, pp. 244–8).

5. In May 1904, Forster also published in the *Pilot*, where Fry had been the art critic in 1900–1, an unreprinted familiar essay called 'A Day Off' (*AE*, pp. 80–5). It describes a Tyrolean walk of fantastic sights on one of those joyous days that the world seems to have taken off and suspended cause and effect. The sights all turn out to have natural explanations. It is not completely surprising that the *Pilot* ceased publication a week after Forster's piece appeared.

6. The narrator seems to have been at Forster's Cambridge. He remarks of Ford's dreams of another earth 'that everything is to be itself, and not practically something else', (*CO*, p. 94) which echoes the epigraph of *Principia Ethica*, yet when Evelyn asks why humanity is here, he says he cannot tell her because he did not take the Moral Science Tripos (p. 115).

7. Forster also helped Julia (Snow) Wedgwood, a friend of his great-aunt Marianne Thornton and a niece of Charles Darwin, revise her book *The Moral Ideal: A Historic Study*. Forster stated that he 'redrafted certain passages with the author's approval' but does not indicate what these were about (Kirkpatrick, *EMF* B2). *The Moral Ideal* might have been called a 'History of Human Aspiration' had the author thought the book historical enough (p. v). As it stands in the revised 1907 edition, there are chapters on Egypt, India, Persia, Greece, Rome, Stoicism (but not Epicureanism), Gnosticism, Augustinianism, and, finally, on an evolutionary moral ideal founded on the sexual union of opposites but collectively expansive enough to include all incomplete historical ideals. Despite the strong evolutionary bent of this moral history, there are no references to Leslie Stephen or any other utilitarian philosophers (as Clive Bell indicated in his *Athenaeum* review of another of Wedgwood's books – see p. 281). But Forster might have liked Wedgwood's basing an evolutionary ideal on love, collectively abstract as it was, and the sections on Indian and Alexandrian moral ideals may have been useful to him later.

8. Several brief posthumously published early Edwardian fragments remain merely suggestive of Forster's intentions. Three of the fragments, 'Simply the Human Form', 'Arthur at Ampelos', and 'At the National Gallery' sketch various situations in which beauty is insufficiently appreciated and understood in art. The most amusing is the first, a science fiction fragment in which a space-traveller tries to understand why humans conceal under absurd, anachronistic clothes their beautiful form, as revealed to him by a Parthenon torso in the British Museum; he learns that art is a universal language and 'more human than humanity' (*AS*, p. 241). The fourth fragment, 'Hassan in England', is a product of Forster's emotional relationship with Syed Ross Masood; it presents a comic encounter between a well-intentioned Indian visitor to England and a practical Englishman named Dickenson whose categorising enthusiasm for mystery puts off the Indian. Still unpublished is an early text entitled 'Pagus Quidam' that

describes some minor misadventures in an inhospitable Wiltshire village (p/KCC).

9. Fry's unpublished letter, dated 19 January 1901 (RF/pKC) refers to Mrs Henry Ady's *Painters of Florence* as borrowing the whole structure and sequence of ideas in his lectures. Oliver Stallybrass, however, identifies the Giovanni da Empoli of the story with Antonio Pollaiuolo and the plagiarising Lady Anstey with Maud Cruttwell (*LTC*, pp. xi, 236). In 1902 Fry was critical of Cruttwell's book on Mantegna in the *Athenaeum* but did not suggest anything about plagiarism (Laing, *Fry*, p. 85).

NOTES TO CHAPTER 3: THE FIRST BOOK OF BLOOMSBURY

1. The identities of the poets of *Euphrosyne* are based on five marked copies of the collection and on the correspondence of Saxon Sydney-Turner. The most completely marked copy, now in the University of Toronto Library, was discovered in a Cambridge bookstore a number of years ago; the initials of each contributor are written in the Table of Contents in purple ink by an italic pen, and Sydney-Turner's contributions are further indicated in pencil, probably in another hand, at the end of each of his poems. The original owner is unknown, but he or she knew that Clive Bell's initials were ACHB and Walter Lamb's WRML. (It is difficult to identify handwriting only by printed initials but Virginia Woolf was partial to purple ink and italic nibs.) The contributions of Sydney-Turner in this copy are all confirmed in a letter, now at Harvard University, from his father to Coulson Kernahan. Harvard also has a copy of *Euphrosyne* presented to Kernahan by Arthur Francis Bell who styles himself part-author. He must be the 'Brighton Bell' referred to by Sydney-Turner in letters to Clive Bell. (I am grateful to John Lancaster for the information about this copy and the letter of A. M. Sydney-Turner.) A partially marked copy in the possession of Quentin Bell is inscribed from Thoby Stephen to V. D. (probably Violet Dickinson) with twenty-eight of the poems' authors identified. Another copy, owned by Barbara Bagenal, has most of the poets identified according to Sydney-Turner. (I am grateful to the late Mrs Bagenal for this information and for the letters to Sydney-Turner from Clive Bell about *Euphrosyne* that are now in the Huntington Library.) There is also a copy in the Cambridge University Library partially marked by Lady Aberconway in 1963 (Laing, *Bell*, p. 33). The attributions in these copies do not always agree, but there is enough evidence in letters and in the most completely marked copies to warrant the identifications in the table of authorship. J. S. R., identified only by his initials in the Toronto copy, is most likely 'the man who contributed a solitary sonnet to *Euphrosyne*', that Sydney-Turner wrote of visiting in Brighton in 1906 (LW/pS).

2. In an unpublished sestina dedicated to Strachey and apparently written after they had gone down from Cambridge, Clive Bell writes in a similar fashion of how their singing days are over, as Strachey had

said, and as the poet now says he demonstrates in his verse; yet love and friendship still make the dying poetic embers blaze (CB/pT).

3. Sydney-Turner in a letter to Bell thought George Manville Fenn, a novelist and journalist, may have written the review for this illustrated weekly (15.ix.05, CB/pKC). Fenn pronounced the contents of *Euphrosyne* to be of unequal value and speculated that they were the work of several undergraduates. Swinburne's influence was mentioned, 'At the Bar' called the most notable poem, Strachey's 'When We Are Dead a Thousand Years' quoted for its sound rather than its sense, and Sydney-Turner's 'PYRRHA' praised (Fenn, *Graphic*, 26 August 1905, p. 278).

4. A more general source for *Orlando* might also be connected with *Euphrosyne*; at a party in 1915 Vanessa Bell and Duncan Grant performed a piece called *Euphrosine ou les mystères du sexe*, in the course of which Vanessa changed into boy's clothing (Spalding, *Bell*, p. 146). *Euphrosyne* also appears at the end of a list of names (which includes Clarissa) that Virginia offered Vanessa in 1918 for the, as yet, unnamed Angelica Bell. And in 'The Messiah of Bloomsbury', a 1925 supplement of the *Charleston Bulletin* devoted to the life of Clive Bell and illustrated by Julian and Quentin, Virginia referred to *Euphrosyne* as the volume that caged the symphonic voices of the Trinity songbirds Clive, Lytton, Saxon, and Walter Lamb, but warned that if, twenty years later, you whisper 'Euphrosyne' in Clive's ear he will retaliate with bread pellets (Q. Bell, *Papers*). A last mention of *Euphrosyne* in Bloomsbury's writings is again ironic; in Desmond MacCarthy's brief dream of John Bunyan, she is one of the daughters of Mr Common Sense, in whose house the dreamer Turnback has chosen to remain (*Portraits*, p. 43).

NOTES TO CHAPTER 4: E. M. FORSTER'S FIRST NOVEL

1. Other prefigurings of later Forster works in *Nottingham Lace*, can be found in phrases such as the description of school as a 'world in miniature' (p. 6), that is emphasised in *The Longest Journey*. Trent's sisters' piano-playing sounds like that in the story 'Co-ordination', and the route Edgar's telegram to his father in India takes is similar to the route in time and space that Forster's *A Letter to Madan Blanchard* follows.

2. There are photographs of Forster and Dent as young men in Francis King's *E. M. Forster and His World*, pp. 35, 39.

3. Leonard Woolf actually gives 'Monterians' (*Sowing*, p. 172) as the title but this must be a misreading or a misprint. 'Monteriano' is the title of the original manuscript now in the British Library.

4. Bernard Harrison associates Forster's criticism of Philip's aestheticism with the retrospective critique of Moore's ethics that Keynes wrote more than thirty years later in 'My Early Beliefs'. For the 'de-rhetoricising' interpretation by Leonard Woolf and others, see *Victorian Bloomsbury*, pp. 215–16.

5. Forster's description of the frescoes indicates their similarity to those Ghirlandaio painted of Santa Fina in San Gimignano (*WAFT*, pp.

180–1). Roger Fry in *Macmillan's Guide to Italy* (1901) described Ghirlandaio's early work at San Gimignano as showing 'an almost Flemish feeling for the literal rendering of interiors and still life' (p. li). Duncan Grant, perhaps under the stimulus of *Where Angels Fear to Tread* (whose title he used for his Apostles memoir), thought San Gimignano a great discovery in 1907 (Shone, p. 50).

6. Philip's reluctance to take moral stands places him clearly in Dante's vestibule with those who have chosen neither good nor evil. The year after *Where Angels Fear to Tread* was published, Forster wrote a Housman-like poem in which he described watchers who are 'not good enough for Heaven/Nor bad enough for Hell. . .' (PNF/EMF, I 137). For connections between *Where Angels Fear to Tread* and *La Vita Nuova* see Purkis.

7. Forster told his mother that Blackwood offered no royalties on the first 300 copies, 10 per cent on the next thousand, 15 per cent up to 2,500, and then a shilling a copy (*WAFT*, p. xi). A total of 1050 copies were printed at six shillings each, and another 526 in January 1906 (Kirkpatrick, *EMF*, p. 3).

8. Forster's influence on Hartley has been noted by Michael L. Ross.

NOTES TO CHAPTER 5: DESMOND MacCARTHY AT THE COURT THEATRE

1. MacCarthy may also have been reviewing for the revived imperialist weekly the *Outlook*, according to Hugh and Mirabel Cecil (p. 68), but I have been unable to identify any reviews by him there.

2. In the undocumented second volume of his Shaw biography, Michael Holroyd includes Leonard Woolf among those (such as Rupert Brooke) who approved of the plays Shaw was putting on at the Court Theatre (p. 149). Woolf, of course, was in Ceylon at the time; the praise Holroyd cites comes from *Sowing*, published in 1960.

3. MacCarthy may owe something here and elsewhere to the lectures on dramatic criticism that Walkley published in 1903, just as MacCarthy began his career as a drama critic. The first lecture is on the Aristotelian ideal spectator whose perfectly open mind receives the impressions he is to evaluate. The lecture on the dramatic critic distinguishes between impressionistic and dogmatic types of critics (Walkley, *Dramatic Criticism*).

NOTES TO CHAPTER 6: LYTTON STRACHEY AND THE PROSE OF EMPIRE

1. Methuen apparently expressed interest in the dissertation when Strachey was first writing it but then suggested that he write a book for them on the Holland House Circle, which included Macaulay (MH/LS, p. 223). The publisher offered little financial inducement for such a

work, so Strachey went on with his dissertation instead. The offer in 1910 to write an introduction to French literature for the Home University Library may have finally led to Strachey's abandonment of his Hastings book.

2. The 370-page typescript of Strachey's dissertation is a fairly accurate transcription of a holograph manuscript of more than 800 pages, except for the introduction. A partly cancelled draft preface to the holograph became the basis for the typed introduction, which is on different paper than the rest of the typescript. The table of contents for the typescript mentions a preface but not an introduction. Though Holroyd and Levy date the introduction as 1905 (LS/SS, p. 232), it seems obvious, as Redford has argued, that it was written sometime later when Strachey was planning to make a book of his dissertation (p. 48). The manuscript, typescript, and nearly 600 pages of notes are now in the Robert H. Taylor Collection in the Library of Princeton University which kindly granted me access to these materials.

3. The first paragraph of the introduction, which Strachey took from his holograph preface, has been deleted without indication from the published version in *The Shorter Strachey*. The other omissions marked by ellipses are statements of Strachey's purpose in the dissertation.

4. Strachey may have written this text in collaboration with his uncle and editor St. Loe Strachey (Sanders, p. 169).

5. Lawrence's painting is reproduced in G. M. Trevelyan's *Illustrated History of England*, plate 109.

6. Leonard Woolf sailed for Ceylon in October, 1904. Strachey appears to have written most of his Apostle papers at the last moment, and it is unlikely he would have sent one to Ceylon for comment before delivering it.

7. Strachey did not mention Keynes's essay at the time but in 1908 he wrote for the *Spectator* a pseudonymous letter entitled 'The Political Wisdom of Burke' in which he supported the editor's contention that Burke was unscrupulously violent in his attacks on Hastings. The letter consists essentially of a series of quotations illustrating again Condorcet's remark about the fatal results of mixing ignorance and enthusiasm.

8. The poems are 'The Mask of Gold', 'The Two Triumphs', 'To Him', 'The Category', 'The Crow', 'The Hoods', 'The Resolution', 'The Specula- tion', 'The Resignation', 'The Conversation', and 'The Exhumation'. MacCarthy also published a 1907 poem called 'Knowledge', mis- takenly stating that it and 'The Exhumation' were part of a series recording 'an emotional experience' (M, p. 41). Holroyd refers to some poems called 'The Situation' and 'The Reappearance' in the 1905 series, but I can find no trace of them in Strachey's papers. Holroyd also quotes excerpts from a long satiric poem in heroic couplets that Strachey wrote while working on his dissertation. The poem describes the martyrdom of a shepherd who has anticipated Pope's strictures on verse in 'An Essay on Criticism', and whose death gives birth to a new religion of bad poetry (MH/LS, pp. 251, 349–50).

NOTES TO CHAPTER 7: VIRGINIA WOOLF: BEGINNINGS

1. Though it is anachronistic, I shall continue to refer to Virginia Woolf by her professional name in this account of her beginnings as a writer.

2. Woolf's juvenilia, including her earliest surviving journals, have been mentioned in *Victorian Bloomsbury* (pp. 77, 281–2). To them should be added a recently published *Hyde Park Gate News* story of Miss Smith, a young would-be writer and advocate of temperance and women's rights who abandons them at thirty for marriage to a wiser, stronger companion. The views reflected appear to be those of Virginia's mother who was opposed to women's suffrage and the story itself is modelled on Charlotte Yonge's *The Clever Woman of the Family* (VW/'Miss Smith'; Q. Bell, 'Who's Afraid for Virginia Woolf', p. 4). Woolf's 1899 'A Terrible Tragedy in a Duckpond', which spoofs provincial journalism by reporting the drowning of a party (it turns out to be only a wetting, according to the concluding note of correction and addition 'by One of the Drowned') was copied out for Violet Dickinson in 1904 and has also now been published.

3. The detached, amused tone of Woolf's early description emphasises one significant aspect of her attitude towards George Duckworth; recent psychological biographers of Woolf such as Louise DeSalvo appear to be unaware of this first embodiment of her half-brother in fiction, however. In quoting from the manuscript I have ignored cancellations and supplied a missing word in square brackets.

4. There are several undated short sketches on Thames expeditions and an essay on marginalia among her papers at Sussex but they seem similar to other short pieces that she wrote in 1906 and will be mentioned with them.

5. Mary Kathleen (Mrs Arthur) Lyttelton is confused with her daughter Margaret by the editors of Woolf's letters, essays, and early journals; both Lytteltons apparently had some share in editing the early reviews of Woolf, however (*L*, I 172).

6. The manuscript of this first essay was preserved by Violet Dickinson. Though there are numerous cancellations, the text is not heavily reworked; its structure and flow are essentially unimpeded (pNY).

7. The Gissing review is listed in Woolf's diary as having been done before Christmas, but it was not published until May. Mitchell Leaska, the editor of Woolf's early journals, confuses this book with the two dull Spanish books that Woolf was reviewing early in May (*EJ*, p. 270).

8. It is not possible to reconstruct much beyond this fee, which was presumably for the Haworth essay and Howells review, to find how much Woolf was paid for her early contributions. Some figures in a list of her contributions at the end of 1905 include nine contributions totalling 5100 words and averaging perhaps £3 9s. (*RN*, p. 176). No correspondence with her early editors seems to have survived, but in the notes for her speech on professions for women, Woolf thought she was paid a guinea per thousand words and earned a total of 50 guineas her first year (*P*, p. 163).

9. An anonymous article entitled 'Spanish Homes and Housekeeping' in

the *Guardian* on 14 June might conceivably be by Woolf. It opens with the sentence, 'On a map a streak of sea looks like a barrier far more formidable than the faint black lines indicating mountains, and only on the south side of the Pyrenees does the truth become apparent of the saying that Spain has been closed to Europe and open to Africa since before history began.' The text describes the heartless homes and difficult housekeeping arrangements of the Spanish, emphasising again at the end that the Spanish girl is more akin to 'her southern rather than her northern sisters' in courting rituals. The prose is carefully structured and well written, but the details about cooking, including the use of Spanish terms, are not characteristic of Woolf's writing; she may have taken some of them, however, from the Spanish travel books she reviewed the previous month for the *TLS*. In July Woolf may have also sent another Spanish sketch to the *Academy & Literature* (*L*, I 202, where it is misidentified as a review Woolf had not yet written).

10. In her paper Woolf transcribed the last entry of her diary on 11 May as 'Our evening: gay Bell, D. MacCarthy and Gerald – who shocked the cultured' (*MB*, p. 186). The diary actually continues until the 31st but all the entries after the 11th were written at the end of the month. In her *Early Journals* the entry of the 11th is transcribed more correctly as 'Gay, Bell', etc., and Leaska suggests plausibly that Gay is a fellow of Trinity named R. K. Gaye. In the final entry of 31 May, however, Leaska's transcription mistakenly omits the ambivalent 'if' from the final clause.

11. Both the six-page manuscript on Cellini and the five-page manuscript entitled 'The Dramatic in Life and Art' are undated but the hand-writing is early.

12. This essay is not recorded in Kirkpatrick's bibliography. Woolf mentions it under the title 'Night Walk' in her reading notebook list of work done for the *Guardian* in 1905 (p. 176). (See my 'Three Unknown Early Essays by Virginia Woolf'.) It has now been included in McNeillie's edition of Woolf's essays.

13. Charles Kingsley's 'The Sands of Dee' is also quoted by Woolf in the entry. The editor of the early journals overlooks the Kingsley allusion and misidentifies Lucy as the heroine of Scott's *The Bride of Lammermoor* (p. 286).

14. The second sentence on p. 35 of Woolf's *Essays* should read: 'It is tempting, in many instances, to use our knowledge of a man's life to interpret his work, and the result may be not only that we lay too great a stress upon the ethical element, *but that we emphasize unduly the personal element* with which it is allied'. The words italicised here have been accidentally omitted from *Essays*, I 85.

15. 'Chippinge' is one of three new 1906 *TLS* reviews identified recently by B. J. Kirkpatrick that Woolf apparently wrote after her return from Greece. The others were of Violet A. Simpson's *Occasion's Forelock* and R. Macaulay's *Abbots Verney* (Kirkpatrick, 'Unrecorded'). They will be included in the last volumes of McNeillie's edition of Woolf's *Essays*.

16. There is a review of *Fenwick's Career* in the *Guardian* for 16 May 1906 but it is far too favourable to be Woolf's. In the *TLS* there is also a review of

the Betham book of letters on 30 June 1905 that corresponds a little to her notes but seems too flat in its writing to be hers.

17. The essay on Gissing was written first but printed last as her penultimate contribution to the *Guardian* in February 1907.

  The last undated entry in her reading notebook (following one dated 9 July 1906) is headed 'Auto. of De Quincey,' and the brief notes correspond to works cited and phrases used in 'The English Mail Coach' published 29 August 1906. The essay on James's *English Hours* is referred to, not in the notebooks, but in a letter to Violet Dickinson probably on 11 August 1906 where, after mentioning in an earlier paragraph of 'that blessed Lyttelton takes every word I write and corrects the spelling', she writes 'read your Guardian carefully, and see if you find anything about Henry James; the first words, like [a] coin with a head on it, will tell you who wrote it' (*L*, I 234, where it is dated 4 August). Both the James and De Quincey essays are unlisted in Kirkpatrick but have now been included in volume one of *The Essays of Virginia Woolf*. (See my 'Three Unknown Early Essays by Virginia Woolf'.)

  At the end of 1906 Woolf said she had been sent five more books of poetry to review for the *Guardian*; the only poetry review to appear there early in the next year was on 6 February when seven volumes of minor verse were disposed of in a manner quite unlike hers, and none corresponds to the one she said took the Almighty for a hero and Satan as the villain (*L*, I 272–3). (A last review by Woolf of seven volumes of poetry in 1907 is discussed in Chapter 13.)

18. The untitled typescript of the story is called 'A Dialogue upon Mount Pentelious' [*sic*] in Woolf's papers at Sussex. Parts of two of the pages are torn off, and one of them is out of order and somewhat overlaps another page, indicating that there must have been at least two typed versions of the story at one time. By rearranging one page and omitting ten repeated words, it is possible to read the story as a complete, though unfinished work (VW/'A Dialogue upon Mount Pentelicus'). The story has now been included in the second edition of Woolf's *Complete Shorter Fiction*.

19. Woolf says first she has three and then four novels to review. The three newly identified *TLS* reviews published in November and December (see note 15) were presumably all written after her return from Greece.

NOTES TO CHAPTER 8: ROGER FRY AND THE EARLY AESTHETICS OF BLOOMSBURY

1. Fry's various undergraduate and postgraduate Cambridge writings are mentioned in *Victorian Bloomsbury* (pp. 251–4). To them should be added a short, anonymous satire written in 1889 for a series that the newly founded *Granta* was running on what men do when they go down. Fry's *Granta* essay, entitled 'What Men Do When They Go Down. No. III. – Art' was discovered by Panthea Reid Broughton, and I am indebted to her discussion of it. Fry's topic was schools of art, like the Ecole des Beaux Arts where students fight sometimes mortal duels

with palettes, brushes and arsenic paint, the Royal Academy where they lose their minds stippling the antique from an old plaster cast for two years, or the Chicago School of Art where the antique is improved before being copied by putting the arms back on the cast of Venus di Milo. One other school, the impressionists, avoid the beautiful altogether in their ugly paintings and conventional dress, but they did not impress the correspondent of *Granta* who, with the help of McTaggart's dialectic, founds his own 'Impressionist–Pre-Raphaelite School' (p. 11). It was another twenty years before the author would find his real synthesis in post-impressionism.

2. Fry was occasionally assisted in this reviewing by C. J. Holmes, while E. A. Gardiner reviewed classical art and archaeology. Fry's reviews in the *Athenaeum* are itemised and described in Laing's bibliography.

3. Ernest Samuels suggests in his biography that one of Berenson's sources was Charles Waldstein's notion of the '*plastic* character of mind' in his *Essay on the Art of Pheidias* (*Connoisseur*, p. 47). Waldstein (later Walston) was a fellow of King's and Slade Professor from 1895 to 1901; it was at his invitation in 1900 that Fry gave the extension lectures on Italian painting which E. M. Forster heard. It seems likely that Waldstein was also one of the sources for Fry's ideas on plasticity in painting. Samuels also states that in 1899 Fry had 'humbly dedicated' *Giovanni Bellini* to Berenson (*Legend*, p. 21), but the book is actually dedicated to 'H. F.' or Helen Fry.

NOTES TO CHAPTER 9: E. M. FORSTER'S REFUTATION OF IDEALISM

1. Ansell's Jewishness also associates him with Sidney Trent, the schoolmaster in *Nottingham Lace* whose relationship to Edgar somewhat resembles Ansell's to Rickie's (the school is also called Sawstone and Sawston). In the original plot for *The Longest Journey* the prototype of Ansell joins the Indian Civil Service after Cambridge, as Leonard Woolf did the Ceylon Civil Service.

2. The interview, parts of which were published in the *Paris Review*, was conducted by P. N. Furbank and F. J. H. Haskell as well as Ian Watt, who has kindly made his notes available to me. Meredith sponsored Forster in the Apostles; Moore participated in his election along with Ainsworth, who later married Moore's sister.

3. Forster may have been reminded of 'The Refutation of Idealism' by Lowes Dickinson's use of it in a review of Edward Carpenter's Idealistic *The Art of Creation* for the *Independent Review* in January 1905, and to which Carpenter, uninformed of Moore's arguments, replied the next month. This was about the time Forster was starting to write his novel (T. Brown, *Longest Journey*).

4. As in *Victorian Bloomsbury* Idealism, Realism, and Materialism are all capitalised when referring to particular philosophies, as distinct from the less technical meanings of these words.

5. The chapter is included in Heine's useful appendix on the manuscripts of *The Longest Journey*. The text of this edition is freer of errors than

other, though a duplicated sentence from Ansell's dining-hall speech at Sawston on p. 225 ('Perhaps he will die . . . accepted from me') remains uncorrected.

6. Desmond MacCarthy recognised Widdrington as Strachey and told him (PNF/*EMF*, I 150). Widdrington's name was that of a family Forster knew, whose daughter Roger Fry proposed to and whose mother undertook, in Virginia Woolf's words, 'to educate him in the art of love' (Spalding, *Fry*, pp. 39, 47–8). Forster's sometimes ironic borrowing of names from people he knew occurs again when Agnes remarries and becomes Mrs Keynes. (Stephen seems too common a name to be connected with the Stephens, however.)

7. In using *world* instead of *crowd* (l. 151) and *sad* rather than *chained* (l. 158) Forster is following an earlier draft of the poem, though he rejects the draft's 'and many a jealous foe' for the 'perhaps a jealous foe' wording of the final version. Forster's choices all suit his use of Shelley better than the alternatives.

8. H. O. Meredith has also been described as a model for Clive Durham in *Maurice*, which makes one wonder how useful such identifications are. J. R. Ackerley thought Forster himself turned out to be 'in some important respects rather like his own creature, that grand philosopher Ansell . . .' (*Letters*, p. 317). Sometimes the specific resemblances between Moore and Ansell at Cambridge appear more than just commonplace or coincidental. Moore wrote an Apostle paper, for example, on whether there was a duty to hate (Levy, pp. 220–2). Again, one of Moore's ridiculing arguments against Idealism held that Idealists on trains forgot there were wheels as soon as they were inside because they could no longer perceive them (the argument was published much later in *Some Main Problems of Philosophy*, p. 151); when Rickie, Ansell, and their friends return to Cambridge once, the wheels of the station tram taking them to college fall off (p. 55).

9. Also germane to Ansell's speech, perhaps, is the evolutionary vitalism of Shaw's *Man and Superman*, where the female carrier of the life force is engaged to a man nicknamed Rickie (Stone, pp. 199, 410).

10. Wiltshire is also related to Cambridge somewhat in the manner of Matthew Arnold's Oxford poems 'Thyrsis' and 'The Scholar Gipsy'. Forster said he liked neither Arnold's scenery nor sentiment, but the poems seem to have been in his mind when thinking about *The Longest Journey* (pp. lxvii, 305–6). Another poem that is interesting to compare with *The Longest Journey* is Wordsworth's *The Prelude*, particular the account of youthful wanderings in Wiltshire and on 'Sarum's Plain' where once his spirit was raised. The end of the passage emphasises epistemologically, like the novel, the mind's balance of outer and inner – 'Both of the object seen, and eye that sees' (*The Prelude*, XIII, 279–378).

11. Perhaps because the historical milieu of Forster's work has received less attention than his biography, critics appear reluctant to read Forster in the philosophical context of his own time. In response to an earlier version of this chapter (Rosenbaum, *LJ*), for example, P. N. Furbank acknowledged that Moore's influence was greater than had he

allowed in his biography, yet thought that Forster's knowledge of Idealism was not much more than that expressed in Knox's well-known limerick about the unperceived tree in the quad (which was probably written after *The Longest Journey* – see below n. 12). But the novel's explicit concern for truth suggests that Forster was quite aware of Moore's fundamental distinction in his various refutations of Idealism between our thinking of something and the truth of what we are thinking. Furbank contends that Moore's analytic methods of arguing arithmetically about such things as organic unities would have repelled Forster. It repelled Moore too, and his influential notion of organic unity was developed to refute the notion of wholes as merely the sums of their parts. (This is the primary meaning of the epigraph to *Principia Ethica*: 'Everything is what it is and not another thing' – see *Victorian Bloomsbury*, pp. 228–30). Moreover, there are distinct echoes of Moore's rigourous analytic method in Ansell's talk. Furbank finds Forster's philosophy to be one of death, resting on a proposition about the idea of death saving man (Furbank, 'Philosophy' pp. 37ff.). Yet in *The Longest Journey*, the importance of death is clearly connected not only with epistemological and moral questions about the existence and non-existence of objects and people, but also with problems about the reality of symbolic moments, time, history, and human continuity. Forster said on various occasions that death for him was largely related to the need for remembering. If Forster can be said to have a 'philosophy' in *The Longest Journey*, it would seem to be more one of secular salvation through emotional openness, social compassion, and human continuity that remembers the unidealised dead.

Bernard Harrison also questions the significance of Moore for Forster, believing that the notion of influence 'suggests a simple transfer of ideas or ideals from one writer to another . . . ' and misconstrues the argument for Moore's influence as making Forster a 'consistent Moorean Realist' and 'a complaisant publicist' of his outlook (pp. 2–4). The workings of Forster's mind are indeed more complicated than that, but the nature of influence need not be just simple transference. My claim again is not that Forster was directly influenced by Moore's epistemological arguments (I quote him saying Moore's thought was mediated to him through friends) but that he understood his conclusions well enough to transmute – with the help of Shelley's poetry – Moore's epistemological point of view into a fictionalised moral one.

12. Woolf's review is among those identified recently by B. J. Kirkpatrick. It is included as an anonymous review in *E. M. Forster: The Critical Heritage*.

13. Wilfred Stone notes Lawrence's similar use of Shelley in *Women in Love* (p. 410), and Forster's symbolic extension of Idealism comes into Birkin's early conversation with Gerald's mother in Chapter 2. In his late poem 'The Ship of Death' Lawrence describes death several times as 'the longest journey towards oblivion' (*Complete Poems*, II 716-177). (Frieda Lawrence wrote to Forster how she loved *The Longest Journey* but did not understand why Forster so disliked the women in the novel – *EMFCH*, p. 97).

NOTES TO CHAPTER 10: DESMOND MacCARTHY AND
THE *NEW QUARTERLY*, CLIVE BELL AND THE
ATHENAEUM

1. MacCarthy did write a reminiscence of Paley for the Memoir Club but
   it is currently unavailable. Mr Hugh Cecil has kindly allowed me to
   examine other unpublished papers relating the *New Quarterly*,
   however.
2. MacCarthy sent Russell proofs of the last section of the work, and
   Russell states in a note that it was published in the September issue of
   the *New Quarterly* – an issue that never appeared (*Papers*, VI 206). When
   Russell printed 'Ethics' in *Philosophical Essays* (1910), he renamed it 'The
   Elements of Ethics', which was the title of the lectures in which Moore
   first worked out many of the ideas of *Principia Ethica*; Russell had read
   Moore's lectures in typescript and made some criticisms of them (see
   my 'Moore's Elements'). The editor of Moore's *The Elements of Ethics*,
   which has recently been published, seems unaware of Russell's
   comments and ignores in his introduction the interrelations of Moore's
   and Russell's early work in ethics.
3. Forster almost certainly read Dickinson's lecture but it does not clarify
   his own ideas about death. (The lecture does quote with approval the
   last lines of Whitman's 'Passage to India', however.) Forster was
   contemptuous of the Society for Psychical Research in his biography of
   Dickinson, and he later published a parody of the Landor epitaph that
   Dickinson quoted as so beautiful:

   > I strove with none, for none was worth my strife;
   >   Nature I loved and next to nature art;
   > I warmed both hands before the fire of life;
   >   It sinks, and I am ready to depart.
   >   (Dickinson, 'Immortality', p. 194)

   Forster wrote:

   > I strove with none, for none was worth my strife;
   >   Reason I loved, and next to Reason, Doubt;
   > I warmed both hands before the fire of life;
   >   And put it out.
   >   ('Landor at Sea')

4. The focus of Fry's essay is indicated in the title of an earlier version
   that he read to a philosophical discussion group at Oxford: 'Expression
   and Representation in the Graphic Arts'. Fry had been asked to discuss
   aesthetics in metaphysical terms but he said his education had already
   revealed to him his incapacity for metaphysics; all he could offer was a
   practical and empirical hypothesis (RF/pKC).
5. Strachey replied he was delighted to have increased Bailey's appreciation of Racine, because French was *sui generis*: 'One has to creep into

its skin as best one can, and then if one succeeds, one's liable to find that one's lost one's balance, and is beginning to consider all other languages with the calm disdain of the average Frenchman' (Bailey, *Letters*, p. 218).

6. Lytton's correspondence with his brother James indicates that the poem (see *Victorian Bloomsbury*, p. 287) may have led to the idea of an article on Giles in which Lytton could use 'one of my well-known pseudo quotations' (23.vii.08, LS/pBL).

7. Some ribald parodies that Strachey later wrote of Waley's translations diminished Waley's 'corporate admiration for the whole Strachey family'; he found them 'very stupid, and Lytton fell off his pedestal' (*Bloomsbury Group*, pp. 303–4).

8. Bell's *Athenaeum* reviews are itemised and described in Laing's bibliography.

NOTES TO CHAPTER 11: LYTTON STRACHEY AND THE *SPECTATOR*

1. The fame of the *Spectator* clung to the Stracheys. In 1914 Leonard Woolf described in a letter to Janet Case how the bearded Lytton, wearing maroon corduroys and a huge broadbrimmed hat, was thought in the village where they were staying to be the editor of a paper with two words in its title – the *Sporting Times*, they said (29.xii.14, LW/pS).

2. Henry Strachey signed his reviews 'H' and Lytton 'Z'. Four reviews on 6 March, 15 May, 19 June, and 26 June 1909 are signed 'G' and may be by the young Duncan Grant. Only one of these, praising a still life of Vanessa Bell's, has been attributed to Grant by Spalding (*VB*, p. 82). One of the others briefly discusses some pastels by Simon Bussy, the husband of Strachey cousin, Dorothy; it was written the year before the first post-impressionist exhibition, and is interesting for its impressionistic formalism. Bussy's pictures will appeal to English nature-lovers, says 'G', but they will not derive all the pleasure they might unless they approach them aesthetically, for their represented trees, hills, and sky 'exist in the picture only for the sake of their relationship to one another, and . . . only that portion of the aspect of an object is chosen which plays its part with other forms, tones, and colours to complete a whole, and reproduce the deliberate impressions of the painter'. To the spectator who looks at these marvellous pictures and exclaims he never saw anything like their natural objects, the reviewer replies 'But that is hardly the point, which is rather: "Are we not glad that M. Bussy has?"' (p. 377).

3. Strachey's *Spectator* texts are itemised in Michael Edmonds's bibliography; mostly quotations of them will be cited from the *Spectator* or the *Spectatorial Essays* selection made by James Strachey in 1964 (SE).

4. Strachey wrote facetiously to his friend Bernard Swithinbank that he did not know what to say about Mrs Inchbald and thought of writing instead on Mrs Barbauld because she at least came into the part of the new edition of the *Dictionary of National Biography* that he had just

bought. He doubted if the public would notice the difference (30.vi.08, LS/pKC).

5. In the summer of 1908 Strachey was playing another letter-game with Keynes and Grant, describing to them an erotic but fictive encounter with a young man named Horace in Scotland. Keynes eventually complained that Strachey's Horation epistles, complete with Swinburnean verse, were a waste of good emotion (LS/pKC, JMK/pKC).

6. The finances of plays provoked a letter signed 'L' from Strachey to the *Cambridge Review* in 1909, after another letter signed 'K' (but not apparently by Keynes) attacked a performance of Ibsen's *Love's Comedy*, which devoted its funds to women's suffrage without saying so. Strachey agreed with 'K' and suggested all productions should declare where their profits go, for after all a conservative churchman might discover his attendance at the theatre would be financially assisting 'an actor who disapproved of the damnatory, minatory, or monitory clauses in the Athanansian creed' (Letter, p. 93). 'K' replied he was concerned only with amateur theatricals and therefore L's sarcasm and sophistry were irrelevant. Lytton admitted his authorship to James. The letter is not included in Edmonds's bibliography.

7. Lytton marked with square brackets St. Loe's interpolations in his own copies of his *Spectator* reviews, and James retained them in *Spectatorial Essays*.

8. Most of chapters one, two, and four of Lord Pettigrew have been printed in *The Really Interesting Question*; for some reason the third chapter has been omitted.

9. The manuscript of the play in the Strachey Trust papers lacks a second act and ends abruptly in the third. In quoting from it I have not recorded Strachey's cancellations.

Another fragment of a Strachey play that may have been written around this time is entitled 'Dr. De Jongh' and is described on the title page as a one-act farce. It is set somewhere in Oceania; Dr De Jongh is an Australian patent-medicine salesman who bears the birth name of Leonard Woolf's mother but there are no other connections with Leonard Woolf or Ceylon in the play.

10. Levy dates 'Will It Come Right in the End' in 1908 or later and 'Art and Indecency' sometime before 1908 (LS/*RIQ*, pp. 71, 82). A comparison of the two papers shows, however, the latter to be a rewritten version of the former.

11. John Maynard Keynes also wrote a later Edwardian Apostle paper on art in 1909 that was not mentioned in the descriptions of Keynes's Cambridge writings in *Victorian Bloomsbury*. Entitling it 'Science or Art', Keynes argued, according to D. E. Moggridge, that the creative processes of scientists and artists were similar; the scientist, for example, also requires insight to understand the significant connections of his data (Moggridge, p. 184)

NOTES TO CHAPTER 12: E. M. FORSTER: ROOMS AND VIEWS

1. The perils of reviewing current fiction in a literary supplement of record are reflected in the review printed just above Virginia Woolf's notice of *A Room with A View* on 22 October 1908. The work reviewed was *The Wind in the Willows*, 'a book with hardly a smile in it', according to the reviewer, 'through which we wander in a haze of perplexity, uninterested by the story itself and at a loss to understand its deeper purpose. The chief character is a mole, whom the reader plumps upon on the first page whitewashing his house. Here is an initial nut to crack; a mole whitewashing. No doubt moles like their abodes to be clean; but whitewashing? Are we very stupid, or is this joke really inferior? . . . Then enters a water rat, on his way to a river picnic. . . . Nut number two; for obviously a water rat is of all animals the one that would never use a boat with which to navigate a stream. Again, are we very stupid, or, is this nonsense of poor quality.' The reviewer concludes 'as a contribution to natural history the work is negligible. . . . Grown up readers will find it monotonous and elusive; children will hope in vain for more fun.'

2. The names of the characters in *A Room with a View* have exercised the ingenuity of critics: Lucy Honeychurch's name seems to echo Matthew Arnold's sweetness and light; Eager and Lavish sound like Restoration comedy characters; Beebe has been identified with asexual bees in Virgil; Cecil means 'blind' in Latin; and poor Charlotte has even been tied to Bartlett's *Familiar Quotations* (see M. L. Ross, H. T. Moore, Meyers, and Summers's, *Forster*).

3. Forster agreed with Peter Burra's suggestion that this more mysterious love might also allude to the couple's coming children (*L*, II 128). There are other references in the novel and elsewhere in Forster's fiction to the power of the love for children and the desire for personal continuation though them.

4. 'HOM', whom Strachey thought the basis for Ansell in *The Longest Journey*, is listed as a character in the Italian sketches for *A Room with a View*, where his role is similar to George's (*LN*, p. 3). In the finished novel, George's personality includes aspects of both Ansell's and Stephen's.

5. In response to some recollections of Henry James by Leonard Woolf in 1959, Forster wrote to the *Listener* about his own, quoting from a diary entry he had made early in 1908. Sidney Waterlow introduced Forster to James (he had been preceded by the daughter of James's old friend Leslie Stephen and her newly married husband Clive Bell, both of whom the master thought grubby) but the meeting was less exciting than expected, perhaps because James mixed up Waterlow's friends and thought Forster was Moore. Forster believed James never got their names entirely separated ('Henry James', p. 103). Forster told his mother that the Waterlows had shown James his story 'The Celestial Omnibus', which they had liked but Forster knew James would not. After the visit, which Forster enjoyed a great deal, he noticed outside

Lamb House a young workingman smoking in the shadows. Forster subsequently wrote a poem in his diary, not quoted in the *Listener*, about the contrast; it ended with the lines, 'For those within the room, high talk,/Subtle experience – for me/The spark, the darkness, on the walk' (PNF/*EMF*, I 165).

6. The American publishers of *Howards End* supplied their own chapter titles for that novel but removed them when Forster objected (Kirkpatrick, *EMF*, p. 16).

7. In quoting from *The Lucy Novels* I have corrected misspellings and omitted passages marked as deletions.

8. Forster wrote to Garnett as well to Strachey, asking if he could have *A Room with a View* reviewed in the *Nation*; it was, but by Masterman not Garnett, who then asked for a copy which Forster sent – for use as a blotter if nothing else (EMF/pT). According to David, the Garnett family all thought *A Room with a View* Forster's best novel, (p. 33), which agrees with the review; so does the suggestion that Forster might now try a play, for Edward was also writing plays at this time.

9. Lawrence began rewriting *The White Peacock* for the third time in October 1908, the month that *A Room with a View* was published. He had, it seems, already chosen the names of George, Laetitia and Cyril for his characters in earlier drafts however. The presence of a gamekeeper in the novel anticipates *Maurice* a little, which in turn influenced *Lady Chatterley's Lover* (Dixie King).

10. Stein's plotless work of prose poetry, which she had printed in 1931, attempts to represent spatially rather than temporally a woman called Lucy Church and her friends, as well as a church and landscape in the French village of Lucey.

11. In 1985 the *Whole Earth Review* reprinted 'The Machine Stops' after discovering it in a Christian magazine, of all places. An editorial note on 'this story of the ultimate electronic cottage' observed that it was written when Forster was thirty and wondered if there were other thirty-year-olds 'now writing with this kind of insight?' (p. 40).

12. Forster revised his 1947 introduction to the American *The Collected Tales* for the 1948 English *Collected Short Stories*.

NOTES TO CHAPTER 13: VIRGINIA WOOLF AND THE PROPER WRITING OF LIVES

1. 'Some Poetic Plays' has not yet been included in Woolf's bibliography. It appeared on 1 January 1908, four months after she wrote to Dickinson 'I have 7 volumes of poetic drama to review for the Guardian . . .' (*L*, I 307). No other reviews of poetic plays appeared in the *Guardian* between August and January. Like her other recently discovered *Guardian* pieces on Cornwall, Henry James, and De Quincey, there is nothing in the unsigned review to suggest Virginia Woolf could not have written it. Even the confusion in the review between Raleigh's biographer William Stebbing and Bacon's editor, James Spedding, is one she could have made, as she would have been familiar with both men's work.

Another drama review has been credited to Woolf by Marjorie Strachey, who wrote the theatre section of *The Englishwoman* at the end of the decade. She told Elizabeth Boyd that Woolf was the reviewer of a modern adaptation of Aristophanes's *Lysistrata* in the November–December issue of 1910 (VW/pS). The reviewer finds the play interesting mainly because of its relevance for suffragists, but she is also amused and irritated by it, for sometimes the modernised Lysistrata's words are right and true but more often they are not.

2. All but four of her fiction reviews in 1907 and 1908 have been discovered since the third edition of Woolf's bibliography. They are listed along with other recently found reviews of biographies, journals, and letters in Kirkpatrick's 'Unrecorded *TLS* reviews', and will be cited here only when quoted.

3. Among the great nineteenth-century English novelists, Thackeray is conspicuously absent from Virginia Woolf's criticism. She never devoted an essay to his work, perhaps because of the family connection, but her various remarks indicate she had serious reservations about his work. In her reading notes for the Sterne review, for instance, she remarks that Sterne is 'much more cynical than Thackeray, as his sentiment is far less repulsive' (*RN*, p. 150; pNY).

4. Woolf quoted in her review the line 'All, all are men – women and all!' from the opening of Hitchener's 'Ode on the Rights of Women'. Twenty years later she remembered it in drafting *Women & Fiction* but deleted it in revision of *A Room of One's Own* (*W&F*, p. 49).

5. A reading list and some notes have survived from 1909–11 in a manuscript book Virginia Woolf later used for writing part of *Night and Day* (*RN*, pp. 147–52). In 1910 Clive Bell asked Virginia Woolf for *Zarathustra*, it being one of the books he supposes one should read (6.ix.1910, CB/pS).

6. Clive Bell wrote to Strachey that 'Virginia has had her Miss Willatt rejected by Reginald, but she sees that he is a fool & doesn't mind' (14.xi.09, LS/pBL). Bell's reference to the text only by its title suggests Strachey's familiarity with it.

7. It was not until 1922 that Trevelyan wrote *British History in the Nineteenth Century*, and his *English Social History* did not appear for another twenty years after that.

8. Quotations from the early journals here and later follow Quentin and Anne Olivier Bell's transcriptions (*VW*, I 138; *D*, III 352–3), which vary at several points from Leaska's versions.

9. The envelope in which the untitled typescript is stored at Sussex has written on it 'VW Reminiscences (Julia/Stella/Vanessa)' – but the handwriting is not Virginia or even Leonard Woolf's.

NOTES TO CHAPTER 14: LEONARD WOOLF'S CEYLON WRITINGS

1. Like Rachel Vinrace of *The Voyage Out*, Woolf was twenty-four at the beginning of his voyage. One of the women he was attracted to in Ceylon is called Rachel in *Growing*, though this was not her real name

(pp. 150ff.). Another Bloomsbury voyage out resembling Woolf's is described briefly by Forster in his biography of Dickinson (pp. 112–13); Forster's contrast of his friends' clique and the clan of the others on board the P&O also fits Leonard Woolf's experience to some degree.

2. 'Memoirs of an Elderly Man', published in *Orion* in 1945, has different dates, names, and places (the voyage out is to India, it takes place in 1900, the narrator is twenty-seven, etc.) but neither narrative of the voyage nor the account of Dutton's character and marriage differ much from the episodes as they are retold in *Growing* – except perhaps for the narrator's kissing a young woman on shipboard and being reproved for it by a middle-aged lady. Several other brief unpublished memoirs, some of which were also used in *Growing*, remain among Leonard Woolf's papers at Sussex.

3. In another letter to Strachey, Woolf explained that his success as a civil servant was entirely due to his use of 'the method' which they had applied aesthetically and theoretically in Cambridge and which he was using practically in Ceylon (*L*, p. 106). This 'method' is not so a much the psychoanalytic third-degree described in *Sowing* (see *Victorian Bloomsbury*, pp. 148–9) as an attempt, in unravelling intrigues, to think or feel what someone else is thinking or feeling.

4. An Edwardian imperialist once described the Russian defeat as 'the first set-back of the Caucasian since the Neolithic period' (Porter, 134). One wonders what Neolithic event he had in mind.

5. An inscribed copy of *Eastern Star-Dust* by 'Bella Sidney Woolf (Mrs. W. T. Southorn)' is among the books of Leonard and Virginia Woolf now at Washington State University. It was published in 1922 and consists of a series of short sketches or essays on the scenery, servants, ceremonies, etc., of Ceylon. Also among the Woolfs' books are her *The Twins in Ceylon* (1909), a children's story about visiting Ceylon, and *From Groves of Palm* (1925), a series of brief descriptive sketches of colonial life in Ceylon. Her *How to See Ceylon*, published in 1914 with an acknowledgement to her brother's 'intimate and introspective knowledge of the people, so strikingly set forth in his book *The Village in the Jungle*', went through four editions in the 1920s.

6. Though Leonard Woolf said in *Growing* (1961) that the description was written forty years before, he had stated in 1921 that it was written 'a long time ago' (*DAW*, p. 89). The only specifically datable reference in the story is to the King's Indian visit of 1911 (p. 22). There are no references to the First World War in it or the other two stories.

7. In 1963, however, the Hogarth Press included at the end of their edition of Woolf's *Diaries in Ceylon*, the three stories, mistitled *Stories from* [*sic*] *the East*, that had been included with the original Ceylon edition of the diaries.

8. Among Leonard Woolf papers at Sussex is another Eastern story, not included in the collection, about an Englishwoman in India who is in love with the narrator; at her death she leaves him her dog who gives birth to dead puppies. The basis for the story is a memoir, also not incorporated in *Growing*, of Leonard Woolf's relations with a German woman in Ceylon who was in love with him. Another fragment of a

story suggests that Woolf was trying at some time to write a number of stories of the East.

9. There is a small but characteristic discrepancy between the two versions of the story as to the amount of the fines and a more significant difference in the headman's question; in *Growing* he demands to know if it was 'fair' but in *The Journey Not the Arrival Matters* if it was 'just'. The headman may have also been complaining about L. S. Woolf's combination of administrative and judicial functions in the levying of fines as Assistant Government Agent and then again as Police Magistrate.

10. *Diaries in Ceylon* includes an extensive historical introduction by S. D. Saparamadu, a general introduction on Leonard Woolf by Mervyn de Silva, and a helpful glossary.

11. L. S. Woolf wrote 'Hic labor, hoc nobis opus est, sunt illa laboris/ Praemia' (*Aeneid*, VI 126). The deleted entry is preserved in Woolf's papers at Sussex.

12. The footnotes are occasionally rather delayed. Words will sometimes appear several times in the text before the footnotes get around to identifying them. This suggests they may have been added later.

13. The early fragment of a story by Virginia Woolf on the life of two jungle monkeys also bears the trace of Kipling's *The Jungle Books* (see p. 184).

14. In *How to See Ceylon*, Bella Woolf comments, 'It is the women who have the poorest time in village life. The ordinary villager cultivates his patch of paddy and then lazes on a cane couch before his door, while his wife pounds the paddy, collects and chops the firewood, fetches water in the heavy chatties, cooks and does every other odd job. Women occupy the traditional oriental subservient position among the village Sinhalese. When they are educated, their influence will do much to elevate the tone of village life' (p. 220).

15. A film of *The Village in the Jungle* entitled *Beddagama* and made in Sri Lanka opened at Colombo early in 1981. I have not seen it but one scene apparently features Leonard Woolf as a magistrate in court; the science-fiction writer Arthur C. Clarke played the bit-part of Woolf in the film (McAleer, p. 294).

16. Various critics and scholars, including the editors of Forster's letters, have confused Leonard's first novel with Virginia's, which was not published until a month after Lawrence's letter. A letter of Frieda Lawrence's to Forster (quoted in PNF/*EMF*, II 11) refers to the pig entering the house at the end of the novel, and thus shows that it was *The Village in the Jungle* the Lawrences were reading and not *The Voyage Out*. Forster and Lawrence would also not have referred, in 1915, to a book by Virginia Woolf simply as 'Woolf's' without her title or given name.

NOTES TO CHAPTER 15: E. M. FORSTER: ENDS AND MEANS

1. The memoir is included as an appendix to the Abinger Edition of *Howards End* and the Penguin edition which uses the Abinger text. A

photograph of the farmhouse is reproduced on the front of the Abinger dust-jacket and Forster's plan of Rooksnest on the back. A story about the inheritance of an estate owned by someone called Howard had been in Forster's mind since at least 1905, when he wrote 'The Purple Envelope' (see p. 57).

2. References to *The Manuscripts of Howards End* are to the page and line numbers, separated by a colon, that key the changes to the Abinger Edition of *Howards End*. References without a colon refer to the page numbers of *The Manuscript of Howards End* itself rather than to the novel. In quoting from the transcribed manuscripts I have ignored Forster's cancellations and added his insertions into text.

3. Margaret maintains to Leonard, for example, the unWagnerian distinctiveness of the arts (*HE*, pp. 36–7). In *What Is Art?* (which Forster had invoked in an early draft of *A Room with a View*) Tolstoy summarised Schlegel's efforts to connect art, nature, and humankind as follows:

> beauty in art is understood too incompletely, one-sidedly, and disconnectedly. Beauty exists, not only in art, but also in nature and in love; so that the truly beautiful is expressed by the union of art, nature, and love. Therefore, as inseparably one with aesthetic art, Schlegel acknowledges moral and philosophic art. (p. 30)

4. The extensive critical literature on *Howards End* has been listed and annotated by McDowell and Summers. Unless otherwise indicated, critical commentary on *Howards End* referred to in the text can be identified in their works. It is a little surprising that there are no discussions of the relation between Chekhov and *Howards End* listed by them. Chekhov's plays were not staged in London until 1912, though Maurice Baring had discussed them in MacCarthy's *New Quarterly* in 1908, and Duckworth had published translations of two volumes of Chekhov's stories. (Constance Garnett's translations of Chekhov's fiction did not begin until 1916.)

5. *Howards End* may be the most frequently misspelled title of any English novel. When Penguin advertised their edition of a novel called *Howard's End*, Forster asked his agent 'to write and tell them there isn't one. I do think that was right once' (18.x. 51, pB).

6. G. E. Moore used Arnold's phrase in an uncharacteristic paper entitled 'Is conversion possible?' that he read to the Apostles on several occasions. Relying on what he called a literary rather than a scientific method, Moore described the experience of rebirth to a new life as one in which one sees life steadily and whole (Papers).

7. A picture had educated Leonard in the past, says the narrator in one of the few allusions not identified by Oliver Stallybrass in his informative notes to the Abinger Edition of *Howards End*. Shortly before the fatal visit to Howards End, Leonard goes into St Paul's to see the picture again: 'the light was bad, the picture ill-placed, and Time and Judgement were inside him now. Death alone still charmed him, with her lap of poppies, on which all men shall sleep. He took one glance,

and turned aimlessly away towards a chair' (p. 316). Then the sight of Margaret and Tibby drives him from the Cathedral. I am grateful to Quentin and Olivier Bell; R. H. Jefferies, the Curator of the Watts Gallery; and Michael Pantazzi of the National Gallery of Canada for help in identifying the painting as G. F. Watts's *Time, Death, and Judgement*, which was presented to St Paul's Cathedral in 1898 and is now on permanent loan to The Watts Gallery. The picture shows a bare-chested Attic youth with a scythe alongside a hooded woman with downcast eyes and an apron full of flowers; looming behind is larger robed figure with a sword on his shoulder. (The painting resembles a little the figures of Hermes and Death escorting Alcestis to the underworld on the column-drum from Ephesus in the British Museum that Forster was very fond of.) The picture has also been identified and one of its various versions reproduced by Garrett Stewart in *Death Sentences: Styles of Dying in British Fiction*. Stewart quotes Watt's description of the picture's allegory: 'Time, represented as the type of unfailing youth and vigour, advances hand in hand with Death, while, poised in the clouds above their heads, follows the figure of Judgment, armed with attributes of Eternal Law' (pp. 179, 381).

8. A ten-page supplement, *The Manuscripts of Howards End: Corrigenda and Addenda*, was published by Stallybrass in 1976 as a result of J. H. Stape's study of the manuscript.

9. Putnam's, for example, priggishly altered Tibby's 'damn' to 'iota', which produced the following absurdity: '"I don't care an iota what people think!" cried he, heated to unusual manliness of diction' (*HE*, p. 251). Nearly fifty years later Forster recalled the change with indignation while testifying along with T. S. Eliot before a parliamentary select committee on obscene publications (*HEMSS*, p. xvi). Putnam's published *A Room with a View* in May, 1911, but the rest of Forster's novels were brought out in America by Knopf, who also reprinted the earlier ones in the 1920s. (The details on sales and royalties of Forster's books can be found in Kirkpatrick's bibliography and in Forster's correspondence with the Society of Authors that is now in the British Library and the New York Public Library.)

Misprints accumulated as *Howards End* went through new editions in England and the United States, to which Forster responded in a 1958 letter, 'Oh the misprints! Do not mention, do not even dream about them'. He said he had a kind of nightmare locker into which he put corrections when they were pointed out to him, hoping someday they would re-emerge; no such locker has been found (*HEMSS*, pp. xvi–ii). Although the two-volume Abinger Edition of the novel records and corrects the various misprints, Knopf's successors have continued to perpetuate theirs in American reprintings of the novel.

10. A different sexual interpretation of the novel's title occurs in the film *Educating Rita*, where *Howards End* becomes a symbol of literary education to which a working-class woman aspires. At the beginning, she cannot understand the book and thinks the title filthy, but eventually she is able to reassure her teacher that she will go to bed 'with cocoa and *Howards End* – if Howard shows up'.

11. Judging from the epigraph alone, the influence of *Howards End* on novelists continues. John Fowles in *Daniel Martin* notes, for instance, the slick come-down from Forster's 'only connect' to the more modern 'only reify' (p. 623), and Renata Adler in *Speedboat* ironically includes Forster and Pound among 'the great dead men with their injunctions. Make it new. Only connect' (p. 73). An unusual testimony to Forster's significance for writers that also perceptively understands how the epigraph epitomises the novel is the interpretation of P. L. Travers in a lecture on the origins of *Mary Poppins* entitled 'Only Connect'. For Travers, the phrase had been precious ever since she had read *Howards End*:

> Perhaps, indeed, it's the theme of all of Forster's writing, the attempt to link a passionate scepticism with the desire for meaning, to find the human key to the inhuman world about us; to connect the individual with the community, the known with the unknown; to relate the past to the present and both to the future.
> (p. 184)

12. Other novelists in the New Directions Makers of Modern Literature series at this time included Gide, Gogol (by Nabokov), Joyce (by Levin), Wolfe, and Woolf (by Daiches).

13. A closer analysis of the passage at the end of Chapter 19 criticised by Leavis, Richards, and Trilling, among others, has been given by Kenneth Graham, who takes into account Helen's ambiguous statement 'One would lose something' at the beginning of the paragraph and also Margaret's later interpretation of her sister's remark (*HE*, pp. 172, 198; Graham, p. 168). The prose of Helen's reaction might also be compared to the description of Margaret's reaction to Leonard's death in which logical connections dissolve in an associative stream before Margaret can reach some diviner consolation:

> Here Leonard lay dead in the garden, from natural causes; yet life was a deep, deep river, death a blue sky, life was a house, death a wisp of hay a flower, a tower, life and death were anything and everything, except this ordered insanity, where the king takes the queen, and the ace the king. (p. 327)

14. This romantic reading of *Howards End* has proceeded under the influence of Northrop Frye, who distinguished not two but four forms of prose fiction: novel, romance, confession, and anatomy. There has been relatively little critical attention given to the autobiographical and satirical elements of the last two in *Howards End*, but they are present in the important role of the narrator and elsewhere. It might be particularly interesting to analyse *Howards End* as an anatomy. (Frye himself dismissed Forster, however, as a refined and finicky minor writer because of his criticism of Dickens – pp. 303–12, 169).

15. *Howards End* was translated into French in 1950 by Forster's good

friend Charles Mauron and given the title, so risible to English readers, of *Le legs de Mrs Wilcox.*

Bibliography

This bibliography is divided into two parts: first, works by members of the Bloomsbury Group, then other works. The place of publication is London unless otherwise stated. Short title references used in the text are given in square brackets at the end of the entry. Uncollected essays by Virginia and Leonard Woolf, E. M. Forster, Lytton Strachey, Clive Bell, Roger Fry, and Desmond MacCarthy have been included only when they have been quoted. Otherwise readers are referred to the bibliographies that have been published of all but MacCarthy.

1 WRITINGS BY THE BLOOMSBURY GROUP

Bell, Clive, *Art*, ed. J. B. Bullen (Oxford University Press, 1987).
——, *Civilization: An Essay* (Chatto & Windus, 1928). [C]
——, 'George Bernard Shaw by G. K. Chesterton', *Athenaeum*, 11 Sept 1909, pp. 291–2. ['Shaw']
——, 'John Keats: A Literary Biography by A. E. Hancock', *Athenaeum*, 2 Jan 1909, pp. 8–9. ['Keats']
——, 'Mad Shepherds, and other Human Studies by L. P. Jacks', *Athenaeum*, 18 July 1910, p. 729. ['Mad Shepherds']
——, 'Nineteenth Century Teachers and other Essays by Julia Wedgwood', *Athenaeum*, 19 June 1909, pp. 723–4.
——, Papers, Huntington Library, San Marino, California. [pH]
——, Papers, King's College, Cambridge. [pKC]
——, Papers, Trinity College, Cambridge. [pTC]
——, Papers, University of Sussex. [pS]
——, *Poems* (Hogarth Press, 1921).
——, *Pot-Boilers* (Chatto & Windus, 1918). [PB]
——, 'Shelley, the Man and the Poet by A. Clutton-Brock', *Athenaeum*, 18 Dec 1909. ['Shelley']
——, 'Strenuous Enthusiasm', *Cambridge Review*, 31 May 1906, pp. 432–3. ['Strenuous']
Bell, Quentin, *Roger Fry: An Inaugural Lecture* (Leeds University Press, 1964).
——, *Virginia Woolf: A Biography*, 2 vols (Hogarth Press, 1972). [QB/VW]
——, Papers, University of Sussex.

Bell, Quentin, 'Who's Afraid for Virginia Woolf', *New York Review of Books* (15 Mar 1990) pp. 3–6.

Bell, Vanessa, Papers, Berg Collection, New York Public Library. [pNY]

——, Papers, King's College, Cambridge. [pKC]

——, Papers, University of Texas. [pT]

Euphrosyne. A Collection of Verse (Cambridge: Elijah Johnson, 1905).

Forster, E. M., *Abinger Harvest* (Edward Arnold, 1936). [*AH*]

——, *Albergo Empedocle and Other Writings*, ed. George H. Thomson (New York: Liveright, 1971). [*AE*]

——, *Arctic Summer and Other Fiction*, Abinger Edition IX, ed. Elizabeth Heine (Edward Arnold, 1980). [*AS*]

——, *Aspects of the Novel and Related Writings*, Abinger Edition XII, ed. Oliver Stallybrass, (Edward Arnold, 1974). [*AN*]

——, 'Breaking Up', *Spectator*, 28 July 1933, p. 119. ['Breaking Up']

——, *The Celestial Omnibus and Other Stories* (Sidgwick & Jackson, 1912).

——, *Collected Short Stories* (Sidgwick & Jackson, 1948). [*CSS*]

——, *Collected Tales of E. M. Forster* (New York: Knopf, 1947).

——, *Commonplace Book*, ed. Philip Gardner (Scolar Press, 1985). [*CB*]

——, 'Conversation with E. M. Forster' by Angus Wilson, *Encounter*, 9 (Nov 1947) 52–5. ['Conversation']

——, *The Eternal Moment and Other Stories* (Sidgwick & Jackson, 1928). [*EM*]

——, *Goldsworthy Lowes Dickinson and Related Writings*, Abinger Edition XIII, ed. Oliver Stallybrass (Edward Arnold, 1973). [*GLD*]

——, 'Henry James and the Young Men', *Listener*, 16 July 1959, p. 103. ['Henry James']

——, *The Hill of Devi and Other Indian Writings*, Abinger Edition, XIV, ed. Elizabeth Heine (Edward Arnold, 1983). [*HD*]

——, 'How I Lost My Faith', *Humanist*, LXXVIII (Sept 1963) 262–6. ['How I Lost']

——, *Howards End*, Abinger Edition, IV ed. Oliver Stallybrass (Edward Arnold, 1973). [*HE*]

——, *Howards End*, dir. James Ivory, screenplay by Ruth Prawer Jhabvala, Merchant–Ivory Productions, 1992.

——, Interview: 'E. M. Forster', *Writers at Work: The 'Paris Review' Interviews*, ed. Malcolm Cowley (New York: Viking Press) pp. 24–35. [Interview]

——, 'Introduction', Giuseppe Di Lampedusa, *Two Stories and a Memory* (New York: Panthon Books, 1962) pp. 13–17. [Lampedusa]

——, 'Introduction and Notes', *The Aeneid of Virgil*, trans. E. Fairfax Taylor, 2 vols. Temple Greek and Latin Classics, ed. G. Lowes Dickinson and H. O. Meredith (J. M. Dent, 1906) I:vii–xviii, 331–50; II:351–63; 'Introduction.' Virgil's *Aeneid*, trans. Michael Oakley (Dent, 1964) v–xii.

——, 'Landor at Sea', *New Statesman and Nation*, 6 Aug 38, p. 219.

——, *The Life to Come and Other Stories*, Abinger Edition, XIII, ed. Oliver Stallybrass (Edward Arnold, 1972). [*LTC*]

——, *The Longest Journey*, Abinger Edition, II, ed. Elizabeth Heine (Edward Arnold, 1984). [*LJ*]

——, 'Looking Back', *Cambridge Review*, LXXXII (Oct 1960) 58.

——, *The Lucy Novels: Early Sketches for A Room with a View*, Abinger Edition, IIIa, ed. Oliver Stallybrass (Edward Arnold, 1977). [*LN*]

Forster, E. M., 'The Machine Stops', *Whole Earth Catalogue*, XXXXIV (Dec 84) 40–55.

——, 'The Man Behind the Scenes', *News Chronicle*, 30 Nov 1931, p. 4. ['Man Behind']

——, *The Manuscripts of Howards End*, Abinger Edition, IVa ed. Oliver Stallybrass (Edward Arnold, 1973). [*HEMSS*]

——, *The Manuscripts of Howards End: Corrigenda and Addenda*, ed. Oliver Stallybrass (Edward Arnold, 1976).

——, *Marianne Thornton, 1797–1887: A Domestic Biography* (Edward Arnold, 1956).

——, *Maurice* (Edward Arnold, 1971). [*M*]

——, Papers, University of Bristol. [pB]

——, Papers, King's College, Cambridge. [pKC]

——, Papers, New York Public Library. [pNY]

——, Papers, University of Texas. [pT]

——, *Pharos and Pharillon*, 2nd edn (Hogarth Press, 1923).

——, *A Room with a View*, Abinger Edition, III, ed. Oliver Stallybrass (Arnold, 1977). [*RV*]

——, *A Room with a View*, adapted from Forster's novel by Stephen Tait and Kenneth Allott (Edward Arnold, 1951).

——, *A Room with a View*, dir. James Ivory, screenplay by Ruth Prawer Jhabvala, 1985.

——, 'The Sahib from Bloomsbury', *Observer*, 5 Nov 1961, p. 29. ['Sahib']

——, *Selected Letters of E. M. Forster*, ed. Mary Lago and P. N. Furbank. 2 vols (Collins, 1983–5). [*L*]

——, *Two Cheers for Democracy*, Abinger Edition, XI, ed. Oliver Stallybrass (Edward Arnold, 1972). [*2CD*]

——, *Where Angels Fear to Tread*, Abinger Edition I, ed. Oliver Stallybrass (Edward Arnold, 1975). [*WAFT*]

——, 'Where Angels Fear to Tread', *The Times*, 12 July 1963, p. 11. ['Where Angels']

Fry, Roger, 'Art and Religion', *Monthly Review*, VII (May 1902) 126–39.

——, *Characteristics of French Art*, see *French, Flemish, and British Art*.

——, 'The Double Nature of Painting', *Apollo* LXXXIX (May 1969) 362–71. ['Double Nature']

——, *Flemish Art*, see *French, Flemish, and British Art*.

——, *French, Flemish, and British Art*, originally published as *Characteristics of French Art* (1932) *Flemish Art* (1927) and *Reflections on British Painting* (1934) (Chatto & Windus, 1951). [*FFBA*]

——, *Giovanni Bellini*, Artist's Library, ed. Laurence Binyon (At the Sign of the Unicorn, 1899).

——, 'Italian Art', *Macmillan's Guide to Italy*, xxxiv–lxxx. (Macmillan, 1901)

——, *Letters of Roger Fry*, ed. Denys Sutton, 2 vols (Chatto & Windus, 1972). [*L*]

——, 'Mere Technique', *Independent Review*, III (Sept 1904) 514–26.

——, 'Mr. Whistler', *Athenaeum*, 25 July 1903, pp. 133–4. ['Whistler']

——, 'The New Gallery', *Athenaeum*, 13 Jan. 1906, pp. 56–7. ['New Gallery']

——, Papers, King's College, Cambridge. [pKC]

——, 'The New Gallery', *Pilot*, 5 May 1900, pp. 291–2.

Fry, Roger, *Reflections on British Painting*, see *French, Flemish, and British Art*.
——, 'The Drawings of Florentine Painters . . ., by Bernard Berenson',
    Athenaeum 12 Nov, 3 Dec, 1904, pp. 662–3, 769–71. ['Drawings']
——, 'The Prado by C. S. Ricketts', *Athenaeum*, 6 Aug 1904, pp. 180–1.
    [Prado]
——, '*Rembrandt von Rijn* by Malcolm Bell and *Rembrandt: a Critical Essay* by
    Auguste Bréal', *Athenaeum*, 16 Aug 1902, pp. 228–9. [*'Rembrandt'*]
——, '*Turner* by Sir Walter Armstrong', *Athenaeum*, 31 Oct. 1903, pp. 587–8.
    [Armstrong]
——, 'The Royal Academy', *Athenaeum*, 11 May 1901, pp. 601–2. ['Royal']
——, 'The Ruskin Drawings', *Pilot*, 16 Feb 1901, pp. 207–8. ['Ruskin']
——, Sir Joshua Reynolds, *Discourses Delivered to the Students of the Royal
    Academy*, ed. Roger Fry (Seeley, 1905). [Reynolds]
——, 'Turner at the Fine Art Society', *Pilot*, 16 June 1901, pp. 482–3.
    ['Turner']
——, *Vision and Design*, ed. J. B. Bullen (Oxford University Press, 1981). [*VD*]
——, 'What Men Do When They Go Down. No. III. – ART', *Granta*, II (17
    May 1889) 10–11.
——'Watts and Whistler', *Quarterly Review*, CCII (April 1905) 607–23. ['Watts
    and Whistler']
Grant, Duncan, Papers in possession of Henrietta Garnett. [pHG]
——, Papers, British Library. [pBL]
[——,] 'M. Simon Bussy's Pastels', *Spectator* (6 March 09) p. 377.
Keynes, John Maynard, *The Collected Writings*, ed. Donald Moggeridge and
    Elizabeth Johnson, 30 vols (Macmillan, 1971–89). [*CW*]
——, Papers, King's College, Cambridge. [pKC]
MacCarthy, Desmond, 'The American Scene', *Albany Review* I (April 1907)
    111–20.
——, 'An Anonymous Autobiography', *Albany Review*, II (Dec 1907) 335–41.
    ['Anonymous']
——, 'The Censorship of Plays', *New Quarterly*, II (Nov 1909) 601–614.
——, 'Court Theatre – "You Never Can Tell"', *Speaker*, XIV (21 July 1906)
    361–2. ['Court Theatre']
——, *The Court Theatre, 1904–1907: A Commentary and Criticism* (A. H.
    Bullen, 1907). [*CT*] Reprint. ed. Stanley Weintraub (Coral Gables, Fla.:
    University of Miami Press, 1966).
——, *Experience* (Putnam, 1935). [*E*]
——, *Humanities* (Macgibbon and Kee, 1953). [*H*]
——, 'The Ideal Husband', *Speaker*, XIII (7 Oct 1905) 11. ['Ideal']
——, 'The Irish Plays', *Speaker*, XIII (9 Dec 1905) 251–2.
——, 'John Donne', *New Quarterly*, I (March 1908) 267–292. ['Donne']
——, *Memories* (Macgibbon and Kee, 1953). [*M*]
——, 'Mr. Waller as Othello. Mr. H. B. Irving as Iago', *Speaker*, XIV (26 May
    1906) 182–3.
——, 'Nietzsche', *Albany Review*, III (April 08) 90–4.
——, 'The New St. Bernard', *Independent Review*, I (Nov 1903) 346–52. ['New
    St.']
——, 'Oscar Wilde [*Salome*] and the Literary Club Theatre', *Speaker*, XIV (7
    July 1906) 315–6. ['Wilde']

518   Bibliography

MacCarthy, Desmond, Papers, Lilly Library, Indiana University. [pM]
——, Papers, Cambridge University Library. [pCU]
——, 'Poetic Injustice', *Speaker*, XIV (21 April 1906) 55–6. ['Poetic']
——, *Portraits*, I (Putnam, 1931). [P]
——, 'Shakespeare [*Antony and Cleopatra*] at His Majesty's', *Speaker*, XV (2
Feb 1907) 524–5.
——, *Shaw* (MacGibbon and Kee, 1951). [S]
——, 'Some Recent Books', *Independent Review*, XI (Nov 1906) 229–40.
['Recent Books']
——, 'The Taming of the Shrew' *Speaker*, XII (12 Aug 1905) 455–6.
——, 'Tears, Idle Tears', *Speaker*, XIV (23 June 1906) 269–70. ['Tears']
——, *Theatre* (MacGibbon and Kee, 1954).
——, 'The Theatre', *Speaker*, XIII (3 March 1906) 522–3.
——, 'Three Books on Russian Literature', *Independent Review*, XII (March
1907) 346–56. ['Russian Literature']
——, 'Verse and the Reverse', *Speaker*, XIII (17 March 1906) 574. ['Verse']
——, *Lady John Russell: A Memoir with Selections from Her Diaries and
Correspondence*, ed. Desmond MacCarthy and Agatha Russell (Methuen,
1910).
MacCarthy, Mary, Papers, courtesy of Mr Hugh Cecil.
Stephen, Adrian, *The 'Dreadnought' Hoax*, Introduction by Quentin Bell
(Chatto & Windus, The Hogarth Press, 1983).
[Stephen, Julian Thoby] 'Euphrosyne', *Cambridge Review*, XXVII (2 Nov 1905)
49.
[——,] 'The Cambridge Muse', *Cambridge Review*, XXVII (19 Oct 1905) 8.
——, Papers King's College, Cambridge.
Strachey, Lytton, 'The Admirable Boileau', *Spectator* (7 Nov 1908) pp. 735–6.
['Boileau']
——, 'The Age of Spenser', *Spectator* (23 March 1907) pp. 457–8.
——, *Books and Characters, French and English* (Chatto & Windus, 1922). [BC]
——, *Characters and Commentaries* (Chatto & Windus, 1933). [CC]
——, '"Comus" at Cambridge', *Spectator* (18 July 1908) pp. 94–5. ['Comus']
——, *Elizabeth and Essex: A Tragic History* (Chatto & Windus, 1928). [EE]
——, 'Elizabethan Drama', *Spectator* (20 June 1908) pp. 975–6.
——, *Eminent Victorians* (Chatto & Windus, 1918). [EV]
——, 'The Follies', *Spectator* (13 Feb 1909) pp. 262–3. ['Follies']
——, 'The Italian Renaissance', *Spectator* (21 Nov 1908) pp. 838–9
——, 'John Milton', *Spectator* (5 Dec 1908) 933–4.
——, 'Lady Epping's Lawsuit', *Spectator* (31 Oct 1908) pp. 673–4. ['Lady
Epping']
——, 'The Late Miss Coleridge's Poems', *Spectator* (4 Jan 1908) p. 19.
——, Letter to the *Cambridge Review*, 11 Nov 1909, pp. 92–3.
——, 'Light Verse', *Spectator* (20 Feb 1909) pp. 304–5.
——, *Lytton Strachey by Himself: A Self Portrait*, ed. Michael Holroyd (Heine-
mann, 1971). [LSH]
——, 'Mediaeval Studies', *Spectator* (17 Nov 1906) pp. 786–7.
——, 'Modern Poetry', *Spectator* (18 April 1908) pp. 622–3.
——, 'Milton's Words', *Spectator*, XCIX (14 Dec 1907) pp. 991–2.
——, 'The Mollusc', *Spectator* (30 Nov 1907) pp. 867–8.

Strachey, Lytton, 'Mr. Sidney Lee on Shakespeare', *Spectator* (1 Dec 1906) pp. 887–8. ['Lee on Shakespeare']

——, 'Mr. Yeats's Poetry', *Spectator* (17 Oct 1908) pp. 588–9. ['Yeats']

——, 'Old Masters at Burlington House', *Spectator* (11 Jan 1908) pp. 61–2. ['Old Masters']

——, Papers, Berg Collection, New York Public Library. [pNY]

——, Papers, Strachey Trust. [pST]

——, Papers, King's College, Cambridge [pKC]

——, Papers, Taylor Collection, Princeton University. [pP]

——, 'A Poet on Poets', *Spectator* (3 Oct 1908) pp. 502–3. ['Poet on Poets']

——, 'The Poetry of William Barnes', *Spectator* (16 Jan 1909) pp. 95–6. ['Barnes']

[——,] 'The Political Wisdom of Edmund Burke', *Spectator* (14 Nov 1908) pp. 774–5.

——, 'The Praise of Shakespeare', *Spectator* (4 June 1904) pp. 881–2. ['Praise']

[——,] 'The Prose Style of Men of Action', *Spectator* (25 Jan 1908) pp. 141–2.

——, *The Really Interesting Question and Other Papers*, ed. Paul Levy (Weidenfeld & Nicolson, 1972). [*RIQ*]

——, 'The Shakespeare Problem' *Spectator* (30 Jan 1909) p. 185.

——, *The Shorter Strachey*, ed. Michael Holroyd and Paul Levy (Oxford University Press, 1980). [*SS*]

——, 'Some Napoleonic Books', *Spectator* (26 Dec 1908) pp. 1100–1. ['Napoleon']

——, 'Some New Carlyle Letters', *Spectator* (10 April 1909) pp. 577–8 ['Carlyle Letters']

——, 'Some New Plays in Verse', *Spectator* (12 Dec 1908) pp. 998–9. ['New Plays']

——, *Spectatorial Essays*, ed. James Strachey (Chatto & Windus, 1964). [*SE*]

——, 'Three New Plays', *Spectator* (6 June 1908) pp. 899–900.

——, 'The Two Triumphs', *New Statesman and Nation*, Literary Supplement (26 June 1937) p. 1045.

——, 'The Value of Poetry', *Spectator* (21 July 1906) pp. 93–5.

——, *Virginia Woolf and Lytton Strachey: Letters*, ed. Leonard Woolf and James Strachey (Hogarth Press, 1956). [*LVWLS*]

——, *Warren Hastings, Cheyt Sing, and the Begums of Oude* (Unpublished Fellowship Dissertation): Strachey Papers, Princeton University. [Hastings]

——, 'Wordsworth's Letters' *Spectator* (21 March 1908) pp. 460–1. ['Wordsworth']

——, 'The Works of W. E. Henley', *Spectator* (8 Aug 1908) pp. 196–7. ['Henley']

Sydney-Turner, Saxon, Papers, King's College, Cambridge.

——, Papers, Huntington Library, San Marino, California.

Woolf, Leonard, 'Arch Beyond Arch', *Nation and Athenaeum* 14 June 1924, p. 354. ['Arch']

——, *Beginning Again: An Autobiography of the Years 1911–1918* (Hogarth Press, 1964). [*BA*]

——, 'Ceylon Folk Tales', *TLS*, 7 Jan 1915, p. 3.

Woolf, Leonard, 'Coming to London: 2, Leonard Woolf' *Coming to London*, ed. John Lehmann (Phoenix House) pp. 27–35. ('Coming')

——, *Diaries in Ceylon,1908 –1911: Records of a Colonial Administrator and Stories from the East*, ed. L. Woolf (Hogarth Press, 1963). [DC]

——, *Downhill All the Way: An Autobiography of the Years 1919–1939* (Hogarth Press, 1967). [DAW]

——, *Empire & Commerce in Africa: A Study in Economic Imperialism* (New York: Howard Fertig, 1968). [ECA]

——, *Essays on Literature, History, Politics, Etc.* (Hogarth Press, 1927). [E]

——, *Growing: An Autobiography of the Years 1904–1911* (Hogarth Press, 1961). [G]

——, *Imperialism and Civilization* (Hogarth Press, 1928). [IC]

——, 'Introduction', *The Village in the Jungle* (New York: Harcourt, Brace, date [1925]). ['Introduction']

——, *The Journey Not the Arrival Matters: An Autobiography of the Years 1939–1969* (Hogarth Press, 1969). [JNAM]

——, *Letters of Leonard Woolf*, ed. Frederic Spotts (New York: Harcourt, Brace, Jovanovich, 1989). [L]

——, 'Memoirs of an Elderly Man', *Orion: A Miscellany* I (1945) 76–87. ['Memoirs']

——'Mr Saxon Sydney-Turner', *The Times* (13 Nov 1962) p. 14.

——, Papers, Huntington Library, San Marino, California. [pH]

——, Papers, University of Sussex. [pS]

——, Papers, University of Texas. [pT]

——, *Sowing: An Autobiography of the Years 1880–1904* (Hogarth Press, 1960). [S]

——, 'Sport in Ceylon', *TLS*, 3 Dec 1914, p. 537.

——, *Stories of the East* (Hogarth Press, 1921). [SE]

——, *The Village in the Jungle* (Edward Arnold, 1913). [VJ]

——, 'Voltaire', *Independent Review*, I (Jan 1904) 680–4.

——, *The Wise Virgins: A Story of Words, Opinions and a few Emotions* (Hogarth Press, 1979).

Woolf, Virginia, '*Abbots Verney* by R. Macaulay', *TLS*, 14 December 1906, p. 417.

——, '*Between the Twilights* by Cornelia Sorabji', *TLS* 11 June 1908, pp. 190–1.

——, '*Chippinge* by Stanley Weyman', *TLS*, 9 Nov 1906, p. 377.

——, *Collected Essays*, ed. Leonard Woolf, 4 vols (Hogarth Press, 1966–7). [CE]

——, *The Common Reader*, First Series, ed. Andrew McNeillie (Hogarth Press, 1984). [CR1]

——, *The Complete Shorter Fiction of Virginia Woolf*, 2nd edn, ed. Susan Dick (Hogarth Press, 1989). [CSF]

——, *Congenial Spirits: The Selected Letters of Virginia Woolf*, ed. Joanne Trautmann Banks (Hogarth Press, 1989).

——, *Contemporary Writers*, ed. Jean Guiguet (Hogarth Press, 1965). [CW]

——, 'A Dialogue upon Mount Pentelicus', ed. S. P. Rosenbaum, *TLS*, Sept 11–17 1987, p. 979.

——, *The Diary of Virginia Woolf*, ed. Anne Olivier Bell, assisted by Andrew McNeillie, 5 vols (Hogarth Press, 1978–84). [D]

Woolf, Virginia, 'Disciples by Mary Crosbie', TLS, 8 March 1907, p. 77.
——, The Early Journals of Virginia Woolf see A Passionate Apprentice.
——, The Essays of Virginia Woolf, ed. Andrew McNeillie, 6 vols (Hogarth Press, 1986–). [E]
——, 'The Feast of Bacchus by E. G. Henham', TLS, 21 June 1907, p. 197.
——, 'Friendships Gallery', ed. Ellen Hawkes, Twentieth Century Literature, 25 (Fall/Winter, 1979) 270–302.
——, 'Lady Huntingdon by Sarah Tytler', TLS, 5 April 1097, p. 111.
——, 'Letters of a Betrothed by Philippine von Griesheim', TLS, 31 May 1907, p. 170.
——, The Letters of Virginia Woolf, ed. Nigel Nicolson and Joanne Trautmann, 6 vols (Hogarth Press, 1975–80). [L]
——, 'Lysistrata', The Englishwoman, VIII (November–December, 1910) 91–3.
——, Manuscripts from the Monks House Papers at the University of Sussex, 6 reels (Brighton: Harvester Press Microform Publications, 1985).
——, 'Mary Christie', TLS, 29 March 1907, pp. 102–3
——, 'Masques and Phases by Robert Ross', TLS, 28 October 1909, p. 398.
——, 'The Method of Henry James', TLS, 26 Dec. 1918 p. 655.
——, 'Miss Smith', Seeds in the Wind: Juvenilia from W. B. Yeats to Ted Hughes, ed. Neville Braybrooke (Hutchinson, 1989) p. 81.
——, Moments of Being: Unpublished Autobiographical Writings, 2nd edn, ed. Jeanne Schulkind (Hogarth Press, 1985). [MB]
——, 'Mr. Henry James's Latest', Guardian, 22 Feb 1905 p. 339.
——, 'Mrs Sellar's Recollections', TLS, 17 May 1907, p. 155.
——, 'Outrageous Fortune by Bak', TLS, 24 Oct 1907, p. 326.
——, Papers, Berg Collection, New York Public Library. [pNY]
——, The Pargiters: The Novel-Essay Portion of the Years, ed. Mitchell A. Leaska (Hogarth Press, 1978). [P]
——, A Passionate Apprentice: The Early Journals, 1897–1909, ed. Mitchell A. Leaska (Hogarth Press, 1990. [EJ]
——, 'Rachel Gurney of the Grove by Sir Alfred Pease', TLS, 2 Jan. 1908, p. 5.
——, Reading Notebooks, see Silver, Brenda, The Reading Notebooks of Virginia Woolf.
——, 'The Red Neighbour by W. J. Eccott', TLS, 16 April 1908, p. 126.
——, Roger Fry: A Biography (Hogarth Press 1940). [RF]
——, A Room of One's Own (Hogarth Press, 1929). [RO]
——, 'Some Poetical Plays', Guardian, 1 Jan 1908, pp. 18–19; reprinted in S. P. Rosenbaum, 'An Unknown Early Review by Virginia Woolf,' The Charleston Magazine, 2 (Autumn/Winter, 1990) 37–41.
——, 'The Sword Decides by Marjorie Bowen', TLS, 9 April 1908, p. 117.
——, 'A Terrible Tragedy in a Duckpond', Charleston Magazine, I (Spring/Summer, 1990) pp. 37–42.
——, To the Lighthouse, Uniform Edition. (Hogarth Press, 1930). [TTL]
——, 'Venice by Beryl de Sélincourt and May Sturge Henderson', TLS, 14 June 1907, p. 186.
——, Virginia Woolf and Lytton Strachey: Letters, ed. Leonard Woolf and James Strachey (Hogarth Press, 1956). [LVWLS]
——, The Waves, Uniform Edition (Hogarth Press, 1943). [W]
——, 'The Wingless Victory by M. P. Willcocks', TLS, 5 April 1907, p. 110.

Woolf, Virginia, *Women & Fiction: The Manuscript Versions of A Room of One's Own*, ed. S. P. Rosenbaum (Oxford: Blackwell 1992).

2 OTHER WRITINGS

Ackerley, J. R., *The Letters of J. R. Ackerley*, ed. Neville Braybrooke (Duckworth, 1975). [*Letters*]

Adler, Renata, *Speedboat* (New York: Random House, 1976).

Annan, Noel, *Leslie Stephen: The Godless Victorian* (Weidenfeld & Nicolson, 1984).

Archer, William, *The Vedrenne–Barker Season, 1904–5. A Record and a Commentary* (David Allen & Sons, no date).

Arnold, Matthew, *The Portable Matthew Arnold*, ed. Lionel Trilling (New York: Viking Press, 1949).

Auden, W. H., *Collected Poems*, ed. Edward Mendelson (New York: Random House, 1976).

Bailey, John C., *The Claims of French Poetry: Nine Studies in the Greater French Poets* (Constable, 1907).

——, *Letters and Diaries*, ed. Sarah Bailey (John Murray, 1935). [*Letters*]

Barron, T. J., 'Before the Deluge: Leonard Woolf in Ceylon', *Journal of Imperial and Commonwealth History*, VI (Oct 1977) 47–73.

Beerbohm, Max, *Around Theatres*, 2 vols (Heinemann, 1924).

——, 'At the Savoy Theatre', *Saturday Review*, MIV (28 Sept 1907) 389–90. ['Savoy']

Bennett, Arnold, *The Journals*, ed. Frank Swinnerton (Harmondsworth, Middx.: Penguin, 1971).

Berenson, Bernard, *Italian Painters of the Renaissance* (New York: Meridian Books, 1957).

Bishop, Edward, *A Virginia Woolf Chronology* (Macmillan, 1989).

Black, Naomi, *Social Feminism* (New York: Cornell University Press, 1989).

Bloom, Harold, 'Introduction', *E. M. Forster: Modern Critical Views*, ed. Bloom (New York: Chelsea House, 1987).

The Bloomsbury Group: A Collection of Memoirs, Commentary, and Criticism, ed. S. P. Rosenbaum (University of Toronto Press, 1987).

Bowen, Elizabeth, 'A Passage to E. M. Forster', *Aspects of E. M. Forster*, ed. Oliver Stallybrass (Edward Arnold, 1969) pp. 1–12.

Bradbury, Malcolm, 'E. M. Forster as Victorian and Modern: *Howards End* and *A Passage to India*', *Possibilities: Essays on the State of the Novel* (Oxford: Oxford University Press 1973) pp. 91–120.

Brewer, Ebenezer Cobham, *Brewer's Dictionary of Phrase and Fable*, Centenary Edition, rev. Ifor H. Evans (New York: Harper & Row, 1970).

Britten, Benjamin, 'Some Notes on Forster and Music', *Aspects of E. M. Forster*, ed. Oliver Stallybrass (Edward Arnold, 1969) p. 81–6.

Brooke, Rupert, *The Collected Poems* (New York: Dodd, Mead & Co., 1961).

——, *The Letters of Rupert Brooke*, ed. Geoffrey Keynes (Faber & Faber, 1968).

Broughton, Panthea Reid, 'Impudence and Iconoclasm: The Early *Granta* and an Unknown Roger Fry Essay', *English Literature in Transition*, XXX (1987) 69–79.

Brown, E. K., *Rhythm in the Novel* (University of Toronto Press, 1950).

Brown, Tony, 'Edward Carpenter and the Discussion of the Cow in *The Longest Journey*', *Review of English Studies*, XXXIII (Feb 1982) 58–62. [*Longest Journey*]

——, 'Edward Carpenter, Forster and the Evolution of *A Room with a View*, *English Literature in Transition*, XXX (1987) 279–300.

Buchanan, Donald W., *James Wilson Morrice: A Biography* (Toronto, Canada: Ryerson Press, 1936).

Burke, Edmund, *The Speeches of the Right Honourable Edmund Burke* IV (1816).

Bussy, Simon, 'Mere Technique: An Answer', *Independent Review*, VI (May 1905) 56–68.

Butler, Samuel, *Erewhon, Erewhon Revisited*, intro. Desmond MacCarthy (Dent, Everyman Library, 1965).

——, *The Note-Books of Samuel Butler*, ed. Henry Festing Jones (A. C. Fifield, 1912). [*Notes-Books*]

Carswell, John, *Lives and Letters: A. R. Orage, Beatrice Hastings, Katherine Mansfield, John Middleton Murry, S. S. Koteliansky, 1906–1957* (Faber and Faber, 1978).

Cecil, Hugh and Mirabel, *Clever Hearts: Desmond and Molly MacCarthy, A Biography* (Victor Gollancz, 1990).

Charteris, Evan, *The Life and Letters of Sir Edmund Gosse* (Heinemann, 1931).

Chesterton, G. K., *G. F. Watts* (Duckworth, 1975).

Clarke, Peter, *Liberals and Social Democrats* (Cambridge University Press, 1978).

Clifford, Sir Hugh, 'Mankind and the Jungle', *Blackwood's Magazine*, CXCIII (Jan–June, 1913) 844–51.

Colmer, John, *E. M. Forster: The Personal Voice* (Routledge & Kegan Paul, 1975).

Conklin, Groff, *17 x Infinity* (New York: Dell Publishing, 1963).

Connolly, Cyril, *Enemies of Promise*, rev. edn (Harmondsworth, Middx.: Penguin, 1979). [*Enemies*]

——, *The Modern Movement: One Hundred Key Books from England, France and America, 1880–1950* (Andre Deutsch, Hamish Hamilton, 1965).

Coward, Noël, 'A Room with a View', *This Year of Grace* (1928).

Crews, Frederick, *E. M. Forster: The Perils of Humanism* (Princeton, New Jersey: Princeton University Press, 1962).

Crowley, Aleister, *The Confessions of Aleister Crowley: An Autohagiography*, ed. John Symons and Kenneth Grant (New York: Bantam Books, 1971).

Dahl, Christopher, 'Virginia Woolf's *Moments of Being* and Autobiographical Tradition in the Stephen Family', *Journal of Modern Literature*, X (June 1983) 175–96.

Das, G. K. and John Beer, eds., *E. M. Forster, A Human Exploration: Centenary Essays* (Macmillan, 1979).

Delany, Paul, 'Lawrence and Forster: Two Rainbows', *D. H. Lawrence Review*, XIII (1975) 54–62. ['Lawrence']

——, *The Neo-Pagans: Rupert Brooke and the Ordeal of Youth* (New York: The Free Press, 1987).

DeSalvo, Louise, *Virginia Woolf: The Impact of Childhood Sexual Abuse on Her Life and Work* (Boston: Beacon Press, 1989).

Dick, Susan, *Virginia Woolf* (Edward Arnold, 1989).

Dickinson, Goldsworthy Lowes, 'Is Immortality Desirable?' *Letters from John Chinaman and Other Essays*, intro. E. M. Forster (Allen & Unwin, 1946).

——, 'Noise That You Pay For', *Independent Review*, III (Aug 1904) 377–90.

Dictionary of National Biography, ed. Leslie Stephen and Sidney Lee *et al.*, 22 vols, Supplements, 1901– (Oxford University Press, 1967 –). [*DNB*]

Donne, John, *The Poems of John Donne*, ed. Herbert J. C. Grierson, 2 vols. (Oxford University Press, 1912).

Dowling, David, *Bloomsbury Aesthetics and the Novels of Forster and Woolf* (Macmillan, 1985).

Edel, Leon, Bloomsbury, A House of Lions (Philadelphia, J. B. Lippincott, 1979).

Edmonds, Michael, *Lytton Strachey: A Bibliography* (New York: Garland Publishing, 1981).

Educating Rita, dir. Lewis Gilbert, with Julie Walters and Michael Cain, 1983.

Eliot, T. S., *The Complete Poems and Plays* (Faber & Faber, 1969).

——, *The Letters of T. S. Eliot*, ed. Valerie Eliot, I (Faber & Faber, 1988).

——, *Selected Essays*, new edn (New York: Harcourt, Brace, 1950). [*Essays*]

——, *To Criticise the Critic and Other Writings* (Faber & Faber, 1965). [*Critic*]

——*The Waste Land: A Facsimile and Transcript of the Original Drafts*, ed. Valerie Eliot (Faber & Faber, 1971).

Ellmann, Richard, 'Two Faces of Edward', *Edwardians and Late Victorians: English Institute Essays*, ed. Ellmann (New York: Columbia University Press, 1960) pp. 188–210, 230–3.

Ensor, R. C. K., *England, 1870–1914*, The Oxford History of England, XIV (Oxford: The Clarendon Press, 1936).

Falkenheim, Jacqueline V., *Roger Fry and the Beginnings of Formalist Art Criticism* (Ann Arbor, Michigan: UMI Research Press, 1980).

Ferns, John, *Lytton Strachey* (Boston: Twain Publishers, 1988).

Fishman, Solomon, *The Interpretation of Art: Essays on the Art Criticism of John Ruskin, Walter Pater, Clive Bell, Roger Fry, and Herbert Read* (Berkeley, University of California Press, 1963).

Fogel, Daniel Mark, *Covert Relations: James Joyce, Virginia Woolf, and Henry James* (Charlottesville, Virginia: University Press of Virginia, 1990).

Fowles, John, *Daniel Martin* (Toronto: Collins, 1977).

Frye, Northrop, *Anatomy of Criticism: Four Essays* (New Jersey: Princeton University Press, 1957).

Furbank, P. N., *E. M. Forster: A Life*, 2 vols (Secker & Warburg, 1977–8). [PNF/*EMF*]

——, 'The Philosophy of E. M. Forster', *E. M. Forster: Centenary Revaluations*, ed. Judith Scherer Herz and Robert K. Martin (Toronto: University of Toronto Press, 1982) pp. 37–51. ['Philosophy']

Gardner, Philip, *E. M. Forster: The Critical Heritage* (Routledge & Kegan Paul, 1973). [*EMFCH*]

Garnett, David, *The Flowers of the Forest*, II of *The Golden Echo* (Chatto & Windus, 1955).

Gillespie, Diane Filby, *The Sisters' Arts: The Writing and Painting of Virginia Woolf and Vanessa Bell* (Syracuse, New York: Syracuse University Press, 1988).

Gooneratne, Yasmine, 'Leonard Woolf's "Waste Land": The Village in the Jungle', *Journal of Commonwealth Literature*, XII (June 1972) 22–34.

Gordon, Lyndall, *Virginia Woolf: A Writer's Life* (Oxford University Press, 1984).

Graham, Kenneth, *Indirections of the Novel: James, Conrad, and Forster* (Cambridge University Press) pp. 156–79, 216–9

Gransden, K. W., *E. M. Forster* (New York: Grove Press, 1962).

Gross, John, *The Rise and Fall of the Man of Letters: Aspects of English Literary Life Since 1800* (Weidenfeld and Nicolson, 1969).

Harrison, Bernard, 'Forster and Moore', *Philosophy and Literature*, XII (April 1988) 1–26.

Harrod, R. F., *The Life of John Maynard Keynes* (Macmillan, 1951).

Hart, Elizabeth, *Where Angels Fear to Tread: A Play in Two Acts* (Samuel French, 1963).

Harvey, John, 'Imagination and Moral Theme in E. M. Forster's *The Longest Journey*', *Forster: A Collection of Critical Essays*, ed. Malcolm Bradbury (Englewood Cliffs, NJ, 1966) pp. 117–27.

Heilbrun, Carolyn G., *The Garnett Family: The History of a Literary Family* (George Allen & Unwin, 1961)

Herz, Judith Scherer, 'The Double Nature of Forster's Fiction: *A Room with a View* and *The Longest Journey*', *Critical Essays on E. M. Forster*, ed. Alan Wilde (Boston: G. K. Hall, 1985). ['Double Nature']

——, 'The Narrator as Hermes: A Study of the Early Short Fiction', *E. M. Forster, A Human Exploration: Centenary Essays*, ed. G. K. Das and John Beer (Macmillan, 1979) ['Hermes'].

——, *The Short Narratives of E. M. Forster* (Macmillan, 1988). [*Narratives*]

——, and Robert K. Martin, eds. *E. M. Forster: Centenary Revaluations* (Macmillan, 1982).

Hillegas, Mark R., *The Future as Nightmare: H. G. Wells and the Anti-utopians* (New York: Oxford University Press, 1967).

Hobson, J. A., *Imperialism: A Study* (Ann Arbor: University of Michigan Press, 1965).

Holleyman and Treacher, Ltd., *Catalogue of Books from the Library of Leonard and Virginia Woolf* (Brighton, 1975).

Holroyd, Michael, *Bernard Shaw*, II, 1898–1918: *The Pursuit of Power* (Chatto & Windus, 1989).

——, 'Bloomsbury and the Fabians', *Virginia Woolf and Bloomsbury: A Centenary Celebration*, ed. Jane Marcus (Macmillan, 1987) pp. 39–51. ['Fabians']

——, *Lytton Strachey: A Biography*, rev. edn (Middlesex: Penguin, 1971). [MH/LS]

——, *Lytton Strachey and the Bloomsbury Group: His Work, Their Influence* (Harmondsworth, Middx.: Penguin, 1971). [MH/LSBG]

Housman, A. E., *Complete Poems* (New York: Holt, Rinehart and Winston, 1959).

Howards End, dir. James Ivory, screenplay by Ruth Prawer Jhabvala, Merchant–Ivory Productions, 1992.

Howarth, Herbert, 'E. M. Forster and the Contrite Establishment', *JGE: The Journal of General Education*, XVII (April 1965–Jan 1966). 196–206.

Howe, Irving, 'Introduction' to 'The Machine Stops', *Classics of Modern Fiction*, ed. I. Howe, 2nd edn (New York: Harcourt, Brace, Jovanovich, 1972) pp. 233–40.

Hudson, Derek, 'Reading', *Edwardian England: 1901–1914*, ed. Simon Nowell-Smith (Oxford University Press, 1964) pp. 305–26.

Hynes, Samuel, *The Edwardian Turn of Mind* (Princeton, New Jersey: Princeton University Press, 1968).

Inchbald, Mrs [Elizabeth], *A Simple Story*, intro. G. L. Strachey (Henry Frowde, 1908).

Isherwood, Christopher, *Lions and Shadows: An Education in the Twenties* (Hogarth Press, 1938).

James, Henry, *English Hours* (New York: Horizon Press, 1968).

——, *Henry James Letters*. VI, *1895–1916*, ed. Leon Edel (Cambridge, Mass.: Harvard University Press, 1984). [*Letters*]

——, Literary Criticism: French *Writers, Other European Writers, The Prefaces to the New York Edition*, ed. Leon Edel and Mark Wilson (New York: The Library of America). [*Criticism*]

Jefferson, George, *Edward Garnett, A Life in Literature* (Jonathan Cape, 1982).

Kallich, Martin, 'Lytton Strachey: An Annotated Bibliography of Writings about Him', *English Literature in Transition*, V (1962) 1–77.

Kenner, Hugh, *The Pound Era* (Berkeley: University of California Press, 1971).

King, Dixie, 'The Influence of Forster's *Maurice* on *Lady Chatterley's Lover'*, *Contemporary Literature*, XXIII (1982) 65–82.

King, Francis, *E. M. Forster and His World* (Thames & Hudson, 1978).

Kirkpatrick, B. J., *A Bibliography of E. M. Forster*, 2nd edn (Oxford University Press 1985). [Kirkpatrick, *EMF*]

——, *A Bibliography of Virginia Woolf*, 3rd edn (Oxford University Press, 1980). [Kirkpatrick, *VW*]

——, 'Unrecorded Times Literary Supplement Reviews by Virginia Woolf', *Modern Fiction Studies*, XXXVIII (1992) 279–283. ['Unrecorded']

Lago, Mary, *Calendar of the Letters of E. M. Forster* (Mansell Publishing, 1985).

Laing, Donald A., *Clive Bell: An Annotated Bibliography of the Published Writings* (New York: Garland, 1983). [Laing, *CB*]

——, *Roger Fry: An Annotated Bibliography of the Published Writings* (New York: Garland, 1979). [Laing, *RF*]

Lamb, Charles, *Essays of Elia* (Dent Everyman's Library, 1977).

Lawrence, D. H., *Aaron's Rod*, ed. Mara Kalnins (Cambridge University Press, 1988).

——, The Complete Poems of D. H. Lawrence, ed. Vivian de Sola Pinto and Warren Roberts, 2 vols (New York: Viking, 1964).

——, *The Letters of D. H. Lawrence*, ed. James T. Boulton *et al.*, 5 vols to date (Cambridge University Press, 1979–).

Lawrence, D. H., *The White Peacock*, ed. Andrew Robertson (Cambridge University Press, 1983).

——, *Women in Love* (Heinemann, 1954).

Leavis, F. R., *The Common Pursuit* (Chatto & Windus, 1953). [*Pursuit*]

——, 'Meet Mr. Forster', *Scrutiny*, XII (Autumn, 1944) 308–9. ['Meet']

Lehmann, John, *A Garden Revisited and Other Poems* (Hogarth Press, 1931).

Levin, Bernard, 'The Shield of Achilles', *The Times*, 23 Oct 1971, p. 5.

Levy, Paul, *Moore: G. E. Moore and the Cambridge Apostles* (Weidenfeld & Nicolson, 1979).

London, Jack, *The People of the Abyss* (Nelson, no date).

Luedeking, Leila and Michael Edmonds, *Leonard Woolf: A Bibliography* (Winchester, 1992).

Macaulay, Rose, *The Writings of E. M. Forster* (Hogarth Press, 1938).

Macaulay, Thomas Babington, 'Warren Hastings', *The Works of Lord Macaulay*, IX (Longmans Green, 1907) pp. 408–547.

Magnus, John, 'Ritual Aspects of E. M. Forster's *The Longest Journey*', *Modern Fiction Studies*, XIII (1967) 195–210.

Mailer, Norman, Interview, *Writers at Work: 'The Paris Review' Interviews*, 3rd series, ed. Alfred Kazin (New York: Viking, 1967) pp. 253–78.

Maitland, Frederic William, *The Life and Letters of Leslie Stephen* (Duckworth, 1906).

Majumdar, Robin, *Virginia Woolf: An Annotated Bibliography of Criticism, 1915–1974* (New York: Garland 1976).

Majumdar, Robin and Allen McLaurin, eds., *Virginia Woolf: The Critical Heritage* (Routledge & Kegan Paul, 1975). [*VWCH*]

Marchand, Leslie A., *The Athenaeum: A Mirror of Victorian Culture* (Chapel Hill, North Carolina: The University of North Carolina Press, 1941).

Marshall, P. J., *The Impeachment of Warren Hastings* (Oxford University Press, 1965).

Masterman, C. F. G., *The Condition of England*, 7th edn (Methuen, 1911).

——, *From the Abyss. Of Its Inhabitants by One of Them* (Brimley Johnson, 1902).

Maugham, W. Somerset, *Of Human Bondage* (Pan Books, 1981).

McAleer, Neil, *Odyssey: The Authorised Biography of Arthur C. Clarke* (Victor Gallancz, 1992).

McConkey, James, *The Novels of E. M. Forster* (New York: Cornell University Press, 1957).

McDowell, Frederick P. W., *E. M. Forster*, rev. edn (Boston: Twayne Publishers, 1982)

——, ed., *E. M. Forster: An Annotated Bibliography of Writings about Him* (De Kalb Illinois: Northern Illinois University Press, 1976).

——, '"Fresh Woods and Pastures New": Forster Criticism and Scholarship since 1975', *E. M. Forster: Centenary Revaluations*, ed. Judith Scherer Herz and Robert K. Martin (Macmillan, 1982) 311–29. ["Fresh Woods"]

McTaggart, J. McT. Ellis, 'Mysticism', *Philosophical Studies*, ed. S. V. Keeling (New York: Books for Libraries, 1968) pp. 46–68.

Merivale, Patricia, *Pan the Goat-God: His Myth in Modern Times* (Cambridge, Mass.: Harvard University Press, 1969).

Merle, Gabriel, *Lytton Strachey (1880–1932): Biographie et critique d'un critique et biographe*, 2 vols (Lille, France: Université de Lille 1980).

Meyerowitz, Selma S., *Leonard Woolf* (Boston, Mass.: Twayne Publishers, 1982).

Meyers, Jeffrey, *Homosexuality and Literature 1890–1930* (Montreal, Quebec: McGill–Queen's University Press).

——, *Painting and the Novel* (Manchester, England: Manchester University Press, 1975).

Mill, James, *The History of British India*, ed. William Thomas (Chicago, Illinois: University of Chicago Press, 1975).

Mizener, Arthur, *The Saddest Story: A Biography of Ford Madox Ford* (New York: World Publishing, 1971).

Moggridge, D. E., *Maynard Keynes: An Economist's Biography* (Routledge, 1992).

Moore, G. E., 'Hume's Philosophy', *Philosophical Studies* (Routledge & Kegan Paul) pp. 147–67. ['Hume']

——, 'Kant's Idealism', *Proceedings of the Aristotelian Society*, n.s. (1903–4) pp. 127–40, rpt. G. E. Moore, *The Early Essays*, ed. Tom Regan (Philadelphia, Penn.: Temple University Press, 1986) pp. 233–46).

——, 'The Nature and Reality of Objects of Perception', *Philosophical Studies* (Routledge & Kegan Paul) pp. 31–96.

——, Papers, Cambridge University Library. [Cambridge papers]

——, *Principia Ethica* (Cambridge University Press, 1922). [*PE*]

——, 'The Refutation of Idealism', *Philosophical Studies* (Routledge & Kegan Paul, 1922) pp. 1–30. ['Refutation']

——, *Some Main Problems of Philosophy* (New York: Collier Books, 1962). [*Problems*]

Moore, Harry T., *E. M. Forster* (New York: Columbia University Press, 1965).

Morley College Magazine, XV (1905–6) XVII (1907–8). [*Morley*]

The New Cambridge Bibliography of English Literature, III: 1800–1900, ed. George Watson; IV: 1900–1950, ed. I. R. Willison (Cambridge University Press, 1969, 1972).

Orwell, George, *Burmese Days* (Gollancz, 1935).

——, 'A Hanging', *Collected Essays, Journalism, and Letters,* I, ed. Sonia Orwell and Ian Angus (Secker & Warburg) pp. 44–8.

——, *The Road to Wigan Pier* (Secker & Warburg, 1973). [*Road*]

——, 'Shooting an Elephant', *Collected Essays, Journalism, and Letters,* I, ed. Sonia Orwell and Ian Angus (Secker & Warburg) pp. 235–42.

The Oxford Companion to English Literature, ed. Paul Harvey and Dorothy Eagle, 4th edn; ed. Margaret Drabble, 5th edn (Oxford University Press, 1967, 1985).

The Oxford Companion to the Theatre, ed. Phyllis Hartnoll, 4th edn (Oxford University Press, 1983).

The Compact Oxford English Dictionary, 2nd edn (Oxford: Clarendon Press, 1991). [*OED*]

Oxon, 'Euphrosyne', *Cambridge Review*, XXVII (27 Nov 1905) 65–6; (30 Nov 1905) 125–6.

Ozick, Cynthia, 'The Room Where Forster Lived', *New York Times*, Pt. 2, 4 March 1990, pp. 8, 12.

Parker, Peter, *Ackerley: A Life of J. R. Ackerley* (New York: Farrar, Straus, Giroux, 1989).

Pearson, Hesketh, *Beerbohm Tree: His Life and Laughter* (New York: Harper & Row, 1956).

Pollock, Frederick, 'Leslie Stephen', *Independent Review*, III (June 1904) 48–60.

Porter, Bernard, 'The Edwardians and their Empire', *Edwardian England*, ed. Donald Read (Croom Helm, 1982) pp. 128–44.

Pound, Ezra, *Literary Essays*, ed. T. S. Eliot (Faber, 1960).

Pritchett, V. S. 'E. M. Forster at Ninety', *New York Times Book Review*, 29 Dec 1968, pp. 1–2, 18–19.

Purkis, John, 'Where Angels Fear to Tread', *The Nineteenth Century Novel and Its Legacy*, Unit 28 (Milton Keynes: Open University Press, 1973).

Putt, S. Gorley, 'A Packet of Bloomsbury Letters: The Forgotten H. O. Meredith', *Encounter*, LIX (Nov 1982) 77–84.

Raverat, Gwen, *Period Piece: A Cambridge Childhood* (Faber & Faber, 1960).

Redford, Bruce B, 'The Shaping of the Biographer: Lytton Strachey's "Warren Hastings, Cheyt Sing, and the Begums of Oude"', *Princeton University Library Chronicle*, XLIII (Autumn, 1981) 38–52.

Rees, Goronwy, *A Chapter of Accidents* (Chatto & Windus, 1972).

Regan, Tom, *Bloomsbury's Prophet: G. E. Moore and the Development of His Moral Philosophy* (Philadelphia: Temple University Press, 1986).

Reynolds, Sir Joshua, *Discourses Delivered to the Students of the Royal Academy*, ed. Roger Fry (Seeley, 1905) [Reynolds]; ed. Robert R. Wark (New Haven, Connecticut: Yale University Press, 1975).

Rice, Thomas Jackson, *Virginia Woolf: A Guide to Research* (New York: Garland 1984).

Richards, Denis, *Offspring of the Old Vic: A History of Morley College* (Routledge & Kegan Paul, 1958).

Richards, I. A., 'A Passage to Forster', *Complementarities: Uncollected Essays*, ed. John Paul Russo (Cambridge, Mass.: Harvard University Press, 1976) pp. 159–166.

A Room with a View, dir. James Ivory, screenplay by Ruth Prawer Jhabvala, Merchant–Ivory Productions, 1985.

Rosecrance, Barbara, *Forster's Narrative Vision* (New York: Cornell University Press, 1982).

Rosenbaum, S. P., 'Aspects of the Novel, and Literary History', *E. M. Forster: Centenary Revaluations*, ed. Judith Scherer Herz and Robert K. Martin (Macmillan, 1982) pp. 55–83. [*Aspects*]

——, 'The Longest Journey: E. M. Forster's Refutation of Idealism', *E. M. Forster: A Human Exploration, Centenary Essays*, ed. G. K. Das and John Beer (Macmillan, 1979) pp. 32–54, 287–9. ['Refutation']

——, 'Three Unknown Early Essays by Virginia Woolf', *Virginia Woolf Miscellany*, XXVI (Spring, 1986) 1–4.

——, *Victorian Bloomsbury: The Early Literary History of the Bloomsbury Group*, I (Macmillan, 1986).

Ross, Michael L. 'Forster's Arnoldian Comedy: Hebraism, Hellenism, and *A Room with a View*', *English Literature in Transition*, XXIII (1980) 155–67.

Ross, Robert, 'Salome', *Speaker*, XIV (14 July 1906) 337.

Russell, Bertrand, *The Autobiography of Bertrand Russell*, 3 vols (Allen & Unwin, 1967–9). [*Autobiography*]
——, *The Collected Papers of Bertrand Russell*, VI, ed. John G. Slater, XII, ed. Richard A. Rempel, Andrew Brink, Margaret Moran (Routledge, 1992; Allen & Unwin, 1988) [*Papers*]
——, 'My Mental Development', *The Philosophy of Bertrand Russell*, ed. Paul Schilpp, 3rd edn, 2 vols (New York: Harper & Row, 1963) I, 3–20. ['Mental Development']
Russell, John, *Style in Modern British Fiction: Studies in Joyce, Lawrence, Forster, Lewis and Green* (Baltimore, Maryland: Johns Hopkins University Press, 1978).
Samuels, Ernest, *Bernard Berenson: The Making of a Connoisseur* (Cambridge, Mass.: Harvard University Press, 1979). [*Connoisseur*]
——, *Bernard Berenson: The Making of a Legend* (Cambridge, Mass.: Harvard University Press, 1987) [*Legend*]
Sanders, Charles Richard, *Lytton Strachey: His Mind and Art* (New Haven, Connecticut: Yale University Press, 1957). [*Strachey*]
——, 'Lytton Strachey's Revisions in Books and Characters', *Modern Language Notes*, LX (April, 1945) 226–34. ['Revisions']
Schoenbaum, S., *Shakespeare's Lives* (Oxford University Press, 1970).
Shakespeare, William, *The Complete Oxford Shakespeare*, 3 vols., ed. Stanley Wells and Gary Taylor (Oxford University Press, 1987).
Shelley, Percy Bysshe, 'Epipsychidion', *Poetical Works*, ed. Thomas Hutchinson (Oxford University Press, 1968) pp. 411–20.
Sheridan, Richard Brinsley, *Speeches of the Late Right Honourable Richard Brinsley Sheridan*, I ed. A Constitutional Friend (1816).
Shone, Richard, *Bloomsbury Portraits: Vanessa Bell, Duncan Grant, and their Circle* (Oxford: Phaidon, 1976).
Skidelsky, Robert, *John Maynard Keynes: Hopes Betrayed, 1883–1920*, I (Macmillan, 1983).
Silver, Brenda, *The Reading Notebooks of Virginia Woolf* (Princeton, New Jersey: Princeton University Press, 1983). [VW/RN]
Spalding, Frances, *Roger Fry: Art and Life* (Berkeley, University of California Press, 1980). [RF]
——, *Vanessa Bell* (Weidenfeld and Nicolson, 1983). [VB]
Spater, George and Ian Parsons, *A Marriage of True Minds: An Intimate Portrait of Leonard and Virginia Woolf* (Jonathan Cape & Hogarth Press, 1977).
Spender, Stephen. 'Elegies for England: E. M. Forster', *Love–Hate Relations: A Study of Anglo-American Sensibilities* (Hamish Hamilton, 1974) pp. 172–81.
Spurr, Barry, 'The Miracle of Order: Lytton Strachey's Essayist's Art', *Prose Studies*, XII (December 1989) 240–58.
Stallybrass, Oliver, ed. *Aspects of E. M.Forster* (Edward Arnold, 1969).
Stape, J. H., *An E. M. Forster Chronology* (Macmillan, 1992).
——, 'Leonard's "Fatal Forgotten Umbrella": Sex and the Manuscript Revisions to *Howards End*', *Journal of Modern Literature*, IX (1981–2) 123–32.

Stape, J. H., 'Myth, Allusion and Symbol in E. M. Forster's "The Other Side of the Hedge"', *Studies in Short Fiction*, XIV (Fall 1977) 375–8. ['Myth']

Stead, C. K., *The New Poetic* (Hutchinson) 1964.

Stebbing, L. Susan, 'Moore's Influence', *The Philosophy of G. E. Moore*, ed. Paul Arthur Schilpp, 2nd edn (New York: Tudor, 1952).

Steele, Elizabeth, *Virginia Woolf's Literary Sources and Allusions: A Guide to the Essays* (New York: Garland, 1983).

——, *Virginia Woolf's Rediscovered Essays: Sources and Allusions* (New York: Garland, 1987).

Stein, Gertrude, *Lucy Church Amiably* (New York: Something Else Press, 1972).

Stephen, Sir James Fitzjames, *The Story of Nuncomar and the Impeachment of Sir Elijah Impey*, II vols (Macmillan, 1885).

Stephen, J. K., *Quo Musa Tendis?* (Cambridge: Macmillan & Bowes, 1891).

Stephen, Leslie, *History of English Thought in the Eighteenth Century*, 3rd edn, 2 vols (New York: Harcourt Brace and World, 1962). [*History*]

——, *The Life of Sir James Fitzjames Stephen*, 2nd edn (Smith Elder, 1895).

——, *Mausoleum Book*, ed. Alan Bell (Oxford: Clarendon Press, 1977).

——, *Studies of a Biographer*, 4 vols (Duckworth, 1910). [*Studies*]

Stevens, Wallace, *Letters*, ed. Holly Stevens (New York, Alfred A. Knopf, 1966).

——, *Opus Posthumous*, ed. Samuel French Morse (New York: Alfred A. Knopf, 1957).

Stewart, J. I. M., *Eight Modern Writers, Oxford History of English Literature*, vol. XII (Oxford: Clarendon Press, 1963).

Stewart, Garrett, *Death Sentences: Styles of Dying in British Fiction* (Cambridge, Mass.: Harvard University Press, 1984).

Stone, Wilfred, *The Cave and the Mountain: A Study of E. M. Forster* (Oxford University Press, 1966).

Strachey, Amy, *St. Loe Strachey: his Life and his Paper* (Gollancz, 1930).

Strachey, Barbara, *The Strachey Line: An English Family in America, In India and at Home 1570–1902* (Victor Gollancz, 1985). [*Line*]

Strachey, John, *The End of Empire* (Victor Gollancz, 1961).

Strachey, Sir John, *Hastings and the Rohilla War* (Oxford: Clarendon Press, 1892).

Strachey, St. Loe, *The Adventure of Living: A Subjective Autobiography* (Hodder and Stoughton, 1922).

Summers, Claude J., *E. M. Forster* (New York: Frederick Ungar, 1983). [*Forster*]

——, *E. M. Forster: A Guide to Research* (New York: Garland, 1991).

Swinburne, Algernon Charles, *Poems and Ballads. Atlanta in Calydon*, ed. Morris Peckham (Indianapolis: Bobbs-Merrill, 1970).

Swinnerton, Frank, *The Georgian Scene: A Literary Panorama* (New York: Farrar & Rinehart, 1983).

Thomson, George H., *The Fiction of E. M. Forster* (Detroit, Michigan: Wayne State University Press, 1967).

Thornton, A. P., *Doctrines of Imperialism* (New York: John Wiley, 1965).

Thwaite, Ann, *Edmund Gosse: A Literary Landscape, 1849–1928* (Secker and Warburg, 198

'The Times Literary Supplement: A Record of Its Beginnings', *Times Literary Supplement* (18 January 1952) pp. 33–9.

Tolstoy, Leo N. *What Is Art?* trans. Aylmer Maude (New York: Liberal Arts Press, 1960).

Toynbee, Arnold J., *A Study of History* 3 vols (Oxford University Press, 1935).

Travers, P. L., 'Only connect', *Only Connect*, ed. Sheila Egoff, G. T. Stubbs, L. F. Ashley (Toronto: Oxford University Press, 1980) pp. 183–206.

Trevelyan, G. M., *Clio, A Muse, and Other Essays Literary and Pedestrian* (Longmans Green, 1914).

——, *Illustrated History of England* (Longmans' Green, 1956).

Trevelyan, R. C., Papers, Trinity College, Cambridge.

——, *Polyphemus & Other Poems*, with designs by Roger Fry (R. Brimley Johnson, 1901).

Trilling, Lionel, *E. M. Forster* (Norfolk, Connecticut: New Directions, 1943; with a new preface, 1964).

Twitchell, Beverly H., *Cézanne and Formalism in Bloomsbury* (Ann Arbor, Michigan: UMI Research Press, 1987).

Virgil, *Aeneid*, trans. E. Fairfax Taylor; introduction and notes E. M. Forster, 2 vols (Dent, 1906).

Waley, Arthur, translator, *A Hundred & Seventy Chinese Poems* (New York: Knopf, 1918).

Walkley, A. B., *Drama and Life* (Methuen, 1907). [*Drama*]

——, *Dramatic Criticism* (John Murray, 1903).

Wedgwood, Julia, *The Moral Ideal: A Historic Study*, rev. edn (Kegan Paul, Trench, Tribner, 1907).

Weintraub, Stanley, 'Editor's Introduction', Desmond MacCarthy's *The Court Theatre 1904–1907*, ed. Weintraub (Coral Gables, Florida: University of Miami Press, 1966).

Wellek, René, *A History of Modern Criticism: 1750–1950*, 6 vols (New Haven, Connecticut: Yale University Press, 1955–86).

Wells, H. G., *Three Prophetic Novels: When the Sleeper Awakes, A Story of the Days to Come, The Time Machine* (New York: Dover, 1960).

Where Angels Fear to Tread, dir. Charles Sturridge, screenplay by Tim Sullivan and Derek Granger, Stagescreen Productions, 1991.

Who Was Who, 1897–1980, 7 vols (Adam & Charles Black, 1920–80).

Widdowson, Peter, *E. M. Forster's Howards End: Fiction as History* (Sussex University Press, 1977).

Wilde, Alan, *Art and Order: A Study of E. M. Forster* (New York: New York University Press, 1964).

——, ed., *Critical Essays on E. M. Forster* (Boston, Mass.: G. K. Hall & Co., 1985).

——, *Horizons of Assent: Modernism, Postmodernism, and the Ironic Imagination* (Baltimore, Maryland: Johns Hopkins University Press, 1981). [*Horizons*]

Wilkinson, Patrick, 'Forster and King's', *Aspects of E. M. Forster*, ed. Oliver Stallybrass (1969) pp. 13–28.

Wilson, Angus, see Forster, 'Conversation with E. M. Forster'.

Wilson, Duncan, *Leonard Woolf: A Political Biography* (Hogarth Press, 1978).

Wood, Christopher, *Olympian Dreamers: Victorian Classical Painters, 1860–1914* (Constable, 1983).

Woolf, Bella Sidney (Mrs W. T. Southorn) *Eastern Star-Dust* (Colombo, Ceylon: Times of Ceylon Co., 1922).

——, *How to See Ceylon*, 2nd edn (Colombo, Ceylon: Times of Ceylon Co., 1922).

Wordsworth, William, *The Prelude, 1799, 1805, 1850*, Norton Critical Edition, ed. Jonathan Wordsworth, M. H. Abrams, Stephen Gill (New York: W. W. Norton, 1979).

Wright, Andrew, '*Howards End* and the Denial of Doom', *Fictional Discourse and Historical Space* (Macmillan, 1987) pp. 58–73.

Yeats, William Butler, *The Collected Poems*, 2nd edn (Macmillan, 1967). [*Poems*]

Zabel, Morton Dauwen, 'E. M. Forster', *Nation*, New York: 22 Oct 1938, pp. 412–3, 416.

Index

Academy & Literature, 157, 161, 169, 172, 173, 177, 340
Ackerley, J. R., 466, 485, 500
Adams, Henry, 392
Addison, Joseph, 285, 349
Adler, Renata, 512
Aeschylus, 143
Ainger, Alfred, 173
Ainsworth, A. R., 230, 499
Albany Review, see Independent Review
Allingham, William, 357
Allott, Kenneth, 334
Antoinette, Marie, 353
Apostles, Cambridge, 3, 4, 9–10, 14, 22, 26–7, 39, 42, 47, 52, 59, 72, 92–4, 132–7, 194, 199–200, 208, 211, 217, 221, 224, 229, 230–31, 236, 237, 243, 244, 245, 247, 248, 252, 259, 262, 266, 290, 308, 309, 311, 316, 395, 396, 412–13, 440, 486, 494, 499, 500, 504, 510
Archer, William, 105, 114, 293
Aristophanes, 507
Aristotle, 39, 155, 159, 160, 164, 166, 210, 252, 288, 295;
Arnim, Countess von, 92, 154, 256, 342–3, 440
Arnold, Matthew, 21, 68, 69, 99, 143, 174, 198, 271, 294, 295, 324, 360, 445–6, 452, 454, 500, 505, 510
Arnold, Thomas, 256
Arthurian legends, 242
Asquith, H. H., 25
Asuph-ud-dowla, 123, 124
Athenaeum, 7, 97, 194, 196, 199–208, 212, 217, 260, 277–83, 285, 331, 351, 440, 474, 491, 502, 503
Auden, W. H., 333, 479
Augustine, St, 28

Austen, Jane, 13, 44, 95, 150, 212, 317, 319, 333, 396, 398, 442, 476
Austin, Alfred, 270

Bacon, Francis, 302–3, 306, 506
Baedeker Guides, 88, 163, 315, 323, 327
Bagenal, Barbara, 363
Bailey, John C., 270–1, 502–3
Baldovinetti, Alesso, 327
Ballet Russe, 222, 448
Balzac, Honoré de, 27, 212, 278, 291, 294
Barbauld, Anna Laetitia, 503
Baretti, Giuseppe, 347
Baring, Maurice, 217, 262, 264–5, 272, 510
Barnes, William, 297
Barrie, J. M., 36, 53, 292
Bartlett's Familiar Quotations, 505
Basileon, 486
Bateson, William, 208
Baudelaire, Charles, 264, 451
Beale, Dorothea, 371
Beardsley, Aubrey, 199–200, 361
Beddoes, Thomas Lovell, 263, 269–70, 276, 295–6, 306
Beerbohm, Max, 6, 101, 105, 114–15, 217, 261, 262, 264, 269, 281, 371
Beethoven, Ludwig van, 320, 326, 331, 442, 469; Fifth Symphony, 21, 211, 441–2, 451–2, 454, 485
Begums of Oude, 119–32
Bell, Anne Olivier, 507, 511
Bell, Arthur Francis, 63–4, 73, 74, 492
Bell, Clive, 3–5, 7, 8, 61–8, 71, 73, 74, 75, 166, 209, 210, 212–14, 217, 219, 220, 224, 259, 260, 267, 268, 277, 278, 281, 286,

Bell, Clive – *continued*
299, 340, 351, 352, 355, 360,
371, 374, 381, 389, 492, 493,
497, 502, 503, 505, 507
art and artists, on: Berenson, 213;
impressionism, 68, 212;
Kelly, 212; Matisse, 213;
Morrice, 212–14; O'Conor,
212–13; Reynolds, 213;
Rodin, 213; Whistler, 68
Athenaeum and, 199–200,
277–84, 351, 491, 503
Bloomsbury and, 4, 218, 219,
221
Bloomsbury relationships: Bell,
V., 3, 4, 62, 172, 213, 217,
218, 419; Fry, 4; Stephen,
T., 4; Strachey, 5, 217–19,
277, 282, 283; Sydney-
Turner, 4, 62; Woolf, V., 4,
213, 217–20, 224–5, 277,
283, 351, 357, 376, 384
Cambridge Review and, 278
Dreadnought Hoax and, 222
Euphrosyne and, 4, 7, 61–4,
67–9, 74
Moore, G. E., and, 212, 214,
278, 281, 283, 435
New Renaissance book, 277, 283
reviewing, conditions for, 279
revisions of essays, 279, 282
significant form and, 203, 206,
281
style, 208, 279, 281, 282
writers other than Bloomsbury
and: Augustine, 280;
Balzac, 278; Beerbohm,
281; Bennett, 213; Boswell,
280; Burr, A. R., 280;
Byron, 281; Carlyle, J. W.,
280–1; Carlyle, T., 280–1;
Chesterton, 282; Clutton-
Brock, 280; Coleridge, 279;
Coleridge, M., 281–2;
Crowley, 214; Darwin, 281;
Dryden, 279; Eliot, T. S.,
213; Estaunié, 278; Ferrero,
301; Flaubert, 278; Gibbon,
280; Jacks, 283; Keats, 279,

280; Mauclair, 205;
Maugham, 213; Maurice,
281; Meredith, G., 278;
Mérimée, 281; Mill, J. S.,
280, 281; Nietzsche, 507;
Pater, 277; Plato, 279;
Rousseau, 280; Sévigné,
281; Shaw, 111, 282–3;
Shelley, 279, 280; Stephen,
J.K., 68; Swinburne, 281;
Synge, 283; Trelawny, 281;
Voltaire, 282; Walpole, 281;
Wedgwood, 281; Wells,
213; Whistler, 208;
Wordsworth, 280;
writers, Bloomsbury, and:
Forster, 5, 283, 474;
Strachey, 132, 492; Woolf,
L., 435; Woolf, V., 218, 283,
371
writings: *Art*, 212, 279;
Civilization, 39, 225; *Old
Friends*, 212; 'Paris 1904',
212; poetry, 4, 61–4, 67–9,
74, 283–4, 381, 492–3; *Pot-
Boilers*, 213, 279, 280, 282
Bell, Julian, 218, 257, 383, 493
Bell, Quentin, 166, 183, 191, 220,
370, 493, 496, 507, 511
Bell, Vanessa, 3, 8, 129, 149, 154,
211, 220, 222, 328, 339, 359,
364, 365, 383, 486
art and artists, on: impressionism, 205; Whistler, 207
biography by Woolf, V., 383–90
Bloomsbury relationships with:
Bell, C., 3, 4, 62, 172, 218,
419; Fry, 4, 199; Strachey, 5,
159, 218; Woolf, V., 143,
149, 151, 183, 375, 376;
383–90, 513
Bellini, Giovanni, 85, 196
Belloc, Hilaire, 9, 11, 25, 30, 36,
49, 217, 262, 264, 442, 469, 472
Bennett, Arnold, 49, 112, 218–19,
263, 472–4, 484, 488; *Books
and Persons*, 213; *Clayhanger*,
472; *Journalism for Women*,
147; *Journals*, 219

Benson, A. C., 26, 29, 448
Benson, E. F., 472
Benson, R. H., 342
Bentham, Jeremy, 281
Berenson, Bernard, 6, 195, 196,
    197, 202–4, 210, 211, 213, 315,
    380, 499
Berenson, Mary, 202, 203, 208
Bergson, Henri, 43
Berkeley, George, 231, 257
Bernhardt, Sarah, 367–8
Betham family, 177
Beveridge, W. H., 254
Binyon, Laurence, 106
Birrell, Augustine, 297
Black, Naomi, 456
Blackwood and Sons, 76, 80, 90,
    254, 255, 332, 494
Blackwood's Magazine, 33, 90, 433
Blake, William, 17, 19–21, 59, 201,
    209, 239, 298, 353, 358, 441,
    450, 452, 469
Bloom, Harold, 482
Bloomsbury Group, 14, 15, 183,
    209, 221, 259, 271, 281, 297,
    313, 384, 413, 440
  aesthetics and aestheticism, 3,
    4, 6, 21, 72, 173–4, 194–214,
    206, 208, 267, 268, 292, 310,
    360, 498–9
  arts, interrelations of, and 105,
    210, 268
  ballet and, 222, 363
  beginnings, 3, 159, 226, 259
  biographical writings of, 37, 41,
    390
  earlier and later Edwardian
    'chapters' of, 3–8, 217–25,
  genres, mixing of, 6, 10, 30, 54
  Gordon Square Thursday even-
    ings, 3, 5, 99, 159, 171, 173
  imperialism and, 24, 117, 118,
    129, 223, 396
  letter game, 220–1, 291, 375
  Old Bloomsbury, 3, 164, 217, 219
  opera and, 222, 363
  Play-Reading Society, 220
  publishing conditions for, 5–6,
    100, 260, 279, 286

style, 19, 92, 479
  values, 3, 7–8, 26–7, 37, 100,
    111, 183, 226, 265, 324, 440,
    446
Boileau, Nicholas Despreaux, 298
Borrow, George 162, 163, 455
Boswell, James, 144, 280, 283, 302,
    351–2, 371
Botticelli, Sandro, 314
Bowen, Elizabeth, 485
Bowen, Marjorie, 341
Boyd, Elizabeth, 507
Boyle, William, 101
Bradley, A. C., 9, 364, 377
Bradley, F. H., 29, 244
Bridges, Robert, 262, 264
British Museum, 32–3, 237, 239,
    248, 294, 491, 511
Britten, Benjamin, 89
Brontë, Charlotte, 156, 372, 488
Brontë, Emily, 148, 156
Brooke, Rupert, 51, 221, 296, 476,
    494
Brooke, Tucker, 288
Broughton, Panthea Reid, 498
Brown, E. K., 331
Brown, Tony, 499
Browne, Thomas, 17–19, 22, 38,
    44, 66, 270, 276, 302, 309, 400,
    489
Browning, Elizabeth Barrett, 176,
    380
Browning, Oscar, 262
Browning, Robert, 64, 72, 165,
    199, 220, 276, 380
Bryce, James, 11
Buckle, Henry Thomas, 433, 436
Buddhism, 410, 411, 412, 425, 426,
    427, 430
Bunyan, John, 302
Burke, Edmund, 19, 120, 125,
    126–8, 131, 137, 302
Burlington Magazine, 201, 203
Burney, Fanny, 13
Burr, Anna Robeson, 280
Burra, Peter, 505
Burroughs, Edgar Rice, 425
Bury, J. B., 126
Bussy, Dorothy, 17, 24, 206, 304

Bussy, Simon, 206
Butler, Bishop Joseph, 233, 451
Butler, Josephine, 149
Butler, Samuel, 6, 25, 99, 228, 238,
    265, 266, 316, 330; *Erewhon*,
    29, 53, 228, 256, 337; *Erewhon
    Revisited*, 228, 256, 265, 323;
    Life and Habit, 265; *Note-
    Books*, 261, 262, 264, 265; *Way
    of All Flesh*, 29, 256, 265, 323
Butler, Samuel ('Hudibras'), 18
Byron, George Gordon, 281, 297

Calverley, C. S., 69
Cambridge Arts Theatre, 334
Cambridge Review, 62, 65, 66, 72–4,
    274, 278, 504
Cambridge University, 3, 4, 5, 8,
    9–10, 11, 14, 20, 28, 36, 38, 39,
    65, 72, 78, 84, 97, 130, 149,
    152, 159, 191, 195–6, 204, 205,
    212, 213, 214, 217, 219, 221,
    224, 231, 236, 239, 254, 255,
    259, 261, 273, 278, 289, 290,
    294, 296, 297, 356, 391, 395,
    396, 419, 437, 508; King's
    College, 132, 138, 244, 257,
    434; Trinity College, 3, 5, 19,
    61, 117, 123, 244, 245, 261, 300
Cameron, Julia Margaret, 207
Canning, George, 299
Carlyle, Jane Welsh, 168, 280–1,
    299, 351, 352, 386
Carlyle, Thomas, 12, 126, 148,
    169, 199, 262, 280–1, 283, 299,
    314, 324, 326, 330, 351, 352,
    357
Carpenter, Edward, 9, 309, 316,
    499
Carrington, Dora, 218, 401–2, 474
Carswell, John, 264
Carter, Elizabeth, 178
Cary, Joyce, 443
Case, Janet, 112, 143, 355
Catullus, 309
Cecil, David, 26
Cecil, Hugh and Mirabel, 25, 277,
    494, 502
Cecil, Nelly, 148, 365–6, 370, 374

Cellini, Benvenuto, 165
Cervantes Saavedra, Miguel De,
    294, 328
Ceylon Historical Review, 419
Cézanne, Paul, 204–5, 208, 209,
    213
Chamberlain, Joseph, 10
Charleston Bulletin, 493
Charteris, Evan, 473
Chaucer, Geoffrey, 295
Chekhov, Anton, 28, 262, 264–5,
    510
Chesterton, G. K., 9, 12, 26, 205,
    262, 263, 264, 282–3
Cheyt Sing, 120–6, 128–9, 131
Chinese Poetry, 273–4
Chirol, Valentine, 152
Christie, Mary, 358–9
Church Times, 36, 48, 49
Churchill, Winston, 174
Clarendon, Edward Hyde, 302
Clark, Peter, 489
Clarke, Arthur C., 509
Clifford, Hugh, 412, 413, 432–3,
    436
Clive, Robert, 129, 302
Clutton–Brock, Arthur, 280
Cole, Horace, 222
Coleridge, Mary, 281–2
Coleridge, Samuel Taylor, 18, 34,
    99, 103, 177, 272, 279, 289,
    296, 297, 298, 299, 307
Collins, Churton, 289, 489
Condorcet, Jean Antoine Nicolas
    Caritat, 135, 302, 495
Congreve, William, 220, 347
Connolly, Cyril, 19, 26, 257–8,
    479–80, 483
Conrad, Joseph, 25, 49, 91, 224,
    264, 396, 397, 398, 400, 401,
    404, 406, 408, 424, 433, 472,
    484; 'End of the Tether', 90;
    'Heart of Darkness', 407; *Lord
    Jim*, 488; *Secret Agent*, 27, 343;
    'Youth', 399
Corneille, Pierre, 288
Cornhill Magazine, 147, 152, 198,
    217, 339, 340, 344, 352, 353,
    358, 362, 364–71

Court Theatre, 97–116, 292, 293, 341, 494
Coward, Noël, 333
Cowley, Abraham, 297
Cowper, William, 377
Crabbe, George, 377
Credi, Lorenzo di, 85
Crews, Frederick, 489
Cromer, Evelyn Baring, 286
Cromwell, Oliver, 302
Cross, Wilbur, 345
Crowley, Aleister, 214
Cunningham, William, 123

Daily News, 91, 472
Daily Telegraph, 472
Dalhousie, James Ramsay, 129
Damien, Father, 381
Dante, Alighieri, 16, 23, 44, 53, 89, 197, 494
Darling, Malcolm, 471
Darwin, Charles, 281
David, Jacques-Louis, 271
Davies, H. H., 292
Davies, Theodore Llewelyn, 208
Davies, W. H., 26
Dawson, A. J., 160
Day, Thomas, 300
De Quincey, 178, 179–80, 347
Degas, Edgar, 208, 268
Delane, John, 366
Delany, Paul, 477
Dent, E. J., 80, 89, 312
Dent, J. M., 260
Deodata, St., 80, 82, 85, 86
DeSalvo, Louise, 496
Descartes, René, 299
Dickens, Charles, 35, 44, 108, 156, 197, 396, 442, 476, 512
Dickinson, Goldsworthy Lowes, 9, 11, 16, 30, 39, 52, 78, 88, 93, 112, 134, 196, 212, 217, 224, 230, 245, 249, 250, 259, 262, 335, 441–2, 455, 490, 499, 502, 508; family of, 440; *Greek View of Life*, 239; 'Is Immortality Desirable?', 266; *Modern Symposium*, 229; 'Noise that You Pay for', 441

Dickinson, Violet, 142, 147, 148, 152, 156, 162, 164, 165, 166, 168, 170, 180, 181, 189, 193, 339, 340, 359, 365, 366, 373, 374–6, 382, 383, 384, 492, 496, 498, 506
Dictionary of National Biography, 126, 152, 344, 351, 354, 365, 503–4
Diderot, Denis, 275
Disraeli, Benjamin, 396
Dobson, Austin, 13, 72, 261, 262, 264, 272
Donizetti, Gaetano, 82, 89, 363
Donne, John, 134, 138, 286, 296, 389
Dostoevsky, Fyodor, 28, 287
Dowden, Edward, 15
Dreadnought Hoax, 159, 222, 225
Dreyfus, Alfred, 229, 396
Dryden, John, 220, 279, 287–8, 289, 297
Du Deffand, Marie, 22
Duckworth, George, 142, 387, 390, 496
Duckworth, Gerald, 142, 387; Gerald Duckworth and Co., 59, 91, 205, 293, 510
Duckworth, Stella, 387

East India Company, 122, 124, 131
Edel, Leon, 205, 213, 214
Edgeworth, Maria 348
Edmonds, Michael, 503
Educating Rita, 511
Edward Arnold Ltd., 332, 424, 436, 470
Edward VII, 410
Elijah Johnson, 61
Eliot, George, 319, 358, 372, 488
Eliot, T. S., 33, 71, 97–8, 106, 274, 297, 298, 384, 436, 452, 511; *Criterion*, 257; *Waste Land*, 213, 360, 476
Elizabeth I, 302, 354
Ellis, Havelock, 299
Ellmann, Richard, 331–2
Elton, Charles, 409

Emerson, Ralph Waldo, 316, 356, 358
Empedocles, 45
Encyclopédie, 18
English Men of Letters Series, 13, 280
English Review, 49, 264, 336, 408
Englishwoman, 507
Estaunié, Edouard, 278
Eugénie, Empress, 412
Euphrosyne, 4, 5, 7, 61–75, 76, 97, 106, 117, 139, 172, 182, 211, 277, 283, 400, 492–3
Euripides, 106

Fabian Society, 100, 111, 264, 415
Fanshawe, Ann, 358
Farnol, Jeffery, 471
Fenn, George Manville, 493
Ferrero, Guglielmo, 300–1
Fielding, Henry, 13, 163
Fisher, H. A. L., 12, 168, 362
Fisher, William, 222
Fishman, Solomon, 195
Fitzgerald, Edward, 72, 76
Fitzroy Square, 218, 221
Flaubert, Gustave, 89, 103, 224, 250, 264, 278, 291, 295, 384, 396, 412, 424
Fontenelle, Bernard le Bovier, 302
Ford, Ford Madox, 49, 99, 264, 336, 343, 443, 472, 484
Forster, E. M., 3, 4, 6–7, 8, 9, 10, 25, 28, 29, 49, 72, 82, 108, 110, 130, 132, 134, 137, 140, 148, 155, 163, 173, 188, 190, 191, 197, 211, 224, 225–6, 259, 260, 264, 265, 272, 276, 279, 281, 283, 295, 340, 344, 384, 391, 396, 401, 403–4, 408, 412, 419, 424, 425, 434, 435, 436, 482, 489, 490, 491, 499, 502
  Abinger Harvest, 32
  Arctic Summer, 487
  art and artists, on: Bellini, 85; Berenson, 315; Botticelli, 314; Credi, 85; Giotto, 314, 326; Michelangelo, 315,

323, 449; Robbia, Della, 314; Signorelli, 85
  Aspects of the Novel, 33, 54, 59, 81, 89, 250, 251, 463, 483
  Blackwood's Magazine and, 33, 42
  Bloomsbury and, 4, 223, 224
  Bloomsbury relationships: Bell, C., 5; Fry, 4, 45, 56–7, 196, 327, 440, 492; MacCarthy, 26, 29; Strachey, 4, 5, 13, 16, 20, 21, 224, 225, 239, 253; Woolf, L., 4, 42, 47, 57, 80, 224, 225, 418, 499; Woolf, V., 47, 154, 223–4, 328
  Cambridge and, 30, 36, 39, 50, 57, 76, 224, 491
  Cambridge University extension lectures, 8, 38
  Church Times and, 36, 48, 49
  Commonplace Book, 84, 461
  Deceased Wife's Husband, 334
  Demeter and, 32, 230, 242, 248
  Dickinson, Goldsworthy Lowes, and, 10, 224, 229–30, 250, 335, 439, 440–1, 442, 470, 502, 508
  English Review and, 49, 336
  films of novels, 95, 258, 322, 334, 485
  Garnett, Edward, and, 91, 254, 331, 336, 462, 472
  genres, mixing of, 30, 59
  Hermes and, 33, 44
  Hill of Devi, 430
  Howards End, 21, 50, 54, 57, 59, 78, 91, 95, 117, 217, 224, 225, 226, 247, 258, 315, 318, 319, 324, 330, 331, 332, 338, 438–85, 506, 509–13; Bell, C., on, 283; Bloomsbury novel, as, 439–40, 470; Dickinson, G. L., and, 439, 440–1, 442, 470; epigraph, 438, 445–6, 451, 470, 476, 512; Forster on, 447, 448, 460, 461–2, 463, 465–6, 470, 473, 510, 511; *Manuscripts of Howards End*, 465, 510, 511; narration in, 440, 444,

Forster, E. M., *Howards End* –
  continued
    463, 479; origins of, 439–43,
    465–6, 509–10; reception of,
    460, 462, 470–85, 511–13;
    revisions of, 465–70;
    Stephen family and, 439,
    441; Strachey and, 441;
    title, 444, 470, 471, 510;
    Woolf, L. on, 400; Woolf,
    V., on, 474–6
  Idealism and, 226–58, 336, 338,
    499–501
  imperialism, and, 34, 36, 44, 45,
    51, 442, 446, 457, 476
  Independent Review and, 9, 10,
    11, 29, 30–7, 41–2, 44, 45,
    441, 442, 490
  Longest Journey, 20, 32, 50, 54,
    56, 57, 60, 76, 77, 85, 95, 223,
    226–58, 259, 269, 311, 312,
    313, 318, 320, 321, 322–3,
    324, 325, 331, 341, 353, 404,
    444, 448, 450, 461, 463, 467,
    480, 481, 482, 493, 499–501;
    Cambridge and, 226–7,
    229–30, 243–5, 248; form of,
    227, 250; Forster on, 226–7,
    228, 231, 233, 238, 243, 247,
    248, 249–51, 253, 254, 255,
    311; Fry on, 252; Keynes on,
    252; MacCarthy on, 252;
    Moore, G. E., and, 226–7,
    230–6, 240–4, 249, 254,
    500–1; narration in, 250, 251,
    257, 258; reception of,
    249–58, 500–1; revisions of,
    238, 246; Shelley and, 226,
    240–3, 244–5, 500; origins of,
    226–30; Strachey and, 133,
    239, 252, 441, 500; Woolf, L.,
    on, 253, 401; Woolf, V., on,
    227, 251–2, 312–13, 341, 353,
    501
  *Lucy Novels, see Room with a
    View*
  Marianne Thornton, 54
  Maurice, 54, 56, 220, 255, 487,
    500, 506

Moore, G. E., and, 36, 44, 96,
    224, 226–7, 230–6, 240–4,
    249, 254, 312, 313–14, 330,
    491, 500–1, 505
  music and: Beethoven, 320,
    331, 441–2, 451–2, 485;
    Gluck, 320; Mozart, 320;
    Schumann, 320; Wagner, 44
  Nottingham Lace, 76–9, 85, 93,
    238, 493, 499
  Pall Mall Magazine and, 49
  Pan and, 35–6, 48, 49, 50, 65,
    323, 448
  Passage to India, 35, 95, 112, 117,
    332, 400, 404, 430, 465, 474,
    481
  Pharos and Pharillon, 33
  Pilot and, 491
  Putnam's Monthly and, 49
  Room with a View, 50, 76, 95,
    223, 226, 235, 299, 311–335,
    341, 343, 363, 379, 419, 440,
    444, 445, 452, 456, 457, 471,
    485, 505–6, 510, 511; chap-
    ter titles, 323; Forster on,
    311, 331; James's *Portrait of
    a Lady* and, 317; *Lucy
    Novels*, 76, 311, 321, 325–30,
    506; Meredith's *Egoist* and,
    318; narration in, 317–20,
    322–4; reception of, 330–4,
    470–1, 506; 'View without
    a Room', 320, 330, 333;
    Woolf, L. on, 312, 314, 419;
    Woolf, V., on, 312, 320, 322,
    341, 343
  Russell, Bertrand, and, 232,
    243, 247, 254
  Temple Bar and, 45
  Trevelyan, R. C., and, 57, 83, 92–3
  Where Angels Fear to Tread, 4, 7,
    42, 60, 76–96, 97, 110, 117,
    227, 228, 238, 249, 254, 255,
    313, 315, 316, 319, 325, 326,
    363, 379, 440, 475, 493–4;
    Forster on, 80, 83, 93;
    James's *Ambassadors* and,
    80–2, 88, 318; reception of,
    90–6; Strachey on, 93–4,

Forster, E. M., *Where Angels Fear to Tread – continued*
253; titles of, 80; Woolf, L. on, 93–5, 400; Woolf, V. on, 88–9, 95
Working Men's College and, 8, 52, 441
writers other than Bloomsbury and: Arnold, 324, 445–6, 454; Austen, 44; Barrie, 53; Belloc, 11, 30, 36, 442; Bennett, 472–3, 488; Blake, 452; Brontë, C., 488; Brooke, R., 51; Browne, 38, 44; Butler, 53, 228, 316, 323, 330, 337; Carlyle, T., 324, 326, 330; Carpenter, 316; Cervantes, 328; *Collected Short Stories*, 33, 48, 506; Conrad, 408, 488; Dante, 44, 52–3, 89; Dickens, 35, 44, 512; Eliot, G., 488; Eliot, T. S., 452; Emerson, 316; Fitzgerald, E., 76; Flaubert, 89, 250; Ford, F. M., 49; France, 41; French symbolist poets, 451; Gibbon, 53, 209; Gissing, 53; Hardy, 53, 488; Homer, 44; Housman, 314, 323; Hugo, 49; Ibsen, 53, 57; Isherwood, 478–9, 484; James, H., 31, 42, 53, 54, 56, 58, 80–2, 88, 224, 317–18, 320–1, 440, 488, 505–6; James, M. R., 57; Keats, 31, 37, 44; Kipling, 53, 256, 335, 408; Lampedusa, 48; Lawrence, D. H., 256, 332, 436, 477; Maeterlinck, 43, 57; Mansfield, 47, 477–8; Meredith, G., 51, 318, 322, 330, 449, 490; Mill, J. S., 488; Pater, 76; Pinero, 53; Poggio, 264; Ruskin, 199, 315, 327; Scott, W., 316; Shakespeare, 327; Shaw, 53, 490; Shelley, 44, 226, 240–3, 244–5, 320, 500; Sophocles, 34; Sterne, 31; Stevenson, 53; Swinburne, 76; Tennyson, 34, 52; Thoreau, 324; Tolstoy, 53, 327; Virgil, 37, 52, 234; Voltaire, 209; Ward, Mrs, 328; Wells, 336; West, R., 49; Whitman, 461; Wilde, 50; Wordsworth, 312; Zola, 53
writers, Bloomsbury, and: MacCarthy, 52; Strachey, 37, 51, 59, 66, 450, 490; Woolf, L., 231, 397, 408, 430, 435; Woolf, V., 34, 37, 51, 54, 87, 223, 225, 234
writings, shorter: 30–60, 334–8, 490–2; 'Albergo Empedocle', 45–6, 59; 'Amateur among the Mountains', 31, 36; *Anonymity*, 384; 'Ansell', 54–5, 56; 'Cardan', 16, 37–8, 490; 'Celestial Omnibus', 41, 44–5, 51, 455, 490–1, 505; *Celestial Omnibus*, 30, 33, 34, 36, 44–5, 477; 'Cnidus', 31–3, 35, 230, 248; *Collected Short Stories*, 33, 48, 336, 506; 'Co–ordination', 493; 'Curate's Friend', 49–50; 'Day Off', 491; 'Eternal Moment', 37, 41–4, 48, 56, 59, 90; *Eternal Moment*, 30, 49, 335; 'Feminine Note in Literature', 487–8; 'Gemistus Pletho', 38–40; 'Helping Hand', 54, 56–7, 59, 492; 'Landor at Sea', 502; *Letter to Madan Blanchard*, 493; 'Macolnia Shops', 30–1, 45; 'Machine Stops', 49, 51, 335–8, 506; Memoir Club papers, 36, 78, 80, 92, 249–50; 'Mr. Walsh's Secret History of the Victorian Movement', 486; 'My Wood', 50; 'Notes on the English Character', 245; 'Other Kingdom', 49, 50–1,

Forster, E. M.: shorter writings –
  continued
  264, 336; 'Other Side of the
  Hedge', 36–7, 44–5, 51, 56,
  59; 'Pessimism in Literature', 53–4, 166, 320–1, 329;
  'Point of It', 51, 66; poetry,
  494, 506; 'Purple Envelope', 54, 57, 59, 510; 'Ralph
  and Tony', 54, 55–6; revisions of essays, 32, 33, 34,
  52, 490; revisions of
  stories, 49; 'Road from
  Colonus', 33–4, 36, 42, 44,
  58, 59, 489; 'Rock', 20, 54,
  57–9; 'Rooksnest', 438, 510;
  'Story of a Panic', 16, 33,
  35–6, 42, 44, 45, 47, 51, 58,
  59, 441; 'Story of the Siren',
  47–9, 51, 55, 478; 'Three
  Generations', 442, 453;
  'Tomb of Pletone', 40–1;
  unpublished writings, 31,
  52, 491–2; Virgil's *Aeneid*,
  Introduction and notes to,
  37, 52
Forster, Lily, 460, 473, 478
Fowles, John, 512
Fox, Charles James, 127, 128
France, Anatole, 41, 183
Francis, Philip, 120, 122, 127, 131
Frazer, J. G., 9
Freeman, E. A., 165
Freeman, Mary Wilkins, 172
Freud, Sigmund, 230, 394, 409
Friday Club, 3–4, 172, 173,
  210–12, 224, 271, 440, 486, 488
Fry, Roger, 3, 4, 6, 7, 29, 39, 45,
  92, 105, 194–214, 217, 224,
  252, 259, 279, 286, 294, 304,
  327, 391, 440, 477, 488, 491,
  492, 498–9, 500,
  art and artists, on: Beardsley,
  199–200; Bellini, G., 196,
  197, 499; Blake, 201;
  Cézanne, 204–5, 208, 209;
  Degas, 208, 268; English
  Impressionists, 199; French
  Impressionists, 207;
  Ghirlandaio, 494; Giotto,
  196, 316; impressionism,
  199, 202, 204, 209, 210, 268;
  John, 205; Michelangelo,
  210; Morris, 205; post-
  impressionism, 194, 200,
  204–5, 206, 499; Rem-
  brandt, 200, 268; Reynolds,
  268; Ricketts, 201; Sargent,
  199; Sickert, 199; Steer, 199;
  Turner, 199; Watts, 200,
  207–8; Whistler, 200, 206–8
  Athenaeum and, 194, 196, 199–
  208, 260, 267, 278, 285, 440,
  492
  Bloomsbury aesthetics and,
  194–210, 267–8
  Bloomsbury relationships: 195;
  Bell, C., 4, 282; Bell, V., 4,
  196, 199; Forster, 4, 45, 47,
  56–7, 488, 492; MacCarthy,
  4, 26, 212, 277
  Burlington Magazine and, 201,
  203
  Cambridge and, 196, 208, 267,
  498
  Dickinson, Goldsworthy
  Lowes, and, 39, 245, 441
  Idealism and, 196, 198, 199,
  204, 210, 212, 267
  illustrations: *Celestial Omnibus*
  end papers, 45, 477, 490;
  poetry of R. C. Trevelyan,
  196
  interrelations of the arts and,
  210, 268
  lectures, 195–7, 268, 499
  McTaggart, J. M. E., and, 39
  Monthly Review and, 196, 327
  New Quarterly and, 204, 217,
  259, 262
  Pilot and, 196, 199, 200, 205
  reviewing, conditions of, 200,
  208
  Reynolds's, Joshua, *Discourses*,
  edition of, 4, 208–10
  Royal Academy, on, 199, 200,
  202, 205, 209, 212, 213
  Russell, Bertrand, and, 267

Fry, Roger – *continued*
style, 195, 196, 202, 204
Woolf, V., on, 194–5, 199, 201,
204, 205
writers and: Aristotle, 210;
Arnold, 198; Blake, 209;
Berenson, 197, 202–4, 210;
Dante, 197; Dickens, 197;
Hazlitt, 209; MacColl, 202;
Mallarmé, 298; Mauclair,
205; Maupassant,; 208;
Pater, 201, 204; Ruskin,
198, 199, 204, 206, 209;
Santayana, 208–9; Shake-
speare, 197; Shaw, 111;
Symonds, 204; Tolstoy, 267,
327; Wilde, 207; Zola, 208
writings: 'Essay in Aesthetics',
203, 204, 262, 267–8, 502;
Giovanni Bellini, 196, 197–8,
499; 'Italian Art', 494; *Last
Lectures*, 195–6; *Macmillan's
Guide to Italy*, and, 196,
494; 'Mere technique', 205;
Vision and Design, 196, 197,
200, 201, 268; 'What Men
Do When They Go Down',
498
Fry, Helen, 499
Frye, Northrop, 512
Furbank, P. N., 237, 479, 499, 500

G. P. Putnam's Sons, 471, 511
Galsworthy, John, 49, 107, 213,
264, 292, 343, 365, 442, 472,
484
Galton, Francis, 153
Gandhi, Mohandas K., 416
Gardiner, E. A., 499
Garnett, Constance, 265, 506, 510
Garnett, David, 91, 506
Garnett, Edward, 59, 91–2, 99,
177, 254, 331, 335, 336, 462,
472, 506
Garvin, J. L., 152
Gaskell, Elizabeth, 148, 348
Gauguin, Paul, 213
Gay, John, 69
Gaye, R. K., 497

George I, 299
George, David Lloyd, 305, 454
Georgian Bloomsbury, 3, 283, 486,
488
Ghirlandaio, Domenico Bigordi,
493
Gibbon, Edward, 18, 53, 126,
128–9, 209, 280, 301, 302, 362
Gilbert, William, 335
Giles, H. A., 273–4, 503
Gillespie, Diane, 143
Giotto, 196, 314, 316, 326, 327
Gissing, George, 25, 53, 150, 178–9
Gluck, Christoph Willibad von,
320, 363
Glyn, Elinor, 472
Goethe, Johann Wolfgang von, 482
Gogol, Nikolai, 265
Goldsmith, Oliver, 13, 349
Gordon Square, 149, 159, 218, 220
Gorky, Maxim, 252
Gospels, 134
Gosse, Edmund, 12, 18, 26, 27,
269, 276, 289, 392, 473, 478,
489
Graham, Kenneth, 512
Gransden, K. W., 490
Grant, Duncan, 5, 136, 212,
218–19, 224, 253, 260, 287,
292, 353, 494, 503, 504;
Dreadnought Hoax and,
222–3; *Spectator* reviews, 503
Granville-Barker, Harley, 104,
105–7, 113, 211, 262, 293
Granta, 498
Graphic, 72
Greek Anthology, 68, 69
Green, J. R., 162, 165
Greene, Graham, 439, 440
Greg, W. W., 288
Gregory, Augusta, 101
Greville, Fulke, 346
Grey, Zane, 472
Grillparzer, Franz, 69
Guardian (Church), 7, 147–51, 153,
155–7, 158, 160, 162, 163–4,
168, 170, 172–3, 174, 178, 180,
185, 340, 352, 382, 497, 498,
506

Hale, William Bayard, 367
Hall, Fielding, 343
Halley's comet, 417
Hammond, J. L., 99, 104
Hankin, St. John, 107
Harcourt, Cyril, 107
Harcourt, Robert Vernon, 107
Hardy, Thomas, 9, 49, 53, 144, 156, 212, 217, 262, 264, 297, 333, 378, 386, 396, 398, 488
Harrison, Bernard, 493, 501
Hart, Elizabeth, 95
Hartley, L. P., 95
Haskell, F. J. H., 499
Hastings, Warren, 13, 24, 117–33, 135, 137, 300, 302, 347, 495
Hauptmann, Gerhart, 107
Hawthorne, Nathaniel, 141, 162, 342, 349, 366
Hawtrey, Charles, 293
Hawtrey, Ralph, 266
Hazlitt, William, 209
Hegel, G. W. F., 236, 246, 273
Heilbrun, Carolyn, 59
Heine, Elizabeth, 257, 403, 499
Henley, W. E., 72
Heretics Society, 308
Herz, Judith, 30, 33, 51, 490
Hewins, W. A. S., 433
Hewlett, H. W. 106–7
Hillegas, M. R., 335
Hills, Jack, 145, 387–90
Hitchener, Elizabeth, 507
Hobbes, Thomas, 426
Hobhouse, Arthur, 136, 137
Hobson, J. A., 99, 129, 418
Hogarth Press, 47, 72, 222, 401, 420, 423–4, 478
Hogarth, William, 292
Holland, Elizabeth, 369–70
Holmes, C. J., 499
Holmes, Oliver Wendell, 349
Holroyd, Michael, 111, 123, 286, 292, 293, 304, 305, 494, 495
Home University Library, 12, 495
Homer, 44, 190, 271, 377
Hooch, Pieter de, 271
Hood, Thomas, 347
Hope, Anthony, 342

Housman, A. E., 6, 72, 314, 323, 324, 452, 466, 494
Howarth, Herbert, 489
Howe, Irving, 335
Howells, William Dean, 148–50
Hudson, Derek, 471
Hudson, W. H., 26, 29, 49
Hueffer, Ford Madox, *see* Ford, Ford Madox
Hugo, Victor, 36, 49
Hume, David, 262, 290
Huxley, Aldous, 338

Ibsen, Henrik, 53, 57, 101, 105, 106, 107, 110, 220, 292, 357, 384, 481, 504
imperialism, 24, 34, 36, 44, 45, 51, 99, 118–132, 134–8, 223, 391–437, 442, 446, 457, 476, 495, 508–9
Impey, Elija, 118, 124
impressionism, 19, 68, 199, 202, 204, 205, 209, 210, 211, 268
Inchbald, Elizabeth, 291
Independent Review, 3, 7, 9–37, 41–2, 44, 45, 52, 59, 79, 90, 91, 97, 99, 110, 120, 126, 129, 137, 191, 205, 206, 230, 239, 254, 259, 261, 269, 275, 285, 295, 303, 393, 412, 441, 442, 455, 489–90, 499
Ingres, Jean Auguste Dominique, 271
Irish Theatre Society, 101
Irving, Henry, 300
Isherwood, Christopher, 258, 478–9, 485

Jacks, L. P., 283
Jackson, Stonewall, 153
Jacobson, Dan, 396
James I, 299
James, Henry, 6, 25, 31, 53, 54, 56, 58, 95, 148, 150, 155, 160, 163, 164, 172, 178, 217, 224, 251, 262, 264, 342, 349, 356, 359, 375–6, 377, 384, 392, 396, 398, 408, 424, 440, 442, 471, 472,

James, Henry – *continued*
484, 488, 505–6; *Ambassadors,*
79, 80–2, 88, 90, 256, 318;
American Scene, 27; *Awkward
Age,* 27; *English Hours,* 180–1,
185; *Golden Bowl,* 27, 155–7,
180; *Portrait of a Lady,* 317,
320, 322; Prefaces, 81, 319–20;
Roderick Hudson, 144; *Wings
of the Dove,* 321
James, M. R., 57
James, William, 266
Japanese theatre, 106
Jebb, R. C., 11
Jefferies, Richard, 153, 455
Jefferson, George, 59, 91, 462
Jenks, Edward, 33
Jhabvala, Ruth Prawer, 334, 485
Job, Book of, 16
John, Augustus, 205, 219
Johnson, Samuel, 13, 17, 18, 21,
73, 129, 144, 194, 209, 273,
288, 289, 302, 303, 347, 489
Jonson, Ben, 220
Jowett,Benjamin, 135
Joyce, James, 33, 69, 256, 384
Jung, Carl, 230

Kant, Immanuel, 21, 231, 244
Keats, John, 31, 37, 44, 165, 190,
270, 279–80, 319, 347, 377
Kelly, Gerald, 212
Ker, Walter, 288
Keynes, John Maynard, 3, 8, 38,
72, 118, 132, 136, 137–8, 217,
219, 224, 233, 252, 260, 262,
263, 269, 294, 305, 334, 400,
500, 504
  Forster, and, 36, 93, 333
  Moore, G. E., and, 84, 138, 290
  New Quarterly and, 217, 259,
  262, 305
  Russell, Bertrand, and, 138
  Strachey and, 5, 23, 84, 99, 117,
  137–9, 211, 269, 495, 504
  writers, and: Austen, 333;
  Hardy, 333; Shaw, 111;
  Wells, 111
  writings: fellowship

dissertation, 138; *Indian
  Currency and Finance,* 117;
  'Moral and Material
  Progress of India', 138;
  'My Early Beliefs', 493
King, Dixie, 506
King, Francis, 493
Kinglake, Alexander, 172
Kingsley, Charles, 497
Kipling, 53, 130, 135, 184, 224,
256, 295, 298, 335, 394, 396,
397, 398, 399, 404, 408, 410,
411, 425–6, 472, 509
Kirkpatrick, B. J., 255, 332, 491,
494, 497–8, 501, 506, 507, 511
Knopf, Alfred A., 511
Knox, Ronald, 501
Köpenick, Captain, 222
Kruger, Paul, 276

La Bruyère, Jean de, 11, 302
La Fontaine, Jean de, 294
La Rochefoucauld, François, Duc
  de, 11
La Vallière, Louise de, 368
Lago, Mary, 332
Laing, Donald A., 492, 503
Lamb, Charles, 18, 20, 28, 153,
157, 177, 182, 199, 293, 295,
349, 359, 443, 444, 489
Lamb, Walter, 63, 64, 65, 72–4,
492, 493
Lampedusa, Giuseppe di, 48
Landor, Walter Savage, 199, 502
Lane, E. M., 160
Lang, Andrew, 22
Lawrence, D. H., 36, 91, 321, 474,
477, 509; *Aaron's Rod,* 332–3;
Lady Chatterley's Lover, 506;
Rainbow, 462, 477; 'Ship of
Death', 501; *Sons and Lovers,*
256, 477; *White Peacock,* 332,
506; *Women in Love,* 256, 436,
477, 501
Lawrence, Frieda, 477, 501, 509
Lawrence, Thomas, 131, 358, 495
Layard, Austin Henry, 153
Leaska, Mitchell, 496, 497, 507

Leavis, F. R., 97, 255, 288, 331, 332, 480, 481–2, 483, 512
Lee, Sidney, 15, 288, 295, 352
Lee, Vernon, 359–60
Leibniz, Gottfried Wilhelm, 299
Leslie, C. R., 370
Lespinasse, Julie-Jeanne-Eléonore, 22–3
Levin, Bernard, 485
Levy, Paul, 495, 500, 504
Lewis, Wyndham, 112, 212
Li Po, 273
Liberalism, 10, 11, 25, 99, 112, 262, 285, 455; New Liberalism, 10, 22, 24, 489
Life and Letters, 263
Lincoln, Abraham, 302
Listener, 505
Locke, John, 18
Lockhart, J. G., 22
London, Jack, 49, 340, 442, 453
Louis XIV, 22, 300, 368
Lounsbury, T. R., 288
Lowell, James Russell, 150, 349–50
Lubbock, Percy, 176, 471
Lucas, E. V., 299–300, 347–8, 455
Luce, G. H., 72
Lugard, F. J. D., 433
Lydgate, John, 186
Lyly, John, 22, 489
Lyttelton, Margaret, 496
Lyttelton, Mary Kathleen (Mrs Arthur), 147–9, 151, 153, 156, 162, 164, 168, 173, 177–8, 271, 496
Lytton, Edward Robert Bulwer, 23–5, 24, 118, 129

Macaulay, Thomas Babington, 13–14, 119–22, 124–8, 130, 131, 198, 296, 303, 351, 362, 369
Macaulay, Rose, 175, 331, 480, 481, 483
MacCarthy, Desmond, 3, 4, 6, 8, 90, 91, 92, 102, 161, 190, 204, 211, 212, 217–18, 224, 252, 281, 283, 293, 304, 340, 391, 493, 497, 502, 510

Bloomsbury critic, as, 25, 27, 108
Bloomsbury relationships with: 4, 5; Bell, V., 183; Forster, 26, 29; Fry, 4, 26, 212, 277; Strachey, 5, 138, 259, 489, 495, 500; Woolf, L., 26; Woolf, V., 26, 28, 102, 183
Court Theatre and, 97–116
Independent Review and, 9, 10, 25–9, 99
Moore, G. E., and, 26, 98, 111, 217, 252, 263, 474
New Quarterly and, 10, 217, 259–77, 263, 502, 510
New Statesman and, 112
Russell, Bertrand, and, 261, 276, 502
Shaw, George Bernard and, Shaw, 7, 9, 12, 25–7, 108–15, 218, 264, 446; *Back to Methuselah*, 111; *Caesar and Cleopatra*, 111; *Candida*, 109; *Captain Brassbound's Conversion*, 109; *Doctor's Dilemma*, 110; *John Bull's Other Island*, 106, 109; *Major Barbara*, 109, 110; *Man and; Superman*, 25, 26–7, 37, 109; *Philanderer*, 110; *You Never Can Tell*, 109
Speaker and, 25, 99–104, 109–10, 112, 114–15, 261, 275, 285, 292
Sunday Times and, 27
writers other than Bloomsbury and: Archer, 114; Arnold, 99; Augustine, 28; Baring, 217; Beerbohm, 114–15, 217; Belloc, 26, 217; Bennett, 472; Benson, A. C., 26, 29; Boyle, 101; Browning, R., 276; Butler, S., 25, 29, 99, 265; Chekhov, 28; Chesterton, 26; Coleridge, 99, 103; Conrad, 25, 27; Davies, W. H., 26; Donne, 276; Dostoevsky, 28; Gissing, 25; Gosse, 26, 27, 276;

MacCarthy, Desmond, and
    writers other than Blooms-
    bury – *continued*
    Gregory, A., 101; Hudson,
    26, 29; Ibsen, 101, 107, 110;
    James, H., 25, 27, 156, 218,
    264; Lamb, 28; Murray, G.,
    106–7; Pater, 103; Phillips,
    101; Ruskin, 99; Shake-
    speare and, 27, 102–3, 104,
    110; Swinburne, 103;
    Symons, 26, 28; Synge, 101;
    Tolstoy, 28; Turgenev, 28;
    Verlaine, 28; Walkley, 114,
    494; Wedekind, 99; Wells,
    26, 29, 217; Wilde, 103–4;
    Yeats, 101; *see also*
    MacCarthy and Shaw
  writers, Bloomsbury, and,
    Forster, 51, 93, 96, 474, 487;
    Strachey, 26, 99, 272;
    Woolf, V., 26, 99, 116
  writings: 28; African writings,
    276; 'Censorship of Plays',
    275–6; *Court Theatre*,
    104–16, 117, 261, 264, 494;
    drama reviews, 97–103;
    'John Donne', 276; 'New
    St. Bernard', 26; Russell,
    Lady John, memoir, 276
MacCarthy, Mary, 217, 261, 265,
    435
MacColl, D. S., 202
Mackail, J. W., 153
Mackenzie, Compton, 256
Maeterlinck, Maurice, 43, 57, 103,
    107
Magnus, John, 255
Mailer, Norman, 258
Maitland, F. W., 145, 151–2, 186,
    193, 382, 386; *Life and Letters
    of Leslie Stephen*, 152, 154,
    160, 162, 193
Mallarmé, Stéphane, 72, 298
Manchester Guardian, 471
Mann, Thomas, 256
Mansfield, Katherine, 47, 264,
    477–8
Marchand, Leslie, 200

Marie Antoinette, 353
Marivaux, Pierre, 262
Marlowe, Christopher, 295
Marsh, Edward, 473
Marshall, P. J., 122, 131
Marvell, Andrew, 66, 297
Marx, Karl, 49
Masefield, John, 49
Masood, Syed Ross, 335, 491
Massingham, H. W. 100
Masterman, C. F. G., 9, 91, 254,
    442, 453, 455, 506
Matisse, Henri, 213
Mauclair, Camille, 205
Maugham, W. Somerset, 163, 256,
    292, 293, 397
Maupassant, Guy de, 208, 424
Maurice, F. D., 52, 281
Mauron, Charles, 257, 332, 512–13
Maxse, Kitty, 147, 152, 153
Maxse, Leo, 147, 152, 153–4, 163,
    340, 365
McConkey, James, 255
McDowell, F. P. W., 440, 490, 510
McNeillie, Andrew, 155, 358, 497
McTaggart, John McTaggart Ellis,
    39, 136, 196, 198, 212, 236,
    248, 259, 262, 266, 267, 499
Medici, Lorenzo, 300
Meleager, 69
Memoir Club, 3, 36, 78, 80, 142,
    162, 212, 219, 221, 223, 226,
    249, 250, 394, 502
Meredith, George, 6, 49, 51, 67,
    72, 93, 95, 156, 159, 162, 185,
    224, 254, 317, 319, 322, 330,
    340, 342, 346, 374, 380, 455,
    472, 490; *Celt or Saxon*, 278;
    Diana of the Crossways, 169,
    442; *Egoist*, 318, 323, 488;
    Harry Richmond, 379; *Modern
    Love*, 278, 449; 'Of Love and
    the Valley', 278
Meredith, H. O., 29, 52, 72, 77, 93,
    99, 230, 253, 317, 499, 500, 505
Mérimée, Prosper, 189, 277
Merivale, Patricia, 49
Merle, Gabriel, 11, 22
Meryon, Charles Louis, 354

Methuen & Co., 90, 494
Metropolitan Museum of New York, 4, 440
Meynell, Alice, 380
Michelangelo, 210, 315, 323, 449
Michelet, 126, 362
Mill, James, 119–23, 125–8, 131
Mill, John Stuart, 280, 281, 392, 419, 486, 488
Milton, John, 62, 67, 127, 144, 207, 220, 270, 287, 288, 294, 296–7, 469
Mind, 231
Mizener, Arthur, 264
Moggridge, D. E., 504
Moir, David, 172
Molière, 17, 294, 377, 413
Monet, Claude, 68
Montagu, Mary Wortley, 23, 169, 412
Montaigne, Michel Eyquem de, 53, 157
Montespan, Madame de, 368
Monthly Review, 196, 327
Moore, G. E. 10, 15, 36, 84, 96, 98, 103, 128, 134, 137, 138, 144, 196, 217, 221, 224, 226–7, 230–8, 241–5, 248–9, 252, 259, 261, 262, 263, 264, 265–7, 272, 273, 278, 283, 304, 308, 312, 313–14, 324, 359, 396, 413, 430, 435, 436, 446, 474, 476, 481, 489, 493, 499–500, 505; *Elements of Ethics*, 502; 'Hume's Philosophy', 266; 'Is conversion possible?', 510; 'Kant's Idealism', 231, 234; 'Nature and Reality of Objects of Perception', 233, 234; *Principia Ethica*, 3, 7, 9, 26–7, 32, 44, 111, 126, 133, 136, 212, 214, 230–1, 233, 238, 243, 256, 266, 281, 289–90, 309, 330, 343, 376, 395, 441, 451, 491, 501, 502; 'Refutation of Idealism', 231–2, 234, 240, 241–2, 499; *Some Main Problems of Philosophy*, 500
Moore, George, 213

Moore, T. Sturge, 103, 261, 262, 264, 333
More, Paul Elmer, 98
Morelli, Giovanni, 203
Morgan, J. P., 440
Morgan, William de, 472
Morley College, 8, 152, 154, 158, 161, 162, 165–8
Morning Leader, 471
Morning Post, 254, 472
Morrell, Ottoline, 221
Morrice, J. W., 212–14
Morris, William, 153, 195, 205
Mozart, Wolfgang Amadeus, 271, 320, 413
Murray, Gilbert, 11, 71, 106–7, 114
Musset, Alfred De, 212

Nation, 100, 200, 254, 261, 440, 442, 472, 506
National Review, 147, 152–3, 154, 157, 163, 340, 365
Neo-Pagans, 221
Nevill, Dorothy, 369
New Age, 263, 472
New Directions Books, 482, 512
New English Art Club, 205, 440
New Quarterly, 100, 104, 204, 217, 259–77, 281, 287, 294, 304, 305, 306, 308, 340, 502–3, 510
New Statesman, 49, 100, 200, 275
Newboldt, Henry, 196
Newman, John Henry, 299
Newton, Isaac, 386
Nietzsche, Friedrich Wilhelm 28, 29, 115, 264, 324, 357, 449
Nijinski, Vaslav, 448
Norris, W. E., 160, 172, 341
Norton, Caroline, 169
Norton, Harry, 211
Nuncomar, 118, 119, 124

O'Conor, Roderick, 212–13
Omega Workshops, 206
Orage, A. R., 28, 263–4
Orion, 508
Orwell, George, 338, 412, 433–4
Outlook, 152, 157
Oxford and Cambridge Review, 336

Oxford University, 19, 65, 73, 196, 231, 294, 356, 376, 450
Oxford University Press, 291
Ozick, Cynthia, 257

Paley, G. A., 261, 262, 263, 276
Paley, William, 261
Pall Mall Gazette, 471
Pall Mall Magazine, 49
Pantazzi, Michael, 511
Parker, Peter, 258
Paston Letters, 170, 185
Pater, Walter, 6, 76, 77, 103, 120, 153, 160, 164, 179, 183, 194–5, 196, 199, 201–2, 204, 210, 277, 309, 360, 361, 371
Pater, Clara, 143
Peacock, Thomas Love, 95, 192
Pearson, Hesketh, 101
Perugino, 379, 386
Phillips, Stephen, 101, 106
Piero Della Francesca, 327
Pilot, 196, 199, 200, 205
Pinero, Arthur, 53, 292
Pitt, William, 355
Plato, 39, 182, 191, 252, 239, 279, 288, 308, 359–60, 482, 487
Platonism, 83, 241, 243, 265
Play-Reading Society, 220, 347
Pletho, Gemistus, 37, 38, 315
Pollock, Frederick, 10, 489
Pope, Alexander, 270, 286, 296, 297, 298, 495
Porter, Bernard, 508
post-impressionism, 85, 107–8, 194, 200, 204–5, 206, 214, 222, 499
post-impressionist exhibitions, 3, 105, 268, 277, 278, 488, 503
Pound, Ezra, 49, 71, 274, 512
Praed, William, 69
Praxiteles, 32
Pre-Raphaelites, 200, 340
Prior, Matthew, 68, 69
Pritchett, V. S., 335
Proust, Marcel, 212
Purkis, John, 494
Putnam's Monthly, 49

Quarterly Review, 207, 261, 340
Quiller-Couch, Arthur, 97

Racine, Jean, 17, 262, 263, 270–4, 287, 291, 294, 296, 413, 502–3
Raleigh, Sir Walter, 302, 506
Raleigh, Walter, Professor, 16, 19, 176, 288, 291, 308
Raverat, Gwen, 92
Rayleigh, J. W. S., 261, 269
Redford, Bruce B., 122, 495
Rees, Goronwy, 476–7
Regan, Tom, 244, 266
Rembrandt, 200, 206, 268
Renan, Ernest, 294
Rendell, Vernon, 278
Renoir, Pierre Auguste, 68, 208
Reynolds, Joshua, 4, 19, 177, 195, 208–10, 211, 213, 268
Rhodes, Cecil, 276
Richards, I. A., 7, 72, 97, 267, 480–2, 483, 512
Richardson, Samuel, 13, 291, 296
Richmond, Bruce, 152, 156, 157, 160–1, 162, 168, 175, 181
Ricketts, Charles, 103, 201, 440
Ritchie, Anne Thackeray, 157, 217, 262, 264, 358
Robbia, Della, 314
Robbins, Elizabeth, 164
Rodin, Auguste, 205, 213
Romanticism, 21, 233, 235, 272, 275, 280, 298, 441
Romney, George, 183
Roosevelt, Theodore, 366–7
Rosenbaum, S. P., 54, 251, 475–6, 497, 500, 502
Ross, M. L., 494, 505
Ross, Robert, 103, 360, 360–1
Rossetti, Christina, 342, 350
Rothenstein, William, 440, 469
Rousseau, Jean Jacques, 12, 275, 280, 297, 392, 426
Royal Academy, 107–8, 199, 200, 202, 205, 209, 212, 213, 294, 499
Rubens, Peter Paul, 19
Ruskin, John, 99, 195, 196, 197,

Ruskin, John – *continued*
  198, 199, 204, 206–7, 209, 267,
  281, 315, 327, 342, 360, 380,
  392, 454
Russell, Agatha, 276
Russell, Bertrand, 9, 32, 93, 99,
  137, 138, 196, 208, 232, 243,
  247, 254, 259, 261, 265–7, 269,
  276, 502
Russell, Lady John, 276
Russian literature, 28, 262, 264–5
Rylands, George, 16

Saint Bridget, 485
Saint-Simon, Louis de Rouvroy,
  302
Sainte-Beuve, Charles-Augustin,
  21
Saintsbury, George, 97, 294
Samuels, Ernest, 203, 499
Sanders, Charles Richard, 12, 15,
  18, 270, 271, 495
Santayana, George, 208–9, 210
Saparamadu, S. D., 509
Sappho, 150
Sargent, John Singer, 199
Saturday Review, 105, 202, 472
Savage, George, 152
Savoy Theatre, 293
Scaliger, Julius Caesar, 38
Schlegel, August Wilhelm von, 440
Schlegel, Friedrich von, 440, 510
Schnitzler, Arthur, 107
Schoenbaum, S., 15
Schopenhauer, Arthur, 28, 109,
  115, 244, 324
Schumann, Robert, 320
Scott, Walter, 22, 89, 156, 294, 316,
  341, 348, 372, 442, 497
Scott-James, R. A., 331, 472
Scrutiny, 481
Seaton, Charles, 489
Seccombe, Thomas, 352, 354
Sévigné, Marie de
  Rabutin-Chantal, 281
Seward, Anna, 299–300, 347–8
Shaftesbury, Anthony Ashley
  Cooper, 18
Shakespeare, William, 14–16, 17,

19, 35, 104, 197, 220, 271, 287,
  288, 290, 293, 294, 295–6, 297,
  303, 319, 364, 366, 417, 469;
  Antony and Cleopatra, 300; *As
  You Like It*, 104; *Coriolanus*,
  15, 16; *Cymbeline*, 14; *Hamlet*,
  102, 166, 293; *King Lear*, 149,
  290, 327, 489; *Measure for
  Measure*, 103; *Midsummer
  Night's Dream*, 15; *Othello*, 16;
  Romeo and Juliet, 364; *Sonnets*,
  295, 303; *Taming of the Shrew*,
  102; *Tempest*, 14, 15; *Twelfth
  Night*, 15, 16; *Winter's Tale*, 14
Shaw, George Bernard, 7, 9, 25,
  53, 100, 103, 105–6, 107,
  108–15, 217, 238, 263, 264,
  265, 282–3, 292, 335, 446; *Back
  to Methuselah*, 111; *Caesar and
  Cleopatra*, 111; *Candida*, 105,
  109; *Captain Brassbound's Conversion*, 109; *Doctor's Dilemma*,
  110, 341; *Heartbreak House*,
  111, 443; *John Bull's Other
  Island*, 106, 109; *Major Bar-
  bara*, 109, 110, 115; *Man and
  Superman*, 12, 25, 26–7, 37,
  109, 115, 500; *Philanderer*, 110;
  Village Wooing, 111; *You Never
  Can Tell*, 109
Shelley, Percy Bysshe, 44, 165,
  226, 227, 233, 236, 240–5, 256,
  269, 270, 279, 280, 320, 350,
  356, 500, 501
Sheridan, Richard Brinsley, 127,
  131, 347, 348
Sichel, Edith, 160, 282
Sichel, Walter, 347
Sickert, Walter, 199
Sidgwick & Jackson, 352
Sidney, Philip, 346, 489
Signorelli, Luca, 85
Silva, Mervyn de, 509
Sinclair, May, 365, 472
Sitwell, Edith, 335
Smith, Reginald, 152, 365, 371, 507
Smyth, Ethel, 487
Society for Psychical Research,
  266, 502

Socrates, 243, 377
Song of Songs, 103
Sophocles, 16, 17, 33–4, 71, 159, 160, 161, 182, 192, 275, 293, 445
Sorabji, Cornelia, 353
Southorn, W. T., 399, 400
Spalding, Frances, 196, 202, 203, 205, 277, 500, 503
Speaker, 7, 12, 18, 22, 25, 91, 99–104, 109–10, 112, 114–15, 129, 172, 173, 175, 176, 177, 254, 259, 261, 275, 285, 292, 293, 489
Spectator, 91, 99, 118, 127, 129, 130, 202, 217, 255, 260, 263, 269, 271, 285–304, 305, 311, 331, 340, 472, 489, 495, 503–4
Spedding, James, 506
Spender, Stephen, 258, 479
Spenser, Edmund, 62, 270, 295
Spingarn, J. E., 288
Spotts, Frederic, 489
Spurr, Barry, 18
St Paul's School, 256, 410
Stallybrass, Oliver, 311, 465, 510, 511
Standard, 471
Stanhope, Hester, 354–5
Stape, J. H., 37, 511
Stead, C. K., 476
Stebbing, Susan, 266
Stebbing, William, 506
Steele, Richard, 285
Steer, Wilson, 199
Stein, Gertrude, 203, 333, 506
Stein, Leo, 203
Stephen family, 24, 118, 170, 385
Stephen, Adrian, 8, 159, 162, 191, 218, 219, 221–3, 364, 385
Stephen, Caroline Emelia, 145, 148, 373, 382
Stephen, J. K,, 69
Stephen, James Fitzjames, 24, 118, 119, 120, 123, 124, 128, 140, 270
Stephen, Julia, 164, 170, 179, 385
Stephen, Leslie, 3, 5, 6, 10, 21, 37, 69, 99, 127, 140, 144–5, 147, 148, 150, 151–2, 153, 164, 165, 168, 173, 182, 186, 196, 207, 219, 270, 272, 276, 278, 299, 318, 351, 357, 359, 365, 366, 382, 384–5, 387, 409, 489, 491, 505; *Fitzjames Stephen*, 118; *Hours in a Library*, 179; *Mausoleum Book*, 145, 383, 385; *Science of Ethics*, 489; *Studies of a Biographer*, 344, 346, 349, 356
Stephen, Thoby, 3, 4–5, 8, 25, 72–4, 99, 140, 149, 159, 167, 172, 191, 193, 211, 217, 218, 377, 385, 404, 441, 492
Stephen, Virginia *see* Woolf, Virginia
Stephens, F. G., 200
Sterne, Laurence, 13, 23, 31, 148, 163, 209, 280, 345–6, 348, 507
Stevens, Wallace, 23, 436
Stevenson, Robert Louis, 31, 53, 160, 179, 295, 455, 473
Stewart, Garrett, 511
Stewart, J. I. M., 108, 256
Stone, Wilfred, 439, 500, 501
Strachey, Amy, 285
Strachey, Barbara, 118
Strachey family, 15, 24, 118, 489, 503
Strachey, Henry, 286, 503
Strachey, James, 12, 129–30, 221, 260, 285, 286, 303, 503, 504
Strachey, Jane Maria, 22, 269, 306
Strachey, John, 131–2
Strachey, John, Sir, 118, 119, 123
Strachey, Lytton, 3, 4, 5, 6–7, 8, 30, 34, 37, 38, 39, 115, 159, 161, 169, 174, 177, 186, 206, 209, 211, 217, 224, 239, 253, 277, 279, 280, 281, 312, 340, 344, 347, 351, 352, 353, 355, 376, 391, 441, 442, 450, 454, 472, 473, 474, 489, 500, 505, 506, 507, 508
art and artists, on: 21; David, 271; Hogarth, 292; Hooch, 271; impressionism, 19, 211, 308; Rubens, 19;

Strachey, Lytton, on art and
      artists – *continued*
   Tintoretto, 271; Velasquez,
      19; Watteau, 413; Watts, 211
   Bloomsbury and, 4–5, 211, 218,
      219–21
   Bloomsbury relationships: Bell,
      C., 5, 61, 218–19; Bell, V., 5,
      218; Forster, 5, 13, 16, 20–1,
      94, 211; Grant, 5, 20, 218,
      287, 292, 504; Keynes, 5,
      23, 84, 99, 117, 136–9, 211,
      269, 495, 504; MacCarthy,
      5, 259–61, 263, 275, 489;
      Stephen, .T, 5, 25; Sydney-
      Turner, 5, 60, 218; Woolf,
      L., 5, 12, 19, 20, 23, 60, 134,
      136, 137, 211, 217, 218, 219,
      253, 287, 307, 395–6, 398–
      400, 401, 403, 404, 405,
      408–13, 419, 433, 504;
      Woolf, V., 13, 20, 137, 217,
      218–20, 272, 304, 348, 351,
      352, 355, 373, 419, 507
   Cambridge and, 118–20, 123,
      125, 132–9, 308–10
   Cambridge Review and, 504
   Chinese Poetry and, 273
   Cunningham, William, and, 123
   Euphrosyne and, 61–6, 71–5,
      492–3
   Gosse, Edmund, and, 12, 18,
      269, 489
   Hastings, Warren, 24, 117–33
      135, 137, 302, 347, 494–5
   Ignotus pseudonym, 292
   imperialism, and, 24, 117–32,
      133, 135–7, 139, 302,
      399–400, 494–5
   Independent Review and, 9–25,
      27–9, 120, 269, 295, 303,
      412, 490
   Moore, G. E., and, 9, 15, 126,
      128, 133, 135, 137, 266, 272,
      273, 289–90, 301, 304, 308,
      309
   music, and: Beethoven, 21, 211;
      Mozart, 271, 413; Wagner,
      271

New Quarterly and, 217, 259–65,
      269–76, 304, 306
reviewing conditions for, 286,
      287, 302, 304
revisions of essays, 15, 18, 270,
      271
Russell, Bertrand, and, 137, 266
Se Lig pseudonym, 274
Speaker and, 12, 18, 22
Spectator and, 12, 29, 118, 255,
      260, 269, 271, 285–304, 305,
      311, 351, 503–4
style, 5, 13, 17, 118, 121, 122,
      125, 270, 273, 291, 294, 301,
      302, 303, 304
writers and writings other than
      Bloomsbury and: Aristotle,
      288; Arnold, 21, 174, 295–6;
      Austen, 13; Bacon, 302;
      306; Bailey, J. C., 271;
      Balzac, 291, 294; Barbauld,
      502–3; Barnes, W., 297;
      Barrie, 292; Beddoes, 263,
      269–70, 295, 306; Birrell, A.,
      297; Blake, 17, 19–21;
      Boileau, 298; Boswell, 302;
      Brooke, T., 288; Browne,
      17–19, 22, 270, 302, 309,
      489; Bunyan, 302; Burke,
      19, 120, 125, 126, 128, 135,
      302; Burney, 113; Butler, S.,
      265; Butler, S. (Hudibras),
      18; Byron, 297; Canning,
      299; Carlyle, J. W., 280,
      299; Carlyle, T., 126, 280,
      299; Carpenter, 309; Catul-
      lus, 309; Cervantes, 294;
      Chaucer, 295; Clarendon,
      302; Clive, 302; Coleridge,
      18, 272, 289, 297, 299;
      Coleridge, M., 282; Collins,
      C., 289; Condorcet, 135,
      302; Corneille, 288; Cowley,
      298; Cromwell, 302; Dante,
      16, 23; Davies, H. H., 292;
      Day, T., 300; Diderot, 275;
      Donne, 134, 138, 296;
      Dostoevsky, 287; Dryden,
      287–8, 289, 297;

Strachey, Lytton, and writers and writings other than Bloomsbury – *continued*
Du Deffand, 22; Elizabeth, 302; Ferrero, 300–1; Flaubert, 291, 295; Fontenelle, 302; Francis, P., 120, 127; Galsworthy, 292; Gibbon, 126, 128–9, 301, 302, 490; Goldsmith, 13; Gospels, 134; Gosse, 18; *Greek Anthology*, 273; Hugo, 35; Ibsen, 292, 504; Inchbald, 503; Job, 16; Johnson, S., 13, 17, 18, 21, 129, 273, 288, 289, 302–3, 489; Keats, 270; Ker, 288; Kipling, 135, 295, 298; La Bruyère, 11, 302; La Fontaine, 293; La Rochefoucauld, 11; Lamb, 18, 20, 293, 295, 489; Lang, 22; Lee, S., 15, 288, 295; Lespinasse, 22–3; Li Po, 273; Locke, 18; Lockhart, 22; Lounsbury, 288; Lucas, E. V., 299–300; Lyly, 22, 489; Lytton, 23–5; Macaulay, 13–14, 119–22, 124–8, 130, 272, 296, 303, 494; Marlowe, 295; Marvell, 297; Maugham, 292, 293; Michelet, 126; Mill, James, 119–23, 125–8; Milton, 270, 287, 288, 294, 296–7; Molière, 17, 294–5, 413; Montagu, Mary, 23; Montaigne, 490; Newman, 299; Pinero, 292; Plato, 288; Pope, 296, 297, 298, 495; Racine, 17, 263, 270–4, 287, 291, 294, 296, 413, 502–3; Raleigh, Prof. W., 16, 19; Raleigh, Sir W., 302; Renan, 294; Richardson, S., 291, 296 Romantic poets, 297; Rousseau, 297; Saint-Simon, 302; Sainte-Beuve, 21; Saintsbury, 294; Scott, W., 22, 294; Seward, A., 300; Shaftsbury, 18; Shakespeare, 14–16, 17, 19, 35, 287, 288, 290, 293, 294, 295, 300, 303; Shaw, 111, 292; Shelley, 270; Sidney, 489; Sophocles, 16, 17, 293; Spenser, 270, 295; Spingarn, 288; Stephen, L., 21; Sterne, 13, 23; Stevenson, 295; Swift, 17, 18, 302, 304; Swinburne, 288, 295, 309; Tacitus, 126, 301; Thackeray, 291; Theobald, 297; Thomson, J., 288, 297; Thucydides, 126, 301; Vauvenargues, 11; Verlaine, 273, 298; Virgil, 270; Voltaire, 12, 16–17, 490; Walpole, H, 13–14; Ward, Mrs, 309; Wells, 310; Wilde, 292; Wordsworth, 272, 287, 288, 289, 296, 297, 298; Yeats, 298–9; Zola, 435
writers, Bloomsbury, and: Forster, 5, 51, 59, 93, 224, 225, 490; Fry, 206; Woolf, L. 435–6; Woolf, V., 37, 355
writings: 'Anthology', 273; aphorisms, 11; Apostle papers, 118–19, 132–7, 211, 252–3, 308–10, 504; *Books and Characters*, 12, 17, 271, 273, 275, 489; diary, 221; 'Dr. De Jongh', 504; *Elizabeth and Essex*, 302, 306; *Eminent Victorians*, 23, 117, 121, 131, 133, 256, 286, 289, 299, 300, 355; *Essex*, 302, 305–7, 504; 'Ethics of the Gospels', 7, 134; 'First and Last Will and Testament', 123; 'Haschish', 307; Hastings undergraduate essay, 117–20; 'He, She, and It', 134–5; 'Historian of the Future', 125–6, 133; Introduction, Rylands's *Words and Poetry*, 16; Introduction, Inchbald,

Strachey, Lytton: writings –
　continued
　　Simple Story, 291, 503–4;
　　*Landmarks of French
　　Literature*, 12, 494; 'Last
　　Elizabethan', 269–70; letter
　　games, 220–1, 504; *Lord
　　Pettigrew*, 304–5; 'Modern
　　Poetry', 71; 'Political Wis-
　　dom of Burke', 495; poetry,
　　61–6, 69, 72, 74, 138, 220,
　　307–8, 493, 495; *Portraits in
　　Miniature*, 125; 'Prose Style
　　of Men of Action', 127,
　　302; *Queen Victoria*, 117;
　　'Racine', 270–4, 502–3;
　　Really Interesting Question,
　　504; 'Rousseau Affair', 263,
　　274; 'Shakespeare's Final
　　Period', 14–16; *Shorter
　　Strachey*, 495; *Spectatorial
　　Essays*, 129–30, 503, 504;
　　'Tragedy Old and New',
　　293; 'Two Frenchmen',
　　11–12; 'Value of Poetry',
　　289; 'Voltaire's Tragedies',
　　14, 16–17, 37, 490; *Warren
　　Hastings, Cheyt Sing, and
　　the Begums of Oude*, 13,
　　117–32, 133, 135, 139, 495;
　　'Wrong Turning', 13
Strachey, Marjorie, 262, 489, 507
Strachey, Richard, 118, 304
Strachey, St. Loe, 91, 99, 131, 255,
　260, 285–303, 309, 495, 504
Sturridge, Charles, 95
Summers, Claude J., 50, 51,
　490–1, 505, 510
Sunday Essay Society, 14, 133,
　134, 136
Swift, Jonathan, 17, 18, 127, 302, 304
Swinburne, Algernon Charles, 6,
　68, 72, 75, 76, 103, 106, 138,
　220, 281, 288, 295, 309, 307,
　377, 438, 504
Swinnerton, Frank, 331
Sydney-Turner, Saxon, 3, 4, 5,
　61–71, 73–4, 94, 168, 218, 221,
　363, 368, 400, 404, 412, 492–3

Symonds, John Addington, 6,
　165, 194–6, 204, 360
Symons, Arthur, 26, 28, 261, 264
Synge, John Millington, 101, 283
Synge, Mrs Hamilton, 175

Tacitus, 126, 301
Tait, Stephen, 334
Temple Bar, 45, 47, 48
Temple, William, 280, 351
Tennyson, 34, 52, 72, 386, 307, 428
Tetrazzini, Luisa, 363
Thackeray, William Makepeace,
　101, 141, 156, 166, 212, 291,
　358, 365, 507
Theobald, Lewis, 297
Theophrastus, 11
Thompson, Francis, 279
Thomson, George H., 47, 239, 255
Thomson, James, 72, 288, 297
Thoreau, Henry David, 324, 455
Thornton, A. P., 130
Thornton, Marianne, 334, 491
Thucydides, 126, 159, 301
Thwaite, Ann, 473
Times, 69, 99, 115, 152–3, 157, 178,
　254, 305, 349, 362–4, 366, 375,
　485
Times Literary Supplement, 7, 23,
　97, 152, 156–7, 160–1, 162,
　172, 173, 174–5, 178, 180, 181,
　217, 251, 260, 280, 283, 285,
　312, 339, 340, 342–54, 356,
　358–62, 365, 415, 425, 470–71,
　497, 498, 507
Tintoretto, 271
Tolstoy, Leo, 28, 53, 210, 264, 267,
　268, 327, 357, 377, 476, 510
Toynbee, Arnold, 436
Travers, P. L., 512
Tree, Herbert Beerbohm, 101,
　102–3, 104, 293
Trelawny, Edward John, 281
Trevelyan, G. M., 9, 99, 126, 167,
　264, 270–1, 276–7, 278, 362,
　374, 507
Trevelyan, R. C., 9, 57, 72, 83,
　92–3, 99, 196, 202, 211, 264,
　311–12, 323, 337

Trilling, Lionel, 50, 82, 255–6, 410, 419, 434, 480, 482, 483, 484, 512
Tristram and Iseult, 186
Trollope, Anthony, 160, 164
Turgenev, Ivan, 28, 262, 264, 476
Turner, J. M. W., 199, 206

Upward, Edward, 478

Van Gogh, Vincent, 99, 107
Vanbrugh, John, 220, 347
Vaughan, Margaret, 165, 182, 184–5, 187, 188–9
Vauvenargues, Luc de Clapiers, Marquis de, 11
Vedrenne, John Eugene, 104, 105, 113, 293
Velasquez, Diego de Silva y, 19
Verlaine, Paul, 28, 72, 273, 298
Verrall, A. W., 262
Verrall, Mrs, 262
Victoria, Queen, 299
Victorian Bloomsbury, 3, 6, 8, 14, 15, 17, 20, 79, 133, 136, 196, 204, 231, 240, 248, 265, 267, 308, 382, 383, 441, 446, 451, 493, 496, 498, 501, 508
Villiers, George, 347
Virgil, 37, 52, 159, 234, 262, 270, 423, 505
Voltaire, 12, 16–17, 209, 282, 392, 393, 489

Wagner, 44, 221, 242, 271, 363–4, 452, 499, 510
Waldstein, Charles, 499
Waley, Arthur, 274, 503
Walkley, A. B., 105, 114
Wallace, Edgar, 472
Walpole, Horace, 13, 19, 281
Ward, Mrs Humphry, 146–7, 148, 152, 177, 309, 328, 359, 369, 488, 497
Warre-Cornish family, 262
Waterlow, Sidney, 505
Watt, Ian, 499
Watteau, Jean-Antoine, 413

Watts, G. F., 154, 200, 205, 207–8, 211, 454, 511
Waugh, Alec, 256
Waugh, Evelyn, 443
Webb, Beatrice, 111, 113
Webb, Sidney, 53, 112, 113
Wedd, Nathaniel, 9, 30, 78
Wedekind, Frank, 99, 107
Wedgwood, Julia, 92, 281, 491,
Weintraub, Stanley, 97
Wells, H. G., 9, 26, 111, 112, 213, 217, 262, 263, 264, 309, 335–7, 442, 472, 484
West, Rebecca, 49
Weyman, Stanley, 175
Wharton, Edith, 172, 472
Whistler, James McNeill, 68, 200, 206–8, 211, 212
Whitman, Walt, 6, 72, 461, 502
Widdowson, Peter, 484
Wilbur, Richard, 257
Wilde, Oscar, 6, 16, 50, 103, 104, 157, 207, 212, 292, 309, 360, 490
Wilde, Alan, 51
Wilhelmina, Margravine, 173
Wilkinson, Patrick, 244
Willcocks, M. P., 341
Wilson, Dover, 489
Wodehouse, P. G., 472
Woolf, Bella Sidney, 399, 508, 509
Woolf, Leonard, 3, 4, 5, 7, 8, 12, 25, 74, 77, 99, 117, 118, 129, 132, 138, 211, 217, 224, 263, 265, 266, 275, 279, 285–6, 312, 325, 394, 396, 400, 438, 439, 457, 474, 480, 493, 495, 499, 504, 505, 507
Bloomsbury relationships with: Forster, 94, 224, 401, 403–4, 408, 418, 419, 439; Keynes, 400; MacCarthy, 26; Strachey, 5, 12, 19, 20, 23, 60–1, 134, 136, 137, 211, 217, 218, 219, 253, 287, 307, 395–6, 398–400, 401, 403, 404, 405, 408–13, 419, 433, 435, 504; Sydney-Turner, 398, 400, 403–4, 412, 419; Woolf, V., 13, 20, 113, 137,

Woolf, Leonard: Bloomsbury
relationships – *continued*
217, 218–20, 272, 304, 348,
351, 352, 355, 373, 393, 411,
419, 434–5, 507
Ceylon, and, 3, 66, 74, 118, 123,
137, 217, 219, 224, 253, 312,
343, 391–436, 457, 499, 504,
507–9
imperialism and, 223, 391–437,
508–9
Independent Review and, 9, 393,
399
Moore, G. E., and, 136, 314,
395, 396, 436
Times Literary Supplement and,
415, 425
writers other than Bloomsbury
and: Austen, 396, 398;
Bennett, 112; Browne, 400;
Carlyle, T., 12; Collins, C.,
289; Conrad, 396, 398, 399,
400, 401, 406, 407; Dickens,
396; Elton, 409; Flaubert,
396, 424; Freud, 394, 409;
Hardy, 396, 398; James, H.,
396, 398, 408; Kipling, 394,
396, 398, 399, 410–11, 425;
Maupassant, 424; Mon-
taigne, 53; Rousseau, 12,
392; Shaw, 112, 238; Tennyson, 428; Virgil, 423; Voltaire, 12, 392, 393; Wells,
112; Zola, 424
writers, Bloomsbury, and:
Forster, 5, 47, 50, 93, 224,
225, 231, 312, 395, 403, 412,
425, 433, 474; Strachey, 19,
74, 123, 412; Sydney-
Turner, 69, 74
writings: *Beginning Again*, 392;
Diaries in Ceylon, 414, 415,
419–24, 426–8, 431–3, 437,
508, 509; *Downhill All the
Way*, 392, 418; *Empire and
Commerce* in Africa, 436;
'Gentleness of Nature',
414; *Growing*, 391–401,
405–19, 420, 423, 427–8,

435, 437, 507–9; *Journey Not
the Arrival Matters*, 53, 392,
413, 509; letters, 93, 253,
312, 395, 398–401, 408–13,
419, 508; 'Memoirs of an
Elderly Man', 394, 400,
508; 'Pearls and Swine',
404, 408; poetry, 61–3, 65–7,
71–3, 419; *Sowing*, 256, 392,
400, 437, 494, 508; *Stories of
the East*, 401–8, 424, 436,
437, 508; unpublished
stories, 508–9; *Village in the
Jungle*, 391, 397, 399, 413,
414, 420, 421, 423–37,
508–9; 'Voltaire', 12; *Wise
Virgins*, 427, 439
Woolf, Virginia, 3, 4, 5, 7, 8, 23,
25, 54, 59, 75, 91, 113, 116,
118, 129, 140–93, 199, 201,
204, 205, 214, 217, 221, 224,
231, 254, 259, 260, 263, 265,
271, 272, 276, 277, 279, 280,
283, 286, 287, 291, 294, 295,
296, 299, 312, 313, 320, 322,
328, 330, 339–90, 391, 413,
419, 438, 461, 462, 471, 473,
478, 479, 480, 481, 483, 484,
487, 488, 490, 492, 494,
496–8, 500, 505, 506–7, 508,
509
Academy & Literature and, 157,
161, 169, 172, 173, 177, 340
art and artists on: Beardsley,
361; Perugino, 379;
Whistler, 207
Bloomsbury, on, 3–4, 5, 217,
219–20
Bloomsbury relationships: 5;
Bell, C., 4, 193, 218, 219,
220, 225, 283, 351, 355, 374,
376, 381–2, 384; Bell, V.,
143, 149, 151, 183, 374, 376,
381; Forster, 47, 154, 223–4,
328, 438, 488; Grant, 219;
MacCarthy, 26, 28, 99, 102;
Stephen, A., 191, 218, 221;
Stephen, T., 5, 73, 191, 193;
Strachey, 5, 13, 20, 159, 193,

Woolf, Virginia: Bloomsbury
relationships – *continued*
217, 218, 219–20, 304, 348,
351, 353, 355; Sydney-
Turner, 222, 363, 368, 419;
Woolf, L., 112, 217, 219,
393, 419, 434
Cambridge and, 5, 223
Cecil, Nelly, and, 148, 364–70,
373–5
Cornhill and, 339, 340, 344, 352,
353, 358, 362, 364–71
Dictionary of National Biography,
354
Dreadnought Hoax and, 222
Duckworth, George, and, 142,
496
Euphrosyne, on, 5, 75, 182
feminism, 144, 151, 160, 223,
353, 355
Friday Club and, 211, 488
genres, mixing of, 344, 370–4,
375, 383, 385, 390
Guardian and, 7, 147–51, 153,
155–7, 158, 160, 162, 163–4,
168, 170, 172–3, 174, 178,
180, 185, 340, 352, 382, 497,
498, 506
history and, 140, 145, 162, 164,
165, 166, 168, 174, 184,
361–2
Moore, G. E., and, 144, 231,
343, 359, 376
Morley College teaching, 8,
154, 158, 161, 164, 165–8;
unpublished lectures, 152,
165–6
opera, and, 182, 363
reviewing conditions for,
146–7, 155, 157, 160, 164,
167, 172, 173, 175, 178,
339–41, 342, 343, 345,
365–6, 496
Speaker and, 172, 173, 175–7
Stephen, Caroline Emelia and,
373, 382
Stephen, Leslie and, 140, 145,
151–2, 164, 174, 179, 344,
349, 351, 384–5
style, 141, 148, 157, 161, 168,
170, 354, 356, 360, 362
Times and, 152–3, 157, 178, 349,
362–4, 366, 375
Times Literary Supplement and,
152, 156–7, 160–1, 162, 172,
173, 174–5, 178, 180, 181,
217, 285, 339, 340, 342–54,
356, 358–62, 365, 497, 498,
507
writers other than Bloomsbury
and: Aeschylus, 143;
Ainger, 173; Allingham, W.,
357; Aristophanes, 507;
Aristotle, 159, 160, 164;
Arnim, 342–3; Arnold, 143,
360; Austen, 476; Baretti,
347; Bennett, 113, 147, 213;
Benson, A. C., 29; Benson,
R. H., 342; Borrow, 162,
163; Boswell, 144, 151–2,
283, 351; Bowen, M., 341;
Bradley, A. C., 377; Brontë,
C., 148–9, 156, 372; Brontë,
E., 148–50, 156; Browning,
R., 165, 380; Browning, E.
B., 176, 380; Butler, S., 265;
Carlyle, J. W., 168–9, 280,
351; Carlyle, T., 169, 280,
283, 351; Cellini, 165, 497;
Christie, 358–5; Churchill,
174–5; Coleridge, 177; Con-
greve, 347; Conrad, 224;
Crabbe, 377; Dawson, 160;
De Quincey, 178–80, 347;
Dickens, 156, 476; Donne,
389; Edgeworth, 348; Eliot,
G., 372; Emerson, 356, 358;
Euripides, 143; Fanshawe,
358; Flaubert, 224; France,
183; Freeman, E. A., 165;
Freeman, M. W., 172; Gals-
worthy, 113; Galton, 153;
Gaskell, 348; Gibbon, 362;
Gissing, 178–9, 496, 498;
Green, J. R., 162, 165;
Greville, F., 346; Hall, F.,
343; Hardy, 144, 156, 378;
Hawthorne, 141, 162, 342,

Woolf, Virginia, and writers
   other than Bloomsbury –
   continued
      349, 366; Holmes, 349;
      Homer, 190, 377; Hood,
      347; Hope, 342; Howells,
      148, 496; Ibsen, 357; James,
      H., 144, 155–7, 163, 172,
      173, 178, 180–1, 185, 224,
      342, 349, 356, 359, 375–6,
      498; Jefferies, 153; Johnson,
      S., 144, 194, 209, 347;
      Keats, 165, 190, 347;
      Kinglake, 172; Kipling, 142,
      184; Lamb, 153, 157, 182,
      359; Lane, 160; Layard,
      153; Lee, V., 359–60;
      London, 340; Lowell, J. R.,
      349–50; Lucas, E. V., 347–8;
      Lydgate, 186; Macaulay, R.,
      175, 497; Macaulay, T., 351,
      362; Maugham, 163; Mere-
      dith, G., 156, 159, 162, 169,
      224, 340, 342, 346, 374, 379,
      380; Mérimée, 18; Meynell,
      380; Michelet, 362; Milton,
      144, 297; Moir, 172; Moli-
      ère, 377; Montaigne, 157;
      Morris, W., 153; Nietzsche,
      357; Norris, W. E., 160, 172,
      341; Paston letters, 170,
      185; Pater, 153, 160, 164,
      179, 183, 194, 201, 360, 361,
      371; Peacock, 192; Plato,
      143, 182, 191, 359–60, 377;
      Raleigh, Prof., 176; Rest-
      oration playwrights, 377;
      Ritchie, A. T., 358; Ross, R.,
      360–1; Rossetti, C., 342,
      350; Ruskin, 342, 380;
      Scott, W., 156, 341; Seward,
      347; Shakespeare, 166, 364,
      377; Shaw, 111, 113; Shelley,
      165, 350, 356; Sheridan,
      346–7, 348; Sichel, 282;
      Sidney, 346; Simpson, V.
      A., 497; Sophocles, 159,
      160, 161, 182, 192; Sorabji,
      353; Sterne, 163, 209, 345,
      348, 507; Stevenson, 160,
      179; Swinburne, 377;
      Symonds, 194; Synge, Mrs,
      175; Thackeray, 156, 166,
      507; Thucydides, 159;
      Tolstoy, 357, 377, 476;
      Turgenev, 476; Villiers, 347;
      Virgil, 159; Ward, Mrs H.,
      146–7, 177, 359, 369; Wells,
      113; Weyman, 175;
      Wharton, 172; Wilde, 361;
      Willcocks, M. P., 341;
      Wordsworth, 171, 175,
      350–1, 356; Yeats, 340;
      Yonge, 496
writers, Bloomsbury, and: Bell,
      C., 281, 376; Forster, 34, 47,
      51, 59, 88–9, 95, 155, 225,
      251–3, 312–3, 320, 322, 341,
      343, 474–6, 478; Fry, 194–5,
      199; MacCarthy, 116;
      Strachey, 37, 220, 355,
      376–7; Woolf, L., 435
writings: 'Andalusian Inn', 163;
      Anon, 371; Bell, C., sketch
      and dialogue, 218, 381–2;
      Bell, V. biography, 218,
      383–90, 507; 'Bluest of the
      Blue', 178; '*Chippinge*', 497;
      Common Reader, 1st Series,
      143, 162, 188, 369; *Common
      Reader*, 2nd Series, 179, 350;
      Complete Shorter Fiction, 498;
      'Covent Garden', 363; Decay
      of Essay–Writing', 157–8;
      'Dialogue upon Mount
      Pentelicus', 191–2, 498;
      diaries, 140, 142, 144–6, 162,
      164, 166, 169, 184–5, 189–91,
      339, 355, 360, 377–81, 497;
      Dickinson, V, sketches of,
      142, 373–4; early sketches,
      142–4, 181–2, 184; 'Dramatic
      in Life and Art', 166, 497;
      Dreadnought Hoax fragment,
      222; 'English Mail Coach',
      179–80, 498; *Essays*, 155, 497;
      Flush, 41, 149, 176, 188;
      Forster reviews, 224;

Woolf, Virginia: writings –
  continued
  Freshwater, 207; 'Friendships Gallery', 373, 380, 384;
  'Haworth', 148–9, 496; 'How
  Should One Read a Book?',
  180; 'Impassioned Prose',
  180; 'Impressions at
  Bayreuth', 363; 'Introduction', 145; *Jacob's Room*, 251,
  313; James's *Golden Bowl*
  review, 155–6; 'Journal of
  Mistress Joan Martyn',
  185–9; 'Journeys in Spain',
  163; 'Leaning Tower', 330;
  lectures, 165–6; letters, 140,
  193, 339, 375; 'Letters of Jane
  Welsh Carlyle', 168–9;
  'Literary Geography', 156–7;
  'Louise de la Vallière', 368;
  Lysistrata review, 507; 'Magic
  Greek', 161–2; marginalia
  essay, 182; *Melymbrosia*, 344;
  Memoir Club Papers, 142,
  162, 'Memoirs of a Novelist', 370–4; *Moments of Being*,
  383; *Monday or Tuesday*, 185,
  398; *Mr. Bennett and Mrs.
  Brown*, 182, 225, 308; *Mrs.
  Dalloway*, 117, 145, 313;
  'Mysterious Case of Miss V',
  184; *Night and Day*, 507;
  novel fragment, 141; 'Novels
  of E. M. Forster', 476; 'Old
  Bloomsbury', 3, 217, 219,
  221, 223; 'On a Faithful
  Friend', 149; 'On Not
  Knowing Greek', 162;
  Orlando, 41, 75, 166, 188, 223,
  305, 374, 493; 'Phyllis and
  Rosamond', 182–3; 'Plague
  of Essays', 157; 'Portraits of
  Places', 180; 'Professions for
  Women', 147; reading
  notebooks, 153, 177, 180, 364,
  377, 498; 'Reminiscences',
  see biography of Bell, V., 218;
  Roger Fry, 195, 199, 201, 205;
  Room of One's Own, 54, 150,
  178, 179, 313, 372, 390, 461,
  507; 'Serpentine', 144; Sichel
  review, 160–1, 162; 'Sketch of
  the Past', 383, 386, 387, 389,
  390; 'Society', 223, 440;
  'Some Poetic Plays', 506;
  Spanish review, 162–3;
  Stephen, C. E. obituary, 382;
  Stephen, L., sketch, 151–2;
  'Street Music', 153–4;
  'Sweetness – Long Drawn
  Out', 177; 'Terrible Tragedy
  in a Duckpond', 496; *Three
  Guineas*, 117, 162, 223, 439; *To
  the Lighthouse*, 170, 313, 409,
  476; '22 Hyde Park Gate',
  142; 'Unwritten Novel', 182;
  'Value of Laughter', 158–9;
  Voyage Out, 75, 117, 162, 218,
  225, 283, 304, 307, 313, 339,
  376, 393, 488, 507, 509; 'Walk
  by Night', 170–1; *Waves*, 28,
  143, 414, 440; *Women &
  Fiction*, 507; *Years*, 117, 143;
Wordsworth, William, 171, 175,
  270, 272, 280, 287, 288, 289,
  296, 297, 298, 312, 318, 350–1,
  356, 370, 381, 386, 500
Working Men's College, 8, 52,
  166, 441
World, 472
Wundt, Wilhelm, 98

Yeats, William Butler, 9, 69, 70–1,
  99, 101, 298–9, 307, 333, 340
Yellow Book, 361
Yonge, Charlotte, 496

Zabel, Morton Dauwen, 480
Zola, Emile, 53, 208, 424